GERMAN FILM AND LITERATURE

Adaptations and Transformations

GERMAN FILM & LITERATURE

Adaptations and Transformations

Edited by

Eric Rentschler

METHUEN   NEW YORK & LONDON

First published in 1986 by
Methuen, Inc.
29 West 35th Street,
New York NY 10001

Published in Great Britain by
Methuen & Co. Ltd
11 New Fetter Lane,
London EC4P 4EE

The collection © 1986 Eric Rentschler
Individual chapters © 1986
the respective authors

Typeset in Great Britain by
Scarborough Typesetting Services
and printed at
the University Press, Cambridge

Library of Congress Cataloging in
Publication Data
German Film and Literature:
Adaptations and transformations.
Bibliography: p.
Includes index.
1. Moving-pictures – Germany.
2. German literature –
Film and video adaptations.
I. Rentschler, Eric.
PN1993.5.G3G36   1986
791.43 '75 '0943   85-25903

ISBN 0-416-60331-9
ISBN 0-416-60341-6 (PBK.)

British Library Cataloguing in
Publication Data
German Film and Literature:
Adaptations and transformations.
1. Moving-pictures – Germany –
History. 2. German literature –
Film and video adaptations
I. Rentschler, Eric.
791.43 '0943   PN1993.5.G3

ISBN 0-416-60331-9
ISBN 0-416-60341-6 Pbk

Contents

Notes on the contributors

RUSSELL A. BERMAN teaches twentieth-century German literature and culture at Stanford University. He is the author of *Between Fontane and Tucholsky: Literary Criticism and the Public Sphere in Wilhelmine Germany* as well as numerous articles and reviews on German literature, critical theory, contemporary cinema, and political culture.

TIMOTHY CORRIGAN is Associate Professor of English at Temple University where he teaches courses on literature and film. Besides many articles on film, literature, and theory, he is the author of *New German Film: The Displaced Image* and the editor of a forthcoming anthology on the films of Werner Herzog.

THOMAS ELSAESSER teaches comparative literature and film at the University of East Anglia. Author of articles on a wide spectrum of topics ranging from melodrama to classical and contemporary German cinema, film theory and the representation of history in film, he is the former editor of *Monogram* and a contributor to *Screen, Positif, Sight & Sound, New German Critique, Wide Angle, Monthly Film Bulletin, October, Framework*, and other journals.

MIRIAM HANSEN teaches literature and film courses in the Department of English at Rutgers University. She is a member of the editorial board of *New German Critique* and author of a book on Ezra Pound. Her most recent work includes studies on early silent cinema in Germany, Adorno and film, recent directions in film theory, the work of Ulrike Ottinger, as well as a series of articles on Alexander Kluge.

JAN-CHRISTOPHER HORAK is the Associate Curator of Film at the George Eastman House. He has just completed a lengthy study of German filmmakers in exile during the Third Reich and the anti-Nazi film genre. His many publications include a book on film and photography in the 1920s and articles on Werner Herzog, Zionist film propaganda in Nazi Germany, progressive film culture in the Weimar Republic, and German films of the Third Reich.

ANTON KAES is Associate Professor of German at the University of California, Berkeley, where he teaches courses on literature, film, and theory. Besides a book study on the reception of German expressionism in America, he has edited the volumes *Kino-Debatte* and *Weimarer Republik: Manifeste und Dokumente zur deutschen Literatur 1918–1933*. He is currently working on a book concerned with the question of national identity as represented in recent New German films.

E. ANN KAPLAN teaches film and literature at Rutgers University in the Department of English. Her books include *Fritz Lang: A Research and Reference Guide* and *Women and Film: Both Sides of the Camera* as well as the edited volumes *Women in Film Noir* and *Regarding Television: A Critical Anthology*. At present she is working on a study devoted to constructions of the mother in literature, film, and psychoanalytic theory.

GERTRUD KOCH is the co-editor of *Frauen und Film* and a film critic and theorist. Based in Frankfurt, she has taught at the Johann Wolfgang von Goethe Universität as well as at the film academies in Berlin and Munich. Her publications include monograph studies on Louis Malle and Carlos Saura, articles on pornography and film, feminist film theory, women directors, critical theory and film, Jacques Tati, Yasujiro Ozu, and other topics.

DENNIS F. MAHONEY is Associate Professor of German at the University of Vermont where he teaches courses on literature and film. He is the author of *Die Poetisierung der Natur bei Novalis* and is presently completing a book on the novel in the Age of Goethe.

JUDITH MAYNE is Associate Professor in the Department of Romance Languages at Ohio State University where she teaches courses on film, literature, and women's studies. She has completed book-length studies on film and literature as well as on Soviet films of the 1920s. Her numerous articles and reviews include work on feminist film theory, Rainer Werner Fassbinder, Helke Sander, *Hiroshima mon amour*, *King Kong*, primitive cinema, spectatorship and spectacle, as well as Roland Barthes.

BRIGITTE PEUCKER teaches film and literature in the Department of Germanic Languages at Yale University where she is Associate Professor. She has published articles on Werner Herzog and Rainer Werner Fassbinder as well as a book on eighteenth-century German poetry.

ERIC RENTSCHLER is Associate Professor of German and Director of Film Studies at the University of California, Irvine. His articles include pieces on Alexander Kluge, Herbert Achternbusch, Hans W. Geissendörfer, film history and reception theory, images of America in New German Film, and German film historiography. His most recent book is *West German Film in the Course of Time*. He is currently completing an anthology in English devoted to the writings of New German filmmakers and working on a book dealing with fantasy production in the Third Reich.

HEIDE SCHLÜPMANN lives in Frankfurt, where she is co-editor of *Frauen und Film* and instructor at the Johann Wolfgang von Goethe Universität. She has published on psychoanalysis and film, *Mädchen in Uniform*, and romantic couples in German films of the 1950s, as well as writing regular film reviews in various German periodicals.

MARC SILBERMAN teaches German and Humanities at the University of Texas at San Antonio. His publications include books on GDR literature and articles on contemporary literature, film theory and history. His work has appeared in *Jump Cut, Camera Obscura, German Quarterly, Quarterly Review of Film Studies*, and *Discourse*. He has received grants from the NEH and the Alexander von Humboldt Foundation to pursue research on the social history of German film.

MAUREEN TURIM teaches in the Cinema Department at SUNY-Binghamton. She has recently completed a book entitled *Flashbacks in Films: Memory Processes and the Subjectivity of History*. Her work on a number of topics has appeared in *Enclitic, Wide Angle, Semiotica*, the AFI monograph *Cinema Histories, Cinema Practices*, and the anthology *New German Filmmakers: From Oberhausen through the Seventies*.

ALAN WILLIAMS teaches film in the French Department at Rutgers University. His articles on cinema have appeared in many magazines and anthologies. His monograph, *Max Ophüls and the Cinema of Desire*, was published by Arno Press. He is currently writing a social history of French film.

KARSTEN WITTE is an author and an independent journalist who lives in West Berlin. His many publications include studies on Nazi cinema, Bernardo Bertolucci, Pier Paolo Pasolini, Robert Bresson, film stars from the 1930s through the 1960s, film historiography, and Siegfried Kracauer. His poetry has appeared in *manuskripte* and *Akzente*; he has also translated works by Jean Cocteau and Christopher Isherwood into German and edited the collected writings of Siegfried Kracauer. His film criticism recently appeared in a volume published by S. Fischer Verlag, Frankfurt am Main.

ERIC RENTSCHLER
Introduction:
Theoretical and historical
considerations

Film history seems to demonstrate that literary adaptations always have less to offer than literature. Looking at results alone – *these are two different media and for this reason their ability to produce expressive richness lies in different areas* – does not show the way out. One must above all go back to the common root of film and books: that is telling stories. People tell a story about something. They do this in an epic, a dramatic way, or in forms not specifically categorizable, always according to the circumstances. This is the *process*.   (Alexander Kluge[1])

Given the problematic nature of the discourse of fidelity, one is tempted to call for a moratorium on adaptation studies. On the other hand, the literary source does affect the production and consumption of the film adaptation and we run the risk of impoverished film studies by ignoring this fact. How can we discuss this phenomenon in more profitable ways? What directions should the study of adaptation take?   (Christopher Orr[2])

Every interpretation is based on displacement, since the interpreter redirects the original object by inserting it into a new frame of reference.
                                                        (Dudley Andrew[3])

This volume presents the first sustained investigation in any language of the historical interactions between German film and literature. There exists, to be sure (as the bibliography at the back of this book attests), a substantial body of scholarship and many anthologies devoted to the relations between German literature and film: studies of film versions of novels and dramas,[4] discussions of various authors' interactions with the cinematic medium,[5] texts documenting the different responses of German intellectuals to the form,[6] a recent compilation of cinemorphic texts demonstrating how crucially the visual art has impressed itself upon the minds of German writers in this century.[7] Given the increasing number of university courses and academic publications on German film and literature, both in the US and Germany,[8] one can hardly complain (as one might have as late as a decade ago) that the sub-discipline languishes in obscurity, that it is a stepchild of *Germanistik*. On the other hand, the way in which film has become integrated into German curricula as well as American departments of German has tended to place the medium in the service of literary studies, more often than not forgoing cinematic specifics and slighting both historical and institutional consider-ations, exactly those questions that have engaged film scholars working in other sectors of the academy during the last two decades.[9]

In discussions of German film and literature by Germanists in the United States and elsewhere, fidelity analysis stands all but unchallenged.[10] One finds in these essays dealing with movies based upon novels and dramas by canonized figures an unwavering insistence on comparing literary sources and filmic renderings. The dominant tendency has been to emphasize the question of adaptation understood in a very narrow manner, to speak of films based on literary sources as *Verfilmungen*, works transposed from one medium into another. Alfred Estermann's *Die Verfilmung literarischer Werke*, a German analogue to George Bluestone's ground-breaking *Novels into Films*, has enjoyed the status of a standard work among Germanists since it appeared in 1965.[11] In this influential study, Estermann remains single-mindedly concerned with the question of adaptation, resolving to describe "the difference between (poetic) 'verbal art' and (optical-moving) 'visual art,' between which every adaptation seeks to effect a synthesis that is not an independent work."[12] The analyses of individual texts proceed along literary lines – to the point that discussions of certain films deal with printed scripts rather than celluloid artifacts. Although Estermann grants that film possesses its own arsenal of formal and stylistic possibility, he forsakes such matters, focusing instead on the thematic shifts that transpire when a book becomes a film. Estermann avoids thorny issues like the potential influence and intervention of the film industry in the process of adaptation, a lesson well documented in Brecht's *The Threepenny Lawsuit*. He intends, so he argues, to maintain "all due neutrality,"[13] the cavalier attitude that will also permit him to leave questions of historical and social import unbroached.

Germanists, both in America and elsewhere, have analyzed the relations between literature (in the main, narrative literature) and film, more often than not coming to conclusions that privilege the former. In recent years, however, various scholars (no doubt affected by advances made by their colleagues in cinema studies programs) have broken out of this conservative mold, stressing the autonomy of the two forms and not always insisting on a hierarchy that casts film into a subsidiary role while practicing the so-called "adaptation-as-betrayal approach."[14] (This can amount to an act of daring for an untenured assistant professor: s/he ventures into a field of study only grudgingly tolerated by many senior colleagues who view film as a watering-down rather than an enrichment of course offerings, a challenge to accepted notions of the literary canon and the departmental domain.) Nonetheless, one still uses the literary source as a "pre-text" in a double sense: as a starting point and as a justification for one's explorations outside accepted boundaries. Even when individuals make a point of stressing the integrity of filmic adaptations, as texts in their own right with distinct formal dimensions, one nevertheless avails oneself of a methodology "where notions of traditional criticism – authorship, aesthetic autonomy – apply."[15] In scrutinizing the process whereby a literary sign system becomes reshaped into a cinematic one, the exegete privileges the literary source as the primary determining factor. By so doing, one overlooks vast reaches of intertextual space to be found between any film and its source(s), space that "includes codes specific to the institution of cinema as well as codes that reflect the cultural conditions under which the film was produced."[16]

This book is about adaptations and transformations. It includes analyses devoted to renderings of classical dramas by Lessing and Kleist, well-known modern plays by Büchner, Schnitzler, Wedekind, and Zuckmayer, reworkings of famous novels by Heinrich and Thomas Mann, Seghers, Musil, Döblin, contemporary prose pieces by Kluge and Handke, a selection that spans the entirety of modern German literary history from the mid eighteenth century through the 1970s. In a number of cases, though, the reader might well wonder how certain texts have found their way into this collection. Why, for instance, consider Stellan Rye's *The Student of Prague*, which, after all, is based on Hanns Heinz Ewers's original script, not a literary source? How does one justify the inclusion of Fassbinder's *The Marriage of Maria Braun*, which like Rye's film provides an example of a book which came about only after the success of the film? Or, perhaps even more puzzling: is a title taken from a poem by Brecht enough to warrant an entire chapter on Helma Sanders-Brahms's autobiographical exercise, *Germany, Pale Mother*? What indeed is being adapted here and what does it have to do with literature?

I use the terms *adaptations* and *transformations* in order to suggest a more dynamic and process-bound notion of the interactions between film and literature. "Every representational film *adapts* a prior conception," argues Dudley Andrew, a conception taken from another context and placed into the experiential horizon of the adaptor.[17] In this way adaptation, in its widest sense, amounts to an act of understanding, the attempt to read one's own meaning into and out of the texted realities that surround us, to shape a personal discourse from the stories and history with which we live. As Andrew puts it, "Adaptation is the appropriation of a meaning from a prior text."[18] Each of the examples discussed in this volume dramatizes a dialogue with tradition, a reworking of certain modes of expression, a play with various cultural givens. Seen in this light, all of the twenty films dealt with in these pages embody adaptations, even the ones that do not seem to fit accepted notions of what constitutes a *Literaturverfilmung*. Ewers's screenplay for

The Student of Prague shuffled romantic motifs so as to provide early German film with a more respectable and – so it was hoped – marketable literary appeal. Fassbinder took recourse to postwar German history as the raw material for *The Marriage of Maria Braun*, a narrative derived from wisps of a collective memory, fragments that Fassbinder reshaped into a critical historical fiction. Sanders-Brahms wanted to explore her own war experience with her mother in *Germany, Pale Mother*. The film not only adapts the director's childhood in the Third Reich; it likewise reckons with the patriarchal use of the mother figure (both literary and literal) in German history.

Each film under discussion here came about as the result of a dynamic interaction. The central question to which the articles in this anthology continually return can be stated simply: why do artists adapt certain material at certain times? What reasons, for instance, conditioned Schlöndorff's turn to Musil's prophetic vision of prefascism (in *Young Törless*) precisely at a time when a young postwar generation was beginning to challenge its parents' shadowy past? What are the ideological stakes involved in Staudte's East German updating of Heinrich Mann's *Der Untertan* (cf. the film's coda), a work that provoked virulent disfavor among officials in the Federal Republic and did not find its way into West German cinemas until many years after its première in the GDR? What transpires when a German-speaking emigrant working in wartime Hollywood takes on a novel written by someone whose Communist allegiances were no secret, as in Zinnemann's rendering of Seghers's *The Seventh Cross*? Why did Nazi cinema so resolutely turn to the classical literary canon in its film production; how does *völkisch* ideology insinuate itself into the works of figures like Lessing and Kleist? And how does one account for the more recent and widespread tendency of German artists to see their work in film and literature as part of a larger endeavor? What sort of institutional considerations pose themselves when a writer like Kluge decides to confront the legacy of yesterday in an independent film when these structures continue to persist today?

The contributors to this project come from a variety of disciplines (departments of German, English, Romance Languages, Comparative Literature, and Film Studies programs); one finds among them journalists working in West Germany as well as academics teaching at universities in Great Britain and the United States. Methodologically, these twenty chapters span an extensive space, reflecting the wide range of discourses to be found in critical studies today. In commenting on these adaptations, each author transforms them into objects of understanding in his or her own play with tradition, an exercise grounded in yet another historical and social space. In the past, Germanists working in film have tended to stress cultural and literary aspects of a given text, at the same time betraying their lack of cinematic expertise by their neglect of formal and medium-specific concerns – much less theoretical questions. (Departments of German in America have by and large displayed a marked resistance to continental theory – what wags variously refer to as "Frenchspeak" or "frogchat" – and the recent directions taken by their colleagues in other literature departments.) Exponents of film studies and cinema programs, on the other hand, turn to German films with an array of sophisticated tools, delving into the "work" of these texts with scientistic fervor and analytical aplomb. Quite often, though, such individuals tend to obscure the contextual exigencies framing these texts, questions of history and cultural significance. Although the variance to some degree is to be encountered in this book, the hope has been to enlist scholars whose backgrounds bridge this gap. The major impetus linking the articles here has been to expand the field of adaptation study so as to include sociological, theoretical, and historical dimensions, to bring a livelier regard for intertextuality to the study of German film and literature. The collection is in fact less interested in adaptations of certain privileged texts (masterpieces or high art) than it is with the ways in which filmmakers in Germany have engaged – and been engaged by – literary history, an exchange conditioned by a larger general history. This history, to be sure, has assumed a prominent role in the precarious course of German film history.[19]

Something needs to be said about the selection of texts. Clearly, the intent was to survey the entirety of German film history and present some of the most dramatic examples of the interactions between film and literature since the onset of narrative features. One finds texts taken from all of the major epochs: the pre-Weimar period, the "golden age" of German cinema, the Third Reich, the postwar era, as well as the more recent New German Film. It was crucial as well that certain aspects of German film history all too often forgotten in popular accounts be included: exile productions made abroad during World War II and the DEFA films from the "other" Germany, both of which demand more than the cursory treatment thus far accorded them. The volume is nonetheless anything but definitive. At best it can be understood as an initial exploration, one that aims to map out territory previously obscured or unappreciated, hoping besides to point in directions that might lead to productive further ventures. Some areas that suggest themselves as sites for future investigations, topics not represented in these pages, include:

– popular literature and its effect on commercial and independent filmmaking (e.g. the *Heimat* novels of Ludwig Ganghofer, Patricia Highsmith's thrillers, the role of Karl May's westerns);

– the dynamics behind TV adaptations of canonized authors, especially as film enters the age of electronic reproduction (take, for example, titles from the last half-decade alone, the renderings of *Berlin Alexanderplatz*, *The Confessions of Felix Krull*, *Buddenbrooks*, *Exile*, and *The Magic Mountain*, all of which were screened as serials on German public networks);

– the question of why certain periods tend to prefer certain historical epochs in their search for sources (why does one find the numerous reworkings of eighteenth-century titles in Nazi cinema; what brought about the wave of adaptations based on nineteenth-century writers during a certain phase of the 1970s; how does one account for the waves of Thomas Mann films during the 1950s as well as the early 1980s and how do these appropriations differ?);

– the thematization of film in German literature, throughout this century, not to mention the formal influence of the cinematic medium on German writers;

– the actual use of books and literature as objects of reference in films (think of the black-market dealer, played by Fassbinder, who hawks a complete edition of Kleist in *The Marriage of Maria Braun,* or the copy of Faulkner's *Wild Palms* we see Bruno read in Wenders's *Kings of the Road*);

– the relations between certain literary movements and their filmic extensions, the best-surveyed of which is expressionism (but what about the exchanges between the postwar literature of shatters and the *Trümmerfilm*, the documentary tendencies of the 1960s and their filmic analogues, the impact of the so-called "New Subjectivity" on the New German filmmakers of the 1970s?);

– the connections between the literary avant-garde and its filmic counterpart (Werner Nekes's *Uliisses* provides only the most obvious starting point).

Among regretted and conspicuous absences in this volume, those due to considerations of space more than lack of interest are adaptations of works by Kafka (any updated version of this volume would include a chapter on Straub/Huillet's 1984 film *Class Relations*, their staging of Kafka's *Amerika*), and in particular a discussion of Fritz Lang's appropriations of literary sources during the Weimar period (taking into account, of course, the role of Thea von Harbou). One could well explore the film versions of Günter Grass and Heinrich Böll more carefully – and critically – than has previously been the case. Likewise, there remain many lessons from Brecht yet to be accounted for, especially exercises in Brecht found in German film history. And certain figures present many different kinds of theoretical and historical challenges yet to be taken up by scholars in the United States concerned with the exchanges between German film and literature, individuals as diverse as Herbert Achternbusch, Konrad Wolf, Ulf Miehe, and Ingemo Engström, to list only a few names from the recent past. The appended bibliography means to give the reader a sense of what has been done in the field of German film and literature; the year-by-year inventory of German films based on literature aims to direct attention to the significant number of adaptations to be encountered in German film history, about which we still for the most know so very little.

This undertaking involved scholars working at a host of institutions. Each contributor no doubt has her or his share of people to credit for their assistance in this endeavor. On this occasion I want to thank the participants for their enthusiasm, support, and, of course, their scintillating essays. For my own part, I am particularly indebted to the Stiftung Deutsche Kinemathek for background information, bibliographical and filmographical references, as well as many of the photographs that appear here. Hans Helmut Prinzler and his colleagues have my gratitude for their gracious and thorough attention to my every request. Thanks go out as well to Ingrid Tabrizian of the Deutsches Filmmuseum Frankfurt who was extremely helpful in locating stills for this book. I appreciate likewise the efforts of the Kommunales Kino Frankfurt to organize a private screening of *The Student of Prague* and the willingness of the Deutsches Institut für Filmkunde to provide a copy of the film. Acknowledgment is also due to New Yorker Films and the George Eastman House for stills that appear with their permission. The editors of *Screen*, *Goethe Yearbook*, and *German Quarterly* kindly allowed me to use essays that originally appeared in the pages of those journals. All of the other contributions were commissioned for this volume and appear here in English for the first time.

The anthology would not have come about as easily had it not been for a generous Alexander von Humboldt-Stiftung fellowship, which I received during 1983 and 1984, enabling me to work on this project in West Germany and Berlin. A University of California Irvine Faculty Research Grant proved invaluable in helping me pay for film rentals, xeroxed materials, books, periodicals, and illustrations. Likewise, a UCI School of Humanities Research and Travel stipend furthered the venture at a crucial juncture. I am indebted to Dean Kendall Bailes and Professor Thomas Saine for their understanding, flexibility, and continuing encouragement.

Finally, I would like to thank Evelyn Ehrlich who worked with me as a reader during important stages of the project. She proved to be an exemplary critic whose many suggestions made a decisive difference in the style and shape of the book's essays.

Notes

1. Alexander Kluge, *Bestandsaufnahme: Utopie Film* (Frankfurt am Main: Zweitausendeins, 1983), p. 436.

2. Christopher Orr, "The discourse on adaptation," *Wide Angle*, 6, No. 2 (1984), 72.

3. Dudley Andrew, *Concepts in Film Theory* (London and New York: Oxford University Press, 1984), p. 154.

4. See e.g. the articles in "Special issue: New German Cinema," *Literature/Film Quarterly*, 7, No. 3 (1979), or a similarly film-oriented issue of *German Life & Letters*, 32, No. 3 (April 1979).

5. Some representative examples include: Helga Belach *et al.* (eds), *Das Kino und Thomas Mann: Eine Dokumentation* (Berlin: Stiftung Deutsche Kinemathek, 1975); Wolfgang Gersch, *Film bei Brecht* (Munich: Hanser, 1976); Wolfram Schütte (ed.),

Klassenverhältnisse (Frankfurt am Main: Fischer, 1984), a volume that includes articles on Kafka's relation to film as well as about adaptations based on the writer's works.

6. There is a plethora of collections concerned with the mixed feelings of German writers about the cinematic medium during the first three decades of this century. See, among other sources, Ludwig Greve, Margot Pehle, and Heidi Westhoff (eds), *Hätte ich das Kino! Die Schriftsteller und der Stummfilm* (Stuttgart: Klett, 1976); Anton Kaes (ed.), *Kino-Debatte. Texte zum Verhältnis von Literatur und Film 1909–1929* (Tübingen: Niemeyer, 1978); two recent volumes edited by Fritz Güttinger, *Der Stummfilm im Zitat der Zeit* and *Kein Tag ohne Kino: Schriftsteller über den Stummfilm* (Frankfurt am Main: Deutsches Filmmuseum, 1984); and, finally, Heinz-B. Heller, *Literarische Intelligenz und Film* (Tübingen: Niemeyer, 1984).

7. Hans Stempel and Martin Ripkens (eds), *Das Kino im Kopf* (Zürich: Arche, 1984).

8. For an initial and by now outdated survey of the inroads made by film into American departments of German, see "German film courses and resources: a special survey," *Monatshefte*, 69, No. 3 (Fall 1977), 305–19. The Stiftung Deutsche Kinemathek has published annual documentations of film courses and publications in Germany since 1978. See the various numbers of *Film und Fernsehen in Forschung und Lehre*, especially No. 7 (1984), which contains Hans-Bernhard Moeller's overview, "Der deutsche Film in amerikanischer Forschung und Lehre," 96–110. Cf. my critical review, "Deutsche Filmgeschichte made in Germany and USA," *epd Film*, September 1984, 12–14.

9. For a discussion of the historical development of this institutional split, see Andrew, pp. 3–9.

10. Cf. Christopher Orr's observations about the state of film and literature scholarship in general: "The concern with the fidelity of the adapted film in letter and spirit to its literary source has unquestionably dominated the discourse on adaptation" (p. 72).

11. Alfred Estermann, *Die Verfilmung literarischer Werke* (Bonn: Bouvier, 1965).

12. ibid., p. 5.

13. ibid., p. 6.

14. The phrase is taken from Andrew Horton and Joan Magretta's introduction to *Modern European Filmmakers and the Art of Adaptation* (New York: Ungar, 1981), p. 1.

15. Judith Mayne, "Introduction: film/narrative/the novel," *Ciné-Tracts*, No. 13 (Spring 1981), n.p.

16. Orr, p. 72.

17. Andrew, p. 97.

18. ibid.

19. For a survey of the problematic and productive role literature has played in German film history, see chapter 5 of my book, *West German Film in the Course of Time* (Bedford Hills, NY: Redgrave, 1984), pp. 129–57.

1

HEIDE SCHLÜPMANN

The first German art film:
Rye's *The Student of Prague* (1913)

Hanns Heinz Ewers, best-selling author, movie-theater owner, and "avowed *Herrenmensch*,"[1] took pride in the continuing success of *The Student of Prague* (*Der Student von Prag*, 1913), for which he wrote the filmscript:

> Films have a very short life, yet this film has survived twelve years and is still being shown throughout the world. It was a huge success, not only in Germany, but abroad as well: the first real art film. It proved to critics, artists, and the public that the cinema could produce art, and to the film industry that art in the cinema could also earn substantial sums of money.[2]

Timely associations guided Ewers, to be sure: art, cinema, and capital. He had become famous mainly for his Gothic horror novels, especially *Mandrake* (*Alraune*), which was brought to the screen in 1928, 1930, and again in 1952. *The Student of Prague* was also remade twice. Ewers worked as an adviser for the second version in 1926, one directed by Henrik Galeen, but apparently he disowned Arthur Robison's 1935 remake.[3]

Ewers was an artist who wanted to turn a profit and yet still not be debased by business. In his 1930 preface to *The Student of Prague: An Idea by Hanns Heinz Ewers*, the writer attacked not only film producers without sensitivity for art, but also scriptwriters who imbued film texts with alien forms – i.e. literary contrivances taken from novels and dramas. At the same time, Ewers bemoaned the way his "idea" had been exploited. He seized the occasion as well to boast of his own accomplishments in the film medium. Ewers did not think much of transpositions from the one medium to another; he was only interested in original screen treatments. These aesthetic principles apparently did not stop him in 1933 from adapting his own novel, *Horst Wessel*. The resultant film, *Hans Westmar* (directed by Franz Wenzler), was, along with *Hitler Youth Quex* (*Hitlerjunge Quex*, directed by Hans Steinhoff) and *SA-Mann Brand* (Franz Seitz), one of three explicit propaganda feature films made in the year of Hitler's rise to power depicting National Socialism's revolutionary phase.

The Student of Prague opened in Berlin on 22 August 1913. A critic present ironically described the event:

> It was a real première. A lot of tuxedoes. The poet sat in a private box, occasionally visible with very pretty ladies. A monocle gave its master the necessary bearing. Goethe, Chamisso, E. T. A. Hoffmann, Alfred de Musset, and Oscar Wilde were also present. They were not averse to the fact that Dr H. H. Ewers, the legendary celebrator of black masses, had achieved a technical masterpiece, which was greeted by an enthusiastic audience. They succumbed to the unique magic of Prague's golden city. Later in the bar they could not forget the unbelievably slender, beautiful, frisky legs of Lyda Salmonova.[4]

The eyewitness – with tongue in cheek – pointed out the array of literary luminaries who had acted as the film's godfathers. In the pundit's opinion, Ewers had sold his literary honor and taken on the role of a buffoon. Movies were still in the process of casting off their fairground origins and gaining the respectability of a bourgeois entertainment. The writer Ewers helped in that endeavor. He belonged to a circle of artists and intellectuals who raised cinema out of its pariah status. In an article, "Der Kientopp," Ewers, as early as 1907, asked: "Where are the poets and painters who will create for the nickelodeon?"[5] A similar statement is to be found in Kurt Pinthus's *Das Kinobuch* of 1914.

The Golden Age of German cinema after World War I had its origins in the years 1912 to 1914 and took many of its impulses from established artists and writers. Not only Ewers was involved in the production of *The Student of Prague*, but the Max Reinhardt actor, Paul Wegener, as well. Furthermore, the crew included the Danish director, Stellan Rye, and the cameraman, Guido Seeber. Rye would die in the first year of the war. Seeber, cinematographer for many Asta Nielsen films, went on to work with G. W. Pabst in the 1920s. The cinema, however, did not only contain artistic ambitions; it also became an object of interest for capital. Art and capital: these amounted to the main forces that would bring about the cooptation of film by the middle class, a process that many intellectuals in Germany would condemn during the Weimar Republic. It may in fact be the participation of numerous other intellectuals which secured cinema a place as a functional part of bourgeois culture in this century.

The Student of Prague was hailed in the credits as "the first German art film," analogous to and yet in contradistinction to the French *Film d'art* movement. The film forced audiences to reconsider the relationship between literature and film, to become aware of how widespread cooperation by artists in the established art forms affected the silent cinema in Germany.

Did these artists impose traditional aesthetic values on the new medium, taking account of film's technical potential? Did they transform the medium and emancipate it from established forms?

The Student of Prague reworks the *Doppelgänger* motif, one of the major preoccupations of German romantic literature from Ludwig Tieck to Heinrich Heine. Subsequent variations on the theme throughout the nineteenth century are found in the works of Guy de Maupassant, Feodor Dostoevsky, Edgar Allan Poe, and Oscar Wilde. Ewers's script borrows particularly from E. T. A. Hoffmann's *The Story of the Lost Reflection* (*Die Geschichte vom verlorenen Spiegelbilde*), Poe's *William Wilson*, and Goethe's *Faust*, especially in the hero's pact with the devil. The film's opening titles explicitly quote a poem by Alfred de Musset, "La Nuit de Décembre." Despite these obvious influences, *The Student of Prague* is not determined by literary sources *per se*, but rather concentrates on a central motif of nineteenth-century literature: the *Doppelgänger*. This sets the film apart from customary patterns of literary adaptation.

In *The Haunted Screen*, Lotte H. Eisner discusses the classical period of German cinema, taking recourse to art history for her formal and stylistic insights. She perceives the German films of the epoch as being highly evocative of German romanticism. For Eisner the relationship between romantic literature and German film is not a simple question of dominance or dependence. She sees similarities in style and the recurrence of certain motifs ontologically, as being grounded in identical world views, as emanations of a distinctly German *Geist*. Eisner does not discuss whether these recurring romantic elements served to reflect contemporary reality or whether they merely served as ideological emanations of bourgeois culture.

This distinction becomes necessary, particularly when one compares the 1913 and the 1926 versions of *The Student of Prague*. Siegfried Kracauer (in *From Caligari to Hitler*, 1947) is – in contrast to Eisner – only concerned with the first version. The strength of Eisner's study lies in its descriptions, in the parallels it draws between art and literary history and film. Her stress is on the role of romantic chiaroscuro and her attention given to the reappearance of the "hybrid, half-real world" of E. T. A. Hoffmann in Rye's film.[6] She also goes on to compare the character and dress of Scapinelli (in the second version) with the archivist Lindhorst in Hoffmann's *The Golden Pot* (*Der goldene Topf*). She juxtaposes a landscape scene in the 1926 film with a painting by Caspar David Friedrich. Yet, while tracing variations on the *Doppelgänger* theme from Robert Wiene's *The Cabinet of Dr Caligari* (*Das Cabinet des Dr Caligari*, 1920) to Fritz Lang's *M* (1931), Eisner loses sight of its importance for *The Student of Prague*.

Kracauer, on the other hand, concentrates on the ideological permutations of this motif and what it means for the cinema of 1913 to appropriate and rework it. To be sure, Kracauer mentions the film's literary origins, but then goes on to analyze *The Student of Prague* as the expression of a socio-historical situation. For him a "people's mentality" is not a fixed national characteristic (Eisner's German *Geist*), but rather a variable disposition bound in socio-psychological determinants. *The Student of Prague* is of fundamental importance for the development of German cinema after World War I, especially for the period between 1919 and 1924:

> *The Student of Prague* introduced to the screen a theme that was to become an obsession of the German cinema: a deep and fearful concern with the foundations of the self. By separating Baldwin [Balduin] from his reflection and making both face each other, Wegener's film symbolizes a specific kind of split personality. Instead of being unaware of his own duality, the panic-stricken Baldwin realizes that he is in the grip of an antagonist who is nobody but himself. This was an old motif surrounded by a halo of meanings, but was it not also a dreamlike transcription of what the German middle class actually experienced in its relation to the feudal caste running Germany?[7]

The Student of Prague, read in this way, implies that the bourgeoisie's opposition to the imperial government was only nominal; in reality it identified with the Kaiser. This revelation is garbed in fantastic forms, because the middle class insisted on withdrawing into the interiority of autonomous individuals, instead of establishing the solidarity with the working class necessitated by strained economic conditions. An external dualism – an ambiguous social identity – thus appears as an inner schism.

As Kracauer continues, this withdrawal into inwardness not only means escape, but a sort of confrontation with historically generated psychic dispositions. The recourse to romantic motifs thus is bound in parallel historical constellations. German romanticism coincides with a period of political reaction during which bourgeois individuals accommodated themselves to feudalism by turning inward. In 1913, the collapse of the German Empire was at hand, yet the emancipation of the individual could only come about if one eradicated those structures which had been created in the place of an unsuccessful bourgeois revolution. In speaking about *The Student of Prague*, Kracauer dwells on the story. But the political importance of the film only becomes clear if one reflects on its form and the filmic articulation of the literary figure of the double.

Upon its première in 1913, *The Student of Prague* appealed to a large audience, and also stimulated the special interests of scientific research, specifically the burgeoning field of psychoanalysis. An extensive study by Otto Rank, "The Double" ("Der Doppelgänger"), published in 1914 in Sigmund Freud's journal, *Imago*, opens with a description of "shadowy, fleeting, impressive images in Hanns Heinz Ewers's film drama."[8] Rank deals with literary configurations of this motif, going on to reveal *volks*-psychological elements by using ethnographic, mythological, and folkloristic materials.

As a psychoanalyst, Rank is concerned with the "original problem (*Urproblem*) of the self . . . which modern adaptors support or which has been obtrusively pushed to the fore by new techniques of representation."[9] Rank in this way addresses the question of new modes of signification made possible by the filmic medium:

> Perhaps it follows that filmic form, which reminds us of dream techniques in more ways than one, expresses certain psychological facts and relationships – which the poet cannot clearly articulate in words – in a distinct and manifest imagistic language and thus makes their meaning more accessible.[10]

Rank demonstrates crucial correspondences between various literary renderings of the double. They all can be rediscovered in the film, reinforcing the fact that the film reflects not a single literary work, but rather the continuity of a certain motif. The correspondences are seen in the way the *Doppelgänger* appears as a complete likeness, as if "stolen from a mirror" (E. T. A. Hoffmann) – which is in fact the case in the film. This likeness causes its model difficulties; catastrophes occur in his relationship to women; a persecution complex results. The outcome is suicide, the murder of the other self. Rank also discusses the psychological disposition of the writers, coming to the conclusion that individual pathology cannot be explained by the representational form of the double, whether as shadow, mirror image, or portrait. It would seem that a "superindividual element subconsciously plays a role."[11]

Films, even so-called *auteur* films, are not the products of individual authors as in literature. Due to their collective production, films reflect – as Kracauer insists – the "collective mentality" of a nation, the "superindividual" layer, much more directly than traditional arts. While it does not seem fruitful to regard the "poet" Hanns Heinz Ewers as the sole shaper of the film's design, it does make sense to bear in mind the contributions of the actor Paul Wegener. Like Ewers, Wegener was also interested in – as the title of his 1916 lecture indicates – "the artistic possibilities of film." In this speech he argues that film technique defines film content:

> Three years ago I turned for the first time to film, because I thought I had an idea which could not be realized in any other medium. I remembered seeing trick photographs in which a man plays cards with himself or a fraternity student duels against himself. I knew that could be done by splitting the image, and I said to myself that it must also be possible to film E. T. A. Hoffmann's fantasies of a *Doppelgänger* or mirror image, as if they were reality, and thus achieve effects which were not possible in any other art form. Thus, I hit upon the idea for *The Student of Prague* which Hanns Heinz Ewers gave filmic form.[12]

Wegener bases his choice of the double motif, of Hoffmann's story of mirror images, on the cinema's specific technical, trick, and montage capacities. Likewise his wish to play with mirror images indicates an aesthetic concern. The question left unstated by Wegener is: what does it mean for the art of the actor when he moves beyond the border of theater into film?

This question is taken up in Walter Benjamin's hallmark essay, "The work of art in the age of mechanical reproduction":

> The feeling of strangeness that overcomes the actor before the camera, as Pirandello describes it, is basically of the same kind as the estrangement felt before one's own image in the mirror. But now the reflected image has become separable, transportable. And where is it transported? Before the public. Never for a moment does the screen actor cease to be conscious of this fact.[13]

The film actor, writes Pirandello, becomes a phantom, a shadow, a disembodied figure present only in absence. The projector plays with the actor's shadow before the public.[14] The penchant for mirrors and shadows in German expressionist cinema is thus not simply a matter of the never completely forgotten "mysterious world" of German romanticism, in which – according to Eisner – "the German cinema found its true nature."[15] Nor is it merely a more direct expression of a national psyche and a reflection of social reality. It may also be based on production strategies which actors, confronted with the new medium, were forced to design. It thus stands as a metafilmic consideration. The recourse to the romantic motif was not simply provoked by film technique, but above and beyond that by film aesthetics.

The role of mirrors is a central concern in recent psychoanalytically oriented film theory. They are particularly germane in discussions of stars, but also in considerations of visual pleasure. Cinema satisfies voyeuristic and ego-bound desires. It grants a narcissistic pleasure, one that originates in the identification with the screen image. Just as a child in its early months perceives itself in a mirror, according to Lacan, as a more complete self, so too does an audience view certain presences on the screen as idealized selves. Film reactivates a child-like joy in experiencing mirrors. Freud claims that repressed experience is transformed from a positive to a negative recollection when it returns to consciousness. The choice of content in early silent films was an angst-laden mirror experience in fantastic and horror literature. Could educated burghers enjoy their regression in the "first German art film," because the screen's play freed them from a potentially threatening situation?

Rank argues that *The Student of Prague* reformulates a motif which is older than literary culture. It originates in an early, animistic phase of human development. Shadows and mirror images gain cohesive meaning in connection with narcissism, a stage in collective as well as individual child development. They act as a defense against danger. Narcissistic self-esteem is threatened by death and sexual love. Duplications of the self through shadows and mirrors represent, within the context of an animistic world view, a form of immortality, achieved through a division of the soul. Yet repressed experience resurfaces without fail in the repressor, transforming the symbolism of the other self: it becomes an angel of death. Rank cites the Dionysus myth (birth and rebirth of the god is connected to mirrors) and the Narcissus fable (unifying eros and thanatos), in order to document the *Doppelgänger*'s erotic importance. Examples of *Doppelgänger* are most prevalent in literature as a narcissistic defense against sexual love.

Repressed experience haunts the repressor, in the same way that the original mirror image as a narcissistic verification of the self turns into an object of fear and loathing. The context of fear is ambiguous; it arises both out of the threat of sexual love and out of sexual love threatened. In his analysis, Rank notes that Narcissus views his reflection ambiguously. However, an historical metareflection seems to be missing: literary culture is no longer caught in an historical stage of animistic world views and unbroken narcissism. It then becomes understandable why the meaning of narcissistic resistance is ambiguous. Is the *Doppelgänger* warding off the sexual love threatening his narcissism, or is his loving half attempting to rid itself of its narcissistic fixation?

The first explanation corresponds within a homosexual context to Oscar Wilde's *The Picture of Dorian Gray*. In the second explanation, Narcissus reappears with a vengeance, in literary representations of lost shadows and mirror images. The narcissistic self becomes a pursuer who stands in the way of the other half's romantic ties. Rank describes how the mirror image of the student in the 1913 film always turns up in erotic situations. Freud explains paranoia as a narcissistic fixation. Based on a guilt complex bound to this repressed fixation, all other reprehensible drives and desires are attributed to the *alter ego*. Balduin's mirror image thus reneges on his word of honor and kills a rival in a duel, despite the student's promise to leave the opponent unharmed.

The *Doppelgänger* in its literary configuration no longer accords with genuine narcissism; it represents an expression of an individual's inability to free himself from the narcissistic phase. Rank also accepts the interpretation presented in the press booklet for the film, namely that the *Doppelgänger* embodies the undetachable past of the student who has advanced overnight to the position of a castle owner. Suicide, then, must be understood as the only way Balduin can divest himself of that past, even though his narcissism hinders him one last time. While writing his suicide note, Balduin senses the *alter ego*'s presence behind him, turns around, and points a pistol at him. Suicide does not occur directly; it takes place as the murder of the hated, feared, and culpable *alter ego*.

Just as Rank does not discuss the changed situation of literature *vis-à-vis* myth, so too does he overlook the historical determinations behind the film. Although a comparison of myth and literature provides similarities and differences in the motif's embodiment, the film seems merely to reproduce literary patternings of the double, even if it surpasses literary prototypes in its clarity. This, however, is not quite the case. Doubles in literature invariably have to do with love, loneliness, and vanity, elements to be found in the film. An additional element in the film, though, is money. The first meeting between Balduin and the magician Scapinelli, centers on the student's financial woes. Half jokingly, half seriously, Scapinelli suggests that only a rich heiress can help him now. The fact that Balduin is enamored of the Count's daughter furthers Scapinelli's scheme. The devil's pact is not signed, however, until the student trades his mirror image for hard cash, the precondition for his becoming an acceptable suitor. In E. T. A. Hoffmann's story, Erasmus Spikher leaves his image with his mistress when he departs from her. If the threat of death is central to the double in its mythic dimension, and if in literature, on the other hand, erotic complications abound, it becomes in film a question of economic survival, with the libidinal component of narcissism simultaneously resurfacing.

Kracauer's reading of *The Student of Prague* as ''a dreamlike transcription of what the German middle class actually experienced in its relation to the feudal caste'' is too abstract. That is in part because he views the *Doppelgänger* state in a vacuum, without referring to its changing contexts. From romanticism to expressionism, this figure parallels the illusory opposition of the bourgeoisie in conflict with the aristocracy. Kracauer not only ignores the differences between filmic and literary traditions, but also, surprisingly, fails to refer to psychoanalytic models, even though they would support his thesis concerning the cinema's relationship to a socio-historical situation. The middle class under capitalism in 1913 suffered from continually worsening living conditions, which became an undeniable reality during and after World War I. Economic deterioration practically caused the petite bourgeoisie to slide down to the level of the proletariat. This led not only to diminished material security, but also to a loss of self-esteem. The inability to react realistically to this situation may be connected to a narcissistic fixation, which, reactivated as a threat from within, obscured external threats at a conscious level. The world view of the petite bourgeoisie, of grey-collar workers, prevented any form of solidarity with the working classes, while at the same time making its members susceptible to fascist *Führer* cults.

The film illustrates the psychic substructure of a threatening socio-political situation. Unconscious forces which systematically distort reality are objectified in this drama of narcissism. Educated, but with empty pockets, equipped with nothing more than the pride of a German fraternity brother, Balduin joins forces during an existential crisis with the conjurer,

Scapinelli. In Balduin's eyes, Scapinelli possesses magical powers, because he makes it possible for Balduin to climb the social ladder to the economic class in which the object of his love is at home. The dream of an aristocratic life comes true. New status, however, demands sacrificing old pride: Balduin is asked not to employ his superior swordsmanship in a duel. His *alter ego*, though, which he has disowned, but not shaken off, takes his place. The dream shatters, attempts at restoration result in a persecution complex. In the end fulfillment is only a certain step towards self-destruction.

The film is not a parable. Its meaning is not exhausted in a symbolic use of images. What does the film communicate by presenting this *Doppelgänger* story, using the language of acting, *mise-en-scène*, photography, and montage? Is the film's distance from the self-delusion of the middle class that of a tragic "prophet"? While the story centers on the problem of threatened self-preservation, the filmic means concentrate on the erotic components of narcissism. The film thus succumbs to the medium's affinity with a non-verbal language of eroticism. It is not merely a matter of sexism when a critic enthuses over "the unbelievably slender, beautiful, frisky legs of Lyda Salmonova." The gypsy Lyduschka impressively personifies the anarchy of carnal instincts. Dancing on a table, she exposes herself to the voyeuristic glances of the students, all the while hoping to impress the one at whose window she waits with flowers. She jealously trails her unresponsive loved one, climbs dexterously and nimbly up steep walls and over balconies, ducks behind columns, crouches at street corners, and invades private bedrooms. She jumps unnoticed onto the carriage of her rival and blocks her path on the way to a nightly rendezvous.

At one point a steep, narrow staircase, a sexual symbol *par excellence*, dominates the frame. Salmonova climbs the stairs in order to thwart the relationship between the social climber student and the Count's daughter. Rank rightfully points out that the gypsy woman serves as the Countess's mirror image. Just as Balduin's real mirror image symbolizes his repressed narcissistically loved ego, so too can Lyduschka be viewed as a *Doppel-gänger*, i.e. as the Countess's repressed sexuality. "I want your love, not your money," says Lyduschka, thus differentiating between herself and her rival, after again approaching Balduin who has been rejected by the aristo-cratic family. The Countess is a pale figure, an actress caught in theatrical conventions. In contrast to Salmonova's expressive body movement, Grete Berger's acting appears awkward and exaggerated.

The free-floating erotic energy embodied by Lyduschka is forbidden in social interaction, degraded like the shadow following her. Balduin ignores her, but becomes inflamed by the unreachable Countess. The film's subject then is not eroticism, but rather its impeding. The breakdown of love through narcissistic fixation creates images: the lovers wander among weed-covered gravestones, vestiges of an old religion. As they finally pause, swaying towards each other for a kiss, the lost mirror image suddenly

Plate 1 Shadowed by the double: one interrupted tryst among many in *The Student of Prague*. Photo courtesy of Stiftung Deutsche Kinemathek.

appears on the other side of a grave, staring silently and motionlessly. The Countess flees. The specter dissolves just as the exasperated Balduin angrily tries to grab it. Another scene: the desperate Balduin steals into the Countess's bedroom at night, throws himself at her feet and implores her to save him from the curse. She lifts him up and kisses him, but a new and final breakdown follows. The Countess faints twice; first, after she and her lover step in front of a mirror, revealing her loneliness rather than her happiness; and a second time after seeing Balduin's mirror image appear suddenly and threateningly at the balcony door: the double stalks her lover rather than her. She capitulates. For Balduin there is no longer any escape. At the mercy of his repressed narcissism, he flees through narrow streets, up and down the stairs of old Prague, searching open terrain, but his *alter ego* turns up everywhere, silent and motionless. His persecution complex bursts forth.

Wegener has no real erotic appeal, neither the subtle flair of Albert Bassermann, nor the obsessive intensity of Fritz Kortner, to name two Reinhardt players who also acted in films. Half child, half domineering master, Wegener in fact projects a narcissistic-macho vitality. He shows off by fencing in front of a mirror. "The best fencer in Prague," without equal apart from himself: "My adversary is my mirror image," a metaphor for the ambivalence of Narcissus towards his ego, antagonism through self-confirmation. If ostentatiousness were all Wegener had to offer, then only his exotic physiognomy would have made him interesting in fantasy films.

Plate 2   "My adversary is my mirror image." The horror of the uncanny as Balduin (Paul Wegener) faces himself. Photo courtesy of Stiftung Deutsche Kinemathek.

Yet he is also capable of something special. He can take on the opposite of self-assured, egocentric appearances and become silent, accusingly sad, a creature excluded from love and life. *The Golem* (*Der Golem*, 1914) and *The Golem: How He Came into the World* (*Der Golem: Wie er in die Welt kam*, 1920), films co-directed by Wegener (with Henrik Galeen and Carl Boese, respectively) after *The Student of Prague*, present this pathos in a monstrous form. Balduin's *alter ego*, his mirror image, cowers behind a column like a hunchback, or like a fairytale frog waiting futilely for his princely redemption. Balduin, the master of the castle, meanwhile dances under the arches, triumphant and in love. At the end the *alter ego* languishes similarly at the grave of Balduin, the former "best fencer in Prague." Even after Balduin's mirror image returns from the duel with a bloodied foil, he does not seem malicious, merely deeply helpless. Through static gestures and mimicry, Wegener manages to play his mirror image, moving far beyond the accomplishments of trick photography. Double exposures and superimpositions only create the conditions which allow the actor to express eroticism's negation in "the one and only and his property."

After World War I, film theorists expressed the hope that cinematic language might become one of eroticism, with a socialist revolution creating the preconditions for such a cinema. In *The Student of Prague*, the confrontation between the would-be *Herrenmensch* and his dehumanized mirror image brought bourgeois cinema to the limits of its expressive possibilities. The final words of Musset's "La Nuit de Décembre," quoted twice at different points in the film, are those of the double sitting on the grave: "Je suis la solitude." The film does not go beyond this literary expression of the middle class's dilemma, its flight into a realm of insularity and isolation. *The Student of Prague*, however, staged this drama of bourgeois individualism in a forum accessible not only to the middle class, but to a mass public.

The uncanny, according to Freud, is the result of resurfaced repression, a narcissistic phase of human development which still persists as an animistic world view. More than just a mere effect of horror, the intimation of the fantastic as something real gains its power when something from that past seems to exist in the here and now. Literature, by dint of its fictional nature, can only produce the effect of horror by first creating the illusion of everyday reality. In the Berlin pubs and middle-class residences of E. T. A. Hoffmann's tales, transformations suddenly take place. A door knob in *The Golden Pot* becomes the grinning face of a market wench; the archivist Lindhorst turns into a grey and white vulture. Nonetheless, the writer never loses track of his realistic setting. No sooner has Dapertutto disappeared in a "stinking fog" (in *The Story of the Lost Reflection*) after a foiled devil's pact, than the scene changes and Erasmus Spikher stands in his conjugal bedroom, his wife nagging him:

> "Please look in the mirror over there, my dear good man!" Spikher looked, shaking all over with a fairly wretched look on his face. The mirror remained empty and clear, no Erasmus Spikher gazed back. "This time," his wife continued, "it's a good thing that the mirror doesn't reflect your image, because you look quite ridiculous, dear Erasmus. You probably realize yourself that without a reflection you will become a laughing stock, and that you can't be a respectable father who enjoys the respect of wife and children. Rasmushen is already laughing at you and wants to draw a moustache on your face with coal, which you won't even notice. So wander about a bit in the world and try occasionally to steal your mirror image from the devil. When you have it, you are welcome to come back."[16]

Such irony thus brings the reader back to pragmatic concerns. Ewers was correct in rejecting comical interludes in the film, an idea which was suggested to him.[17] His means of mitigating the fantastic are different.

It takes no special effort for the cinema to create the illusion of reality, other than to emphasize the documentary quality of the camera. The filmmakers refrained from building sets around Balduin and his *Doppelgänger*. Instead they sought out real locations which seemed to suit their fantastic undertaking: the old city of Prague with its narrow alleys, stairs, and arches, the medieval Jewish cemetery (reconstructed in a natural forest), the Hradčin,

Prague's palaces and villas and the surrounding countryside. The film is lavish in its use of location shots: for example, the hunt. Again and again the camera searches out riders and dogs on wooded trails, in open fields, along the banks of a pond. The scene manages to create interest solely through its images of reality, instead of through plot-motivated suspense. The old Jewish cemetery is filmed just as intriguingly. The film's real charm lies in its opening up of reality, making us receptive to the uncanny. The opening scene in the beer garden with the boisterous students is broadly drawn. Suddenly, a carriage pulls up, for a moment separating Balduin, in the foreground, from his colleagues. The carriage moves on. The image seems restored, but a thin, grey man with a top hat and pointed nose remains behind. He sits down opposite Balduin: the uncanny has arrived.

If photography offers a world devoid of subjective and projected meaning, as Kracauer once suggested,[18] if it demythicizes, then the cinema can achieve an uncanny effect *par excellence* by inserting subjective images of an animistic world view into photographic reproductions of reality, e.g. by making a mirror image become the image of a soul. The film in this way connects a despiritualized world to its forsaken primeval past.

The 1926 version of *The Student of Prague* avoids this confrontation. Despite a large budget (200,000 RM), the direction of Galeen, and the excellent acting of Conrad Veidt and Werner Krauss, the remake accomplished nothing more than to reaffirm the quality of its predecessor, whose virtues are, first, a depiction of narcissistic fixation which reflects the socio-political dilemma of the German middle class; second, its presentation of impeded eroticism; and, finally, its portrayal of the uncanny by blending realistic and fantastic elements. What transpired in the 1926 remake does, however, deserve some brief note.

The representation of the double no longer communicates a projection or even the appearance of subjective mania, because Veidt plays his role as mirror image all too independently. The precise logic of narcissistic fixation gives way to mere straining for effects. The mirror image no longer inheres as an object of love–hate bound up in the past (replete with student cap and jacket), but rather appears as Mr Balduin, who opens the castle door for his disturbed master. When Balduin flees to his former student quarters, the dust-covered furniture and broken windows exude a sense of penury and desperation. Economic survival becomes more crucial a consideration than in the first version. Material exigency has to do with Jewish profiteers. Scapinelli appears as a ruthless skinflint who carefully counts a huge pile of money, coin by coin, in what amounts to unabashed anti-Semitic propaganda. Werner Krauss is convincing in the role by virtue of his expressive body movement. The remake reserves for him a big scene where he controls a boar hunt with his magical powers.

The expansion of Scapinelli's role, however, militates against the mirror thematics. The motif is similarly de-emphasized by no longer having

Plate 3   Conrad Veidt in a diminished version of *The Student of Prague* from 1926. (Yet another remake was to follow in 1935 directed by Arthur Robison.) Photo courtesy of Stiftung Deutsche Kinemathek.

Lyduschka function as a female *Doppelgänger*. At times it is in fact Scapinelli who interrupts romantic encounters. His huge shadow wipes a compromising note from the balcony into the hands of Lyduschka. Erotic tension is weakened, because Lyduschka appears now as a sweet girl with neat curls who may well be able to swing her legs over a wall, but who cannot master more difficult acrobatic tasks. She is a jealous and weak rival; eroticism in general is denigrated to a ripe play of tormented renunciation and refusal. Nothing remains of the subtle visualization of instincts and their rampant extremes. Wegener's mirror image, a motionless, deeply sad creature, becomes in Veidt's portrayal a somnambulistic apparition. Cesare returns, an extension of Scapinelli/Caligari, rather than Balduin's *Doppelgänger*. The repressed, narcissistic ego becomes the subconscious, controlled by foreign and magical powers.

The uncanny has thus sunk to the level of penny dreadfuls; the tension between realism and fantasy is lost. Most of the film was shot in the studio. The sets appear heavy and pompous: high rooms with satin curtains, overbearing chandeliers hanging from the ceiling. The medallion as a love-token becomes a cross, a prop straight out of Gothic novels. The quotation from de Musset disappears, as does the reflection on the self-acknowledged despair and isolation of the bourgeois. Only a frightening perspective of self-destruction persists. In 1926, after the stabilization of the Weimar Republic, *The Student of Prague* amounted to an opportunistic exercise in a fashionable fatalism.

Translated from the German by Jan-Christopher Horak

Notes

1. See "Hanns Heinz Ewers während der Nazizeit. Erinnerungen von Josephine Ewers," in Michael Sennewald, *Hanns Heinz Ewers. Phantastik und Jugendstil* (Maisenhain am Glan: Hain, 1973), p. 204.
2. Hanns Heinz Ewers, "Anfänge des Films," in Ludwig Greve, Margot Pehle, and Heidi Westhoff (eds), *Hätte ich das Kino! Die Schriftsteller und der Stummfilm* (Stuttgart: Klett, 1976), p. 106.
3. Cf. Bernd Kortländer, "Vom *Studenten von Prag* zu *Horst Wessel* — Hanns Heinz Ewers und der Film," in *Düsseldorf Kinematographisch. Beiträge zur Filmgeschichte* (Düsseldorf: Triltsch, 1982), pp. 137–8, 140.
4. Alfred Richard Meyer, writing in the periodical *Die Bücherei Maiandros*, quoted in *Hätte ich das Kino!*, p. 111.
5. Quoted in Kortländer, p. 140.
6. Lotte H. Eisner, *The Haunted Screen*, trans. Roger Greaves (Berkeley: University of California Press, 1969), p. 109.
7. Siegfried Kracauer, *From Caligari to Hitler: A Psychological History of the German Film* (Princeton: Princeton University Press, 1947), p. 30.
8. Otto Rank, "Der Doppelgänger," *Imago* (1914), 98.
9. ibid., 101.

10. ibid., 97.

11. ibid., 134.

12. Paul Wegener, "Die künstlerischen Möglichkeiten des Films" (1916), in *Paul Wegener und seine Rollen: Ein Buch von ihm und über ihn*, ed. Kai Möller (Reinbek: Rowohlt, 1954), p. 110.

13. Walter Benjamin, "The work of art in the age of mechanical reproduction," in *Illuminations*, ed. Hannah Arendt, trans. Harry Zohn (New York: Schocken, 1969), pp. 230–1.

14. ibid., p. 229.

15. Eisner, p. 17.

16. *E. T. A. Hoffmann: Werke in 4 Bänden*, ed. Herbert Kraft and Manfred Wacker (Frankfurt am Main: Insel, 1967), I, 231–2.

17. See Kortländer, p. 146.

18. Siegfried Kracauer, "Die Photographie," in *Das Ornament der Masse*, ed. Karsten Witte (Frankfurt am Main: Suhrkamp, 1977), pp. 21–39.

Script

Der Student von Prag. Ed. Helmut H. Diederichs. Stuttgart: Fischer, Kress, Wiedlroither, 1985.

Selected Bibliography

Brennicke, Ilona and Joe Hembus. *Klassiker des deutschen Stummfilms 1910–1930*. Munich: Goldmann, 1983.

Eisner, Lotte H. *The Haunted Screen*. Trans. Roger Greaves. Berkeley: University of California Press, 1969.

Elsaesser, Thomas. "Social mobility and the fantastic: German silent cinema." *Wide Angle*, 5, No. 2 (1982), 14–25.

Greve, Ludwig, Margot Pehle, and Heidi Westhoff (eds). *Hätte ich das Kino! Die Schriftsteller und der Stummfilm*. Stuttgart: Klett, 1976.

Kaes, Anton (ed.). *Kino-Debatte. Texte zum Verhältnis von Literatur und Film 1909–1929*. Tübingen: Niemeyer, 1978.

Kortländer, Bernd. "Vom *Studenten von Prag* zu *Horst Wessel* – Hanns Heinz Ewers und der Film." In *Düsseldorf Kinematographisch. Beiträge zur Filmgeschichte*. Düsseldorf: Triltsch, 1982, pp. 137–48.

Kracauer, Siegfried. *From Caligari to Hitler: A Psychological History of the German Film*. Princeton: Princeton University Press, 1947.

Möller, Kai (ed.). *Paul Wegener und seine Rollen. Ein Buch von ihm und über ihn*. Reinbek: Rowohlt, 1954.

Rank, Otto. *The Double: A Psychological Study*. Trans. and ed. Harry Tucker Jr. Chapel Hill, NC: University of North Carolina Press, 1971.

Sennewald, Michael. *Hanns Heinz Ewers. Phantastik und Jugendstil*. Maisenhain am Glan: Hain, 1973.

Wegner, Hart L. "Literary influences on the earliest expressionist film: *Der Student von Prag*." *Philological Papers*, 26 (August 1980), 1–6.

2

JUDITH MAYNE

Dracula in the twilight: Murnau's *Nosferatu* (1922)

Were it not for the actual acknowledgment of Bram Stoker's 1897 novel *Dracula* in the credits, it might be easy to forget that F. W. Murnau's film *Nosferatu* has any direct connection to a literary source. Stoker's novel has been the most influential literary version of the vampire legend, but because that legend is so well-known, one tends to discount the importance of this particular novel for the first screen version of Dracula's tale.

Is anything to be gained from an analysis of *Nosferatu* as an *adaptation* of the Stoker novel? Some of the temptation to dismiss a comparison between the two texts has less to do with this particular novel and this particular film than with the limitations of adaptation analysis itself. Critics of film adaptations of literary works may no longer insist, again and again, that "the novel (or play) was better," but the very notion of source (sacred or otherwise) and adaptation (faithful or not) is problematic. Many film adaptations have been little more than illustrated comic-book versions of the classics. But even more complex and sophisticated adaptations are evaluated more often than not according to how certain scenes and techniques were "translated" into film language. It is as if literature provides the unquestioned master code for which cinematic equivalents must be found.

That literature has a central place in the history of the cinema, and of the classical cinema in particular, is certain. But it is precisely the historical perspective which is so often lacking in the study of adaptations. By "historical perspective" I mean some obvious questions – why certain kinds of works were adapted at certain periods in film history, for example, or how the turn to literary sources was often an attempt to attract middle-class audiences to movie theaters, thus giving the cinema a certain legitimacy. An historical perspective on the relationship between literature and film also suggests that the relationship between two texts, one literary and one cinematic, is a dynamic encounter rather than a static rendering of a story line from one medium to another.

It could be argued that the acknowledgment of Stoker in Henrik Galeen's screenplay is more strategic than substantial. The acknowledgment might well be a gesture of legitimation, an identification with a literary source so as to validate Murnau's own contribution to the development of an art cinema.[1] The problem with such a view, however, is that Bram Stoker is not an author one immediately associates with such validation. When an American producer like David O. Selznick turns to an author like Charles Dickens, the validative strategy is clear. Stoker, however, is more of an anomaly in nineteenth-century fiction, and many of the features of *Dracula* – its Gothic themes, its epistolary form – are characteristic of earlier periods of literary history. Praise of the novel as a literary gem seems to require a certain defensiveness. One critic describes this anomalous status of *Dracula*: "The book appeared in 1897, at the height of literary Realism and Naturalism. Had it been written in 1820, I suspect that it would have been hailed, as *Frankenstein* is, as a Romantic milestone."[2] Perhaps Stoker was less a romantic cast out in a sea of realists and naturalists than he was symptomatic of changes taking place in the very scope and function of narrative. The sheer number of film versions of *Dracula* do not necessarily attest to some fundamental affinity between Stoker's handling of the vampire legend and the nature and appeal of the cinema. Yet that *Dracula* was published in 1897, during the very years that the cinema was emerging, may well be, as the saying goes, "no coincidence." Stoker provides Murnau not only with a source for the film version of *Dracula*, but also with a set of reflections and meditations on the very nature of story-telling itself. There are numerous suggestions, in Murnau's film, that the vampire story as it is plotted in Stoker's novel is not just being transformed, but commented upon as well.

Dracula may be divided into three major parts, each focusing on Dracula's relationship to a victim. In the first section, Jonathan Harker has traveled from England to Transylvania to make a real-estate transaction with the Count. His experiences in the bizarre castle are described in his journal and in his correspondence with his fiancée Mina. Jonathan is attacked by the vampire, and in addition he encounters three female vampires, part of the Count's "family," who are anxious to make Jonathan their victim as well. The second part of the novel takes place in England where the Count has now purchased his house. Here the major voices of the novel are Mina, her friend Lucy, and Dr Seward, a rejected suitor of Lucy, who is director of an insane asylum. Lucy becomes Dracula's next victim. Dr Van Helsing is brought in to assist the group of men – including Jonathan, Dr Seward, and Lucy's fiancé – in destroying the vampire. Lucy herself becomes a vampire and preys on children.

The Count's attacks on Jonathan and Lucy presage what is to come in the final section of the novel, in which Mina becomes his next intended victim. Van Helsing and the group of men now involved in the case successfully destroy the vampire and save Mina. Mina returns to her normal way of life, and Jonathan, by this time Mina's husband, informs us in an epilogue that the couple had a son and lived happily ever after.

These three sections of the novel correspond to the progressive stages of the central conflict of *Dracula*, which is not between Dracula and his victims, but rather between Dracula and Van Helsing. The struggle is between two different cultures and two different orders: between good and evil, between the forces of civilization and the forces of nature, between reason and passion. And the contested terrain, on every count, is the body of the woman, Mina. The structure of *Dracula* is a striking illustration of what is commonly referred to as classical narrative. Order is restored by the victory of the good patriarchal figure. The object of struggle, the woman's body, returns to its "normal" functions of marriage and child-bearing, while the husband Jonathan implicitly assumes the patriarchal role of Van Helsing (even though he does so in a way that is nondescript).

The manner in which Stoker and Murnau plot and resolve their material is quite different, but both work within a similar field of oppositions. Attention is drawn in both the novel and the film to the excessive contrasts which construct these fictional universes. In the opening pages of the novel, the opposition between east and west establishes a geography, as it were, for the oppositions which will develop in the course of the novel: good versus evil, science versus mysticism, and so on. So too does the beginning of Murnau's film suggest a field of oppositions, with Jonathan and Nina (Mina becomes Nina in the American print of Murnau's film) first seen within a tranquil context of domesticated nature denoted by flowers and kittens, soon contrasted with the wild and barbaric nature associated with Nosferatu.

Now *Dracula* and *Nosferatu* can hardly be singled out for their reliance on a set of binary oppositions – these are, after all, rather classic oppositions in western literature and film. What does seem particular to these texts, however, and perhaps to the art of horror in general, is the obsession not only with oppositions, but with the hypothetical area between opposing terms. In the opening pages of *Dracula*, for instance, Jonathan speaks of the twilight, and of the "great masses of greyness" characteristic of Transylvania.[3] The fascination which Count Dracula holds might have less to do with his incarnation of evil than with the impossibility of categorizing him according to dualistic categories of thought. Central to both *Dracula* and *Nosferatu*, then, is a dangerous territory where opposing terms are not so easily distinguishable.

The basic material of Stoker's novel is present in Murnau's film, if plotted differently. We begin in Germany (rather than England) where Jonathan's employer Renfield (a conflation of the realtor and the madman in the novel) sends him away to arrange for Nosferatu's purchase of a house. Jonathan's trip is represented in the film, and after a brief stay in the castle (where he also becomes the vampire's victim), his return to Germany is shown at some length, alongside of the Count's simultaneous journey on board a ship where all of the crew members are killed, one by one. With the arrival of the Count in Germany, a plague erupts. Jonathan's wife Nina puts an end to the plague by sacrificing herself. Having read in *The Book of the Vampires* that the vampire will perish if a pure woman spends the night with him, she does so. At the conclusion of the film, Nosferatu vanishes into thin air, and Nina dies. Much more so than the novel, the film is concerned with that hypothetical area between west and east, between the land of reason and the land of passion, between self and other. The sheer amount of screen time devoted to passage, to voyage, suggests precisely the central function of the space "between" in the film. Whereas the novel, by its conclusion, dispels any possibility of an identity between opposing terms, the film remains, almost resolutely, in that twilight.

Murnau's stress on that twilight area emerges from a rereading of Stoker's novel. To speak of *Nosferatu* simply as an adaptation does not do justice to this process of rereading. More suggestive are the terms proposed by the Russian formalist Boris Eikhenbaum in a 1926 essay on the relationship between film and literature:

Cinema is not simply a moving picture, but a special photographic language. This language, in all its "naturalism," does not materialise literature as theatre does. What results, rather, is something analogous to a dream: a person approaches; now you see only the eyes, now the hands – then everything disappears – another person – a window – a street, and so on. Just as if, having read a novel, you saw it in a dream.[4]

That there are important analogies between film and dreams has been argued in film theory and criticism, and perhaps certain transformations of literary sources are particularly well described through the language of the dream work.[5] Specifically, the changes which most set *Nosferatu* apart from Stoker's novel appear to be the result of a process of displacement, not unlike that dream mechanism whereby disturbing associations are stripped of their intensity.

Two such displacements occur in *Nosferatu*. First, Van Helsing is in no way the protagonist of the film. Instead of a conflict between two patriarchal figures, we have an encounter between a man and a woman. The vampire is destroyed, but so is the woman – there is no happy ending here. Yet Van Helsing is not eliminated from the film. His role is, rather, purely metaphoric: he is shown giving a lecture on carnivorous plants. Second, any trace of female vampirism is erased from the film. In Stoker's novel, the presence of female vampires – the three women at Dracula's castle, Lucy after her initiation, and even Mina for a brief time – allows the opposition between good and evil to take the specifically female form of a conflict between chastity and sexuality. It is through vampirism that female sexuality is represented in the novel. Here, for instance, is how Jonathan describes the approach of one of the female vampires:

The girl went on her knees, and bent over me, simply gloating. There was a deliberate voluptuousness which was both thrilling and repulsive, and as she arched her neck she actually licked her lips like an animal, till I could see in the moonlight the moisture shining on the scarlet lips and on the red tongue as it lapped the white sharp teeth. Lower and lower went her head as the lips went below the range of my mouth and chin and seemed to fasten on my throat.[6]

At first sight, the erasure – or censorship – of female vampirism with its attendant implications seems much more absolute than what happens to Van Helsing. However, there is an ambivalence in the representation of Nina.

In a famous scene which occurs early in the film, images of Jonathan being attacked by Nosferatu alternate with images of Nina, at home in her bedroom, suddenly awake. A title informs us that Nina sensed the danger to her husband. Yet in this alternation between the vampire's castle and the Harker home, an eyeline match between the vampire and Nina suggests not only Nosferatu's attraction to Nina, but her own arousal as well. In Stoker's novel, the poles of attraction and repulsion are confused in Jonathan's

Plate 4 Nina's two "husbands" (Max Schreck and Gustav von Wangenheim) scrutinize her image. "Is this your wife? What a lovely throat!" Photo courtesy of Stiftung Deutsche Kinemathek.

reaction to the three women vampires. In *Nosferatu* the poles are also confused, albeit more subtly, in Nina's reaction to the vampire. The ambivalence is more pronounced later in the film, when Jonathan (and Nosferatu) are about to return. Robin Wood describes the scene as follows:

> The two men are exactly paralleled as Nina's two husbands; Nina sits by the shore . . . looking out to sea, ostensibly for Jonathan, whose mode of travel is by land; in the sleepwalking scene she exclaims "He is coming! I must go to meet him!" after a shot, not of Jonathan, but of the vampire's ship.[7]

These two key elements, Van Helsing and female vampirism, are not simply "left out" of the film version of the novel – there are many elements which are omitted, for whatever reasons. These are elements which are, rather, displaced, and hence reworked in such a way as to be enormously significant for the film as a whole. That Van Helsing appears at all in Murnau's film, and in such a purely metaphoric way, suggests that the forces of science, reason, and civilization can no longer successfully wage battles against the Draculas of the world, but exist only to give illustrated lectures. In the novel *Dracula*, narrative closure can still be achieved through the positive force of a figure like Van Helsing. However, the fact that such a colorless and drab figure as Jonathan Harker is designated as van Helsing's successor could be read easily as a weakness within that narrative coherence. Murnau seizes upon that weakness in his rereading of *Dracula* as an encounter between male and female.

What then happens to the representation of woman in this encounter? The disappearance of female vampirism suggests that the dichotomy which characterizes the representation of female sexuality in the novel is replaced, in the film, by a profound ambivalence – stressing, again, the "twilight" which characterizes *Nosferatu* as a whole. As is the case of the function of Van Helsing, female vampirism can be read as a weak link in the novel. As Robin Wood points out: "It is the woman that the work is really about." In the second half of the novel, it is Mina who is central, with Dracula appearing very rarely.[8]

Whenever we speak of binary oppositions, we refer above all to a separation between the self and the other, and it is precisely that separation which is closed in Murnau's rendering of the novel. This is ultimately a reading against the grain of the novel, attentive to those symptoms that reveal "otherness" as not so easily separable after all. One might ask then what perspective informs this reading against the grain. Here we encounter another problem, peculiar not to adaptation analysis but to many German films of the 1920s. Siegfried Kracauer's reading of German cinema in *From Caligari to Hitler*[9] has so overdetermined reception of a film like *Nosferatu* that it has become almost *too* simple to understand the guiding perspective of Murnau's reading of Stoker. If Van Helsing is reduced to pure decoration, and if sexual dichotomy becomes sexual ambivalence, the rationale must be the obsession with tyrants and evil that – according to Kracauer – so possessed the German imagination. Thus Murnau takes the conventions of an essentially Victorian novel and turns them upside down to portray a world obsessed with dark, omnipotent forces which form an integral part of our so-called rational universe. It would appear from this vantage point that Murnau's adaptation of *Dracula* amounts to so much superstructure built upon the base of German angst.[10]

A critique of Kracauer's notion of film as a barometer of collective fears and fantasies is beyond the scope of this essay. In any case, one could argue for a Kracaueresque reading of *Nosferatu*, particularly if one's inquiry is defined by reflection theory – however simple or sophisticated. To address historically the relationship between film and literature does not mean simply re-creating the dominant panorama of given ages. Such an engagement requires, in the case of *Nosferatu*, exploration not only of how Dracula is so easily shaped by the context of Weimar Germany, but also of how the very substance of a novel like Stoker's responds so directly to our very conception of the cinema.

Along these lines of inquiry, Eikhenbaum's suggestion that in a filmic adaptation we see a novel as if in a dream, is again useful. Central to the dream analogy is the relationship between a subject and discourse – between, that is, the organizing intelligence of a text and the modes through which it is revealed, such as point of view and perspective. In other words, the issue of *narration* is crucial in the transformation of *Dracula* into a film. Here the characteristic of *Dracula* which is most striking is its epistolary structure. The use of journals and letters to create multiple points of view is unique in Stoker's novel, for this predominantly eighteenth-century literary form is coupled with a nineteenth-century technological imagination. Both Jonathan and Mina keep their journals in shorthand, and write to each other in shorthand as well. They share a secret code, suggesting intimacy, but it is a curiously efficient and machine-like form of intimacy. When Mina writes in her journal, ''I am anxious, and it soothes me to express myself here: it is like whispering to one's self and listening at the same time,'' we can easily imagine ourselves in the company of many an eighteenth-century heroine who has retired to the closet. But Mina then continues: ''And there is also something about the shorthand symbols that makes it different from writing.''[11] *Different* from writing: Mina describes a tension in language, between self-expression and imposition of a code, which parallels the overall tension in the novel between opposing terms.

Surely the most unusual voice in the novel is that of Dr Seward, director of the insane asylum. For Seward's journal is kept on phonograph records! On the one hand, the function of the phonograph is to give a certain naturalism to the voice of the doctor. But more important, the phonograph suggests, even more strongly than the shorthand used by Jonathan and Mina, a technological arsenal at the disposal of this narrator. Herein lies one of the supreme ironies of the novel. No matter how refined and complex the technological means might be, they fail to elucidate the enigma of Dracula.

There is, in *Dracula*, a problem of narration. For all their obsessive recording and interpretation of what is going on around them, these narrators cannot put the pieces together. The differing points of view on the Count's invasion are first presented in the novel in a relatively isolated way, but as the plot thickens, the characters read each other's diaries in their attempt to decipher the phenomenon of Dracula. The final showdown with the Count is prepared by piecing together all the diaries, as well as a variety of documents, concerning, for example, the sale of the house. Dr Seward observes that the goal of such a collation is the emergence of a "whole connected narrative." The assumption is that a story must be told, that the various fragments must connect, that a narrative structure and coherence must be achieved before any direct battle with the vampire can be initiated. Narrative is, then, the supreme form of understanding in the novel.

The emergence of the "whole connected narrative" is also riddled with ironies. The men decide that it will be better for all concerned if Mina does not participate in their plans. What they do not realize at first is that Mina is quickly becoming Dracula's next victim. Mina travels, let us say, the distance separating the world of these men from the world of Dracula. As a result, she has more of a finely tuned narrative intelligence, and is able to interpret more successfully the facts which the men have compiled about their enemy.[12]

The epistolary technique of *Dracula* assures that the vampire remains the object of knowledge, even if an elusive one.[13] Hence the distinction between subject and object remains fixed and absolute. The distinction is also one of speech and writing. For the narrators of *Dracula*, with their shorthand and their phonographs, all seek to make their writing as direct an imitation as possible of direct speech. Of Dracula, however, it is pointed out very early in the novel that his knowledge of the English language – the speech of the text – comes only from books. Yet that Mina, who is a bridge between the two poles of the novel, should emerge as the most clever of story-tellers is a sign that even the distance between subject and object is not as great as the triumphant conclusion of the novel would lead us to believe.

It seems to me a mistake, however, to conclude that Mina therefore emerges as the central narrator within the novel, as the authoritative narrative voice. There is, rather, a single *technique* which allows Mina and the men to solve the mystery. That technique is hypnosis. When Van Helsing hypnotizes Mina, she reveals information about her seduction by the Count which later, in a conscious state and with the assistance of Van Helsing, she interprets. The argument could thus be made that it is Van Helsing, as hypnotist, who is the supreme narrative authority in the novel. More important, it seems to me, is that a process beyond the realm of discursive language is required to complete the story, to solve the problem of narration that is posed in the novel.

The assemblage of first-person narrations in *Dracula* means that there are several narrators, yet one – Van Helsing – emerges as the most authoritative. Thus the narrating intelligence of the novel is, if not reducible or identical to the point of view of Van Helsing, then at least aligned with it. A fundamental difference between narrative in film and the novel concerns just this relationship between narrator and narrating intelligence. In film, narration need not be – indeed, most often is not – identified with any particular narrator. Now at first glance, *Nosferatu* seems to simplify the epistolary structure of the novel by maintaining the device of a narrational journal, but from only one person's point of view. Titles at the beginning of the film are ostensible reproductions of the journal of the city scribe, Johann Cavallius: "From the diary of Johann Cavallius, able historian of his native city of Bremen: NOSFERATU! That name alone can chill the blood! NOSFERATU! Was it he who brought the plague to Bremen in 1838?" This narrator is more or less the equivalent of an omniscient point of view, since he is not a character within the film, and supposedly recounts the story of Nosferatu with all the salient details intact. This narration appears only in written titles, along with snippets of dialogue. There is not really a visual point of view which can be called that of the narrator, unless it be the high-angle long shot of the city which opens the film. The role of this narrator is defined, then, primarily in terms of language.

Now there is nothing particularly striking about the function of this narration; indeed, it is quite conventional. The narrator's interventions are more than conventional, however; they are so literal as to be uninsightful. The kind of information he provides – informing us why the vampire always travelled with coffins of earth, for instance – is not exactly useless, but not particularly pertinent either. The narrator almost always intervenes in those passages of the film where cross-cutting creates strong thematic and visual associations. We have discussed the scene, early in the film, where images of Jonathan being approached by the vampire in his castle alternate with images of Nina, awakened suddenly in the night. There is a moment of intense identification between Nina and the vampire. But the narrator comments only on the literal significance of the scene – that Nina was aware of a threat to her husband's well-being.

The narrator intervenes in a similar way when Dr Van Helsing is introduced. Given the purely metaphoric function of Van Helsing, this is perhaps the only moment in the film where some kind of introduction is necessary to assure narrative coherence. An alternation occurs between Van Helsing lecturing, and Renfield catching flies in his cell at the asylum. The narrator may be said to introduce the analogy between vampirism in the plant world and in the human world. But as in the previous scene, he fails to comment on any of the more subtle analogies. For each scene contains point-of-view shots from the perspective of the scientist as well as the madman. Hence an affinity is implied between the scientist and the madman in terms of the looks they bring to bear on their objects of study, and passion, respectively. That affinity, that identification, is not unlike the pull between Nosferatu and Nina suggested, also by cross-cutting, in the previous scene.

Something happens on screen, then, that eludes the written commentary of the narrator. The figure of the narrator is pulled in two directions. He represents narration, of course; and he also represents written language. There is, in *Nosferatu* as well as in *Dracula*, a problem of narration. Here, the problem of narration is also a failure of language. Within the fictional universe of the film, language is as limited as it is in the narrator's commentary. Jonathan sees the marks of the vampire on his throat when he looks at himself in a mirror, but neither *The Book of the Vampires* nor the letter he writes to Nina can decipher them. Officials turn to the log of the ship to seek some explanation of the similar marks on the neck of the ship's captain, but the mystery of Nosferatu still eludes them. Language is limited, that is, until Nina reads *The Book of the Vampires*. Suddenly the language of books, of the written text, has become endowed with narrative potency. How, then, has this problem of narration been resolved?

In silent film, written titles represent one possible form of narration, among many others. Narration is understood most often in film in visual terms, for obvious reasons. We often equate, in fact, point of view as a narrative device with the camera eye. If the first image following the titles of *Nosferatu* – the high-angle long shot of the city – suggests that definition of narration, with the eye of the camera imitating somehow the omniscient text of the narrator, the images which follow trace another conception of narration in the cinema. Nina and Jonathan are presented in turn – from the very start, one notes that cross-cutting, here in a more restrained spatial environment than later in the film, is the primary narrative mode of the film. Cross-cutting only becomes narration when a specific relationship is articulated. That relationship is defined in terms of differing perceptions of the screen surface. We first see Jonathan in front of a mirror, a window at his side. We first see Nina through a window, as she plays with a kitten. The frames of these images will be significant as the film progresses. Jonathan will gaze into a mirror as he attempts to comprehend the bite marks on his neck. He cannot comprehend them, indicating, as does the mirror, a failure of recognition in general. Indeed, the mirror is a dominant motif throughout *Nosferatu*, and is a form taken by the theme of the double underscored by Lotte Eisner in her discussion of this and other films of the period.[14]

In virtually all of the scenes involving cross-cutting, a mirror effect is established. For the identification between Nina and the vampire, between Van Helsing and Renfield, is a mirror effect; and, more important, is a form of narration in which *surface* is key: the screen as mirror surface, the film

Plate 5 Gazing into the mirror: Jonathan Harker meets his double under the arches – the return of the repressed. Photo courtesy of Stiftung Deutsche Kinemathek.

as projection. Nosferatu indeed functions as a mirror for all of the characters in the film. In this sense he is a narrating presence within the film. Only Renfield and Nina recognize themselves in the mirror of Nosferatu. Thus, prior to the conclusion of the film, cross-cutting links the demise of Renfield, escaped from the asylum and caught by the townspeople, with Nina's decision, after reading *The Book of the Vampires*, to sacrifice herself. Nina crosses a threshold; she goes through the looking-glass. In narrational terms, the screen surface has become both mirror and passageway. That passage is marked by her beckoning to Nosferatu through the window, from which the vampire's house has been visible in the Harkers' bedroom. The cinema screen becomes, then, mirror and window simultaneously.

The problem of narration in *Nosferatu* is the disjuncture between narrator and screen, and that problem is resolved by the development of film narration as surface and projection. Whereas *Dracula* resolves its problem of narration through hypnosis in order to produce a classical (if somewhat weak) resolution, *Nosferatu* affirms, rather, the fragility and the tenuousness of narrative. This is narrative which embraces ambiguity, by positing the film screen as both mirror and passageway. Theorized conversely as a window open onto the world, or as a mirror in which we see and project idealized images of ourselves, the film screen in *Nosferatu* is both. German angst notwithstanding, *Nosferatu* designates the cinema as a form perfectly suited to the embrace of that ambiguity, to the lure of the twilight which in Stoker's novel is dispelled. Between the novel *Dracula* and the film *Nosferatu* a dialogue takes place, one on the nature of the narrative experience.

There remains a missing link in the common narrative concerns of *Dracula* and *Nosferatu*. An imagination informs both works, an imagination that it is altogether appropriate to describe as a narrative imagination in its own right. This is psychoanalysis. That hypnosis should have such a strategic role in the novel indicates one correspondence between psychoanalysis and questions of narrative. But hypnosis is only one of the symptoms of the psychoanalytic influence. *Dracula* has been read as a variation on a number of Freudian themes, from the group killing of the father (elaborated in *Totem and Taboo*) to the Oedipus complex, from Van Helsing as ego and Dracula as id to sexual symbolism.[15] What is striking about the novel is not that psychoanalytic readings "apply," but that they are so embedded, almost to excess, within the text. One could note, of course, that *Dracula* is a text contemporary with Freud's writings. More important, the novel is the fictional construction of the fascination of psychoanalysis.

The fiction of psychoanalysis thus presented in *Dracula* invites speculation on the cinema. Here, for instance, is a scene, early in the novel, where Jonathan writes of the vampires:

Something made me start up, a low, piteous howling of dogs somewhere far below in the valley, which was hidden from my sight. Louder it seemed to ring in my ears, and the floating motes of dust to take new shapes to the sound as they danced in the moonlight. I felt myself struggling to awake to some call of my instincts; nay, my very soul was struggling, and my half-remembered sensibilities were striving to answer the call. I was becoming hypnotised! Quicker and quicker danced the dust; the moonbeams seemed to quiver as they went by me into the mass of gloom beyond. More and more they gathered till they seemed to take dim phantom shapes. And then I started, broad awake and in full possession of my senses, and ran screaming from the place. The phantom shapes, which were becoming gradually materialised from the moonbeams, where those of the three ghostly women to whom I was doomed. I fled, and felt somewhat safer in my own room, where there was no moonlight and where the lamp was burning brightly.[16]

If it seems excessive to suggest that Jonathan might well be describing the cinema, compare the passage to Maxim Gorky's famous and much-quoted reflection on the early Lumière film, *L'Arrivée d'un train en gare*.

Yesterday I was in the kingdom of the shadows.
If only you knew how strange it was to be there. There are no sounds, no colours. There, everything – the earth, the trees, the people, the water, the air – is tinted in the single tone of grey: in a grey sky there are grey rays of sunlight; in grey faces, grey eyes, and the leaves of the trees are grey like ashes. This is not life but the shadow of life, and this is not movement but the soundless shadow of movement.
. . . A railway train appears on the screen. It darts like an arrow straight towards you – look out! It seems as if it is about to rush into the darkness in which you are sitting and reduce you to a mangled sack of skin, full of crumpled flesh and shattered bones, and destroy this hall and this building, so full of wine, women, music and vice, and transform it into fragments and into dust.[17]

The point here is not that "becoming hypnotized" in *Dracula* somehow anticipates the cinema, but rather that narrative takes shape as the posing of certain questions which will be taken up by the cinema – at, as the Gorky citation suggests, a kind of founding mythic moment.

I have kept psychoanalysis waiting in the wings, saved it as the punchline, as it were, to the dialogue between *Dracula* and *Nosferatu*. This might be read as a somewhat coy gesture. For psychoanalysis is as omnipresent in contemporary film studies as it is in Stoker's novel. That the basic elements of the cinema – the screen, image projections, dream analogies – interlock with the language of psychoanalysis has become a given in film theory. Murnau's film may not evoke psychoanalytic themes in quite the explicit fashion of *Dracula*, but in its meditation on a Victorian novel, *Nosferatu* suggests how questions of narrative and questions of psychoanalysis intertwine. If narrative is the supreme form of knowledge in *Dracula*, it is a form of knowledge served by hypnosis. Put another way, the function of hypnosis is to harness the unconscious to the desire for narrative resolution. But narrative in *Nosferatu* is not so well-served by the insights of psychoanalysis. For *Nosferatu* explores the other side of the connection between narrative and psychoanalysis, where the disruption of that supreme form of knowledge is acknowledged. Between *Dracula* and *Nosferatu*, then, between the novel and the cinema, between voice and screen, between the desire for resolution and the embrace of ambiguity, is that "kingdom of the shadows" where phantom shapes have become the reigning figures of narrative.

Notes

1. A case for such a reading is made by Lane Roth, "Dracula meets the *Zeitgeist: Nosferatu* (1922) as film adaptation," *Literature/Film Quarterly*, 7, No. 4 (1979), 312.

2. James B. Twitchell, *The Living Dead: A Study of the Vampire in Romantic Literature* (Durham, NC: Duke University Press, 1981), p. 132.

3. Bram Stoker, *Dracula* (1897; repr. New York: Dell, 1974), p. 15.

4. Boris Eikhenbaum, "Literature and cinema," in *Russian Formalism*, ed. Stephen Bann and John E. Bowlt (New York: Harper & Row, 1973), p. 123; the article was translated by T. L. Aman.

5. See in particular Thierry Kuntzel, "The film-work, 2," *Camera Obscura*, No. 5 (1980), 7–69; an article translated from the French original by Nancy Huston.

6. Stoker, p. 48.

7. Robin Wood, "Burying the undead: the use and obsolescence of Count Dracula," *Mosaic*, 16, Nos 1–2 (Winter/Spring 1983), 184.

8. ibid., 177.

9. Siegfried Kracauer, *From Caligari to Hitler: A Psychological History of the German Film* (Princeton: Princeton University Press, 1947), esp. pp. 77–9.

10. Lane Roth develops his interpretation of Murnau's adaptation using categories taken from Kracauer. See note 1.

11. Stoker, p. 84.

12. Nina Auerbach makes a convincing case for the emergence of female power in what appears to be a classically oppressive situation in her analysis of *Dracula*, Freud's "Dora," and du Maurier's *Trilby*. See "Magi and maidens: the romance of the Victorian Freud," *Critical Inquiry*, 8, No. 2 (Winter 1981), 281–300.

13. As Wood writes in "Burying the undead," 178: "The diary form is a means of excluding from any apparent control over the narrative the two most powerful presences of the novel: Count Dracula himself and Bram Stoker."

14. Lotte H. Eisner, *The Haunted Screen*, trans. Roger Greaves (Berkeley: University of California Press, 1969), esp. pp. 109–13.

15. As James Twitchell (see note 2) writes, the reading of *Dracula* through *Totem and Taboo* has become "almost a donnée of *Dracula* criticism" (p. 135). For a survey of psychoanalytic readings of *Dracula*, see *The Living Dead*, pp. 134–41.

16. Stoker, p. 55.

17. Cited in Richard Taylor, *The Politics of Soviet Cinema 1917–1929* (Cambridge: Cambridge University Press, 1979).

Script

In Roger Manvell (ed.). *Masterworks of the German Cinema*. New York: Harper & Row, 1973, pp. 52–95.

Selected Bibliography

Barlow, John D. *German Expressionist Cinema*. Boston: Twayne, 1982.

Eisner, Lotte H. *The Haunted Screen*. Trans. Roger Greaves. Berkeley: University of California Press, 1969.

—— *Murnau*. Berkeley: University of California Press, 1973.

Elsaesser, Thomas. "Film history and visual pleasure: Weimar cinema." In *Cinema Histories, Cinema Practices*. Ed. Patricia Mellencamp and Philip Rosen. Frederick, Md.: University Publications, 1984, pp. 47–84.

—— "Social mobility and the fantastic: German silent cinema." *Wide Angle*, 5, No. 2 (1982), 14–25.

Guillermo, Gilberto Perez. "F. W. Murnau, an introduction." *Film Comment*, 7, No. 2 (Summer 1971), 13–15.

—— "Shadow and substance: Murnau's *Nosferatu*." *Sight & Sound*, 36, No. 3 (Summer 1967), 150–3, 159.

Jameux, Charles. *Murnau*. Paris: Éditions Universitaires, 1965.

Kracauer, Siegfried. *From Caligari to Hitler: A Psychological History of the German Film*. Princeton: Princeton University Press, 1947.

Patalas, Enno. "Unterwegs zu *Nosferatu*: Brief an Lotte H. Eisner." *Film-Korrespondenz*, 13 March 1984, 20–4.

Prawer, S. S. *Caligari's Children: The Film as Tale of Terror*. New York and London: Oxford University Press, 1980.

Prodolliet, Ernst. *Nosferatu: Die Entwicklung des Vampirfilms von Friedrich Wilhelm Murnau bis Werner Herzog*. Freiburg (Switzerland): Universitätsverlag, 1980.

Roth, Lane. "Dracula meets the *Zeitgeist: Nosferatu* (1922) as film adaptation." *Literature/Film Quarterly*, 7, No. 4 (1979), 309–13.

Wood, Robin, "Burying the undead: the use and obsolescence of Count Dracula." *Mosaic*, 16, Nos 1–2 (Winter/Spring 1983), 175–87.

—— "F. W. Murnau." *Film Comment*, 12, No. 3 (May–June 1976), 4–19.

3

THOMAS ELSAESSER

Lulu and the meter man:
Pabst's *Pandora's Box* (1929)

The figure of Lulu that Frank Wedekind portrayed in his dramas *Earth Spirit* (*Der Erdgeist*, 1895) and *Pandora's Box* (*Die Büchse der Pandora*, 1904) superficially belongs to the tradition of the *femme fatale*, the sexually alluring but remote woman, through whom men experience the irrational, obsessional, and ultimately destructive force of female sexuality. Many of the literary and visual embodiments of the figure, especially in the late nineteenth century, projected onto the desired woman an aggressiveness and destructiveness whose subjective correlative is guilt and self-punishment: for transgression, for violation, perhaps for desire itself. With Wedekind, a specific social milieu, marked by class division, comes into view.

More explicitly than anyone else, he locates the question of sexuality within an ideological field. The repression of almost all manifestations of female sexuality entails an intense eroticism suffusing everything that is asocial, primitive, instinctual, according to a *topos* that sees nature as devouring whenever its nurturing function has been perverted. At the same time, Wedekind saw very precisely the relationship between social productivity and sexual productivity which the bourgeoisie had fought so hard to establish, and which lay at the heart of its "sexual repression": it was the energy that had to be subjected to the labor process, regulated and accounted for. The bourgeois subject, for whom sexual passion is nothing but the reverse of all the frustrations that make up its social and moral existence, is contrasted with the members of the *Lumpenproletariat* − those outside, unassimilable or scornful when it comes to the bourgeois dialectic of renunciation and productivity.

By locating a deviant, instinctual, and liberating social behavior among circus people, *artistes*, petty criminals, and calling it sexual passion, Wedekind built a fragile bridge to another class that also felt itself outside the bourgeois order, the declining aristocracy against whose notions of libertinage, of productivity and non-production, of waste and display, the codes of the bourgeoisie once developed. A non-repressive sexuality thus becomes the utopia where the *lumpen*-class and the aristocracy meet in mutual tolerance and indulgence: the cliché situation of so many Viennese operettas and popular literature fantasies, the ones that served film directors from von Stroheim to Ophüls.

This kind of identification cannot maintain itself other than as a projection that also invests the "other" with the attributes that the self lacks. The attraction of the bourgeois for the *Lumpenproletariat*, however, arises out of an opposition. Wedekind's Lulu is without family ties, without social obligations, without education or culture. Her psychological existence is free of guilt and conscience, her physical existence the very image of beauty, youth, and health. Being outside the social order, she belongs to "nature" – the only non-social realm that the plays can envisage. Sexuality here becomes a product of negative categories, where non-family equals amorality, and the non-social becomes the "wild" on the animal level, or the tropical plant in the vegetal realm. Several layers of self-projection are superimposed, yet it is the sympathy of the aristocrat for the *lumpen* (one outcast for another) that provides the basis for the glamorization of these negative, somewhat demonic categories.

For Wedekind, Lulu is a construct, not a sociological portrait: she represents in all her manipulative deviousness the only constant value, set against the relativity and dissolution of the so-called absolute and transcendent values. Wedekind endows her with a kind of articulacy and energy that makes her the next of kin of another outcast altogether: the artist, traitor to his class – whether aristocratic or bourgeois. She voices not only the artist's disgust with the members of all classes, but with himself, which is why her predatory lust vents itself against members of all constituted classes and convictions.[1] As an artist she remains distant and alluring, devouring and irresistible. As a woman, she represents *terra incognita*. For Wedekind, the conflict between class and productivity, between class and sexuality, resolves itself through the intermediary of art, and of an art that understood its own productivity as a form of elemental, natural expressivity. Lulu is characterized by her *ex*pressivity, because she is conceived in response to a social *re*pressivity.[2]

The space where such an expressivity could articulate itself is the theater. Voice and gesture, thought and body, could be unified in the performance and thus represent what one might call an image of non-alienated existence, the enactment of "destiny as pure present,"[3] even if Wedekind is careful to relativize the tragic pathos of his figure by such "epic" devices as the prologue, the ringmaster, and the animal imagery of the circus, as well as stating in the preface that Geschwitz, not Lulu, is the tragic figure.[4]

The cinema, however, is still silent. Its expressivity, the way it speaks to the mind and the senses is different, and different affective values attach themselves to gesture, decor, or face. With it, the relation of expression to repression changes; conflict and contrast, antinomies and argument are suggested, and perceived by an audience, in forms specific to the cinema. When Leopold Jessner staged *Pandora's Box* in 1911, he wrote:

Lulu is honest, because she is woman, *only* woman, who, however, has succumbed to the pleasure of the *senses*, in an elementary form that cannot but bring disaster to us civilized beings, removed as we are from animal instincts.[5]

In 1923 he made a film entitled *Erdgeist*, with Asta Nielsen in the lead role. Louise Brooks, who would portray Lulu in Pabst's rendering, described Jessner's film in these terms: "There was no lesbianism in it, no incest. Loulou the man-eater devoured her sex-victims – Dr Goll, Schwarz, Schoen – and then dropped dead in an acute attack of indigestion."[6] For her, *Erdgeist* is pure camp, because the relationship between theatrical and cinematic body language is so different: Jessner's conception of cinema is clearly felt to be inadequate, even though his conception of the figure ("Lulu is honest") would be completely endorsed by Louise Brooks in *Pandora's Box*.

In Pabst's film, Lulu becomes a childlike creature. Her attraction resides in the incorruptibility, the lack of guile, menace, calculation, the simple pleasures she enjoys, among which are sex, but which could be the bulging biceps of a trapeze artist, the sight of old Schigolch in the doorway, the fashion page of an illustrated journal, or mistletoe at Christmas. Her sexual ambiguity and indeterminacy, however, have nothing to do with puberty. Just as Pabst seems concerned to redefine active and passive, so he is at pains not to take up Wedekind's paradigm of the antisocial as identifiable with animal nature or tropical vegetation.

She is modern. The film gives us a Lulu practically without origin, or particular cultural associations. No doubt this allows for a much more "symbolic" configuration. Pabst's Lulu, in her relation with the Schön father and son, as well as on the gambling boat, acts as a stake in male/male power play. Her role is circumscribed by a double male fantasy: she is the woman that father and son both want to possess; she is also the phallic mother whom they want to destroy, the father by demanding that she kill herself, the son by wishing her to act out his own parricidal desire, so that his guilt feelings become her crime. In this respect, the film takes up in elegantly condensed figurations some of the main themes and motifs of Siegfried Kracauer's portrayal of the paranoiac male German soul in *From Caligari to Hitler*.[7] But the very elegance and sophistication of Pabst's narrative and visual solutions indicate that *Pandora's Box* is not primarily about the secrets of this (German) soul, but is more a knowing allusion to homosexual latency and a deconstruction of the pathos of repression/expression. A central complex of German expressionism is inspected with serene indifference, an indifference to which Lulu gives a (provisionally) female form.

Pabst's particular strategy is strikingly demonstrated in the film's opening scene. A man's back is turned to us. He seems to be noting something in a book. It is the meter man, reading the electricity in Lulu's apartment. We first see her as she comes from the living-room into the hall, to give the man a small fee and to offer him a glass of liqueur. Torn between looking at the bottle and looking at Lulu's revealing dress, the man drops some coins, but before he can pick them up, the bell rings, and grandly, he volunteers to answer the door for her. Outside is a shabby old man, holding his bowler hat with self-deprecating humility. With another grand gesture, the meter man takes a few coins from his waistcoat pocket, to give to the old man and be rid of him. But Lulu, peering past his back, recognizes the visitor, rushes out, and flings her arms around the old man. She pulls him into the apartment and past the meter man into the living-room, shutting the door. The meter man, not hiding his surprise and disappointment, stoops to gather up the lost coins, goes over to the chair and picks up his peaked cap and battered brief-case. He gives the closed door an indignant look and exits by the front door.

The scene plays on a number of ambiguities. The meter man (whom the spectator only gradually perceives as such: without his official uniform cap and with his back turned, he typifies just a kindly old gentleman) is caught in both a class and a sex fantasy, which allows him, even if only for an instant, to place himself in the position of owner of the apartment and desirable suitor. He becomes Schön, the master, by the very appearance of someone socially inferior to himself, whom he can patronize by giving him alms. Mirroring himself in the smile of a ravishing young woman, he becomes young and handsome himself, and the fact that his attention is further divided between sexual allure and alcohol, allows him the illusory choice between two kinds of transgressions, of which the one he chooses, namely alcohol, may well be the consolation he seeks for the unattainability of the other.

In this brief episode, remarkable for giving us virtually no plot infor-mation, the normal social relations implied by master and servant (or mistress and servant), of favors rendered and money received, of alms, fees, and gratuities – in short, the conditions of exchange and value – are comically suspended. But it is not only the meter man's illusions that are shattered when the mistress of the house and the beggarly tramp fall into each other's arms. The spectator, too, has no time to get his/her visual bear-ings, for the scene is staged and edited in a very complex succession of camera movements, glance-glance shots, and glance-object shots, which create a very mobile point-of-view structure. It establishes hierarchies and relations between the characters, only then to undo them.

There is, for instance, a very noticeably false continuity match – Lulu looks offscreen right, when the logic of the glance-glance cut demands that she look offscreen left – which increases the sense of an imaginary space, not quite destroying, but also not quite confirming, the realistic space of the hallway and entrance lobby. The two doors, front door and apartment door, suggest a rather theatrical proscenium space, but it is the effect of editing and the dynamic of the point-of-view shots which establish the illusion of a real space, while at the same time undercutting it, making it imaginary. Juxtaposed to this imaginary space, and counteracting the spectator's disorientation (one shared with the meter man), is the image of Lulu, framed by the door and offering the spectator, too, a radiant smile and the promise of pleasure and plenitude. The disorientation increases the fascination, the dependence on the image, yet the very excess of the smile (excessive because it does not register or respond to the meter man's lowly social status or Schigolch's shabby clothes) breaks the strictly narrative function of her presence within the frame, and makes her a figure of desire for the spectator.

The scene is a kind of emblem for the film itself: first, in its view of social relations, since Lulu, at the end, when back in the world of Schigolch and beyond all sense of bourgeois decorum, flings herself into the arms of another outcast, Jack the Ripper, with the same unbounded smile. Second, it is also a scene that initiates cinematic identification, by placing the spectator in the fiction, via the meter man, whose lack of plot function turns the episode into a parable of movie watching as a paid-for pleasure. With his exit, the petite bourgeoisie, Kracauer's white-collar workers (*Angestellten*),[8] exit from the fictional space of the film, and yet they are the historical audience that the film addresses. They may take pleasure in seeing themselves portrayed on the screen, but – according to Kracauer – they take even more pleasure (and thus open themselves up to the play of pleasure and anxiety) in identifying with their "betters." The meter man waiting in the hall of Lulu's apartment, is in some sense also the office-worker waiting in line at the entrance lobby of the Gloria Palast in Berlin for the star to appear or the show to begin. The prologue points out, lightly, how fragile his class identity is, and the play on the man's uniform and status recalls F. W. Murnau's *The Last Laugh* (*Der letzte Mann*, 1924), of which it is in a sense a parody. The presence of Lulu makes it impossible for sexuality to be the repressed signified of the scene, as it remains throughout Murnau's film. Lulu's total indifference to class and status renders the predominant anxiety of the early Weimar cinema – *déclassement* and proletarianization – a comic rather than a tragic motif. The meter man's humiliation or disappointment derives from the total reversal and reversibility of the social positions, as Lulu demonstrates.

This opening scene leads to a cautious hypothesis about sexuality in the film and its power of attraction: sexual desire constitutes itself for Pabst in the hesitation between two roles, between two glances. Lulu's "essence" – or that of femininity in the realm of the sexual – is nowhere except in these moments of choice and division, in the reversibility of the order of exchange. Lulu is an object of desire in the imaginary of men and women, old and young, but her symbolic position is never fixed; it criss-crosses both class and gender, both the law and moral authority.

In fact, Lulu is desirable whenever her appearance is caught in the crossfire of someone else desiring her as well, and her sexual attractiveness always stands in relation to someone experiencing a crisis in their own sexual identity. An example is the encounter between Dr Schön and his son Alwa. The father, having decided to give up Lulu as his mistress, realizes that his son is sexually interested in her. Suddenly his passion is once more inflamed by anger, hatred, and jealousy. But the son, too, experiences desire via someone else. He falls in love with Lulu only after having seen the jealous and passionate glances that Countess Geschwitz casts at Lulu in his studio.

Such a triadic structuration suggests a psychoanalytic reading: Lulu's murder by Jack the Ripper merely completes the homosexual fantasy that is centered on Alwa. After the father has died in his son's arms, killed by the mother figure, on whom the son has projected the guilt for his incestuous desire, Alwa appears to have freed himself from his obsession. But Lulu's escape, thanks to Countess Geschwitz, and the appearance of Casti-Piani on the train, trap Alwa once more in a masochistic, self-punishing role. He is powerless against the father figures and displaces his masochism onto Lulu, with whom he identifies. In the London scenes, the regressive – oral and anal – aspects are heavily underscored: Lulu, Alwa, and Schigolch live in filth, and their abode is penetrated by wind, rain, fog, and cold. All three are exclusively preoccupied with oral gratification, Alwa greedily devouring the piece of bread that Lulu breaks off for him in disgust, and Schigolch sucking his brandy bottle like a baby. He finally settles down to a Guinness and a big Christmas pudding – a return to the beginning, where both he and the meter man preferred oral pleasures to sex. Alwa's infantilism – he is in turn enraged and petulant – represents the sadomasochistic stalemate of his unresolved Oedipal dilemma. Emerging from the fog is Jack the Ripper who is also Alwa's double: for in the encounter between him and Lulu, the two sides of Alwa's personality are fully played out – the tender, yielding, and seductive side, and the punishing, castrating, and destructive side. It is a scene without violence and struggle, hence disturbingly archaic, where the very tenderness indicates a phantasmic and also regressive quality. As the Ripper leaves and meets Alwa at the front door, a sign of recognition seems to pass between the men which sets Alwa free and allows him, too, to disappear into the fog, having found his sexual salvation from ambivalence.

Such a reading concentrates on Alwa – problematic in terms of plot, but suggestive of a possible male spectator position. Conversely, a feminist reading might argue that Lulu, after challenging Oedipal and patriarchal logic by placing herself outside it, had succumbed to it the very instant she herself manifests sexual desire, as she clearly does for the Ripper. In this sense, her death inscribes itself in a hysterical reassertion of patriarchy: the woman is sacrificed so that the order of men can continue, an order cemented

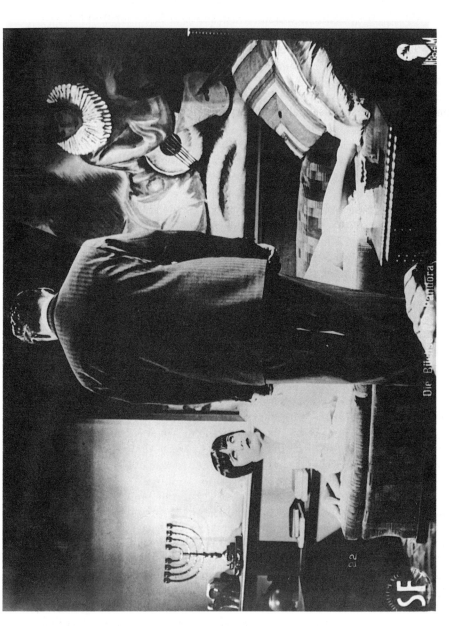

Plate 6 The massive back of Dr Schön (Fritz Kortner), the agile and light body of Lulu (Louise Brooks). Photo courtesy of Deutsches Filmmuseum Frankfurt

by a perpetually displaced homosexuality and a desexualization of women as represented by the Salvation Army female in the episode.[9] Yet it seems doubtful whether this reading is wholly satisfactory either. However poignant the tenderness, it is without pathos or the element of horror one might associate with such a scene. The tenderness stays, but a cool irony ensures that the end is anticlimactic, a dream that is already faint, and fading into the darkness that envelops all.

I would prefer to see in the ending another way in which Pabst distances himself from the socio-sexual imaginary described by Kracauer. He shows the events as if he were citing them, thus holding up for inspection a certain form of patriarchy, or more precisely, a particular vision of sexuality – at once ecstatic and apocalyptic – as it might be said to characterize Wedekind's plays, Oskar Kokoschka's *Murderer Hope of Women* (*Mörder Hoffnung der Frauen*, 1907), or Bertolt Brecht's *Baal* (1918).

The dynamism of the film – and its fundamentally different eroticism – comes in large measure from the stark, but always modulated, and often subtly shaded contrast between Lulu's agility, the diaphanous and transparent quality of her body in motion, and the solidity, the heavy dark bulk of the men who block her way. Just as Lulu smiles, and one hesitates to say why, or at whom, so her body moves without necessarily inflecting her gestures with intentionality. About the men in the film, every move, every finger and eyebrow is heavy with significance. As Dr Schön, Fritz Kortner fills the frame, quite often with his massive back. Pabst stresses the bull-necked, looming, and cowering nature of his physiognomy. Such a body conveys to perfection the complex interplay of willpower and instinctual drive, of anger and repression, of frustrated, barely controlled, finally flaring aggression and masochistic, suicidal despair, which makes Dr Schön the quintessential opposite of Lulu, an opposition paradigmatic for all the men in the film. As the opening scene shows, Fritz Kortner's back is not even the first in the film, among the long line of backs that finally (in the London scene) spread blackness everywhere.

Countess Geschwitz, in her sexually ambiguous role, is a good example of how what is male and what is female is defined by its physical and gestural support, the always changing contrast between two kinds of bodies and body languages. She, Alwa, and Schigolch can appear as one or the other, depending on how the dynamics of the visual composition define and redefine their symbolic positions in the narrative. In comparison to Dr Schön and other males, it is much more difficult to assign Lulu a similarly consistent psychological essence. Schön's back and its doubles are the very image of motive, design, intentionality, the world of cause and effect, of self-realization as self-imposition, to which correspond self-abasement and self-pity as their negative mirrors.

Lulu, on the other hand, is always in between: between the meter man and Schigolch, Schigolch and Schön, Rodrigo and Schigolch, Alwa and

Die Buchse ... ...ndora

Plate 7   Lulu typically caught in the middle, this time between Countess Geschwitz and Dr Schön. Photo courtesy

Countess Geschwitz, Alwa and Schön, Rodrigo and Alwa, the stage manager and Schön, the State Prosecutor and Countess Geschwitz, Casti-Piani and Alwa, Casti-Piani and the Egyptian. . . . If it were simply a matter of sexual desire, the sexual would indeed emerge as the elemental, irrational, asocial force that it is in Wedekind. Yet almost invariably an economic motif disturbs the symmetry. It accompanies the sexual link between the characters, but it also crosses it in the opposite direction. This may seem obvious if one simply sees Lulu as a prostitute, who trades sex for money. But sex and money stand in a much more complex relationship in the film. Lulu appears as a kept woman, but she also gives money – to the meter man and then to Schigolch. Dr Schön finances Alwa's theater revue as a way to stop Lulu's involvement with his son. Schigolch introduces her to Rodrigo, because "men like Schön won't always pay the rent," but Rodrigo has no sexual interest in her. Countess Geschwitz supports Lulu financially because she is in love with her, but the favor is not returned. Casti-Piani blackmails Alwa, but he is not interested in Lulu sexually. On the boat, Rodrigo tries to blackmail her, and it is only with a complicated sexual ploy that Lulu can get rid of him. By this time, Alwa is no longer interested in her sexually, yet he constantly demands money from her. The police offer a reward for her arrest, and the Egyptian quotes a price for her body. Casti-Piani simply calculates which is the better deal. In the London scenes, where Lulu most explicitly becomes a prostitute, we never see her with clients or in a financial transaction. She gives herself to Jack the Ripper precisely because he has no money.

Sexual desire is thus part of a more generalized structure of exchange. In the case of men, it seems wholly bound up, but not identical, with money and finance. Male desire, in other words, has a precise exchange value, for which either money or sex serve as accepted currency. Lulu is that which allows both desire and money to circulate. The reward offered in the name of the law, for instance, opens up an unbroken chain between police, Alwa, Casti-Piani, the Egyptian slave trader, Rodrigo, and Geschwitz: it is as if the law fixes Lulu's price, and everyone else enters into an exchange in order to trade most favorably with the same stock.

The scenes on the gambling ship make these relations explicit. In a sense, the gambling ship can be seen as a fictional metaphor for the economic chaos of the Weimar Republic, a demonstration of the mechanics of inflation, de- and re-evaluation as it inflects and transforms sexual difference, and with it the symbolic position of women within a patriarchal society. Pabst has another emergent institution in mind as well, one that is radically transforming society. The symbolic logic that ties together subjectivity and representation, sexuality and the image, belongs to an institution which can be called the order of the spectacle. It appears in *Pandora's Box* as the critique of theater in the spirit of the cinema, this time not focused on acting but on *mise-en-scène*.

At the center of the first part and as its climax, Pabst has placed a scene in the theater – in terms of the narrative, it is the point where all the threads so far introduced are tied into the proverbial Gordian knot, which Lulu undoes at a stroke. It is the opening night of Alwa's revue. Lulu suddenly refuses to go on stage, because she has seen Dr Schön enter with his official fiancée, the daughter of the Prime Minister. Despite everyone's entreaties, Lulu remains adamant. The tension mounts; the stage manager is frantic. Eventually, Schön agrees to see Lulu in her dressing-room. But no amount of aggression, verbal or physical, appears to move Lulu to change her mind. Dr Schön, eyes blazing with hatred, cannot resist the seductive force of her defiance. Sexually aroused, he embraces her at just the moment when Alwa, frantic, and Schön's fiancée, worried about his absence, enter the dressing-room. Profound consternation all round, except for the theater manager and Lulu, who, triumphant, sweeps past the shocked assembly and leaves the dressing-room in the direction of the stage. The scene ends with a brief exchange between father and son – a meeting that rhymes with the one where they struck a bargain over Lulu's appearance in the revue – to the effect that Schön will marry Lulu, even though (because?) it will be his ruin.

What gives the scene its force is primarily the editing, the cross-cutting between the effervescence and mounting chaos on- and back-stage, and the more and more single-minded determination of Lulu to provoke a show-down. But determination is perhaps the wrong word, because it makes her seem too active, when in fact it is the strength of her refusal, her negativity, the control she keeps on her absence, which makes the events take shape in her favor. Pabst recasts and reformulates here the central "moral" issue of the play: is Lulu active or passive, evil or innocent? The answer that the film gives is that she is neither, that it is a false dichotomy. Instead it becomes a matter of presence or absence, of spectacle, of image and *mise-en-scène*. Lulu puts on a show of her own disappearance – and reappearance. The spectacle of her person, about which she controls nothing but the cadence and discontinuity of presence, is what gives rise to desire and fascination.

The battle of the sexes, the question of possession, of who belongs to whom and who controls whom, becomes a battle for the right to the look and the image, the positionality of the subject as seeing or seen. Dr Schön's undoing, in the film's terms, is precisely that he, supreme possessor of the right to look (emphasized by his glittering monocle and his scowling, piercing eyes), becomes himself the object of the gaze: in other words, an image, which in terms of classical narrative means feminized. Such is the logic of the visible which underpins the general position of women who are encouraged to objectify their narcissistic self-image as that which regulates their lives. In order to be and to assure themselves of their existence, they seek a gaze in which to mirror themselves. Lulu has no gaze, hence the fascination of her smile. It is so open as to appear empty, unfocused, mirror-like. The few times she frowns or looks puzzled, Pabst neutralizes her gaze by inserting a cut that disperses, disorients the direction, as in the deliberate mismatch of the opening scene.

Lulu is forever image: framed in the doorway or by Rodrigo's biceps, dancing in front of Schigolch, or painted in a Pierrot costume hanging from the wall. In the jealous encounter between Geschwitz and Alwa she is present as the costume sketches that the Countess has drawn. With an emphatic finger, Schön stabs at the same sketches when he tells Alwa that one does not marry women like Lulu. In court she is on display in the witness box – the very image that Count Casti-Piani recognizes in the newspaper when her face appears from behind the compartment door on the train. Finally, the Egyptian settles on a price after he has shuffled through a pack of photos, which catch the spectator in a significant hesitation about how to read the image: as "real" (within the fiction), when in fact it is "merely" a photo (within the fiction).

The nature and function of the look thus appear to be subject to the same divisions and ambiguities which structure the signifying materials of the fiction: class, gender, body, motion, frame. In strictly cinematic terms, an analysis of the relation of the close-up shots head-on into the camera, and other types of point-of-view shots, or the relation of offscreen space to onscreen space, would probably confirm the systematic use of these markers of difference in order to keep the narrative in the register of hesitation and ambivalence. It is tempting to identify a typically male look, the look of patriarchy, of which Schön's is evidently the paradigm. It is the look of and through the monocle, a withering look that hits Lulu, Schigolch, Alwa, Geschwitz. We might call it the look of the Father, the Law, and its force is never broken or subdued. After Dr Schön's death, it is merely passed on – to the State Prosecutor's monocle, to Alwa's scowl and Rodrigo's frown. Of all the sexualized men in the film, only Jack the Ripper's eyes are as unfocused as Lulu's. The film establishes sexuality through the disavowed and hidden power of this look. For the spell to be broken, Lulu would have to return the look in defiance rather than acknowledge its force by constituting herself as picture and image. One would have to imagine Lulu turning around and sticking out her tongue at Dr Schön in order to imagine how this would change the film, break the fascination, because it would upset the delicate and invisible balance that has displaced the opposition between active and passive. The peculiar ambivalence that surrounds the encounter between Jack and Lulu resides not least in the fact that here both characters transgress the logic of the look specific to their symbolic role in the fiction. This logic gone, the paradigm of fascination on which the narrative was built is broken.

It would seem that only one reading is possible: the moment Lulu, representative of "the woman," manifests desire and appropriates the look defined by the film as "male," she suffers death at the hand of a severely psychotic male, tormented by evident castration anxieties. But the direction of my argument, the systematic difficulty of making units of the represented (men and women, the one who looks and the one who is being looked at) coincide with the act of representation (editing, point-of-view shots, framing), suggests that it would be rash to reduce the fiction to a fable where characters act out ideological types or gender-specific positions. Could one not see the ending as a "disenchantment," the breaking of a spell, and seek from there an answer to the question: what is desire, sexuality, and fascination in this film?

This distinction seems particularly crucial, since it is logical to ask whether there is opposed to the characters' look in the fiction an inscribed gaze of the spectator, who after all, looks at all the characters and is free to draw his or her own conclusion and assume the proper distance. Is the spectator's look identical with the act of representation? Can one juxtapose to the "castrating look" the pleasurable look of the voyeur? In aligning these different types of look, it seems possible to see Lulu as the intermediary, the figure that allows for the commutations and exchange of different specular positions. For her response to the look of the Father is not to return the look with a suitably aggressive one, but to constitute herself as image and spectacle for the same or another subject's visual pleasure. An obvious example is on the train, when, in response to Alwa's sullen frown, Lulu, as if by chance, attracts the interested and pleased eye of Count Casti-Piani. Similar reversals structure the entire courtroom scene, where Countess Geschwitz, in order to divert attention from Lulu, makes a spectacle of herself, which leads directly to the business of the staged fire alarm and Lulu's escape.

This division, however, cannot be shown to work throughout. On the contrary, Pabst's use of the point-of-view shot and his editing establish a constant slippage or transfer between the various characters' points of view and that of the camera. Since for the spectator characters are stand-ins, markers of position, whose function it is to split — systematically and in constantly changing dramatic contexts — the attention of the viewer, Pabst's textual system here introduces subtle but significant variations on the "norm" of classic realism. A brief reminder of the role played by the meter man in the opening scene: the spectator participates in his point of view, "moral" as well as physical. Yet, although he is on the screen for no more than a minute or so, his gaze, his back, and his preference for liquor are all "preserved" for the fiction, as his semantic attributes are split between Schigolch, Schön, and the mobile, hovering, alternating point of view — making hesitation and indeterminacy part of the very definition of spectatorship and its pleasure in this film. Pabst's insistence on Lulu as image, framed picture for the characters in the fiction as well as for the spectator, renders even more ambiguous any distinction between the characters' look and that of the spectator.

By far the most disturbing, because virtually unreadable scene — unreadable not in its narrative logic, but in the logic of glance–glance, facial expression, space, and gesture – is the death of Dr Schön. Schön presses Lulu to kill herself, after he has surprised her in the conjugal bedroom with Alwa's head cradled in her lap. Pabst stages the scene in a series of medium shots, with Lulu and Schön cut off at the waist. As Schön tries to force the gun into Lulu's hand, both of them appear in the bedroom mirror. From then on, it is impossible for the spectator to decide whether he sees Schön or his mirror image, whether Schön looks at Lulu, the camera, or himself. On their faces, as they struggle, the expressions subtly and continuously change; from surprise, anger, anxiety, they modulate until the emotive quality or intentionality of their looks become indecipherable. Finally, a faint column of smoke rises between their faces, Schön looks pleased, Lulu surprised, but then Schön's features become rigid, as his body begins to slide out of frame, and blood trickles from his mouth. Lulu's face glazes over, but also shows intent curiosity as the camera pulls back to reveal her holding the smoking gun. As she turns from the mirror, her body is broken up by a rapid succession of shots before it is virtually smothered by Schön's slumped body. The scene ends with Alwa re-entering the room, looking fascinated and horrified at his father's dying face.

The very discrepancy between the highly dramatic, but nonetheless coherent narrative situation and the elaborate manner of its staging splits the spectator's perception and points of view in ways that subvert actantial (who does what to whom) and gender identification, in favor of a sliding, reversible, difficult identification of face and gesture. Its effect is to make the scene imaginary, which is to say, it allows us to talk about the scene as a fantasy, be it a primal scene fantasy or Alwa's own wish-fulfilling fantasy. What is important is that such a reading is not a metaphoric interpretation of a diegetically realistic scene. It is a specifically filmic elaboration of the signifying elements which renders the scene imaginary.

One might, however, just as convincingly construct the scene as "narrated" from Dr Schön's point of view. In which case, it would represent his struggle, and ultimate failure, to "possess" Lulu, to fix, limit, and define her – if necessary by the act of marriage – in order to impose on her the negative identity of his obsessions. Schön at the wedding is depicted as a man whose life is suddenly and dramatically getting out of control, and ultimately only a pistol shot can put an end to the chaos. Since the wedding is in some important aspects a repetition of the chaos at the theater, it would seem that the way he stopped the first one, namely by the proposal of marriage to Lulu, and the second one, the proposal that Lulu commit suicide, are structurally identical: a caustic comment on the bourgeois institution of marriage.

The problem with this reading, however, is that it is impossible to ignore how the filmic narration in the scene remains considerably more complex, making it unlikely that the narrative point of view is Dr Schön's. What the systematic ambiguity of the point-of-view structure does allow is speculation on the conditions of cinematic perception and fascination. In the staging of

Schön's death, the act of viewing becomes an activity of the imaginary: presented as a series of views of "real" or identifiable objects or part-objects (hands, faces, backs, etc.). Their sequence is, however, organized in such a way that they constantly imply what we do not see, or evoke a space where we are not. The cinema here is never what is shown: it is always also what the shown implies or demands in the way of the not-shown or not-seen. The many different systems that Pabst develops in this film for splitting perception, in order to create hesitation, indeterminacy, or ambiguity, are ultimately in the service of producing out of real perceptions imaginary sights. Being an object of desire for everyone in the film, Lulu preserves herself by being nothing and everything, a perceptual oscillation in the dramaturgy of conflict and aggression. Pabst transforms the cinema into an institution that turns the desire for possession into an obsession with the image, and the obsession with the image into a mirror maze of divided, discontinuous, and partial views, whose identification and interpretation always entail a fine and final doubt – for me indicated by the different readings of the symbolic structure I have given, none of which "settles" the issue.

I said earlier that the meter man never returns. That is not quite accurate. We first see him studying a book. He turns around and sees Lulu, *as* the spectator sees her and *when* he sees her. The meter man is thus the first spectator, turning from writing/reading to looking. In a different guise, he returns as the last spectator. After Jack the Ripper kills Lulu, he steps out of a doorway, glances at Alwa, tightens his raincoat, and walks off into the night fog. After a brief hesitation, Alwa, too, begins to walk off, disappearing into the night. They look like men leaving the cinema – not the Gloria Palast, but the sort of cinema that caters to men in raincoats. Both look disappointed, disenchanted, as if the spectacle had finally revealed its emptiness, its nothingness, had proven to be "a masquerade that shows that there is nothing there." Jack the Ripper, as long as he looks into Lulu's eyes, is held by her image, the smile that fascinates with its radiant openness and indeterminacy. It is only when, in the embrace, he looks *past* Lulu, that the knife appears – the object of his own obsessions, like the "knife phobia" of the hero in Pabst's *Secrets of a Soul* (*Geheimnisse einer Seele*, 1926). Past the image, past the smile, he encounters once more only himself, only his own anxieties. Jack the Ripper, as a stand-in for the spectator, wanting to grasp the presence that is Lulu, finds that he is distracted/attracted by the flickering candle and the glittering object: oscillating between the source of light and its reflection, his gaze traverses the woman, making her an image, a phantom, a fading sight.

This would suggest that the pleasures of spectatorship are voyeuristic in nature, that they enact a fetish fixation. But sexuality in this film is not simply linked with the woman's body alone. It is not a matter of degrading acts committed on women or titillation or pornography: all these positions, moral and ideological, Pabst seems to have anticipated and significantly restated. Sexuality in the cinema, at least in *Pandora's Box*, is the infinitely deferred moment of the constantly renewed movement away from identity. The film sustains this movement by the creation of a specifically cinematic imaginary that has no equivalent in either literature or the theater. Pabst called his film not *Earth Spirit*, but *Pandora's Box*. Pandora's Box is the cinema machine, the machinery of filmic *mise-en-scène*. The achievement of the film is for Pabst to have represented sexuality *in* the cinema as the sexuality *of* the cinema, and to have merely used as his starting point the crisis in the self-understanding of male and female sexuality which characterized his own period. Yet Pabst is far from implying an ontology of cinema; nor does he posit an essence of film, any more than he believes in an essence of sexual identity. The very play on *"Büchse"/*"Box" on the level of the signifier – can of film, camera, Freudian "symbol" of the female sex – disperses any notion of the fixity of the signified, be it sex or the cinema.

This is why in some respects the Louise Brooks of *Pandora's Box* can be compared with the Maria of Fritz Lang's *Metropolis* (1926) – the man-created robot-woman. Significantly enough, the figure of Lulu cannot be conceived as a mother. Her eroticism is constructed on the paradigmatic opposition to all the traditionally female roles. In Pabst's other film with Louise Brooks, *The Diary of a Lost Woman* (*Das Tagebuch einer Verlorenen*, 1929), the heroine does have a child – illegitimate and taken away from her – and this fundamentally changes the character, making the film more of a melodrama, the woman becoming the victim and the film a sociological tract. With the introduction of the biological function of women, we immediately have sociology and morality, whereas in Lulu, it is precisely the absence of these motifs that makes the erotic shine so brilliantly but also so coldly. Indeed, Lulu's hint of a maternal feeling for Jack the Ripper is that which makes her fallible and vulnerable. The film thus becomes a parable of the new woman, created by man, whose fatal weakness is her maternal "memories."

The eroticism of Lulu is paradoxically that of the creature that comes to life, the auto-eroticism of the creator and the narcissism of the creature – a relationship only too familiar with the Sternberg–Dietrich myth, which Pabst very nearly anticipated with Louise Brooks three years earlier. This eroticism plays, however, on a concomitant anxiety, that of the creature which emancipates itself from the creator, the sorcerer's apprentice, a motif which might be called the key motif of the German cinema since Robert Wiene's *The Cabinet of Dr Caligari* (*Das Cabinet des Dr Caligari*, 1920) itself, in a tradition where the robot of *Metropolis* constitutes the decisive transformation, from "medium" or Golem to vamp and woman.

It is this genealogy that might give a clue to the mysteriously truncated subsequent career of Louise Brooks. In her essay on Pabst, she reports how at the end of her work with him, he took her aside:

"Your life is exactly like Lulu's," he said, "and you will end the same way." At that time, knowing so little of what he meant by "Lulu," I just sat sullenly glaring at him, trying not to listen. Fifteen years later in Hollywood, with all his predictions closing in on me, I heard his words again – hissing back to me.[10]

What Pabst meant by "Lulu" is perhaps this: a woman, an American actress, created by the film industry into a star, becomes an object among objects, alive only in front of the camera. Louise Brooks's struggle with the film industry bore out exactly what it meant for an intelligent articulate woman to be a thing among things.

It is as if, at the very threshold of becoming a star, Louise Brooks made a film which had as its subject the psychopathology of this very star system, against the background, not of Hollywood or its ideological critique, but of a very specifically German argument about expressionism, theater, modernism, and cinema. The film testifies to the degree of abstraction that the German cinema, in its commercial output, was capable of. The enigma of Louise Brooks is thus in part the enigma of Hollywood filmmaking, and the very film that might have made her a star allowed her to see what being a star entailed, in the mirror of a film that dramatized and contrasted the liberating pure externality of the "American" character – the hope of modernism for most of the 1920s – with the contorted inwardness of the German psyche. Against its obsessiveness, but also its moral essentialism, her externality is seen to be not objectivity, and certainly not New Objectivity, but the object-status and objectification of a subjectivity and sexuality – that of women – that still had no name and no place. It was as if in the debate between patriarchy on the one side, and technological modernism on the other, Louise Brooks had glimpsed, albeit at first unconsciously in her defeats by Hollywood but later with full lucidity, the blank that both left for women as a site of representation and being.

The central thematic and fictional support in Pabst's film is sexual desire. Male obsessions – repressed homosexuality, sado-masochism, an urge to possess, capture, limit, and fix – confront feminine androgyny and feminine identity in a play of presence and absence, masks and appearances, in a display of spectacle and image as the expression of a freedom from all teleology and essentialism. But, conversely, this androgyny, this ambiguity on the level of sexual definition and identity is only the support, the metaphoric matrix that points in the direction of a whole series of other abstract and conceptual registers of ambiguity – in this case, those that have to do with cultural and ideological stereotypes of active and passive, subject and object, but also with the cogency of Oedipal narratives and the symbolic roles they assign to male and female subjects, on the basis of which the spectators construct their individual subject positions, structures of identification and visual pleasure.

The source of all these ambiguities, and that which manifests them as differentiation, structure, and semiotic system, is the cinema itself, with its infinite capacity of divisions, based as it is on the total divisibility of its materials (the visible world) and the intermittence of its *physical* material, the individual frames of the celluloid strip, and its *optical* material, the beam of light. Lulu, the "free woman," living without memory or regret, without guilt or volition, is a pure invention of the cinema. That she seems so modern and so real, is a sign of how much modern reality and the cinema have become interchangeable.

Pabst perceived this perhaps more clearly than most of his contemporaries. His emphasis on the cinema creating its own time (that of the motion of the camera whose signifiers the characters become and to which they lend their gestures, faces, and expressivity) and its own space (that of editing and lighting, of the cut on movement or the cut according to the dynamics of the gaze) makes Louise Brooks embody the principle of the cinema itself, in its distinctiveness from literature, the theater, and the other arts. But in this very principle lies an objectification of human beings and a humanization of technology such as the cinema has developed for itself and – through its institutions – has rendered autonomous. For this intelligence is the principle of divisibility and division itself, of exchange and substitution, as it can be observed in the symbolic logic of Western culture and society. By contrast, it is a sign of Louise Brooks's intelligence that she decided not to become the objectified commodity which the logic of this process demanded of her. What Pabst could not prevent in any case was the momentous shift, whereby the film industry, seizing on the woman's body, and focusing gratification so much on the voyeuristic look, turned the cinema into an obsessional, fetishistic instrument, and thus betrayed in some sense its modernist promise, by making this modernism instrumental and subservient to the logic of capital and the commodity.[11]

Notes

1. In the play, Alwa Schön makes the following observation: "The curse on our literature today is that it is much too literary. We know of no other questions and problems than those that crop up among writers and intellectuals. We see no further in our art than the limits of our interests as a class. To find our way back to great and powerful art, we would have to move much more among people who have never read a book in their lives, and for whom the simplest animal instincts serve as a guide to their action. I have tried to work along these lines in my play *Earth Spirit*." From *Die Büchse der Pandora*, act I (my translation).

2. See Wedekind, quoted in Artur Kutscher, *Wedekinds Leben und Werk* (Munich: List, 1964), p. 128: "When writing the part of Lulu, the main problem was to depict the body of a woman through the words she speaks. With every line of hers I asked myself, does it make her young and beautiful?"

3. Georg Lukács, "Thoughts on an aesthetic for the cinema," trans. Barrie Ellis Jones, *Framework*, No. 14 (Spring 1981), 3.

4. Wedekind, according to Kutscher (p. 127), declared Geschwitz the tragic figure because he hoped to deflect the legal objections to his plays, raised at three successive

trials in Berlin, Leipzig, and again Berlin. However, it is very important that his conception of Geschwitz is seen as "non-nature," i.e. outside the binary opposition of social/natural and of gender-based sexual difference: "What the courts did not object to was that I had made the terrible fate of being outside nature [*Unnatürlichkeit*] which this human being has to bear, the object of serious drama. . . . Figures like her belong to the race of Tantalus. . . . I was driven by the desire to snatch from public ridicule the enormous human tragedy of exceptionally intense and quite fruitless inner struggles. . . ." From the Foreword to *Die Büchse der Pandora* (my translation).

   5. Leopold Jessner, *Schriften*, ed. Hugo Fetting (Berlin (GDR): Henschel, 1979), p. 213.

   6. Louise Brooks, *Lulu in Hollywood* (New York: Praeger, 1982), p. 94.

   7. Siegfried Kracauer, *From Caligari to Hitler: A Psychological History of the German Film* (Princeton: Princeton University Press, 1947). What Kracauer argues in this famous study is that the depictions of Oedipal conflicts and their modes of narrative resolution in German films of the Weimar era are so paranoid and perverse because they are a "screen," a field of projection and a compensation for objectively insoluble political contradictions and immovable class barriers. Sexuality – always an overdetermined cultural code – becomes the site for the representation of highly ambiguous fears about any social existence outside the bourgeois order, outside the law, outside the hierarchical markers of identity and difference recognized by the middle class. The bourgeois film of the Weimar period does indeed have a narrative structure whose symbolic code remains remarkably constant throughout the 1920s: it is Kracauer's achievement to have pointed this out.

   8. See Siegfried Kracauer, *Die Angestellten: Aus dem neuesten Deutschland* (Frankfurt am Main: Suhrkamp, 1971). The book originally appeared in serial form in the *Frankfurter Zeitung* during the course of 1929.

   9. This reading owes a great deal to a discussion with Mary Ann Doane and a seminar paper she gave at the University of Iowa during the spring of 1979.

   10. Brooks, pp. 105–6.

   11. A longer version of this article appeared as "Lulu and the Meter Man: Louise Brooks, Pabst and *Pandora's Box*," *Screen*, 24, Nos 4–5 (July–October 1983), 4–36. It appears here with the permission of the *Screen* editors.

Script

Pandora's Box (Lulu): A Film by G. W. Pabst. Trans. Christopher Holme. New York: Simon & Schuster, 1971.

Selected Bibliography

Amengual, Barthélemy. *G. W. Pabst*. Paris: Seghers, 1966.
Atwell, Lee. *G. W. Pabst*. Boston: Twayne, 1977.
Aubry, Yves and Jacques Petat. *G. W. Pabst*. Paris: Anthologie du Cinéma, 1968.
Brennicke, Ilona and Joe Hembus. *Klassiker des deutschen Stummfilms 1910–1930*. Munich: Goldmann, 1983.
Brooks, Louise. "Actors and the Pabst spirit." *Focus on Film*, No. 8 (n.d.), 45–6.
—— *Lulu in Hollywood*. New York: Knopf, 1982.
—— "Pabst and Lulu." *Sight & Sound*, 34, No. 3 (Summer 1965), 123–7.
Buache, Freddy. *G. W. Pabst*. Lyon: SERDOC, 1965.

Davidson, David. "From virgin to dynamo: the 'amoral' woman in European film." *Cinema Journal*, 21, No. 1 (Fall 1981), 31–58.

Eisner, Lotte H. *The Haunted Screen*. Trans. Roger Greaves. Berkeley: University of California Press, 1969.

Kracauer, Siegfried. *From Caligari to Hitler: A Psychological History of the German Film*. Princeton: Princeton University Press, 1947.

Krasna-Krausz, A. "G. W. Pabst's *Lulu*." *Close Up*, 4, No. 4 (April 1929), 24–30.

4

GERTRUD KOCH

Between two worlds:
von Sternberg's *The Blue Angel* (1930)

Josef von Sternberg belonged to that group of directors who insisted that
their films were a product of their own fantasies, their own expressive
capacities. In short, he claimed for himself the status of an *auteur*. His autocratic point of view led to a situation where Sternberg tried to prove obsti-
nately and repeatedly – verifying his facts with threatening and sarcastic
statements – that his most famous myth, the transformation of Maria
Magdalena Sieber, *née* Dietrich, into the *objet d'art* Marlene Dietrich, was
exclusively a product of the director's art. "Marlene, c'est moi," he
proclaimed, in analogy to Gustave Flaubert's famous pronouncement,
"Madame Bovary, c'est moi."

Filmed in 1930 by Sternberg in Berlin, *The Blue Angel* (*Der blaue Engel*)
gained its reputation as the film in which "Svengali Joe" led Marlene
Dietrich to fame in their first film together. Just how Marlene Dietrich, who
had previously appeared in a number of silent films with varying degrees of
success, was discovered by the filmmaker remains open to debate, one that
depends on considerable hearsay, legend, and fabrication. Marlene's
entrance into Sternberg's pandemonium, however, only superficially
describes her relationship to the director's *oeuvre*. The difficulty in analyz-
ing *The Blue Angel* within an historical framework lies in the way various
film-historical perspectives, each making its own slice into the web of film
history, cut out different and differing interpretive contexts. Clearly, a film
cannot escape the hermeneutic problem of bias, of preconceived socio-
cultural and theoretical frames of reference, all of which structure both
interpretation and taxonomy.

The Blue Angel and its reception history provide a striking example of
how various historically defined interpretive parameters result in totally
different aesthetic judgments. Theodor W. Adorno, for example, deals
harshly with Sternberg's film by playing off the literary qualities of Heinrich
Mann's novel, *Professor Unrat* (1905),[1] against the film's deficiencies,

coming to the conclusion that the film softens Mann's biting social critique and thus operates like a typical commodity produced by the culture industry. In 1952, on the occasion of a paperback edition of the novel (published now as *Der blaue Engel*), Adorno spoke again of the differences between film and novel, commenting as well on the change of title which ensued after the film's success:

[T]he film, which today is looked upon as an heroic feat, voluntarily reflected a conviction in the pre-Hitler days, which, without the censors having had to intervene, was institutionalized after Hitler's rise, and only the pretty legs of Marlene Dietrich belie that fact. Enraptured by the care-fully doled-out portions of sex appeal, the viewer overlooks the fact that the committee making the film removed every social jab, turning a petit bourgeois demon into a sentimental comedy figure. In Heinrich Mann's novel, Unrat ends up in a paddy wagon. He rises to greatness as a degener-ate due to his obsessive vendetta against a world of contumacious students. His antisocial acts are legitimized once he turns around the absurd precepts of society's own notion of authority and fights back. The hero of the film, on the other hand, drags himself – his pedagogical *eros* can no longer stand it – into his former classroom and dies there broken-hearted and transfigured. The real woman who destroys him is turned into a splendid creature who seems to take care of the old man, rather than turning him into a procurer. This venerable blockbuster is one of those detestably mendacious and – except for the famous legs – quite boring commodities which captures ticket-buyers with its "life-as-it-is" come-on, while simultaneously filtering its view through the very hypocrisy attri-buted to the audience by the gentlemen hoping to force feed them. The very humanism that *The Blue Angel* elicits through its softening touch-ups, allowing for an all-too-human chuckle, has no other purpose than to silence a denunciation of inhumanity evident in Heinrich Mann's novel, and twenty years after its publication still so unbearable to the novel's beneficiaries that they sought their fortune in a patched-together film script.[2]

In his polemic, Adorno relies on a method which had long served as a standard procedure in discussions of filmed literature. The aesthetic stan-dards of the literary original become the touchstone by which one measures the veracity of the transformation. Seldom does one consider that film criticism has its own immanent criteria. Adorno's method conceals a socio-cultural bias, one that proceeds from the assumption that cinema is part of the "culture industry," thus emphasizing film's commodity and commercial status, and in doing so, obstructing any intrinsic or aesthetic perspective.

While Adorno categorically damned cinema because of the universality of its commodity forms and the character of its producers from Hollywood to

Babelsberg, the film critic and theoretician, Siegfried Kracauer, came to a more measured diachronic reading of the film in two separate reviews. In looking at the relationship between novel and film, Kracauer was less concerned with the question of the film's fidelity to the novel. In 1930 he noted in *Die neue Rundschau*;

> Crucial is not whether Heinrich Mann's novel has been misused, but rather that this prewar book was even chosen. What motive guided film producers to the dark side of Professor Unrat's psyche, and to his relationship with the singer, Lola, rather than to Mann's *The Subject* [*Der Untertan*]? Precisely because, should its topicality be criticized, such reproaches could be effectively countered. Whether the selection of subjects and forms for public consumption is conscious or unconscious, it is in any case geared towards repressing and disguising reality, as the case of *The Blue Angel* paradigmatically demonstrates. The personal fate of Unrat is not an end in itself, but rather a way of escaping reality. It can thus be compared to a painting on a theater curtain which is supposed to simulate the play itself.[3]

Kracauer's contemporary criticism of *The Blue Angel* turns away from the novel to an independent view of the film. Even though Kracauer's verdict is no less harsh than Adorno's, he does deal with the film's own idiom, drawing attention to certain aspects of the film which will become important in Sternberg's subsequent work. Kracauer speaks not only of the successful use of sound, the film's technical perfection in general, but also of Sternberg's lack of both social and psychological realism. Kracauer emphasizes the film's artificial quality, the vacuum created by Sternberg, a deflation of reality:

> Neither Unrat nor Lola have enough air to breathe. The conclusion can thus be supported that the film does not attempt to prove the reality of their existence as much as it conceals the existence of reality.[4]

Sixteen years later, Kracauer, now in exile in the United States, once again turns to *The Blue Angel*. In his psychological history of German film, *From Caligari to Hitler*, he expands his socio-psychological critique to an *a posteriori* apocalyptic prophecy:

> It is as if the film implied a warning, for these screen figures anticipate what will happen in real life a few years later. The boys are born Hitler youths, and the cockcrowing device is a modest contribution to a group of similar, if more ingenious, contrivances much used in Nazi concentration camps.
>   Two characters stand off from these events; the clown of the artists' company, a mute figure constantly observing his temporary colleague,

and the school beadle who is present at the professor's death and somehow recalls the night-watchman in *The Last Laugh*. He does not talk either. These two witness, but they do not participate. Whatever they may feel, they refrain from interference. Their silent resignation foreshadows the passivity of many people under totalitarian rule.[5]

While Adorno views the specific difference between *The Blue Angel* and *Professor Unrat* in terms of the unspecific abstraction of commodity fetishism, connecting Babelsberg to Hollywood, Kracauer sees things from another perspective altogether. For him *The Blue Angel* is the product of a specific set of constellations bound up in the rise of National Socialism. After grounding his first analysis of the film's escapist attributes in a moral tenor, he uses a much more measured tone in the second critique. Kracauer not only speaks of the film's aesthetic virtues, but likewise grants the work a certain – and possibly unwitting – clairvoyance. The portrayal of a typical petit-bourgeois rebel, a character who in the end returns broken and repentant to that place where his rebellion began, communicates escape and ultimate subordination to authority.

Kracauer interprets the film, and especially Emil Jannings's performance, in terms of its social psychology, an approach which would have seemed inappropriate for the first critique. It remains an open question whether Kracauer's reading of the film convinces – or whether it is simply a matter of the exiled author's projected experience of National Socialist rule and annihilation. Sternberg seems to have been astonished by Kracauer's interpretation of the film as a foreshadowing of fascist terror. The theme of sadism, which Kracauer also identifies in the film, matches no doubt the sadomasochistic contours of many Sternberg films. This strain, however, probably owes more to the specific psychological features of the film's sexual politics than to fascism. Adorno does address the question of the film's national relevance – and just as quickly does away with it. Unlike Kracauer, he nonetheless gets stuck in the same framework when he recalls Mann's specific social criticism as a basis for comparison between film and novel. The question poses itself: how German is *The Blue Angel*?

As is well known, the film was shot in two versions, an American and a German one. Sternberg emphasizes that he had never previously visited Germany, that he had no knowledge of conditions there, and was not even curious. He apparently declined an offer from his producer, Erich Pommer, to visit Lübeck, the North German town where Mann had situated the novel. If we discern aspects of German history and a commentary on Weimar society, these would have to have evolved in defiance to Sternberg's self-image as an autocratic filmmaker, an *auteur* who maintains the right to mold the German team according to his own designs. It would seem to follow that one should be able to distinguish elements in *The Blue Angel* which reflect the divergent experiences of an American director of Austrian birth and a production team caught in transition from the Weimar Republic to the Third Reich.

Concerning the script, Sternberg states that he discussed his ideas for a "free" adaptation with Heinrich Mann, whose novel had been published in 1905. He lists as scriptwriters Robert Liebmann, who later received credit for dialogue and lyrics, and Karl Vollmöller, who, according to Sternberg, received credit as a friend, although his contribution to the film's conception and composition was negligible. Finally, the name of the famous playwright, Carl Zuckmayer, appears in the credits. To be sure, Zuckmayer ironically plays down his participation. Sternberg's claim that the script was largely his own can therefore not be so easily ruled out of hand. Zuckmayer describes how the large team of writers slowly produced the script:

> In this office real work was accomplished. A detailed exposé was produced, what professionals call a treatment, followed by a first draft, and then the director did what he wanted to. And because he was a really productive director, who internalized and assimilated all those suggestions coming from others, giving them artistic form, instead of deforming them, everything was OK.[6]

Sternberg himself insists that the figure of the professor stemmed from his childhood experience, and the extremely illusory, fictitious, and unreal character of Sternberg's films makes it plausible to see in the pedagogue traces of Sternberg's personal history, rather than of the Third Reich. If we assume for a moment that the *auteur* theory, to which Sternberg readily subscribes, is correct, then it might pay to look a bit closer at a few of Sternberg's biographically related themes.

Sternberg was born on 19 May 1894 in Vienna, the son of Moses and Serafin Sternberg, and was given the name Jonas. His childhood in an impoverished, orthodox Jewish family was apparently shaped by his father's brutal strictness and by the repeated journeys his father made to America in search of fortune. Little Jonas was 3 years old when his father left for the States; at 7 he saw his father again in the US, returned to Vienna three years later, and finally emigrated at 14 to America. Sternberg's contradictory and fragmentary autobiography only allows a partial reconstruction of his troubled childhood. His battle for survival was apparently accompanied by a struggle with language. As a child of 6 years, Sternberg received religious instruction in Hebrew, "without knowing the meaning of a single word."[7] His Hebrew teacher became the model for Professor Unrat in *The Blue Angel*:

> The instructor was a terror. We dared not open our mouths, with the result that the entire class developed loose bowels. Stalking the room with a ruler in his hand, sniffing at each pupil in turn, our persecutor would soon

discover the culprit, and with a triumphant exclamation haul him out of his seat to escort him to a platform which never served any other purpose. On this pedestal he then transfixed the victim with a petrifying glare, made him extend his small hand, smacked it with his ruler, and made sarcastic reference to inadequate sphincter control. Then he allowed the scholar to seek the sanctuary of a toilet that was never reached in time to do any good.[8]

The sadistic traits spoken of by Kracauer are certainly sadomasochistically refined in *The Blue Angel*. They are transformed into the professor's masochistic subjugation rituals and gestures, and the students' revenge fantasies, ones involving the sexual distress of their teacher. The controlled austerity with which Sternberg drapes, channels, and overloads symbols of excess in his films can be explained by early sadomasochistic punishment rituals. His usage of language as aural material, as a flow of word sounds, rather than as a medium of communication, is also typical of his films. The actors in *The Blue Angel*, especially, are known to have complained bitterly about Sternberg's despotism, his prodding efforts to get the right tone in a language in which they felt themselves to be more competent and at home than the visitor from across the ocean.

One of the most striking characteristics of the films of Josef von Sternberg – formerly little Jonas, now spewed forth from a whale called the New World – is the transformation of unintelligible signs into aesthetic form, mythological signs whose meanings are coded in formal design, their signification embodied exclusively in such designs. The majority of his films take place in exotic and imaginary spaces: Morocco, Macao, Shanghai, Spain, Russia, Japan, and, yes, a small town in Germany. *The Blue Angel* is probably the first film in which Sternberg produces a merely illusory reality of a place, one whose reality originates wholly in his fantasy. His last film, *The Saga of Anahatan* (1952), has Japanese dialogue while Sternberg narrates in English. Rather than translating a foreign language, he relates the story he hears in the film's sounds. Josef von Sternberg's imaginary dream world reaches the viewer's eyes and ears infinitely quietly, transported by a magic carpet made up of foreign sounds, including Marlene Dietrich's *Berlinerisch*, full of symbolic mystery. Sternberg spells languages according to a symbolic rhythm of mythic signs associated with them: his cinematic universe is a completely synthetic translation of linguistic sounds into images, thereby completely detouring reality. As Kracauer notes regarding *The Blue Angel*, Sternberg's talent for sound film was made of such stuff. The artificial and synthetic component in Sternberg's mythology which drains the prevailing realistic mythology – a mythology which pretends to be natural, evoking what Alexander Kluge calls "average realism" – has been discovered by camp culture (cf. Susan Sontag) as raw material for narcissistic-imaginary masks and costumes, as a fetish for partial instincts. By

Plates 8 and 9 Before and after: Professor Rath changes costumes and identities in *The Blue Angel*. Photos courtesy of Stiftung Deutsche Kinemathek.

constructing a completely synthetic mythology, Sternberg suggests that masks and roles are totally interchangeable. In many of his films, his characters change identities more than once: e.g. Unrat in *The Blue Angel*, who appears chameleon-like in a series of costumes. Masked balls and stage shows are privileged events in the Sternbergian empire and seem to take place continuously. Clothes are changed either in the isolated jungle surrounding the shipwrecked (*The Saga of Anahatan*) or in the dressing-room and bedroom of *The Blue Angel*. Costumes are tailored out of plants, turning a woman into a costume, a man into a rooster, in other words, effecting the complete metamorphosis of nature. Sternberg's costumes and sets, his feathers, fur, helmets and hats, lace, veils, his obliquely gabled roofs, and attic rooms with bed and bookcase, all function as language: they are signs of a mythology.

The elements of kitsch, bombastic and flamboyant touches for which critics have taken Sternberg to task since *The Blue Angel*, have been too seldom seen as self-sufficient aesthetic forms. Sternberg's overbearing narcissism certainly awakens fear of contamination. A quick comparison with reality guarantees a quicker appeal to a questionable common sense than do the affirmative traits in Sternberg's films, ones critics claim to perceive. Sternberg's films, however, are only good when they are overextended, when steamy eroticism radiates from the ice-cold narcissism of

Plate 9

Marlene Dietrich or Gary Cooper in *Morocco* (1930). His films are unbearable when, for example, Jannings thunders his "Oh Lord!" pathos in *The Last Command* (1928) or in *The Blue Angel*.

Sternberg is not interested in human beings *per se*, except in terms of their form, their larva-like design. As in the case of Lola and Unrat, many couples in Sternberg's films simply do not match; they chase rather than hold each other. The feeling of discrepancy found in many Sternbergian women points toward a sadistic component: he turns his women into fetishistically exaggerated *dominas*, who, like Lola, cruelly stage their adultery in front of humiliated husbands. Sternberg imagines his men as more or less sculptured, masculine men of extreme physical or – like Unrat – moral austerity and rigor, except when they are transformed into narcissistic objects, e.g. Gary Cooper's sexually provocative indolence. Such images make it easy to reconstruct psychoanalytically the family drama of little Jonas: the father whom he describes as a strict wild man, the teacher a sadistic tormentor, bound in a hatred of anal catastrophe. The many years during which Sternberg stood under his mother's authority never allowed him to believe in the myth of the "weaker sex." Thus Marlene Dietrich wears the signs and insignia of a phallic mother, of a strong woman. Such elements move far beyond simple vampness: Sternberg's fissured erotic wishes become images and lead an independent life in the panerotic cosmos of his fictions. Transvestism and transsexuality in his films defy one-dimensional symbolic connections because they communicate and signify via visual design. The indignation his films have provoked stems no doubt from those same disorderly desires, the ones Emil Jannings overstates.

The Blue Angel sets the tone for the imaginary within Sternberg's *oeuvre*, one transported by women. *The Blue Angel* is therefore not unjustly famous as a Marlene Dietrich vehicle. She embodies a new acting style, the style of Sternberg's subsequent work, one contrasting with Jannings's naturalism, the dominant idiom at the time. There are, of course, a number of aesthetic breaks caused by the incompatibility of the two aesthetic conceptions. In the film world of Sternberg, *The Blue Angel* is a transition film in the true sense of the word.

This can be best observed in the different acting styles of Marlene Dietrich and Emil Jannings. Jannings remained tied to the conventions of a naturalistically tinged psychology, presenting the deterioration of a psyche, acting "in character" as theater people call it. He utilizes a full range of mimicry, gestures, and intonations; inner decay is visualized through outward behavior. What gets lost in the process is exactly that which Sternberg is striving for, namely the dissolution of an individual in an aestheticized and illusory universe. Jannings's rolling eyes, exaggerated gesticulation, child-like grin when spying on Lola, his trembling cheeks, nodding head, open hands, fearful looks, quaking voice with its false solemnity, finally his concealed insanity: they document Jannings's vain attempts to give his all, rather than demonstrate an internal connection to Sternberg's aesthetics. Jannings's erotic obsession – the film's actual theme – fades to the degree that it can no longer be distinguished from the pubescent crushes of his students. They at least know that Lola's erotic mythology promises more than hearth and home.

Marlene Dietrich as Lola knows better how to present herself as a type rather than a character, defining herself through body movement, her choice of lingerie and dresses, avoiding a humanistic portrayal. Her often-mentioned legs (usually covertly denounced) are in fact much more impressive as metaphors of erotic promise than all of Jannings's suffering pyrotechnics. The latter merely hopes to expose underneath all that erotic decline a valuable character in conflict with himself. Jannings wishes to appear moral in Sternberg's unabashedly amoral universe.

Just how little Sternberg cares for the psychic make-up of his characters can be demonstrated by the fact that he borrows the film's socio-historical ambience from German expressionist cinema rather than from reality. A number of street sets in *The Blue Angel* are direct quotes from other expressionist films, clearly indicating that Sternberg was a totally synthetically oriented director who viewed artificiality as his own reality. The classical opening shot, localizing the film's story, consists of an expressionistically chaotic landscape of rooftops and chimneys: a stylistic quotation, placing the film firmly in a film-historical context. Sternberg also stages his interiors theatrically, continually creating narrowed perspectives, ones that establish relationships between characters in terms of beholder and object viewed: a screen behind which Lola changes clothes; a spiral staircase to her bedroom, good for theatrical entrances and exits, allowing Lola to seduce and simultaneously guide Unrat's glances; a tiny balcony for the chosen one, where Unrat can take in the show; jealous looks through half-closed doors; curtains and stage sets which sometimes function as carriers of images, sometimes as visual barriers. In *The Blue Angel* Sternberg undoubtedly tests a whole series of later stylistic idiosyncrasies.

The most interesting aspect of *The Blue Angel* is the use of sound. Not because Marlene Dietrich is really a good singer – her musical offerings are modest to be sure – but rather because Sternberg makes original use of the new possibility. It is noteworthy that he develops his own approach to sound, disregarding the prevailing awkward usage. He creates a wall of sound. Lotte Eisner describes the sound aesthetics of *The Blue Angel* in her famous study of Weimar cinema:

Sternberg had made only one sound film before *Der Blaue Engel* (*The Blue Angel*), but his work in the American studios had taught him how to use sound more effectively than the German filmmakers of his day. An example to note is the play on doors, from which snatches of laughter or singing escape as soon as they are opened. In these early days of the talkie

Plates 10 and 11 The beholder and the beheld: Rath's initial encounter with Lola. A spectator from the start enthralled by the spectacle of her, he will soon become a captive audience. Photos courtesy of Stiftung Deutsche Kinemathek.

he has still to learn how to lap-dissolve or fade out sound as doors or windows are closed. But Sternberg succeeds in associating a sparkling, dazzling ''Impressionism'' with the German chiaroscuro; and this Impressionism is joined by a visual eroticism as soon as the footlights come on and Marlene Dietrich delivers her loaded, ambiguous songs.[9]

What Eisner calls ''impressionistic'' is in fact an ongoing characteristic of Sternberg, namely his dissolution of space, his flowing transitions and movement.

The success of *The Blue Angel* in Germany can be explained by the fact that the film was less successful in the United States. Studio executives indeed held the film back from release until after *Morocco* had won an American audience for Dietrich. The objective reason for such divergent receptions lies in the film's own hybrid quality, in its utilization of contradictory film-aesthetic paradigms, which do not necessarily produce a unified whole. *The Blue Angel* plays an important role in Sternberg's *oeuvre* because

Plate 11

it foreshadows his later – and more accomplished – artificial and exotic worlds, without however achieving the aesthetic density of this later work.

Translated from the German by Jan-Christopher Horak

Notes

1. Theodor W. Adorno, "Ein Titel," *Die Neue Zeitung*, 25 January 1952, 4. The editors of *Die Neue Zeitung* changed Adorno's original title to "Warum nicht *Professor Unrat*? Zu einem geänderten Titel." The article is included in Theodor W. Adorno, *Gesammelte Schriften* (Frankfurt am Main: Suhrkamp, 1974), XI, 656–7.
2. ibid.
3. Siegfried Kracauer, "*Der blaue Engel*," *Die neue Rundschau* (1930), published in *Von Caligari zu Hitler: Eine psychologische Geschichte des deutschen Films*, trans. Ruth Baumgarten and Karsten Witte (Frankfurt am Main: Suhrkamp, 1979), pp. 418–21. This volume, the second in Witte's planned complete edition of Kracauer's writings, includes a new and more accurate translation of *From Caligari to Hitler* as well as an appendix containing Kracauer's collected film criticism written during the years 1924 to 1939. It is not only in the case of *The Blue Angel* that the writing from two different periods – in Weimar Germany and in exile – poses interesting possibilities for comparison.

4. Kracauer, p. 419.

5. Siegfried Kracauer, *From Caligari to Hitler: A Psychological History of the German Film* (Princeton: Princeton University Press, 1947), p. 218.

6. "Aufmarsch der Filmautoren. (Das Arbeitskollegium des Films *Der blaue Engel*.)" Program (from the archives of Deutsches Institut für Filmkunde, Wiesbaden). Reproduced in *Joseph von Sternberg: Eine Darstellung*, ed. Alice Goetz and Helmut W. Banz with the assistance of Otto Kellner (Mannheim: Verband der Deutschen Filmclubs, 1966), p. 54.

7. Josef von Sternberg, *Fun in a Chinese Laundry* (New York: Collier, 1973), p. 7.

8. ibid.

9. Lotte H. Eisner, *The Haunted Screen*, trans. Roger Greaves (Berkeley: University of California Press, 1969), p. 314.

Script

The Blue Angel: The Novel by Heinrich Mann: The Film by Josef von Sternberg. Ed. Stanley Hochman. New York: Ungar, 1979.
Der blaue Engel. Ed. Hart Wegner. New York: Harcourt Brace Jovanovich, 1982.

Selected Bibliography

Baxter, John. *The Cinema of Josef von Sternberg.* London/New York: Zwemmer/Barnes, 1971.
Baxter, Peter. "On the naked thighs of Miss Dietrich." *Wide Angle*, 2, No. 2 (1978), 18–25.
—— (ed.). *Sternberg.* London: British Film Institute, 1980.
Firda, Richard Arthur. "Literary origins: Sternberg's film *The Blue Angel*." *Literature/Film Quarterly*, 7, No. 2 (1979), 126–36.
Kracauer, Siegfried. *From Caligari to Hitler: A Psychological History of the German Film.* Princeton: Princeton University Press, 1947.
—— *Von Caligari zu Hitler: Eine psychologische Geschichte des deutschen Films.* Trans. Ruth Baumgarten and Karsten Witte. Frankfurt am Main: Suhrkamp, 1979, pp. 418–21.
Sarris, Andrew. *The Films of Josef von Sternberg.* New York: Museum of Modern Art, 1966.
Sternberg, Josef von. *Fun in a Chinese Laundry.* New York: Collier, 1973.
Wagner, Geoffrey. *The Novel and the Cinema.* Cranbury, NJ: Fairleigh Dickinson University Press, 1975.
Wegner, Hart. "*Der blaue Engel*: a feature film in foreign language instruction." *Unterrichtspraxis*, 12, No. 2 (Fall 1979), 30–6.
Weinberg, Herman G. *Josef von Sternberg.* New York: Dutton, 1967.
Willis, Don. "Sternberg: the context of passion." *Sight & Sound*, 47, No. 2 (Spring 1978), 104–9.

5

ALAN WILLIAMS

Reading Ophüls reading Schnitzler: *Liebelei* (1933)

The work of Arthur Schnitzler was important to Max Ophüls, both as vehicle and as cultural reference point. In interviews and writings, Ophüls referred to Schnitzler frequently, comparing and contrasting the Austrian writer's work and attitudes with his own. Ophüls adapted a Schnitzler text as his last project in pre-Nazi Germany (*Liebelei*, 1933) and another as his first project on his return to Europe after World War II (*La Ronde*, 1950). But both these events are more the result of happenstance than of conscious design. Out of all the unrealized projects that punctuate this director's professional history, two Schnitzler works were actually produced as films. Change almost anything about the ever-shifting state of European cinema production (at least the economically marginal sectors in which Ophüls typically worked) and we might have had three filmed Balzacs and no Schnitzlers in the Ophülsian canon.

We must be wary, in fact, of seeing only a marriage of compatible sensibilities in *Liebelei*. Ophüls liked some Schnitzler works and not others, and those he liked he saw in differing ways:

There's a nice thing about Schnitzler's life itself. He wrote *La Ronde* at 23 and *Liebelei* at 40, and you'd think it was the other way round. [Indeed! These "facts" are wrong: *Liebelei* was written before *Reigen* (*La Ronde*), though not by much. – A.W.] But when you know his work well, you understand. *La Ronde* is opposed to love and its cynicism is not the fruit of lived experience. But at 40 or 45, Schnitzler is nostalgic for purity and that's why – because he's experienced it – the purity in *Liebelei* is genuine. If he'd written *Liebelei* at 23, he would have infused it with far too much romantic melancholy, whereas at 40 he could view his subject from the necessary distance. That's why I find that *La Ronde*, despite the cynicism of a 23 year old, has a splendid purity and freshness.[1]

To judge by deed rather than by word, Ophüls seems to have had far less quarrel with his supposedly young, cynical Schnitzler than with the putatively more mature playwright: *La Ronde* is strikingly more faithful to its original text than is *Liebelei*.[2]

One can find in these remarks of Ophüls's a kind of willful paradox that is typical of his public statements, and that is more significant than his mangling of the chronology of Schnitzler's life. Ophüls's public statements are dominated by a figure that one can call the "union of opposites." Another example that crops up often is that comedy is only effective when there is tragedy within it, and vice versa.[3] This *topos* also makes its way into the film scripts: "Our marriage is only superficially superficial," says Monsieur de . . . This is merely the apparent form of a profound understanding.

The union of opposites *topos* links Ophüls, in my reading of his work at least, to the French *moraliste* tradition, and particularly to Pascal and to La Rochefoucauld ("Nos vertus ne sont que nos vices déguisés"). It also separates him from Schnitzler, for whom, no doubt, such thinking would seem fatally to miss the point of human existence. Schnitzler is Freud's contemporary in ways that Ophüls simply is not, and it is likely he would have rejected dichotomies of innocent/decadent, tragedy/comedy, and so on in favor of a deep structure-surface-structure configuration akin to that of psychoanalysis. It is a question, for Schnitzler, of instincts versus convention, energetics versus hermeneutics, as in this passage, chosen from *Beatrice*:

In a few moments the set was ended. Both couples met at the net, racquets in hand, and stood there, chatting. Their features, earlier made tense by the excitement of the game, now melted into vacuous smiles; their eyes, which before had followed the spring of the balls so keenly, now met dreamily. Beatrice realized this with strange uneasiness: it was as if the atmosphere, formerly so clean and pure, had suddenly become stormy and misty, and she could not help thinking: How well this evening would end if suddenly, by some magic, all the inhibitions of society should be done away with, and these young people might follow without hindrance the secret, perhaps even unsuspected urge which impels them. And suddenly she realized that there was a lawless world — that she had just stepped out of just such a one, and that its breath still hung around her. It was only because of that, that she saw today what otherwise would have escaped her innocent eyes.[4]

Similar passages can be found elsewhere in Schnitzler's prose fiction, and though the idea is less explicit in the plays, it seems crucial to them. *Reigen* (*La Ronde*) is a study of how the "urges" of the "lawless world" break through the surface in encounters among varying social types. Ophüls, while keeping most of Schnitzler's text, displaces its interest in his 1950 film adaptation. In the film, desire is always already embodied in the social system, which is there, not to repress it, but *as its expression*. Ophüls does not see desire and the social system as representing two warring levels, but as necessarily implying one another. (But let the reader beware. The film is notoriously open to a variety of other readings – most curiously to the "neo-Christian" interpretation of its subject as "the vanity of the flesh and the absurdity of life without faith."[5])

Another way of looking at Ophüls and Schnitzler is to see the latter as speaking from and of turn-of-the-century Vienna, the former from the edge of the industrial German provinces several decades later. Even today Ophüls is sometimes erroneously identified as a "Viennese" filmmaker. Nothing could be farther from the truth. Vienna was the Other. Ophüls did make several films set there (three features out of twenty-one) not because of nostalgia but, to borrow his own words about Schnitzler, because "he could view his subject with the necessary distance." Vienna seems to have had only one tangible effect on his life: he married a well-known young Viennese actress, Hilde Wall, whom he had directed at the Burgtheater. To believe his somewhat malicious account of the place, they would have been virtually the only two people there under the age of 65. During the few months he spent in the city in 1926, Ophüls found Vienna lifeless and hopelessly tradition-bound. Engaged as a director at the very same Burgtheater that was so important to Arthur Schnitzler throughout his life, Ophüls found that:

Unfortunately, [my colleagues'] imagination did not flow from the same source as did mine. Their cultivated, brilliant minds flourished in a dying city that could only contemplate its own past, whereas mine had undergone the experience of urban industrial life. Of course, I was fascinated by the melancholy charm of Vienna . . . I would have liked to have been a painter and to capture it on canvas. But then I would have wanted to run away. As fast as I could.[6]

It is of course true that Schnitzler himself also saw turn-of-the-century Vienna as a dying culture, turned in upon itself. Yet there is a peculiar quality to Schnitzler's Vienna, because he saw this culture from the inside, as a virtual prisoner. Thus he could cry out against it, but he could only *criticize* it in severely limited ways. The same seems to have been true for Ophüls, though for quite different reasons: he does not seem to have cared *enough* about the city (or, for that matter, to have known it at all well). His Vienna differs only anecdotally from his Paris in *Madame de . . .* (1953) or the Munich of *Lola Montes* (1955). What little historical specificity there is in the portrayal of Vienna in Ophüls's films seems rather distilled from media images of the city – and hence largely from Schnitzler. Gertrud Koch argues that Ophüls had an *imago* of Vienna long before going there, and that the city, as it were, never had a chance to be anything else for him.[7] Ophüls seems to have adapted many of the elements and much of the tone of Schnitzler's view of Vienna, but in the service, as we shall see, of his own rather different purposes.

Ophüls recalls rereading *Liebelei* before accepting to do a film of it, and finding it charming, if "a little dusty."[8] He and his collaborators seem not to have hesitated, in any event, to make major structural changes in the work. Schnitzler's play is in three relatively short acts, for a limited cast, and uses only two simple sets and a few props. It could be described as largely Racinian, in that the vast bulk of the plot does not occur on stage, but rather is described. Ophüls, Hans Wilhelm, and Curt Alexander have chosen to dramatize most of what Schnitzler merely has his characters discuss. And so they have multiplied the number of sets, actors, and episodes. Merely the dramatizing of the exposition in act I – how the characters meet, who they are – results in a film that is one-third over before it even hits a scene taken directly from the work on which it is based.

In the play, act I takes place in the front room of Fritz Lobheimer's flat; he and his friend Theodor Kaiser are not roommates as in the film. The young men enter and, in an exposition that is at times a bit clumsy, establish that Fritz has been having an affair with a married woman, that Theo does not approve, and that the latter has introduced Fritz to Christine, a friend of his lady friend Toni (Mizzi in the film), in the hope of distracting him from "that woman." The two young women, invited by Theo without Fritz's knowledge, arrive. A candlelit supper party ensues, interrupted by the unexpected appearance of The Gentleman (Herr von Eggersdorf in the film). Fritz sends his friends into another room and is confronted with proof of his illicit affair (love letters). He is challenged to a duel by the jealous husband. The latter departs and the party recommences briefly, with Fritz concealing everything from Christine, before the guests leave Fritz alone and the curtain descends.

The long and beautifully handled exposition of the film *Liebelei* is much too complicated even to outline here. Things that are merely alluded to in the play get fleshed out, in many cases more than is strictly necessary to explain what is spoken of in the Schnitzler text. Characters get not only complete names, but visible social backgrounds. We see the opera orchestra in which Christine's father plays, the millinery shop where Mizzi works (where Toni used to work, in the play), the home of the von Eggersdorfs, and so on. The Gentleman's wife becomes a character. There is a sequence to illustrate the husband's suspicions (he comes home early from the opera in hopes of finding his wife with Fritz).

Although the rest of the play is not quite as strikingly expanded in the film version, the same process obtains. There is an added scene for the fatal duel (which is very reminiscent of later Ophüls duels, particularly in *Madame de . . .*), for the setting of conditions for the duel, reactions of various

Plate 12   A shot from the galvanizing opening sequence in the opera house. At the center of the image are Christine (Magda Schneider) and Mizzi (Luise Ullrich) – and a soon-to-be-dropped pair of binoculars. Photo courtesy of Stiftung Deutsche Kinemathek.

additional minor characters to the conditions, and so on. The last event in the narrative, Christine's suicide, is only predicted in the play but gets full dramatic treatment in the film.

In addition to this sort of change, and presumably to make for a less "stagy" film, things that Schnitzler has happen in one of the play's two sets – Fritz's flat and the much shabbier Weiring home – get shifted around to a variety of locations. This "opening up" of the play entails creating still more minor characters, social situations, and bits of behavior than are introduced merely by visualization of events referred to in Schnitzler's narrative. Ophüls and his collaborators have taken a play that seems to exemplify the notion of economy of means – a "classical" text – and multiplied its entities well beyond necessity.

There are many ramifications of this process, but perhaps the most characteristic of Ophüls's film work is the way in which dramatic space is modified. *Liebelei* the play exemplifies what for André Bazin was the essential, intense, inward-directed space of the stage:

Whether as a performance or a celebration, theater of its very essence must not be confused with nature under penalty of being absorbed by her and ceasing to be. Founded on the reciprocal awareness of those present, it must be opposed to the rest of the world in the same way that play is to reality, concern to indifference, or liturgy to the common use of things. Costume, mask, or make-up, the style of the language, the footlights, all contribute to this distinction, but the clearest sign of all is the stage, the architecture of which has varied without ever ceasing to mark out a privileged spot actually or virtually distinct from nature. . . .

Just as the picture is not to be confounded with the scene it represents and is not a window in a wall, the stage and the decor where the action unfolds are an aesthetic microcosm inserted by force into the universe but essentially distinct from the Nature which surrounds them.[9]

Max Ophüls's film shifts dramatic action from Schnitzler's two constricted sitting-rooms to a succession of hallways, doorways, streets, stairs, windows, balconies. Focused dramatic space cedes to *transitional* space, to spaces *between* things. A crucial scene between Fritz and Baron von Eggersdorf, for example (their last encounter before the film's version of act I of the play), is played on a broad staircase, one of many in the film. Theo first meets Christine and Mizzi at the concierge's box inside the stage door to the opera. Many scenes are set between two places, as with Christine and Fritz's walk through the streets of Vienna on the night of their first meeting. Even the centered dramatic spaces of what remains of Schnitzler's play text have been somewhat displaced. In the play, The Gentleman throws a packet of love letters at Fritz as proof of the liaison. In the film, Baron von Eggersdorf fits a key he has found in his wife's dressing-room into the door to Fritz's flat (itself in an anteroom) and turns it back and forth, his face contorted in silent fury. (Surely this is one of the best uses of sound in this remarkably inventive early talkie: the sharp click of the bolt sliding home is repeated as the Baron's anger grows.)

In addition to this shift in dramatic space, another correlate of Ophüls's structural expansion of the play is a multiplication of accessories, costumes, and bits of dramatic business associated with them. Things that happen in Schnitzler's play happen only once; things that happen in Ophüls's film happen, in various guises, repeatedly. One might even suggest that for Schnitzler's unity of time, place, and action (the unities of classical drama),[10] Ophüls and his scriptwriters have substituted a unity of props and behavior. Consider items of clothing, for example, or musical performances, or going through doors and up and down stairs. It would be tedious and ultimately unrevealing to map out the film in terms of its micro-level dramatic devices, but it could easily enough be done – and a complicated map it would be. (Elsewhere I have given a demonstration, with a rather different sort of film, of this level of analysis.[11]) The point to be retained here is that nothing of the sort happens in Schnitzler, or in any classical dramatic text. But it does happen routinely in the so-called "classic" sound cinema. (This is a very different sort of "classicism" than that of classical drama. "Classical Hollywood cinema" is – alas! – the label most widely used to designate dominant sound film practices from the early 1930s to the present.) In the early 1930s, dominant narrative film practices were not wholly codified, at least not in Europe. *Liebelei* is a bit ahead of its time in terms of commercial screen dramaturgy, on this level of the deployment of dramatic devices.

All of this expansion, specification, and structuration has the effect of profoundly modifying the context of Schnitzler's dramatic vision. Questions left open in the play are answered in the film (for example, the quality of Christine's vocal technique). In choosing to spell out what Schnitzler most often only alludes to, the film's authors have been forced – have forced themselves – to *read* the play, to interpret it, to do some of the work that its original author left to the audience. I do not mean this necessarily as a criticism: a film of *Liebelei* as Schnitzler wrote it would be claustrophobic, pedantic, and (unlike the play) probably doomed to commercial failure. What one can sell in the theater is not, clearly, what one can sell in the cinema. *Liebelei* as a play was one of its author's box-office triumphs. A "faithful" rendering of it would possibly be interesting as minimal cinema, but would be entirely different from the original in terms of audience reception.

What I have said so far could easily be stated as part of a defense against possible charges of infidelity to Schnitzler. But there is another area of modifications performed by the filmmakers which cannot be classified so easily, if at all, as correlates of the change from play to commercially viable film. Ophüls's work substantially modifies the emotional tone of the original play, and Schnitzler's ferocity seems to dissolve in a kind of generalized sentimentality. Octave's famous remark in Jean Renoir's *Rules of the Game* (*La Règle du jeu*, 1939) that "everyone has his reasons," could not be applied to any work by Arthur Schnitzler without adding, "though of course these reasons are always patent self-deception." But it might just apply, unmodified, to Ophüls's rendering of *Liebelei*. Or perhaps – and this is a view I am happier with – the film has been consciously made ambiguous on the question of the moral responsibility of most of its characters.

In Schnitzler's play, there are two sorts of people: Christine and everyone else. She is the only character capable of awareness of her own feelings, and of expressing these to others. Her polar opposite is Theo, who believes only in social gamesmanship and the pleasures of the senses. He thinks that Fritz should forget his dreams of forbidden passions and devote himself to *flirtation* (which is the literal meaning of the word *Liebelei*):

THEODOR: It's not the business of women to be interesting, but to be agreeable. You must seek happiness where I have sought it and found it – where there are no grand scenes, no dangers, no tragic entanglements – where the beginning has no special difficulties, and the ending has no torments – where you take your first kiss with a smile, and part with *very* gentle emotion.[12]

Schnitzler's Theo does not believe that Christine has any real feeling for Fritz, though he changes his mind when he sees her reaction to the latter's death. Ophüls and his collaborators, on the other hand, make Theo aware of and supportive of Christine's feelings. And Fritz himself is also emotionally shifted towards Christine, in the film, though perhaps not as much. At the very end of Schnitzler's act II, Fritz looks around the Weirings' shabby rooms – which Ophüls will make much less shabby – and says to Theo, "I'm *almost* ready to believe that my happiness is here, that this sweet girl . . . but this hour is a tremendous liar!" (p. 65, my italics). Ophüls's Fritz not only knows that his happiness lies with Christine, he pledges eternal love to her in the film's most sentimental scene, an idyllic sleigh ride complete with romantic background music score.

But this is not to say that the cynicism, the alienation from true feeling, characteristic of all persons but Christine in the play is wholly absent from the film. Rather, it has been shifted onto most of the additional characters

Plate 13 Christine (Magda Schneider) and Fritz (Wolfgang Liebeneiner) during their idyllic ride in the snow, evidence of Ophüls seeking to open up Schnitzler's play and shift tonalities. Photo courtesy of Stiftung Deutsche Kinemathek.

devised for the screenplay, such as the Baroness von Eggersdorf, her brother-in-law Major von Eggersdorf (a character not mentioned in Schnitzler's text), Fritz and Theo's commanding officer, and so on. In Ophüls's film, the emotional dividing point seems placed between the two central couples and everyone else. The Others are those who believe in honor over love, appearance over emotion.

Paradoxically, this shift makes the film both less and more bleak than the play. Less bleak because love and good will are possible. People can be nice to each other across class lines: Theo does not automatically make snide remarks about Christine's home as he does in the play (p. 64), nor does he wait until after the funeral to tell her about Fritz's death (p. 75). Fritz can say that he loves Christine. But these changes can also be seen as making matters worse. Fritz is still unworthy of Christine, though now for a different reason. He goes to what a very brief scene identifies as certain death (the Baron is a crack shot) despite his feelings for her and though he must or at least *should* know how she will react. Unlike Theo, he will not opt out of his social surroundings to go to South America (!) out of love and a sense of decency. But one need not read the film this way, and many viewers do not. To see Fritz as an emotional and moral weakling, and Christine as his trusting victim, does not make for a good cry *à la West Side Story*. Yet Theo seems to have been strengthened emotionally in the film precisely in order to offer this contrast with Fritz.

But for any defense of the film, there remains the problem of its ending, the ghostly reuniting of the lovers after death on the soundtrack. Schnitzler would have been appalled: his play ends with Christine's father sobbing "She won't come back," while Ophüls's film returns to the scene of the lovers pledging their troth, accompanied by the same musical theme, dripping with easy sentiment, while their words of love are heard once more. Some viewers like this, and take it at face value (Andrew Sarris, for example).[13] My own reaction is that the carefully ambiguous mood of the work has been broken, and that the end must be taken as ironic – an interpretation that may be supported by the fact that prominent in this "happy" image is a snow-covered graveyard.

But I would argue that the film has been deliberately crafted to support both an empathetic and a judgmental reading of its characters (except Christine), both a straight and an ironic reading of its conclusion. Is this not "success" in the commercial cinema, to leave a work open to as wide a range of audience response as possible (and thus to as large a number as possible of happy, paying customers)? To some extent, how one reads the film will be inflected by whether or not one knows the play on which it is based, or at least the play's author. This is presumably the case here to a greater extent than for most filmed theater. *Liebelei* would not have posed the same problems to its first audiences that it does today, since Schnitzler's play was a semi-classic of the German-language stage in 1932, only one year after its author's death. Ophüls and company, I think, wanted to have it both ways: to craft a double-faced text that can be seen as a sentimental love story or as a critique of emotional dishonesty and inadequacy. (The latter is Schnitzler's recurring stance towards his characters.) That the film was a commercial success in some widely different *milieux* – with German Nazis and with Parisian leftist intellectuals – is at least some evidence that they succeeded.

There are two remarkable aspects of *Liebelei* considered solely for a moment as a film: it is a remarkably adept early talkie (with one exception – see below), and it seems to contain practically all of the motifs that will characterize Ophüls's great cinematic works, particularly those to come after World War II. The two points are not always easy to separate, nor is either easily disengaged from the question of who did what in a collaborative medium.

Ophüls almost overwhelms Schnitzler with music. *Liebelei* is typical of the director's work in that it quotes an opera. As with the other classic opera sequences in the Ophüls canon, from *La signora di tutti* (1934) to *Madame de . . .*, the quotation is ironic in a variety of dramatic and rhetorical senses. The fate of the happy lovers in Mozart's *The Abduction from the Seraglio* (*Die Entführung aus dem Serail*) does *not* foreshadow Christine and Fritz's destiny. And we do not ever *see* the work performed. We hear it while an almost associative-seeming flow of images furthers the (offstage) plot. These images have a free-floating feeling to them, as if they ride on a wave of music that both engulfs them and flows independently past them. From this opening sequence on, the film is periodically characterized by a wide variety of musical materials, from a tinkly player piano to a Beethoven symphony. One result – and in this Ophüls may well have profited from the early work of René Clair – is that the visuals are not continually tied down to any fixed dramatic center. It is easier to cut freely or move a camera in an unusual way if continuity is assured by the soundtrack. Compared to any other play adaptation of the early 1930s, for example Pagnol and Korda's *Marius* (1931), *Liebelei* seems remarkably un-stagebound.

In a broad sense, the fusion of music with play text that Ophüls and his collaborators created for *Liebelei* can be called *operatic*, and it will continue to characterize his later works, even those done with other collaborators. What is remarkable is that it emerges, so to speak, wholly formed in *Liebelei*. The same can be said of the film's ruling opposition, between the worlds of the military and the theater. This will remain a dominant, if not *the* dominant dichotomy in all of Ophüls's work, and again it seems to have emerged fully formed, down to details that will recur in later films such as the various bits of business with soldiers' hats and swords. Now this theme, like so much in the film, is only latent in Schnitzler. Theo and Fritz are reserve officers in the play, but this is only mentioned. Christine sings, and her father plays in the opera orchestra, but again these details are given only as background. Related to the military/theater opposition is the film's loving attention to social hierarchy, which is always on the "military" side of the dichotomy. Ophüls's films give much attention to what can be termed, broadly speaking, master–slave relations. Hence all the servants, obsequious shopkeepers, and so on, that people his films. The constant military presence in his work seems a concretization of his concern for hierarchy in general.

Were these Ophüls's ideas, or did he only admire them after having gotten them from Wilhelm and Alexander? It matters very little. Either way, the director seems to have harked back continually to *Liebelei*, formally and thematically, every time he treated a *belle époque* subject. (Two years later in Italy, Ophüls, Wilhelm and Alexander wrote the script for Ophüls's other master text of the 1930s, *La signora di tutti*. What little of the director's later work cannot be traced to *Liebelei* can be found there.)

Cinematographically, *Liebelei* sets the Ophüls style for the 1930s. Like almost all directors, Ophüls changed his style over time, and like so many others, he seems to have made a major shift immediately after World War II – probably in part as a response to Orson Welles's *Citizen Kane* (1941) and *The Magnificent Ambersons* (1942). (*Caught* (1949) frequently seems a sort of affectionate parody, visually, of *Citizen Kane*.) But the Ophüls style of the 1930s has a bit larger range than that of the later works. The long take, generally with intricate camera movement, is present but does not dominate – as it will seem to in works like *La Ronde*. *Liebelei* manifests an extraordinary range of formal experiment, from classic shot/reverse-shot dialogue sequences to the more recognizably Ophülsian long takes. Again, much will be repeated, as for example a complicated above-the-table tracking sequence-shot of a conversation among the officers, which will reappear with little change in *La Tendre Ennemie* (1936) at a wedding banquet. It seems to me that Ophüls must have made a careful study of a variety of sound-film styles and come up with a broad synthesis of what he had seen. Later in his career, he will eliminate some of this 1930s' synthesis and emphasize other elements, developing the style of what are now considered his mature masterpieces.

In this area I think there is evidence that we are considering something specifically Ophülsian. It is unlikely that the 1930s' Ophüls cinematic style came from anyone other than Ophüls because in this first manifestation, *Liebelei*, we find one of his weaknesses. The amazing thing about *Liebelei* is how such a visually sophisticated film can be filled with occurrences of a trivial error: "bad" directional matches. In the opening sequence, particularly in the shots of the audience, one finds errors that no first-semester film student is allowed to make. People look offscreen left, and the next shot shows what they are supposedly looking at on the right. Later in his career, when convinced of the importance of this problem, Ophüls supposedly wore buttons on his lapels labeled "left" and "right." For the director was, according to his son Marcel, mildly dyslexic – which is, ironically, one explanation of his liking for long takes, in which screen direction is not crucial.[14] Although not conclusive, the inclusion of marked directional mismatches in *Liebelei* seems to be strong circumstantial evidence that visually the film is primarily an expression of its director's way of seeing things. This is important historically because *Liebelei* is one of the earliest examples of what I propose calling "classic" European *découpage* of the 1930s, a style that dominates commercial cinema in France and, perhaps to a lesser degree, elsewhere on the continent. This style is more inclusive and flexible than the so-called "classic Hollywood cinema" of the 1930s, but it is in most senses its functional equivalent.[15] When Ophüls arrived in Paris in 1933, he found somewhat to his surprise that *Liebelei* alone sufficed to give him *entrée* to the French film industry. It seems unlikely that this was accidental. All of Europe, and France in particular, was still adapting to and arguing about the introduction of sound to cinema. *Liebelei* was one of a few privileged works that integrated and deployed early sound practices in a manner that was satisfactory to the European film community and that also seemed to promise commercial success. (Perhaps this was also the reason for the great interest that the Soviet film industry showed in Ophüls during this period.) In any event, the film undoubtedly either sets or anticipates later commercial practices (which is not, of course, to say that later films were as good).

But a curious and basically unresolvable question remains: how important is it that it was *through Schnitzler* that Ophüls discovered "himself" and also possibly a major style of the commercial sound cinema? To some extent, the dramatist may be incidental in these important historical matters. Or perhaps not. What seems certain is that the contemporary interest in *Liebelei* the film is largely due to the meeting of two strong and not always totally compatible artistic sensibilities, and that of their "meeting" came a seminal work in the history and aesthetics of cinema.

Notes

1. Jacques Rivette and François Truffaut, "Interview with Max Ophüls," in *Ophüls*, ed. Paul Willemen (London: British Film Institute, 1978), p. 23.

2. See my article, "Keeping the circle turning: Ophüls's *La Ronde* (1950)," in *Modern European Filmmakers and the Art of Adaptation*, ed. Andrew S. Horton and Joan Magretta (New York: Ungar, 1981), pp. 38–50.

3. See, for instance, *Max Ophüls par Max Ophüls* (Paris: Laffont, 1963), p. 91.

4. Arthur Schnitzler, *Beatrice*, trans. Agnes Jacques (New York: Simon & Schuster, 1926), pp. 46–7.

5. This is Richard Roud's formula (and label), summarizing the attitude of the *Télé-Ciné* group, in *Max Opüls: An Index* (London: British Film Institute, 1958), p. 3. I must confess that I find the idea of Ophüls and Schnitzler as premature Jews for Jesus a bit unsettling.

6. *Max Ophüls par Max Ophüls*, p. 92. I have translated from this version but corrected it in two instances to follow the German text cited by Gertrud Koch (see note 7).

7. Gertrud Koch, "Positivierung der Gefühle: Zu den Schnitzler-Verfilmungen von Max Ophüls," in *Arthur Schnitzler in neuer Sicht*, ed. Hartmut Scheible (Munich: Fink, 1981), pp. 309–29. The article, working from initial theses on Ophüls, analyzes *Liebelei* and *La Ronde* as literary adaptations. It can profitably be compared with the present analysis of many of the same issues.

8. Rivette and Truffaut, p. 17.

9. André Bazin, "Theater and cinema," in *What Is Cinema?*, ed. Hugh Gray (Berkeley: University of California Press, 1971), pp. 104–5. I have modified Gray's translation in the interest of greater fidelity to the original text. (*"Locus dramaticus,"* for example, is not in Bazin's article.)

10. Clearly *Liebelei* is not quite as restricted as Racinian drama, taking place in two locations rather than one, and over several days rather than twenty-four hours. But this is a matter of degree compared to, for example, Shakespeare.

11. Alan Williams, "Narrative patterns in *Only Angels Have Wings*," *Quarterly Review of Film Studies*, 1, No. 4 (November 1976), 357–73.

12. I cite, with occasional very slight modifications, the translation by Bayard Quincy Morgan in *The Drama*, 7 (August 1912). This citation is from p. 19; subsequent page references are given in the text.

13. Andrew Sarris, "The most dangerous game," *Village Voice*, 7 June 1983, 45.

14. Interview with James Blue, Rice University Media Center, 7 March 1973.

15. Classic European *découpage* is more flexible than the American style(s) of the same period: integrating travelling movements *within* sequences routinely, rather than only at beginning or end; having the alternative of the sequence shot for dialogue scenes (in Ophüls, typically combined with camera movement in or out at crucial points); and other peculiarities which remain to be classified. I propose the term based on Bazin's description of *découpage classique* (which Hugh Gray translated, somewhat misleadingly, as "classical editing"). The attentive reader of Bazin's text (note 9) will note that the sequence imagined by the critic (see *What Is Cinema?*, p. 31) is more likely to occur in a European film of the 1930s than in an American one, where the camera movements proposed would probably not occur, and where variation in shot type and length would be smaller and more regular. All this is an important area for future research in the history of cinema.

Selected Bibliography

Beylie, Claude. *Max Ophüls*. Paris: Seghers, 1963; repr. Paris: Lherminier, 1984.

Chamblee, Robert Livingston. "Max Ophüls' Viennese trilogy: communication styles and structures." Dissertation. New York University, 1981.

Fritz, Walter. "Arthur Schnitzler und der Film." *Journal of the International Arthur Schnitzler Research Association*, 5, No. 4 (1966), 85–92.

Grafe, Frieda and Enno Patalas. "Theater, Kino, Publikum. *Liebelei* und *Lola Montez* von Max Ophüls." In *Im Off. Filmartikel*. Munich: Hanser, 1974, pp. 244–8.

Kammer, Manfred. *Das Verhältnis Arthur Schnitzlers zum Film*. Aachen: Cobra, 1983.

Koch, Gertrud. "Positivierung der Gefühle: Zu den Schnitzler-Verfilmungen von Max Ophüls." In *Arthur Schnitzler in neuer Sicht*. Ed. Hartmut Scheible. Munich: Fink, 1981, pp. 309–29.

Ophüls, Max. *Spiel im Dasein: Eine Rückblende*. Frankfurt am Main: Fischer, 1959.
Sarris, Andrew. *"Liebelei." Film Comment*, 9, No. 2 (March–April 1973), 50–3.
Willemen, Paul (ed.). *Ophüls*. London: British Film Institute, 1978.
Williams, Alan Larson. *Max Ophüls and the Cinema of Desire: Style and Spectacle in Four Films, 1948–1955*. New York: Arno, 1980.

6

MARC SILBERMAN

Kleist in the Third Reich: Ucicky's *The Broken Jug* (1937)

Directed by Gustav Ucicky with the artistic collaboration of Emil Jannings, the 1937 film adaptation of Heinrich von Kleist's comedy *The Broken Jug* (*Der zerbrochene Krug*) was hailed by contemporary critics as a masterful entertainment, remarkably distinctive for the strength of the acting ensemble and the unusual camera work.[1] Recent critics too have commented positively on the "faithful" transposition of this literary text into the film version.[2] Moreover, this film is frequently chosen for classroom use as an "illustration" of Kleist's classic comedy and/or as a film classic in its own right.[3] My guiding hypothesis is that National Socialist ideology permeated all artistic production within the Third Reich. Furthermore, there is no such thing as an ideologically free reading of a text. This raises the question, then, whether the Ucicky/Jannings adaptation is simply a successful reshaping of a popular dramatic text into the filmic medium, or whether precisely this kind of highly artistic production demonstrates that fascist ideology – even more so a fascist film aesthetic – had much to gain in the marriage of propaganda to art.

The Broken Jug as an entertainment seems to resist propagandistic intentions. Moreover, as a classic literary text, raised by tradition and convention into the canon and approved even for inclusion in school curricula, it hardly seems to promise fruitful ground for ideological manipulation. Nonetheless: in adapting a classic text such as Kleist's comedy, a complex process of ideological colonization is at work, a process that goes beyond coopting the literary heritage for overtly propagandistic aims.

Ideology consists of a system of re-presentation. Film engages in a process of transforming social and political anxieties and desires into narrative forms which utilize rhetorical devices such as closure, irony, and repetition. Ideology permeates all areas of cultural production, not simply as theme, motif, or symbol, but rather as a constitutive factor of the imagination. Apologists for the cinema of the Third Reich frequently stress the distinction between propaganda and entertainment films or between political and non-political films.[4] Such an understanding of propaganda and politics, however, excludes much of what is ideological. An entertainment film such as *The Broken Jug* is political despite its seeming lack of blatant propagandistic messages. Therefore, I take exception to assertions that Jannings and Ucicky, in this case, were merely indulging their artistic impulses.[5] Such views disregard (intentionally or unintentionally) the economic forces at work in the film industry at that time. They also betray a level of understanding about the nature of film art far below that of Josef Goebbels. Analyses of the type surrounding Ucicky's and Jannings's film tend to close off critical discussion on cultural developments in the Third Reich. They short-circuit the possibility of posing questions of potential theoretical importance, such as the following: what features of National Socialist ideology can we identify in a film adaptation of a classic literary text? What contradictions arise between the historical conditions under which Kleist originally conceived his text and those of the filmmakers 125 years later? A brief survey of the cultural context in which Gustav Ucicky and Emil Jannings first conceived and carried out their project sheds light on their political motivations and necessarily precedes a discussion of the specifics of the film.

The history of German studies in its scholarly pursuits has its own social history, and certainly its status during the Third Reich figures as one of the more calamitous chapters in this scholarly tradition.[6] K. O. Conrady detailed several implications for literary scholarship resulting from the general post-1933 ideological "coordination" (*Gleichschaltung*). Among those implications, he points out that the distinction between friend and enemy led to an ideological rewriting of literary history in which certain authors and works were either disqualified or rehabilitated.[7] Paul Alverdes, one of the more sophisticated literary critics and theorists of the time, proposed in 1934, for example, a process of transforming tradition which would lead to the creation of a truly popular culture (*"eine völkische Kultur"*) based on traditional values (*"Bildungsvoraussetzungen"*).[8]

Heinrich von Kleist did not escape vandalism of the sort widely perpetrated on German literary classics. Indeed, quite early he became one of the showpieces in the selective cooptation of the bourgeois cultural heritage. Renewed interest in Kleist had already been registered during World War I. Critics seeking historical parallels to Germany's hour of trial found in their idiosyncratic readings of Kleist's tragedies a source for glorifying militaristic values and heroic resignation. The 150th anniversary of the author's birth in 1927 marked a veritable Kleist renaissance. And after 1933, Josef Nadler characterized Kleist in his standard literary history as a full-blooded Prussian Junker who represented the renewal of German mysticism in the eastern provinces.[9] Although a Kleist scholar like Gerhard Fricke never resorted to such questionable categories, even he found it convenient to discover that Kleist returned "to the fateful and mature community, to the reality of the

Volk."[10] Finally, Georg Minde-Pouet's second, revised edition (1938) of Kleist's complete works echoes a familiar sentiment in National Socialist cultural policy. Here he reclaims what he calls the "isolated and misunderstood genius in his own time" as a hero for the New Age: "He is the first and greatest poet of the New Germany, in whom the national and political will powerfully spoke at the same time. For this reason it is not until now that his works have become increasingly vital."[11]

It is against this backdrop of fervent revisionism, of a transfigured Kleist, that the initial steps were taken to put his comedy on film. The idea of adapting Kleist's text must be traced back to Emil Jannings, who had a twofold interest in filming it: first, he had played Judge Adam twice in successful theatrical stagings of the play (Das königliche Schauspielhaus, Die Volksbühne), and second, he considered the film project to be an aesthetic experiment in which he could demonstrate a way of adapting literature to film so that neither medium would be betrayed.[12] As early as 1935, trade journals announced that Karl Valentin was scheduled to direct a film version of *The Broken Jug.*[13] Valentin, however, was dropped when Jannings learned of the project and that in particular Valentin was not planning a "faithful" adaptation. Jannings was in a position which allowed him to intervene in such a decisive manner. He had established his reputation in the 1920s as a serious and talented film actor, most notably in F. W. Murnau's *The Last Laugh (Der letzte Mann,* 1924). His success brought him an offer from Hollywood, where he spent three years in the late 1920s, winning an Oscar for his acting in the process. With the advent of sound films, Jannings – whose English was never very exact – found himself in the difficult situation of many European émigrés in Hollywood. He returned to Germany in 1929 and quickly reclaimed his popularity in the role of Professor Rath in one of the most highly acclaimed German sound films, *The Blue Angel (Der blaue Engel,* 1930).

Documentation on Jannings's response to political changes in 1933 is scarce. His autobiography touches only briefly on his reactions, indicating that he responded positively to the new sense of order and optimism in the cultural sphere.[14] Initially he remained with his family in their residence in Austria, but soon he accepted important positions with Tobis, one of the four largest film production companies in Germany: first as head of the film company's artistic committee and then as chairman of the board. In addition, Jannings received the State Award (*Staatspreis*) for his lead role in Veit Harlan's film *The Ruler (Der Herrscher,* 1937) and was subsequently appointed Cultural Senator of the Reich and a member of the governing board of the Reich's Film Committee.[15] Altogether he played major roles in nine films produced during the Third Reich. From a political point of view, his role in *The Ruler* comes closest to serving an overt function as propaganda. In an adaptation of Gerhart Hauptmann's *Before Sunrise (Vor Sonnenaufgang),* under Harlan's direction, the family drama was transformed into a social drama in which Jannings plays an industrial magnate who proves the efficacy of the *"Führer* principle.'' Contemporary reviews acclaimed the film as one of the first to reflect the new artistic policies of the Third Reich: a political film without swastikas, raised arms, and *Führer* portraits, but nevertheless one with a subtle ideological message.[16] Nothing shows more clearly Jannings's ties to the official political establishment than the fact that in 1939 he received – from the hand of Hitler himself – the highest state cultural award, the Goethe Medal, on the occasion of the twenty-fifth anniversary of his first film role.

If Jannings's professional stature and administrative connections could guarantee a prestigious film, director Gustav Ucicky's qualifications were no less important for the success of the project. The alleged illegitimate son of painter Gustav Klimt, Ucicky entered the movie industry at the Viennese Sascha Studios during World War I. (He worked there as cameraman with Mihaly Kertesz, alias Michael Curtiz, in the early 1920s.[17]) In 1928 he left Austria for Germany where he capitalized on his reputation as a director of light comedy and made some of the first sound film operettas. With the grand success of *The Flute Concert at Sans Souci (Das Flötenkonzert von Sanssouci,* 1930), one in an increasingly popular film series about Frederick the Great, Ucicky became known as a director of films with nationalist themes. There followed, among others, *Yorck* (1931, about the anti-Napoleonic wars in Germany), *Dawn (Morgenrot,* 1933, about a World War I submarine crew which prefers to die for the Fatherland rather than to be defeated), *Refugees (Flüchtlinge,* 1933, about German immigrants in China rediscovering their "Germanness"), *The Girl Joan (Das Mädchen Johanna,* 1935, an anti-British story in which Joan of Arc foreshadows Hitler as a military leader who can unify the people). After the annexation of Austria, Ucicky returned to Vienna where, in addition to making the virulently racist and nationalistic film *Homecoming (Heimkehr,* 1941), he specialized in romantic comedies.[18] Although Ucicky has nearly been forgotten in Germany and Austria, two French historians of Nazi cinema, Pierre Cadars and Francis Courtade, insist with good reason that he should be counted among the five most important directors of the Third Reich.[19]

This quick historical outline of Jannings's and Ucicky's careers is necessary if we wish to understand the film's ideological thrust. That is not to argue, however, that the ideological content of a film, or of any aesthetic construct, can be read out of its creators' biographies or intentions. Rather, we must first investigate the historical conjuncture of such a creation, the context of its production, in order to recognize it as a historical product. As head of the Propaganda Ministry, Joseph Goebbels was fully aware that overtly political films were a less effective instrument for ideological hegemony than so-called "entertainment" films. In an important speech at the annual conference of the Reich's Film Committee in

1937, he formulated succinctly the artistic values of the National Socialist State:

I do not wish an art that proves its National Socialist character purely by means of exhibiting National Socialist emblems and symbols but rather an art which demonstrates its position by its National Socialist character and by taking up National Socialist problems. These problems will penetrate the emotional life of Germans and of other peoples more if they are handled unobtrusively. An essential characteristic of effectivity is the fact that it never appears to be intentional. If, however, it remains in the background as propaganda, as tendentiousness, as character, as position, and only comes to life through story, plot, action, contrasting individuals, then it will be effective in every way. You cannot tell me that such a development will damage German art.[20]

Goebbels's demand for "quality" films was prompted by political aims, for films dealing "filmically" with popular themes would not only fulfill a covert ideological function but would also fill the cinemas, thus strengthening the industry, and act as an instrument to legitimate the "cultural" credibility of the young state at home and abroad. For Goebbels, then, the ideological, artistic, political, and economic considerations were intimately linked, and he cogently articulated the linkage. His insistence on films devoid of obvious, stated, political messages was part of a general program instituted in 1936–7 to enhance the quality of film art. In particular, a striking number of films based on classical or well-known literary sources was produced in 1937,[21] owing in part to the assumption of inherent quality in the literary sources and in part to the expectation of absorbing that quality by mere contagion. Yet despite the rhetoric and even the administrative measures taken to assure the priority of art over commerce, the film industry during the Third Reich was managed as a profit-oriented, capitalistic enterprise, not as a subsidized arm of the Propaganda Ministry. Ideologues and artistic councils did play a role in planning and executing projects, but ultimately the commercial demands of the market-place dominated, and the advisory board for questions of film finance, which had the final say on budgets, consisted only of managerial and financial experts.[22]

Jannings, as has been noted, was a member of the artistic committee at Tobis and played an instrumental role in making the decision to film a Kleist play, a choice which coincided with general cultural policies. The fact that it was a Kleist comedy was in itself not surprising. Indeed, three of the best-known German literary comedies were all filmed during these years (see footnote 21). *The Broken Jug* is constructed around the motif of mistaken identity, a strong element in burlesque comedy of the 1920s and equally popular after 1933. Moreover, statistics verify that film comedies and musicals represented a major part of film investments; they account for nearly 50 per cent of the annual production during the Third Reich.[23] In general the humorous element in such films was limited to visual gags with the humor directed toward the comical aspects of the social hierarchy.[24] Ucicky's adaptation is unusual because of its mixture of physical comedy (Jannings's acting), visual comedy (camera work), and verbal comedy (Kleist's dialogues). Yet characteristic in these comedies is the avoidance or suppression of political themes so that any critical resonance is subdued.

Plate 14 Physical comedy: Emil Jannings, playing Judge Adam, strikes a pose in *The Broken Jug*. Photo courtesy of Stiftung Deutsche Kinemathek.

Jannings, who received credit as the film's artistic supervisor, exerted his influence by casting himself in the lead role and personally choosing Ucicky as director. The production team included some of the most competent technicians around, among them Thea von Harbou as scriptwriter, Fritz Arno Wagner as cameraman, and Robert Herlth as costume and set designer. All of them had extensive experience in film production and enjoyed reputations going back to the classic films of the 1920s. The cast too was hand-picked by Jannings, who drew on experienced actors, some of whom had shared the stage with him in an earlier theater production of Kleist's comedy at Die Volksbühne in 1934 (Lina Carstens, Gisela von Collande, Elisabeth Flickenschildt). Jannings – who described the film as the "favorite child" among all his works[25] – was responsible for the larger question of how to transpose a quintessentially theatrical text, which comes alive through its dialogue, into a medium distinguished by its visual qualities. In fact, the film's artistic achievement can be attributed in large measure to the technical virtuosity of the camera and the superb acting. Although the film action is limited almost exclusively to one room (Judge Adam's chamber), frequent camera pans, zooms and travelling shots explode the sense of confinement in this restricted stage-like setting. Furthermore, the editing – Ucicky claims there were not less than 529 shots[26] – reinforces the visual fluidity and detail. Thus, Jannings and Ucicky succeeded technically, for each scene comes to life visually and not solely as a result of Kleist's verse. Yet their cinematic accomplishment is ultimately vitiated by the superficial transference from one medium to another. *The Broken Jug*, as adaptation, is a highly polished example of canned theater.

The source for Kleist's comedy goes back to a painting he had seen in Switzerland. Le Veau's *The Judge, or The Broken Jug* (*Le Juge, ou La Cruche cassée*) portrays the six characters we know from the play positioned around the broken jug in a moment of captured tension. Each face displays a different emotion while the glances directed at one another structure the painting's formal unity. Kleist's interpretation of this moment gives shape to an analytical play, a trial which finally unravels the mystery of who broke the jug. The point of departure for the dramatic dialogue, or better, cross-examination, is the fact that two characters (Adam and Eve) are trying to hide the answer for opposite reasons while four others (Marthe, Ruprecht, Licht and Walter) are trying to discover the secret, each again for different reasons. The result is a verbal burlesque in which the characters encounter one another like performers in a highly structured circle dance: meeting, changing partners, and returning to each other. First staged by none other than Goethe at the Weimar Hoftheater in 1808, the play – divided as it was into three acts, which shattered the suspense – was a flop. Kleist subsequently revised it, deleting an entire lengthy scene (the variant of scene xii which constitutes 20 per cent of the complete play, and in which Kleist raises the conflict between Eve and Ruprecht to a more general and abstract crisis of trust). After several years of neglect, the play was rediscovered and has since come to be regarded as one of the few and most popular comedies in German stage history.

Kleist himself named his play a comedy, but just as in his other dramatic comedy, *Amphitryon*, he pushes structures and conventions to the limits of the genre. The tragic potential of star-crossed lovers, of broken trust, and lost authority is just barely disguised under an abrupt happy ending. For this reason, I feel justified in reading this play – both in the context of Kleist's serious dramas and within his specific experience of Prussian bureaucracy – as a serious critique or subversion of comic closure as well as of political reform efforts. The jug of the title assumes the symbolic value of the delicate condition of justice, in this case its broken condition indicating the corrupt state of earthly justice and the betrayal of truth. Marthe Rull's lengthy and central description of the historical scene depicted on the broken jug discloses an (ideal) image of social wholeness and harmony. And just as the jug cannot be made whole again, that system of personal trust and hierarchical relations cannot be fully re-established. The comedy, then, reflects a

Der zerbrochene Krug

Plate 15   The broken jug as a symbol – at least in Kleist's play – for a precariously ordered world. Frau Marthe (Lina Carstens) demands that the shattered vessel find justice. In the Nazi reshaping of the comedy, all ends neatly and it appears likely that her wish will be granted. Photo courtesy of Stiftung Deutsche Kinemathek.

more general and serious theme in Kleist's writing: his preoccupation with uncertainty and the lack of absolutes in a world characterized by the individual's alienation from an integral self. The comedy also projects this imbalance onto a broader social level. The polemical satire exposes the imperfection of state authority which can be restored only by means of a *deus ex machina*: Walter, who assures a happy but fairytale-like closed ending for Eve and Ruprecht and an open but fragile one for the jug.

Kleist's thematic reference – the tenuous nature of authority, the potentially tragic dimension of absolute demands – obviously could have become explosive material in the hands of a filmmaker during the Third Reich. What did Ucicky and Jannings make of the material? First of all, on a superficial level, the dialogue and even the strict cadences of Kleist's verse remain intact. Most of the omissions can be explained by the exigencies of visual or plot economy, and the few notable exceptions will be discussed later. Second, the comic dimension of the film derives almost exclusively from the plot's burlesque elements and the inept attempts by Judge Adam to hide his own guilt. In other words, the satire on state authority recedes behind the personal buffoonery so well played by Jannings. Here the camera's precision is especially important in directing the spectator's attention to visual detail for comic effect. Close-ups of the wounds on Adam's head, zooms onto platters of food and bottles of wine, and quick shots of the Judge's wig, a door handle, a clock, a black cat, interrupt the flow of images in a kind of counterpoint to the dialogue. At the same time, the camera's humor invites the spectator to become a collaborator, who, along with the camera, can see more than any one of the characters. Finally, the film version introduces a framing device – prologue and epilogue sequences – which creates an emphatic effect of closure that Kleist's delicately satirical happy ending eschews.

What a director chooses to cut and to add when adapting a literary text to the film medium often provides a key to the more general interpretive scheme at work. Several passages omitted from the film appear significant for the film's general ideological message.[27] One such passage is Veit Tümpel's argument with his son Ruprecht over whether the son was lying about his activities on the night of the "crime"; it culminates in his curse on Ruprecht:

What now of flight, what now of treachery
Is being heaped on my gray head, high Sirs,
That's all as new to me as 'tis to you.
In that case may the devil break his neck.

(p. 50)

The opposition between parents and children within the character constellations set up by Kleist constitutes an important dimension in the progressive disintegration of trust. Marthe Rull and Veit Tümpel are characterized by their honesty and moral rectitude. Indeed they are both willing to sacrifice their children, even to disrupt the family's unity and trust, should they discover that the children rebelled against the authority of the prevailing moral code (dishonest conduct, desertion). The film version undermines this dimension through the deletion of key passages such as Veit's curse as well as Marthe Rull's appeal to the memory of Eve's dead father to force her confession:

> Her father said when he passed on: 'Hear, Martha,
> Get for your girl an upright husband, dear.
> Should she become a good-for-nothing wench,
> Then give the man who digs the graves a coin
> And let him lay me on my back again;
> My Soul, I think I'd turn me in my grave!
> . . . If you, Eve,
> Would honor father and mother and keep the fourth
> Commandment well and good, then say: Into my chamber
> I let the cobbler or some other man.
> But not the man I am to wed. You hear?

(p. 43)

Moreover, Ruprecht – in the play, a role with much sensitivity and poetry, the wronged suitor who pleads his case eloquently at times – becomes in the film a stupid rustic, inarticulate, and denied most of his lines.

An important aspect of the play's social criticism is invested in the opposition between parents and children. The children assert their independence *vis-à-vis* the parents' authority and thus throw into question the foundations of that authority within the family, a microcosm of the crisis of state authority threatened by Judge Adam's dissimulation.

Another problem elided in the film version concerns the resolution. Kleist's text proposes a happy ending in the penultimate scene. Necessary for this resolution is the clarification of how Judge Adam gained access to Eve's bedchamber. Eve reveals Ruprecht's conscription order, which Adam forged to read that he will be sent to the East Indies rather than serve with the national militia to defend the country's borders ("service within the boundaries of this land," p. 71). Walter recognizes the fraud and, to regain Eve's trust, he personally vows to buy Ruprecht's freedom from military service if he is proven wrong.

The film condenses and rearranges this dialogue. First of all, the denouement of Adam's structure of lies, directly preceding the resolution, is accorded much more visual space than it is given in the play's dialogue. The camera follows the stage directions by focusing on the physical confrontation between Ruprecht and Adam as the latter flees the court. (Interestingly, in the film version, Ruprecht does not tear off the Judge's robe in the fray, a clear, symbolic act in the play where the deception is uncovered and

Adam is denied the last remnants of his authority.) But at the same time the camera includes in its frame the public peering in dismay through the courtroom windows. As the camera follows Adam, who struggles to get away, the anonymous crowd of peasants (as well as the main characters) laughs gleefully. Once outside, the camera watches as Adam slips into a canal where he splashes helplessly as a group of children enjoy his humiliation before he pulls himself out and disappears into the distance. Whether the jocular dunking might be viewed as symbolic baptism, anticipating a new beginning and the restoration of order, is less noteworthy than the stress placed on Adam's humiliation. In effect, the film trivializes the wider issue of trust by extending this scene and playing it for laughs so that the following dialogue about the details of the deception pales in significance. Moreover, the very dialogue of that following scene is condensed in such a way that the problem of conscription as well as the issue of serving in overseas colonies rather than defending the country diminishes to one of fraud and taking advantage of Eve's innocence. The reconciliation between Eve and Ruprecht and Marthe's insistence on restitution, the action of scene xiii in the play, seem to be mere footnotes to the burlesque, and the issue of who serves in the military for what reasons – a sensitive matter in 1937 as Hitler was mobilizing Germany for war in violation of the articles of the Versailles Treaty – is lost in the laughter.

The framing sequences in the film shift the emphasis of Kleist's resolution in another way. The film runs ten minutes before we hear the first word of dialogue from scene i. The credit sequence contains a series of still lifes, among other things, a drawing of a pile of law books and a feather pen which suggests the legal framework of the story to follow. The film proper opens with a shot from behind a windmill (an index for the Netherlands, the locale of Kleist's play). A lengthy tracking shot leads us to a village street where children frolic, the same children who will later watch gleefully when Adam falls into the canal. The camera then cuts to a clock tower. In the meantime we hear carillon chimes.[28] The camera tilts down to the clock face and we see moving carved figures, members of a medieval court, bowing to their lord in the center. The camera then cuts to the icy village, and moving through the town's structures, finally halts at a building in the Dutch style, at a sign announcing the daily session of court. We are in front of Judge Adam's residence. A cut later and we are inside Adam's private chambers, in front of his canopied bed where the official snores loudly. The rest of this lengthy sequence concerns Adam's *levée*, the discovering of his wounds and Licht's entrance, all without spoken dialogue but accompanied by a soundtrack of yawns, burps, groans, and other noises. The establishing shots localize the film action and set the burlesque tone for what is to come: Adam is a vulgar, all-too-human, but funny figure who will probably get into trouble because of his excessive appetites.

For our purposes, however, it is the detail of the clock tower with its chimes that attracts attention, for in the film's coda it is once again seen and heard. As Walter's carriage pulls away, the film cuts to the clock face and focuses on the figures as the clock strikes twelve. We hear the same tune of the chimes and the figures emerge from the door, but now rather than carved figures they are none other than the film actors in their costumes, taking their bows to the audience and at the same time paying deference to the figure of blindfolded justice as they pass by. Kleist's text, of course, does suggest a return to balance and the promise of justice.

Walter represents the state and its interest in a reform of the justice system. Ironically he is forced into a position of upholding the questionable authority of the state in the figure of Adam, a judge who sits in judgment on his own crime and denies it. To preserve the appearance of the court's honor and to prevent a scandal, Walter is willing to indulge Adam's lapse out of an unprincipled collegiality and to accept, if only temporarily, the condemnation of the innocent victim Ruprecht. In other words, he is intent on restoring the status quo at any cost. His reform effort is not radical in that it responds to an injustice suffered by the people, but rather it aims at continuity.[29] Yet the fact that each character experiences a personal crisis and the disintegration of the social fabric – family ties disrupted, bride and groom relationship dissolved, subject-authority hierarchy exposed as corrupt – undermines the very denouement dictated by the comic genre. The film's final sequence gives a different weight, however, to the denouement. Here there is no sense of uneasiness or irony in the fragile justice hurriedly secured by Walter, who in scene xii of the play even gets tipsy, a fact noticeably absent in the film. Walter impatiently continues on his journey of reform, with no acknowledgment that the foundations of the justice system have been jarred: nothing is out of order. On the contrary, the final shot celebrates a triumph of justice and underscores it in the gesture of obeisance – disguised as a curtain call – paid by each character to that symbol.

This film adaptation is *not* a misreading of Kleist's text. In the process of adapting a literary source to the film medium, an act of interpretation is involved; thereby certain choices have to be made, and their consequences play themselves out. Whether these choices are conscious or unconscious, imposed by a censor or voluntary, is not of primary importance. In the case of the film version of *The Broken Jug*, Ucicky and Jannings opted for a slapstick approach and integrated that choice effectively on all levels – gesture, expression, camera, framing, editing, soundtrack, etc. That is a legitimate and in its own way artistically defensible interpretation of Kleist's comedy. But identifying the ideological system of representation in a film (or any other text, for that matter) can never derive simply from reading out a set of textual characteristics. It is the function of that text within a particular situation as a collectively produced and consumed product that reveals its ideological use or "politics." In this particular case, both Jannings and Ucicky, the two individuals primarily responsible for the final "look" of the film, were actively engaged in the cultural life and film politics of the Third Reich.

Moreover, choosing a classical literary source in 1937 fit well within the larger planning to increase the legitimacy of the National Socialist idea by demonstrating cultural continuity. On the other hand, by stressing the burlesque and buffoon qualities, the filmmakers transformed a "dark," ironic comedy with somber and acerbic overtones into a comic intrigue. In Kleist's play every character and every relationship is threatened by the irrational law of the tyrant Adam. If the action of the comedy moves toward restoration of the community – inherent in the comic genre – then it does so only by purging itself of an irritant which is by no means always harmless. The speed and arbitrariness with which Kleist dispels Adam and implements the happy ending resembles the feeling of waking from a nightmare more than the ritual festivity which generally closes a comedy. Yet in the film, Adam, and secondarily Ruprecht, are consistently debased in their functions as impostor and witness by means of comic devices in acting, expression, and camera work. As a result, Kleist's interest in problems of autocratic power, liberal reform, and the contradictions in each shifts in the film to a story of personal decline, strongly accented in the catharsis through ridicule. By glossing over the original text's contradictions and potentially tragic undertones, then, the filmmakers foreground specific ideological choices – paternalistic statism, cult of the leader, hierarchical authority – and above all they exclude any discrepancy that would undermine the image of a harmonious status quo. Here the anti-juridical moment formulated in Kleist's exposure of injustice and corruption is neatly folded back into an argument for sustaining state control despite systemic and existential crises.[30]

Notes

I would like to thank Hermes Coassin and Russell Berman for helping me locate obscure sources and Sheila Johnson for her comments on an earlier draft of this essay.

1. Erwin Bare, "Kleists Lustspiel würdig verfilmt," *Der Völkische Beobachter* (Munich edition), 3 December 1937; and Albert Schneider (*Licht Bild Bühne*, 20 October 1937) and Günther Schwark (*Film-Kurier*, 20 October 1937), both quoted in *Preussen im Film*, ed. Axel Marquardt and Heinz Rathsack (Reinbek: Rowohlt, 1981), p. 262.

2. Cf. Karsten Witte, "Die Filmkomödie im Dritten Reich," in *Die deutsche Literatur im Dritten Reich*, ed. Horst Denkler and Karl Prümm (Stuttgart: Reclam, 1976), p. 350.

3. *The Broken Jug* (*Der zerbrochene Krug*) is available in the US from Trans-World and West Glen Films. All references to the play are from Heinrich von Kleist, *The Broken Jug*, trans. John T. Krumpelmann (New York: Ungar, 1962).

4. Cf. David Stewart Hall, *Film in the Third Reich* (Berkeley: University of California Press, 1969; New York: Simon & Schuster, 1973) and Erwin Leiser, *Nazi Cinema*, trans. Gertrud Mander and David Wilson (New York: Collier, 1975).

5. Such was Jannings's view in his autobiography. Cf. *Theater-Film – Das Leben und ich* (Berchtesgaden: Zimmer & Herzog, 1951), p. 209. Such also was the thrust of

Tobis's publicity campaign for the film. See a reproduction of the film program from *Illustrierter Film-Kurier*, ed. Eberhard Mertens (Hildesheim and New York: Olms, 1982), I, n.p.

6. Cf. Uwe Ketelsen, *Völkisch-nationale und nationalsozialistische Literatur 1890–1945* (Stuttgart: Metzler, 1976); and Klaus Vondung, *Völkisch-nationale und nationalsozialistische Literaturtheorie* (Munich: List, 1973).

7. K. O. Conrady, "Deutsche Literaturwissenschaft und Drittes Reich," in *Germanistik – eine deutsche Wissenschaft* (Frankfurt am Main: Suhrkamp, 1967), pp. 94–5.

8. Paul Alverdes, "Rede vom Inneren Reich der Deutschen," quoted in Bernd Peschken, "Klassizistische und ästhetizistische Tendenzen in der Literatur der faschistischen Periode," in *Die deutsche Literatur im Dritten Reich* (see note 2), p. 209.

9. Josef Nadler, *Literaturgeschichte des deutschen Volkes. Dichtung und Schrifttum der deutschen Stämme und Landschaften* (Berlin: Propyläen, 1938), II, 584.

10. Gerhard Fricke, "Über die Aufgabe und die Aufgaben der Deutschwissenschaft," quoted in Conrady, p. 95.

11. Heinrich von Kleist, *Werke*, 2nd edn (Leipzig: Bibliographisches Institut, 1938), I, 62–3. This is a revision of the 1904/1905 Erich Schmidt edition, which was edited by Schmidt, Georg Minde-Pouet, and Reinhold Steig.

12. Jannings, p. 206.

13. Goswin Dörfler, "Gustav Ucicky" (Anthologie du cinéma, No. 108), in *L'Avant-Scène*, No. 278 (16 December 1981), 254.

14. Jannings, p. 204. It should be noted that Jannings's autobiography was to have been published in 1941, but after the censor deleted large portions of the text referring to Jewish personalities in the theater and movie world, Jannings withdrew it. Not until ten years later, after his death in 1950, did his wife arrange for publication. It is unclear to what extent Jannings became his own censor when writing the autobiography during the late 1930s.

15. Herbert Ihering, *Emil Jannings. Baumeister seines Lebens und seiner Filme* (Heidelberg: Hüthing, 1941), p. 55.

16. Cf. Jerzy Toeplitz, *Geschichte des Films 1934–1939*, trans. Lilli Kaufmann (Berlin (GDR): Henschel, 1982), III, 266.

17. Dörfler, pp. 243–5.

18. After 1945, Ucicky was "denazified" and able to re-establish himself quickly in Vienna. None of his films, however, proved to be successful. In 1952 he returned to Germany and made increasingly commercial and routine productions. When he died in 1961, he was known as a specialist for well-made *Heimatfilme* (cf. Dörfler, pp. 264ff.).

19. Pierre Cadars and Francis Courtade, *Le Cinéma Nazi* (Paris: Losfeld, 1972). Cadars and Courtade focus justifiably on Ucicky's strong visual sense and his solid technical grasp of film production. Interestingly, they suggest that he – along with other greats of the Nazi cinema – would have had little trouble fitting into the American studio system of the time.

20. Joseph Goebbels, "Rede bei der ersten Jahrestagung der Reichsfilmkammer am 5.3.1937 in der Krolloper, Berlin," in Gerd Albrecht, *Nationalsozialistische Filmpolitik. Eine soziologische Untersuchung über die Spielfilme des Dritten Reiches* (Stuttgart: Enke, 1969), p. 456.

21. Besides Ucicky's *The Broken Jug*, there were adaptations of Hermann Sudermann's *The Cat Walk* (*Der Katzensteg*), Gerhart Hauptmann's *The Beaver Coat* (*Der Biberpelz*) and *Before Sunrise* (*Vor Sonnenaufgang*, under the title *The Ruler/Der Herrscher*). Other important adaptations during the Third Reich include *Wilhelm Tell*

(1934), *The Girl Joan* (*Das Mädchen Johanna*, 1935), the biographical film *Friedrich Schiller* (1940) – Schiller was especially popular for what were considered his nationalistic and "Germanic" qualities, Lessing's *Minna von Barnhelm* (*Das Fräulein von Barnhelm*, 1940), Ibsen's *An Enemy of the People* (*Ein Volksfeind*, 1937), and Storm's *Immensee* (1943), to mention just a few.

22. Julian Petley, *Capital and Culture: German Cinema 1933–1945* (London: British Film Institute, 1979), p. 78; for more detail, see Jürgen Spiker, *Film und Kapital* (Berlin: Spiess, 1975), pp. 164ff.

23. Witte, p. 348.

24. ibid., p. 350.

25. Jannings, p. 206.

26. Gustav Ucicky, "Rund um den zerbrochenen Krug," in *Mein Film* (Vienna), 29 October 1937.

27. Among the excluded lines: 35–40 (on Adam's face wound), 200–15 (on Walter's carriage accident), 380–8 (on the borrowed wig), 900–13 (Ruprecht's personification of his fear at discovering Eve in someone else's arms), 926–34 (Ruprecht's curse on Lebrecht), 1558–1606 (Walter's interrogation of Marthe about her relationship to Adam), 1770–5 (Adam's "monument" left behind in the garden).

28. The tune of the chimes, the only music in the film, is the Papageno flute motif from Mozart's *The Magic Flute* (*Die Zauberflöte*). The choice of this particular melody was probably motivated by several considerations: the motif is related to the general quest for truth and goodness; the opera's story is identified with a fairytale world; and the music has a distinctly folklike quality.

29. It is also possible to read this play as Kleist's response to the Prussian Reform Movement which lasted from approximately 1795 to 1805. His initial hopes for a reorganized civil service and reformed judiciary more sensitive to the people's needs were sorely disappointed by 1803 when he began to write *The Broken Jug*.

30. This essay appears in this volume with the kind consent of Henry Schmidt, editor of *The German Quarterly*, where it first appeared in the fall 1984 number.

Selected Bibliography

Cadars, Pierre and Francis Courtade. *Geschichte des Films im Dritten Reich*. Trans. Florian Hopf. Munich: Hanser, 1975.

Holba, Herbert. *Emil Jannings*. Ulm: Knorr, 1979.

Hull, David Stewart. *Film in the Third Reich*. Berkeley: University of California Press, 1969; New York: Simon & Schuster, 1973.

Jannings, Emil. *Theater-Film – Das Leben und ich*. Berchtesgaden: Zimmer & Herzog, 1951.

Kurowski, Ulrich (ed.). *Deutsche Spielfilme 1933–1945. Materialien*. 3 vols. Munich: Filmmuseum, 1978ff.

Leiser, Erwin. *Nazi Cinema*. Trans. Gertrud Mander and David Wilson. New York: Collier, 1975.

Marquardt, Axel and Heinz Rathsack (eds). *Preussen im Film*. Reinbek: Rowohlt, 1981.

Petley, Julian. *Capital and Culture: German Cinema 1933–45*. London: British Film Institute, 1979.

Welch, David. *Propaganda and the German Cinema 1933–1945*. Oxford: Clarendon Press, 1983.

Witte, Karsten. "Die Filmkomödie im Dritten Reich." In *Die deutsche Literatur im Dritten Reich*. Ed. Horst Denkler and Karl Prümm. Stuttgart: Reclam, 1976, pp. 347–65.

Wulf, Joseph (ed.). *Theater und Film im Dritten Reich. Eine Dokumentation*. Frankfurt am Main: Ullstein, 1966.

7

KARSTEN WITTE

How Nazi cinema mobilizes the classics: Schweikart's *Das Fräulein von Barnhelm* (1940)

Film adaptations address readers and promise familiar images from the literary canon. Like every translation – known in French since the Renaissance as *belles infidèles* – film adaptations necessarily betray that canon. The classical heritage is engaged and the reader is transformed into a spectator. As spectators, however, forget the readers in themselves, their awareness of tradition tends to fade correspondingly. Little room remains for critical response; the spectator becomes a member of a captive audience.

In Joseph Goebbels's 1941 speech, "The Film as Educator," the Propaganda Minister inaugurated the Hitler Youth Film Works Program. He spoke candidly about his strategic goals, the same goals he had already implemented in the nationalized German film industry:

A national leadership, which aspires to such a lofty title, must make it a duty to care for the people, lovingly and helpfully, not only in their worries and burdens, but also in their joys and recreations. Film in this respect is one of the most valuable factors, contributing to beautifying those few hours remaining to the individual German citizen after work, ones necessary to replenish his soul. Beyond that, however, the modern cinema is a national educational tool of the first order. The scope of its effect is almost comparable to that of primary schools.[1]

Goebbels not only *spoke* as if he were the father of the German film industry – in fact, he *was*. If one translates the familiar tone of his speech, geared to address the everyday reality of his audience, then "worries and burdens" meant the world war he failed to name. At that point – October 1941 – the Russian winter threatened to bring the German invasion of the Soviet Union to a standstill. Film art was no longer perceived in terms of Schiller's theater as a "moral institution," but rather had become an intensive care unit for the regeneration of military fighting spirits. The film artist, whether director or actor, was, according to Goebbels's appeal, to become a nurse, who "lovingly and helpfully" cared for the moviegoer. Films were now placed in the service of "beautifying those few hours remaining" to both soldiers at the front and citizens at home. Goebbels did not ask for aesthetic endeavor in film production. He demanded instead the medium's functionalization for recreational purposes, for "beautification." If one reads Goebbels's pharisaic appeal correctly, then it becomes clear that he cannot mean freedom of choice in programming or the audience's aesthetic education. The audience is not supposed to kill time in the cinema, but rather to make use of it, because, as Goebbels concludes, film is "a national educational tool of the first order. The scope of its effect is almost comparable to that of primary schools." If primary schools are educational tools of the first order, then the Propaganda Minister can hardly favor secondary and higher education in the mass media. In fact, he is talking to Hitler Youth. And, of course, he wants to keep film-production ideology at this level of reception.

He succeeded.

He did not succeed, however, despite his call for more "recreational" films, in redressing an imbalance in German film production. Since the declaration of war in 1939, the production of entertainment films had dropped from 50 to 36 per cent of the total German output. Political propaganda films, on the other hand, rose from an average 10 per cent to the substantial number of 25 per cent in 1942, the year of the Nazis' greatest military expansion in Europe. Goebbels rejected overt propaganda and encouraged more indirect forms. His call for "more entertainment" in 1941 was a production goal which the indecisive and long-term-oriented film industry apparently did not take to heart until 1943. After the turning point in the war, the Battle of Stalingrad, the output of political films sank to 8 per cent while entertainment films, now recognized as "politically" of special value, rose far above the average to 55 per cent.

If one considers the substantial output of the industry – almost one hundred films a year for the German-speaking and European market between 1939 and 1945 – the number of literary adaptations seems minute. The tradition of the Viennese (not Parisian) operettas enjoyed a sure-fire mass base and as a result made up a larger percentage of film entertainment. Dressing up the social luster of yesteryear in the film studios, the majority of Nazi comedies hardly go beyond operetta. They are louder, more expensive, but scarcely more contemporary. Only during the transitional phases 1933–4 and 1944–5 do films reflect a critique of the operetta's clichés. Especially in the late war phase, Nazi goals are carefully built into these productions. These literary adaptations represent an exception to the rule of everyday Nazi film production. Even so, they hardly deserve an exemplary status when one regards these mediocre works in terms of their film aesthetics, as media transformations, and in relation to the literary canon. They only become relevant when one measures their production ideology, i.e. their thematic concerns and the degree of correspondence to the *Zeitgeist*. Nordic authors predominate, Henrik Ibsen being the favorite. Four National Socialist films drew from his dramas: *Peer Gynt* (1934), *Pillars of Society* (*Stützen der Gesellschaft*, 1935), *An Enemy of the People* (*Ein Volksfeind*, 1937), and *Nora* (1944). Just how scriptwriters went about reading Ibsen becomes clear when one sees how the enemy of the people is rehabilitated by a Film Minister, or how Nora locks the door from inside rather than fleeing her doll's house. Naturalism is modernized, but not its aesthetic framework, as evidenced in an acting style based on a naturalist aesthetic. The preference for Nordic themes accompanies a racist attitude towards humanity as well as a fair amount of fatalism, both being visible in the large body of films meant as positive orientations for their audience. According to these productions, escape from the fatalism in which blind individuals are caught more often than not comes from above, from the state, whose activity invariably brings about a political happy ending.

Selma Lagerhöf and Knut Hamsen also supplied textual sources that satisfied the German yearning for the myth of an omnipotent nature. Such yearnings not only failed to disappear after 1945, despite their fascistic resonance; they in fact became a major genre, the so-called "*Heimatfilm*" in the Federal Republic of Germany. Another "Nordic" writer was Hermann Sudermann, whose *The Cat Walk* (*Der Katzensteg*, 1937), *Homeland* (*Heimat*, 1938), *The Journey to Tilsit* (*Die Reise nach Tilsit*, 1939), and *St John's Fire* (*Johannisfeuer*, 1939) were adapted for the screen.

Oddly enough, the Englishman Oscar Wilde, hardly an examplar of the Nazi ideal, was also frequently represented on Nazi screens: *An Ideal Husband* (*Ein idealer Gatte*, 1935), *Lady Windermere's Fan* (*Lady Windermeres Fächer*, 1935), and *A Woman of No Importance* (*Eine Frau ohne Bedeutung*, 1936). Such films merely attempted to capitalize on Berlin stage successes, often with the same actors. Another example was the comedy *Pygmalion* (1935) by George Bernard Shaw, who refused to authorize the film version.

Reinhold Schünzel's *Amphitryon* (1935) demonstrated a marked schism between original and adaptation and only with some difficulty can one discern Kleist's serious comedy in the Ufa production. The film musical had about as much to do with Kleist's play as Kleist's version did with the original by Plautus. The film nonetheless remains noteworthy for its breaking away from literary tradition and its leaning on the conventions of Hollywood musicals.

Once the war broke out, the production of literary adaptations all but came to a halt. *Das Fräulein von Barnhelm* (1940) was an exception because it lent itself readily to the needs of psychological warfare. Standardized products were much needed in a film market that had expanded immensely due to Hitler's conquest of foreign countries. Literary adaptations, however, specifically made for a literate German audience became inappropriate within the ideological framework of the Greater German Reich, since the Reich had taken control of most "dream production" in occupied Europe. *Das Fräulein von Barnhelm* passed the rating board on 9 October 1940, judged "suitable for young audiences," and premièred in Vienna on 18 October, opening in Berlin four days later. The Bavaria-Film Company produced and distributed the film. Its head of production, Hans Schweikart, also directed. The script, "based on Lessing's comedy," was written by Bavaria's chief dramaturges, Ernst Hasselbach and Peter Franke. Schweikart was hired as head of production personally by Goebbels shortly after the enforced nationalization of the film industry in 1938. After the war Schweikart took over the Munich Kammerspiele, making a point of not mentioning the significant role he served within the Nazi culture industry. He also made no mention of his directorial efforts during this period.[2]

In fact Schweikart had had more than a little experience. He made his directorial debut with *The Girl with the Good Reputation* (*Das Mädchen mit dem guten Ruf*, 1938), followed by *Freed Hands* (*Befreite Hände*, 1939), in which a woman sculptor suppresses her desires in the name of art. Other titles included: *Fasching* (1939); *The Girl from Fanö* (*Das Mädchen von Fanö*, 1940); *Comrades* (*Kameraden*, 1941), about German rebellions against Napoleonic occupation; *The Neverending Road* (*Der unendliche Weg*, 1943), a bio-pic about the Pennsylvanian railroad man, Friedrich List; *In flagranti* (1944); and finally, the comedy *Insolent and in Love* (*Frech und verliebt*, 1945). His postwar films included *That Can Happen to Anyone* (*Das kann jedem passieren*, 1952) and *A House Full of Love* (*Ein Haus voll Liebe*, 1955).

The Allied commission reviewing Nazi film productions after the war banned *Das Fräulein von Barnhelm* in Germany. Today – despite the fact that the ban has never officially been lifted – the film is a regular attraction in German cinemas, especially in those with programs for senior citizens, as well as on television. The German Second Channel (ZDF) broadcast the film in 1974, followed by a screening on the First Channel (ARD) in 1978, on both occasions without special commentary. Even the liberal *Frankfurter Rundschau* did not complain about the broadcast. On the contrary, the reviewer certified that the director had stuck closely to the original and created a "watchable film" and "a successful adaptation."[3] Such an evaluation could easily have been culled from David Stewart Hull's historical account, *Film in the Third Reich* (1969), which notes in blatant ignorance of Lessing the following:

Hans Schweikart's *Das Fräulein von Barnhelm* (*The Girl* [sic!] *from Barnhelm*), (October 18, 1940), represented an exceptionally happy attempt to adapt a literary classic, in this case Lessing's comedy *Minna von Barnhelm*, to the screen. It is an attractive and sympathetic film, with a young cast full of enthusiasm for their roles. Despite the opportunities for propaganda inherent in the setting of the Seven Years' War, the battle scenes are effective and simple, and the sequences of returning troops pacifistic.[4]

Just how scenes from a war can at the same time be effective and pacifistic for one and the same audience remains Hull's secret.

The Nazis labelled the film "artistically valuable," and its director received, at Goebbels's suggestion, an under-the-table, tax-free "donation for artistic achievement" from the *Führer*, some 40,000 RM. Veit Harlan received 10,000 more, Wolfgang Liebeneiner 10,000 less.[5] So much for Schweikart's official position in 1940.

At the time, Lessing's comedy was one of the most often staged plays in Germany. It was performed, for example, no less than 280 times during the 1934–5 season:

> Emmy Göring, in the role of Minna von Barnhelm, retired from the stage in a festival performance on April 20, 1935 [Hitler's birthday] at the Berlin State Theater. She remained however as the State's first lady of the theater, competing only with Magda Goebbels.[6]

Minna von Barnhelm also remained associated with the theater of the Third Reich, primarily as a cultural attachée in occupied Europe. In 1941 Hamburg's Schauspielhaus did a guest performance of the play in Oslo; in 1943 a Croatian translation premièred in Zagreb; in 1944 it was added to the Greek repertoire. Schweikart's film rendering no doubt found receptive audiences between Narvik and Tripoli, Brest and the Crimea, in all of those places where the film strengthened the fighting spirit of German occupation troops. In the film a war council prods the indecisive Prince Heinrich of Prussia (whom Lessing ignored altogether), the matter at hand being the Seven Years War and the conflict between Prussia and Saxony: "As long as our enemies force us to fight, we will take violent countermeasures." The film's own violent countermeasures included forcing the historical backdrop to fit present concerns, thus justifying the ongoing world war. The film is not so much indebted to Lessing's classical play as it is bound in a topical undertaking. The film perforce must commit "treason" in order that its source maintain a contemporary relevance.

Lessing's comedy reflects the aftermath of the Seven Years War. The year of its inception is emphasized in the play's subtitle: "completed in the year 1763." Schweikart's film begins, unlike Lessing's play, in 1761, the fifth year of the Seven Years War, at the moment when the Prussian king, Frederick II, attacks neighboring Saxony, an ally of Prussia's enemies, Austria and France.

Historically, the driving force precipitating Prussia's war was King Frederick's lust for glory and his struggle to create a European superpower.

Economic interests played their part as well: colonization of the Oder River basin, the annexation of the province of Saxony, the prosperity of iron and linen industries through expansion into new markets. Prussia's power struggle for hegemony in Europe came as the product of a militant philosophy of history and an equally militant praxis of war. The military "New Order" for Europe as envisioned by Adolf Hitler likewise sought and found its legitimization in the magical analogy with old Prussia.

The film opens with an establishing shot of a landscape in which two warring armies face off. The Prussians wear black, the Saxons white. Soldiers march diagonally through the film, their antagonisms accentuated through the contrasting colors and the starkly opposing lines. One-third of the film deals with the play's "pre-history." The Prussians occupy Saxony and Major Tellheim quarters his troops at Minna von Barnhelm's estate, Schloss Bruchsal. Not until forty-five minutes into the film, almost half-way through it, do Minna and her chambermaid Franziska travel to Berlin, where Lessing's play actually begins. The film's pre-history – unlike that in the drama – is not presented in flashback. Instead the film adopts the linearity of a straightforward narrative, whose hidden director is not Minna's power of reason but rather, from early on, Tellheim's sense of honor.

As a counterbalance for Tellheim's drama of degradation in the Berlin hotel (where he is evicted from his rooms to make way for more lucrative guests), the film has the Saxon women being forced to furnish rooms for Prussian officers. Characterized at first as a "Prussian hater," Minna can all the better appear later as someone who has heroically gained control over herself when she becomes the mistress of a Prussian officer. From the beginning Minna possesses such masculine attributes as caution and strength, fearlessness and rationality. When enemy troops requisition her palace, she persists in holding her "position." Even more, to the horror of various Saxon noblewomen, she collaborates with the occupiers. Their horror is demonstratively visualized. It does not suffice to show Minna's compeers as old maids; a visual metaphor is thrown in for good measure, signifying that they are walking anachronisms. When they in chorus shriek "Scandal," their reservations are denounced as low and beastly. The five noblewomen are seen putting their heads together, and in a matching shot the camera cuts to a shot of five piglets in a sty. It then pans to the pair who have come to a quick agreement, Tellheim and Minna (Ewald Balser and Käthe Gold).

At the estate the couple work together as conspirators. Fräulein von Barnhelm nurses the Prussian wounded while Major Tellheim detaches his soldiers to work in the estate fields. Lessing's alliance of reason and skepticism no longer propels the comedy. Here the collaboration of nobility and military takes care of business. Collaboration in the private sector finds a public counterpart in political cooperation. Tellheim's decision to lend the Saxon nobles 10,000 thalers so that they can pay the war reparations demanded by Prussia is presented as a "greater German" act, something

Plate 16   The occupation of *Minna von Barnhelm*: Major von Tellheim (Ewald Balser) recruits the *Fräulein* (Käthe Gold) just as Nazi cinema pressed G. E. Lessing's classical comedy into the service of a nation at war. Photo courtesy of Stiftung Deutsche Kinemathek.

that looks far beyond the story. In doing so, Tellheim sets himself apart from the narrow regionalism endemic to a Germany which at his time consisted of a collection of separate political entities. Tellheim defends Saxony in these terms: "They speak our language. We are one people." In essence Tellheim ignores all political borders – Hitler's own strategy – in order to define the state implicitly as the manifestation of all German-speaking peoples. In the same way Hitler brought the Volga Germans and the Siebenburger Swabians back home from the Soviet Union and Romania "into the Reich." Tellheim serves here as Hitler's teleologist.

Prussia threatens while Tellheim negotiates. If he had not lent the Saxons the outstanding sum (which later becomes the object of his injured honor), the Prussians would have burned down three Saxon villages. In 1940 this would have amounted to an everyday act of reprisal, experienced in wartime Poland and France and carried out by German troops. The Saxon refugees gather in the courtyard of Schloss Bruchsal, worrying about their homes, crying while they wait with their few remaining belongings. The soundtrack underscores the scenes with lamenting choruses and wailing music redolent of catastrophe. The suspense at work here is not let down until Tellheim's "act of grace," a gesture that elevates the figure into an ethereal realm. On the other hand, the scene anticipates the war suffering of *German* refugees. The audience must perforce experience the film with mixed emotions, since the scene also prefigures later civilian air raid maneuvers in the wake of Allied bombings. At least cinematic misery offers a savior, Major Tellheim, while at the same time Minna distributes bread to the homeless like a bivouac angel.

Tellheim's first line in the film is: "War is tough. It must be endured." That is a striking hypostatization of war. No commanding general here gives the order to fight to the end. It is war itself, as a fatalistic god, that commands Prussian soldiers through an inner voice, one that bypasses all military chains of command. Without a moment's hesitation, Major Tellheim hangs a looter who has stolen a watch: "A soldier who acts dishonorably has no right to live." Honor becomes the law of war and Tellheim acts as its enforcer. Such a hanging strengthens the "morale" of occupation forces. Franziska, a representative of a less noble station, protests against Tellheim's measures. Her mistress, whose good sense gives way to a belief in Prussian necessity, defends the act: "Tellheim must be [tough] that way."

After sixty minutes of film time, the Prussians leave the Saxon estate and go to war against Austria. A violent battle ensues between the Austrian cavalry and the Prussian infantry, an altercation, like the opening sequence, staged linearly in a huge panorama shot. Tellheim is responsible for only a small portion of the troops. Low-angle shots, however, make it look as if he were controlling the battle. His friend, the officer Marloff, a character who does not appear in Lessing's drama, falls in action. The film, curiously and tellingly, drops the character of the *Widow* Marloff, an important minor figure in the original drama, but a role that could only carry a negative connotation in 1940, at a time when war widows were being mass produced. The figure is no longer needed to demonstrate Tellheim's generosity because his heroism has already been clearly demonstrated in the heat of battle.

The war sequence is framed by a scene in which Minna plays a harpsichord and sings the popular tune, "If you want to give me your heart, do it secretly." Her heart of course belongs to Tellheim. Minna plays in the palace and at the same time is on the battlefield. Flames of foreboding flicker around her head. Superimpositions effect the transposition. The woman has her place: the soundtrack. And the man has his place: the image. Minna von Barnhelm is thus transported spiritually to the man's place. That means that her own sounds and feelings, her own wishes, are unable to create their own visual space. Even her desire to create music for peace is transformed into an ode to war.

The Prussian troops return home victoriously. Women in the streets cheer. The *Präsentiermarsch* is played; a *Te Deum* is sounded at a thanksgiving service in the Charlottenburg Palace church. The film has finally reached Berlin. Before the congregation of victors becomes visible, however, a giant

Plate 17   An imposing and solitary Fridericus Rex struts down a wide aisle: inexorable authority and its distance from the world of mortals. Photo courtesy of Stiftung Deutsche Kinemathek.

shadow is thrown from the church stairs to the center aisle. The shadow casts the outline of the true victor, whose image previously appeared on the wall of the War Treasury, where Tellheim's claim (the Saxon loan) is being processed. The Prussian king's shadow reaffirms the myth of the lonely *Führer*, Fridericus Rex. By 1940 the figure of the jovial, eccentric Prussian king, as embodied by the actor Otto Gebühr in countless films before and after 1933, had lost its appeal. Death and transfiguration were now what was in demand.

In order to avoid completely transforming Lessing's comedy into a melodrama *à la* Veit Harlan, the scriptwriters expanded the supporting role of Riccaut (Theo Lingen) by modernizing it as a negative stereotype. Lessing has the figure carry the news from the War Ministry that Tellheim's case looks as if all is going well; Schweikart's Riccaut weaves intrigues of the most odious sort in the Ministry, aiming to blackmail Tellheim. In Lessing's play Riccaut represents a comic figure who has become an anachronism. In Schweikart's film, he serves as a negative mirror image of Tellheim, as a useless officer who after the war advances to the position of a military informer. Riccaut is clearly depicted as a cliché version of the "French hereditary enemy." He threatens the fortune of his Prussian counterpart. Riccaut acquires Tellheim's ring after the latter's servant, Just, pawns it to the innkeeper. The mercenary Riccaut, in Prussian service, profits from Tell-heim's suffering – for the officer pays much more for the ring than its cash value.

The first reunion between Minna and Tellheim takes place in a Berlin café. In this sequence Minna savors his every word. The camera perspective consistently shows Minna a head smaller than Tellheim. The proportions confirm the hierarchy of their relationship. Tellheim acts more like Minna's commanding officer than her lover. Minna herself no longer seems to be "the lover graced with reason" that she was in Lessing's comedy, but merely the Major's mistress.

Tellheim's misgivings and second thoughts, crucial moments in the play (such as the long speech in act V, scene v) where he questions his actions and identity as an officer and a man, are missing in the film. What remains is his declaration of love: "You are the sweetest, most charming creature under the sun." For Lessing love is not simply a private affair; the crucial point is that love is not only articulated verbally but borne out in human interaction. The Tellheim of the film cannot accept defeat. He ceases to be a war-weary skeptic, whose loving companion makes him see the light of reason. He becomes a heroic figure who has been displaced in a romantic comedy, some-one who at the war's end must take leave of the battlefield. Only war has allowed him to see reason.

In the play Tellheim rejects the royal offer of a complete rehabilitation and a resumption of his military career. "My whole life is dedicated to your service alone," he swears to Minna in scene ix of the final act. Tellheim wants to become "a calm and contented human being," attributes Lessing ascribes to civilians only. Such resignation, however, has no place in a German film of 1940. No sooner is Tellheim completely rehabilitated by the king, with full military honors, than he is seen mounted on his horse, leading his regiment in a parade. Flowers, cheering women, children in the streets: a military demonstration concludes the film, a scene marked by balanced compositions, one that presents a resounding, whirling, rolling apotheosis of Prussianism. With the peace treaty of Hubertusburg in 1763, the Seven Years War had come to an end. Which war, then, was Tellheim marching off to? With the world war expanding on all fronts in Europe during 1940, the reactivation of a dishonorably discharged officer might be taken as a hint to all those ex-army officers who still had not stepped onto the fields of battle occupied by the Greater German Reich. *Das Fräulein von Barnhelm* appealed to them too.

In the film Minna points out the "so-called Brandenburg Gate" to Tell-heim as they take a carriage stroll through Berlin. Built by Langhans some thirty years *after* the Seven Years War, the structure points ahead into the distant future. In 1940 the audience readily associated the image of the Brandenburg Gate, one of the film's more modest historical falsifications, with the victory parades of the Nazis.

Lessing politicized? In 1938 Ernst Suter posed the same question in the *Zeitschrift für Deutschkunde*:

We are not looking for literary history's National Socialists. The numerous historical novels in which Caesar, Cromwell, Hannibal, or who knows who else, appear as a disguised Adolf Hitler, cannot be models for our studies. No, Lessing too was not a National Socialist, and anyone who tries to turn him into one, is not pursuing National Socialist research, but rather presenting an ideologically deranged masquerade.[7]

If philologists deny searching for Nazis in history, did the film industry acknowledge such intentions more openly? As early as 1933, Goebbels, the self-styled protector of German cinema, articulated an official guideline, which for all practical purposes banned images of Nazis from film: "As I have said elsewhere, we by no means want to have our storm-troopers marching across the screen and stage. They are to march in the streets."[8]

That is Goebbels's interpretation of the *art* of taking power which he, as a *metteur-en-scène* of the masses, understood well. Film should consolidate the Nazi takeover of Germany, not rework it as art. Just how this process of transmogrification became legitimized can be seen in a report on National Socialist film dramaturgy. Edmund Th. Kauer, comparing lines from Lessing's play with an excerpt from the film script, writes: "We are offering the reader an example of a free adaptation of a theme shaped by a classical writer, by contrasting the same scene in Lessing's original version with the film rendering."[9]

It is worthwhile to read this statement carefully. It contrasts "Lessing's original" with the film version, "a theme shaped by a classical writer" with the "free adaptation." Literature, according to this juxtaposition, is the original form, possessing a creator, Lessing, while the film unites author and medium. The director, Schweikart, the production and distribution companies, the scriptwriters: all remain invisible, reduced to the status of anonymous technicians not worthy of mention, to the role of producers of industrial commodities. Once one does this, the notion of authorship can be reduced to the simple terms of "a classic." The connection to the "original" dissolves completely; a "theme" at best remains as a vestige of this source, one shaped by the classical author. The result of this radical taking of leave from literature becomes a "free adaptation."

Lessing is pushed aside, but such an ideological undertaking does not want to do without the "classical author" altogether. Its radicalism is half-hearted because it still needs the legitimizing sanction of this authority of bourgeois aesthetics, Lessing. It needs his stamp of approval in order to justify the cinematic appropriation and political functionalization of *Minna von Barnhelm*. Given all of this, it is only logical that the Nazis eradicated the humanistic elements of Lessing's enlightenment, falsifying his works: his drama, *Nathan the Wise* (*Nathan der Weise*), was banned; *Miss Sara Sampson* was retitled *Clarissa* after the outbreak of war in 1939. Lessing is relieved of his authorship in the same way that Tellheim is freed from his skepticism. Designed by Lessing as an individualistic character and a vehicle of topical critique, the Tellheim of 1940 is de-individualized and becomes an exemplary officer who allows himself to be remobilized for the Prussian cause. The film no longer criticizes historical reality from an historical perspective, but rather calls into question Lessing's criticism and its aesthetic form. Lessing's art of comedy is neither recognized nor respected. Its main theme, the injustice present in the wake of war, undergoes radical reshaping.

Das Fräulein von Barnhelm is in fact the antithesis of Lessing's *Minna von Barnhelm*. No longer does an individualized character stand at the center of interest, but rather a stereotypical representative of a social class, the noble *Fräulein*. Minna is deposed as a "lover graced with reason" and graced instead with the Prussian ethos of duty. She must forget the Minna "within her" so that she may become the future lady of the house. She marries *Major* Tellheim in the same way that he remarries the Prussian Army, which responding like a jealous lover, had once left him sitting with the Saxon debts. It is inevitable that Minna joins the nobility just as Tellheim rejoins the military. He will take her into his service so that he no longer has to serve her reason. Lessing's comedy closed with a double-edged locution directed at Franziska, Minna's servant: "Ten years from now she will either be the wife of a general or a widow!" This is, however, a possibility which in the film version of 1940 much more readily seemed to apply to the *Fräulein* von Barnhelm.

In closing, let us turn to the film director and a few thoughts of his on film aesthetics published in 1963, thoughts which include no mention of his own film, *Das Fräulein von Barnhelm*. Hans Schweikart writes: "Fifty years of cinema have not ruled out the possibility that stage plays can be filmed time and again, sometimes in fact well." The attempt to legitimize the transformation process from one medium to another by the author Schweikart is revealing. "A dramatic work is only apparently complete; it either lives on, further developing itself, or it fades away."[10] Again the dramatic work's author is neatly pushed to the side and the work's aesthetic character denied. The process of change in history, one governing each and every work, likewise has no authors, names no special interests, and knows no manipulators of history's contemporary relevance. The work itself lives and evolves. Such a hypostatization of art contains an evolutionary *Weltanschauung*, one that denies a work its aesthetic character and at the same time seeks to confer upon it a natural status.

Thus the author of a work becomes that which Edmund Th. Kauer termed in 1943 the primordial form (*Urform*), a form which "makes" art history out of its own power, taking on new forms (to use Schweikart's phrases: living on, developing itself), or, lacking this power, perishing (fading away).

Following this logic, when Schweikart adapted Lessing's comedy for the cinema in 1940, he shattered the aesthetic illusion surrounding Lessing, reactivating and thus further developing the play. A more concise definition of Nazi film aesthetics cannot be found. In every manifestation of reality, the National Socialists sought to fortify the status quo ante. Schweikart took the Fräulein von Barnhelm into his service and she him. To the very end he remained caught in her spell.

Translated from the German by Jan-Christopher Horak

Notes

1. Joseph Goebbels, "Der Film als Erzieher. Rede zur Eröffnung der Filmarbeit der HJ." Berlin, 12 October 1941. Quoted in Gerd Albrecht, *Nationalsozialistische Filmpolitik. Eine soziologische Untersuchung über die Spielfilme des Dritten Reiches* (Stuttgart: Enke, 1969), p. 430.
2. Hans Schweikart's life spanned the years 1895 to 1975; in his autobiographical portrait "Wie wird das Fernsehen dem traditionellen Drama und der Theateraufführung gerecht?" one finds no account of the years 1938 to 1945, much less any reference to *Das Fräulein von Barnhelm*. See *Vierzehn Mutmassungen über das Fernsehen*, ed. Anna Rose Katz (Munich: dtv, 1963). Other renderings of Lessing's *Minna von Barnhelm* include two West German productions, Dietrich Haugk's *Heroines* (*Heldinnen*, 1960) and Franz Peter Wirth's *Minna von Barnhelm* (1966), and the DEFA adaptation of 1962 by Martin Hellberg.
3. TV program in the *Frankfurter Rundschau*; author identified by the initials "mwr," 24 May 1978.
4. David Stewart Hull, *Film in the Third Reich* (Berkeley: University of California Press, 1969; New York: Simon & Schuster, 1973), p. 203.
5. Cf. Boguslaw Drewniak, *Das Theater im NS-Staat. Szenarium deutscher Zeitgeschichte 1933–1945* (Düsseldorf: Droste, 1983), pp. 162–3.
6. ibid., p. 48.
7. Ernst Suter, "Lessing politisch gesehen," *Zeitschrift für Deutschkunde* (1938), as quoted in Joseph Wulf (ed.), *Literatur und Dichtung im Dritten Reich* (Reinbek: Rowohlt, 1966), pp. 401–2.
8. Josef Goebbels, "Rede in den Tennishallen Berlin, 19 May 1933," as quoted in Albrecht, p. 442.
9. Edmund Th. Kauer, *Der Film: Vom Werden einer neuen Kunstgattung* (Berlin: Deutsche Buch Gemeinschaft, 1943), p. 240.
10. Schweikart, pp. 19–20.

Selected Bibliography

Albrecht, Gerd (ed.). *Der Film im Dritten Reich. Eine Dokumentation*. Karlsruhe: Schauburg & Doku, 1979.
—— *Nationalsozialistische Filmpolitik. Eine soziologische Untersuchung über die Spielfilme des Dritten Reiches*. Stuttgart: Enke, 1969.
Cadars, Pierre and Francis Courtade. *Geschichte des Films im Dritten Reich*. Trans. Florian Hopf. Munich: Hanser, 1975.

Hull, David Stewart. *Film in the Third Reich*. Berkeley: University of California Press, 1969. New York: Simon & Schuster, 1973.

Kurowski, Ulrich (ed.). *Deutsche Spielfilme 1933–1945. Materialien*. 3 vols. Munich: Filmmuseum, 1978ff.

Leiser, Erwin. *Nazi Cinema*. Trans. Gertrud Mander and David Wilson. New York: Collier, 1975.

Marquardt, Axel and Heinz Rathsack (eds). *Preussen im Film*. Reinbek: Rowohlt, 1981.

Petley, Julian. *Capital and Culture: German Cinema 1933–45*. London: British Film Institute, 1979.

Welch, David. *Propaganda and the German Cinema 1933–1945*. Oxford: Clarendon Press, 1983.

Wolff, Udo W. *Preussens Glanz und Gloria im Film*. Munich: Heyne, 1981.

Wulf, Joseph (ed.). *Theater und Film im Dritten Reich. Eine Dokumentation*. Frankfurt am Main: Ullstein, 1966.

8

JAN-CHRISTOPHER HORAK

The other Germany in Zinnemann's *The Seventh Cross* (1944)

During the era of the *Front Populaire*, between the Spanish Civil War and World War II, German refugees from Hitler living in Paris could often observe a woman, not yet quite middle-aged, sitting in a café, writing intensely, enveloped in a cloud of cigarette smoke and walled in by noise. The writer, Anna Seghers, herself a German émigrée, had already collected countless stories from her fellow countrymen, many newly arrived, tales of life inside the Third Reich, of Gestapo terror, concentration camps, and a prisoner hung on a cross after an unsuccessful escape attempt.[1] In Paris she remembered and imagined the fields around her native Mainz, the sounds of the town market and Gothic cathedral, the images of the Rhine and Main rivers, the talk of the local farmers and factory workers, recognizing their essential human attributes, but also remaining aware of what had happened to them under German fascism.

Anna Seghers's novel, *The Seventh Cross* (*Das siebte Kreuz*), was a labor of love, written by a German exile on the run. No sooner had the first chapter appeared in July 1939 in a German émigré literary journal, *Internationale Literatur* (Moscow), than World War II broke out. Forced to flee from the *Wehrmacht*'s invasion of France, Seghers burned her completed manuscript for fear of being caught and identified. Fortunately, while Seghers and her family arduously sought visas and passports, slowly making their way from Vichy France to Martinique to San Domingo to Ellis Island, and finally after almost two years to Mexico City, a single surviving copy reached New York, where a fellow German writer, F. C. Weiskopf, found an American publisher. *The Seventh Cross* became an American bestseller and "Book of the Month Club" selection in October 1942, eventually attracting over 600,000 American readers (many of them GIs who received a special Armed Forces edition in 1944). On the other hand, until the defeat of fascism allowed for its dissemination in Germany, only a handful of German speakers read the German edition published in Mexico.[2]

The incredible commercial success of *The Seventh Cross* was no doubt connected to the US entry into World War II a mere ten months earlier. By late 1942 a flood of anti-Nazi fiction and non-fiction swamped the book market, attempting to answer the question just what was America fighting for. Propagandistic and commercial intentions were thus indivisibly intertwined. Hoping to cash in on *The Seventh Cross*'s success, Otto Preminger, an Austrian émigré, planned a dramatization for the New York stage.[3] In Hollywood, Metro-Goldwyn-Mayer, the most politically conservative of the great studios, paid $100,000 for the film rights.[4] Working from a script by Helen Deutsch and with the German cameraman Karl Freund, director Fred Zinnemann, another Austrian, completed shooting in March 1944. Apart from such stars as Spencer Tracy and Signe Hasso, the cast featured no less than thirty German refugee actors, including Felix Bressart, Kurt Katch, Alexander Granach, John Wengraf, Ludwig Donath, Helene Thimig, Gisela Werbesick, Helene Weigel, Otto Reichow, Lisl Valetti, and Edgar Licho, a fact which MGM's publicity department emphasized to demonstrate the film's verisimilitude.[5] The German look was also to be guaranteed by the presence of technical adviser Felix Bernstein, formerly head of MGM's Berlin distribution office. For MGM producer Pandro S. Berman, commerce and propaganda were at stake. As early as December 1943, he noted in an interview that *The Seventh Cross* was being filmed with "an eye to securing a market in post-war Germany."[6]

For Anna Seghers, on the other hand, politics in postwar Germany, not commerce, were at stake. A Kleist Prizewinner in 1928, the same year she joined the Communist Party (KPD), Seghers left Germany in May 1933 after being arrested, then released, by the Gestapo, her books banned and burned. Like many other German writers of repute, from Friedrich Alexan to Carl Zuckmayer, she emigrated to France, hoping to continue the battle against fascism with the means at her disposal: the written word. German writers in exile were well aware that they represented "the other Germany," the humanistic tradition of Goethe and Humboldt, that, in the words of Heinrich Mann, they were "the voice of a silenced people." In the years before World War II, they published novels, pamphlets, and articles in host countries and on German exile presses, reaching audiences inside Germany (illegally), as well as German and foreign anti-fascists. As Seghers noted in a letter to critic Georg Lukács: "Our enemy is fascism. We fight against it with all our physical and intellectual powers. It is our enemy, as feudalism was Lessing's enemy."[7]

In keeping with this perspective, Seghers's political and literary activity was of a piece, each sphere in turn mitigating the other, often leading her to the fringes of acceptable KPD practice. Between 1933 and 1935, she was a member of the editorial board of the German émigré literary magazine, *Neue Deutsche Blätter* (Prague), which published works by both leftists and bourgeois anti-fascists (e.g. Walter Mehring and Stefan Zweig), thus anticipating the Popular Front politics of the Communists instituted after the seventh Comintern conference in July 1935.[8] Simultaneously, Seghers's fiction in exile turned away from the exotic locales of *The Revolt of the Fishermen of St Barbara* (*Der Aufstand der Fischer von St Barbara*, 1928), towards German subject matter, specifically the rise of fascism and its effects. Her first post-Weimar novel, *The Bounty* (*Der Kopflohn*, 1933), described the growth of Nazism in a country village, explicitly noting the anti-fascist left's failure to win over the agricultural proletariat, or even to contain the political successes of the Nazis in the farming sector.[9] *The Way Through February* (*Der Weg durch den Februar*, 1935) detailed the inability of the Austrian Social Democratic rank and file to organize effectively during the revolt against the crypto-fascists in February 1934, while at the same time identifying Social Democrats as potential allies of the Communists in the battle against fascism, thus implicitly negating the Comintern's "Social-Fascism" theory.

In 1935 Seghers suggested and helped to organize the "International Writers' Conference for the Defense of Culture" in Paris. Seghers's speech at the conference, "Patriotism" (*"Vaterlandsliebe"*), was of seminal importance not only for Popular Front politics, but also for her own work. In it she espoused the theory that nationalism was a human emotion born out of the bourgeois revolution, which working-class parties had ignored, creating a vacuum for the perverting influence of imperialist and fascist ideologies:

> Every cheer in their mother tongue, every bit of dirt between their fingers, every hand operation of their machines, every smell in the forest confirms for them once more the reality of their community. Today's usufructuaries of this community call it god-given. . . . Let us deprive supposed superintendents of our really national cultural values. Let us writers help reconstruct new mother countries; then the old pathos of the poets of truly national freedom will, surprisingly, become valid once again.[10]

Such concepts, suggested in the spirit of the Popular Front's unification of all anti-fascists from Catholic conservatives on the right to anarcho-syndicalists on the left, had a formative influence on Seghers's subsequent novels, especially *The Seventh Cross*, which presented an epic view of German society. By 1939 Seghers could only hope that her novel would function prominently in the democratic re-education of Germany. Accordingly, she identified those German characteristics worth saving, and attempted to place the burden of guilt for fascism on the system, rather than on individuals.

In this light it is not surprising that *The Seventh Cross* should contain both realistic and mythic dimensions, its prose characterized both by intensely descriptive passages of everyday reality and dreamlike flights of fancy, its narrative points of view and interior monologues creating an objective view by the very nature of their multiplicity, its epic scope searching out only minor heroes and villains, rather than larger-than-life fictions. In contrast, Fred Zinnemann's film, especially its plot structure, appears not only to reduce the novel's narrative complexity, a fact which may be excused as a necessary condition of adaptation, but also to be much less dense in its characterization, even while lifting numerous scenes almost verbatim from the novel. Whereas Seghers's (anti-?) hero, George Heisler, and other characters are nearly ambiguous, displaying both strengths and weaknesses, Zinnemann's *The Seventh Cross* ideologically sanitizes them, drawing much more obvious lines of demarcation between good and evil persons, while simultaneously depoliticizing their conflicts. Furthermore, Seghers draws complex portraits of her German fascist characters, pointing out the social origins of their mentality, while the film merely provides a few short scenes of Nazi brutality involving stereotypical Gestapo characters. Still, a number of important themes in the novel do survive in the film adaptation, e.g. the strength of the weak, and Seghers's view of the relationship between love and politics. Furthermore, Zinnemann's *mise-en-scène* emphasizes expressionism rather than realism, ultimately capturing the mythic dimensions apparent in Seghers's novel.

The Seventh Cross is, at its simplest level, a chase story (which may have encouraged MGM to produce the film, since such a narrative structure constitutes the backbone of the anti-Nazi-film genre).[11] Seven concentration camp prisoners escape early one morning in 1936 from Westhofen. One by one six of them are recaptured, tortured, hung on crosses, and finally murdered. After seven days the last prisoner reaches the safety of a Dutch boat heading down the Rhine to freedom. Basing her character on such contemporary escapees as Hans Beimler and Gerhart Seger, to whom she specifically refers (p. 131),[12] Seghers allows Heisler to survive not because he possesses superhuman qualities, but because he finds both committed political activists and previously apolitical fellow travelers in Nazism willing to help him, even at the risk of their own lives.

Seghers develops an ever more complex narrative structure (inspired by Alessandro Manzoni's historical novel, *I promessi sposi*, which presents a cross-section of Italian society), allowing her to introduce many different kinds of characters from all strata of society; all in all, there are thirty-two major characters. Although Heisler's flight defines the temporal and spatial parameters of the novel, Seghers makes no attempt to psychologize his character, his previous life, or his actions. In fact, only about one-third of the narrative deals directly with Heisler. All the reader learns is that Heisler is a conscientious party functionary who has become a legend in the underground, but whose personal life is relatively disorganized, what with an abandoned wife, countless ex-girlfriends, and deserted buddies. One gets the sense that, like the functionaries in Seghers's earlier novel, *The Comrades* (*Die Gefährten*, 1932), Heisler places the concerns of the party over any personal matters, a position Seghers rethinks in *The Seventh Cross*. Seghers utilizes Heisler's character and predicament as a kind of acid test, indicating what percentage of the German populace has been poisoned by fascism, and what percentage can be counted upon to defy Nazi terror. Subsequently, the characters around Heisler show signs of internal development; they overcome their fear to find new strength in collective action; they once again discover the love of their spouses. Meanwhile, Heisler seems unchanged by the experience, a catalyst unaffected by chemical reactions.

Quite the opposite is true in Zinnemann's *The Seventh Cross* where Spencer Tracy (Heisler) is on screen throughout much of the film. The story begins with a voice-over narration: the narrator's words explain that Heisler is a broken man who, after countless beatings, has lost faith in humanity, and whose flight becomes a quest for lost faith:

> George Heisler, before I die I must tell you this. I must tell you that there is in men an instinct for good which cannot be destroyed. It isn't dead. Even in this nation of beasts, it still must live somewhere. If, in this Germany, among the cruelest people on earth, you find one man with a spark of good still in him, then there's hope for the human race.

At first Heisler apparently only discovers Nazis: the storm-troopers and their bloodhounds, a rabid pack of Hitler Youth, his nazified fiancée, a neighbor with a portrait of Hitler in her living-room, a *Blockwart* (the local Party informer). He then meets his old friend Paul Roeder and other good Germans. By the end of the film Heisler realizes that his own escape is a symbol for the good faith of many. Spencer Tracy, who, according to a number of commentators in the German émigré press,[13] looked right for the part, played a German everyman whose only connection to the political underground is an address he receives from his fellow inmate, Wallau. Heisler is portrayed as a politically nondescript, nebulously anti-Nazi character, rather than as a professional revolutionary. Simultaneously, the film places him closer to traditional bourgeois moral norms: Heisler's past personal life is reduced to a single fiancée, who, unknown to Heisler, has married a storm-trooper, and refuses to help him. His relationship to the waitress, Toni, is expanded in the film (possibly to increase the obligatory Hollywood love interest) and is characterized as genuine, even though its permanence is precluded. Seghers in fact handles the character similarly. Before boarding the boat, Heisler tells Toni why he must leave her:

> I have a debt. Not only for their help but for what they taught me. . . . I know that, no matter how cruelly the world strikes at the souls of men, there is a God-given decency in them that will come out, if it's given half a chance. And that's the hope for the human race. That's the faith we must cling to. The only thing in our lives that's worth living for. . . .   (p. 391)

Plate 18 A romantic relationship – however transient – as a revolutionary act: the fugitive George Heisler (Spencer Tracy) and the waitress Toni (Signe Hasso). Photo courtesy of George Eastman House.

The Seventh Cross thus presents a quest for faith and its positive resolution. Such themes are indicative of the way the film adapts and simultaneously depoliticizes Seghers's thematic concerns. Even the propagandistic usage of such phrases as "nation of beasts" and "the cruelest people on earth" emphasizes the theological juxtaposition between demonic Nazis and the forces of hope. "Faith in man" takes on religious connotations, because without it, life "is not worth living," because man's decency is "God-given." Fascism, on the other hand, does not appear to be the result of a specific set of political and economic circumstances, but rather a moral illness, a genetic weakness in the national body politic. The film thus misinterprets Seghers's text, which champions "the strength of the weak," the power of the persecuted to survive despite all odds, ultimately to resist actively and to abide against the forces of fascism. The novel ends with a comment by a prisoner at Westhofen:

We all felt how deeply and terribly outside powers could penetrate man, touching his innermost being, but at the same time we felt that in man's innermost being there was something which was untouchable and invincible.   (p. 393)

That core of resistance common alike to concentration camp prisoners and anti-Nazis in the larger prison of the Third Reich, represents for the author the hope for a democratic and humanitarian Germany after the war. Heisler's escape becomes the occasion for finding that innermost core, untouched by fascism's power to instill fear. Accordingly, Seghers draws characters who simply refuse to denounce Heisler, and thus become elements of passive resistance, e.g. the priest in Mainz Cathedral, the doctor Loewenstein, and the artiste Frau Marelli. Loewenstein and Marelli both appear in the film, the former treating Heisler's badly infected hand, the latter giving him a fresh set of clothes. In each case they are unaware of Heisler's plight, but their suppressed suspicion leads Heisler and the viewer to believe that they are indeed silent accomplices. Other characters actively resist fascism after years of timidity. Heisler's escape precipitates both a working-class character (Fiedler) and a middle-class character (Kress) to join the fight once again. This second group especially contributes to the reformation of underground resistance. In keeping with the KPD's Popular Front strategies, Seghers implies that it is the revolutionary *élan* of the still active Party cadre which has the power to form a broad anti-Nazi coalition inside Nazi Germany.

In Zinnemann's *The Seventh Cross* at least two characters are similarly transformed by their contacts with the anti-Nazi underground: the blue-collar worker, Roeder, and the white-collar worker, Sauer. Paul Roeder is an apparently average German worker who, after years of unemployment in

Plate 19   Political activity in a collapsed public sphere: Heisler (Spencer Tracy) meets in secret with Roeder (Hume Cronyn) and Fiedler (Paul Guilfoyle). Photo courtesy of George Eastman House.

the Weimar Republic, now works in an armaments plant, earns a steady income, has a wife and three children, is satisfied with his private fate, and is unconcerned with politics in any form (p. 228). However, the act of helping Heisler, his contacts with the underground leader Marnet, and his direct confrontation with the fascists politicize him. After being arrested and released by the Gestapo, Roeder realizes that the power of fascism is indeed limited: "They threatened terrible things would happen to me if I didn't tell them everything. And do you know what I discovered? They only know what you tell them. They want us to think that they know everything" (p. 372). Roeder's professed intention to keep in touch with Marnet indicates that he will join the anti-Nazi resistance.

Bruno Sauer, a middle-class architect, refuses at first to help when Heisler sends Roeder to him. The scene in Sauer's bathroom, where his face is disguised by shaving cream (p. 259), illustrates Sauer's fear of showing his true face, of losing his government job after being unemployed for five years. In the film, though, Sauer changes his mind and keeps his word to help "when something serious comes up." He goes to his former comrades in the resistance, informs them of his meeting with Roeder, and is asked to stay. The decision to fight rather than cower not only gives Sauer new self-esteem, but also improves his marital relations, since his wife had previously chastised him for being a coward. This development of Sauer's character parallels that of Kress in the novel (p. 341), and touches upon a central issue in Seghers's story.

Whereas in her previous work, specifically *The Comrades*, Seghers views work for the Party as incompatible with a personal love life, in *The Seventh Cross* she sees personal and political life as being interdependent. Both in the case of the working-class couple, Fiedler and his wife, and the middle-class couple, Kress and his wife, the decision to resist actively gives their respective marriages new impetus. When Kress hides Heisler for a night, Seghers describes his wife's reaction: "The eyes of the wife glazed over. She lifted her head. Only once at the beginning of their life together had her face been so bright. . . . 'I really didn't believe you could do it!'" (p. 347). Seghers seems to be saying that love under fascism is impossible, because of its perverting influence on all human relations; love and fascism are antithetical. In the same way that exiled German writers believed that there can be no true art and literature under the aegis of fascism, because art is by definition humanistic and fascism barbaric, so too there can be no expression of love among exponents of National Socialism, whether active or passive, because fascism represents hate, distrust, and violence. That Bruno Sauer will resist and so regain his wife's love is indicated in the film through decor: an example of the kind of modern art banned by the Nazis as degenerate hangs prominently in Sauer's living-room, a stark contrast to the Hitler portrait seen earlier. As Zinnemann surely knows, the preservation of exiled literature and art is itself an act of resistance under German fascism.

In the novel another character undergoes a change of heart: the Hitler Youth, Fritz Helwig. The problems of German youth, educated by two-hundred-percent Nazis, are of particular concern to Seghers, specifically in regard to postwar Germany. Time and again she refers to the issue in *The Seventh Cross* (p. 158), worrying that the youngest generation may be incorrigible. In the film, Helwig's development is only barely hinted at in a moment of self-doubt, before he disappears from the story, while, on the other hand, the Hitler Youth are depicted as particularly ardent bounty hunters.

The anti-Nazi underground appears in Zinnemann's treatment as a well-oiled clandestine organization, headed by level-headed professionals, like Leo Hermann. Its members come from all walks of life, outwardly pretending to be law-abiding citizens of the Reich. Understandably, the resistance movement exists above party politics, and no mention is made of the Communists. This is in keeping with Seghers's Popular Front strategy, which also never overtly names the KPD, but rather identifies the Party by proxy, referring to known figures and events, e.g. Hans Beimler or the revolts in Saxony in 1923. Zinnemann's characterization of the German underground by way of an anecdote translates Seghers's concept of "the strength of the weak." The delicatessen owner, Poldi Schlamm, relates to Heisler: "Yesterday the ants emptied a sugar bowl and moved it to the other end of the shop. Each little ant doing his part. See what I mean? They can't kill all the ants, can they?" The powerless multitudes are thus characterized as truly potent, if they work together for a democratic society. The anecdote also implies, however, that the Nazis are a minority in Germany, a terroristic and totalitarian dictatorship of storm-troopers.

In terms of onscreen time, the Nazis indeed appear to be a minority. The concentration camp wardens are presented briefly as brutal animals who take pleasure in murder. With closely shaven heads, brown storm-trooper uniforms, black boots, whips, and other paraphernalia of terror, these Nazis embody the stereotypical German fascists in Hollywood anti-Nazi films. Gestapo commissar Overkamp bears out another kind of Nazi stereotype: the small, methodical bureaucrat who works with cool professional efficiency. Overkamp too appears only briefly to interrogate Wallau and later to review the course of the manhunt. Seghers's handling of these Nazi types is much more detailed. Concentration camp commander Fahrenberg, for example, is shown to be a member of the impoverished petty bourgeoisie, an unsuccessful intellectual who joins the Nazis out of opportunism. Zillich, a character first appearing in Seghers's *The Bounty*, is a brutish farmer who loses his farm to the banks and subsequently joins the Nazis, where he can legitimately vent all his pent-up hatred on supposed enemies of the state. The important difference between novel and film is that whereas Seghers sees these characters as merely agents of a fascist ruling élite, bent on maintaining power at all costs, the film mistakes these henchmen for the system.

Apart from a few Nazis at the beginning of the film, almost all of the ordinary people in *The Seventh Cross* are upright anti-Nazis or at least sympathizers with the Resistance. The film thus openly belies the fact that in 1936 the German government enjoyed widespread popularity, despite concentration camps, police state tactics, and persecution of the Jews. Given the dearth of knowledge about fascist Germany in America, such a thesis may have been tenable in the prewar years, but by late 1944, when the film was released, enough facts were known to make the film's point of view a clear distortion of history. Not only were the death camps by then a matter of public record, but also the German people's will to wage war to the bitter end could no longer be discounted as a fantasy of Nazi propagandists. Not surprisingly, a number of critics perceived the film as a plea for a "soft peace." Bosley Crowther wrote in the *New York Times*: "Without any question, it creates human sympathy for a people of a nation with whom we are at war."[14] Exiled German writers also criticized the film, even though they were usually most willing to champion the vestiges of "the other Germany." Manfred George, a former editor for the Berlin publisher Ullstein, wrote in *Aufbau* (New York):

> In this film there are only Gestapo on the one side, and Germans on the other side who help the anti-fascists. American soldiers who see this film must get the impression that the German population is basically waiting to help anti-fascism. Anna Seghers may have believed that in 1936, but a film which confirms such a belief through its images in 1944 is guilty of a gross crime: not because of what it shows, but because of what it neglects to show.[15]

Although such criticism is surely justified in terms of America's war goals, it fails to consider Hollywood's genre strategies. Zinnemann's *The Seventh Cross* merely utilizes those conventions developed since the beginning of the war by the industry for its anti-Nazi film genre. Whereas in the years 1942–4 countless French, Czechoslovakian, and Norwegian underground fighters were being chased across the screen by villainous German SS officers, the victims here are German nationals. Anti-Nazi films portrayed America's allies in occupied Europe through genre-specific narrative and visual codes, signified as "the underground," attributing to them democratic and essentially American values, which were now transferred to images of the enemy. The film's representation of Nazi characters also follows contemporary genre conventions: shots of Nazis and their sympathizers invariably incorporate such identifying codes as swastikas or Hitler portraits; public spaces implicitly controlled through such manifest symbols represent danger for Heisler and are juxtaposed to private spaces, e.g. the Roeder home or the waitress Toni's quarters, where traditional, middle-class values are still intact. Such genre conventions imply a totalitarian theory of fascism, which places the blame on a Nazi élite, without criticizing the economic and social conditions leading to fascism, while simultaneously valorizing American democratic values.

In point of fact, though, the film's distortion is also a consequence of its reduction of Seghers's complex narrative. Within the context of the totality of German history, Seghers describes Nazis, anti-fascists, and those who have managed to survive in ideologically free spheres. Her narrative returns repeatedly to the farmers of the Rhine and Main valleys, the Marnets and Mangolds, who till their fields, pick their apples, and tend their flocks, regardless of the political system in power. Like Ernst, the shepherd, they are never directly connected to the chase narrative, but are elements of a landscape outside time, a natural world, representing a German tradition much older than the Third Reich. The only time the film picks up on this point is a short scene where a farmer's wife complains to her husband that he should be picking grapes, instead of chasing after fugitives (p. 46). The Rhine itself becomes another symbol of continuity in Seghers's work: "How many coats of arms, how many flags had already been washed away by her?" (p. 15).

In her 1941 article, "Germany and us," published in the German exile journal, *Free Germany (Freies Deutschland/Alemania Libre)* (Mexico City), Seghers attempts to explicate ideas first articulated in her 1935 "Patriotism" speech, and given aesthetic form in *The Seventh Cross*. She states that Germany is not a unified construct of people and landscape, language and art, as propagated by the purveyors of fascist *"Volkstum,"* but nevertheless still constitutes a unity: "It is not our country which is wild and barbaric, the only thing wild and barbaric in our country is fascism, and in which country is fascism not wild and barbaric?"[16] Seghers presupposes that fascism is an alliance against the working class combining monopoly capitalism, militarism, and a reactionary bureaucracy. She prophesizes a denazified German society in which everyone can develop a unified social and national consciousness, expressing true patriotism, *sans gêne*. Compared with the Morgenthau planners in the State Department, who envisioned postwar Germany as a de-industrialized, agricultural hinterland, Seghers's call for a democratic, anti-fascist German republic can indeed be interpreted as a "soft peace" proposal.

But Seghers's book also transcends propagandistic and political concerns, conveying archetypal and mythic dimensions. The passages where Seghers describes the centuries-old Rhine landscape exemplify her archetypal prose. Another passage celebrating a ritualistic German Sunday afternoon in and around the Marnet farm (pp. 373ff.) symbolizes a little bit of heaven, contrasted to the hell of nearby Westhofen.[17] Sunday, the seventh day of biblical creation, the seventh day of Heisler's flight, becomes the day of his secular salvation in the seventh chapter of Seghers's book. Obviously, Seghers quite consciously plays with the mythical number seven and its

Christian connotations, as well as with cross symbolism. For those still incarcerated in the camp, the seventh cross symbolizes their hope for redemption, a positive indication that the Nazi terror machine is not omnipotent. Heisler, who is identified with the seventh cross, is by extension a source of redemption for all those helping him, recalling Christ and his benefactors. In the same vein, the six inmates martyred on the cross give their lives for the future life of all in an anti-fascist Germany.[18]

Fred Zinnemann captures this Christian symbolism, while transporting other mythical dimensions through his *mise-en-scène*. The cross symbolism is not only visualized in the opening shot, to which the film returns periodically, but also in the image of the artiste Bellini jumping to his death, his arms stretched out to form a cross. The film's opening escape scene consists of purely expressionist imagery: the camera dollies past seven crosses, while an invisible speaker's voice narrates the flashback. Out of the dense fog seven shadows appear, moving horizontally along a barbed wire fence; shadows of men, dehumanized by a fascist system. A guard is killed, he too nothing but a shadow. Seven men walk in turn directly towards the camera, out the camp's gate, and into the high-key light of a lamp-post. This movement literally from the darkness of their own shadows into the light, where they take on recognizable human features, can be read in terms of Christian mythology, i.e. the human soul's redemption from darkness (sin) to light (grace) through Christ. However, the direction of movement, distinguished on the one hand by an exact horizontal movement within the barbed wire perimeter, and, on the other, by vertical movement towards the camera, can be understood politically as a movement away from the world view of the camp, fascism, and towards the values of the audience. Only then are they introduced to the audience by the narrator as individuals, not as nameless victims or oppressors: Pelzer, Bellini, Aldinger, Beutler, Fullgraber, Heisler, and Wallau look directly at the audience. The scene's dreamlike, almost somnambulistic quality, its expressionist light and shadow, relate the point of view of its heavenly narrator, never attempting a conventionalized, realistic depiction of a prison break.

Even Heisler's subsequent flight through the marshes is determined by pauses rather than movement, his figure frozen while fascist guards who remain shadows even outside the camp move on a horizontal axis above him. Although the *mise-en-scène* switches to more realistic modes as Heisler's escape is chronicled, he is seen again and again waiting for danger to pass, waiting for others to help him while he hides; pauses rather than movement define the narrative. Unlike other anti-Nazi heroes, Heisler kills no Nazis, is rarely seen running, and is dependent on the active help of others. Here then, the film implies a need for a Popular Front against fascism which includes Germans and, by invitation, the Americans in the audience.

The political dimension of this reading is however mitigated by Wallau's de-politicization and spiritualization. Wallau, the real hero of Seghers's story,[19] continues to narrate the film after his capture and death, taking on the role of Heisler's guardian angel: "George Heisler, before I die I must tell you this. . . ." Virtually nothing remains in the film of the interrogation scene central to the novel, where Wallau remains steadfastly silent, answering Overkamp only by way of a moving interior monologue (p. 175ff.). Seghers's symbol of the indefatigable proletarian movement is transformed in Zinnemann's film into an image of fatherly Christian goodness.

Ironically, Zinnemann's dream sequence in Mainz Cathedral secularizes a religious image: the camera pans up to a subjective shot of the Madonna, then dissolves to Heisler and his fiancée lying in an open field. Leni's long flowing hair in the dream is later juxtaposed to the tight bun she wears, symbolizing her conversion from freedom to the strict confines of National Socialism. In contrast, Seghers's image of Heisler gazing at the crucified Christ must be understood in terms of religious faith: "One can be consoled not only by the suffering of contemporaries, but also by the suffering experienced by others in earlier times" (p. 77).

The final shot in the film, a broad view of the Rhine river flowing into the sea, once again hints at Seghers's archetypal imagery, carrying with it associations of freedom and new beginnings. Thus, Fred Zinnemann's *The Seventh Cross*, while relying heavily on anti-Nazi film genre conventions, does manage to incorporate elements of Seghers's mythologizing. Whereas, though, Seghers's use of Christian symbolism is a function of her Popular Front politics, the film's intentions are more attuned to an American audience and its religious and ideological horizon. From an historical perspective, it is clear that both Seghers and Zinnemann tend to overemphasize the effectiveness and power of German anti-fascist resistance. Ironically, *The Seventh Cross* was banned in Berlin after the war, American occupation forces fearing that the film might encourage German resistance against the Allies. It is strange that the victors should identify with their erstwhile enemies.

Notes

1. Kurt Batt, *Anna Seghers: Versuch über Entwicklung und Werke* (Leipzig: Reclam, 1980), p. 120.
2. Anna Seghers, *The Seventh Cross*, trans. James A. Galston (Boston: Little, Brown, 1942); and Anna Seghers, *Das siebte Kreuz* (Mexico City: El libro libre, 1942).
3. *The War and Films* (United Nations Information Office), 15 January 1943.
4. *Aufbau*, 12 March 1943.
5. *Lion's Roar*, 3, No. 4 (July 1944).
6. *Aufbau*, 3 December 1943.
7. Anna Seghers, *Über Kunstwerk und Wirklichkeit: Die Tendenz in der reinen Kunst* (Berlin [GDR]: Akademie, 1970), p. 183; trans. and quoted in Lowell A. Bangerter, *The Bourgeois Proletarian: A Study of Anna Seghers* (Bonn: Bouvier, 1980), p. 179.

8. Peter Roos and Friedericke J. Hassauer-Roos (eds), *Anna Seghers Materialien-buch* (Darmstadt: Luchterhand, 1977), p. 67.

9. Werner Roggausch, *Das Exilwerk von Anna Seghers 1933–1939, Volksfront und antifaschistische Literatur* (Munich: Minerva, 1979), pp. 107–41.

10. Seghers (1970), pp. 64–6.

11. See Jan-Christopher Horak, *Die Anti-Nazi-Filme der deutschsprachigen Emigration von Hollywood 1939–1945* (Münster: MAKS, 1984), pp. 365–70.

12. All references in parentheses are taken from Anna Seghers, *Das siebte Kreuz* (Berlin and Weimar: Aufbau, 1982).

13. Henry Marx, *New Yorker Staatszeitung und Herold*, 1 October 1944; *The German-American*, 15 January 1945; Joe Gassner (Karl Jakob Hirsch), *Neue Volkszeitung*, 14 October 1944; *Freies Deutschland/Alemania Libre*, 5 April 1945.

14. *New York Times*, 29 September 1944.

15. Manfred George, "Ein guter Film mit zweifelhafter Wirkung," *Aufbau*, 6 October 1944.

16. Seghers (1970), p. 187. Cf. Kathleen A. Bunten, "Isolation and solidarity in the early works of Anna Seghers" (dissertation, Ohio State University, 1976), pp. 130–1.

17. Erika Haas, *Ideologie und Mythos: Studien zur Erzählstruktur und Sprache im Werk von Anna Seghers* (Stuttgart: Heinz, 1975), pp. 68–99.

18. Batt, p. 129.

19. Bangerter, p. 89.

Selected Bibliography

Elsaesser, Thomas. "Pathos and leave-taking: the German émigrés in Paris during the 1930s." *Sight & Sound*, 53, No. 4 (Autumn 1984), 278–83.

Engström, Ingemo and Gerhard Theuring. "Dossier: *Escape Route to Marseilles*." Trans. Barrie Ellis Jones. *Framework*, No. 18 (1982), 22–9, and No. 19 (1982), 40–5.

Heilbut, Anthony. *Exiled in Paradise*. Boston: Beacon, 1983.

Hilchenbach, Maria. *Kino im Exil: Die Emigration deutscher Filmkünstler 1933–1945*. Munich: Saur, 1982.

Horak, Jan-Christopher. *Die Anti-Nazi-Filme der deutschsprachigen Emigration von Hollywood 1939–1945*. Münster: MAKS, 1984.

—— "The palm trees were gently swaying: German refugees from Hitler in Hollywood." *Image*, 25, Nos 3–4 (September–December 1982), 29–37.

Roos, Peter and Friedericke J. Hassauer-Roos (eds). *Anna Seghers. Materialienbuch*. Darmstadt: Luchterhand, 1977.

Schürmann, Ernst (ed.). *German Film Directors in Hollywood: Film-Emigration from Germany and Austria*. San Francisco: Goethe Institute, 1978.

Taylor, John Russell. *Strangers in Paradise: The Hollywood Émigrés 1933–1950*. London: Faber & Faber, 1982.

Zinnemann, Fred. "Different perspective." In *Hollywood Directors 1941–1976*. Ed. Richard Koszarski. London and New York: Oxford University Press, 1977, pp. 144–7.

9

JAN-CHRISTOPHER HORAK

Postwar traumas in Klaren's *Wozzeck* (1947)

In December 1947, Germany consisted of little more than a vast stretch of ruins, its cities and transport systems almost totally destroyed by three years of Allied bombing, its political, social, and economic infrastructures only minimally reconstructed by the victors after twelve years of National Socialism. For the average German, survival meant a black market for even the most basic goods and an Allied military government dictating public life. The Morgenthau Plan envisioned a future Germany as an agricultural hinterland, its heavy industry disassembled to prevent the nation from ever again creating a war machine. Moreover, Germany ceased to exist as a nation: the four zones (American, British, French, and Soviet) represented four different legislative, executive, and judicial entities. Germans thus faced a loss of national identity, aggravated by a loss of faith in the monolithic fascist system which they had actively or passively supported and which was now held accountable for the genocide of 6 million European Jews and a world war that had cost over 50 million lives.

Allied public policy in postwar Germany was one of re-education. On the one hand, re-education entailed public disclosure of the manifold crimes of fascism; on the other, it meant political propagation of the principles of egalitarian democracy. Just what defined democracy, though, depended on whether one lived in the Soviet zone, where a people's democracy under the leadership of the Communist party was instituted, or in one of the three western zones, where democracy was understood to be liberal and capitalist. Similarly, east and west differed on their choice of media for the purpose of re-education. The west relied more heavily on the power of the press, leaving film – as an entertainment medium – in Hollywood's domain. After 1948, American capital controlled the German film market, while Allied military bureaucrats sought to take apart the giant Ufa film combine. The Soviets preferred cinema as their most potent public information medium. Consequently, the newly founded DEFA (*Deutsche Film-AG*) received a Soviet license in spring 1946 and public funding for the production of educational, documentary, and fiction films. By the end of 1947, the DEFA had produced seven strikingly anti-fascist features, including such international successes as Wolfgang Staudte's *The Murderers Are Among Us* (*Die Mörder sind unter uns*, 1946), Gerhard Lamprecht's *Somewhere in Berlin* (*Irgendwo in Berlin*, 1946), and Kurt Maetzig's *Marriage in the Shadows* (*Ehe im Schatten*, 1947).[1]

On 17 December 1947, *Wozzeck*, based on Georg Büchner's play, and written and directed by Georg C. Klaren at the DEFA studios, reached the German screen as the first postwar literature-to-film adaptation.[2] For the still shell-shocked German cinemagoer, the question might have arisen: of what value was a nineteenth-century drama in times like these? In fact, Klaren's adaptation had much to offer, for it not only explored explanations for the Nazi-created débâcle, but also positive traditions for the creation of a non-fascist, German national identity.

Klaren's *Wozzeck* attempted to re-establish German intellectual ties to a radically democratic and socially conscious literary tradition, one that had been eradicated from public memory by officials in Joseph Goebbels's Ministry of Propaganda after 1933. Beyond that, Klaren utilized a film style reminiscent of expressionist and progressive German cinema, thus re-establishing links to the film heritage of the Weimar Republic. Further, by attacking Prussian militarism and ruling-class oppression of the masses, *Wozzeck* revealed the forces that had led to the rise of the Third Reich. Finally, by presenting a sympathetic portrait of a murderer, who is simultaneously the victim of class oppression, *Wozzeck* at least in part exonerates all those Germans who, fearing Gestapo terror and concentration camps, had failed to resist German fascism. Despite its many allusions to themes concerning postwar Germany, however, Klaren's interpretation may be considered a faithful rendering of Büchner's play – or at least of the incomplete fragments of a drama which Büchner never shaped into a final form.

Büchner wrote *Woyzeck* in 1836–7, basing his drama on the historical murder case of Johann Christian Woyzeck, who, in a jealous rage, had stabbed his mistress to death. Although there were grave doubts about Woyzeck's sanity, he was executed in Leipzig in 1824, causing a public outrage. Büchner made extensive use of published documents.[3] He was also apparently influenced by at least two other murders, ones involving men stabbing their lovers.[4] Büchner also created the characters of the Captain and the Doctor (based on Büchner's professor in medical school at Giessen), and made Woyzeck's mistress a much younger and more sensual woman than she in fact was. Unfortunately, Büchner died in 1837, barely 23 years old, before completing the final draft of *Woyzeck*.

The estate contained four different manuscripts, identified by modern historians as H_1 H_2, H_3 and H_4, which were apparently so illegible that Ludwig Büchner, Georg's younger brother, refused to include *Woyzeck* in the *Collected Works* (*Nachgelassene Schriften*), published in 1850.[5] In 1879 Karl Emil Franzos published *Wozzeck* (*sic*) in his first complete edition of Büchner's works, misreading the title, and unfortunately taking an extremely liberal view of his editorial license. For example, Franzos added his own stage directions and mixed scenes from various manuscripts.[6] Franzos's version formed the basis for Alban Berg's famous opera, *Wozzeck*, as well as the first stage rendering, which premièred in Berlin in 1913. Finally, Fritz Bergemann edited the first critical edition of the *Woyzeck* text in 1922; this again re-arranged scenes from H_1 and H_4, but was considered an improvement over earlier versions.[7] Various new editions have appeared in the past fifteen years, which chronologically present the four manuscripts, and create a "playable" stage version, each editor in turn interpreting the play differently through the scene arrangement.[8]

This uncertainty regarding the original text has of course led to a flood of philological treatises on questions of veracity, Büchner's intentions, and legitimate editions of the text(s). Rather than getting involved in a necess-arily complicated discussion of various *Woyzeck* critiques, suffice it to say that Büchnerians are basically divided into two main camps. Conservative, aesthetically oriented critics see the character Woyzeck as a tragically isolated individual, caught in an irrational universe, and driven to murder by jealousy and a "terrible inner force." These critics tend to conclude that Büchner meant Woyzeck to commit suicide or drown, rather than to bring him to trial and execution. They de-emphasize Büchner's protests against social injustice, interpreting Woyzeck rather as a nihilistically tainted tragic hero. At the other end of the ideological spectrum, opposing critics view Woyzeck as a victim of class oppression, a loving father whose degradation at the hands of the ruling class leads him to commit murder. Following this line of thought and basing their reading on $H_1$21 (the post-mortem examin-ation of the corpse), they argue that Büchner intended to have Woyzeck con-demned to death by ruling-class justice. The play therefore becomes an expression of Büchner's metaphysical and socio-political revolt.

Primarily based on Bergemann's edition, Georg C. Klaren's film version, *Wozzeck*, opts for a socially critical point of view. Klaren not only includes scenes of Wozzeck's trial and execution; he also introduces Büchner as a character in the action. The film's first scene shows the writer at Wozzeck's autopsy, where he immediately gets involved in an argument with the Professor (the Doctor in the play) about whether Wozzeck is in fact guilty or not. This frame story continues, while the actual play is presented as a series of flashbacks, again with Büchner sometimes appearing as an observer of Wozzeck's agony. Klaren's decision to integrate Büchner into the plot is well motivated, considering his overall purpose. Georg Büchner was indeed a political activist, not merely an armchair revolutionary, and is thus suited to act as a positive example for denazified Germans.

In 1896, Ludwig Büchner had published an article identifying his brother

Georg as a socialist.[9] In 1937 Georg Lukács, the doyen of left-wing German literary critics, characterized Büchner as a "plebeian revolutionary" and precursor of socialist ideals.[10] Appearing in an anti-fascist journal, Lukács's article attempted to protect Büchner from certain Nazi philologists who feebly hoped to identify Büchner as one of their own.[11] In this light it seems only natural that Klaren should conjure up Büchner's ghost to legitimize the goals of German anti-fascists in postwar Germany.

Wozzeck opens in fact with a quote from *The Hessian Messenger* (*Der hessische Landbote*, 1834), Büchner's political pamphlet calling the peasants to arms against the ruling classes: "Peace to the cottages! War on the palaces!" In the following confrontations between the student/dramatist Büchner and the Doctor, the former is presented as a dedicated, socially critical observer. The frame story also indicates Büchner's relationship to the intellectuals of his time. In *The Hessian Messenger*, Büchner identifies the peasants as the initiators of revolutionary change, not the educated social reformers of his own class, who were united under the banner of "Young Germany." In a letter to Karl Gutzkow (1835), Büchner notes: "I am convinced that the educated and well-to-do minority, however many concessions it demands from those in power, will never abandon its antagonism towards the masses." Similarly, Büchner argues in *Wozzeck* for equal opportunity and education for the masses, while the Doctor and his students remain for the most part arrogant and élitist. Büchner verbally assaults the Doctor and prophesies: "Today you can still say: riff-raff. Soon you will have to say: the people!"

Thus, the frame story affords Klaren the possibility of clearly articulating his anti-fascist interpretation of the play, simultaneously legitimizing that interpretation through his mouthpiece, Büchner. In the scene between Wozzeck and the Captain, Wozzeck articulates his perception of social reality: "I believe that if us poor people go to heaven, we would have to help make thunder." Moments later Büchner observes Wozzeck and relates how the latter experiences the schism between rich and poor. Klaren visualizes the scene as a juxtaposition between a bourgeois family sanctimoniously praying, before consuming a sumptuous meal, and a dejected proletarian family, starving in their basement tenement. The frames' hazy edges signify the subjective view, but more importantly, the juxtaposition is followed by a reaction shot of Wozzeck sadly shaking his head in anger, while Büchner goes on to explain on the soundtrack: "He can't comprehend his apparitions, he is too simple to understand them. He sees only the way things are, and he feels they can't, mustn't go on like this."

The juxtaposition between rich and poor, ruling class and underprivileged, harks back to film conventions from the 1920s (more on that below), but is also a key device in Büchner's *The Hessian Messenger*, which begins:

The life of the rich is a long Sunday: they live in beautiful houses, they wear elegant clothes, they have well-fed faces, and speak their own language; the common people however lie before them like fertilizer in the fields. . . . The life of a peasant is a long workday; before his eyes strangers eat from his fields, his body consists of welts, his sweat is the salt on the table of the rich.

In *Wozzeck*, then, Büchner is presented as the first in a line of literary prophets of the socialist revolution. Büchner concludes: "If Wozzeck would have risen against the truly guilty, his action would have awakened the people. It would have been committed in the name of freedom and for the countless downtrodden." Büchner stands as a symbol for a democratic and egalitarian Germany which has yet to come into existence. With the victory over German fascism, this literary tradition could now be revitalized in the campaign to further the creation of such a democracy.

Klaren's intentions are similar when he refers the viewer to the traditions of the German cinema before Hitler, specifically the socially critical films of the Weimar left. Films with working-class subjects, e.g. Werner Hochbaum's *Brothers* (*Brüder*, 1929) or Slatan Dudow's *Whither Germany?* (*Kuhle Wampe*, 1932), disappeared completely after 1933 – just as did for the most any expressionistic experiments. The juxtaposition between rich and poor mentioned above, for example, is a convention borrowed from Soviet films, one used extensively in Dudow's *How the Berlin Worker Lives* (*Wie der Berliner Arbeiter wohnt*, 1930), and other films made by the Prometheus Film Collective in Berlin.[12] At another point Wozzeck is seen clenching his fist in anger. Because the camera conspicuously pans down to this fist, the image simultaneously reminds the viewer of the sign's traditional meaning in Weimar cinema as a call for revolutionary action. Coding redolent of the Weimar cinema appears elsewhere in the film, in the interpolated drill scene, where Klaren creates a rhythmic montage, cutting on form and movement, or in the whipping scene, where expressionistic shadows suggest Wozzeck's suffering. Klaren recalls these conventions in order to link his film to a progressive, non-fascist German film legacy.

On the other hand, Klaren sometimes refunctionalizes these codes, transforming their meaning to allow the viewer to sense Wozzeck's intense suffering. The carnival scene is strongly reminiscent both in style and content of German films from the 1920s like Phil Jutzi's *Mother Krause's Trip to Happiness* (*Mutter Krausens Fahrt ins Glück*, 1929). Whereas earlier film carnivals generally signify a liberation from everyday troubles, the carnival here develops into a hideous nightmare. Searching for Marie, Wozzeck is confronted with a terrifying array of masked dancers, death's-heads, chaotic light and shadows, and ever faster movement. Similarly, Klaren later inserts a series of multiple exposure of pairs of lovers to express Wozzeck's confusion after discovering Marie and the Drum Major dancing happily in a pub. In a daze, with Marie's words, "Don't stop!" ("Immer zu!"), ringing in his ears, Wozzeck stumbles through a wood, where he is threatened by grotesquely gnarled trees.

Plate 20   Marie (Helga Zülch), Wozzeck's obsession and great disappointment:
"With her he was a human being, while everyone else took him for a creature." Photo
courtesy of Stiftung Deutsche Kinemathek.

As Büchner clearly states, the loss of Marie would not have been quite as tragic, if Wozzeck had not lived in abject poverty, if Marie had not been his sole means of defining himself as a human being: "With her he was a human being, while everyone else took him for a creature." In keeping with this thesis, Wozzeck's dehumanization is repeatedly projected through animal imagery, a device found both in the play and the film. A monkey in uniform, and a donkey who is a professor at the university, represent at the carnival the two poles of Wozzeck's degradation. The images suggest that not only the victims but also the oppressors are dehumanized by the system. In the drill scene the Drum Major is visually compared with a barking dog. After Marie disappears with the Drum Major, Wozzeck "grows" donkey ears, signifying at one level his being a cuckold, at another his loss of human dignity. Similarly, the Doctor "proves" Wozzeck's kinship to a donkey by having him wiggle his ears – a favorite trick of one of Büchner's own medical professors. Such animal imagery can again be related to German expressionist cinema, e.g. Professor Unrat desperately crowing in Josef von Sternberg's *The Blue Angel* (*Der blaue Engel*, 1930).

Wozzeck becomes capable of murder because the authoritarian and repressive mechanisms of class society have literally turned him into an animal, i.e. ruling-class representatives actually perceive Wozzeck as little more than a beast. In numerous scenes Wozzeck is presented as a loving father and spouse, who has been dehumanized by poverty and an authoritarian system, but who also remains a docile underling. Thus, according to Büchner, Wozzeck's murder is a desperate revolt, committed because his socialization prevents him from attacking his true enemies. Whereas in the play the Doctor and the Captain share the responsibility for Wozzeck's dehumanization, in *Wozzeck* it is the Drum Major who most often torments him. This shift allows Klaren to emphasize anti-militarist elements. By interpolating a number of scenes, Klaren transforms the Drum Major from a mere sexual rival into a symbol for both military oppression and sexual degradation.

Wozzeck is first introduced to the viewer during a drill, while Büchner comments: "This is how the Wozzecks are bred." The staccato "one-two" commands of the Drum Major, the oblique camera angles, showing Wozzeck and his company exercising in a field of mud, the rapid editing (approximately sixty shots in a minute and a half), together reinforce the exceeding harshness and brutality of Prussian military training. One image in particular foreshadows the themes of domination and authoritarianism: shot through the Drum Major's legs, the image shows Wozzeck in the mud, framed by shiny black boots. The Drum Major's rank allows him to dominate Wozzeck both socially and personally in their sexual rivalry. At the carnival he abuses Wozzeck while making eye contact with Marie, who is visibly impressed. Marie, for her part, is drawn to the Drum Major because of his stature and imposing uniform. Klaren emphasizes the fetishistic quality of the uniform, by having a lackey polish the Drum Major's boots, while the martinet taunts Wozzeck, boasting of his sexual conquests. Although this scene in the drill square has been interpolated by Klaren, it is in keeping with Büchner's intentions in $H_4$11, the only scene in the play where the rivals directly confront each other. The Drum Major tries to pick a fight with Wozzeck, who, despite his anger, cannot raise a hand against his superior. To vent his anger, Wozzeck must turn against himself or some weaker victim.

This point is also demonstrated in two scenes ($H_4$5, $H_4$9) involving Wozzeck's Captain. In the first scene, the Captain derides Wozzeck for his stupidity, and for "living in sin" with Marie and his child. Wozzeck counters that only rich people can afford to be moral, while barely containing his anger. Ironically, Klaren repeatedly cuts away to Wozzeck's razor blade gliding over the Captain's throat, possibly suggesting that Wozzeck has indeed the means to bring down the system, just as the Captain, ignoring the blade while he abuses Wozzeck, embodies the blind complacency of his class. In a later scene, the Captain maliciously intimates that Wozzeck is being made a cuckold. Again, Wozzeck's blood begins to boil, but, unable to express his true feelings, he talks about the weather: "A nice gray sky. One could get the urge to drive a rod into it and then hang oneself." The violence with which Wozzeck speaks this line, his fist thrust explosively into the sky, expresses his boundless frustration. According to the film, then, military order, as an element of a rigorously authoritarian system of class repression, simultaneously dehumanizes men, and suppresses any form of resistance.

The Doctor, the other representative of class oppression, appears both as Büchner's antagonist in the frame story, and as Wozzeck's tormentor. Forced to eat nothing but peas and deliver a daily urine sample, Wozzeck functions as a guinea pig for the Doctor's experiments. When Wozzeck fails to deliver the fruits of his labor, the Doctor vigorously reprimands him for surrendering to nature's call. Wozzeck is not perceived as a human being, but as raw material for the Doctor's scientific work. The Doctor treats him in much the same way as the cat he callously throws from a balcony to demonstrate an obtuse theory. Wozzeck ironically catches the cat, thus "impeding research," as the Doctor notes. Wozzeck endures the physical torture, because he desperately needs the meager payment he receives as compensation.

The relationship between the Doctor and Wozzeck, then, is that of capital to labor, exploiter to exploited. Wozzeck's labor is part of a productive process, of experiments which he neither understands nor benefits from. The Doctor's scientific speech only further confuses Wozzeck, thereby demonstrating once again that language too can be used as a weapon for class oppression – a point made by the play as well. The laboratory scenes are shot at extremely oblique angles, a further indication of Wozzeck's confusion. When Büchner takes the Doctor to task for abusing Wozzeck, the latter replies that he is acting purely in the interest of science. Moments later though, the Doctor reveals his self-serving motives, exclaiming with apparent self-satisfaction: "O my theory, my reputation. I will become famous, I will be immortal."

Such statements are, of course, the stuff of caricature, and Klaren satirically emphasizes the fact by having the Doctor complain to Büchner that he has made a comic figure of him. In point of fact, Büchner's *Woyzeck* presents the Doctor, the Captain, and the Drum Major as stereotypes, denying them the personal names he gives his other characters. They merely represent their respective classes. The film treats them in much the same way, exaggerating their symbolic significance through camera angles and lighting. The Drum Major is consistently shot from a low angle which corresponds to his subjectively perceived physical volume and importance. The Doctor is lighted from below, giving his face a demonic quality. They are presented as symbols of a social system that seeks only to preserve power for the ruling élite.

The ultimate historical product of such a system, according to the film, is evident in the lessons of twentieth-century German history. A repressive system must — if it is to keep in check those social forces which are set free in an industrialized mass society — resort to fascism and war. Klaren consequently inserts images which resonate with meaning for all those who had just survived the rise and fall of Nazi Germany. The drill scene, for example, ends with a dissolve to Wozzeck's little boy, marching with a wooden gun and paper soldier's cap. The image signifies that even children are bred for war, but also relates to Germany's "Hitler Youth," possibly the most blindly obedient generation in German history. In the last year of the war it was 12- and 13-year-old Hitler Youths who defended the "Fatherland" against the Allied armies. Wozzeck forbids the boy to play with guns, because he is plagued by visions of war and destruction. At the end of the film his parting words to the boy are, "Do a better job," a bit of advice also directed at Germany's postwar youth.

The scene in the open field (H₄1), where Wozzeck imagines a mass conspiracy of Freemasons slowly undermining the earth with a network of tunnels, is transformed by Klaren into an anti-fascist and anti-war image. While Wozzeck exclaims, "A fire comes up from the earth to heaven and a deafening noise like trumpets comes down," a series of superimpositions show a monstrous executioner with an ax (a favorite tool of the Nazis for eliminating political foes), followed by a vision of the war dead rising up to haunt the nation from under a vast field of white crosses. In another scene, a military parade ends with a lonely, crippled war veteran. The uniforms and helmets belong in fact more to the twentieth century than the nineteenth, while the image of the war victim, culled from countless postwar films which followed World War I, again makes the point that militarism in any form leads not to glory, but only to death and destruction. The experience of Germany in the Third Reich only substantiates that fact.

Other allusions to Nazi Germany abound in the film. The Doctor's inhuman experiments, carried through without the slightest regard for human suffering, recall the perverse horror of Dr Treite's sterilization experiments in Ravensbrück, Dr Karl Gebhardt's and Dr Fritz Fischer's experiments in bone grafting at Auschwitz, and the work at Professor August Hirt's Anatomical Institute in Strasbourg, crimes which were brought to public attention during the "doctors' trials" at Nuremberg in 1947. Likewise, the medical students attending the Doctor's lectures later taunt Wozzeck in the pub (they are wearing fraternity caps and sashes), a reminder how university fraternities were among the first and most ardent supporters of the Nazis.

Finally, the court of law where Wozzeck is condemned to death resembles less a traditional court than it does the Nazi-created "people's court" (*Volksgerichtshof*). In the frame story, Büchner provokes the Doctor with a statement, quoted by Klaren from *The Hessian Messenger*: "The judiciary? It has become the whore of power." The same can be said of the so-called "people's court," an *ad hoc* committee of unscrupulous judges and Nazi party officials, which was instituted in order to mete out death penalties more swiftly, without due process of law. These examples demonstrate how *Wozzeck*, while reflecting ruling-class structures in nineteenth-century Germany, also alludes to their radical and perverted extension under fascism.

Georg C. Klaren's *Wozzeck* condemns the system that created the conditions for the Holocaust, yet, at the same time, it seeks to rehabilitate individuals in that system. By negating the theory of "collective guilt," the film attempts to mitigate the trauma gripping postwar Germany. Wozzeck commits murder, yet the audience is given to understand that he should not be morally condemned, but must rather be perceived as a victim of class oppression. As Büchner notes: "First you turn human beings into animals, then you condemn them for acting like animals." Time and again, Wozzeck is shown receiving corporal punishment: he is whipped, kept under arrest, and made to run the gauntlet. Ironically, the birch rods used to beat him are cut by Wozzeck and Andreas in an earlier scene. Wozzeck becomes the producer and the victim of the instruments of his own repression.

The visualization of such a predicament strikes close to home for many Germans. Even today most Germans who experienced the Nazi period consider themselves as having been not so much active participants, as victims of a brutal dictatorship. Fearing the kind of punishment Wozzeck receives, i.e. Gestapo torture and concentration camps (1 million Germans died in these prisons), the great mass of working-class and lower-middle-class Germans stood by idly rather than actively resisting, as their neighbors were beaten in the streets or transported to the death camps. That Klaren, himself a silent fellow traveller of German fascism, wishes to communicate sympathy for this paralyzed majority is expressed in a number of scenes where Klaren cuts away to working-class types sadly looking on while Wozzeck is being abused. Like Wozzeck, they are caught in the system, aware of its brutal injustice, but unable to act against it.

Wozzeck's comment to the Doctor, modified from H_48, also illustrates this point: "When the world becomes so dark that one must grope about, how dark it is; and only a red gleam, as if the world were going up in flames. What can one hold on to?" The imagery of darkness and a world in flames is typical of postwar German descriptions of their own fascist war. The use of such apocalyptic imagery, however, also acts to depoliticize: fascism thus becomes a kind of natural catastrophe, rather than the product of a specific set of political and social forces, willfully conspiring to maintain power at any cost. Another scene communicating this sense of catastrophe is the grandmother's parable. Although the allegory is taken almost verbatim from Büchner's original ($H_1$14), German audiences most certainly could relate it to their own fascist episode. The lonely child surrounded by death stands for the isolated citizen in Nazi Germany; the world upturned becomes an image for Germany's obliterated cities; the child's flight a symbol for Germany's criss-crossing refugee caravans.

Given this materialist interpretation of *Woyzeck*, it is indeed surprising to find Klaren utilizing such depoliticized imagery. It is in fact a dangerous interpretation, because it presupposes that most Germans were indeed victims of the system, innocents lost in the fascist woods, rather than active, albeit reluctant, participants in an aggressive campaign against humanity. Such inconsistency is not uncommon in anti-fascist German literature. One need only recall Bertolt Brecht's attack on Lion Feuchtwanger, who uses similar non-political symbols in his anti-fascist *Waiting Room Trilogy* (*Wartesaal-Trilogie*).[13] Furthermore, Klaren is primarily concerned with gaining the support of his audience, which for the most part thought in such terms. Finally, Klaren attempts to counteract the collective guilt theory propagated by the western allies. That theory sought to make each and every German personally responsible for the crimes committed under National Socialism. In contrast, the film firmly states that it is not individuals but rather an authoritarian and class society that is at fault for the rise of totalitarianism. Once individuals recognize this, they can hopefully overcome the trauma of defeat and move towards the creation of a truly democratic society, destroying in the process those ruling élites at the root of fascism. This, then, is the ultimate message of Klaren's *Wozzeck*.

Whether or not Klaren is justified in adapting Büchner's *Woyzeck* almost exclusively in socio-political terms, while de-emphasizing existentialist elements central to the work, is open to debate. Undeniably, though, *Wozzeck* can claim to be both a legitimate interpretation – given the confusion regarding the original text – and a timely adaptation, the emanation of a *Zeitgeist*. Whether the film is aesthetically valid as a formal transformation from stage to screen is another question. Lotte Eisner's comment that the film is "an over-picturesque stylization of Büchner's violent drama,"[14] is not totally unjustified. The carnival scenes, especially, seem too ornate for Büchner's minimalist language and stage design. One can imagine that the style of other early DEFA films, similar to Italian neorealism, might have been more appropriate. Modern audiences will also miss that element which Büchner delivers more than a century ahead of his time: modernism. *Wozzeck* manages to fill all those narrative and psychological holes which make *Woyzeck* such a startingly modern play.

In this light, Werner Herzog's rendering, *Woyzeck* (1979), seems both closer to the spirit of Büchner, and at the same time an almost prototypical Herzog film. A deep hatred of professors and other ruling élites unites Büchner and Herzog, as manifested in *The Mystery of Kaspar Hauser* (*Jeder für sich und Gott gegen alle*, 1974) and *Woyzeck*. The former in fact ends with a paraphrase from *Woyzeck*.[15] Herzog emphasizes the existential nausea of his protagonist in *Woyzeck*, simultaneously softening the explicit social criticism, even though he remakes Klaren's drill scene. Woyzeck, however, is not a dwarf in a mass of muddied soldiers, but rather a lonely private, following the orders of an invisible guard-god. In keeping with his modernist interpretation, Herzog also inserts obvious narrative inconsistencies, such as when Marie admires the beard of the beardless Drum Major. Furthermore, Herzog leaves his film open-ended: the audience loses sight of Woyzeck in haze and darkness, recalling Kaspar Hauser's disappearance in the earlier film. In Klaren's film, the hero's fate is sealed, as Wozzeck marches to the executioner, the camera freezing on Wozzeck's face. Ironically enough, in the modern cinema a freeze frame signifies that the story has no end.

Notes

1. Cf. Roger Manvell and Heinrich Fraenkel, *The German Cinema* (New York: Praeger, 1971), pp. 99–107.

2. *Wozzeck* was only screened in the Soviet and French zones. The film was not shown in West Germany until the late 1950s. Georg C. Klaren, born 10 September 1900 in Vienna, had been a scriptwriter during the silent era, continuing to write and occasionally direct films throughout the 1930s and early 1940s, producing "entertainment" fare. After 1945, he was appointed chief dramatic producer (*Dramaturg*) of DEFA.

3. Dr Johann Christian August Clarus, "Die Woyzeck Gutachten," *Henkes Zeitschrift für die Staatsarzneikunde*, No. 4 (1825), and No. 5 (1826), reprinted in Hans Mayer, *Georg Büchner, Woyzeck. Dichtung und Wirklichkeit* (Frankfurt am Main: Ullstein, 1967), pp. 75–137.

4. The Schmolling and Diess murder cases are described by Maurice B. Benn in *The Drama of Revolt* (Cambridge and New York: Cambridge University Press, 1976), p. 219.

5. Georg Büchner, *Nachgelassene Schriften*, ed. Ludwig Büchner (Frankfurt am Main: Sauerländer, 1850).

6. Georg Büchner, *Sämtliche Werke und handschriftlicher Nachlass*, ed. Karl Emil Franzos (Frankfurt am Main, 1879). Cf. Gerhard P. Knapp, *Georg Büchner: Eine kritische Einführung in die Forschung* (Frankfurt am Main: Athenaion, 1975), p. 32.

7. Georg Büchner, *Sämtliche Werke und Briefe: Auf Grund des handschriftlichen Nachlasses*, ed. Fritz Bergemann (Leipzig, 1922; Frankfurt am Main, 1962 [9th edition]).

8. See, among many others, Georg Büchner, *Woyzeck: Eine kritische Lese- und Arbeitsausgabe*, ed. Lothar Bornscheuer (Stuttgart: Reclam, 1972). For a particularly original recent reconstruction of the manuscript in English translation, see *Georg Büchner: The Complete Collected Works*, trans. and ed. Henry J. Schmidt (New York: Avon, 1977), pp. 177–228.

9. Ludwig Büchner, "Georg Büchner, der Sozialist," *Zukunft*, 16 (1896), 598–601. An excerpt from this article is reprinted in Dietmar Goltschnigg (ed.), *Materialien zur Rezeptions- und Wirkungsgeschichte Georg Büchners* (Kronberg: Scriptor, 1974), pp. 183–242.

10. Georg Lukács, "Der faschisierte und der wirkliche Georg Büchner," *Das Wort*, 2, No. 2 (1937), 7–26. Reprinted in Georg Lukács (ed.), *Deutsche Realisten des 19. Jahrhunderts* (Berlin and Berne: Dietz, 1953).

11. Josef Magnus Wehner, "Georg Büchner zum 100. Todestag," *Münchener Neueste Nachrichten*, 19 February 1937; reprinted in Goldschnigg, pp. 297–300.

12. See Jan-Christopher Horak, "Prometheus film collective (1925–1932). German Communist *Kinokultur*, Part 1," *Jump Cut*, No. 26 (1981), 39–41; and "*Mother Krause's Trip to Happiness*: Kino-Culture in Weimar Germany, Part 2," *Jump Cut*, No. 27 (1982), 55–6.

13. Cf. Sigrid Schneider, *Das Ende Weimars im Exilroman: Literarische Strategien zur Vermittlung von Faschismustheorien* (Munich: Saur, 1980), p. 151.

14. Lotte H. Eisner, *The Haunted Screen*, trans. Roger Greaves (Berkeley: University of California Press, 1969), p. 339.

15. See Jan-Christopher Horak, "Werner Herzog's *Écran Absurde*," *Literature/Film Quarterly*, 7, No. 3 (1979), 223–34. *Kaspar Hauser* concludes with the town clerk noting: "A beautiful protocol, an exact protocol," paraphrasing Büchner's phrase (from H$_1$21), "A good murder, a real murder, a beautiful murder. . . ."

Script

"*Wozzeck.*" In Peter Pleyer. *Deutscher Nachkriegsfilm 1946–1948*. Münster: Fahle, 1965, pp. 255–83.

Selected Bibliography

Jansen, Peter W. and Wolfram Schütte (eds). *Film in der DDR*. Munich: Hanser, 1977.

Kotulla, Theodor. "*Wozzeck.*" *Filmkritik*, 2, No. 8 (August 1958), 175–6.

Pleyer, Peter. *Deutscher Nachkriegsfilm 1946–1948*. Münster: Fahle, 1965.

Walker, William. "GDR film in cultural context." *Die Unterrichtspraxis*, 15, No. 2 (1982), 194–206.

Walker, William. "Georg Klaren's *Wozzeck*: the adaptation of drama to East German cinema and socialist realism." In *Purdue University Fifth Annual Conference on Film: Proceedings*, 30 October–1 November 1980, West Lafayette, Indiana: Purdue University, 1980, pp. 75–80.

Weiss, Wolfgang (ed.). *Film- und Fernsehkunst der DDR: Traditionen, Beispiele, Tendenzen*. Berlin (GDR): Henschel, 1979.

10

MARC SILBERMAN

Semper fidelis:
Staudte's *The Subject* (1951)

Although Wolfgang Staudte had already scripted several literary texts for film adaptations, *Der Untertan* was the first feature-length literary adaptation he directed.[1] Later he went on to film, among others a fairy-tale by Wilhelm Hauff, the Dutch novel *Ciske de Rat* (1955) and such classics as Gerhart Hauptmann's play *Rose Bernd* (1956), Bertolt Brecht's musical *The Threepenny Opera* (*Die Dreigroschenoper*, 1963), and Jack London's *The Sea Wolf* (*Der Seewolf*, 1971). Of all Staudte's adaptations, *Der Untertan* resembles its literary source most closely in tone, and of all his films it contains the most daring and imaginative *mise-en-scène*. To appreciate fully how Staudte implemented his cinematic know-how in this adaptation, we must first briefly examine the source and inspiration.

As the author of *Professor Unrat* – the novel which Josef von Sternberg adapted for *The Blue Angel* (*Der blaue Engel*, 1930) – and *Der Untertan*, Heinrich Mann (1871–1950) provided the source for two of the most successful literary adaptations in German film history. He had become quite a popular author by World War I, characterized by Gottfried Benn as the mentor of an entire literary generation and by Georg Lukács as the greatest German master of satire and caricature in his time.[2] Mann's radical critique of the bourgeoisie and his rejection of German tradition places him in the company of his contemporaries Frank Wedekind and Carl Sternheim. *Der Untertan* is the first part of a trilogy which Mann began to write after 1905. In the tradition of Zola's social tableaux, it paints a panorama of German society during the time of William II (hence the subtitle of the trilogy: *The Imperial Reich. The Novels of German Society at the Time of William II*).[3] Each novel concentrates on a single social class: the bourgeoisie in *Der Untertan*, the proletariat in *The Poor* (*Die Armen*, 1917) and intellectuals in *The Head* (*Der Kopf*, 1925). Mann completed *Der Untertan* in 1914, only to see its publication in serialized form interrupted – due to the publisher's anticipation of censorship – when war broke out in August.

The complete text appeared in book form after the fall of the Second Reich in 1918.

The novel provided Staudte with the basic plot and its motifs. It gave him a model for the satiric tone, the characters, and the fictional space they inhabit. Therefore, if we consider the novel's narrative strategies, we can recognize many of the film's characteristics. *Der Untertan* finds its roots in the satiric novel of the eighteenth century but combines this comic vision with elements of social realism popularized by the French novel of the late nineteenth century.[4] Mann molds his protagonist in a series of quick episodes which portray the psychology of the *Untertan* type. Cowardly, foolish, brazen, ambitious, racist, chauvinistic: Diederich Hessling is the exemplary Wilhelminian to the point that he at times imagines himself to be the Emperor's mouthpiece.

The novel consists of six chapters and is divided into two distinct parts. The first two chapters portray the stations of Hessling's maturation in the tradition of the German *Bildungsroman*: raised "properly" in his family, trained to respect authority in social institutions like school, and finally initiated into patriarchal ways in a love affair. At the end of this process – an inversion of the classical ideal of *Bildung* – the anti-hero has learned to extinguish his personality by imitating his masters' behavior and appearance rather than developing his individuality and true inner self. After Hessling abruptly withdraws from a love affair and prepares to leave Berlin at the end of his studies, the narrator sums up his growth to this point:

> Diederich was proud and glad of his excellent training. The students' corps, his military service and the atmosphere of imperialism, had educated him and made him fit. He resolved to give effect to his well-earned principles at home in Netzig, and to become a pioneer of the spirit of the times. (p. 74)

Having come of age at the very time when William II ascended to the throne, Hessling decides to serve the new "spirit of the times" and becomes a loyal subject of the new emperor.

The second part of the novel – the last four chapters – shifts the action to Hessling's home town and onto the plane of the social novel. In this microcosm of bourgeois society, the other figures are choreographed around Hessling like dancers on a stage as he undertakes the conquest of Netzig. Here he externalizes the lessons of his *Bildung*, inspired not by inner conviction but by his fear of authority. He takes over his father's newsprint factory, helps establish the conservative, nationalistic "Emperor's Party," gradually incapacitates the city's liberal forces in a conspiracy with other reactionaries representing the Army, the Church, and the State bureaucracy, marries a wealthy heiress, makes political deals with the Junker governor and the Social Democratic workers' representative and becomes ultimately

Netzig's most powerful and most feared citizen. The novel originally carried the title of *History of the Public Soul under William II*, clearly conveying Mann's concept of his anti-hero: Hessling comes to embody the quintessence of Wilhelmine society, the public soul inscribed with the loss of bourgeois identity.

Mann situates his critique of Wilhelmine society in the crisis of bourgeois values and democratic liberalism during the last quarter of the nineteenth century. He traces the ascendancy of a new bourgeois type who, subjected to rapid industrialization and social change, transfers the traditional values of individual self-realization within a community to the cult of the great personality. In Mann's eyes this industrial bourgeoisie shared responsibility with the military and state leaders for the imperialist expansionism under William II which eventually led to the Great War. Translated into the novel, this Bonapartism becomes pure theater. Politics are staged as Wagnerian opera, and ethics are practiced with a Nietzschean will to power. This framework determines both the novel's dramatic form and the narrative topos of role playing. The dominant behavioral pattern of the *Untertan* type is the role or mask, and Diederich Hessling maneuvers himself into a powerful position by reproducing, both physically and expressively, the image of his idol, Emperor William II. Wolfgang Buck, the author's fictional *alter ego* as well as a young lawyer-aesthete who gives up his profession to become an actor, describes Hessling in the following way: "What . . . makes him a new type, is simply the gesture, the swaggering manner, the aggressiveness of an alleged personality, the craving for effect at any price, even at the expense of others" (p. 177). In addition, theater situations literally organize the dramatic highpoints: the two trials initiated by Hessling are stage shows par excellence; the dilettante production of *Die heimliche Gräfin* (*The Secret Countess*) by the local governor's wife (a travesty of Goethe's play *Die natürliche Tochter*) and the *Lohengrin* performance satirically punctuate and at the same time confirm Hessling's ruthless rise; and finally the climax, the unveiling of an equestrian statue of William II, places the protagonist in the limelight for his apotheosis as mime of power.

Within this novelistic structure, Mann establishes a tension between the intoxication of success and the anxieties which accompany it, between a satire of the society which tolerates, even breeds the *Untertan*, and a punitive comedy. There is no balance here, for the extreme is typical. Characters represent types, like sketches or caricatures by George Grosz. *Der Untertan*, in short, is a satirical novel with a political message, written by an author whose work more than any other's reflects Germany's political, social, and cultural developments during the Second Reich. The critique of the *fin-de-siècle* bourgeoisie aims at exposing its complicity with the power structure of a decadent society. Mann mocks the false interiority and bankrupt romanticism of a dreamer, of a not entirely unsympathetic scoundrel. This is the novel's material and the substance out of which Staudte fashioned his film.

Staudte's biography had not predestined him for the role he would play in the postwar German cinema. Born in 1906, he chose engineering and drafting as a career until the 1920s, when he broke off his studies and followed his father into the theater. Because Staudte was identified with leftist cultural circles (his work with director Erwin Piscator and at the leftist Volksbühne theater), Nazi authorities denied him permission to work in 1933. As they gradually relaxed such controls, he was able to act in films and even direct commercials and shorts. Staudte's break came in 1942 when he was given the opportunity to direct a film independently. Before Germany's capitulation in 1945, two Staudte films were released, both of them unexceptional comic fare with stereotypical romantic plots (two other films were never released). Germany's defeat brought also the collapse of the film industry. By 1946, however, the Soviet Military Authority had set up a central film company, DEFA (Deutsche Film-AG) in the eastern zone that was producing newsreels and cultural films under primitive physical and material conditions. Although Staudte was living in the western sector of Berlin (as were many film people), he became one of the pioneer members of the original DEFA crew. Neither tainted by a Nazi affiliation nor directly engaged in socialist politics, Staudte was for the Soviet authorities one of the "critical bourgeois intellectuals" with technical skills whom they wanted to enlist in the cultural re-education of the Germans.

Basing it on an exposé he had already conceived before the end of the war, Staudte directed the first postwar German feature-length film, the DEFA production *The Murderers Are Among Us* (*Die Mörder sind unter uns*, 1946). It focuses on a military doctor who after the war tries to come to terms with his own guilt by seeking vengeance on a former SS officer who executed hostages in Poland while he stood by and watched. What would become a characteristic Staudte theme already surfaces in this film – the caricature of petty-bourgeois mentality in the factory owner, alias SS-guard, and his tendency toward violence. The film was widely acclaimed and established the director's international reputation. Staudte's next two DEFA features also addressed political themes and the German past. *The Strange Adventures of Mr Fridolin B.* (*Die seltsamen Abenteuer des Herrn Fridolin B.*, 1948) is a satire on German bureaucracy, both in content and form anticipating many aspects of *Der Untertan*. *Rotation* (1949) retraces the daily life of an unemployed, apolitical working-class family which in 1933 looks for nothing more than law and order and work, only to discover later that they have become Nazi victims. *Rotation*, more clearly than any other film of the time, denotes a break with the characteristic "Ufa style" of the 1930s and 1940s. Rejecting gaudy visual ornamentation and conventional thematic clichés, Staudte's signature came to mean fluid editing and visual originality with political conviction, an unusual combination in postwar German cinema.

Der Untertan was Wolfgang Staudte's fourth film project with the DEFA studios. He explains in an anecdote how he came to make the film:

I went to London for the première of *The Murderers Are Among Us* and afterwards an English critic, Hans Wollenberg, said to me: 'This Paulsen [Wolfgang Paulsen, the lead actor] is really an extraordinary figure. You ought to make *Der Untertan* with him.' At that time I didn't even know Heinrich Mann's novel. When I got back to Berlin, I casually mentioned to the DEFA people: 'Someone ought to film *Der Untertan*, really great material, with Paulsen.' They jumped right on the bandwagon, but the rights were held in America, and in the meantime I lost track of the project. Then one day I heard – we got the rights, Staudte's next film will be *Der Untertan*. The first thing I did was to read the book.[5]

What Staudte read fit his interest and temperament: the historical reconstruction of the Wilhelmine burgher with all his vanities and social parasitism was a film idea made to order. Diederich Hessling, one of the herd, consumed by his instinct for self-preservation, was precisely the type of figure that Staudte had used as a critical foil in his previous DEFA films. Mann's work also excited Staudte's camera eye. The novel's cinematicity – its privileging of action, its episodic structure, the assimilation of appearance and reality – undoubtedly appealed to Staudte whose reputation as an optical director was by that time well established. More than that, however, the novel challenged him to devise visual solutions for the nuances of its satiric language and expression. On the whole Staudte's adaptation works its source hard and well. The filmmaker condensed Mann's novel, eliminated or rearranged characters and deleted episodes, transforming the rest into cinematic terms. Yet, although the novel and the film achieve their effects with very different means, both the reader and the spectator share in similar imaginative experiences.

Plot, character, and narrative editing all contribute to the film's satiric structure. Staudte was forced to compress radically the novel's plot to make it manageable for the film version. He cut out everything that was not directly germane to the power relationship forming and controlling Hessling's development as an exemplary symbol of his class. The essence of role playing as a social metaphor – the interpersonal and interspatial relations which reveal social stratification – became the film's central concern. As a result, Staudte changed some of the characters. The State Attorney Jadassohn, a caricature of the careerist, anti-Semitic Jew, becomes Mennicke, simply a careerist. Kienast, to whom Hessling manages to marry his sister Magda, disappears, and the point of the entire subplot – marriage as an economic contract – is collapsed into that of Hessling's own marriage to Guste. Other secondary characters are deleted (the mayor Scheffelweis, the patriotic teacher Kühnchen) or reduced in importance (old Buck and his son

Wolfgang Buck). Finally, Staudte streamlined his plot by excluding a series of characters and subplots revolving around hypocritical sexual attitudes: Käthchen Zillich, the pastor's daughter who becomes an expensive prostitute kept by highly regarded citizens such as Hessling and Jadassohn; Hessling's recourse to a slanderous rumor about incest in order to snatch Guste from her fiancé; the series of mysterious, obscene letters which even threatens to destroy the fragile system of trust between family members; and Hessling's sadomasochistic relationship with his wife. Whereas Mann incorporated this dimension of sexuality – hate for women, perversion of feelings – as a primary element in the structuring of the authoritarian personality, Staudte stresses the social consequences of the *Untertan* mentality so that sexuality becomes simply another instructive lesson about dominance and role playing. What changes from scene to scene are the power relations between Hessling and the other figures: victim becomes victimizer becomes victim. Everyone is corrupted or corruptible in this decadent social structure, and Hessling, the loyal subject of his emperor, is one of the most adept at changing roles.

The skeletal plot offered Staudte enough scenic material to create satirical arrangements. One device was to structure repetitive but contrasting situations. When his mistress's father comes to ask him to marry her, Hessling basks in the feeling of power he experiences because he can cruelly humiliate the man by throwing him out. Later Hessling finds himself opposite Lieutenant von Brietzen, his sister's lover, making a similar request, and ironically the lover repeats verbatim Hessling's own hypocritical sentiments from that earlier encounter while showing him the door. Moreover, in a caricature of his own "disgrace," he even expresses his respect for the Lieutenant:

Whoever trampled others under foot must be prepared to be walked on, that was the iron law of might. After his attack of resistance, Diederich again felt the secret thrill of the man who is trampled upon. . . . In spite of everything Diederich rejoiced in the fresh, chivalrous young officer. 'Nobody can duplicate that for us,' he said with conviction.   (pp. 266–7)

Another time Hessling discovers a sick worker and her husband, resting behind a ragpile in his factory. He accuses them of lewd behavior and fires them. Later he seduces Guste behind the same ragpile, telling the story of the workers to excite her. Such repetition exposes through satirical contrast Hessling's inept actions. Sometimes his obvious self-disgrace, accentuated by the narrator's calm explanations, is enough to generate a ridiculous impression. We see Hessling in hot pursuit of a suspected assassin of the Emperor only to watch him end up in a cloud of white powder when the man turns out to be an artist carrying a can of pigment. Or in the last sequence, he ducks like a scared rabbit under the speaker's lectern when thunder breaks during his warmongering speech. In such cases the scenic structure reveals the discrepancy between pompous façade and the emptiness behind it.

As instrument and prototype of the authoritarian state, the film's protagonist appears distorted and larger than life. His exaggerated looks and behavior are eminently suited to visual language. Although the then unknown actor Werner Peters was not originally considered for the lead role, the choice to engage him turned out to be a fortunate one. He appears in almost every scene, either as visual object or as the voyeur through whose eyes we implicitly see. Indeed, the few sequences without Peters – such as exposition scenes for Emmi's love affair and for Guste's indignant rejection of her fiancé – are among the least memorable in the film because they lack the striking combination of banality and intensity which typifies his presence. Peters's achievement as an actor lies in his ability to project the schizophrenic behavior both of a bullied child, frightened and cowering, and of an arrogant parvenu, strutting and vain.

Staudte's cameraman, Robert Baberske, knew how to translate these satirical distortions into a matter of perspective. He employs the camera to organize the hierarchically defined world as the protagonist perceives it, alternating between high and low angles. Thus, in the reversed repetition of the sequences described above, Hessling's triumph over his mistress's father is shot from a low angle, whereas the rebuff at the lieutenant's hands frames him from a high angle. Similarly, when Hessling, one of the recruits in military training, dares to step out of line and address the captain of the regiment, we see first the captain from an extremely low-angle shot, and then in a reverse shot, a tiny Hessling from an exaggeratedly high angle. Here the soundtrack reinforces the visual satire: as the camera focuses in close-up on the captain's lips, a long string of incomprehensible gibberish spews from his mouth, sounding like indignant scolding and commands, together with fife and drum music in the background, all playing increasingly faster.

Such visual comic effect is nowhere more cleverly achieved than in the extended montage sequence for Hessling's Roman encounter with the Emperor, the film's best executed scene. Hessling abruptly decides to interrupt his honeymoon in Switzerland to be in Rome to applaud and "protect" his beloved Emperor during a state visit. The quick montage focuses on small details from dramatic camera angles in a series of sketchbook-like takes accompanied almost solely by the narrator's calm explanations about what happens. From a low angle, black military boots descend a monumental flight of stairs; cut to a close-up of Hessling's feathered hat and then a slow crane up to a bird's-eye shot of borsalinos crowding next to a straight line of military caps while a feathered hat pushes its way through to the street. The feathered cap finally breaks through the crowd of hats to the street, and the camera cuts to a shot of a carriage from behind. Only two heads are visible, one topped by a helmet with a shining eagle, the Prussian *Pickelhaube*, the other topped by an Italian military dress cap. Once again a bird's-eye shot catches Hessling as he runs alongside the carriage wheel shrieking "Hurrah," and then we see him from a low angle, parallel pan through the spokes of the carriage wheel as he frantically bows from the waist and waves his hat, all the time running with the carriage. The camera catches the *Pickelhaube* from the side, again from a high angle, as it slowly turns a bit to the right. The narrator ends his comments: "For one moment under the clear blue sky they were alone with each other, the Emperor and his subject. They looked at each other, and the Emperor nodded." The separation of narrative elements — here dramatic action, camera movement, narrator's voice — functions not unlike the Brechtian notion of distanciation (*Verfremdung*). The overdrawn image of the protagonist approaches hyperbole, but without didacticism Staudte exposes to ridicule Hessling's self-deception.

The details which distinguish figures and roles in the montage sequence constitute a classic example of metonymy. The hats stand for the characters. In a similar way, Staudte uses caricature throughout the film to amplify foibles or negative traits as if seen under a microscope. As a result the characters tend to be flat, no more than ciphers for different facets of bourgeois philistinism. Yet that is part of the satire's strategy, for by isolating and reducing the figures, their actions, and their modes of behavior, it deforms them so grotesquely that they assume allegorical dimensions. In an almost documentary way, Staudte "quotes" fragments of reality that will reveal the characters' socio-cultural profile: a painting, a statuette, a song, a uniform, a verbal cliché. Frequently he makes use of close-ups to frame such details for unusual visual effects. The atavistic faces of the drunken fraternity brothers seen through their glass beer mugs or the reflection of the recruits in the polished metal of a bugle are two instances. Gestures too can be quotes, as when Hessling is discharged from the army and leaves the barracks twirling his cane and strutting like Charlie Chaplin, or when his self-righteous blustering recalls Werner Krauss's interpretation of the philistine Theobald Maske in the film version of Sternheim's *Royal Scandal* (*Die Hose*, 1927).

Caricature, then, is a radically economical device which minimizes discrete features to produce instant recognition. It requires the viewer to fill in the gaps and organize configurations or relations from visual detail. The first sequence, the "exposition" or introduction to the film's social milieu, employs most consistently visual detail in constructing a meaningful *mise-en-scène*. A long, lateral tracking shot from left to right surveys the quintessentially Wilhelmine parlor: Biedermeier furniture with its ornamental ruffles and carved feet, bric-a-brac on every horizontal surface, a framed still life, until finally the camera comes to rest on a portrait of baby Diederich posed on a white fur rug. The image freezes and the credits follow, accompanied by light waltz and march music. Then, the camera pan continues to the floor where Diederich sits on the same fur rug crying helplessly, and the narrator speaks the novel's first lines: "Diederich Hessling was a dreamy, delicate child, frightened of everything. . . ." This opening sequence, as well as a similar tracking shot in the Göpels's parlor, suggest that Staudte learned something from G. W. Pabst's descriptive, naturalistic interiors and camera rhythms, with the difference that here the naturalism is undercut by the interaction of camera, music, and narrator.

More literal and crudely done in this respect are two comic scenes which verge on the burlesque in the incongruous disparity between form and subject matter. During his studies in Berlin, Hessling visits a vaudeville show where we witness a dance number that could be a parody of a 1930s Erik Charell musical: an inept chorus line of chubby women, dressed scantily but enough to suggest soldiers, marches in a circle singing, "The whole world knows our deeds, we are the nation's élite. . . ." In a later scene, Hessling uses his wedding party to introduce his newest invention, "World Power," a brand of toilet paper with patriotic slogans printed on each tissue. As the couple sneaks out to leave for their honeymoon, the camera fades on the distinguished guests reading slogans with great interest as they unwind the rolls. The narrator explains that this invention was designed to "carry triumphantly German spirit, supported by German technology, to the remotest corners of the Reich."

The presence of an off-camera narrator is a structural device which Staudte introduced to underscore the grotesque exaggerations and visual distortions. In the novelistic tradition the third-person, omniscient narrator has generally come to be accepted as the most "natural." In the cinema, however, a disembodied narrator is more pronounced than in a written text. In *Der Untertan*, Staudte follows the novel and retains the narrator as an ironic vehicle. The neutral male voice is the first to speak in the film and returns at crucial junctures to summarize, provide transitions, and give access to the characters' inner thoughts. His understated, matter-of-fact explanations for the most outrageous and unexpected situations produce a constant flux between the narrator's irony and the cinema's impression of reality. Hessling behaves as if his world were continuous and rational, and so it appears. Lurking behind him, however, is the narrator's voice which invites the viewer to laugh and – as a rhetorical mechanism – draws the viewer's attention to the very artifice of story-telling. Stylized camera work also highlights the ironic distance between narrator and action, between viewer and characters. Static images are often so perfect that they draw attention to themselves. The symmetry in the interiors of Hessling's home, the *Ratskeller*, and the doctor's office stresses the way in which characters are entrapped in their public behavior. Other devices such as painted portraits and freeze frames serve as metaphors of confinement. When Hessling discovers that his sister Emmi wants to commit suicide after being jilted by the Lieutenant, the camera joins the two: we see Hessling in profile, watching Emmi who, framed in the mirror, is seen lying on her chaise longue. If this close, blocked-off frame conveys a sense of social rigidity and domination, then the frame within the frame – which avoids the classical

Hollywood reverse-angle shot for showing emotional reactions – emphasizes Hessling's inability to comprehend his sister's emotions.

The film's editing and visual style encourage the spectator to participate in its playfulness and artifice. The ironic point of view with the sudden changes in Hessling's fate demands an episodic structure. The film narrative exploits and expands this pattern, already present in the text, in order to rationalize motivations. Instead of a clear plot, Staudte condenses episodes in pointed situations only loosely connected by chronology. As a result the transitions become more pronounced. Although antiquated devices like irising out, fades to white, and dissolves with gauzes are transition techniques which went out of fashion in the 1920s, here they are consciously used to create distance between the film as fiction and the time historically represented. In other cases, Staudte uses complementary or contrasting image sequences to clarify connections and to create temporal transitions, as in the change of portraits from one emperor to the next or the change of seasons as Hessling's affair with Agnes Göpel sours. Sound too is an important means for establishing continuity and defining context. In the school sequence – a series of five quick vignettes demonstrating young Hessling's progress in adapting to the demands of authority – a mixture of voice and music overlies, connects, and ironically comments on the content of school learning. Most striking about the film, however, is its momentum. No matter how compelling each scene is, the viewer is carried along – by the narrator, by the music, by the cinematography, by the editing.

The entire process pushes toward the last scene which provides the structural climax as well as declares the lesson of the entire film. As in any satire, *Der Untertan* carries a moral message. Staudte wisely waits until the end of the spectacle to draw the full consequences. At the pinnacle of his career, Hessling delivers an oration before the assembled townspeople and dignitaries for the unveiling of a statue of William the Great, a monument which serves to crown Hessling's precarious conniving with the town's political factions while at the same time marking his triumph as the vanguard of the new "spirit of the times." His speech is a wild mixture of fragments from actual speeches by William II, patriotic slogans, and battle cries. Language and gesture reflect his total self-alienation, expressed in the fetishization of nation, military, emperor, and success. He juxtaposes unrelated ideas – spiritual and material values, feudal ideology and industrial imperialism – culminating in a call for war: "Only on the battlefield will the greatness of a nation be forged with blood and iron. . . ." But this is also Hessling's day of fate, for at that very moment stormy music swells up, lightning rends the sky, thunder rolls, and a mighty rainstorm interrupts the ceremony. Abandoned ignominiously by the crowd, Hessling is left alone with, towering over him, the monument before which he bows down in awe.

Mann's novel prophesies in the image of an apocalyptic downpour the real catastrophe of war that would befall Germany in 1914. The novel follows

Plates 21 and 22   Two views of Diederich Hessling (Werner Peters), from above and below, as dutiful subject bowing to his Emperor, as authoritarian personality savoring the taste of power. Photos courtesy of Stiftung Deutsche Kinemathek.

Hessling one step further, though, as he witnesses the death of his political arch-rival, Old Buck, who in a last vision sees Hessling transformed into Satan. Whereas in the novel the elder Buck represents the memory and broken spirit of the glorious democratic impulse of 1848, in the film Staudte reduces him to a minor supporting role. Consequently, the film has to render differently the novel's closure which is, in fact, an open end, for the triumph of Hessling's false values leaves the outcome to the reader's imagination. Staudte's ending makes explicit the fact that history turned Mann's satire into reality; it thus undermines the comic distance of the textual satire. Yet in this respect he did not apparently contradict Mann's own retrospective evaluation:

> At that time the 'Untertan' seemed to exaggerate the Germans. The Germans have caught up with him; in essence they haven't left him behind, only in means of expression. A comic figure, the German 'Untertan' of his Emperor William became deadly serious for the first time under him, only then to be in Hitler the brutal parody of himself.[6]

The last frame of Hessling gradually fills up with black smoke as we hear a sound montage of sirens, strains from the Nazi "Horst Wessel Song" and the trumpet fanfare for Nazi newsreels. Then there is a cut to the same

Plate 22

square destroyed by bombs with only the statue standing among the rubble. The narrator repeats Hessling's last call to war, adding: "– and so have many others called and they still do to this day." Staudte's ending shows the monstrous results of accommodation to power. He makes a direct connection between the moral of his tale about adaptation to repression and to social violence and the destruction brought upon Germany by the reign of fascism. *Der Untertan* is a satirically blistering glance at provincial Germany and one of its most corrupt types, an outrageously defiant film whose comedic vision has not lost its bite.

A postscript must mention the film's reception, for by no means did critics perceive unequivocally the qualities of Staudte's work.[7] The filmmaker and the lead actor both received in 1951 national awards in the GDR for their accomplishments, and other international prizes followed. The film was generally praised by East German journalists as a success. Nonetheless, other critics saw in the film a tendency toward formal experimentation at the expense of pedagogical values, and some expressed concern about the lack of a strong proletarian figure to counterbalance Hessling's negativity. Such criticism can be accounted for by the general swing of GDR cultural policies in the early 1950s toward a program of anti-formalism and contemporary proletarian subjects. The result for Staudte meant that he found fewer and fewer opportunities to make films with DEFA. In 1955 his last project in the GDR, an adaptation of Brecht's *Mother Courage and Her Children* (*Mutter Courage und ihre Kinder*), was suspended during shooting when irreconcilable differences arose with the dramatist. Today film critics in the GDR count Staudte's films among the early DEFA classics.

With the Cold War already well under way and anti-Communist hysteria entrenched in West Germany, Staudte's film hardly had a chance to get a showing in the Federal Republic. The government officially prevented the film from being imported for a festival in Heidelberg in 1951, and in the press it was presented as a cynical piece of propaganda for the Soviet system. Not until 1957 did authorities allow the film to be shown officially in West Germany, and even then the censor for films imported from socialist countries required that the credits include a disclaimer about Diederich Hessling as a fictional character. In contrast, Helmut Käutner's West German production *The Captain of Köpenick* (*Der Hauptmann von Köpenick*, 1956), a mild satire about the Prussian penchant for obedience, won the highest prizes and critical eulogies. Unwelcome in the east and variously slandered in the west for "dirtying the nest" and being a "protégé of Goebbels," Staudte found it increasingly difficult to produce any films at all during the 1950s. Despite a series of undistinguished commercial productions, he was able to continue his social critique in such films as *The Muzzle* (*Der Maulkorb*, 1958), *Roses for the Prosecutor* (*Rosen für den Staatsanwalt*, 1959), *Carnival* (*Kirmes*, 1960), and *Stag Outing* (*Herrenpartie*, 1964). Thereafter Staudte was involved almost exclusively with West German television productions. At his death in 1984, he represented one of the few links between a critical tradition of German filmmaking that was wiped out in the early 1930s and its rebirth among directors of the New German Cinema. But curiously, Staudte has yet to be recognized as one of the most important mentors of postwar cinema.[8]

Notes

1. Heinrich Mann, *Der Untertan* (Leipzig/Vienna: Wolff, 1918). The novel was published in the English translation of Ernest Boyd under several different titles: *The Patrioteer* (New York: Harcourt Brace, 1921); *Little Superman* (New York: Creative Age, 1945); *Man of Straw* (London: Hutchinson, 1947); and is in press once again (1985) as *The Patrioteer* (New York: Fertig). Page references in this essay are to the 1945 edition; to avoid confusion I will refer to the film and to the novel by the German title *Der Untertan*.

2. Gottfried Benn, "Rede auf Heinrich Mann," in *Gesammelte Werke* (Wiesbaden: Limes, 1968), IV, 98; and Georg Lukács, *Skizze einer Geschichte der deutschen Literatur* (Berlin [GDR]: Aufbau, 1955), p. 126.

3. Cf. Mann's "Zola" essay originally published in 1915, shortly after he had finished *Der Untertan*, in Heinrich Mann, *Macht und Mensch* (Munich: Wolff, 1919), pp. 35–131.

4. The most comprehensive introduction to the novel can be found in Wolfgang Emmerich, *Heinrich Mann: "Der Untertan"* (Munich: Fink, 1980), and David Roberts, *Artistic Consciousness and Political Conscience: The Novels of Heinrich Mann* (Berne and Frankfurt am Main: Lang, 1971), pp. 84–124.

5. Eva Orbanz (ed.), "Wolfgang Staudte über die Produktionsbedingungen seiner Filme" (interview) in *Wolfgang Staudte* (Berlin: Spiess, 1977), p. 70–1; translation by M.S. This volume, commemorating the filmmaker's 70th birthday, is the most important and sole extensive survey of Staudte's career. It includes three essays about his film and television work, a lengthy interview with the filmmaker, excerpts from reviews of the most important films, a biography, the complete filmography through 1976, and a selective bibliography. The only other book-length study is a very brief East German volume to commemorate the filmmaker's 60th birthday: Horst Knietzsch, *Wolfgang Staudte* (Berlin [GDR]: Henschel, 1966).

6. Heinrich Mann, *Essays* (Berlin [GDR]: Aufbau, 1962), III, 551; translation by M.S.

7. For a selection of representative reviews, see Orbanz, pp. 116–30.

8. See Christian Ziewer's obituary, "Eingedenken," *epd Film*, February/March 1984, 3–4. See also Helma Sanders, "Wir haben ihn allein gelassen: Für Wolfgang Staudte," *Jahrbuch Film 84/85*, ed. Hans Günther Pflaum (Munich: Hanser, 1984), 23–32.

Selected Bibliography

Gerber, Margy. "Looking for the roots of fascism: Wolfgang Staudte's *Der Untertan.*" In *Purdue University Fifth Annual Conference on Film: Proceedings*, 30 October–1 November 1980, West Lafayette, Indiana: Purdue University, 1980, pp. 88–93.

Jansen, Peter W. and Wolfram Schütte (eds). *Film in der DDR*. Munich: Hanser, 1977.

Knietzsch, Horst. *Wolfgang Staudte*. Berlin (GDR): Henschel, 1966.

Orbanz, Eva (ed.). *Wolfgang Staudte*. 3rd rev. edn. Berlin: Spiess, 1977.

Sanders, Helma. "Wir haben ihn allein gelassen: Für Wolfgang Staudte." *Jahrbuch Film 84/85*. Ed. Hans Günther Pflaum. Munich: Hanser, 1984, pp. 23–32.

Weiss, Wolfgang (ed.). *Film- und Fernsehkunst der DDR: Traditionen, Beispiele, Tendenzen*. Berlin (GDR): Henschel, 1979.

Witte, Karsten. "Ein deutscher Traum vom Realismus: Wolfgang Staudte wird 75 Jahre alt." *Die Zeit*, 9 October 1981.

Ziewer, Christian. "Eingedenken." *epd Film*, February/March 1984, 3–4.

11

RUSSELL A. BERMAN

A return to arms: Käutner's
The Captain of Köpenick (1956)

When Wilhelm Voigt rushes away from Wormser's uniform shop in Potsdam at the end of the second sequence in Helmut Käutner's *The Captain of Köpenick* (*Der Hauptmann von Köpenick*, 1956), the careful viewer can notice a sign in the window proudly proclaiming that the establishment was founded in 1856. For the audience of 1956, the year of the film's release, this precise centennial reference sets up a temporal matrix calling for an obvious contrast: the film claims to offer the modern public a story from another age, or, as the remarks that introduce the film announce, a story that truly happened "once upon a time" but will, so one hopes, "never happen again." Yet while the film apparently thrives on the distance between the actual present of post-World War II West Germany and the represented past of the pre-World War I Wilhelmine Empire, it simultaneously operates with techniques of identification and anachronistic projections which transform the cinematic version of turn-of-the-century Berlin into an ideological mirror of the 1950s and the Cold War. In order to dissect the film's ideological content and to untangle the complex knot of continuities and discontinuities in its account of German history, it is necessary to begin by separating the important three levels in the Köpenick material itself: the real event of 1906, the drama of 1931, and the film of 1956.

On 18 October 1906, the unemployed cobbler and ex-convict Voigt, wearing the uniform of a captain of the Imperial Army purchased in a second-hand-clothing store, took command of ten soldiers in the streets of Berlin, travelled with them to Köpenick, a nearby suburb, occupied the town hall, seized the cash-box containing some 4,000 marks, arrested the mayor and the treasurer and sent them off to Berlin under guard as prisoners. Voigt escaped, but, with the help of an informer who had known him in prison, the police arrested him on 26 October. He received a four-year sentence but was pardoned by the Emperor after twenty months. Later Voigt was able to capitalize on the sensation his case had caused by peddling autographed

Plate 23   Berlin nostalgia, remilitarization, an individual's search for a place in his homeland: Käutner's *Captain of Köpenick* reflects postwar German dispositions. Photo courtesy of Stiftung Deutsche Kinemathek.

postcards of himself, appearing abroad on stage in a captain's uniform and publishing his autobiography in 1909.

For many contemporaries, the ease with which Voigt had carried out his masquerade pointed out the unhealthy consequences of the rampant militarism and the unquestioning obedience to uniformed authority which characterized Wilhelmine society. This predominance of the military, in which the conservative landowning aristocracy, the *Junker*, played the leading role, depended on a variety of factors. Historically, the rise of the army had paralleled the ascendancy of Prussia since the end of the seventeenth century. Although defeated by the French in 1807, the Prussian army, thanks to a series of reforms, was crucial in the final victory over Napoleon, after which Prussia began to emerge as the major German power precisely because of its military prowess. Politically, this military strength excluded Habsburg Austria from internal German affairs in 1866 and overwhelmed the French again in 1871. The significance of these external victories lay above all in the domestic political course charted by the Prussian minister Otto von Bismarck; once the combined German armies, led by the Prussians, defeated the French, a unified German empire could be founded in which the Prussian King became the German Kaiser. The subsequent "Prussianization" of Germany implied the extension of the *de jure* and *de facto* privileging of the military in society and culture to those regions in the west and south where liberal elements had once been more viable and influential. Socially, this militarism reflected the relative underdevelopment of a liberal culture in which civil rights and civilian values received respect. Unlike England, France, or the United States where, during the seventeenth or eighteenth centuries, bourgeois revolutions radically overturned traditional patterns of power and privilege, no successful revolution marked a clean break with Germany's feudal and aristocratic past. National unification was achieved not by a democratic uprising – the last such attempt fizzled out in 1848 – but by a conservative fiat at the conclusion of the Franco-Prussian War. After 1871, military ideals of obedience and discipline began to pervade all spheres of social life, not least of all by way of an extensive system of reserve officers, as seen in the film in the figures of Dr Obermüller and Friedrich Hoprecht.

Wilhelm Voigt, the unemployed ex-convict, became a *cause célèbre*. With his modest coup, he provided a rallying point for the many voices, socialist and liberal, hostile to the prevailing militarism and the social order in general. Still the other side did not surrender quickly: the Emperor himself was said to have been both amused and impressed by the extent of German discipline – the episode is included at the end of the film – and the right-wing press even tried to turn the tables on the liberal critics. It is neither surprising nor objectionable, argued the conservative *Neue Preussische Zeitung*, to find soldiers with soldierly discipline, but while the military has no reason to apologize after Köpenick, the civilian administrators who so readily capitulated had better account for their poor judgment. Who then was the real loser in the affair? The military or the civilians, the right or the left? The ambivalence in the historical material itself continues in both the dramatic and cinematic treatments.[1]

The revolution of 1918–19 transformed the social status of German litera-ture. More explicitly than their predecessors, the writers and intellectuals of the Weimar Republic were called upon to participate in contemporary debate and to address crucial matters of public concern. The ivory-tower aestheticism of the turn of the century, having passed through the expressionist crucible of World War I, gave way to a recognition of litera-ture's potential as a vehicle for social criticism or political agitation. This political character of literature could be emphatically leftist, as in the case of Bertolt Brecht, or moderately liberal, as with Thomas Mann, or even radically conservative and protofascist, e.g. one of the bestsellers of the Weimar Republic, Hans Grimm's *Landless People* (*Volk ohne Raum*, 1926). The political dimension of literary life, in all its competing varieties, seemed irrefutable, and during the late 1920s this political consciousness turned its attention increasingly toward the question of war and militarism. Despite the surfeit of international treaties which promised to preserve the European peace, writers from the left to the right sensed a threat of war and addressed it in their works: the Communist Johannes R. Becher denounced war as imperialist genocide in *Levisite or The Only Just War* (*Levisite oder Der einzig gerechte Krieg*, 1926), Arnold Zweig's *The Battle around Sergeant Grischa* (*Der Streit um den Sergeanten Grischa*, 1927) examined the inhu-manity of military bureaucracy, and Erich Maria Remarque's world-famous *All Quiet on the Western Front* (*Im Westen nichts Neues*, 1929) described the senselessness of war, while, on the right, Ernst Jünger's *The Total Mobiliz-ation* (*Die totale Mobilmachung*, 1931) presented modern war as a heroic, beneficial, and desirable experience. Carl Zuckmayer's play, *The Captain of Köpenick* (1931), with its own portrayal of an army discipline gone haywire can only be understood within this literary context of a widespread thematiz-ation of militarism.

The literary discussion reflected a real remilitarization of political life in the late phase of the Weimar Republic. The right wing had never accepted the military defeat of 1918, attributing it instead to a domestic betrayal, a "stab in the back," by Communist workers, Jewish agitators, and treason-ous politicians of the left. The Republic itself was regarded as the expression of this duplicity, a political form foisted onto Germany by the Western democracies but innately foreign to the authentic German tradition. Mean-while centrist and leftist voices complained of the presence of precisely this anti-democratic, chauvinist sentiment within the army. In 1918–19, the young Republic, weak and besieged by many opponents, had been forced to rely on the state apparatus of the Empire, the civil service bureaucracy, and the military. Yet the individuals in that apparatus had been trained within the hierarchical Wilhelmine world and were often rabidly hostile to the egalitarian principles of the new democratic state which they were now asked to serve. This animosity toward the Republic was particularly strong in high levels of the army where the restrictions on the size of the German military dictated by the Versailles Treaty were deeply resented. The overt cult of military values combined with clandestine efforts to circumvent the limitations on the army drew increasingly sharp attacks from the press, most notably from the left-liberal journal *Die Weltbühne* and its editors, Kurt Tucholsky and Carl von Ossietzky.

With his *Captain of Köpenick*, Zuckmayer took his stance against the forces of militarism and the conservative opponents of the Weimar Republic. For not only did he demonstrate the absurdity of the obsequiousness inherent in the military cult, he also recalled the reality of social hierarchy and mass poverty in the Wilhelmine Empire which the anti-republican propagandists were eager to obscure with their own fictions of halcyon good old days. In response to nostalgic descriptions of the prewar world, Zuckmayer underscored the distance between the military élite and the impoverished underclass, so that "friend and foe alike understood the play as the political act it was meant to be," as he remarked later in his autobiography.[2] Zuckmayer leaves no doubt as to the political and socio-critical intention behind the play:

For although the story was more than twenty years old, it was highly pertinent at this very moment, in the year 1930, when the Nazis were entering the Reichstag as the second strongest party and thrusting the nation into a new craze of uniforms. The story was an image, a farcical mirror image, of the evils and dangers that were growing in Germany, but also of the hope that they could be overcome as the shoemaker had overcome his difficulties by native wit and humane insight.[3]

The play was a stupendous success. After its première on 5 March 1931 in the Deutsches Theater in Berlin under the direction of Heinz Hilpert, it continued to run for two years in more than one hundred theaters throughout Germany. With Hitler's accession to power in 1933, the play was banned, and Zuckmayer was forced into exile. In fact, the Nazis had opposed Zuckmayer since the mid-1920s, objecting to his often explicit treatment of sexuality as well as to the satirical elements in his works. It was however the Köpenick play which angered them the most, as Zuckmayer reports:

The Nazi press waxed rabid over the play, especially the Berlin *Angriff*. Referring to one scene in prison, that paper – edited by Goebbels – predicted that I would soon have the opportunity to become acquainted with a Prussian prison from the inside. I was even then threatened, in anticipation of the coming seizure of power, with expatriation, exile, or simply the hangman.[4]

While the far right decried Zuckmayer's anti-militarism, the left expressed a much more tempered criticism. Herbert Ihering, theater critic of the influential *Berliner Börsen-Courier* and an important exponent of Brecht's epic theater, complained that Zuckmayer's anti-militarism did not go far enough, that the humor often undercut the criticism and that the ambivalence of the historical material was carried over into the play itself. It certainly could not be argued that the play defended the army but, in the context of a perceived danger of military adventurism, the left-wing critic suggested that Zuckmayer had pulled too many punches: militarism is nothing to laugh about.

The Captain of Köpenick was destined for the screen.[5] The sound film was still new, and representatives of the film industry, scouting for material, were in the audience at the première. Richard Oswald directed the first adaptation in 1931, and, ten years later, he directed a remake in his Hollywood exile, released both as *The Captain of Köpenick* and as *I Was a Criminal*. These adaptations as well as Käutner's 1956 version relied heavily on Zuckmayer's play. Many of the scenes, themes, and motifs as well as much of the dialogue were borrowed directly from the theatrical text. Yet in Käutner's film, to which we will turn in a moment, important revisions indicate an intention to rephrase the basic story within a very different historical context. One caveat: the mere fact that the film diverges from the original text is no grounds for complaint. Any adaptation interprets its text and pushes it in one way or another, i.e. there is never a perfectly transparent adaptation. And in this case, an accusation of disloyalty to the original is particularly inappropriate, since Zuckmayer himself collaborated on the screenplay. Nevertheless even Zuckmayer's authorship and seal of approval do not provide an authenticity which is impossible to attain. The character of the reproduced cinematic narrative cannot escape the metamorphosis induced by the changed socio-political setting, just as the director of the adaptation makes a statement to his chronological contemporaries and not only a statement about a historical text. The discovery of differences between the 1931 play and the 1956 film should not be surprising, nor can one denigrate the film simply because of these differences. The critical task is rather to ask why precisely these revisions were made in order to determine how the work functions within its own ideological environment.

In 1906 Voigt illicitly appropriated the military symbolism of the Wilhelmine Empire by donning the uniform and transforming it into a real-life costume. Zuckmayer retold the story in 1931, using the turn-of-the-century material in order to participate in the political controversies of the late Weimar Republic. Käutner's filming of Zuckmayer's account is embedded in the world of 1956 and bears the marks of the intervening history. In 1945, World War II came to an end. Germany, forced to accept an unconditional surrender, ceased to exist as a sovereign state, and its military forces were dissolved. In the belief that it had been the Prussian element in German society which had unleashed two world wars, the victorious powers abolished Prussia as an administrative unit in 1947. More importantly, the Junker class of the landed aristocracy, the traditional backbone of the officers' corps, lost its economic base, since most of its holdings lay east of the Elbe river where the Soviet occupation forces soon carried out major land reforms. The collapse of the wartime alliance between the United States and the Soviet Union and the intensification of the Cold War had a particularly strong impact on the German situation. For Zuckmayer, Berlin in 1931 was merely the capital of the Germany where the Voigt episode had once taken place; in 1948, Berlin became the center of world attention when, in the wake of growing disputes over economic policies, the Soviets imposed a blockade on West Berlin, cutting off the supplies from the western occupation zones. The American airlift ensued, and Berlin became a symbol of the hardening fronts between east and west: in 1949 the two separate German states were founded.

The defeat of the Third Reich, the massive destruction of German cities, and the collapse of the German armed forces fostered an anti-military sentiment throughout the population, and, in 1949, the Chancellor of the young Federal Republic, Konrad Adenauer, stated clearly:

I want to clarify once and for all that I am fundamentally opposed to a rearming of the Federal Republic and am therefore also opposed to the establishment of a new German army. In two world wars we Germans have already spilled so much blood and we have far too few people to carry out such a project.[6]

Nevertheless Adenauer himself soon began to test the waters regarding the establishment of a West German army, and the western allies – despite the resistance of France which had suffered most directly during the war – were hardly reluctant to pursue the proposal. The Korean War indicated the likelihood of a military confrontation in Europe as well, where a West German army would certainly prove a welcome ally against an aggressive Soviet Union. Nor were such plans solely defensive in nature. The American Secretary of State John Foster Dulles envisioned a "roll-back" of the Soviet Union, i.e. a strategy designed to force a retreat of Russian forces from eastern Europe. In either case, a remilitarized West Germany had to be quickly integrated into the western military alliance. In 1954, the Paris treaties put an end to the Federal Republic's occupied status and planned its membership in NATO. After the ratification by the *Bundestag* on 27 February 1955, the path was clear for the establishment of a West German army, the *Bundeswehr*. In response, the Warsaw Pact was established in May, and the division of Europe into two military camps was complete.

The remilitarization of Germany did not proceed without opposition. As early as 1950, a popular resistance emerged in the form of the *Ohne-mich-Bewegung* ("without-me movement"), an amorphous community of opinion hostile to participation in a new army. In 1951–2, a plebiscitary movement attempted to poll public sentiment as a demonstration against the impending alliance with the west and for a peace treaty on the basis of a reunified nation and military neutrality. In a final effort to block the remilitarization and to keep the Federal Republic out of NATO, the Social Democrats and the unions launched the *Paulskirche* movement in early 1955 in opposition to the Paris treaties. Undoubtedly the problem of rearmament was the overriding political issue in the first half of the 1950s. The failure of the anti-militarist movements, attributable in part to Adenauer and in part to American influence, reflected the domestic West German response to the Cold War. Communism appeared to be a dangerous threat. The anti-Russian propaganda of the Nazi regime still had a lingering effect, and the violent establishment of Soviet-style societies in neighboring Poland and Czechoslovakia, despite local opposition, only exacerbated West German fears.

With this background in mind, one can proceed to an analysis of Käutner's film. An important deviation from the original becomes apparent immediately. The play opens in Wormser's shop with a humorous parody of the prevailing uniform fetishism: i.e. the uniform, which will pass from Schlettow to Obermüller, Auguste Viktoria, and finally Voigt, is introduced as the main issue. The film, however, begins with Voigt, portrayed by the well-known actor Heinz Rühmann, returning to Berlin, resisting the evil Kalle's temptation to enter the world of crime, and insisting that all he wants is an honest job. The audience is thus asked to identify with his struggle to reintegrate himself into society, and this problem eclipses the critical analysis of militarism which had been at the center of the play. Where the original had described the general character of society, the film presents a personal (and often sentimental) fate, and one, moreover, that clearly echoed the conservative self-understanding of West Germany: an ambiguous guilt in the past has robbed Voigt of a proper place in the established order, yet he would be willing to forget his crimes, work hard, and become a responsible citizen if he were only given the opportunity. On an individual level, the structure of dislocation and desired reintegration could particularly appeal to former soldiers, prisoners-of-war, and the many refugees from eastern Europe who, having lost their former homes, were compelled to enter West German society as outsiders. Käutner emphasizes this matter by tracing Voigt's steps in the first series of scenes through unsuccessful job interviews to equally unresponsive bureaucrats: society has closed him out, and he can find no home. When in the shelter called "Heimat" (i.e. "home" – the name is borrowed from the play), Voigt lies down on his bunk, the camera captures words scrawled on the wall behind him, identifiable as the opening verses from the famous poem "The Joyful Wanderer" (*"Der frohe Wandersmann"*) by the early-nineteenth-century romantic author Joseph von Eichendorff: *"Wem Gott will rechte Gunst erweisen/Den schickt er in die weite Welt."* ("He to whom God would show his favor/Is sent off into the wide world.") The literary citation restates with bitter irony the film's central theme: Voigt's homelessness as a cipher for postwar dislocation.

The description of the individual wandering aimlessly through an apathetic society which offers no comfort but from which there is no escape draws on the existentialist philosophy popular during the 1950s. While Zuckmayer addressed a social problem, i.e. militarism, Käutner presents a general account of the human condition as a fundamental loneliness. Despite the bureaucrats' various excuses, the narrative refuses to provide a substantial explanation for Voigt's isolation, which is intentionally presented as an absurd situation. He is cast into the world for no apparent reason and must submit to irrational forces: the letter which expels him from Rixdorf and compounds his dislocation seems to appear from nowhere. Voigt eventually overcomes his alienation, not however through an act of rebellion as the French existentialism of Albert Camus and Jean-Paul Sartre might have suggested, but rather by accepting the absurd order – the uniform – without inquiring into its political ramifications. This quietistic conformism corresponds to the conservative existentialism propounded by Martin Heidegger during the Adenauer era.

The play concludes when Voigt, seeing himself in uniform in a mirror for the first time, recognizes the absurdity of the affair and cries out, "Impossible." Käutner appends a significant coda which ends with a positive acceptance of the new designation as "Captain of Köpenick," i.e. the displacement with which the film opens is ultimately resolved. Instead of presenting a denunciation of obsequiousness and servility in a militarist society, the film describes Voigt's reconciliation with the established order: in the final analysis, the bureaucrats, the prison warden, the police officers, and even the Kaiser turn out to be friendly fellows. One detail exemplifies how the adaptation affirms the hierarchy in a manner the play does not. In the play, only one passing mention of the police chief of Berlin, Traugott von Jagow, is made. In the film, he appears as the personable and humorous *Polizeipräsident*, anxious to grant his prisoner's each and every wish. Historically Jagow was notorious for ordering violent attacks against demonstrators in turn-of-the-century Berlin. Because of his abuse of his office as chief censor, he was transferred to Leipzig under a barrage of criticism from the left-liberal press. In 1920 he took part in the Kapp *Putsch*, a *coup d'état* against the Social Democratic government carried out by right-wing elements in the military, which was quickly crippled by a general strike. Käutner's depiction of this representative of the anti-democratic forces of the Empire and the

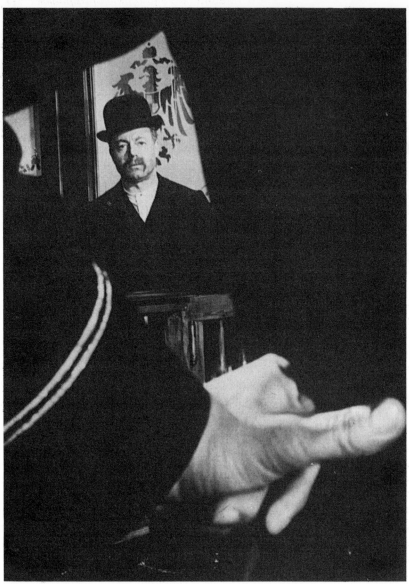

Plates 24 and 25   Voigt (Heinz Rühmann) is circumscribed by a harsh and un-yielding order. His act of rebellion does not expose the evils of authority, though, or call the status quo into question. Even when striking out, Voigt has no sub-versive intention: he simply appeals to a society all too ready to worship uniforms and power, a society that remains intact at the film's end. Photos courtesy of Stiftung Deutsche Kinemathek.

Plate 25

Weimar Republic as a likeable if not fully attractive figure is symptomatic of the fundamentally conservative character of the film.

This conservatism means above all an acceptance of the military order. The problem is no longer the predominance of the army and its values. On the contrary, the ubiquitous columns of soldiers, marching down tidy avenues to the accompaniment of upbeat music and followed gaily by happy citizens, constitute indisputably positive images. The viewers in 1956 could plausibly look forward to a time when the newly formed *Bundeswehr* would similarly adorn their streets and serenade an increasingly prosperous public. The critique of the military is reduced to one issue alone: not the excessive influence of the uniform but its irrational exclusivity, i.e. the difficulty to join the ranks, and, once enlisted, the difficulty to succeed. Voigt must resort to a trick to get into uniform, Schlettow is expelled because of a peccadillo, and Hoprecht is unfairly denied advancement. The shots of Schlettow, compelled to return the new uniform, capture his heroic profile, his downcast eyes, and his shocked view of himself in the mirror: the audience is exhorted to sympathize with the noble officer denied his uniform. In the play, Schlettow was the object of caricature; in the film he becomes the object of sympathy and identification. Thus the Prussian military is shown to have erred only by having separated itself too radically from society. Had it renounced traditional privilege and opened its ranks, all the dislocated Voigts would have eagerly rushed in. In fact, precisely this vision of a purportedly democratic army underlay the contemporary conceptions of the *Bundeswehr*.

This radical reversal of the traditional Köpenick material, the film's presentation of an attractive militarism, could be rendered plausible only with the help of a series of auxiliary thematic devices. Most obvious is the explicit derision of anti-militarist figures, especially the Mayor of Köpenick, Dr Obermüller. Presented as foolish, indecisive, and something of a careerist, he proclaims his membership in the left-liberal Progressive People's party, opposes tax breaks for industry, and – as the footsteps of Voigt's soldiers echo on the stairway – declares his contempt for the army. In order to leave no doubt as to Obermüller's political affiliation, Käutner has one of the aldermen express the suspicion that the Mayor is a clandestine Social Democrat. Later, when he is released from military custody, the contrast between the blustering helplessness of the civilian politician and the bemused superiority of the officers is striking. In line with the conservative press's interpretation of the 1906 affair, the film's humor thrives on the humiliation of the left-liberal politician vis-à-vis the representatives of an unchallenged military authority.

There is however a real threat to order in the film. As Voigt's foil, Kalle represents an alternative path, diametrically opposed to the desired social integration. His criminal intentions link him to a hoi polloi antagonistic to the images of prosperity and hierarchy: while Voigt's shabby derby signifies a modest effort to achieve respectability, Kalle's proletarian cap indexes an anti-bourgeois identity. Voigt claims he wants to work, but it is Kalle who wears the clothing of the working class, expresses contempt for "bourgeois society," and misbehaves in public. The political corollary to this radicalism emerges in the appended 1956 conclusion: Voigt's pardon provokes a leftist demonstration outside the prison, replete with reporters from *The Progressive Worker* and Communist rhetoric. "A dark day for the ruling class!" shouts one scoundrel in the mob. The precise motive for the demonstration is left unclear, but Käutner constructs a significant constellation: a working-class crowd, ugly, angry, and riotous, indistinguishable from criminals, demonstrates against the freedom of lovable Heinz Rühmann who has made his peace with an avuncular warden, a *gemütlicher* Chief of Police, and in the background, a friendly and affectionate Kaiser. If the Communists oppose such a splendid order and its glorious military, then – this is the film's suggestion – the rearmament of West Germany can hardly be wrong.

The film also argues for the *Bundeswehr* by presenting the values of a sentimental nationalism. When Voigt, in the police station in Rixdorf, describes his love for his homeland, the camera focuses on his face, thereby lifting the statement out of its conversational context and lending it an absolute quality. Furthermore Käutner employs Berlin imagery in a nostalgic manner in order to recall the former capital of the united nation. The street musicians outside the Hoprecht home – Käutner in a cameo role with Erica Balqué – sing "Homesick for Berlin" (*"Heimweh nach Berlin"*) and "Berlin, I Can't Forget You" (*"Berlin, ich kann dir nicht vergessen"*).

In the café scene, the cognac which Kalle and Voigt drink in the play is changed by the magic of film into symbolic *Berliner Weisse* – during the Cold War even libations have political meaning. The collective memories of Berlin and the good old days correspond to Voigt's search for a *Heimat*, and in the background looms the new army as the guarantor of this homeland. Käutner touches another nationalist nerve by presenting the secondhand-clothing-store owner as a *Sudetendeutscher*. These ethnic Germans who were forced to flee from Czechoslovakia after 1945 constituted a political lobby in the Federal Republic against any reconciliation with the east and for efforts to re-establish German control over the lost areas, i.e. Dulles's roll-back project. Käutner's introduction of this detail into the film implicitly suggests a potential function for the new military forces, the reconquest of the old *Heimat*. This detail deserves particular attention because the film has intentionally transformed the ethnic identity of the figure: in the 1931 play he is Jewish and the shop is explicitly located in the Grenadierstrasse, the historical ghetto/slum near Alexanderplatz. Käutner purges the Jewish material from the story and thereby avoids any reference to anti-semitism or the holocaust which had decimated Germany's Jewish population. Any such reference would have disturbed the process of identification and nostalgia for the past, consequently impeding the ideological mechanism of the film: in order to restore the traditional power structure, the crimes of those powers had to be forgotten. This forced amnesia regarding Nazi genocide, the repression of the past, was a key feature of West German consciousness during the Adenauer era, and this detail in Käutner's adaptation demonstrates well the political character of the process, which is furthermore mirrored in Voigt's plight. Just as he would prefer to forget his criminal past and get on with the business of life, so too does postwar society, plunging into reconstruction and *Wirtschaftswunder*, attempt to deny the past. For if one began to mourn the victims of Auschwitz, the legitimacy of the new military machine would quickly collapse.

The film's thematic cohesiveness and the potential for the viewer's identification rely on a fundamental ideological economy: the homeless individual can overcome alienation and enter the warm embrace of the social order by donning one of the snazzy uniforms Käutner incessantly marches across the screen. The liberal, i.e. Social Democratic, opponents of rearmament are spineless, and the Communist opponents are a clear and present danger. (In 1956 the German Communist party was declared illegal and many of its members arrested.) A new army will protect the new fatherland and perhaps even regain the lost territories in the east, all to the tunes of a former age with plenty of free beer for all. And best of all, national pride is freed from any allegations of collective guilt since there never was a Jewish question since there never were any Jews: at least not in this film. Yet this political message of the *Captain of Köpenick* also relies on a sexual economy. The defense of the army succeeds by investing the images of male bonding with a barely subliminal homosexual eroticism: Voigt sleeps on top of Kalle, strokes Hoprecht's hand with loving affection and lets Jagow wine, dine, and nearly seduce him. The tailor scenes show how men enjoy dressing each other, and in the prison inmates have a grand time romping about in uniforms that look like pyjamas. If sexuality is never explicit, the film is all the more suggestive regarding the potential pleasure men can find in exclusively male groups: in prison, in the police force, or in the army. The only man with explicit heterosexual desire is the proletarian criminal Kalle, the sign of an anti-social resistance to submissive participation in the organizations of male power.

The corollary to this sexual logic is the pejorative representation of women. For Schlettow and his friend in the café, they are all syphilitic whores. The caricature of Obermüller is intensified by the fact of his marriage, since his stronger wife easily overpowers this weak-kneed liberal, and Hoprecht, worried about leaving his thoughtless spouse alone, even prefers asking the ex-convict Voigt to mind the store, rather than relying on a scatterbrained female. The sexism is intentional: in the play Obermüller insists that he needs the uniform in a hurry because his mother, from a military family, is coming for a visit, but in the film Käutner shifts the blame to an impending visit by a mother-in-law. The new excuse derives its plausibility from the repressive family morality of the 1950s in which mothers were respectable but mothers-in-law were fair game for bad jokes. The female threat is finally made explicit in the figure of Wormser's daughter. Käutner presents her as a calculating vamp, playing devious games with the naive men she attracts, although in the play she was the carrier of the exuberant and healthy sexuality often found in Zuckmayer's works. In an interpolated scene which borders on soft-core pornography, she appears half-undressed, with her undergarments and the military cap. The image underscores the immanent eroticism of the uniform and relies on a rhetoric of transvestism: the representation of the female sex-object in the army uniform heightens the desirability of participation in the male bonding of the military.

This transference of erotic interest away from the female body and into the uniform indicates a further divergence from the literary original. Zuckmayer's play was based on the tension between civilian and military power, expressed via the problem of the uniform understood as a symbol. This symbolic mechanism disappears in the film, which shifts attention to the conflict between the uniform as such and the body. Be it in the case of Wormser's daughter, undressed and intoxicated, or of Obermüller, who has grown too fat to button his jacket, the exposure of the body is presented as humiliating. The individual body becomes an object of shame which must be hidden and protected by the uniform in which however by definition individuality disappears. This disembodiment culminates at the top of the military hierarchy in the representation of the Kaiser who appears as an abstract voice, without concrete corporeal existence. The principle of the fetishized uniform induces the destruction of the body; the generalizing category suppresses the living particularity.

By the end of the film, the military principle is as firmly established as the newly founded *Bundeswehr*. Innocent children joyfully declare Voigt the Captain of Köpenick and then mysteriously disappear behind still one more platoon of soldiers on parade. But one can rest assured, there is no danger, not even from the Communist mob on the other side of the prison. For the uniform, set up as a scarecrow, stands guard over the fields of West Germany and the free world, protecting the crops, defending the soil and ensuring that the old order, reinstated as the remilitarized new order, will never succumb to disorder.

Notes

1. Cf. Siegfried Mews, *Zuckmayer: Der Hauptmann von Köpenick* (Frankfurt am Main: Diesterweg, 1977), pp. 10–12.
2. Carl Zuckmayer, *A Part of Myself*, trans. Richard and Clara Winston (New York: Harcourt Brace Jovanovich, 1970), p. 315.
3. ibid., p. 312.
4. ibid., p. 315.
5. Prior to the play and sound film versions, the actual historical event had been adapted numerous times for the screen: three versions appeared in 1906 and another one in 1926. See Heinz Rathsack, "Preussen im Film," in *Preussen im Film*, ed. Axel Marquardt and Heinz Rathsack (Reinbek: Rowohlt, 1981), pp. 20–1.
6. Cited in Ulrich Albrecht *et al.*, *Beiträge zu einer Geschichte der Bundesrepublik Deutschland* (Cologne: Pahl-Rugenstein, 1979), p. 319.

Selected Bibliography

Bandmann, Christa and Joe Hembus. *Klassiker des deutschen Tonfilms 1930–1960*. Munich: Goldmann, 1980.
Hembus, Joe. *Der deutsche Film kann gar nicht besser sein*. Bremen: Schünemann, 1961.
Koschnitzki, Rüdiger (ed.). *Helmut Käutner*. Wiesbaden: Deutsches Institut für Filmkunde, 1978.
Kreimeier, Klaus. *Kino und Filmindustrie in der BRD. Ideologieproduktion und Klassenwirklichkeit nach 1945*. Kronberg: Scriptor, 1973.
Kurowski, Ulrich *et al.* (ed.). *nicht mehr fliehen: Das Kino der Ära Adenauer*. 3 vols. Munich: Filmmuseum, 1979ff.
Marquardt, Axel and Heinz Rathsack (eds). *Preussen im Film*. Reinbek: Rowohlt, 1981.
Patalas, Enno. "Autorität und Revolte im deutschen Film: Nationale Leitbilder von Caligari bis Canaris." *Frankfurter Hefte*, 11, No. 1 (January 1956), 19–27.
Schmieding, Walther. *Kunst oder Kasse: Der Ärger mit dem deutschen Film*. Hamburg: Rütten & Loening, 1961.
Weinberg, Herman G. "The Captain from Koepenick." *Film Quarterly*, 13, No. 1 (Fall 1958), 52–3.

12

ERIC RENTSCHLER

Specularity and spectacle in Schlöndorff's *Young Törless* (1966)

Volker Schlöndorff's *Young Törless* (*Der junge Törless*, 1966) occupies a privileged position within postwar German film history as *the* work that initiated the rise of Young German Film. Shown at the Cannes Film Festival in the spring of 1966, it received overwhelming approval, the International Critics' Prize, and considerable notoriety at home. After twenty years of floundering and ineptitude, of second-hand fantasies and quickly produced travesties meant to imitate Hollywood, of *Heimatfilme*, serial productions, and sundry other attempts to profit in a film economy lorded over by American occupiers and controlled by foreign distributors, German cinema, so it was proclaimed in 1966, had once again found a voice of its own, a distinct identity. Seen together with a host of ambitious contemporaneous debut features – Alexander Kluge's *Yesterday Girl* (*Abschied von gestern*), Peter Schamoni's *Closed Season on Fox Hunting* (*Schonzeit für Füchse*), and Ulrich Schamoni's *It* (*Es*) – *Young Törless* was a seminal work announcing a new German cinema of worldwide stature, formal assurance, and critical incisiveness.

In this regard *Young Törless* has much in common with two vanguard films that marked new beginnings at other junctures in German film history, decisive reckonings with the past. Robert Wiene's *The Cabinet of Dr Caligari* (*Das Cabinet des Dr Caligari*, 1920) and Wolfgang Staudte's *The Murderers Are Among Us* (*Die Mörder sind unter uns*, 1946), like *Törless*, amount to dramatic leave-takings from a traumatic legacy, be it a world war or a difficult era of reconstruction. At the center of each film stands the dialectics of victim and victimizer. *Caligari* recycled the World War I front experiences of a generation of soldiers, their feeling that they had played the role of pawns in the hands of a capricious leadership. They had been reduced to the status of Cesares at the beck and call of megalomaniacal Caligaris.[1] Mertens (in Staudte's film) cannot escape his war memories, images of a retributive slaughter ordered by a cold-blooded superior on the Polish front.

When Mertens later finds this officer alive and flourishing in the ruins of Berlin, he tracks the criminal down, calling him to justice, and nearly murdering him. Both films – and, as we shall see, *Törless* – portray situations in which arbitrary and insidious powers are seen through by an individual who has suffered under them. All three works leave the spectator with an unsettling sensation, however, for none of them concludes with the exorcism of these frightening specters.

The doctor – or his benevolent double, we do not know for sure – stares into the camera in the final shot of *Caligari*, just as the mountebank does during his initial appearance. The ex-officer Brückner stands accused during the final chilling moments of Staudte's film, but what does this mean in a work that has consistently called into question the functioning of institutions in a shattered city? All three films, ones seen as crucial and dramatic junctures in German film history, share a punitive fantasy involving a fluidity between victim and victimizer, a perverse relationship between the oppressed and the oppressor. Each film ends with certain alarming constellations exposed, but still operative. The doctor's gaze remains unanswered and his authority intact while the audience wonders whether Francis is not correct, after all. The murderers still roam the streets of Berlin, indeed are "alive and kicking" (Brückner) in the postwar landscape. The military academy that spawned the brutality and sadism displayed in *Young Törless*, the product of a tradition and reflection of a larger political order, continues to educate future officers and state officials as the protagonist rides off in the final sequence.

In a sense, *Young Törless* meant taking leave from yesterday, from the fatal constellations of the Adenauer era, its impersonal and mindless film productions, its evasions of a tragic heritage of totalitarianism and genocide, its circumventions of a fledgling democracy's difficult present in an era of Cold War and reconstruction. In another sense, though, it meant reverting to a more distant past, to a legitimate and critical legacy, one embodied in Robert Musil's penetrating novel of 1906, *Die Verwirrungen des Zöglings Törless*, and a venerable mode of filmmaking which harked back to the Weimar Republic and another epoch in German film tradition.[2] *Young Törless* took part in the definitive postwar project in Germany, that of "coming to grips with the past" (*Vergangenheitsbewältigung*), in an oblique, yet decisive manner, portraying with its study of young cadets in an Austrian military academy predispositions that would become dominant structures during the Third Reich. Volker Schlöndorff gained renown with the debut feature, a work lauded for its well-crafted precision and its accessibility, attributes many critics otherwise would come to miss in the larger body of reflexive, discursive, and formally demanding Young German films.

Over the years Schlöndorff has maintained the reputation of a critical yet popular filmmaker, someone who produces historically minded works with a conspicuous social engagement which actually pay off at the box office, occasional failures notwithstanding. At the same time, he has become the object of skepticism and attack for many popular commentators and some scholars. (Actually, reservations soon became apparent in the wake of the initial raves of *Young Törless* in the Federal Republic.) If Alexander Kluge represented Young German Film's Godard, its most compelling exponent of an alternative and anti-illusionist cinema, then Schlöndorff figured as, according to one's level of discontent, either its Louis Malle or Claude Chabrol, an entertaining and sometimes critical talent, but decidedly lightweight when compared with the more uncompromising likes of the director of *Yesterday Girl*. For all of his liberal humanism – few doubted his goodwill – the director lacked analytical rigor and formal daring. The indifference and distance of the troubled young Törless, argued one particularly vociferous pundit, reflected in fact the filmmaker's own wishy-washiness, the position of the quintessential German aesthete fascinated by the bloody spectacle of history, but unmoved by the real suffering it causes. Schlöndorff replicated for this journalist "the apolitically indifferent stance of those intellectuals who, like the rabbit hypnotized by the snake, do not realize that the problem is not the snake, but the rabbit."[3]

Beyond this, it was argued that Schlöndorff all too uncritically worked within the patterns of dominant cinema, never finding a radical formal expression for his ostensibly progressive political content. He may very well present subject matter with disturbing contours, an intention repeatedly stressed by the director in public declarations, in his claims that his films partake in a dialogue with German history. Nonetheless, insist his detractors, he packages things too neatly, in seamless and well-honed narratives. The spectator does not feel compelled to complete these films in his/her head, to continue thinking about them upon leaving the cinema. Schlöndorff, maintains John Sandford, "is not given to technical experiments, avant-garde mannerisms or innovations"[4] – precisely the transgressive and deconstructive praxis which has endeared more "difficult" talents like Fassbinder, Syberberg, Kluge, and Straub/Huillet to serious cineastes. The director's films, in the mind of Timothy Corrigan, "have a strikingly conventional look to them, stylistically unextravagant and narratively bound to clear, novelistic development that employs traditional strategies of suspense and climax,"[5] a description that would seem to characterize *Young Törless* exactly.

And yet, *Young Törless* is not as conventional a film as it might appear at first glance. The work has all too readily been dismissed as pure *histoire* (in the Metzian sense[6]), as a self-enclosed narrative that unfolds with a self-evident forthrightness, providing a smooth flow of events which sweeps the spectator into the fiction, making the observer identify uncritically with the onscreen presence. Outside of occasional references to the subversive and Brechtian dynamics of Schlöndorff's *The Sudden Wealth of the Poor People of Kombach* (*Der plötzliche Reichtum der armen Leute von Kombach*, 1971), a work that virtually turns the generic patterns of the *Heimatfilm* inside out,[7] commentators have failed to find much *discours* in Schlöndorff's cinema. Is this not the director who – together with Margarethe von Trotta – eradicated the painstakingly exacting narrative persona of Heinrich Böll's *The Lost Honor of Katharina Blum* (*Die verlorene Ehre der Katharina Blum*, 1975) and turned the ironic documentation into a melodramatic and shrill passion play? Was it not the same director who insisted on divesting Günter Grass's *The Tin Drum* (*Die Blechtrommel*) of its arresting framework, that of a madman telling his tale retrospectively from behind the doors of an insane asylum, in the celebrated 1979 production? (In Schlöndorff's defence, one must say that he worked closely with the respective authors and effected these changes with their agreement.) *Discours* means for Metz a type of address that establishes a link between a sender and a receiver, a narrative that draws attention to its workings as the product of a certain intelligence and a distinct context. It speaks in a way that keeps spectators awake, aware of their participation in an exchange, cognizant that what they attend to has an originating source outside of themselves, an identifiable one. *Young Törless* is not the "straightforward narrative"[8] most critics have claimed it to be, unadulterated *histoire*. Indeed, the film operates on manifestly discursive lines, (1) in its relation to its source, (2) in its dialogue with German history, and (3) in its reflections on the dynamics of the film medium, three considerations we will broach in turn before discussing how they interact.

Schlöndorff's film and Musil's novel

In the late fall of 1978, Schlöndorff travelled with a package of his films on a Goethe Institute tour through France. He reflected on his work in a journal entry dated 30 November 1978, notes made during the planning of *The Tin Drum*:

> My theme is once again literary adaptation. I read a lot, gladly, reading is a way of experiencing reality.
> I look for the *reality* behind the book, the reality with which the author began.
> Screenings of *Törless*, *Baal*, and *Katharina Blum*. I'm forced to reflect on my films. It is always literature serving as information about German history.[9]

Schlöndorff acquired the rights to Musil's novel while still an unknown assistant director working in France. (Luchino Visconti likewise had at one point planned an adaptation of *Törless* with Horst Buchholz in the lead role.[10]) Numerous factors made the work attractive to the tyro, not the least of which were his own deep regard for Musil as well as the receptivity a script based on the well-known novel could expect from subsidy officials. Schlöndorff vividly recalled his own experiences in a boarding school. Further, he was drawn by the exemplary character of the story, its "incarnation in such a 'German' setting as a cadet academy, which allowed me a certain linkage to German film traditions – Stroheim and Lang. . . ."[11] At no juncture did he intend a loyal rendering of the novel; it just happened that he and his actors found themselves "reacting at all of the essential points exactly as Musil had described things."[12]

Herbert Linder, in his 1966 review of *Young Törless*, could not have been more mistaken when he claimed that Musil's novel basically lacked cinematic elements. To enjoy the film, Linder argued, spectators would be better off if they knew nothing of Musil or his novel[13] – a finding quickly called into question by even a fleeting acquaintance with the book. Musil's novel abounds with visual images. One critic has pointed out that there are some 240 similes to be found in the relatively short work, ones expressing Törless's unrealized aspirations and the circumscribed character of his everyday life, comparisons with nature and natural objects, analogies between the cadet's emotions and the outside world, figures of war and hunting.[14] The inventory, however, leaves out the most crucial signifying chain in the novel, namely the continual references to sight, vision, and special ways of seeing.

In the first section of the novel, the central importance of this discourse about vision becomes readily discernible. The novel begins with a descriptive passage containing wan colors, fixed points, mechanical movements, a sense of established patterns and set ways of seeing. Törless, left by the parents to whom he is fiercely attached, views "everything only as through a veil."[15] The narrator flashes back to Törless's unfortunate friendship with a young prince, a relationship depicted in manifestly specular terms:

> In the prince's company he felt rather as though he were in some little chapel far off the main road. The thought of actually not belonging there quite vanished in the enjoyment of, for once, seeing the daylight through stained glass; and he let his gaze glide over the profusion of futile gilded agalma in this other person's soul until he had absorbed at least some sort of indistinct picture of that soul, just as though with his fingertips he were tracing the lines of an arabesque, not thinking about it, merely sensing the beautiful pattern of it, which twined according to some weird laws beyond his ken. (p. 7)

Walking back from the train station, Törless muses about life in general, perceiving it as one big unreeling, a cinematic event: "Life went on revolving, churning out ever new and unexpected happenings, like a strange and wonderful wheel" (p. 14).

The initial passage exudes a sense of waiting, a hunger for experience yet to come which will bring resolution to the schoolboy's uncertainties. Törless recalls standing before paintings in a museum, likening his present restlessness with the expectations felt in front of the images:

> He had always been waiting for something that never happened. What was it . . .? It must be something surprising, something never beheld before, some monstrous sight of which he could not form the slightest notion; something of a terrifying, beast-like sensuality; something that would seize him in its claws and rend him, starting with his eyes.   (pp. 16–17)

Wilfried Berghahn has commented extensively on the way Musil repeatedly spoke of certain situations bound up in vision: standing at a window and looking into the night or into a threatening world, for instance.[16] A crucial experience encountered often in Musil's writing is the "other state," a way of looking beyond the surface of reality and perceiving the possibilities behind initial appearances. This type of gazing and preoccupation with questions of vision will become a central element in Schlöndorff's rendering of the novel just as the numerous visual figures take on distinctive shape in the film adaptation.

Young Törless and German history

The director chose Musil's novel, among other reasons, for its exemplary quality, the way it disclosed certain contours in German history. Berghahn, a regular contributor to *Filmkritik* and author of an influential monograph on Musil, acted as an adviser for the project. (Another *Filmkritik* adherent, Enno Patalas, in fact was the one who urged Schlöndorff to adapt *Törless*.[17]) In his book, *Robert Musil* (1964), Berghahn characterized the singular and prophetic nature of Musil's early novel:

> Musil is writing, unwittingly, the prehistory of the twentieth century's dictatorships. He illuminates the psychological tensions and sexual aggressions of a few adolescents and finds therein the complete arsenal of brutality which will go on to make history.[18]

The work in essence depicts the collapse of certain bourgeois foundations and shows the abyss lying beneath the thin veneer of civility and culture.

When the film first appeared, Schlöndorff averred that he neither intended an analysis of the fall of the Habsburg empire nor did he have in mind an allegorical depiction of recent German history. Instead he wanted "to portray an 'atmosphere' and certain modes of behavior *an sich* – not through abstractions, but rather solely with plastic and acoustic means."[19]

Most critics, nonetheless, read the film allegorically, despite the director's disclaimers. Take Peter M. Ladiges's review for example: "Schlöndorff wanted things to be understood more strictly and categorically. Basini the Jew, Reiting and Beineberg the dictators, and in between them Törless, the German people."[20] He went on to argue that such an interpretation breaks down, proceeding to fault Schlöndorff in the process. Törless does not just look on; he participates. Basini is not just the victim; he commits a crime before he is forced into that role. If one is to accept the parable, Basini and Törless must be viewed as different aspects of the German people, variations on a common passivity, be it the lack of volition or a fatal fascination with the spectacle of evil.[21] Interestingly, one finds Schlöndorff later repeating this interpretation almost verbatim – with an added nuance. Contrary to what critics have maintained, Schlöndorff does not identify with Törless; the overall perspective of the film does not sympathize with the protagonist, but rather condemns him:

> Törless embodies the German people, about whom one could say that they are more guilty than the tyrants. More guilty because they had the possibility of recognizing things. In a certain way this angel Törless is a dirty dog (*Schweinehund*).[22]

Clearly, one cannot overlook the historical resonance of Schlöndorff's adaptation, the way in which various characters embody behavioral patterns well known in National Socialism, but ones with a long tradition in Germany as well. Beineberg's idle sadism, his inexorable zeal to delve into the limits of the human condition, and the religious mysticism in which his pursuits are garbed: all recall the wanton exploits of physicians in concentration camps, the abuse of inmates in medical experiments for the sake of a moot science, as do, still more, the convoluted torture scenarios.[23] Schlöndorff did not include in the film an utterance of Beineberg in the novel which would have made the connection between the cadets' wanton acts and what was to come all too explicit for any postwar spectator: "We are young," Beineberg tells Törless while speaking of their parents, "we are a generation later, and perhaps things are destined for us that they never dreamt of in all their lives. At least, I feel that it is so" (p. 178). Reiting, the other tormentor of Basini, recalls power-hungry ruffians, someone, as Musil describes him, with "day-dreams of *coup d'état* and high politics" (p. 52), a martinet who well knows the importance of having a mob behind him.

In the school, where "each class constitutes a small State in itself" (p. 52), Törless plays a complex and fluctuating role. He is alternately determined to have Basini punished like a common criminal, complicitous in Reiting and Beineberg's schemes as participant and observer, fascinated and in turn repulsed by what he sees, and in the end, involved in a last-minute protest against the class beating of the school-mate. Törless gets caught up in the abuse of Basini, yet he has different stakes from those of Beineberg and Reiting. He takes part, he watches, fearing the same fate could befall him, that the world could vanish from under his feet. At times he sees Basini as his double. The nocturnal thrashings of the fellow cadet become a mirror reflection for the incipient intellectual, an imaginary for the still unshaped subject who identifies with the tormented captive standing in front of him. Törless, so troubled by the prospect of imaginary numbers, the insight that one can effect real things with non-existent phenomena, has a decidedly imaginary investment in the spectacle at the center of the novel. It remains to be seen how this specular perspective figures in Schlöndorff's reflections on German history and the possibilities of the filmic medium.

Schlöndorff's reflection on the film medium

Central to Musil's novel and the dilemma it depicts is the problem of seeing, of Törless's awareness of a multifaceted, inscrutable, and in many ways monstrous reality, one that takes on elements of the uncanny for him. As Tzvetan Todorov notes, one aspect of the uncanny is the "experience of limits," a sense of being at the margins or the boundaries of human life and nature.[24] Following Freud, Todorov maintains that "the sense of the uncanny is linked to the appearance of an image which originates in the childhood of the individual or the race."[25] Certain images overwhelm the young Törless, the presentiment, for instance, that he lives in the near vicinity of a transgressor, someone with whom he shares things in common he would rather not acknowledge:

> He himself no longer knew whether it was only his imagination that was like a gigantic distorting-glass between him and everything, or whether it was true and everything was really the way it uncannily loomed before him. (p. 65)

Later, he continues to think about Basini, mirroring images of the class- and soul-mate in his head. A telling formulation characterizes the special – and specular – terms in which Törless casts these projections:

> And the next moment this Basini would vanish, only to come again, and yet again, as a small and even smaller figure, tiny and sometimes luminous against a deep, very deep background. . . . (p. 72)

This is how Basini is screened in Törless's mind in the novel – what about the film?

From the film's opening sequence on, one finds numerous subjective shots that mirror Törless's explorations of the world around him. Particularly striking is the passage where he and his class-mates walk back from the train station through the village. A subjective camera captures his gaze, peering through windows and courtyards, watching women bent over at work, eyeing a man slaughtering a pig, an ominous image that points ahead to the treatment the hanging Basini will receive at the hands of his class-mates – as well as prefiguring Törless's own relationship to this spectacle.[26] Later, while sitting in a café with Beineberg, Törless, again in subjective takes, peers with erotic interest at Beineberg's lithe fingers as they roll a cigarette and gazes hungrily at the neck and hands of a waitress.

Nonetheless, so critics have insisted, there is no real radical will behind this film. If anything, Schlöndorff all too readily aligns the perspective of the film with that of the protagonist – and this is problematical. What the director has not done is to distance himself from the novel, to find an impetus of his own. This was a repeated contention in the first German notices about the film: Schlöndorff ultimately was unable to find a subjective relationship to Musil's novel, to create a diegesis of his own. The film-maker, claimed detractors, retains Musil's stylized dialogue verbatim, exchanges that impart an artificiality at odds with the director's attempts to shape a credible milieu and environment. If one follows this line of thinking, it would seem to indicate a half-baked and in the end compromised adaptation, a collision between the young director's attempt to find a personal relationship to the material and his deference to the novel.

Young Törless is, however, a reflection *on* – not a reflection *of* – its sources, Musil's novel and modern German history. It is, further, a radicalized reflection, for all the film's apparent stylistic assurance and formal grace. Schlöndorff does not identify with his protagonist as critics have maintained – neither did Musil, for that matter. Nor does he ultimately grant Törless, as one reviewer would have it, "a certain moral triumph in his withdrawal, his sense of superiority over both sides,"[27] i.e. over Basini as well as Reiting and Beineberg. It is hardly gratuitous that Schlöndorff at crucial moments reverts to the usages of expressionism, that seminal German formal heritage. In so doing, he reflects in a double sense on German tradition, revisiting a legitimate film legacy, the "haunted screen" of the 1920s. At the same time he reflects on a fatal tendency within German intellectual history to reduce the exterior world and other people to narcissistic projections of oneself, to make reality into a playground for one's imagination. A reflection of a venerable German film tradition, *Young Törless* simultaneously provides a metareflection on the dynamics of dominant cinema.

In what ways is *Young Törless* marked by cinematic expressionism? The open fields we see in the film's opening shot (quite unlike the formed and circumscribed space pictured in the novel's first lines) stand as an objective correlative to the still unshaped Törless. The propensity for using landscapes and the exterior world as extensions or functions of a character's psyche is, of course, one of the main earmarks of expressionism. In Lotte H. Eisner's words, this artistic vision was one in which:

> The world has become so 'permeable' that, at any one moment, Mind, Spirit, Vision and Ghosts seem to gush forth, exterior facts are continually being transformed into interior elements and psychic events are exteriorized.[28]

But not just the landscape appears as an extension of the young cadet. Schlöndorff's equally expressive framing in the opening sequence groups constellations in telling ways, ones that foreshadow psychic tensions to come. Törless at one point is framed between his mother (on the right) and Beineberg/Reiting (on the left), in essence between the world of security and nurture he has thus far known and the sinister realm he will soon enter under his companions' tutelage. Behind Törless — as if he were an outgrowth of Törless — Basini lingers, a double, as it were, for the student enamored of his mother and tormented by his class-mates. (This, to be sure, is Schlöndorff's addition, for the novel makes no mention of Basini being present at the train station.) Expressionistic touches include as well the quintessential spaces characteristic of the "haunted screen," the long and eerie corridors, the imposing arches, the shadowy hallways, and secret hiding places.

Musil continually suggests parallels between Törless's frenzied reflections and cinematic seeing, speaking of the youth's rehearsal of reality as a grand unreeling, an attending to a bizarre spectacle. The outside world becomes alternately a dream, an hallucination, a distortion. The actions against Basini take on the quality of an experiment and a psychodrama for young Törless, one in which he mirrors himself, wondering what it is like to walk in a world that has lost its foundations. The whole situation calls into question his previous sources of solace and certainty, causing everything to whirl and become distorted:

> He never at any time "saw" Basini in any sort of physically plastic and living attitude; never did any of all this amount to a real vision. It was always only the illusion of one, as it were only the vision of his visions. For within him it was always as if a picture had just flashed across the mysterious screen, and he never succeeded in catching hold of it in the very instant that this happened. Hence there was all the time a restlessness and uneasiness in him such as one feels when watching cinematographic pictures, when, for all the illusion the whole thing creates, one is nevertheless unable to shake off a vague awareness that behind the image one perceives there are hundreds of other images flashing past, and each of them utterly different from the picture as a whole.   (p. 135)

The capacity cannot be called upon at will; it simply overcomes Törless at times, an "illusion that was, moreover, by an immeasurably slight degree always just insufficient" (p. 136).

The "restlessness and uneasiness . . . one feels when watching cinematographic pictures": this sensibility assumes a key importance in Schlöndorff's film. We watch the trio Reiting, Beineberg, and Törless interrogate Basini in the attic, the latter standing – like the murderer in Fritz Lang's *M* before the underworld tribunal – in a spotlight, the center of the midnight spectacle. As Reiting and Beineberg commence beating Basini, we watch Törless watching the performance. Above him – a form placed at the center of the image – is a reel-like shape. He gazes with horror and interest at the scene, closes his eyes, then opens them. Next to him is a mirror into which he also looks. The show over, he turns to his comrades and asks: "Isn't this like looking into a strange world?" In a subsequent nocturnal torture scene, Törless – now weary of the whole business – will rise and retreat from the attic, making his way out of the space just as a displeased filmgoer who has lost interest in a movie might exit from the cinema.

Throughout the film, but especially in these attic scenes, Törless watches the scenes of persecution like a voyeur, casting them off as reflections of his inner tensions, refusing for the most to accept their real consequences until it is too late. He harbors a decidedly imaginary relationship to the spectacle, one that bothers and fascinates the unsure subject, a drama, though, that Törless visits and leaves with a marked unawareness of its real repercussions. Schlöndorff decorates the otherwise sparse and shadowy attic space with significant props: a reel that suggests the links between the onscreen spectacle and the one experienced by us in the cinema, and, further, a mirror that indicates how Törless, like the real spectator in most filmgoing situations, envisions this event as a reflection of his own psyche. The sequence, in striking, indeed literal ways, illustrates Christian Metz's discussions of the film image as an imaginary signifier, something beheld by a spectator who both knows what s/he sees is not real, yet at the same time attends to it as if it were.

Törless sits at the edge of the frame, in the background, pretending not to be implicated in the violence. In previous scenes we have seen him linked in decisive ways to each of the three actors who stand in front of him. He, like Beineberg, philosophizes and indulges in metaphysical speculations, wondering what goes on in Basini's head. Like Reiting, Törless at times dominates and terrorizes Basini, prompting the latter to exclaim how Törless has a particularly harsh way of tormenting him. Basini likewise becomes a double in Törless's eyes, the victim of others he himself might become, the site of projection for Törless's own punitive fantasies. In the attic sequences and elsewhere in the film (where he watches Beineberg fondle Božena, for instance), Törless peers at the world in the way of fish in an aquarium, the spectator creatures spoken of by Metz who take in "everything with their

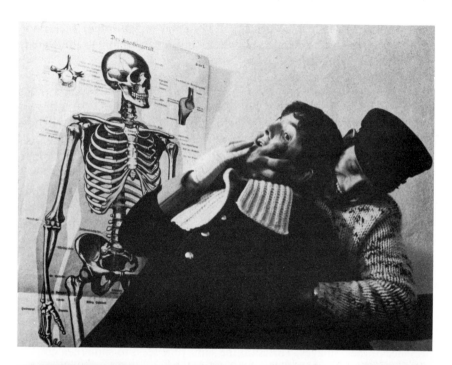

Plates 26 and 27 Victim and victimizers; random acts of violence, physical and psychological, in the school corridor and in the attic. Törless sits at frame's edge, the dispassionate observer. Photos courtesy of Stiftung Deutsche Kinemathek.

eyes, nothing with their bodies.''[29] His relation to the brutal exhibition before him is one of fascinated, but disembodied participation – much like that of the normal spectator in the cinema:

> The institution of the cinema requires a silent, motionless spectator, a *vacant* spectator, constantly in a sub-motor and hyperperceptive state, a spectator at once alienated and happy, acrobatically hooked up to himself by the invisible thread of sight, a spectator who only catches up with himself at the last minute, by a paradoxical identification with his own self, a self filtered out into pure vision.[30]

The attic scenes are metafilmic reflections: we watch Törless watching scenes of horror as if they were private fantasies. Our relation to the screen spectacle is doubled by Törless's relation to the drama unfolding in front of him. He too sits in the dark, apart from the players in front of him, yet involved in the play, identifying with its participants. He too thinks he can leave the space at any time and thus cease the unreeling of events. His relation to the spectacle, like the average filmgoer's, involves a mixture of semi-slumber and heightened attentiveness. He, like we, is a cinema fetishist, a private person enchanted by the possibilities before him, captivated by the theater of shadows transpiring in front of him. And yet: while revelling in the presence of these images, Törless at the same time seeks to shun their consequences, to disavow their reality. Törless's relation to what he sees may be an imaginary one; nonetheless – and this is the crucial insight of Schlöndorff's reflection on Musil, German history, and narrative cinema – what Törless partakes of has not just come out of the dark. This spectacle takes shape as the result of certain pre-existing structures, a symbolic order. The grand achievement of Schlöndorff's reworking of Musil was to elucidate these dynamics against the backdrop of postwar German experience.

The attic scene thus replicates and simultaneously analyzes the workings of dominant cinema, that mode of presentation so vehemently attacked by Young German filmmakers as "Opas Kino." This is the key to Schlöndorff's subtle subversiveness at its best: the director uses the possibilities of the dominant cinema eloquently and professionally, at the same time problematizing these usages by foregrounding their workings, doubling the otherwise unacknowledged relationship between spectator and spectacle in the diegesis itself. This, though, is not just a case where a young German filmmaker sought to transcend the linear and self-enclosed character of classical filmmaking. The tradition of disembodied gazing, of blithe partaking of horrendous spectacles, is a seminal experience in modern German intellectual history. In the novel Musil flashes forward at one point to give the reader a sense of what sort of individual Törless will become as an adult:

> By that time he was one of those aesthetically inclined intellectuals who find there is something soothing in a regard for law and indeed – to some

extent at least – for public morals too, since it frees them from the necessity of ever thinking about anything coarse, anything that is remote from the finer spiritual processes. (p. 169)

True to a cultural heritage of self-cultivation at the expense of society and history, a legacy of apolitical dreamers, Törless grows up to become the German aesthete *par excellence*, a self-indulgent spirit who views the outer world as a laboratory, a testing site for his private musings.

Schlöndorff does not include this flashforward to the mature dandy. His adaptation as a whole updated the novel, however, providing an incisive contemplation on a problematic German tradition of watching the world go by, be it by enraptured spectators surrounded by images of violence who deny these realities, be it by an intellectual who not only partakes of such spectacles, but in doing so, takes part in them. Törless victimizes Basini and in the end becomes a victim as well. His fate is that of his double: he, like Basini, leaves the academy and returns to his mother. "Retrogression assumes the character of resignation" in Törless's case, a resignation indexed by the symbolic return to his mother's womb in the final shots of the film, one similar to the retreats of various "street film" protagonists in Weimar productions discussed by Kracauer.[31]

Törless is the most compelling specular hero in Schlöndorff's cinema, a body of film abounding with such individuals. The character is the dominant figure in the director's *oeuvre* – from the trencherman Baal who acts out his fantasies on others as if they were merely coincidental extras to the brutal newsman Tötges (*The Lost Honor of Katharina Blum*) who transforms the sufferings of others into material for his exploitative articles. Or one can take the family of nobles in *Coup de Grâce* (*Der Fangschuss*, 1976) which exists within the insular realm of the spectacle it has created, doing everything it can to ward off the intrusion of an outside perspective.[32] One can pinpoint the midget Oskar (*The Tin Drum*) who watches the world from below, experiencing German history during the Third Reich from a low-angle purview. And, of course, the reporter Laschen in *Circle of Deceit* (*Die Fälschung*, 1981) plays out his mid-life crisis in the midst of a war-torn foreign landscape, rendering the intense turmoil and factionalism of Beirut, its explosions and carnage, as an expression of his inner torments. Most recently, the rarefied protagonist of *Swann in Love* (*Eine Liebe von Swann*, 1984), Proust's famous *flâneur*, stands as another variation on this specular theme.

The majority of Schlöndorff's films does not contain the self-awareness and reflective aplomb of *Young Törless* and *The Sudden Wealth of the Poor People of Kombach*. In *Törless*, the director left imprints in the text, marking the film as a reflection on a novel, a history, and a medium. One looks in vain for such discursive traces in the later films, evidence that Schlöndorff wanted to reach out to audiences and establish a link between the filmic text and the context in which it is consumed. In *Young Törless*, the last shot makes such an appeal in a chillingly understated way. The camera records the subjective impressions of the ex-cadet as he rides with his mother in a coach, leaving the school behind him. The camera then cuts away from the Oedipal pair and in the closing image looks down train tracks that recede inexorably into the distance as bells chime. Törless's story may have come to an end; the history that produced it has not, however. And this history will have fatal consequences that reach far beyond the life of one young cadet and the world of one military academy in the provinces.

Notes

1. See Siegfried Kracauer, *From Caligari to Hitler: A Psychological History of the German Film* (Princeton: Princeton University Press, 1947), p. 62.

2. Most critics tend to stress the formal lessons learned by Schlöndorff as an assistant director for Alain Resnais, Jean-Pierre Melville, and Louis Malle, claiming that the technical and stylistic precision of *Young Törless* owes great debts to the French models. Cf. Schlöndorff's own self-assessment in *"Die Blechtrommel"*: *Tagebuch einer Verfilmung* (Darmstadt: Luchterhand, 1979), p. 37: "Since *Törless* I have consciously made German films." The director's first film, the short *Who Cares* (*Wen kümmerts*, 1960) carries a dedication to Fritz Lang, "the greatest living German film artist."

3. For a representative compilation of press responses to *Young Törless*, see *Neuer Deutscher Film: Eine Dokumentation*, ed. Verband der deutschen Filmclubs (Mannheim: Internationale Filmwoche, 1967), pp. 78–86. The quotation is taken from Karsten Peters's notice that appeared in the Munich *Abendzeitung* on 20 June 1966 (reprinted on p. 83): "Törless is the exact mirror image of his director. Both are interested only in the phenomenon, not the question, why Beineberg and Reiting both became sadists, nor the problem why Törless himself feels attracted to the atrocities. Schlöndorff said to me in a conversation: 'I couldn't make the film against my hero.' If only he had."

4. John Sandford, *The New German Cinema* (Totowa, NJ: Barnes & Noble, 1980), p. 37. Sandford, it must be noted, is basically positively disposed toward Schlöndorff.

5. Timothy Corrigan, *New German Film: The Displaced Image* (Austin: University of Texas Press, 1983), p. 71. Note Corrigan's particularly apt formulation later in the same essay, where he relates how Schlöndorff's "putative confidence in cinematic realism and its conventional discourse becomes a kind of political plea-bargaining, the accessible look of the representation being the acceptable vehicle for a more subversive tenor" (p. 74).

6. See Christian Metz, "Story/discourse (a note on two kinds of voyeurism)," in *The Imaginary Signifier*, trans. Celia Britton and Annwyl Williams (Bloomington: Indiana University Press, 1982), pp. 91–8.

7. See Eric Rentschler, *West German Film in the Course of Time* (Bedford Hills, NY: Redgrave, 1984), pp. 103–28.

8. Sandford, p. 37.

9. Volker Schlöndorff, *"Die Blechtrommel"*: *Tagebuch einer Verfilmung* (Darmstadt: Luchterhand, 1979), p. 48.

10. Rainer Lewandowski, *Die Filme von Volker Schlöndorff* (Hildesheim and New York: Olms, 1981), p. 54.

11. "Tribüne des Jungen Deutschen Films: Volker Schlöndorff," *Filmkritik*, 10, No. 6 (June, 1966), 309.

12. ibid.

13. Herbert Linder, *"Der junge Törless," Filmkritik*, 10, No. 6 (June 1966), 323–4.

14. Marilyn Gaddis Rose, "Musil's use of simile in *Törless*," *Studies in Short Fiction*, 8 (1971), 295–300.

15. Robert Musil, *Young Törless*, trans. Eithne Wilkins and Ernst Kaiser (New York: Pantheon, 1955; repr. 1982), p. 3. Page numbers of all subsequent citations from the novel appear in the text.

16. Wilfried Berghahn, *Robert Musil* (Reinbek: Rowohlt, 1963), p. 16.

17. This was related to me in a conversation with Frieda Grafe.

18. Berghahn, p. 28. This passage was quoted expressly in the February 1966 issue of *Filmkritik* which introduced the film with stills and selections from the screenplay (76).

19. "Tribüne des Jungen Deutschen Films," 309.

20. Peter M. Ladiges, "Diskussion: *Der junge Törless*," *Filmkritik*, 10, No. 7 (July 1966), 398.

21. ibid.

22. Lewandowski, p. 54.

23. Cf. Alexander Kluge's prose piece, "Ein Liebesversuch," in *Lebensläufe*, 2nd rev. edn (Frankfurt am Main: Suhrkamp, 1977), pp. 156–9.

24. Tzvetan Todorov, *The Fantastic: A Structural Approach to a Literary Genre*, trans. Richard Howard (Ithaca, NY: Cornell University Press, 1975), p. 48.

25. ibid., pp. 46–7.

26. Cf. Lewandowski, p. 55.

27. Ernest Callenbach, *"Young Törless,"* *Film Quarterly*, 20, No. 2 (Winter 1966–7), 43.

28. Lotte H. Eisner, *The Haunted Screen*, trans. Roger Greaves (Berkeley: University of California Press, 1969), p. 15.

29. Metz, p. 96.

30. ibid.

31. Kracauer, p. 122. See, as well, still number 22 in the volume, where the hero of *The Street* rests on his mother: "This gesture," claims Kracauer, recurs in many German films and "is symptomatic of the desire to return to the maternal womb."

32. Corrigan, p. 83.

Script

Volker Schlöndorff. *Der junge Törless*. Film (Velber), 4, No. 7 (July 1966), 45–56.

Selected Bibliography

Berghahn, Wilfried. *Robert Musil*. Reinbek: Rowohlt, 1963.

Bronnen, Barbara and Corinna Brocher. *Die Filmemacher. Zur Neuen deutschen Produktion nach Oberhausen 1962*. Munich, Gütersloh and Vienna: Bertelsmann, 1973.

Callenbach, Ernest. *"Young Törless."* *Film Quarterly*, 20, No. 2 (Winter 1966–7), 42–4.

Fischer, Robert and Joe Hembus. *Der Neue Deutsche Film 1960–1980*. Munich: Goldmann, 1981.

Gmür, Leonard H. (ed.). *Der junge deutsche Film*. Munich: Constantin, 1967.

Ladiges, Peter M. "Diskussion: Der junge Törless." *Filmkritik*, 10, No. 7 (July 1966), 397–8.

Lewandowski, Rainer. *Die Filme von Volker Schlöndorff*. Hildesheim and New York: Olms, 1981.

Linder, Herbert. "*Der junge Törless.*" *Filmkritik*, 10, No. 6 (June 1966), 323–4.

Neuer Deutscher Film: Eine Dokumentation. Ed. Verband der deutschen Filmclubs. Mannheim: Internationale Filmwoche, 1967.

Sandford, John. *The New German Cinema*. Totowa, NJ: Barnes & Noble, 1980.

Schlöndorff, Volker. *"Die Blechtrommel": Tagebuch einer Verfilmung*. Darmstadt: Luchterhand, 1979.

Schmidt, Eckhart. "Der Filmemacher Volker Schlöndorff." *Medium*, June 1973, 15–18.

Stenger, Karl-Ludwig. "Robert Musils *Die Verwirrungen des Zöglings Törless* and Volker Schlöndorffs *Der junge Törless*." *Neue Germanistik*, 3, No. 1 (Fall 1982), 7–16.

Thomson, Barry and Greg Thomson. "Volker Schlöndorff: an interview." *Film Criticism*, 1, No. 3 (Winter 1976–7), 26–37.

13

MIRIAM HANSEN

Space of history, language of time: Kluge's *Yesterday Girl* (1966)

Kluge's first venture into film practice suggests the circuitous plot of one of his stories. Having just published his doctoral dissertation in law and dreading the prospect of a legal career, Kluge discussed his interest in filmmaking with Adorno, a philosopher not exactly known as a champion of the mass media. Adorno in turn wrote a letter to Fritz Lang, a Los Angeles acquaintance suggesting that Kluge be hired as an assistant in the production of the two-part spectacle, *The Tiger of Eshnapur/The Indian Tomb* (*Der Tiger von Eschnapur/Das indische Grabmal*, 1958–9), for which the director had returned to Germany. Lang declined but agreed to admit the neophyte onto the set. As soon as shooting began, Lang's ideas were systematically short-changed by the producer, Artur Brauner, who interfered directly with decisions of lighting and set design and on the whole preferred the advice of his sister-in-law to that of the director. Mildly disgusted with this situation, Kluge spent much of his time in the cafeteria, writing stories; these were the beginning of a collection entitled *Lebensläufe* (*Curricula Vitae*), published in 1962. The story of Anita G. in that collection subsequently became the basis for Kluge's first feature film, *Yesterday Girl* (*Abschied von gestern*, 1966).[1]

This introduction to commercial filmmaking not only turned Kluge into a writer – whose fairly substantial oeuvre has since secured him a reputation independent of (though not unrelated to) his work in film – but also provoked his long-term involvement with the project of *Autorenkino* (uneasily translated as *auteur* cinema). Lang's desire to resume his place in German film history was foiled by a producer who combined the worst of the Hollywood studio system with the mediocre taste of the Ufa tradition. Seeing that the resulting film, a compromise at best, nonetheless achieved a certain quality, Kluge drew a twofold conclusion: one, that there was a distinctly cinematic mode of authorship which manifested itself despite and precisely through the struggle with the prevailing conditions of production;

two, that these conditions had to be reorganized on a large scale if Germany was to develop a new creative tradition in film.

Clearly this position echoes the French *politique des auteurs* which, along with the first films of Godard, Malle, Truffaut, and Resnais, provided a major impulse during the formation of the Oberhausen group of which Kluge was a member and spokesman. Like the director-critics associated with the French *nouvelle vague*, the proponents of "young" German cinema maintained that film was a medium of personal expression, deriving their notions of authorship from literary paradigms while rejecting any subordination of film to established literary works (e.g. adaptations of classics). The provincial status of West German film culture, however, inevitably gave such a position a more pragmatic slant; questions of individual style or a new film language appeared less urgent than the need to improve the economic, legal, and professional support structure of independent film-making, a long-range strategy that eventually – albeit temporarily – succeeded in instituting an elaborate public funding system, including access to TV stations, as well as the founding of film academies, most notably the one at Ulm.

The juncture of film and writing which crucially shaped Kluge's career in both media has to be considered in relation to a third term, i.e. the function and scope of the cinema as well as literature as institutions in a particular social and cultural context. For Kluge, the "politics of authorship" has always been synonymous with film politics, media politics, politics of the public sphere – all of which he actively pursues as a lawyer, lobbyist, teacher (at Ulm and Frankfurt), and theorist/critic. If Kluge can be said to promote a "literarization" of the cinema, such as Brecht recommended for the theater, then this refers to certain textual devices structuring his films (written titles, voice-over, foregrounding of discursive activity) as well as to the institutional confrontation of cinema and literature in the context of the public sphere. Opposing the division of labor by which the traditional arts strive to preserve their "purity," the remnants of aesthetic autonomy, Kluge emphasizes instead the material heterogeneity of film as a medium, a heterogeneity that tends to get suppressed in both commercial and so-called art cinema. Radical filmmaking, as Kluge insists, has to work from the basic tension between discursive elements and visual/aural particularity because it is the very "impurity" of the medium which lends processes of cinematic signification an affinity with the way experience is organized in the human mind ("the film in the head of the spectator") and thus offers a potential alternative to the dominant structures of the public sphere.

In Kluge's writings, the emphasis on non-exclusionary modes of experience and communication takes the form of a systematic transgression of traditional delimitations of genre, media, and authorship. Maintaining what deceptively resembles a logic of narrative, Kluge's stories tend to interweave fragments of non-"literary" (e.g. colloquial, legal, administrative, medical, military) discourse with little or strongly restrained authorial intervention. More conspicuously, Kluge's non-narrative texts, in particular his two most recent collaborations, *History and Obstinacy* (*Geschichte und Eigensinn*, 1981) and *Taking Stock: Cinema as Utopia* (*Bestandsaufnahme: Utopie Film*, 1983), as well as the books accompanying his last two films, *The Patriot* (*Die Patriotin*, 1979) and *The Power of Emotion* (*Die Macht der Gefühle*, 1983), assemble a vast variety of materials – photographs, contact sheets of stills, (once) popular and (now) esoteric illustrations, newspaper clippings, maps, scientific diagrams, sheet music – thus defying conventional divisions between the media. In Kluge's films, finally, the transformation of material heterogeneity into a textual "plurivocity" depends upon particular techniques of montage and *mise-en-scène*, elements crucial to an understanding of *Yesterday Girl*.

When *Yesterday Girl* was released in 1966 – following a spectacular première at the Venice Film Festival – it was hailed by the press as a new beginning, as the rebirth of German cinema. Now that this "new" German cinema is said to have come of age, Kluge's first feature film can hardly be viewed as a product of its infancy, a mere prelude to the internationally acclaimed works of the 1970s. From a distance of almost two decades, *Yesterday Girl* both captures the historical moment and exceeds it, suggesting a whole new range of readings from the perspective of recent film history, developments in film theory and analysis as well as changes in political and cultural contexts of signification. With its amazingly flexible potential of meanings, the film points to a tradition of cinema whose promises have yet to be fulfilled.

Moreover, *Yesterday Girl* undercuts evolutionist conceptions of film history within its own textual framework, on a formal as well as thematic level. Telling the story of Anita G. (played by Kluge's sister Alexandra/ Karen), the film investigates constellations of continuity and discontinuity in West German society and culture. Anita G., born in 1937, is introduced as a displaced character, a person "on the run": daughter of Jewish parents (who, as she asserts in court, returned to Leipzig in 1945 to resume ownership of their factories), she leaves the German Democratic Republic for the Federal Republic in 1957; commits petty theft and is sentenced in 1959 (which is the beginning of the plot); violates parole; goes through a series of jobs, residences and lovers, mostly married; gets pregnant and finally gives herself up. Anita, running away from a past of which she has been twice dispossessed, moves through West German society like a "seismograph," to use Kluge's phrase,[2] registering "non-synchronicity" (Ernst Bloch) – pockets of "yesterday" – in people's diction, behavior, gestures, and faces. While anticipating the Auschwitz trial and the student movement – the two events between which it was made – the film evokes the atmosphere of the Adenauer era, with its tacit continuation of social practices and attitudes underneath its official stance of having accomplished the break with the Nazi past. Hence the film's title, *Abschied von gestern* ("Farewell to Yesterday"), inevitably assumes ironic if not oxymoronic connotations: the persistence of the past in the present is so strong – precisely because it has succumbed to collective repression – that simply to resume the agenda becomes ideological; a real "farewell to yesterday" would involve reversing the flight from history, thus changing the course of the present.[3] *Yesterday Girl* explores this peculiarly German constellation of past and present on a number of levels: through the relationship of discourse and subjectivity as well as that of narrative and history and, finally, through particular spatial and temporal figurations.

The film opens with an epigraph that attacks one of the most common forms of historical amnesia in West German culture, the myth of the "zero hour": "We are separated from yesterday not by an abyss but by the changed situation."[4] As throughout the film, this quotation remains uncredited, emphasizing the fact of enunciation while suspending the question of authorship. The second shot then introduces the discrepancy of discourse and speaking subject as a theme, prior to narrative and diegetic anchoring; more surprisingly, it establishes this discrepancy as a focus of cinematic pleasure. From a slightly high angle, the protagonist is shown reading a text of unidentified origin:

> Did he separate the daughter from the mother? Did he separate the mother from the daughter? Did he not release a prisoner nor set him free? Did he not allow a prisoner to see the light? Did he say "catch him" of one who was already caught?

The text's meaning at this point is irrelevant, although it anticipates key motifs of Anita's story such as persecution, captivity, separation of mother and child. To gauge the distance between Anita and the text, the viewer does not need to know that it is a priests' poem from ancient Egypt. What matters in this shot is the material quality of enunciation: the repetitive interrogatory style, the mock declamatory intonation, its rhythm and upward pitch, the "grain" of the voice, as Barthes puts it, "the encounter between a language and a voice";[5] but also the grain of the image, the shadow that doubles Anita's figure on the wall, her laughter and expression of amused curiosity, her eating with her hands while she reads, the cheerful orality of both.

The following sequences develop the gap between character and discourse in both its spatial and its temporal dimensions. Still from a high angle, a long shot pans with Anita as she enters the old Café Kranzler, approaching a table with six armchairs. Moving from the first to the second to the third she seems to be testing the space with the same air of self-conscious nonchalance that her voice applied to the Egyptian text. The space is marked as a social and historical one: the bourgeois *intérieur* with a small band playing a tango tune of the 1930s or 1940s evokes a world in which Anita used to be at home (as a montage of family photographs accompanied by similar music will shortly show) but from which she has been separated, literally displaced, just as she is spatially segregated from the other guests who look a bit like part of the furniture; fittingly, the film's title is superimposed on this tableau. As Anita orders a piece of cake in the next shot, her hands indicating a span of about a foot, the hyperbolic gesture again associates the pleasure of enunciation with the pleasure of eating and the waitress seems to understand. This moment of speechless communication, however, is immediately counterpointed by a close-up of a stubbly neck: it belongs to a judge who accuses Anita of having stolen a sweater from one of her colleagues.

The subsequent trial scene – the first actual sequence of the film – transposes the discrepancy between protagonist and the discourses surrounding her from the playful into the realm of the reality principle. Besides reducing Anita to an object of criminal law, the judge not only questions the authenticity of her own speech (she doesn't speak the dialect of the region she claims to come from) but also, more importantly, engages in an exercise of token acknowledgment involving Anita's Jewish background (an argument she herself does not advance in defense) only to dismiss all the more authoritatively any connection between the past (her childhood experience as a historical one) and her present situation. The discourse of legality exceeds the individual act of enunciation – thus Anita's case – which is underlined by a mismatched shot showing the judge silent while his voice continues on the soundtrack. The position offered to the spectator, therefore, is not one of unqualified identification with the protagonist as victim; rather it is split by the more discursive pleasure the judge provides as a satire on the legal profession, especially when he rattles off a lengthy commentary on the criminal code, his face and both hands forming a pyramid around the book.

Skipping the verdict, the next sequence shows Anita in prison, inexpressively staring toward the camera. This sequence extends the configuration of space, time, discourse, and subjectivity to the terms of enunciation of the film itself. A discontinuous cut from a long shot (through the open door of the cell) of Anita resting her head against the bedstead to a direct overhead close-up of her face, now flat on the bed, prepares the leap into an imaginary space, initiated by electric-organ Christmas music on the soundtrack (*"leise rieselt der Schnee"*). In a series of shots varying in scale and level, we see an illustration from an 1920s children's book (Heinrich Hoffmann's *Visit at Frau Sonne's/Besuch bei Frau Sonne*) showing a mammoth dancing with one of two boys while the other plays the fiddle, a pile of disproportionately large ladyfingers and a cup of vanilla ice-cream between them. While the music continues, animating the still shots, a male voice-over recites the verse that makes the image legible, recounting little Walter's resurrection of the mammoth, their merry dancing and subsequent craving for the giant delicacies brought along from the Ice Age.

Plate 28 Another kind of German interior, a social and historical one, which the Jewish emigrant from the east gets to know well during her peregrinations through the Federal Republic. Photo courtesy of Stiftung Deutsche Kinemathek.

The verse envisions a prehistoric utopia, articulating the desire for a non-monstrous, non-alienating past. This desire, however, is not spoken from a position of transcendence, addressing the listener over Anita's head, as it were.[6] While the body as point of origin remains invisible, the voice-over is by no means immaterial: through idiosyncrasies of speech, it is associated with Anita's voice, her own pleasure in the non-functional, perverse aspects of language. Moreover, the voice is knowable as that of the filmmaker and, as such, it projects the materiality of the film's enunciation into the viewing process. The effect is one of Brechtian distanciation, but also one of greater intimacy. Not quite as relentlessly personal as Godard whispering into the spectator's ear in *Two or Three Things I Know About Her* (*Deux ou trois choses que je sais d'elle*, 1967), Kluge's voice tropes on a familiar, indeed familial, sound. The childhood memories invoked are far from innocent: the adult voice and implementation of the gaze reactualize the nursery rhyme as a pre-Oedipal fantasy, just as the whole sequence – especially with the disorienting shot preceding the insert – is not without a certain incestuous charm. The subliminal brother–sister relation, however, inscribes the childhood reference with biographical and historical particularity, contextualizing its nostalgic appeal within a field of discursive practices.

Devices that draw attention to the film's status as production abound in *Yesterday Girl*. In addition to the rather infrequent (and rhetorically disjunctive) voice-over, the diegesis is again and again invaded by written titles (either quotations or narrative transitions reminiscent of silent film), commercial illustrations and illuminations (e.g. Christmas imagery), fast motion and other trick photography (often but not always attached to subjective states of consciousness) as well as semi-documentary footage (intersecting the protagonist with non-fictional characters and events). The very notion of diegesis – involving the segregation of screen and spectator spaces, the suppression of the conditions of enunciation, the classical "fiction effect"[7] – becomes problematic in a film that largely avoids editing conventions designed to absorb the viewer into an illusionist space (shot/reverse shot, point of view, etc.) and, by the same token, often acknowledges the offscreen presence of the camera team. Accordingly, the spectator's absorption remains incomplete and fragmentary, all the more since it depends, for narrative motivation, upon a barely compelling plot and a self-consciously unreliable protagonist. The place of the spectator therefore oscillates between a rudimentary kind of identification on the one hand and more indeterminate, pragmatic positions on the other, provoked by the film's stress on discursive activity and plurality.

Considering the formal strategies of self-reflexivity and distanciation in *Yesterday Girl*, it is important to note that the film not merely foregrounds the fact of discourse (as opposed to an imaginary transparency of meaning) but that it focuses its address on the particular quality of language, on particular nuances of diction, dialect, and delivery. As the opening sequences illustrate, discursive performances tend to exceed both narrative motivation and functional subordination to dialogue; they remain semi-autonomous and fragmentary, assuming the status of quotations. Often associated with positions of institutional power, they inevitably reverberate with traces of the German past, regardless of individual speaker and intention. While the film asks us to decipher the political implications of its textual bricolage, it does so, paradoxically, by deflecting spectatorial pleasure towards these discursive performances, in particular their materially contingent yet deeply historical qualities.

One set of discursive performances is motivated by Anita's encounters with official agencies of uplift and correction – e.g. the judge (introduced earlier), a pious and pedantic woman probation officer, a university professor who praises the discipline of reading and listening while ignoring Anita's request for advice. Such characters, with their professionally distorted, abstract rhetoric, are clearly marked as targets of satire, an effect enhanced by the actors' direct address of the camera and hyperbolic style of articulation. Yet there are other characters, equally delineated by their particular diction, who cannot be that easily placed – thus barring the spectator from a position of critical superiority (as an alternative source of identification). What are we to make, for instance, of the appearance of the late Dr Bauer, prosecutor general, whose professed liberal humanism and anti-fascist persona might convince us that the legal establishment is not so unreconstructed after all, whose function for Anita's story, however, is that owing to his fame as well as her lack of aggressiveness he remains inaccessible to her? What of the hotel manager whom we encounter when Anita briefly works as a chambermaid, who digresses from an inventory of his employees through an account of his career to a story about the Russians liberating the concentration camp he was in? Throughout the film, documentary characters are mixed in with actors, professional as well as nonprofessional ones who in turn keep sliding from a Brechtian demonstration of their roles into playing themselves, extemporizing as it appears within an aleatory *mise-en-scène*. This diversity of characters and acting styles lends the web of discourses an empirical impurity, pitting positions of enunciation against each other at oblique angles or conflating them in such contradictory ways that they rarely fall into neatly identifiable ideological slots.

While registering discursive differences with an amazing degree of openness and flexibility, the film nonetheless retains a partisan perspective, urging the spectator to make connections and distinctions. A case in point are the many strands relating to the discourse of education, beginning with the probation officer's lesson in moral semantics. Asked to define general concepts such as the "good" in "doing good," Anita responds, deadpan, "[good is] what does you good." The grotesque tenor of the enterprise, underscored by Anita's punning, is resumed by a variation on the theme, the selling of foreign-language teaching records to young workers and employees, one of Anita's many ephemeral jobs. At a later point in the film, Anita herself is shown buying into a petit-bourgeois belief in upward mobility through self-improvement, albeit on a more idealistic scale: her resolve "to begin a new life" (voice-over) takes her to the university, a move that is doomed from the start given the incompatibility of her high-school degree with West German admission requirements. Anita's visits to classrooms and professorial offices occasion a further parade of institutional discourses, again varying in their degree of reification and mode of enunciation. In addition to the professor already mentioned, there is, on the one hand, Alfred Edel's superb carica-ture of an academic assistant, subservient and self-aggrandizing, who makes Anita's confidence game look harmless by comparison; on the other hand, we overhear part of a lecture by Professor Patzer, a Frankfurt classicist, elaborating on a minor sophist's argument on injustice with an outmoded and touching pedagogical passion.

Yet another aspect of the discourse on education is developed in Anita's relationships with her lovers (i.e. two out of the three). After a brief encoun-ter with a high-school student with whom she discusses the difficulty of "learning not to learn," she gets involved with Pichota, an official in the Hessian Ministry of Culture who eventually – as a written title says – attempts to educate her, since he cannot really help her. The irony of the authorial comment appears fully deserved by the three-part curriculum that follows – reading the train schedule, interpreting a Brecht story, singing an aria from Verdi's *Don Carlos* – yet this irony is effectively subverted by the internal dynamics of the sequence, in particular Anita's responses to Pichota's efforts. Through and against the institutional discourse on education, this sequence redeems the desire to learn, not only as a major source of Anita's strength, but also as a spectatorial disposition encouraged by the textual movement of the film.

Crucial in this respect is the way the film constructs the relationship between the protagonist and the discursive activity motivated by her vagaries. Anita's presence is essential in lending the film a modicum of continuity, in giving the viewer an instance of secondary identification, an emotional, cognitive, intentional focus that partly compensates for the otherwise fragmented organization of the look. At the same time, Anita represents a highly mercurial and artificial character, counteracted only to some extent by the autobiographical affinities the actress brings to the role (GDR background, incomplete assimilation to West German codes of behavior). If she were the heroine of a classical narrative, we would indeed be asked to identify with her as a victim of social indifference and historical insensibility, an object of discursive practices that attempt to position her while actually displacing her all the more thoroughly. Since, however, the textual terms of the film work against such closure, Anita's alienation (*Entfremdung*) functions rather as a strategy of estrangement (*Verfremdung*) in the Brechtian sense. Like the outsider who enters the scene of a family quarrel and, interrupting it, makes the situation legible – and thus change-able – Anita's appearance throws into relief particular discourses that cut across Germany, past and present, East and West. These discourses are not reduced to their function for Anita's story; nor is her character presented as outside or above them – she demonstrates their workings even as she herself participates in them.

Illuminating the peculiar amalgamation of discourses by her ambiguous status (as both inside and outside the fiction), Anita's textual function is to provoke associations that run counter to established patterns of remember-ing and forgetting, associations that are not fully claimed by any particular discourse but depend upon the viewer to fill in the gaps. In the course of her relationship with Pichota, for instance, Anita is seen accompanying him on an official function, a visit to a dogtrainers' club under review for subsidy by the Ministry of Culture. The sequence offers a satire on what Kluge in another context refers to as "the diction of public events."[8] A medium shot shows Anita next to Pichota reading a brief speech from a manuscript, when a slight pan left reveals the audience, i.e. the representative of the club (playing himself) who reciprocates in kind with a speech delivered in a typically Hessian mode of high German. The subsequent demonstration features German shepherd dogs, a detail that, especially in conjunction with Anita's Jewish background, might trigger concentration-camp associations in American audiences, though not necessarily in German ones. Anita's own comment – "the one breed I cannot stand are these bloodhounds" – is unspecific enough, but assumes historical significance precisely because of the way it is denied resonance within the diegesis. The dogtrainer responds, maintaining the imperturbable tone of a dyed-in-the-wool specialist – "Bloodhounds, yes; you're confusing them with the Rottweilers; you see here ten different breeds . . ." – only to slip, almost imperceptibly, in the following sentence ("We would be pleased if more dogs were to come to the club to get information . . ."). The repressed connotation is further twisted by the fact that the demonstration casts the dog in the role of rescuer, troping on (or, actually, literalizing) the 'wolf-in-sheepskin' motif which runs through Anita's encounters with the denizens of Adenauer Germany.

The cognitive dissonances inspired by Anita's presence vacillate between the fictional level of the film and the level of enunciation, this distinction being in itself a fluctuating one. As a fictional character, Anita's responses waver between protest and acquiescence. While the latter offers a partial explanation for her "failure" in narrative terms, the moments of rebellion seem more relevant considering the formal terms by which the spectator is offered access to the film. Anita's first active response – following the evasions into childhood memory and indiscriminate eating – takes the form of verbal mimicry. Besides punning, she resorts to aping the probation officer's pep talk, sanctimoniously intoning: "Don't worry, we will make it. Let us look brightly towards the future!" The next sequence shows a group of people – among them the probation officer and a clergyman – in the living-room of Anita's landlady, Frau Budek, the three talking past each other without listening. From the well-choreographed anarchy of voices emerge fragments of Christian and pseudo-philosophical smalltalk, including speculations on the meanings of homophonic words. With this collage (reminiscent, in its canon effect, of *Last Year in Marienbad/L'Année dernière à Marienbad* [1961]), the soundtrack takes its cue from Anita who is present but silent. More than the obvious point of view of the narrative, she is thus established as an "aural" point of view, sharpening the spectator's ear for the inflections and distortions of social speech while enhancing the overall eroticization of the soundtrack.

Although the notion of an aural point of view is inevitably metaphoric, if not catachrestic, it seems useful in understanding the peculiar way in which the film relays and mediates subjectivity. Given the relative abstention from visual techniques of spectator absorption – *Yesterday Girl* has perhaps less than a handful of actual POVs[9] – the soundtrack takes over this function to some extent, though in a necessarily more differentiated/differentiating fashion, given its emphasis on the heterogeneous (and therefore antithetical) qualities of speech, noise, and music.[10] Moreover, to stay with the disanalogy for yet another moment, images of Anita listening and speaking are far more frequent – and more memorable – than those involving her merely looking or being looked at within the diegesis. As the soundtrack assumes a more active, independently signifying role, the image is in turn set free to comment, question, or counterpoint. This is what lends such interpretive force to Anita's facial expressions and minute gestures, to her many-nuanced look that occasionally, half-accidentally, grazes the camera – material subtleties that foreground the double structure of enunciation, thus setting into play the difference between actress and role.

In its "dual production" of character, *Yesterday Girl* invites a comparison with *Two or Three Things I Know About Her*. While Godard makes the distancing device explicit, introducing first Marina Vlady quoting Brecht ("Actors should quote") and then, over the same footage, the fictional character of Juliette Janson, Kluge presents us with a character whose two parts are both more discrepant and more intertwined. This is an effect not only of different acting styles but also of a different conception of character in relation to narrative and *mise-en-scène*.

Like the story underlying Godard's film, that of *Yesterday Girl* goes back – via the literary version – to an authentic case which Kluge came across when working as a law-clerk. While Godard's interest in his source focused on the practice of prostitution as an extended metaphor of social relations in consumer capitalism, Kluge was preoccupied with the genre of *Lebenslauf*, or life story, as a crossing of narrative form and historical document. Hence Anita appears much less determined by the social, sexual, and economic

terms within which she is constructed and to which she reacts than Godard/
Vlady's Juliette, but remains a more contingent and unpredictable figure –
even (and, perhaps, above all) in relation to the discourse of self-reflexivity
that informs the textual strategies of both films.

The frame of reference that contextualizes the degree of determination as
well as contingency in the narrative of *Yesterday Girl* is as large, contradictory, and overdetermined as that of German history. In Kluge's words:
"Anita and her story are specifically related to the Federal Republic. Her story
[*Geschichte*] would be different if she were living in a different society. And it
would be different if the Germans had a different history [*Geschichte*]."[11]
These are the parameters that demarcate the narrative field, but nothing
more. Anita does not come across as a "type" – in the sense of organic
theories of realism (Engels, late Lukács) – nor do the characters that cross
her path represent a cross-section of German society (in the manner of more
traditionally narrative films like, say, *The Grand Illusion*, *Stagecoach*, or
Open City). While closer to Godard's allegorical pun juxtaposing Juliette
and the Paris region (the "Her" in the film's title), the relationship between
Anita and the Federal Republic rehearses a more complex dynamics of invol-
untary non-identity and disavowed common heritage.

The narrative of *Yesterday Girl* consists of a series of loosely connected
episodes, de-emphasizing a conventional logic of cause and effect, of
enigma, conflict, and closure. The style of narration is highly elliptical,
sketching out a rudimentary plot that allows for a number of barely motivated digressions (many involving documentary characters). Moreover,
there are some minor inconsistencies that are not sufficiently explained by
the possibility, asserted at one point by Pichota in direct address, that Anita
might be lying. In a montage of family photographs, for instance, we
discover among the guests, all *haut bourgeois*, a man wearing the uniform of
the German *Wehrmacht*. Obviously the filmmaker used photographs of the
actress's – and therefore his own – family. Whether a mere blunder, autobiographical indulgence or distancing device, such a "moment of irri-
tation," as Enno Patalas calls it,[12] produces a cognitive constellation that
exceeds narrowly defined standards of realism: the incongruous detail
reflects upon the tragic penchant of German Jews for the social and national
values of a country that was never prepared to accept them.

At this point, a look at "Anita G.," the short story underlying the conception of *Yesterday Girl*, might further elucidate the character's position vis-à-
vis narrative and history. With the opening sentence – "The girl Anita G.,
crouching under the staircase, saw the boots when her grandparents were taken
away"[13] – the story's protagonist is motivated to a far greater degree than that
of the film, grounded in the link between childhood experience and historical
catastrophe. Even the rhetorical questions that conclude the introductory
section rather affirm the foregone determination of the character ("Why does
she constantly infringe on private property as she travels? . . . Why doesn't

this intelligent person regulate her affairs in a satisfactory manner? . . . Why doesn't she behave sensibly? Why doesn't she stay with the man who is making a play for her? Why doesn't she face facts? Doesn't she want to?" [p. 16]). Accordingly, the story's covert narrator endows Anita with a greater degree of pathos, though stylistically suppressed, leaving the reader little choice but to drift with the protagonist toward confinement and nervous breakdown.

Compared to the story, the film minimizes the causal status of Anita's background, focusing instead on its denial as an aspect of contemporary social discourse. Thus her being Jewish is less a matter of narrative/histori-cal motivation than an emblem of absence, a negated term of social and cultural identity. Moreover, the palpable co-authorship of the actress to some extent undermines the pathos emanating from the single authorial voice, resituating it at a more reflective angle, in the interplay of the fictional and the enunciatory elements of the character. When toward the end of the film Anita is supposed to give birth in prison and Alexandra Kluge refuses to simulate this event, the emotional appeal is effectively decentered, leaving the spectator free to absorb the energy and resilience inspired by the actress while acknowledging the impossibility of a happy ending – in narrative as well as historical terms.

Nonetheless, it would be misleading to make "Anita G." sound like a conventional short story that promises its reader a significant insight into the protagonist's life or character. While loyally narrated from Anita's point of view, the story includes a lengthy digression on the famous attorney whom she fails to enlist for her cause (just as he fails to enlist her as his protégée). Moreover, the text rather abruptly shifts in tone and rhythm, from the matter-of-fact terseness of legal reports to microscopic descriptions of physical details (mostly relating to male bodies), from the melancholy slapstick routine of doomed assignations to the dispassionate diagnosis of the state of Anita's health. Finally, the motives listed to account for each of the protagonist's moves do not quite add up to a motivation that would unify the narrative – except for the historical-biographical etiology quoted above.

The fundamental discrepancy between narrative standards of plausibility and actual life stories is raised as an issue early on in the story when, describ-ing a night with her lover, the narrator remarks of Anita: "She gave herself with a simplicity that simple people do not possess either and took care that the stories concerning her past sounded natural" (p. 18; translation modi-fied). Far from characterizing Anita as a liar in a moral sense, this remark aims at the difficulty of telling coherent, conclusive stories about anyone's past without lying, given the way history – and German history in particular – imposes patterns of interruption and discontinuity upon individual lives while dressing up senselessness as fate. The fragmentary, reductive, pseudo-logical account of Anita's case to some degree imitates these patterns, trans-posing them into the fictional yet hybrid genre of *Lebenslauf*; implicitly, it denounces any narrative regime that suppresses the arbitrary and contingent qualities of history, thereby naturalizing the falsely integrated relationship of Germans to their past.

But the desire to tell stories that "sound natural" is not only ideological; it harbors a utopian dimension, through and beyond the fetishistic yearning for a happy end. While "Anita G." refuses the reader the consolations of more traditionally realist types of narrative, it also eludes a fictive sense of inevitability, of fate, suggesting instead the possibility of an alternative course of events. "Don't you have a more cheerful story?" ("Haben Sie nicht eine erfreulichere Geschichte?") says the epigraph preceding the story, in a variation of the Brechtian motto, "It can happen this way but it can also happen in quite a different way." The option implied and rejected in the rhetorical question points beyond textual practices to the realm of historical praxis – the German word *Geschichte* plays on the double meaning of story and history – just as the "you" exceeds the ironic self-address of the narrator to include the reader, singular and plural. When at the end of *Yesterday Girl* Alexandra Kluge's Anita returns the camera's look in an extended close-up, she seems to resume the story's epigraph with precisely that connotation, asking the spectator to conceive of a different history, one in which human life-stories can aspire towards making more sense.

The dialectical mediation of narrative, history, and social praxis incipient in Kluge's first book of stories (*Lebensläufe*) informs not only *Yesterday Girl* but much of his subsequent work as well. As indicated above, Kluge's critique of conventional narrative form, foremost that of the classical Hollywood film and its weak German derivatives, is strongly motivated by a sense of continuing historical catastrophe; this critique notwithstanding, he asserts that the fictional desire which seeks to structure the world according to personal, i.e. the primary relationships (Freud's "family romance"), contains a radical potential, provided the fantasy is contextualized as one among other discursive practices. Undercutting the Metzian opposition of "*histoire*" and "*discours*,"[14] Kluge holds to the basic conception of the cinema as a medium for "telling stories" – "What else is the history of a country but the vastest narrative surface of all?"[15] – despite and in the face of history's masquerading as fate. "Either social history continues to tell its fiction of reality [*Real-Roman*], regardless of human lives, or human beings tell their own story, i.e. counter-history [*Gegengeschichte*]."[16] Although the one participates in the other, there remains a pragmatic difference between textual practice and historical praxis. For Kluge, this gap translates into that between the individual film and the cinema's function within the public sphere, which overlaps with the gap between a textually inscribed cinematic subject and the experience of actual spectators in a given social, political, and cultural context. One obvious strategy towards bridging these multiple gaps has been the "filling-in of the orchestra pit" (Benjamin on Brecht[17]), the breaking down of the illusionist barrier between screen and spectator spaces by means of formal devices as described in connection with *Yesterday Girl*.

The "politics of form," however, cannot be an end in itself, nor is it a guarantee for the cinema's access to history. If *Yesterday Girl* succeeds in asserting its political significance to this day, it is owing to the way the film not only reflects upon its own historicity but also takes up a stance toward history in its particular spatio-temporal figurations. As this is the point at which the film inevitably departs from the literary source, it also urges analysis to go beyond the terms inherited from the model of literary modernism and address the question of figurative modes specific to the cinema. This does not preclude borrowing from other disciplines of interpretation, but it involves a shift in focus from the problem of codes and their subversion to that of tropes and their revision.

In its articulation of space, *Yesterday Girl* does not just subvert the classical continuity system on a formal level – in its refusal of diegetic coherence and closure – but opposes to the fictional purity of classical narrative space an intermittently documentary, historical, and intertextual space. More specifically, this space is developed in the movement between two dominant spatial tropes: on the one hand, the image of *Flucht* (both flight and escape), with its highly traumatic, contradictory resonances in the experiential context of postwar Germany (the term *Flüchtlinge* was reserved for refugees from areas liberated/occupied by the Soviet Army, later from the GDR, though hardly ever used for refugees from Hitler Germany); on the other hand, the magic, untranslatable notion of *Heimat*, the feeling of home which the Nazis literalized into an expansionist politics of space, and which survived, in sentimental disguise, through the 1950s, most palpably in the popular genre of the *Heimatfilm*. Both tropes contain a strong temporal element, involving historical loss and absence; culturally, however, each in its way works to suppress this historical inscription, dehistoricizing the experiential residue.

On the most manifest level, *Yesterday Girl* organizes its spatial and temporal representations along the lines of the plot, following Anita's attempts to escape arrest, to lead a human life and to deal with the consequences of her pregnancy. Thus, Anita's flight describes a circular movement beginning and ending in prison, accelerating in rhythm as her situation seems increasingly hopeless. Cutting across the linear sequence of locations, however, the film visits a series of spaces that often defy narrative rationalization even as flashbacks: images of bourgeois interiors, of a Christmas fair, of painted buildings illuminated from inside, of a hospitable table looking out from a restaurant rotating above the city; in a similar vein, the memory space evoked by the nursery rhyme about the mammoth. Animated by highly emotional music, these images connote a sense of inside versus outside, of safety, protection, warmth, childhood, home – *Heimat*. Moreover, to the extent that they are previously reproduced materials, such inserts, like the music, display the traces of historical usage, and with it the connotation of pastness, of loss. Undoubtedly, a number of them border on the sentimental, the trivial, even kitsch; but they are clearly invested with the protagonist's memory and desire and, more surprisingly, are allowed to appeal to the viewer without the intervention of authorial irony.

At the same time, these imaginary spaces of a seemingly better past are clearly marked in their cultural construction, reflecting upon a peculiarly German tradition of interiority. When Anita seeks out comparable places within the diegesis (in the narrow sense of space denoted by the narrative), she only finds poor copies, empty shells: the Café Kranzler, Frau Budek's and Pichota's living-rooms, a Silesian restaurant, a deserted villa. The obvious discrepancy of hope and reality only sharpens the view for the imaginary quality of the absent idyllic spaces, thus initiating a figurative analysis of a particularly fatal variant of the public/private split.

The social polarization of public and private ("Inside it is warm, outside it is cold"[18]) not only represses the conflicts of those inside to the point of violent eruptions, but also refuses recognition to anything or anyone marked as outside. It is a commonplace of German history that the idealization of the private sphere in terms of eternal human values has as its counterpart the denial of otherness to the point of depersonalization and annihilation. On the basis of her class and cultural background, Anita is part of the tradition that turned its energies on the cultivation of interiority while exploiting those who had neither space nor time of their own; displaced in the name of that same tradition, however, she experiences the public/private distinction as a mechanism of de-privation and alienation. The places she does not seek out but is either unable to maintain or forced to use are structured by a progressive reduction of private space, from the unpaid hotel rooms and the room rented from a landlady who sniffs through her belongings, via the public toilet in which she is seen taking a pregnancy test, to the prison whose receptionist makes an exhaustive inventory of everything but Anita's unborn child. The reduction of private space is epitomized in frequent images of Anita running along with her suitcase(s) as the last of the territories she inhabits. But this trope also evokes a radical sense of freedom and new beginnings, nowhere as poignantly as in the shot in which she opens her suitcase to change clothes, cutting to another in which she washes her shoes in the river, the suitcase standing guard in the foreground to the right.

Nonetheless, why doesn't she try to return to the other side of the public/private division? Why doesn't she find a man to marry, so as to carry out her anarchistic rebellion – like her successor in *Part-Time Work of a Domestic Slave* (*Gelegenheitsarbeit einer Sklavin*, 1973), Roswitha Bronski (also played by Alexandra Kluge) – from within the overheated space of the post-bourgeois nuclear family? The closest Anita gets to this possibility is in her relationship with Pichota. Not coincidentally, their arguments crystallize around issues of space: she would like to stay in his apartment after he leaves,

Plate 29 Stopping to wash her shoes in the Rhine: a poignant moment in Anita G.'s odyssey through West Germany. Photo courtesy of Stiftung Deutsche Kinemathek.

just for ten minutes, and he refuses; he reprimands her for not having a proper residence ("You cannot live like a gypsy") and she takes him to a construction site of which she, in vain, pretends to have bought a share; he vows her unconditional love, in front of a map partly visible on the wall, promising to go with her "to Africa or Alaska, wherever, and start a new life," to which she replies, "Why don't you?" – of course, he doesn't.

Besides his being a married man (whose wife is rather confidently waiting out the end of the affair), the prohibition against Anita's settling down with Pichota is linked to her compulsion to repeat, as suggested by the prominent position of circular figures at certain points in the film. This repetition compulsion revolves around the authority and social status attached to the father. Significantly, she meets Pichota in a *paternoster* lift, a rotating elevator to be found in office buildings or factories. Through the end of their relationship, Pichota, incapable of becoming a husband to her, assumes a paternal role ("educating" her; urging her to find work and an apartment; giving her money as they say goodbye). The image of Anita's father, first introduced in the montage of her family photographs, where it is already emphasized as an excerpt (with only the *Wehrmacht* officer behind him), reappears in an imaginary sequence following her ill-fated efforts to find help in the university. This sequence, with its night-for-night lighting, fast motion and trick photography raises the sense of psychic and political over-determination to a nightmarish, absurd, and apocalyptic pitch (intertitle: "Does yesterday come tomorrow?"), relating the authoritarian structure of the private sphere – a mother consents to choosing which of her two children is going to have his brain-pan emptied – to the increasingly refined persistence of totalitarian systems. Yet this is also the only sequence in which Anita effectively directs any aggression against her pursuers (e.g. stepping on the hand of the probation officer); still on the run, though furious, she concludes the imaginary revolt by directly addressing the viewer with a quotation from Jean Cayrol, cheerfully asserting the intention to arrange oneself in the present, deficient as it may be.[19]

Outside this episode, however, Anita neither breaks the circle nor retreats, but moves on, into ever more open, more public and impersonal spaces – spaces whose distance from anything resembling a home is underscored by a predominantly long-shot range. After leaving Pichota (who remains leaning against an octagonal booth while the camera pans with Anita walking away), a long sequence, intermittently accompanied by tango, Christmas, and pop music, shows her in different German cities, crossing bridges, rushing through streets, dashing into and out of a hotel (fast motion) as well as a movie theater, temporarily resting in the middle of a large, partly wooded traffic circle near Frankfurt airport. The last shot is taken from a car travelling around the area at relatively fast speed, encircling Anita sitting on her suitcase, blurred and immobilized; in the subsequent close shots we see her looking upward, her gaze following the departing airplanes.

Nothing could be further away from the images of idyllic interiority that are concentrated in the first half of the film, building up a critique of the public sphere by their systematic absence in the second, which is counter-pointed in turn by the continuation of the music. Yet in the cinematic exploration of the public/private split, the figure of flight and the figure of the circle are intertwined to suggest two sides of one and the same predicament. Historically, this predicament can be attributed to the combination of "being elsewhere" with "the desperate wish to 'be at home' in a manner at once intense, fruitful and destructive" which Gershom Scholem considered as the clue to the relationship of the Jews to the Germans.[20] In a key image of *Yesterday Girl*, the dualistic tension observed by Scholem becomes emblematic, when Anita and the high-school student are shown talking and making love on a November Sunday and the radio starts playing the *Deutschlandlied* at which point the image track, quoting from their previous walk in a Jewish cemetery, inserts depictions of hares on Hebrew-lettered gravestones; the conflicting connotations of the tune are further compounded by the young man's humming along in a modified West German version ("Unity and justice and liberty for the *whole* fatherland") while Anita contributes a line from the Becher/Eisler version ("Happiness and peace . . .").

If *Yesterday Girl* envisions the painful contradiction of "being elsewhere" combined with the wish to "be at home," this has less to do with the fictional Jewishness of the protagonist than with an elective affinity on the part of the filmmaker for the intellectual tradition most strongly associated with the attempt to analyze and revise that contradiction – the tradition of Critical Theory and the Frankfurt School.[21] Kluge's indebtedness to the philosophy of history of Benjamin and Bloch, each with their own peculiar blend of Jewish messianism and Marxism, is widely recognized and cannot be elaborated here. Suffice it to illustrate this influence by pointing out that the spatial figurations discussed in *Yesterday Girl* do not have any primacy as spaces (an obvious contrast would be the American western), but are functions of an intense and complex temporality. This sense of time is predicated on the experience of the diaspora, on being displaced in history; to compensate for this displacement by social status (as part of Anita attempts) inevitably marks a spatial short-circuit, the regressive illusion of being at home. On the other hand, since history itself is a falling away from paradise, accumulating catastrophe in the degree that it proceeds as if it were linear progress, we have no choice but to turn around and confront the wreckage left behind, hoping to read meaning in the spatialized fragments of time. Anita's contradictory movement answers to Benjamin's backward-flying angel of history, just as Kluge's montage clusters aspire to the epistemological status of Benjamin's "dialectical image," an image "in which the past and the now flash into a constellation."[22] Though Anita is not as professional an assistant to Benjamin's angel as history teacher Gabi Teichert in *The Patriot* (*Die Patriotin*, 1979), she likewise unhinges historical/cinematic fictions of a coherent vision, offering instead cognitive and affective constellations that engage the spectator in a process of revision.

The more difficult aspect of Kluge's commitment to the Frankfurt School, especially Adorno, relates to his concept of representation, which is defined by the paradoxical ambition to undermine the very mechanism of representation. With respect to this ambition, Adorno's writings on film music (together with Hanns Eisler), on the philosophy of modern music, and on aesthetic theory have to be considered at least as influential as his lifelong indictment of the false immediacy of the photographic image in the context of the mass media. The distinction between *Bild* (image) and *Abbild* (mirror image), essential to this indictment, hinges upon an antithetical conception of aesthetic form. On the one hand, Adorno takes Nietzsche's definition of art as the desire to be different, to be elsewhere, to the extreme, assimilating it to the Jewish taboo on representation; on the other hand, he (like Benjamin) rehabilitates the concept of mimesis, in opposition to Marxist theories of reflection (*Widerspiegelung*): works of art are "images that do not image" (*bilderlose Bilder*) in so far as they are "sediments of the subject's experience beyond conscious will and identity,"[23] containing a secular promise of happiness in their very difference of form. Whenever Adorno discusses the aesthetic possibilities of film in a context other than polemical, he grants the medium a potential for such mimetic experience, provided it dissolves the patterns of a superficial narrative realism and instead derives the construction of cinematic material from its formal affinity with the stream of associations in the human mind.[24]

Yesterday Girl, like all of Kluge's films, testifies to Adorno's aesthetics of negativity in its self-conscious ambivalence toward the power of representation. There is hardly a filmmaker whose images claim so little presence in themselves (diametrically opposed to Werner Herzog, for instance). Whether by means of sound (music as much as verbal resonances), associational montage, or the crossing of fictional and documentary *mise-en-scène*, the individual image is consistently split in its temporal connotations, evoking disparate layers of time and experience, thus enacting the thematic disjunction of past and present by a systematic deferment, dispersal, fragmentation of specular unity. Despite this subversion of visual pleasure, the meaning of such images cannot be reduced to their discursive construction, nor should they be explained away as exercises in self-reflexivity. The emphasis on temporality is linked – through the negation of space as the domain of sight – to the eroticization of the soundtrack discussed earlier, its reclamation as a relatively autonomous, potentially antithetical force of signification. By figuring the split into the film's sound/image relations, Kluge attempts nothing less than to exorcise as well as contain the fetishism, the mechanism of ego-splitting that is the basis of classical representation. Fascination is to be redeemed by its mediation through the ear, enabling the cinema to convey mimetic experience of a second degree while avoiding the pitfalls of the *Gesamtkunstwerk*.[25]

This tension between distanciation and fascination, between the pain of knowledge and the knowledge of pleasure, characteristically animates all of Kluge's films. It is no coincidence that the lovers' curriculum in *Yesterday Girl* features both Brecht and Verdi. Brecht's story about Herr K. ("What would you do if you were in love with someone?") addresses the basic split of erotic – and hence all – image-making; at the same time, and especially in Pichota's rendering of the story, it reseals this split with didactic irony. Anita's response to this exercise, her friendly and perhaps unwitting refusal to understand the message, effectively deconstructs the ethics of distanciation, while Pichota's impassioned rehearsal of Philip's aria from Act II of *Don Carlos* ("*Ella giàmmai m'amò*") undercuts the melodramatic impact of the music by the very terms of enunciation, including Anita's half-absorbed, half-knowing look as she sings along. In its multiple layers of irony and reflexivity, this ensemble nonetheless conveys a unique affective appeal, a moment of reconciliation under and against untenable conditions.

The scene of instruction is not only Anita's but that of the filmmaker as well. The confrontation between film and literature which crucially shaped Kluge's career has always been counterpointed, in his films, by references to opera, a cultural institution a radical filmmaker starting out in the 1960s could only have viewed with ambivalence. If in his most recent film, *The Power of Emotion* (*Die Macht der Gefühle*, 1983), opera assumes a paradigmatic function for exploring the institution of cinema, this does not necessarily mean a rejection of literary paradigms. It merely resumes and develops the dialectics of mimetic-expressive and discursive-reflective elements that inform Kluge's best work from *Yesterday Girl* on, suggesting a more complex conception of radical cinema than film theory has provided thus far.

Notes

1. Enno Patalas and Frieda Grafe, "Alexander Kluge" (interview), *Filmkritik*, No. 117 (September 1966), 490ff.; on Lang's significance for the new generation of German filmmakers see Alexander Kluge and Klaus Eder, *Ulmer Dramaturgien: Reibungsverluste* (Munich: Hanser, 1980), p. 31. For more biographical background on Kluge, cf. Rainer Lewandowski, *Alexander Kluge* (Munich: Beck/Edition Text und Kritik, 1980), pp. 7–14.

2. Patalas/Grafe, 487.

3. The English title, *Yesterday Girl*, reduces a complex historical constellation by putting the burden of discontinuity on the protagonist; the French title, like the Italian, "Girl without (Hi)story," also personalizes but from the opposite angle. The point these translations miss is that both Anita and the people she encounters are products of the same history, albeit on different sides, and that neither she nor they have access to – or engage in a meaningful relationship with – that history. For an elaborate analysis of the German relationship to history, cf. Alexander Kluge and Oskar Negt, *History and Obstinacy* (*Geschichte und Eigensinn*) (Frankfurt am Main: Zweitausendeins, 1981), part II, pp. 361–769.

4. Reinhard Baumgart in an essay from *Merkur*; quotation identified in: Alexander Kluge, *Abschied von Gestern: Protokoll*, ed. Enno Patalas (Frankfurt am Main: Filmkritik, n.d.), p. 7.

5. Roland Barthes, "The grain of the voice" (1972), in *Image-Music-Text*, ed. and trans. Stephen Heath (New York: Hill & Wang, 1977), p. 181.

6. The "politics of the voice" and the problem of an alternative use of voice-over are discussed by Mary Ann Doane, in "The voice in the cinema: the articulation of body and space," *Yale French Studies*, No. 60 (1980), 33–50. A more explicitly feminist focus on some of the same issues can be found in Kaja Silverman, "Disembodying the female voice," in *Re-Vision: Essays in Feminist Film Criticism*, ed. Mary Ann Doane, Patricia Mellenkamp and Linda Williams (Frederick, Md.: University Publications, 1984), pp. 131–49. B. Ruby Rich's critique of Kluge as a "patriarchal modernist" is partly based on her understanding of his voice-over in terms of a conventional discursive authority. See "She says, he says: the power of the narrator in modernist film politics," *Discourse*, No. 6 (Fall 1983), 31–47; for an implicit reply to such charges see my comments on Kluge's voice-over in *Germany in Autumn* (1978), in the same issue, 66ff.

7. Cf. Christian Metz, *The Imaginary Signifier: Psychoanalysis and the Cinema*, trans. Celia Britton and Annwyl Williams (Bloomington: Indiana University Press, 1982), parts I–III. On the historical formation of diegesis as process and effect cf. Noël Burch, "Narrative/diegesis – Thresholds, limits," *Screen*, 23, No. 2 (July–August 1982), 16–33.

8. Chapter heading in Kluge and Edgar Reitz's "City Symphony" on Frankfurt, *In Danger and Extremities the Middle Road Leads to Death* (*In Gefahr und grösster Not bringt der Mittelweg den Tod*, 1974).

9. The few optical point-of-view constructions to be found in *Yesterday Girl* are invariably related to either a failure in narrative terms (e.g. a scene on the stairs showing Anita getting thrown out by a landlady, or the one in which she is seen missing her chance to approach Dr Bauer) or a lack of positive results when the expectation of authentic vision was previously raised (e.g. when Anita claims to have bought a share in an apartment building and makes Pichota drive all the way to a construction site). The trope of the failed or failing POV runs through a number of Kluge's films, usually attached to a will, a desire, or a project that defies a linear-positivist conception of aims, means, and results; cf. Miriam B. Hansen, "Alexander Kluge, cinema and the public sphere: the construction site of counter-history," *Discourse*, No. 6 (Fall 1983), 68–70.

10. For a descriptive analysis of music in Kluge's films see Rudolf Hohlweg, "Musik für den Film – Film für Musik: Annäherung an Herzog, Kluge, Straub," in *Herzog/Kluge/Straub*, ed. Peter W. Jansen and Wolfram Schütte (Munich: Hanser, 1976), pp. 52–61.

11. Patalas/Grafe, 624.

12. Enno Patalas, "*Abschied von gestern* (Anita G.)," *Filmkritik*, No. 119 (November 1966), 624.

13. Alexander Kluge, *Attendance List for a Funeral*, trans. Leila Vennewitz (New York: McGraw Hill, 1966), p. 15; the German original first appeared in *Lebensläufe* (Stuttgart: Goverts, 1962).

14. Christian Metz, "Story/discourse (a note on two kinds of voyeurism)," *The Imaginary Signifier*, pp. 89–98.

15. Alexander Kluge, *Die Patriotin* (Frankfurt am Main: Zweitausendeins, 1979), p. 40; trans. by Thomas Y. Levin and Miriam B. Hansen in *New German Critique*, Nos 24–5 (Fall/Winter 1981–2), 206.

16. Alexander Kluge, *Gelegenheitsarbeit einer Sklavin: Zur realistischen Methode* (Frankfurt am Main: Suhrkamp, 1975), p. 222. Cf. Hansen, *Discourse*, 64ff.

17. Walter Benjamin, *Understanding Brecht* (London: NLB, 1973), p. 1.

18. Voice-over comment, *Part-Time Work of a Domestic Slave* (*Gelegenheitsarbeit einer Sklavin*, 1973); sequence description in Kluge, *Gelegenheitsarbeit*, p. 143; also cf. pp. 150, 176–8, 188–94.

19. "To make up with a friend after a quarrel, to take the rotten eggs that they throw at you with a grain of salt, to uphold human dignity even in the face of an unkempt housewife or a stone-deaf old man . . ." (Jean Cayrol, *The Cold Sun*), Kluge, *Abschied von gestern*, p. 59.

20. Gershom Scholem, "Jews and Germans" (1966), repr. in *On Jews and Judaism in Crisis* (New York: Schocken, 1976), p. 82.

21. In *Ulmer Dramaturgien* (note 1, above), p. 116, Kluge lists Jewish theology as one of his "sources," along with Critical Theory. Unlike most of the younger generation of the German left, Kluge has not purged Critical Theory of its Jewishness but recognizes this Jewishness as one of its crucial radical dimensions.

22. Walter Benjamin, *Das Passagen-Werk*, N2a, 3, vol. 1 (Frankfurt am Main: Suhrkamp, 1983), p. 576; translation of the whole section N (Epistemology, Theory of Progress) by Leigh Hafey and Richard Sieburth in *The Philosophical Forum*, 15, Nos 1–2 (Fall/Winter 1983–4), 1–40. Also see his "Theses on the philosophy of

history," *Illuminations*, ed. Hannah Arendt, trans. Harry Zohn (New York: Schocken, 1969), pp. 253–64.

23. Theodor W. Adorno, *Ästhetische Theorie* (Frankfurt am Main: Suhrkamp, 1970), p. 422. For an alternative translation of this passage see Adorno, *Aesthetic Theory*, trans. C. Lenhardt (London: Routledge & Kegan Paul, 1984), p. 396.

24. Theodor W. Adorno, *Minima Moralia* (Frankfurt am Main: Suhrkamp, 1951), p. 266; and, especially, "Transparencies on film" (1966), trans. Thomas Y. Levin, *New German Critique*, Nos 24–5 (Fall/Winter 1981–2), 199–205; 201. On the relationship between Adorno and Kluge see my introduction, "Theodor W. Adorno, 'Transparencies on film': an introduction," *New German Critique*, Nos 24–5 (Fall/Winter 1981–2), 186–98.

25. Kluge, following Adorno on Wagner, is much aware of the pitfalls of film's synaesthetical potential, warning against the "dangers of the '*Gesamtkunstwerk*'" in the early essay (co-authored with Edgar Reitz and Wilfried Reinke), "Wort und Film," *Sprache im technischen Zeitalter*, No. 13 (1965), 1020. Kluge's soundtrack is clearly indebted to the paradigm of modern (atonal, serial) music as proposed for the cinema by Adorno and Eisler in *Composing for the Films* (1947), though the individual musical material used is hardly ever modern in that narrow sense. Cf. David Bordwell, "The musical analogy," *Yale French Studies*, No. 60 (1980), 141–56, and Philip Rosen, "Adorno and film music: theoretical notes on *Composing for the Films*," ibid., 157–82.

Script

Alexander Kluge. *Abschied von gestern*. Ed. Enno Patalas. Frankfurt am Main: Filmkritik, n.d.

Selected Bibliography

Bechtold, Gerhard. *Sinnliche Wahrnehmung von sozialer Wirklichkeit. Die multimedialen Montage-Texte Alexander Kluges*. Tübingen: Narr, 1984.
Böhm-Christl, Thomas (ed.) *Alexander Kluge*. Frankfurt am Main: Suhrkamp, 1983.
Dawson, Jan (ed.). *Alexander Kluge & The Occasional Work of a Female Slave*. Perth: Perth Film Festival, 1975.
Hansen, Miriam B. "Alexander Kluge, cinema and the public sphere: the construction site of counter-history." *Discourse*, No. 6 (Fall 1983), 53–74.
—— "Alexander Kluge: crossings between film, literature, critical theory." In *Film und Literatur: Literarische Texte und der neue deutsche Film*. Ed. Sigrid Bauschinger, Susan L. Cocalis, and Henry A. Lea. Berne and Munich: Francke, 1984, pp. 169–96.
—— "Collaborative *auteur* cinema and oppositional public sphere: Alexander Kluge's contribution to *Germany in Autumn*." *New German Critique*, Nos 24–5 (Fall/Winter 1981–2), 36–56.
Jansen, Peter W. and Wolfram Schütte (eds). *Herzog/Kluge/Straub*. Munich: Hanser, 1976.
Kluge, Alexander. "On film and the public sphere." Trans. Thomas Y. Levin and Miriam B. Hansen. *New German Critique*, Nos 24–5 (Fall/Winter 1981–2), 206–20.
—— and Klaus Eder. *Ulmer Dramaturgien. Reibungsverluste*. Munich: Hanser, 1980.

Kötz, Michael and Petra Höhne. *Sinnlichkeit des Zusammenhangs: Zur Filmarbeit von Alexander Kluge*. Cologne: Prometh, 1981.

Lewandowski, Rainer. *Alexander Kluge*. Munich: Beck/Edition Text und Kritik, 1980.

—— *Die Filme von Alexander Kluge*. Hildesheim and New York: Olms, 1980.

Neuer Deutscher Film. Ed. Verband der deutschen Filmclubs. Mannheim: Internationale Filmwoche, 1967.

Patalas, Enno. "*Abschied von gestern* (Anita G.)." *Filmkritik*, 10, No. 11 (November 1966), 623–5.

14

BRIGITTE PEUCKER

The invalidation of Arnim: Herzog's *Signs of Life* (1968)

The mode of adaptation to which Herzog resorts in *Signs of Life* (*Lebenszeichen*) can best be characterized as what Dudley Andrew calls cinematic "borrowing."[1] Although there is a rough correspondence between the basic narrative situations of Achim von Arnim's *The Mad Invalid at the Fort Ratonneau* (*Der tolle Invalide auf dem Fort Ratonneau*, 1818) and *Signs of Life*, similarities of plot can never be the focus of interest in any attempt to locate the intersection of literary models with this or with any of Herzog's films. In cinematic borrowing, as Andrew says, "the main concern is the generality of the original, its potential for wide and varied appeal; in short, its existence as a continuing form or archetype in culture."[2] As we know, the archetypal or mythological is Herzog's mode; not one to submit easily to the imagination of others, for him the appeal of the archetype lies partly in its impersonality and partly in its availability for continuous and radical revision. Herzog also prefers borrowing – thus defined – because it reflects his conviction that film shares the status of the other arts and is, as they are, a legitimate form of cultural expression.[3] In fact, the rhetorical thrust of Herzog's *oeuvre* extends far beyond the attempt merely to legitimize film; he attempts to undermine the parity of the arts and assert the superiority of film over literature. In declaring that film is the "art of illiterates,"[4] Herzog wishes to claim both for himself – as a truly "illiterate" filmmaker – and for what he would consider to be "genuine" filmmaking, an astonishingly thorough-going independence from literature.[5] Since he does not wish to repudiate all of the arts as sources of inspiration – he is quick to acknowledge the influence of music – Herzog's rhetoric against literature and other written texts is worthy of special attention. In considering the extent of Herzog's independence from Arnim (among others), I think the object of his repudiation is not so much literature as verbal language in general, which is treated everywhere in his work as an untrustworthy mediation.

Critics have often correctly cited Herzog's concern with a "primordial innocence of vision'';[6] his films do strive for new images, for a new cinematic vocabulary. As all his films indicate, Herzog is more interested in the visual code of cinema than in its narrative code. However – and here the matter is complicated somewhat – although the films generally express disapproval of the written text precisely as that which is merely narratable, throughout Herzog's work there are nevertheless traces of literary indebtedness. By proclaiming the ''primordial innocence'' of his imagination – and not least its innocence of literary influence – Herzog by no means extricates himself from the snares of literary concerns and literary history. Indeed, Herzog's proclamation of his originality and his claim to have achieved a more direct, less mediated vision than the literary one are in themselves the ideological signals that align him most closely with the literature of visionary romanticism. This does not mean that Herzog is being somehow ''dishonest'' when he makes use of the rhetoric of romanticism. Rather, it indicates how his literary inheritance must necessarily manifest itself in his films, how a hostility toward the written text – and more fundamentally toward language itself – is at least in part an effort to draw the spectator's attention away from the literary influences that a given film may reflect.

Signs of Life is an interesting case in this regard, because rather uncharacteristically Herzog has never denied having based his screenplay (which won the prestigious Carl Mayer Prize in 1964) on Achim von Arnim's novella. A practical reason for Herzog's overt borrowing at this early point in his career may be that in Germany it is easier to fund films whose screenplays are ''legitimized'' by their connection with works of ''high culture.'' (It is understandable, incidentally, that a culture that requires film to dignify itself in this way might provoke hostility on the part of some filmmakers toward that culture's literature.) But there are aesthetic reasons as well. It is hardly surprising that Herzog should have felt the appeal of the novella form. The preference among German directors in general for a selective imagery, and also, ultimately, for allegory, may be traced, both as an ethical and an aesthetic preference, to the literature of German romanticism and to the narrative forms of the nineteenth century. These strains are met most clearly in the German novella, whose tight construction and highly allegorical quality distinguish it from the ''slice of life'' that grew to dominate the short story and other forms in England and France. (A similar distinction can be made between the Anglo-French novel of manners and the more allegorical German novel.) Ultimately ethical in its message, which nearly always concerns the relation of the individual to society, the novella makes its point by means of symbols which dominate and control the reader's interpretation of the narrative. It is, then, often an object-oriented, in some sense *visual*, literary form. In choosing, for instance, to adapt Heinrich von Kleist's novella, *The Marquise of O . . .* (*Die Marquise von O . . .*, 1808) for his 1976 German film, Eric Rohmer recognized the potential of a novella aesthetic for film; this film differs from Rohmer's French ''moral tales'' precisely in that it is allegorical and image-oriented.

Arnim's *The Mad Invalid* shares with other novellas the tendency to be centered upon one or two image complexes that govern the reader's interpretation of the tale. Arnim's opening passages immediately mark the image of fire as the privileged one: the commander of Marseilles, lost in a reverie while gazing into the fire ablaze in his hearth, imagines the fireworks display with which he intends to commemorate the birthday of the king. Involved as he is in his daydream, the commander does not realize that his wooden leg, with which he has been pushing olive branches into the blaze, has caught fire. From this short sequence alone it is apparent that the "fire" complex of images governs the theme of imagination, exemplified here by the commander's reverie itself and by its content: the imagined fireworks, the "art form" which the commander practices. In fact, in his daydream the commander designs – and "watches" – the progression of the fireworks display in its entirety, culminating in a "grand finale." What the commander imagines, then, is an arranged sequence of images, complete with "soundtrack": an abstract film, in short, without a narrative line.

The opening sequence presents, in a minor key, the issues surrounding the main character, the mad invalid Francoeur, who, like his commander, is a passionate "fire artist" (*Feuerkünstler*). The dangers of the imagination, presented in a comical vein in the case of the commander, are more serious in the case of Francoeur, whose madness allows him no control over his passions. Francoeur is excitable to the point of extreme violence; the actual fireworks display which he sets off, punctuated by cannon-balls and fire-bombs, is an act of aggression, a siege of the city as well as a visual display. When the commander sees entwined olive leaves burning in his fire, he is reminded of hearts united in love. Francoeur's murderous passion, by contrast – his very "art" – is inspired by the unjustified suspicion that his wife has been unfaithful. Arnim implies that the perverted art practiced by Francoeur is the result not only of his madness, but of improperly interpreted and channeled libidinal impulses. Herzog tends to downplay this kind of motivation in his characters, in whom the libido is in general wholly sublimated into more visionary pursuits. (Ironically, this is so even in the case of the vampire, Nosferatu.) But in fact the passion of Arnim's Francoeur also has its sublimated element – which is to say, an allegorical dimension: it is a rebellious assertion of the Self against the World. When Francoeur claims at one point that he feels as though he could devour the world, he is not merely describing his physical hunger. The explosion of fireworks signals the transformation of physical *and* metaphysical passion into the highly concentrated art of the megalomaniac, an art which is also a "play" for power: Francoeur, mediated by Herzog's protagonist in *Signs of Life*, is a precursor of Aguirre, the visionary solipsist who wishes to "direct history as others direct plays."

Herzog's images, themes, and ethos, as critics have repeatedly pointed out and Herzog has repeatedly denied, find their origins in the literature and painting of German romanticism. It should therefore come as no surprise that Herzog should have gone to the literature of romanticism in order to find a text upon which to base the screenplay for his first feature-length film. However this may be, the differences between Arnim and Herzog remain more important than the similarities. It has been remarked that a burgeoning realism is present in Arnim's novella.[7] It contains a wealth of literary detail, so much so that the reader is more aware of the author's pleasure in representation than of the ideas his representation is meant to concretize. Furthermore, the novella's treatment of Francoeur's madness is clinical rather than visionary: it was caused, we learn, by a splinter that remained in his head-wound. And if the cure of his madness is magical – his wife's faith and love lead to the removal of the splinter – it is a magic of the most conventional and non-visionary kind. In this and other ways, the restoration of social order in Arnim's novella vitiates the theme of imagination, and demonstrates a conventionality and optimism quite foreign to Herzog. From *Signs of Life* on, the theme of madness is closely and unflinchingly connected with the theme of imagination. Repeatedly, Herzog has portrayed the negative side – the "night side" – of the romantic imagination; both Francoeur and Stroszek, his counterpart in *Signs of Life*, are figures of negative romanticism, but in Herzog this negativity is never redeemed or rationalized.[8]

Herzog adds to his preoccupation with the inward-turning imagination another concern not shared by Arnim's novella, one that is generally more pronounced in the literature of the English romantic tradition than the German. This is the concern for the doubly alienated situation of man within nature – a nature that is, on the one hand, sublime and indifferent, and is represented, on the other, by the relentless cycle of generation and decay characteristic of the organic world. Herzog's man, in other words, is belittled by the indifference of nature and at the same time degraded by his identification with it. Nature itself becomes a kind of language, a set of "life signs" as inscrutable as hieroglyphics.

Loosely following the plot of *The Mad Invalid*, Herzog's film begins as the central character Stroszek, his Greek wife, and two other German soldiers are sent to a fortress on the Greek island of Kos so that Stroszek may recover from war injuries. As the Seven Years War forms a distant – and rather insignificant – backdrop for Arnim's narrative, so *Signs of Life* takes place during World War II, but this war never intrudes upon the world of the film. (The specificity of social and historical detail is rarely Herzog's concern, and, as if to document this unconcern, he has put some of the soldiers in his film into inappropriate uniforms.) Stroszek's initial view of the island, described by a lurching shot through narrow streets, ends in 180-degree pans back and forth that already suggest his disturbed vision, his inability to find an object upon which to focus.

The isolated and enclosed fortress, an island within an island, seems to exist apart from time itself, and the feeling of being hermetically sealed off from the world generates tensions among its four inhabitants. Stroszek wanders about aimlessly, while Meinhard, one of his companions, takes on the task of terrorizing the animal kingdom. Meinhard invents traps for cockroaches and concocts schemes for making caterpillars crawl in circles. His cruelty stems from a revulsion at the teeming organic world around him, accentuated by the relentless buzzing of bees and chirping of cicadas one hears on the soundtrack. By creating a microcosm of which he is the director, Meinhard avenges himself on the process world. There are other life signs within the citadel as well, signs of a past civilization embodied in ruins: these are the votive tablets and crumbling statues of ancient Greece, all nearly covered over with grass and flowers. Becker, the third soldier, reacts to the sense of timelessness he experiences in the citadel by seeking refuge in these evidences of the past. A philologist, he attempts to decipher the tablets, as though to find in their inscriptions the solution to the riddle of existence.

Whether it is manifested in the ciphers and scrawls of its own process or in the course of taking revenge on the memorial ciphers of past culture, nature is a relentless adversary in this film. The sun seems always to be at high noon, the hour of Pan and pandemonium. The camera lingers over the details of the

Plate 30   Herzog's fascination with even the smallest signs of life: Meinhard (Wolf-gang Reichmann) and Stroszek (Peter Brogle) attend to a tiny insect caught in a figurine. Photo courtesy of Stiftung Deutsche Kinemathek.

landscape, visible through a flickering veil of heat. Herzog's narrative is punctuated with a series of close-ups of flowers, rocks and insects. Shot through a wide-angle lens, man seems reduced and trivial against an impassive landscape. Like Meinhard, Stroszek feels horror at the relentlessness of natural process, which seems determined to obscure the traces of human culture. On the other hand, the sublimity of the sun and sea threatens his sense of self, already in the process of deterioration. When Stroszek's loss of identity becomes acute, he and Meinhard request permission to leave the fortress. While on patrol to the center of the island, the two men arrive at a hilltop from which a singular sight is visible. A panorama shot that lasts an entire minute reveals 10,000 turning windmills in the valley below.[9] These whirling windmills resemble insects on slender legs and thus seem to be gigantic equivalents of the vermin marshalled by Meinhard. The sight of them drives Stroszek mad, and, in a gesture undoubtedly meant to evoke Don Quixote, he fires his rifle in their direction. Many of Herzog's characters will live, like Don Quixote, in the world of their imaginations, and will set out, as he did, on a solipsistic quest. The turning windmills generate the central image of Herzog's *oeuvre*, circular motion, and place it in the context of Don Quixote's inward-turning imagination, madness, idealism – and their futility.

Plate 31 Stroszek runs amok, chasing the others out of the fort and challenging the elements. He becomes a fanatic, taking his own preventive measures against a world that threatens him. Photo courtesy of Stiftung Deutsche Kinemathek.

Overwhelmed and oppressed by nature's vast inscrutability, Stroszek is determined in his madness to take up its challenge, to "make the earth tremble." He evicts the others from the fort and assumes command, terrorizing the town. Unable to interpret the life signs that surround him, he determines now to see "what really lay beneath the surface of things." In his rebellion against nature, Stroszek hopes to compete on equal terms with it. He wishes literally to unearth answers to his questions just as an earthquake had earlier unearthed the ancient statuary and tablets, and he seeks to rival the sun with his fireworks. Like the great rebel angel, Lucifer, he feels that he must "counteract light with light." As night falls, Stroszek's fire-signs reillumine the darkening sky in seeming victory, but as day breaks the sun resumes its position of supremacy. Nature is confirmed once for all as a merely indifferent antagonist; the cycle – the circling – of day and night goes on, and Stroszek, whose rage has resulted in the death of no more than a donkey, and whose search for answers has only "unearthed" a chair, concedes defeat. The film ends with an image of a small truck as it progresses along a dusty road in a vast landscape, carrying Stroszek away. Echoing the film's opening image, it imposes a sad circularity upon the film as a whole.

Herzog tends to stress pictorial representation – the image – in his films at the expense of verbal narrative. In fact, voice-over narration is often undermined by the visual narration that takes place on the screen; *Fata Morgana* (1970) and *Aguirre, the Wrath of God* (*Aguirre, der Zorn Gottes*, 1972) are notable examples of this technique. What we *see*, Herzog feels, is what we should believe – it is the non-deceptive component of the narrative. In *Signs of Life*, however, there is as yet little sign of a disjunction between the image and the word. Herzog's narrator, who is characterized by a flat, distanced monotone, comments upon Stroszek's behavior – sometimes negatively – with more or less unquestionable authority. He tells us, for instance, with inevitable irony, that Stroszek "failed to set the sun on fire," but concedes fairly on the other hand that "there is something titanic in his rebellion against everything." In this film, far from being ridiculed by what occurs on screen, the narrator is more conventionally presented as the sole available guide to the spectator's reading of Stroszek's experience. One reason for Herzog's trust in the voice-over narration on this occasion may lie in the fact that the narration is not based upon a written text, as it will be later, for example, in *Aguirre*.

Arnim's tale is told by a third-person, omniscient narrator whose presence is barely felt until the final paragraph of the narrative. There, we notice the narrator primarily in his struggle to end his story. His attempts at closure are rather conventional. He claims, among other gestures, that after events such as the ones he has described, few human beings experience anything further that is worth the telling. On the whole, however, the reader is unaware of the narrator, whose point of view is presumably expressed by the moral he appends to his tale. It is the light tone of the novella, the counterpoint created by its humorous details, that act as a more continuous commentary on the actions of the central character.

So far, then, we have observed that Herzog's adaptation of Arnim, while it makes use of the skeletal plot of the novella and is likewise image-oriented, manifests few of the stylistic transpositions on which theoreticians thrive. We have also begun to suggest a reason for Herzog's divergence from his source: like the obscured inscriptions in the citadel, Arnim's text is itself part of the frustration with which Herzog's film is concerned, the frustration at the way even life itself is mediated by "signs," by its own indecipherable appearances. What Herzog does inherit from Arnim, however, is the suggestion of the diabolic in his predicament. Arnim's novella is not only centered upon the multivalent image of fire, but is also characterized by the repeated, self-conscious play on the word "devil." While film cannot render linguistic tropes as such, it can create visual metaphors in their place, and Herzog does transpose this aspect of Arnim's text. In *The Mad Invalid*, the word "devil" stands in for the daemonic as well as the demonic forces that are ultimately exorcized by human and divine love, as also for the imagination gone awry. In Herzog, the demonic lingers in nature, while the governing trope of the film, that of circular movement, is expressive both of the solipsistic imagination and of the pointlessness and absurdity of human existence. For Herzog, signs of all kinds lie within – indeed, constitute – this unredeemable condition.

If Herzog is not at pains to repudiate his indebtedness to Arnim, that is because it is of a relatively insignificant kind. Arnim is merely subsumed in the problem of cultural inheritance in general. *Signs of Life* is the film in which Herzog launches his campaign – the high point of which is achieved in *The Mystery of Kaspar Hauser* (*Jeder für sich und Gott gegen alle*, 1974 – against linguistic signs and written texts. When the philologist Becker becomes obsessed with gaining access to the mysteries of the stone tablets, he is presented as someone for whom the meaning of life is semiotic, for whom decoding the text means penetrating the mysteries of existence. For Herzog, Becker's quest is necessarily a futile one. Not only is he far from any such ultimate knowledge – which, for Herzog, can only be intuitive – but he cannot decipher the hieroglyphs in a rudimentary way; literacy is an insufficient preparation even for that. But the dilemma cannot simply be stated in terms of Lessing's distinction – in *Laocoön* – between natural and arbitrary signs. The statuary ought to exist safely within the realm of natural and thus directly intelligible signs, but it is broken, overgrown, and incorporated into walls, and seems to redouble Herzog's mockery at Becker's attempts at reading. In a rare moment of humor, the camera focuses on a stone foot protruding from a wall. For Herzog, these bits of cultural detritus are decidedly not signs of present life. They are, rather, remnants of a dead world, traces of nothing beyond the dissolution of their own meaning.

Though equally futile, Stroszek's defiance is much grander than Becker's. When Stroszek challenges the sun with his fireworks, fighting light with light, he is attempting to speak the language of nature. In seeking to oppose nature's signs with natural signs of his own, Stroszek is a true romantic, seeking to create as nature creates. It is not mere visual self-indulgence on the part of the director that shot after shot is devoted to Stroszek's fire-signs against the dark sky. These sequences evoke the love of spectacle one recalls in the German directors of the 1920s, who took particular delight in portraying the play of lights against a nighttime sky. Herzog makes no attempt to mask the reference to an earlier cinema here; in fact, he makes a point of flaunting this occasion of filmic quotation. It should be clear, then, that Stroszek's fireworks, his "fire-signs" (*"Feuerzeichen,"* as the film was originally to be called) are meant favorably to contrast the visual signs of cinema with the linguistic signs of writing.

It is hardly surprising that Herzog's attitude toward writing should be a negative one when one considers that, for him, language itself is secondary, inexpressive, and often incomprehensible. *Signs of Life* contains several moments in which the insufficiency of speech is featured. A little boy asks the camera plaintively: "Now that I can talk, what shall I say?" A little girl, who has not actually learned to understand language, is forced to recite a poem whose words are meaningless to her. While wandering through the town, Stroszek comes upon a pianist playing Chopin and he listens with rapt attention. When the pianist stops playing in order to harangue Stroszek about the composer, Stroszek cannot effect a connection between the music he has heard and the pianist's words, between the immediacy of the music and the secondariness of language, and can only respond with a painfully long silence. The film clearly wishes to connect Stroszek's response with that of the two naïfs, and to claim that their relation to experience is more direct, and therefore more "true," than that of those who resort to language. In this way, Stroszek anticipates Kaspar Hauser and the other Stroszek (*Stroszek,* 1977).

Earlier I suggested that Herzog wishes generally to repudiate literary influences on his work – and we have seen that this anxiety does not seem to extend to the influence of other films. Herzog pays his debt to F. W. Murnau quite willingly in *Nosferatu* (1978) and elsewhere, and Buñuel is an obvious antecedent in *Even Dwarfs Started Small (Auch Zwerge haben klein angefangen,* 1970); one would be hard put, though, to find many other directors who owe so little to so few of their predecessors. I would suggest, indeed, that Herzog is quite genuinely original as a filmmaker – he has created as novel a filmic vocabulary as has any living director – but that his relation to the literary tradition is, paradoxically, rather more encumbered. It is precisely because so many of his films have a literary subtext that Herzog is at such pains to denigrate written texts.[10] But how does this square with what I have said about the superficiality of Arnim's influence? Since Arnim is an acknowledged source of *Signs of Life*, but, as we have seen, the correspondences between the novella and the film are not of great significance, are there not perhaps other literary texts that *Signs of Life* has absorbed in a more telling way?

One can make an argument for the deeper presence of Heinrich von Kleist in Herzog's film. This would not be wholly surprising, as it is commonly acknowledged that Arnim's *The Mad Invalid* was itself written under the influence of Kleist. This being so, Herzog's subversion of Arnim can consist in replacing Arnim's borrowings from and transformation of Kleist's texts with his own. In other words, while overtly claiming to "adapt" Arnim's novella and actually remaining at some distance from it both stylistically and formally, Herzog rejects Arnim's adaptations from Kleist and substitutes his own references to him.

While Arnim does not model his text on one Kleist novella exclusively, but rather imitates aspects of Kleist's style in general, *The Mad Invalid* can be most obviously referred to *The Marquise of O. . . .* This text is constructed around the reader's – and, finally, the Marquise's – antithetical interpretations of the Count, the second of which is repressed by the Marquise and comes to light only after much delay and narrative innuendo. The struggle between revelation and suppression, masterfully controlled by the narrator, is what propels the plot forward. This movement between understanding and the repression of understanding is mirrored in the attitude of the Marquise's parents, who effectively banish her from their home, only to receive her again later. The movement of the narrative parallels the movement of the characters from house to house and from room to room. One might say that the end of the novella, in which the Marquise describes the Count as both angel and devil, resolves the dialectic that forms both the center of the narrative and its momentum. At the moment of articulation, delayed until the last sentence, sublimation is achieved and both conflict and narrative are terminated.

In *The Mad Invalid* the many wordplays on "devil," while they invest the novella with at least a suggestion of secondary significance, remain on the whole a surface phenomenon lending a cheerful formalism to the style. The mother's curse – that Francoeur's wife "go to the devil" – carries over to Francoeur, so that his wife wonders whether his madness is a result of his being "possessed by the devil." It is the wife's task – and the reader's – to learn to distinguish between literal and metaphorical thinking, and in that regard this strand of the novella contributes to its ultimate didacticism, especially because the final sentence of its summary moral takes up the theme once more: "Love drives out the devil." But in no sense can it be said that the inner structure of the novella is expressed by any latent dictum to the effect that we must recognize the metaphoricity of language.

In the case of Kleist, the angel–devil antithesis, while it epigrammatizes the uneasy conflict that shapes the novella, is understood to be but a feeble approximation of its existential import. The typical Kleistian character "loses consciousness," both literally and figuratively, in the face of the antithetical nature of the universe, because the possibility of coming to terms with it – let alone expressing it in language – is so remote. At moments of crisis, the mind cannot reconcile a radically self-divided reality with the conjunctive and unitary rules of language. Kleist's characters often experience a failure of language, and this failure does not lie exclusively in man's inability to understand reality; it lies also in the inherent insufficiency of language, the neatness of its paradoxes and the imprecision of its predications. Paradox of a more flexible kind may be said to describe Kleist's narrative style. Ellipses between narrative units, what Wolfgang Iser calls the "blanks" in a text,[11] point to the impossibility of narrative completeness, while a masterful control of language (ironically) characterizes his representation of linguistic – and conceptual – difficulty.

For this control, with its attendant irony, Herzog substitutes a pattern of cinematic language. In making use of Arnim's novella, Herzog does not attempt to find a cinematic equivalent for the linguistic web that Arnim weaves, although he could have found one in a very close-knit series of juxtaposed images. Instead, he chooses to thematize Kleist's more radical attitude toward language. And, as a filmmaker whose own language is imagistic, he has the opportunity to carry that attitude to an even greater extreme.

The crisis of language to which Kleist's characters so often fall prey indeed constitutes a central concern of Herzog's film. The little girl who attempts to recite her poem loses the power of speech only moments before Stroszek sees the windmills to which he can only respond by shooting off his rifle, and ultimately, by setting off his fireworks. It is significant that while Stroszek shoots his rifle at the windmills, "natural," diegetic sound – the ominous whirring of the windmills – is gradually usurped by the non-diegetic sound of a Greek melody. As Jonathan Cott has pointed out, the most privileged moments in Herzog's films seem to take place in silence, or to the sole accompaniment of music "that seems to represent audible silence."[12] In this sequence the "loss of consciousness" that Stroszek symbolically experiences is marked by the "silence" that the non-diegetic music successfully creates for the spectator. In effect, Stroszek's rifle shots – the punctuated signs of protest that we cannot hear – thus underscore his inability to formulate his experience by means of any semiotic code. The same is true of the fireworks – we hear no salvo of explosions, only the music that replaces all other sound. Again the moment is marked as a moment of silence.

The little boy who does not know what to say; Stroszek, who is so perplexed by the pianist who discourses upon Chopin that he cannot speak: Herzog intensifies the crisis of language and in the process re-evaluates it. The characters for whom the world is not readily accessible in language are privileged beings who experience the world in its immediacy. Like Kaspar Hauser, they are the "natural men" of romanticism. But this we can only infer. The problem of signification, apart from the charmed sphere of silence, is a central Kleistian problem, and it is Herzog's central problem as well. Unable to dismiss it, that is, in favor of the visionary immediacy that visual signs go only a small way toward achieving, he too presents the spectator with a disjointed narrative, like Kleist's, full of "blanks," or ellipses, and scrambles his codes in a way that postpones decoding. This problematic is at once most dominant and most extreme in a short film shot as a kind of study for *Signs of Life*, *Last Words* (*Letzte Worte*, 1968). This is a non-narrative yet also non-documentary film constructed – though not very convincingly – around the problem of the non-referentiality of language. The people who appear before the camera – two policemen, an old man in a boat, two musicians in a taverna – respond to the questions of an offscreen voice by repeating their assertions over and over again, in Greek, unencumbered by subtitles. It is the images alone that are comprehensible to most members of the audience.

If a film called *Signs of Life* properly takes the tricks of mediation for its theme, then it is equally fitting that its literary origin be mediated and in the process masked by an intervening text. And it is even more fitting, perhaps, that textuality in general mediate the origin of "life" itself, to which we can never stand present except in "signs." *Signs of Life* is in fact a film about its maker's origins. The film is set in 1942, the year of Herzog's birth, on the Greek island of Kos, where Herzog's grandfather did archaeological excavations (Stroszek wants to see "what really lay beneath the surface of things"). As Gideon Bachmann has written of Herzog: "He admires his grandfather, an archaeologist who excavated the Esculapiaeon on the island of Kos. When Herzog was 15, he went off to Greece to retrace the old man's steps, and finally shot his first feature there."[13] The central character's name, Stroszek, evokes Stipetič, Herzog's actual family name; Herzog admits to having been driven nearly mad by 10,000 windmills.[14] Like his grandfather, Herzog digs into his cultural heritage – returns to literary history – in order to discover his origins there. It suits Herzog's purpose admirably, whether he is fully aware of that purpose or not, that the scene of his grandfather's excavations should be that place where so many literary Germans have sought both the origins of European culture and the renewal of their own inspiration. But Herzog himself can be relied upon to say of his marvelously devious and mischievously entitled film, *Signs of Life* – and he *has* said it: "It's my only innocent film."[15]

Notes

1. Dudley Andrew, "The well-worn muse: adaptation in film history and theory," in *Narrative Strategies: Original Essays in Film and Prose Fiction*, ed. Syndy M. Conger and Janice R. Welsch (Macomb, Ill.: Western Illinois University Press, 1980), p. 10.

2. ibid., pp. 10–11.

3. ibid., p. 11.

4. Leticia Kent, "Werner Herzog: film is not the art of scholars, but of illiterates," *New York Times*, 11 September 1977.

5. I argue this point at length in "Literature and writing in the films of Werner Herzog," in *Film und Literatur: Literarische Texte und der Neue Deutsche Film*, ed. Sigrid Bauschinger, Susan Cocalis and Henry Lea (Berne and Munich: Francke, 1984), pp. 156–68.

6. Lawrence O'Toole, "'I feel that I'm close to the center of things,'" *Film Comment*, 15, No. 6 (November–December 1979), 48.

7. Bernd Haustein, *Romantischer Mythos und Romantikkritik in Prosadichtungen Achim von Arnims* (Göppingen: Kümmerle, 1974), p. ix.

8. Jonathan Cott, "Signs of life," *Rolling Stone*, 18 November 1976, 55.

9. The windmill sequence was filmed on the Lasithi Plain on Crete, where there actually are 10,000 windmills.

10. Herzog's *Woyzeck* (1978) is the obvious exception. See my article cited in note 5.

11. Wolfgang Iser, *The Act of Reading: A Theory of Aesthetic Response* (Baltimore: Johns Hopkins University Press, 1978), p. 182.

12. Cott, p. 55.

13. Gideon Bachmann, "The man on the volcano: a portrait of Werner Herzog," *Film Quarterly*, 31, No. 1 (Fall 1977), 5.

14. Herzog speaks of this experience in an interview in the German edition of *Playboy*. He also mentions that his grandfather went mad shortly before dying. See Raimond Le Viseur and Werner Schmidmaier, *"Playboy* interview," *Playboy* (German edn), January 1977.

15. Werner Herzog, in *"Images at the Horizon": A Workshop with Werner Herzog*, ed. Gene Walsh (Chicago: Facets Multimedia Center, 1979), p. 5.

Script

Werner Herzog. *Lebenszeichen*. In *Drehbücher I*. Munich: Skellig, 1977, pp. 7–104.

Selected Bibliography

Benelli, Dana. "The cosmos and its discontents." *Movietone News*, No. 56 (November 1977), 8–16.

Combs, Richard. "Werner Herzog." In *Cinema: A Critical Dictionary*. Ed. Richard Roud. 2 vols. New York: Viking, I, pp. 486–7.

Herzog, Werner (ed.) *Werner Herzog: Eine Dokumentation seines filmischen Gesamtwerks*. Biberach/Munich: Urania-Filmkunsttheater/Filmverlag der Autoren, 1977.

Horak, Jan-Christopher. "Werner Herzog's *Écran Absurde*." *Literature/Film Quarterly*, 7, No. 3 (1979), 223–34.

Jansen, Peter W. and Wolfram Schütte (eds). *Herzog/Kluge/Straub*. Munich: Hanser, 1976.

—— *Werner Herzog*. Munich: Hanser, 1979.

O'Toole, Lawrence. "The great ecstasy of the filmmaker Herzog." *Film Comment*, 15, No. 6 (November–December 1979), 34–9.

—— "'I feel that I'm close to the center of things.'" *Film Comment*, 15, No. 6 (November–December 1979), 40–50.

Peucker, Brigitte. "Literature and writing in the films of Werner Herzog." In *Film und Literatur: Literarische Texte und der neue deutsche Film*. Ed. Sigrid Bauschinger, Susan L. Cocalis, and Henry A. Lea. Berne and Munich: Francke, 1984, pp. 154–68.

—— "Werner Herzog: in quest of the sublime." In *New German Filmmakers: From Oberhausen through the 1970s*. Ed. Klaus Phillips. New York: Ungar, 1984, pp. 168–94.

Perlmutter, Ruth. "The cinema of the grotesque." *Georgia Review*, 33, No. 1 (1979), 169–93.

Walsh, Gene (ed.). *"Images at the Horizon": A Workshop with Werner Herzog*. Chicago: Facets Multimedia Center, 1979.

15

MAUREEN TURIM

Textuality and theatricality in Brecht and Straub/Huillet: *History Lessons* (1972)

Maps, monuments, memoirs, financial accounts, interviews: the resources of the historian and the lessons one might draw from them are presented in Danièle Huillet and Jean-Marie Straub's *History Lessons* (*Geschichtsunterricht*, 1972) by way of a complex investigation of textuality. In order to have lessons about history, a text, a film, is fabricated. That text in images and sounds is a reading of another text, a novel, a fragment by Bertolt Brecht, *The Business Deals of Mr Julius Caesar* (*Die Geschäfte des Herrn Julius Caesar*) written during 1938–42, while Brecht was in Hollywood. Film/play/novel: different textualities collide and inform each other as Brecht's theories of cinema, theater, and literature loom in the margins, in the wings, between the frames. What kind of text have Straub and Huillet made? What does their film text make of Brecht?

One way to begin answering these questions is to note that Straub and Huillet chose one of Brecht's novels (there are only two, the other being *The Threepenny Novel/Der Dreigroschenroman*), rather than one of his plays as the source for their film. This immediately differentiates their undertaking from that of G. W. Pabst with *The Threepenny Opera (Die Dreigroschenoper*, 1931), the Tobis-Klang-Film and Warner Brothers co-production that drove Brecht to court in protest at the cinematic rendering. This early negative experience in adapting epic theater to film was to inform Brecht's subsequent writing on cinema.

In 1931 Brecht published an essay called *The Threepenny Lawsuit* (*Der Dreigroschenprozess*), with the subtitle "A Sociological Experiment" and the motto "Contradictions are our hope!"[1] In that essay he repeatedly speaks of the trial as a kind of self-consciously undertaken demonstration of the ways in which commercial cinema limits the creative political gestures of the writer. Judicial judgments circumvent the enforcement of the studio's official contracts guaranteeing authorial control over filmic production by evoking the greater right of the cinematic producer to make films that exploit cinematic style for the greatest profit. "We have often been told (and the court expressed the same opinion) that when we sold our work to the film industry we gave up all our rights; the buyers even purchased the right to destroy what they had bought; all further claim was covered by the money," is the way Brecht states the problem at the beginning of the essay.[2]

Brecht goes on to say that he knew ahead of time that he had no hopes of winning his suit against Nero-Film, especially since he could never block the exhibition of Pabst's *The Threepenny Opera* which was in distribution long before the case came to trial. Further he explains why, knowing of the inevitable loss of the suit, he declined an out-of-court cash settlement. The suit for him was a "theatrical" event from which his audience could learn; the essay became the means of consecrating and preserving this lesson:

> This trial had as its goal to show the impossibility of a collaboration with the film industry, even when the contract carried guarantees. The goal was attained — it was achieved when I lost the trial. This trial clearly showed, for all those who wished to see, the defects of the film industry and those of the system of jurisprudence.[3]

This object lesson, however, is not meant to show that film itself is any less important as a new apparatus for the future of "literary" expression, though Brecht does see cinema as an "increasingly complex" medium that forces writers to speak "by increasingly inadequate means."[4] He primarily faults cinema for eliminating interaction between audiences and actors. He also says, "The essence of cinema is the dissolution of dramatic processes in so many individual images, resulting in the disappearance of the word and the fact that everything is contained in short scenes filmed independently of one another."[5] As Brecht sees it, the commercial film finishes off the activity of the *Lehrstück*, the learning play, never achieving distanciation (*Verfremdung*), Brecht's invitation to active and critical, rather than empathetic, participation.

Yet if Brecht does *not* denounce all cinematic expression, it is because "the mechanization of literary production cannot be thrown into reverse"; literature will begin to borrow techniques from cinema and cinema will supersede literature.[6] Brecht expresses hope in his essay for *another* cinema, a future cinematic practice, which will be the extension of literature and theater in an age when mechanical reproduction of sounds and images dominates expression. Cinema will have taught a new manner of "reading," for better or for worse. Brecht hopes to see cinema learn to speak better. In what ways does the filmic practice of Straub/Huillet answer to this desire for another cinematic practice, particularly one which will not abet the "disappearance of the word?"

The question is posed in the context of a long inquiry on the possibility of Brechtian cinema. In his book, *Bertolt Brecht, Cahiers du Cinéma and*

Contemporary Film Theory, George Lellis gives a lengthy account of the debate that appeared in *Cahiers du Cinéma* in the last two decades about the applicability of Brecht's theatrical theory of film.[7] The positions range from an early contention by Louis Marcorelles that the "admirable theatrical theories of Brecht are not transportable to the cinema," except as a stimulus to find cinematic equivalents, to the later position taken by Jean Narboni that self-conscious theatricality is a crucial element of a contemporary Brechtian approach to cinema. Lellis summarizes as follows:

> The recognition of theatricality is a way of acknowledging the means whereby cinematic illusion is produced, of acknowledging the symbolic nature of the film medium, of bringing about an active reading on the part of the viewer. This is entirely compatible with the influence of Brecht; from the position (previously held in *Cahiers* by Louis Marcorelles) that Brecht and the cinema are incompatible because of the anti-theatrical nature of cinema, we reach a resolution of the problem by a condemnation of the supposedly anti-theatrical nature of traditional film language.[8]

To be fair to Marcorelles, he also suggested as early as 1957 that Bresson was the most Brechtian director working at that time (which Lellis notes in passing). One must sort through the ambiguities surrounding the word "theatricality" in its various usages in this debate. Sometimes it refers to a specifically Brechtian notion of theater, in which exaggerated gestures entertain and yet deconstruct realism, while in other contexts it means the theatrical tradition, or signifiers that indicate theater, in either its realist or expressionist modes.

It is possible then to see that the film theorists of *Cahiers* have been looking for cinematic correlates to Brechtian theory in a cinema that in one way or another maintains a meta-commentary on theatrical and cinematic illusions of reality and conventions of expression. In Straub/Huillet's use of Corneille's text for the film *Othon* (1969), Narboni thinks he has found an equivalent. The film refuses a traditional staging of classical French drama, in favor of a reading of the text eschewing customary theatrical gesture and spatio-temporal unity and clarity. The text of *Othon* was written for the theater, but is rarely performed. This makes it an intriguing choice for this reworking of theater and film through Straub/Huillet's minimalist cinematic practice. This emphasis on textuality favors the choice of embedded texts whose own history will highlight the issues of theatrical representation once they are "translated" to film. *History Lessons* makes explicit the aspirations Narboni claims for *Othon*: to achieve a Brechtian equivalent in a new form of textuality.

To achieve this new form, recitation is brought to the surface whenever a character speaks. Like Straub/Huillet's *Fortini Cani* (1976), where author Franco Fortini is shown reading long passages from his essay, *I cani del Sinai*, the characters in *History Lessons* recite a text associated with their name within Brecht's novel. The film is a formal reading, a performance of the act of reading that cannot be termed "dramatic" in that it systematically eliminates the intonations of drama. What remains is the literary, written text in confrontation with images that time and punctuate readings. The visual image becomes a temporal marker supplying and dividing duration; a graphic background for the soundtrack establishing the way it is to be heard.

History Lessons points out that the sharp distinctions one might draw between the following categories of language can be undermined in a new cinematic textuality: written words printed on pages, text in recitation, spoken language, are less rigidly distinguishable from one another than one might suppose. In using the middle element of the triad, the text in recitation, *History Lessons* puts the ironic connection between printed text and spoken language into a new light, the one provided by a Derridean theory of textuality. Words no longer present us with the illusion of reconstituting the past. Instead, they are themselves reconstituted as textual "traces" seen from the vantage point of our current position in history and theory; "traces" are presences that hide absences.[9] History can be seen as the deciphering and reinscription of these textual traces. This is presented in the film not by anything anyone in the fiction says, but by the way these speakers of a fiction say the history they speak.

The strategy devised by Straub/Huillet to create film texts that place active demands on the spectator is therefore not simply an adaptation of Brecht's notions of epic theater to film. Straub and Huillet share implicitly the critique of traditional modes of filmic representation voiced by Brecht, but their counter-proposal is a form of image/sound composition whose correlation with Brechtian theory resides primarily in its own version of distanciation and an active audience role in formulating lessons. It leaves behind Brecht's concern with accessibility, entertainment, the traditional resources of theater to please a large audience. Next to Brecht's amusing satire, his clever plot movements and orchestrated scenes, their scripts are intellectual, dry, difficult.

The sacrifice of a certain form of entertainment value seems crucial to their strategy in film. Unlike theater, which, because of its physical presence and live audience, can employ entertainment then reverse its flow, using distanciation to throw the members of the audience back in their seats, while alternately gripping them, traditional film has a greater tendency to grab and hold. The filmic spectator is a more passive witness to an unchanging, "absent" spectacle; the actor confined to the filmic image can "speak as if quoting" but, even so, the iconographic fixity of cinema makes a Brechtian performative mode more difficult to sustain. Jean-Luc Godard's solution is to frame his characters looking out at the camera to make pronouncements that exceed what might be expected within a set of naturalistic character traits. He interrupts the fictional flow with graphic signs and juxtaposes narrative and extra-narrative sequences. Nagisa Oshima splits characters into multiple personalities inhabiting the same icon. In addition, his characters "speak" through a disturbing combination of silence and the acting-out of symbolic violence. Rainer Werner Fassbinder retains more of a directly Brechtian acting ensemble, but as a result, his films are also closer to cinematic realism with expressionist overtones. G. W. Pabst and Fritz Lang are among the ghosts wandering through Fassbinder's filmic stages. While Fassbinder has brought forth the display of social gestures in a context that remains enjoyable for a mass audience, it is not clear, even when read allegorically, that his films markedly deviate from Hollywood melodrama in their effects on most audiences.

Straub/Huillet make films that are harder to assimilate and recuperate from than those of Fassbinder (of whose work they are extremely critical); harder, even than Godard or Oshima. They slice further into the notion of filmic *mise-en-scène*. Their formal system of shot patterning and montage played off against direct sound recording deeply disturbs the mechanisms of filmic fiction. The form this takes in *History Lessons* is to violate the fiction built by Brecht even as they quote whole passages of the text directly. Brecht's novel-fragment is divided into four "books" called respectively, "Career of a Young Man of Distinction," "Our Master C," "Classical Administration of a Province," and "The Monster with Three Heads." In the first book, we are introduced to the young man who wishes to document the life of his hero, Caesar, twenty years after Caesar's death. In first-person narration, this fictive historian living in Ancient Rome tells us of gathering material. He relates his interviews with Mummulus Spicer, a banker, with a peasant who was a former legionary, and with the jurist, Afranius Carbon, whom the young man meets at Spicer's villa. At the end of the first section, Spicer gives the historian the diary of the slave, Rarus. This diary forms the body of book two. A second visit to Spicer provides the young man with a second volume of the slave's diary which comprises most of book three. Book three terminates with the young man's encounter at Spicer's villa with the poet, Vastius Alder. At the end of their conversation, Spicer gives the young man the remaining volume of Rarus's diary, which makes up the fourth and final book.

The montage of testimony about Caesar is presented within fictional frames of characterization, repeated visits to the villa, the thoughts of a first-person narrator. The voices comment ironically on each other's view of Caesar. The young man's notion of the great man's history and Spicer's economic support of Caesar's regime are undercut by the diary accounts of the slave. The fiction is obviously a set-up, a construct that brings into play these testimonies. Brecht said that his own point of view lies in the montage of these accounts. Still, literary fictional conventions are for the most part followed. The novel fragment deviates by indulging the long monologues of the banker, the jurist, and the poet, but even such extended monologues are common devices in the novel, as are the inclusion of diary entries. Brecht includes passages that chronicle the young man's comings and goings from his home to the villa: an effect of a fictional reality is built into this allegorical conceit. This internal coherence within a fictional reality establishes an entirely metaphorical reading. Caesar, for Brecht, is Hitler.

A reading as contemporary allegory is also suggested in Straub/Huillet's film by the opening shots of three maps. The first, the Roman Empire at its acme, is held for five seconds, while the next, a diminished Roman Empire after the Punic Wars, lasts less than one second. The third, the Mediterranean world after the fall of the Empire and the appearance of Italy, lasts one and a half seconds. The noise of the Viale dei Fori Imperiali that accompanies these maps prepares us for the fourth shot, a statue of Julius Caesar erected by Mussolini just off Fori Imperiali. The fall of the Empire, the monumentalization of its architect by a modern fascist dictator: this preface shifts the context of the novel by establishing the place as contemporary Rome. Rome is to learn lessons about its past, the epoch of Caesar and the reinscription of an imperial vision for the purposes of fascism. The maps and statue only ambiguously present a narrative space. For the first-time viewer, these shots are only obliquely meaningful as the beginning of a fiction. They call on our resources as an audience, challenging us to decipher these signs. They are presented too enigmatically for us to read them as we would maps, monuments, and inscriptions in a documentary. Rather than clearly communicating information, these shots function in a way like the diagrams and schemata of conceptual art, presenting various textual forms as images. Unlike the maps of documentaries and newscasts, these images are not simply supplements; they have a life of their own. A text (a map) is presented as an image.

The next shot has a different conceptual function. It introduces the young man of Brecht's story transformed into a contemporary Italian driving into Rome. The shot is taken from behind this historian/driver so that the windshield frames his vehicular perambulations. Our frame of vision on the contemporary city is constricted by the auto, confined to its temporality, its condition as witness of daily life. However, due to the image's flattening of the car-framed perspective, the view we get as spectators of this image is not just that of a back-seat observer. The open sun-roof and side windows multiply the image frames within the image, presenting a view as unlike the view from a real car as it is unlike an ordinary cinematic image. The image thus framed is conscious of the contradictions in representation (an image is never of reality) and fascinated with multiple perspectives. This driving shot lasts nearly nine minutes and is echoed by two other shots that later punctuate the film with identically framed driving scenes. These later shots, shots thirty-five and forty-eight, each last approximately ten and a half minutes, so that in this film of fifty-five shots, the three dispersed driving shots total almost exactly thirty minutes of film time. They form a repeated insertion of

Plate 32   Framing the driving sequence in *History Lessons*: a scene from the
production of the text. Photo courtesy of Stiftung Deutsche Kinemathek.

the contemporary space and time within the ancient story. They also
chronicle in "real" time and synchronous sound the entrance of a character
(the young man) into the fiction by way of contemporary realities.

The driving segments have been interpreted metaphorically by several commentators on the film. Gilberto Perez has taken these frames within frames to
represent camera and perspectival representation, while Martin Walsh has
suggested that the journey through the streets represents in the circulation of a
car the very notion of "circulation" in a contemporary urban society.[10] These
metaphorical readings are indeed present. The car segments offer references to
modes of transportation and the framing of vision in contemporary existence.
Yet the information we receive is sparse. Metaphor does not have an
explanatory function in this case. Instead it draws out a reference, through
insistent framing extended over time, to our knowledge of these issues outside
the text. They might even suggest a comparison with Brecht's concept of the
contemporary city, expressed so poignantly in his poetry. Consider the second
stanza of his poem from the mid 1920s, "Of the Crushing Impact of Cities":

Suddenly
Some of them fled into the air
Building upwards; others from the highest rooftops

Flung high their hats and shouted:
Next time so high!
But their successors
Fleeing from night frost after the sale of familiar roofs
Pressed on behind them and see with a haddock's eyes
Those tall boxes
Successors to houses.
For within the same walls at that time
Four generations at once
Gulped down their food
And in their childhood year
Had never seen
On a flat palm the nail for the stone in the wall.
For them metal and stone
Grew together.
So short was time
That between morning and evening
There was no noon
And already on the old familiar ground
Stood mountains of concrete.[11]

Like Brecht's other city poems, this poem expresses a nostalgic sense of loss for a perspective that existed prior to the modernization of urban life. The driving scenes in *History Lessons* only give us relentless perspectives of the contemporary motorist, a haddock's-eye vision limited to the stream along which a car can move. Nostalgia and criticism are less overtly stated by the shots of driving than by Brecht's poems, however. The film's audience is left to fill in meanings for these ambiguous contemporary punctuations of the Caesar investigation. Due to this puzzlingly "empty" quality of the driving shots, they can also be seen as anasemic signs, signifiers whose meaning is not inherent, but rather relational. They call on the sociological theories of the city, notions of circulation and commerce, but they also serve as punctuations for the rest of the film, time to think about filmmaking and the image. The driving segments encourage us to confront the richness of a "minimalist" style in a manner similar to other avant-garde films. By holding on a frame, Straub/Huillet reduce the effects of montage. By circulating within the frame similar types of signifiers, shapes, and references to objects, the directors magnify subtle changes, transforming them into new, important occurrences. The spectator is challenged visually, asked to derive pleasure as well as meaning from these elements. Just as the text (a map) earlier became an image, now an image becomes a text, a mysterious discourse decipherable only by means of other discourses. This image is a text only by way of tropological readings.

The remaining shots in *History Lessons* contain the interviews and monologues gathered by the young man. In a sense, the verbal text seems to be primary, simply because there is so much of it and so little action within the lengthy, mainly static shots. This is a film about characters talking. Yet it is also about innovation in film characters talking. The camera work and editing are extremely systematic. Each dialogue is presented in a series of oblique angles whose montage produces surprising spatial articulations. This systematic movement through a fragmented space surrounding the speaking subject is an alternative to standard shot/reverse shot editing. In the standard dialogue pattern, shot/reverse shot, each shot is usually taken from an angle thirty to forty-five degrees from an imaginary line running between the speakers. If the first shot is of speaker A from a position forty-five degrees from the line and to this speaker's right, then the reverse shot parallels and inverts this angle by staying forty-five degrees from the line but with the camera aimed in the opposite direction and moved over to the left. This can be seen in a simple diagram:

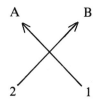

Jean-Pierre Oudart has analyzed this shot/reverse shot pattern in his essay, "La Suture," as a primary means by which cinema binds its discourse, concealing its construction.[12] This shot/reverse shot pattern provides for a clear depiction of who is talking to whom, as it assures a continuity of character direction within the image. The viewer is allowed an imaginary entrance into the scene, seeing each character from a position approximating but rarely exactly equal to the point of view of the other character. The system minimizes spatial surprises and the audience's awareness that cuts are taking place. Dialogue flows across these sutured images, rendering the cuts nearly invisible. Expression on the characters' faces, gestures, expressive lighting can all be developed to provide nuances to the dialogue and further distract audience attention from the editing process. The audience is allowed to enter into the scene of a dialogue as a natural event, witnessed from a privileged space that does not define or call attention to itself. As a result, the textuality of dialogue and the textuality of film as an edited, constructed series of signs is covered over by the flow of events within an illusionary space that the viewer imagines as real. Textuality is effaced in favor of a participatory vision. But on another level, textuality is systematically operating. One realizes this by watching the shots analytically. In some films such deconstructive, vigilant reading is a rewarding revelation of the dialogue scene as text, carefully timed and varied even within the shot/reverse shot system. But standardization also means that often the cutting patterns display no particular rigor as textual *découpage* of verbal enunciations.

In *History Lessons* Straub/Huillet develop an alternative to the shot/ reverse shot dialogue scene which is both a rigorous, thoughtful punctuation of verbal enunciations and a system which, through its obvious spatial fragmentation, calls attention to itself as system, to the process and effects of camera angles and montage. As such, Straub/Huillet's systematic camera work and editing continue the experimentation of Robert Bresson, who developed different systems as alternatives to traditional patterns in several of his films. In *Le Procès de Jeanne d'Arc* (1961), the courtroom scenes lack establishing shots. Each speaker is framed tightly, in an isolated space whose relationship to the preceding and following spaces is unknown. This strategy was cited in Oudart's essay as a prime example of a non-sutured alternative. Bresson's *Au hasard, Balthazar* (1965) is looked on less favorably by Oudart in that essay, but in fact, the recurring conversations on the bench and the seduction scene in the front seat of the car provide an interesting comparison to Straub/Huillet's conversation scenes in *History Lessons*, for they too isolate each character, enunciation, and gesture in space with great deliberateness. Straub/Huillet choose a higher angle for their framing in a shot which emphasizes the space between the hand of the young man resting on the bench and the banker fragmented in close-up at the lower right-hand portion of the image (shot twelve), than did Bresson in very similar shots in *Au hasard, Balthazar*, but the similarity is striking. Straub and Huillet do go further, though, in exaggerating the angles, increasing the difference from angle to angle, in refusing ever to repeat a previously seen angle and in holding each of these emphatic framings for a much greater duration. So the film reveals its concern with the graphic disposition of the character represented as speaking. Graphic composition of each shot emphasizes bold diagonals achieved through canted and/or oblique angles. In these diagonal compositions the character's glances are directional, away from the audience, and away from the listening character. Glances do not meet; they point to a space beyond the frame, suggesting that the speaking character is reciting from memory, speaking a text rather than performing a part. The characters are emblematic graphic representations of their textual lines in the novel—nothing more.

Here we must pause to note how this strategy answers one of Brecht's complaints about cinema, discussed earlier. By using camera angles and cutting that hold insistently on a lengthy recitation of dialogue, while also emphasizing spatial disjunction and creating an arbitrary, formal quality to montage, the film style of Straub and Huillet foregrounds the verbal text. It is due to the extremely designed quality of the cinematic expression that one is told to *listen*. The visual style of the image track strategically foregrounds the voice. The highly patterned, bold, graphic configurations each last a long time without much internal change, while the changes from image to image are also bold graphically, as well as in terms of spatial signification. The spectator is placed and repeatedly displaced into new spaces where auditory attention is demanded. The rapid delivery and lack of intonation that characterize the speaking style further increase this demand for concentrated listening.

In the first conversation between the young man and the banker, the camera angles are selected from a "path" that crosses from behind the bench to circle the banker, and then moves from the bench in the opposite direction. The camera work and editing of this sequence and other key sequences of the film have been analyzed in detail by Martin Walsh.[13] The sequence begins with shot six, taken from behind the bench with the young man in the lower-right foreground and the banker in the upper-left, with the bench diagonally between them. It ends with shot thirteen which inverts the spatial disposition of the characters so that the banker is now in the lower-right foreground and the young man is above (though more to the center of the frame than the banker in shot six). Each of the shots six to thirteen varies distance and angle so as to create a maximum of difference between each one of the images taken from these stationary positions along this trajectory. The result is both to emphasize the banker visually, rather than his interlocutor, the young man, who appears in only three of the shots and then is only seen from behind, or in long-shot, or through the metonymy of his hands resting on the bench. The cumulative effect of such patterned graphic editing is to portray the banker speaking from a separate space, from which he does not gaze at, nor interact with his fictional listener. The voice is the only gesture that counts here, and even its expressive qualities are minimized. The scene is a forceful attack on the "realism" of expression in much cinematic fiction. Recital of dialogue cut into deliberate fragments situates each passage of dialogue as a semi-autonomous "episode" – as Brecht used the term when he called for an episodic structure in epic theater.

Dialogue between the young man and the banker dominates the film. Besides this conversation on the bench, there is a dialogue that takes place on the villa terrace (shots seventeen through twenty-six) that is punctuated by black leader of uneven length at irregular intervals, and another long monologue addressed to the young man on the terrace of the villa (shots forty-five through fifty-four). The banker opens the film and closes it. He provides an economic explanation for political events, even to the point of contradicting the version of Caesar's battle with the pirates that the young man recites upon his request. In the banker's version, Caesar's smashing of the pirates is not a defensive act that proves his valor, but a move that secures Rome's domination of the slave trade. The brief interview with the peasant (shots twenty-eight through thirty-six), the short monologue of the poet (shot forty-three), and the longer monologue of the jurist (shots thirty-nine to forty-one) are sandwiched within the banker's discourse. The diaries of the slave Rarus which constitute a large portion of Brecht's novel are entirely eliminated. As the summary outline of *The Business Affairs of Mr Julius Caesar* above indicates, the diaries of the slave are doled out, section by section, by the banker after each visit of the young man to his villa. Straub/ Huillet have dropped this counterpoint narration, this written artifact whose form so differs from the others. Since Rarus's narration emphasizes the personal daily life of Caesar, dropping the diaries all but eliminates this side of Brecht's text from the Straub/Huillet film. Rarus tells of Caesar's affairs with both men and women, and how these affairs affect his marriage to Pompeia and figure in his political life. This level of melodrama is pursued ironically by Brecht, but with a certain perverse gusto; we also learn of Pompeia's affair with her sister's lover, Claudius, for example, in an amusing passage that includes a clandestine encounter aided by a transvestite disguise. Indiscretions on the part of the ruling Romans are part of Brecht's mockery, but he also entertains the notion that Caesar's lust for sexual gratification, his political ambition and the economic strategies for the domination of the Roman State coalesce into a multidimensional configuration of a will to power.

Rarus is himself in love with a free Roman citizen, Caebio, of whom Rarus writes:

This evening a walk with my beloved Caebio, my one and only love, in the gardens along the Tiber. Nothing to be done: he can't find work. He is a perfume maker and, in this line of work as others, only slaves are now employed. From Syria, Pompey sends us thousands. These are qualified men who in their own country once possessed perfume stores. Everywhere Caebio looks for work he is sent away with the statement that it makes no sense to employ workers who could be drafted the next day. Caebio is a Roman citizen. He is filled with despair.

He tells me he doesn't know what would become of him if I didn't keep him afloat.

Brecht seems in passages such as this to delight in the imbrication of intimate details and economic factors. The political economy of Rome is portrayed as affecting every aspect of daily life from the amorous encounter to the perfume boutiques. But if economic factors permeate all levels of activity, the implied analysis is not a mechanistic economic determinism.

In the film, on the other hand, the spoken accounts that are selected from the novel emphasize the economic causes of war, the bartering of votes to sustain power, and the insecurity of any "democratic" principles. Whatever mention of personal intrigue remains is subordinated to this economic causality. Some commentators on the film see this selection as providing a greater clarity and rigor to the analysis. As Stephen Heath puts it, "The film 'de-anecdotalises' Brecht's text, retaining even in those sections it includes only historico-economic explanation," explanation that is "clear, posed, proffered."[14] While it may be true that clarity is gained in the film's abridgment of Brecht's novel, some of the play and ambiguity is lost. Brecht denounced strict economic determinism in other contexts, and it is possible to see his text as investigating this Marxist construct, suggesting a modification that would also consider the vicissitudes of psychology, although certainly not a "psychology of character" typical of the bourgeois novel. If these aspects are diminished in the film, the elements of Marxist analysis are still presented with great irony and humor. The play with point of view within these monologues and dialogues makes the blunt admissions of corruption and class interest into "impossible" enunciations. Yet they flow with no hesitation from the banker and jurist; they are even spoken with a low-key pride. The film's minimalist style accentuates the humor of this impossible discourse. Brecht's wit is already dry and sardonic; Straub/Huillet's presentation makes it more so.

The peasant's account differs the most from the others. His replies are terse, while the others are mostly extended explanations. Yet even the comments from this former legionary who has returned to farming, and who saw Caesar only from a distance, echo the economic analysis of the banker. The poet is the most critical voice, for he seems to disapprove of the way Caesar's policies were but a series of trade-offs for votes. His monologue ends, "Look at his Senate: a market-hall." The jurist compliments the economic analysis of the banker, with the same "unconscious" irony. He contends that the expansion of trade through bloodshed is a heroic victory for the upwardly mobile element of the plebeian class.

From these multiple ironies emerge individual lines that strike with great impact. For example, close to the end of the film, the banker says:

However, the invasion of his Roman troops followed only when, after C's arrival, it became known that in these regions even human sacrifices were offered. The liquidation of such barbarous conditions called for speedy and merciless intervention. It may lead to loss of human life, but will be worth it in the end. Those Roman cohorts who, in the absence of any roads, thinking it was a dried-up river bed, marched into an arm of the sea and were washed away by the rising tide with all war equipment and baggage, didn't lose their lives in vain. On the same slopes stand today the villas of native and Roman merchants; and the mountain valleys, which at that time were filled with the noise of weapons and the moans of the wounded, resound today once more with peaceful hammering in the ore quarries and the merry cries of the slaves.

Not all of this dialogue is intelligible upon a single viewing of the film, though a German audience certainly can grasp more than a foreign one reading inadequate subtitles. But like other Straub/Huillet films, *History Lessons* benefits greatly from this kind of background information, provided in articles such as the present one, or by the filmmakers' commentaries, by a reading of the script (which has appeared in German, French, and English), and by repeated viewings of the film. Part of the textual play is to invite intertextuality, a demand for other texts. And so the last shot presents us with a fountain (as does *Othon*) accompanied by a passage from Bach's *Passion According to St Matthew*, not only evoking the Straub/Huillet film, *The Chronicle of Anna Magdalena Bach* (*Chronik der Anna Magdalena Bach*, 1967), but asking us to see Caesar as a "false betrayer" of "innocent blood." Once again we are reminded that the film's obsession with Caesar asks for linkages with other murderous betrayers – not only Mussolini as suggested at the film's start, but any leader of whom one might say the things the banker does above, and throughout the text. Those who try to convince us that soldiers did not die in vain may not provide us with such direct Red Sea imagery, momentous washings-away by the tides of history; for this reason film text extends its witty metaphors into the present.

Notes

1. Bertolt Brecht, *Schriften zur Literatur und Kunst I*, Vol. XVIII of the *Gesemmelte Werke in 20 Bänden*, ed. Werner Hecht (Frankfurt am Main: Suhrkamp, 1967), 139–209. Two sections of the essay are excerpted as "The film, the novel and epic theatre," in *Brecht on Theatre*, ed. John Willett (New York: Hill & Wang, 1964), pp. 47–51.
2. Brecht, p. 156.
3. ibid., p. 149.
4. ibid., p. 156.
5. cf. pp. 157–8, 171.
6. ibid., p. 156.
7. George Lellis, *Bertolt Brecht, Cahiers du Cinéma and Contemporary Film Theory* (Ann Arbor: University of Michigan Press, 1982).
8. ibid., p. 132.
9. I use the term "trace" in the Derridean sense. See Jacques Derrida, *Of Grammatology*, trans. Gayatri Chakravorty Spivak (Baltimore and London: Johns Hopkins University Press, 1976).
10. Gilberto Perez, "Modernist cinema: the history lessons of Straub and Huillet," *Artforum*, October 1978, 51; Martin Walsh, "*History Lessons*: Brecht and Straub/Huillet," in *The Brechtian Aspect of Radical Cinema* (London: British Film Institute, 1981), pp. 61–2.
11. Bertolt Brecht, *Poems 1913–1956*, trans. John Willett (New York: Methuen, 1977), p. 109.
12. Jean-Pierre Oudart, "La Suture," *Cahiers du Cinéma*, No. 211 (April 1969), 36–9; No. 212 (May 1969), 50–5.
13. Walsh, *The Brechtian Aspect of Radical Cinema*, pp. 60–77.
14. Stephen Heath, "From Brecht to film: theses, problems (on *History Lessons* and *Dear Summer Sister*)," *Screen*, 16, No. 4 (Winter 1975/6), 42.

Script

Straub, Jean-Marie and Danièle Huillet. "Scenarios of *History Lessons* and *Introduction to Arnold Schoenberg's Accompaniment to a Cinematograph Scene*." *Screen*, 17, No. 1 (Spring 1976), 54–83.

Selected Bibliography

Bennett, E. "The films of Straub are not 'theoretical.'" *Afterimage*, No. 7 (Summer 1978), 4–11.

Brewster, Ben. "Brecht and the film industry (on *The Threepenny Opera* film and *Hangmen Also Die*)." *Screen*, 16, No. 4 (Winter 1975/6), 16–33.

Byg, Barton Benjamin. "History, narrative and film form: Jean-Marie Straub and Danièle Huillet." Dissertation Washington University, 1983.

Gregor, Erika and Ulrich (eds). *Brecht und das Kino. Dokumentation.* Berlin: Freunde der Deutschen Kinemathek, 1973.

Heath, Stephen. "From Brecht to film: theses, problems (on *History Lessons* and *Dear Summer Sister*)." *Screen*, 16, No. 4 (Winter 1975/6), 34–45.

—— "Lessons from Brecht." *Screen*, 15, No. 2 (Summer 1974), 103–28.

Jansen, Peter W. and Wolfram Schütte (eds). *Herzog/Kluge/Straub.* Munich: Hanser, 1976.

Lellis, George. *Bertolt Brecht, Cahiers du Cinéma and Contemporary Film Theory.* Ann Arbor: University of Michigan Press, 1982.

Orr, Christopher. "The adventures of the signifier: the driving sequences in *History Lessons*." *Purdue University Fifth Annual Conference on Film: Proceedings*, 30 October–1 November 1980. West Lafayette, Indiana: Purdue University, 1980, pp. 250–5.

Perez, Gilberto. "Modernist cinema: the history lessons of Straub and Huillet." *Artforum*, October 1978, 46–55.

Turim, Maureen. "Jean-Marie Straub and Danièle Huillet: oblique angles on film as ideological intervention." In *New German Filmmakers: From Oberhausen through the 1970s*. Ed. Klaus Phillips. New York: Ungar, 1984, pp. 335–58.

Walsh, Martin. *The Brechtian Aspect of Radical Cinema.* London: British Film Institute, 1981.

Witte, Karsten. "Brecht und der Film." In *Text und Kritik. Sonderband Brecht I* (1972), pp. 81–99.

16

DENNIS F. MAHONEY

A recast Goethe: Günther's
Lotte in Weimar (1975)

On 6 June 1975, the film version of Thomas Mann's *Lotte in Weimar* was premiered in Weimar, East Germany, in recognition of both the showplace of the novel and its author's 100th birthday. All signs pointed to the importance allotted to this production by DEFA, the East German film company. Earlier that year, *Lotte in Weimar* had become the first film ever to represent the German Democratic Republic (GDR) at the Cannes Film Festival. Director and scriptwriter was Egon Günther, a novelist already known for his proficient cinematic adaptations of literary works.[1] In a move designed to make the film equally suitable for West and East German distribution, the West German actress Lilli Palmer was selected for the title role. GDR screen favorites Jutta Hoffmann and Katharina Thalbach played the duo of Adele Schopenhauer and Ottilie von Pogwisch, while the actors portraying the young Goethe of Lotte's imagination (Hilmar Eichhorn) and the Goethe she actually encounters in Weimar (Martin Hellberg) embodied to a startling degree the images of Goethe we possess from contemporary portraits. Shot partly on location in Weimar and making ample use of Mann's descriptions of the characters' clothing, mannerisms, and even ways of speaking, the film vividly evoked Weimar life in the years around 1816. Even the prestigious Gewandhaus-Orchestra of Leipzig contributed to the production, playing selections from Mahler's Sixth Symphony for the soundtrack.

Dismissed as a "heavy-handed period piece"[2] by the correspondent for *Variety* at the Cannes Film Festival, *Lotte in Weimar* received a more positive rating in the *International Film Guide 1976*. Even there the praises dealt more with details such as costuming and individual acting performances than with the intrinsic quality of the film itself: "Certainly *Lotte in Weimar* demonstrated that the GDR can now offer films with production values the equal of any country's."[3] In West Germany, *Lotte in Weimar* met with great critical disfavor, being perceived as a costume film designed to increase the prestige of the GDR by documenting its interest in "culture."[4]

One exception in this regard was the reviewer for *Der Spiegel*; while entertaining no particularly high regard for the film, he did wonder "whether Günther, seen rightly, has not made an anti-Goethe film on top of the textual carpet of Thomas Mann. At least a film against the blind cult of personality as was typical in Weimar and still is today in the GDR."[5]

This position, expressed as a provocative question in *Der Spiegel*, had in fact already been advanced in part by the East German journal *Film und Fernsehen*, whose June 1975 issue devoted three articles to *Lotte in Weimar*.[6] Dieter Schiller, in particular, commenting on the satiric depiction of the circle around Goethe in Weimar, offered the following interpretation:

> She [Lotte] sees herself confronted with the confessions and fates of people who hide the inability to develop their own personalities by a fixation on the great Goethe. Here lies the focus of the film, it seems – and this is good, because it thereby raises the question as to the origin of the Goethe cult in the city, the social reality, and the individual dispositions arising from it.[7]

To be sure, Dieter Schiller does not make it clear why a contemporary East German director should be interested in exploring the origins of the Goethe cult: his references to the "tradition and heritage of classical humanism"[8] are not likely to mean much to western readers unschooled in GDR cultural politics, nor does this critic consider the possibility that a socialistic Goethe cult might exist.

Before examining the questions as to whether Egon Günther has made an anti-Goethe film, and if so why, I first propose to take a close look at *Lotte in Weimar*, examining differences between the Goethe depicted by Thomas Mann and the image of Goethe imparted by the film. Thereafter attention will be directed to the reception of Goethe in the GDR, both by the official promulgators of cultural politics and by the younger generation of writers in the years immediately preceding the issuance of *Lotte in Weimar*. Seen in this greater context, the film proves paradigmatic for a new approach to Goethe in the appropriation of the cultural heritage by the German Democratic Republic.[9]

In terms of plot, *Lotte in Weimar* follows its literary antecedent closely. Günther's major innovation here is to begin the film, before the credits are shown, with a scene showing a young man pursuing his beloved through a field, dropping to her feet indoors and beginning to kiss and caress her thighs. As she, gently panting, raises his head to hers for a kiss – the scene abruptly shifts to the interior of a coach containing an old woman purring in her sleep like a cat. She is soon identified at her destination, the inn Zum Elephanten in Weimar, as Charlotte Kestner, *née* Buff, and is besieged by townspeople eager to catch a glimpse of "Werther's Lotte." But as Lotte must sadly admit to herself after a similar dream sequence at the inn, where

Plates 33 and 34   The passionate young Goethe (Hilmar Eichhorn) embraces the object of his devotion, Lotte (Martina Wilke). "Storm and stress" reminiscence pales in the face of staid Weimar reality: the classical Goethe (Martin Hellberg) sits in a coach many years later with Charlotte Kestner (Lilli Palmer). Photos courtesy of Stiftung Deutsche Kinemathek.

she has already written a note requesting an audience with Goethe: "Alas, I have not had that experience myself! It wasn't at all that stormy. He only wrote it all like that!"[10] Not only has Goethe's *The Sorrows of Young Werther (Die Leiden des jungen Werthers)* brought people like Mager and the buxom Miss Cuzzle to mistake Frau Councillor Charlotte Kestner for the Lotte of the novel, it has also caused Charlotte's recollections of her youthful encounter with Goethe to be altered by its literary representation.

Still another function of these dream sequences prior to Lotte's conversations with members of Goethe's Weimar entourage, though, is to demonstrate the strength of forty-four years' fascination with the charming egotist and man of letters who came within a shade of winning her away from her fiancé with a single kiss – and then wrote a book about it. In her conversation with Riemer, Goethe's famulus, Lotte expresses her resentment at Goethe for having intruded in the tender relationship between bride and bridegroom in such a fashion; she questions the integrity of a person who could do this. By way of answer, Riemer provides a statement by Goethe: "'A poem,' I have heard him say, 'is actually nothing at all. A poem is like a kiss which one gives to the world. But no children come of kisses'" (p. 90).

At this point in the film, one might still have expected an exposition of the antagonism between life and art, central to so many of Thomas Mann's works. But as the film progresses, it becomes clear that its focus is on Goethe the person, not Goethe the artist. The workings of Goethe's creative mind, such as Mann explored in chapter VII's interior monologue, remain *terra incognita* in the film. Apart from a few mutterings which the barber overhears while Goethe talks to his reflection in the mirror, only the opening of this monologue is spoken in a voice-over narrative, accompanied by a shot of Goethe's profile in his dimly lit green bedroom which makes him look more like a mummy than the "blithe oldster" (p. 281) alluded to in the corresponding scene in the novel. Since Günther has already demonstrated his ability to make effective use of dream sequences – and will do so again in the visionary conversation between Lotte and Goethe at the end of the film – it can be assumed that Günther's excisions are motivated less by fear of undertaking the transposition of stream-of-consciousness narrative into moving pictures than by a deliberate decision to emphasize certain aspects of the novel at the expense of others.

Significant in this regard is the omission of any reference to Marianne Willemer, and only the most fleeting allusion to the *Divan* poems on which Goethe had been working at the time of Charlotte Kestner's visit in September of 1816. In a letter to Karl Kerényi on 16 February 1939, Thomas Mann underscored the importance of these aspects of the novel:

> One of the major themes of *The Beloved Returns* is the repetition of life in a *spiritually enhanced* although also less vital form; for the Hatem infatuation with Marianne Willemer involves just such a repetition of the Lotte experience. She is even called Jung [i.e. "young"]. The beloved is always young; but what is somewhat bewildering is that, alongside the ageless one, the Lotte who has grown old is also still here and presents herself.[11]

It is thus only logical that Thomas Mann should "complete" his montage of verses from Goethe's *Divan* poem "Phenomenon" (*"Phänomen"*) not with the concluding lines "Though the hair may be white, / Yet still shalt thou love,"[12] but rather with Goethe's recollection of "Venus and Adonis" (p. 281) – a sign of both his undiminished erotic sensibilities and their transmutation into art. In the film, however, Goethe's inner monologue is interrupted by a shot of "the Lotte who has grown old" walking past Goethe's Weimar residence, with the lush "Alma Mahler" theme from the soundtrack suggesting Charlotte's determination to re-establish herself as the great love in Goethe's life.[13] But as subsequent events will show, love is precisely what she is *not* going to receive in her reunion with Goethe!

Rather than focusing on the Hatem-Marianne relationship, Egon Günther devotes nearly one-third of the film to Adele Schopenhauer's account of the Ferdinand Heincke–Ottilie–August von Goethe love triangle, establishing this as a parodistic "repetition of the Lotte experience," as portrayed in Charlotte's dreams and flashbacks during her conversation with Riemer. In the process, August appears as a spineless puppet manipulated by his father, who is thus to marry by proxy a copy of the youthful love from whom

Goethe himself fled. "Ottilie is your image," Adele concludes her narrative, "as such she is beloved. As a mother protect Ottilie from being sacrificed to a fascination" (p. 218). This appeal to Charlotte proves fruitless; *Werther* is soon to be re-enacted, with Goethe's son forced into the role of Albert, Lotte's dutiful but dull husband.[14]

Throughout the film, only August's subservience to his father is depicted, for Günther has also chosen to elide the conversation between Lotte and August in chapter VI of the novel, where the son's devotion to his father had been established. On the other hand, where Thomas Mann, through Adele's narration, indirectly reports on Goethe's machinations designed to keep August away from military service, Günther dramatically depicts Goethe's tyrannical behavior toward his son. August, attempting to play the same "poetic" role as Ferdinand, his rival for Ottilie, has joined the volunteers against Napoleon. As the camera focuses on the gigantic bust of Juno, in front of the room where August is revealing his decision to his father, the following storm on Olympus erupts:

GOETHE: You've enlisted after all? Voluntarily stepped forward? As the fiftieth infantry rifle? Without my consent?

AUGUST: I just couldn't avoid joining! It is the fashion, father.

GOETHE: Feebleminded and unfilial! I shall write letters; I shall write to Minister von Voigt! You won't get away from me! That would be −! I shall throw my whole weight into the scale!   (pp. 191–2)

As the tirade progresses, it becomes clear that Goethe's sole concern is to keep August at home to take care of his business affairs and correspondence, regardless of August's own desires or the effects his father's decision will have on Ottilie's opinion of her suitor. August eventually rushes out of the back room and sets himself down, sobbing, in a chair near the foreground of the scene, while the unseen Goethe rages on, behaving very much like the Zeus against whom Goethe's poem "Prometheus" had once inveighed. In the final sharpening of the critical ax, Günther includes a scene outside the house where a woodchopping servant, hearing the tumult inside, turns to his companion and asks: "How long have you been with the great know-it-all of Weimar?" Up until this point in the film, the audience has only heard *about* "Goethe in Weimar." This is the first occasion where one actually hears him speak, and the experience is bound to leave a markedly negative impression.

Nor is the great man shown in a more favorable light in the dinner party scene, where Charlotte finally gets the chance to meet Goethe again face to face. He monopolizes the conversation, recounting anecdotes which his hangers-on can now reproduce word for word, though they still pretend to find them fascinating. Here too one can discern a sharpness in tone greater than that found in the book. In Mann's presentation, Goethe's tale of the crystal he discovered by the side of the road brings "love and pleasure" (p. 409) to the faces of all the dinner guests; in the film, Mines Superintendent Werner echoes Goethe's punchline "Well, how did *you* get here?" (p. 408) before the latter can repeat it himself. And as the guests choke with false laughter – while Riemer pounds the table with a look of unspeakable self-loathing and August, an alcoholic, drinks another glass of wine as his response – the words "the great man is a national misfortune" (p. 418) attain an explicitness not present in Thomas Mann's subtly ironic banquet scene. Indeed, with the exception of the concluding coachride scene, where of course the question arises as to whether or not Goethe is actually there,[15] the aging Goethe is shown to be a thoroughly disagreeable individual. But while this may be one of the points of Thomas Mann's novel, it is hardly the sole message, nor necessarily even the more important of the two poles in Goethe's nature – the genial and the all-too-human – in Mann's presentation of his artistic predecessor.

Rather than faulting Günther, though, for an incomplete and imperfect reproduction of Mann's novel, one is better advised to ask why he has presented Goethe in such a fashion. In his discussion of Luchino Visconti's *Death in Venice* (*Morte a Venezia*, 1971) and the Thomas Mann novella, Hans Vaget speaks of considerations very pertinent for *Lotte in Weimar*:

Language is implicit and does not restrict the reader's imagination to the degree a picture does. Moving pictures, on the other hand, are explicit because they have to show, for instance, a particular person and a specific hotel. It follows that film by the requirements of its medium narrows down and thus changes our perception even when it strives for the utmost fidelity to the literary model.[16]

When dealing with a personality of such mythic proportions as Goethe, however, this inevitable narrowing of the viewer's perception through the medium of film can serve as an artistic benefit. In her analysis of the image of Goethe in Thomas Mann's *Lotte in Weimar*, Charlotte Evans argues that Mann's efforts to provide a counterbalance to the traditional, idealized conception of Goethe were ultimately defeated by the strength of this same preconception.[17] By demystifying Goethe so utterly, then, Günther is in effect preparing the viewer for a fresh perspective on the writer and his works.

Vaget has suggested another useful guideline for the analysis of literary adaptations: a consideration of the respective cultural and historical contexts of the works in question.[18] Very early in *Lotte in Weimar*, Günther supplies the audience with a clue as to the film's perspective. Between the opening scene and Lotte's arrival at the inn Zum Elephanten, the credits are given, with a background establishing shot of Weimar. As the camera pans over the ducal palace in the direction of the Duke Carl August monument, the audience sees not coaches, but rather automobiles whizzing through the main square. Like the ending of Horst Seeman's *Beethoven – Days From a Life* (*Beethoven – Tage aus einem Leben*, 1976), where Beethoven is seen pulling a cart through the streets of East Berlin, this sequence reminds its viewers to consider *Lotte in Weimar* not a costume film hermetically sealed in a past era, but rather an examination of a great artist and his surroundings from a contemporary vantage point.[19]

In this regard, Günther follows a procedure common to Thomas Mann, whose novel clearly bears marks of the late 1930s. During the banquet scene, for example, Goethe's recounting of a pogrom in medieval Eger is intended as a commentary on the atrocity of *Kristallnacht* ("Crystal Night;" cf. pp. 410–11). Likewise, Goethe's reflections on his relationship to the Germans thinly mask Thomas Mann's own attitudes during his exile from Germany: "They think they are Germany – but I am. Let the rest perish root and branch, it will survive in me. Do your best to fend me off, still I stand for you" (p. 331).[20] As scandalous as Mann's image of Goethe might have been to Goethe idolators, it did represent a model of German humanism as an answer to the barbaric developments in Nazi Germany, and was interpreted as such by the Marxist critic Georg Lukács in an essay written in 1945:

> But this novel of Goethe [*Lotte in Weimar*] is more than a monumental song of consolation for a drunken people hurling itself nihilistically into the abyss of fascism. It returns to the past in order to give promise for the future. By re-creating the best that German bourgeois culture had achieved, Mann seeks to awaken its buried, aberrant and brutalized potentialities. Mann's appeal rang with a primal moral optimism; what was possible once could always be realized again.[21]

But with the establishment of the GDR in 1949 – the 200th anniversary of Goethe's birth – the official East German position was that bourgeois West Germany had forfeited any claim to its humanistic heritage. As Johannes R. Becher, the writer of the new national anthem for the GDR, proclaimed in his speech "Goethe the Liberator" in Weimar on 28 August 1949: "Rediscovering the realm ["Reich"] that is Goethe means at the same time that we must liberate Goethe, the Liberator, from the hands of those who have so shamefully misspent and shamelessly misused his heritage."[22] Goethe became official state property, so to speak, in East Germany, whose self-proclaimed mission was to make real the hopes expressed by Goethe at the conclusion to *Faust II:* "The free man, the free people on a free soil, a challenge raised during the Age of Goethe, has become the challenge of our era."[23] And what the poet Becher had expressed as a challenge was soon portrayed as a reality by party ideologues, whose appropriation of Goethe as a means of legitimizing conditions in East Germany often assumed grotesquely comic forms. Consider, for example, Socialist Unity Party theoretician Kurt Hager's musings on what Goethe might say today, were he a party member:

> Johann Wolfgang Goethe reportedly said of the people in this part of Thuringia that they had a quiet, moderate economic striving. If Goethe

were living today and perhaps had even participated in this conference of district delegates as a representative from Rudolstadt or Jena, he would certainly say: Here in the district of Gera live people who distinguish themselves through a quiet, but utterly diligent striving toward high economic achievements.[24]

Egon Günther may well have had such pronouncements in mind when he had his Goethe say "The great man is a national misfortune!"

In the area of East German cultural politics, as well, where Lukácsian aesthetics played a dominant role as late as the 1960s, the prevailing official tendency was to absolutize Goethe and to label his artistic and political viewpoints as being the only appropriate ones for the age in which he lived.[25] But about the same time that western Germanists began to challenge the "Classicism Legend," a younger generation of East German writers and scholars – among them Stephan Hermlin, Günther Kunert, Günter de Bruyn, Klaus Träger, and Christa and Gerhard Wolf – attempted their own re-evaluation of Goethe and his era. Very often their advocacy of writers like Jean Paul, Heinrich von Kleist, or Friedrich Hölderlin was coupled with a criticism of Goethe's egocentricity and intolerance of other artistic directions.[26] No wonder, then, that Egon Günther took care to include in *Lotte in Weimar* Adele Schopenhauer's declaration of cultural independence in favor of the romantic painters and writers, as a parallel to the current re-evaluation of German romanticism in GDR literary scholarship:

ADELE: We [Adele and friends] know and love painters like the pious Cornelius and Overbeck – at whose pictures he [Goethe], as I myself have heard him say, would dearly like to shoot with a pistol.
LOTTE: With a pistol?
ADELE: Caspar David Friedrich's pictures, he feels, can just as well be hung upside down. "It should not be allowed!" he thunders. We let him thunder. We read poems by Uhland and the splendid grotesque tales of Hoffmann – with *de*light! (p. 138)

Seen in this greater context, the film *Lotte in Weimar* becomes part of a widespread effort in East Germany to take Goethe off his pedestal and conduct a critical evaluation of his person and his surroundings. Paradoxically, this analysis succeeds in winning sympathy for Goethe by the end of the film, when he and Lotte conduct their coachride discussion on "impairment" (pp. 449–51). The physical deterioration in Charlotte Kestner is readily apparent in her trembling face and shaking hands; but at least she can still fit into her Lotte dress from *Werther* days! The change in Goethe is even more striking; in Weimar, he has become a tyrannical pedant who uses Frederick the Great's words as a means of telling his entourage: "I am tired of ruling over slaves" (p. 420).

But to a large degree this impairment (*Verkümmerung*) can be ascribed to Goethe's constricted Weimar surroundings, where he is not only the constant center of attention, but also the subject of so much gossip. By means of a subtle filmic device, Günther has implanted this suggestion in the viewer's mind long before the aging Goethe makes his first appearance. Placed very prominently in the room where Charlotte conducts her conversations with Riemer and Adele Schopenhauer is a glass fishbowl containing a goldfish almost the length of the bowl. As the fish twists and turns in its narrow confines, it becomes apparent that it is not the fish which is monstrous or distorted, but rather the discrepancy between its dimensions and the constraints of its environment. Thus the viewer can well believe Goethe's response to Lotte's reproach that all the people in his vicinity are victims of his greatness: "Dear childlike old soul, I, first and last, am the sacrifice, and he that offers it" (p. 451).

In Thomas Mann's treatment of the coachride scene, Goethe's sublimation of personal tragedy through its depiction in art is fortified by references to the "Trilogy of Passion" ("Trilogie der Leidenschaft") and the conclusion to *Elective Affinities* (*Die Wahlverwandtschaften*). In Günther's edited script, only references to the characters Werther and Tasso remain, suggesting the theme of the individual overwhelmed by isolation – the principal concern of his film version of *The Sorrows of Young Werther* (*Die Leiden des jungen Werthers*, 1976):

> GOETHE: Wouldst thou ask of me repentance? Only wait! I see her ride towards me, in a mantle grey. Then once more the hour of Werther and Tasso will strike. Leave-taking for ever, death struggle of feelings, frightful pangs such as probably for some time precede the hour of death. Death, final flight into the flame – the All-in-One – why should it too be aught but transformation?   (p. 452)

It is only fitting that whereas Mann's novel ends on a conciliatory note, the film's coachlight candle illumines a bitterly weeping Lotte, devastated by her vision of "Goethe in Weimar."

In conclusion, a few words should be said about the music that is heard during this coachride scene and at moments throughout the film when Lotte is reliving her memories of Goethe: again and again one hears the ardent second theme from the opening movement of Mahler's Sixth Symphony. Hans Günther Pflaum regards this use of Mahler as unmotivated, or at best a reference to Visconti's *Death in Venice*.[27] Although this use of Mahler is doubtlessly intended as a reference to Visconti's film (which was received enthusiastically in East Germany upon its showing in 1973), it also serves a thematic function. This "Alma Mahler" theme acts as a signal of Lotte's longing to see herself as the great love of Goethe's life. Only one other theme grouping from this symphony is employed, and only on two occasions: both the dream sequence where Goethe/Werther is kissing Lotte passionately and Goethe's final words in the coach, as quoted above, are accompanied by the principal theme of the first movement. In so doing, Günther achieves two effects. He makes it clear that Lotte's final coachride vision is as much a poetic fabrication as was her initial one; and he suggests the fate overtaking even the greatest of poets by sounding the strident march opening Mahler's "Tragic" Symphony.[28]

Conventional GDR treatments of Goethe, while paying all due respect to Marx and Engels's caustic references to "the wretchedness of German life" (*die deutsche Misère*), at the same time heap praises on Goethe for his achievement of the balanced, well-developed personality that is the avowed goal of East German society.[29] But in transcending the cult of personality in the GDR by showing the pain and frustration in Goethe's being, Egon Günther has in fact made *Lotte in Weimar* an exemplification of Friedrich Engels's pronouncement on Goethe's ambiguous relation to German society:

It is the persistent struggle in himself [Goethe] between the poet of genius, disgusted by the wretchedness of his surroundings, and the Frankfurt alderman's cautious child, the privy councillor of Weimar, who sees himself forced to make a truce with it and to get used to it. Thus Goethe is now colossal, now petty; now a defiant, ironical, world-scorning genius, now a calculated, complacent, narrow philistine. Even Goethe was unable to overcome the wretchedness of German life; on the contrary, it overcame him, and this victory over the greatest German is the best proof that it cannot be conquered by the individual.[30]

Made for a society whose young readers had only recently responded enthusiastically to Ulrich Plenzdorf's *The New Sufferings of Young W.* (*Die neuen Leiden des jungen W.*, 1973) and its reworking of *Werther* in a GDR setting,[31] *Lotte in Weimar* demonstrates that a recasting of past literature and literary traditions can result in challenging and provocative film as well – when the director is as critical and imaginative as Egon Günther.[32]

Notes

1. Egon Günther's filmic adaptations of novels include versions of Johannes R. Becher's *Farewell* (*Abschied*, 1968), and Arnold Zweig's *Young Woman of 1914* (*Junge Frau von 1914*, 1970) and *Education before Verdun* (*Erziehung von Verdun*, 1973). Since *Lotte in Weimar*, he has directed *The Sorrows of Young Werther* (*Die Leiden des jungen Werthers*, 1976), *Ursula* (1978) – an adaptation of Gottfried Keller's novella which was co-produced by Swiss Television – and, more recently, the multiple installment television productions, Lion Feuchtwanger's *Exile* (*Exil*, 1981) and Uwe Timm's *Morenga* (1985). For further information on Günther's career,

see Hans Günther Pflaum, "Egon Günther: Bekenntnis zu Gefühlen," in *Film in der DDR*, ed. Peter W. Jansen and Wolfram Schütte (Munich: Hanser, 1977), pp. 115–34.

2. Gene Moskowitz, "Summary of 1975 at Cannes fest," *Variety*, 28 May 1975, 42.

3. Peter Cowie (ed.), *International Film Guide 1976* (London: Tantivy, 1975), p. 187.

4. Cf. Wolfram Tichy and Liz-Anne Bawden (eds), *rororo Filmlexikon* (Reinbek: Rowohlt, 1978), IV, p. 1027. Cf. also Elisabeth Uhländer (ed.), *Filme 1971–76. Kritische Notizen aus sechs Kino- und Fernsehjahren* (Cologne: Bachem, 1977), p. 189. See also Rainer Gansera's polemical article, "Stehen Sie nicht so krumm, Brecht, und nehmen Sie die Hände aus der Tasche," *Filmkritik*, 19, No. 3 (March 1975), 102–4, which condemned *Lotte in Weimar* in advance on the basis of a televised interview with Günther.

5. "DDR-Film: Personenkult mit Popanz-Goethe," *Der Spiegel*, 3 November 1975, 175. Another critic, in a much more favorable review of *Lotte in Weimar*, has gone so far as to call Günther's film a political parable about the cult of personality in socialist countries. See Hans Drawe, "Literatur im Film," in *Die Literatur der DDR*, ed. Hans Jürgen Schmitt (Munich: Hanser, 1983), pp. 222–3.

6. See in particular Dieter Schiller, "Charlotte contra Goethekult: *Lotte in Weimar* – ein Film nach dem gleichnamigen Roman von Thomas Mann," *Film und Fernsehen*, 3, No. 6 (1975), 2–8. Günther Rücker's "Jupiter tritt auf: Gedanken um einen Film von Egon Günther," (ibid., 8–10, 12–13, and 46–7) is above all an impressionistic review of the achievements of Günther, production crew, and principal actors. Martin Hellberg, in "Goethe – das ist nicht spielbar! Zur Gestaltung einer Rolle" (ibid., 10–11), recounts the personal preparations and the suggestions from Günther and Lilli Palmer which finally allowed him to master this "unplayable" role.

7. Schiller, "Charlotte contra Goethekult," 4.

8. ibid., 8.

9. For a brief discussion of the appropriation of "cultural heritage" – specifically Goethe's life and works – through the medium of films such as *Lotte in Weimar*, see Wolfgang Weiss (ed.), *Film- und Fernsehkunst der DDR: Traditionen, Beispiele, Tendenzen* (Berlin [GDR]: Henschel, 1979), pp. 407–10. By way of contrast, see Rolf Richter, "Egon Günther: Der Mensch ist veränderbar," in *DEFA-Spielfilm-Regisseure und ihre Kritiker*, ed. Rolf Richter (Berlin [GDR]: Henschel, 1981), I, 32–56. Richter, while not discussing or even mentioning *Lotte in Weimar*, understands all of Günther's filmic adaptations of literary works as a denunciation of bourgeois life (p. 46).

10. Quotations in this essay, unless otherwise stated, refer to the soundtrack of the film *Lotte in Weimar*. For the analogous section in the novel, see Thomas Mann, *The Beloved Returns: Lotte in Weimar*, trans. H. T. Lowe-Porter (New York: Knopf, 1940), pp. 27–8. For purposes of comparison, quotes from the film will be followed by parenthetical page references to the corresponding scene in the novel. As Egon Günther's filmscript itself employs great chunks of the novel's dialogues, I have followed the Lowe-Porter wording as far as possible in my translation of the soundtrack.

11. *Mythology and Humanism: The Correspondence of Thomas Mann and Karl Kerényi*, trans. Alexander Gelley (Ithaca and London: Cornell University Press, 1975), pp. 88–9.

12. *Goethes Werke*, ed. Erich Trunz (Hamburg: Wegner, 1960), II, 13. The translation is mine.

13. For a further discussion of Günther's use of Mahler's music, see the conclusion to this essay.

14. Hilmar Baumann (August) and Katharina Thalbach (Ottilie), interestingly enough, play the roles of Albert and Lotte in Günther's subsequent film, *The Sorrows of Young Werther*.

15. See Thomas Mann's letter to Fritz Grünbaum on 16 February 1947 in *Briefe: 1937–1947*, ed. Erika Mann (Frankfurt am Main: Fischer, 1963), pp. 527–8.

16. Hans Vaget, "Film and literature: the case of *Death in Venice:* Luchino Visconti and Thomas Mann," *German Quarterly*, 53 (1980), 163–4. Cf. Siegfried Kracauer's fundamental distinction between film as a material continuum and the novel as a mental continuum in his *Theory of Film: The Redemption of Physical Reality* (New York: Oxford University Press, 1960), pp. 237–9.

17. Charlotte Evans, "Das Goethebild in Thomas Manns *Lotte in Weimar*," *Monatshefte*, 63 (1971), 113–14.

18. Vaget, 163.

19. Heinz Kersten's essay "Entwicklungslinien" discusses the indirect treatment of GDR problems in film adaptations of literary works and biographies, citing as examples Seeman's film and Günther's *Lotte in Weimar* and *The Sorrows of Young Werther* (in *Film in der DDR*, p. 53). Dieter Schiller likewise sees the opening of *Lotte in Weimar* as a signal to the audience (in "Charlotte contra Goethekult," 3).

20. Compare the reflections of Thomas Mann's Goethe – which reach their height in the remarks on "Humanity universal, ubiquitous; parody secretly directed against itself" (p. 331) and conclude in the German text with Faust's rhymed response to Helen of Troy – with Goethe's less exalted ruminations in the film: "Do your best to fend me off, still I stand for you – even when you have shit on my poetry with all your bellies gave out!"

21. Georg Lukács, "In search of bourgeois man," in *Essays on Thomas Mann*, trans. Stanley Mitchell (London: Merlin, 1964), p. 41.

22. Johannes R. Becher, "Goethe der Befreier," in *Werke in drei Bänden*, 2nd edn (Berlin and Weimar [GDR]: Aufbau, 1976), III, 426–7.

23. Becher, p. 426.

24. Cited by Joachim Nawrocki, "Hager, Honecker und J. W. V. Goethe," *Die Zeit*, 10 April 1981.

25. Cf. Walter Hinderer, "Die Regressive Universalideologie: Zum Klassikbild der marxistischen Literaturkritik von Franz Mehring bis zu den *Weimarer Beiträgen*," in *Die Klassik-Legende*, ed. Reinhold Grimm and Jost Hermand (Frankfurt am Main: Athenäum, 1971), pp. 141–75, esp. 158–75.

26. See Bernd Leistner's article "Zum Goethe-Bezug in der neueren DDR-Literatur," *Weimarer Beiträge*, 23, No. 5 (1977), 86–120 – itself a prime example of a differentiated, sophisticated approach to the question of "literary heritage" in the GDR. See also Patricia Herminghouse, "Coming to terms with classicism: Goethe in GDR literature of the 1970s," *German Quarterly*, 56 (1983), 273–84.

27. Pflaum, *Film in der DDR*, p. 133.

28. Cf. Henry Raynor's discussion of the programmatic aspects to the themes of Mahler's Sixth Symphony: "Both Mahler and his wife saw the work as intensely personal; its first movement is a resolute, persistent march. The second group themes grow out of a proudly soaring march which, according to the composer, was a musical portrait of his wife." In *Mahler* (London: Macmillan, 1975), p. 96.

29. Cf. Becher, pp. 412–23.

30. Friedrich Engels, "German socialism in verse and prose" ("Deutscher Sozialismus in Versen und Prosa"), here cited from the selected writings of Marx and Engels on the topic of *Literature and Art* (New York: International Publishers, 1947), p. 80. For the German original, see *Marx/Engels Werke* (Berlin [GDR]: Dietz, 1959), IV, p. 232.

31. For further information on Ulrich Plenzdorf's novel, see Kenneth P. Wilcox's introduction to his translation of *The New Sufferings of Young W.* (New York: Ungar, 1979), pp. v–xii.

32. This essay is an expanded version of a talk presented at the 1981 MLA Convention, in connection with the theme "The image of Goethe in our time." My thanks go to Valters Nollendorfs, who helped arrange a showing of *Lotte in Weimar*, and to Claus Wolf, Cultural Attaché of the GDR Embassy in Washington, DC, who generously provided a copy of the film for this session and for a later screening. Thanks also to my colleagues at the University of Vermont for the insights I gained through discussing the film with them. Above all, I would like to acknowledge my appreciation to Thomas P. Saine, editor of the *Goethe Yearbook*, where this article first appeared, for allowing me to publish it in revised form within the present volume.

Selected Bibliography

Belach, Helga *et al.* (ed.). *Das Kino und Thomas Mann: Eine Dokumentation.* Berlin: Stiftung Deutsche Kinemathek, 1975.

Drawe, Hans. "Literatur im Film." In *Die Literatur der DDR.* Ed. Hans Jürgen Schmitt. Munich: Hanser, 1983, pp. 187–228.

Gansera, Rainer. "Stehen Sie nicht so krumm, Brecht, und nehmen Sie die Hände aus der Tasche." *Filmkritik*, 19, No. 3 (March 1975), 102–4.

Herminghouse, Patricia. "Coming to terms with classicism: Goethe in GDR literature of the 1970s." *German Quarterly*, 56 (1983), 273–84.

Leistner, Bernd. "Zum Goethe-Bezug in der neueren DDR-Literatur." *Weimarer Beiträge*, 23, No. 5 (1977), 86–120.

Pflaum, Hans Günther. "Egon Günther: Bekenntnis zu Gefühlen." In *Film in der DDR.* Ed. Peter W. Jansen and Wolfram Schütte. Munich: Hanser, 1977, pp. 115–34.

Richter, Rolf. "Egon Günther: Der Mensch ist veränderbar." In *DEFA-Spielfilm-Regisseure und ihre Kritiker.* Ed. Rolf Richter. Berlin [GDR]: Henschel, 1981, I, pp. 32–56.

Schiller, Dieter. "Charlotte contra Goethekult: *Lotte in Weimar* – ein Film nach dem gleichnamigen Roman von Thomas Mann." *Film und Fernsehen*, 3, No. 6 (1975), 2–8.

Vaget, Hans. "Film and literature: the case of *Death in Venice*: Luchino Visconti and Thomas Mann." *German Quarterly*, 53 (1980), 159–75.

17

TIMOTHY CORRIGAN

The tension of translation: Handke's *The Left-Handed Woman* (1977)

Left-handed woman, you've given yourself away!
Or did you mean to give me a sign?

The debate about fiction-into-film will doubtless continue in as many directions and with as many conclusions as it has sustained since Vachel Lindsay and Sergei Eisenstein addressed the question. Few filmmakers or films, however, focus that debate as explicitly and rigorously as Peter Handke and his much-acclaimed *The Left-Handed Woman* (*Die linkshändige Frau*, 1977). Hailed as "that rare thing, a genuinely poetic movie,"[1] *The Left-Handed Woman* is the second feature film by this dramatist, novelist, and poet whose reputation has been based primarily on his literary achievements[2] but whose entrance into filmmaking brought immediate comparisons with the likes of Jean Cocteau and André Malraux.[3] Handke's success with this film was not, though, unprepared. Together with Wim Wenders, he made *3 American LPs* (*3 amerikanische LPs*, 1969). In 1970 he directed the TV-film *The Chronicle of Current Events* (*Die Chronik der laufenden Ereignisse*), a self-styled allegory about two years of recent West German history. The next year he provided the novel and the script for Wenders's film version of *The Goalie's Anxiety at the Penalty Kick* (*Die Angst des Tormanns beim Elfmeter*, 1972). In 1974 he collaborated with Wenders once again, this time on *Wrong Move* (*Falsche Bewegung*), a loose adaptation of Goethe's classical *Bildungsroman*, *Wilhelm Meister's Apprenticeship* (*Wilhelm Meisters Lehrjahre*).[4]

Handke's literary texts have always been peopled by notorious cinephiles and voyeurs, and, not surprisingly, in *The Left-Handed Woman*, a film produced by Wenders, the novelist's vision is realized by the cinematographer Robby Müller and the editor Peter Przygodda, important contributors to Wenders's lyrical tales of men seeking a language in a world of images. In *The Left-Handed Woman*, however, the dialectic between the visual and the verbal, so dominant in Handke's career and literary work, becomes concentrated and emphasized as never before. Unlike *The Goalie's Anxiety at the Penalty Kick*, this film was first conceived as a film and only then written as a novel. This reversal of the usual pattern of adaptation affects both the fiction and the film in crucial and telling ways – ways well beyond the obvious omissions, additions, and alterations which here and elsewhere often describe the main differences between a novel and its filmic adaptation. (In the film of *The Left-Handed Woman*, some of these simple changes include the moving of the setting from Germany to Paris, and the inclusion of a scene from an Ozu film.) Specifically, because of its filmic conception, Handke's literary version of the story contains an unusually cinematic grammar and prose in which the lack of adjectives and adverbs reduces the characters and their actions to unusually flat (even for Handke) representations. Little is attributed to the characters through the connotative force of language, and, throughout the novel, any emotional depth in or between the characters appears only as the indirect product of the static independence of the images. The strictly imagistic quality of the language and the literal significance of the words thus join in the novel across the image's resistance to any narrative or symbolic meaning and the word's insistence that that meaning be made. Ultimately one might argue that the inadequacy of this particular novel follows from just these austere limits which Handke chooses to impose on his language – for it seeks to convey an imagistic order which, by definition, can never really be made apparent in the novel and which, as a function of the work's conception, has preceded it.

At one point in the novel, for instance, the text reads:

That night the woman sat by the window with the curtains drawn, reading; a thick dictionary lay beside her. She put her book aside and opened the curtains. A car was just turning into one of the garages, and on the sidewalk an elderly lady was walking her dog. As though nothing escaped her, she looked up at the window and waved.[5]

As with much of the novel, the visual dynamics of this scene are its center: as she replaces her reading and dictionary with a gesture as simile, what does not escape the woman is precisely the discrete images which the window as frame makes available to her; she reacts to and with gestures and images, and the prose of the text accordingly seems tensely abstracted from the real drama. The film, moreover, enacts this same tension between an imagistic independence and the languages that seek to appropriate it. But, in the film, the reality of the images and their materially given and authentic status introduce the absent member of the novel's drama, and so make *actually* present the dramatic tension that is at the heart of this and most other works of literature/film adaptation: the dramatic tension of translation itself, of the impossible adaptation of language to image and image to language.

Plate 35 A moment of true feeling: silent until this moment, Marianne (Edith Clever) tells her husband (Bruno Ganz), "I suddenly had an illumination that you were going away, that you were leaving me. Yes, that's it. Go away, Bruno.

From the beginning of the film, the central image and measure of this authenticity are clearly the woman herself. In the book and film, she suddenly announces her break with her husband by saying that she has "had a strange idea. Well, not really an idea, more like an – illumination" (p. 13); and her distinction is especially appropriate since what she is claiming is herself as image, not her position as an abstraction in some larger discourse. In this announcement, there is none of the verbal explaining, none of the social and psychological rationale that generally define (in literature and film) this kind of decision to break with a husband and the social world he represents. Her crisis does not concern any search for identity but simply and plainly a claiming of an identity already possessed but unacknowledged. Like the home where she continues to live, her "leaving" is, more accurately, a staying. In this way, *The Left-Handed Woman* is both less than and more than a feminist film, involving little of the social and psychoanalytic work associated with a feminist position today and instead defining her mainly and quite idealistically in terms of her stoic resistance to *any* typing or social positioning.

The course of the film, in fact, could be described as a series of negations or resistances through which Marianne holds off different individuals and different discourses which attempt to coopt her (image) into their language. In the opening of the film, she picks up her husband, Bruno, at the airport and listens passively as he talks continuously about his trip to Finland where, ironically, he had been completely isolated by the language he could not speak. Later, speaking of "the mature beauty of master/servant relationships," he takes her to dinner in order that they may luxuriate in being served by others. After being confronted with her decision to live alone, he explains it with a terminology that has no real bearing on the act, calling her a "mystic." Finally, when Marianne and their son visit him in his office, Bruno acts out the "stare" with which he hopes to exercise enough power to become a member of the board, the stare through which one controls another's image. Several other men whom she encounters come to represent similar versions of this need to appropriate and dominate Marianne: the publisher who hires her uses the opportunity to court her, and, when she resists, he tries to coerce her by telling a tale of a lonely writer whose isolation eventually made it impossible for him to use words at all; her father visits her in a confused and half-hearted effort to reconcile her to a world that grows more hostile with old age; and even the strange unemployed actor she meets one day pursues her with a silent and romantic passion that, for all the two seem to have in common, is entirely inappropriate to a woman whose ultimate desire is not to get entangled with the objects and desires of the world.

Despite its usually male character, this is not, however, only a patriarchal order that threatens her. Marianne's close friend Franziska, while allowing Bruno to live with her, urges Marianne to join her feminist group so that she may locate an image of herself outside the one forced on her by the dominant male culture. Yet, what Franziska does not realize is that for Marianne the feminist circle offers only another socially and subjectively made image, not one independently isolated in its own integrity. Marianne consistently and stoically remains apart from *any* discourse that attempts to encroach upon her; her placid expression and extraordinarily silent manner are peculiarly non-aggressive and undemanding, bearing witness to a claim for self-possession and nothing more. As Stanley Kauffmann has remarked, she is not violently mute like Elisabet in Bergman's *Persona* (1966) but verbally restrained and sparing in a manner that makes her separation a more confident and less dependent break with the social world around her.[6] If she is part of a woman's film tradition, it is not that of Paul Mazursky's *An Unmarried Woman* (1978) or Agnès Varda's *One Sings, the Other Doesn't* (*L'Une chante, l'autre pas*, 1977), but that of Chantal Akerman's *Meetings with Anna* (*Les Rendez-vous d'Anna*, 1978). This is not a flamboyant assertion into or against another social order but a quiet departure from the abstracting terms of any social discourse.

In this resistance to discourse, Marianne becomes almost pure image, a negation of social languages.[7] It is more than twenty minutes into the film before this central character utters her first word, and for the remainder of the film she says extremely little, a passive listener in most of her conversations with others. After her husband accuses her of mysticism, she regards herself in the mirror and says, "Say whatever you want; the more you say the freer I'll be of you." This confrontation is, on the one hand, directed at her absent husband and his attempt to bully and manipulate her with language. On the other hand, it is aimed at her own divided self as an image produced by that patriarchal discourse and as an image independent of those words, more distinguished in its difference the more those words attempt and fail to claim that image. The scene becomes a metaphoric reversal of a Freudian mirror state, a negation in every sense, as she identifies an image of herself present before that infantile mirror stage when social/linguistic transformations produced a socialized image of her. She identifies herself, in short, as a left-handed image: free of language and logic *because* she can see herself as an isolated and singular image. Here as throughout the film, she lives according to negations, not contraries; ultimately, her efforts are to claim herself not as an opposite discourse but as an entirely separate presence.

Formally, the film is most striking in its dramatization of just this imagistic isolation. Assisted here in large part by Müller and Przygodda, this use of the image as a discrete entity and value follows almost too patently Wenders's sensibility from his first student films to the more recent *The State of Things* (*Der Stand der Dinge*, 1982). But, as in the case of Wenders, and as Handke makes quite clear in this film, the true source of this sensibility is the Japanese filmmaker Yasujiro Ozu. Cited several times in *The Left-Handed Woman*, Ozu is most noticeably acknowledged when the camera pans from a dimly lit shot of the woman silently crouched against the

Plate 36   The woman and her child, scribblings on an otherwise blank Metro wall: an example of Handke's imagistic isolation. Photo courtesy of New Yorker Films.

wall to a poster of Ozu and then back to the woman. The importance of Ozu to Handke and Wenders is mainly the manner in which Ozu's films valorize the image in itself and formally isolate it from both human and diegetic significance. In Noël Burch's words about Ozu, images and objects as images often appear in his narratives as "pillow shots," and, like his mismatching, they reflect "a culturally and complexly determined sign of dissent from the world-view implicit in the Western mode. This mode, of course, is profoundly *anthropocentric*."[8] In Ozu's films these shots "intervene in a certain kind of discourse, and each de-centering effect possesses its own specificity. These shots cause a suspension of the diegesis. . . . The *space* from which these references are made is invariably presented as outside the diegesis, as a pictorial space on another plane of 'reality'."[9]

Despite these clear connections with Ozu and his compositional methods, there is a difference. The sequence with the poster of Ozu follows shortly after a sequence in which Marianne, seated between her son and his friend, watches an Ozu movie, *Tokyo Chorus* (*Tokyo no Gassho*, 1931). In the sequence from the Ozu film, a family is seated in a circle apparently playing a clapping game of some sort; but, while pretending to enjoy herself, the mother-wife is secretly crying. In one important sense, this sequence describes the tragic isolation of the woman from the familial and social circle around her, and it thus partially reflects the predicament of Handke's own woman. Yet, Handke's woman falls asleep during the sequence, and one way of reading this would be that the predicament of the insert film contains nothing filmically or fictionally interesting (or provoking) for Marianne because she has, at this point, moved outside the tragic pathos of that circle (just as Handke's film recontextualizes Ozu's). Significantly, this image of the mother asleep on the shoulder of her son is one of the two images that Handke says is the source of the film.[10] The image suggests a negation (eyes shut, asleep, and uninterested) of the social bind Ozu's mother represents and, at the same time, it enacts a perfectly passive overturning of the traditional gestures of support in a family hierarchy. Handke's perspective is not, therefore, merely a recreation or appropriation of Ozu's world; rather, his heroine and the discrete images about her describe a different drama, since Marianne has already achieved and now only works to maintain the internal authenticity and harmony that Ozu's characters constantly struggle towards. She inhabits the pillow shots that beckon from afar to Ozu's men and women.

The connection between Handke's woman and Ozu's film is therefore not between the characters of the two worlds but between the extra-human images around Ozu's individuals and the human reality of Handke's woman. Quite systematically, *The Left-Handed Woman* establishes an equation between its protagonist and the extra-human realm of the discrete objects and images that tragically evade Ozu's all-too-human characters. The film opens with a series of these shots: grass rustling as a train rushes by, newspapers blowing across an empty station platform, a motionless urbanscape, the woman's home depicted in a symmetrically flat frontal shot, and a still life of fruit. Throughout the film, these kinds of static images punctuate its course with a logic which, while breaking with the diegesis, establishes concomitantly a connection with the woman herself. The montage that develops around these shots paradoxically separates them from the realm of human discourse while linking them to Marianne's independent status as discrete image. Among the many examples of this action, perhaps the most explicit are the shots of tulips (at the restaurant meal, for instance) with trembling or falling petals which, after being pictorially disconnected, are graphically linked to the woman herself. As Eric Rentschler notes, these "pillow shots suggest a concrete world existing outside our everyday consciousness, a world waiting to be discovered, a living world beyond the compositional center of the film's narrative."[11] And the strange irony that permeates and controls this film is that this external consciousness is exactly what defines the new subjectivism that Marianne has claimed as her own and works to maintain through the course of the film. She is at once the compositional center of the film and an image at odds with that center.

The imagistic singularity of Marianne also helps explain her imperviousness to the temporal pressures directed at her. Several times in the film different characters attempt to remind her of how her retreat into a new subjectivism will be eroded and destroyed by time. In a speech that Marianne deflates as rehearsed posturing, an overdetermined social discourse, her husband taunts her with the fact that she will "grow older and older and then hang herself." The publisher tells her of the "ghastly old age" that awaits an author who has inexplicably stopped writing. The theme of her father's visit is primarily the pathos of growing old and the struggles of memory. Likewise, the narrative of the film itself is marked with titles announcing the changes in months from March through May – months of birth but, as T. S. Eliot has made us aware, also months of cruel growth. Against these movements stands the woman in her imagistic isolation, resisting temporal patterning just as she resists social and patriarchal discourses. She retreats into herself against the pressures of time and, more importantly, against the action of a narrative temporality which necessarily threatens to inscribe her in its own conventional scheme.

In this dialectic with narrative itself, one sees the most significant connection between *The Left-Handed Woman* and other feminist films which, in their different ways, confront the patriarchal order in the very structure of narrative cinema, whose temporal ordering purportedly reflects a male mode of seeing and organizing experience.[12] Specifically, these films aim at a nonnarrative disengagement from the fetishizing action of the male perspective which has dominated filmmaking since its historical beginnings; and the resistance of Handke's pillow-shot woman to a temporal composition thus takes on a larger political character as it works to separate the image of the woman (and her image-making activity) from the formal temporality of another order.[13] For her, the fears of an old age must be incidental threats; for her, the imagistic stasis of an extra-human perspective always detaches itself from the human (and male) dynamics of narrative film. Like the windows seen from the inside and the outside of the speeding trains in the film, the perspective of this woman and this film places such a radical emphasis on the frames of the image that its course through time becomes a truly secondary and separate context.

Where then is this woman's place in the public sphere? Does she in fact have such a place, and is it defined only by her separation from the other discourses (of men, of temporality, of any group consciousness) that surround her? Here lies the central tension in the film. For, if this woman defines and maintains herself through an imagistic isolation in the extra-human, the second direction of the film is her translation of herself slowly and subtly back into the human realm, a translation of the image she has claimed into a language for its communication.

Appropriately, her first foray into the matters of the social world is to take a job as a translator, and much of the film evolves around this first assignment of translating Flaubert's *A Simple Heart* (*Un Coeur simple*, 1876). The signs and significance of this movement from a state of singularity to that of human discourse appear again when she pulls her husband from the path of a truck after he has been pleading "I exist too"; and later in the film a shot of her in a café shows her face partially covered by a newspaper, the first she has read for some time and one aptly titled *Le Quotidien*.

The image of another woman and child which drifts now and then across Marianne's course is an equally crucial symbol of a potentially less enclosed relation with the world, and Marianne's own strange son comes to dramatize both the problems and possibilities of a social relationship which could preserve her own image while communicating it with others. As a natural bond that potentially both constricts and opens her, this son represents and crystallizes a dialectic with an outside order which she must separate herself from yet needs to respond to, which she moves toward but only in the tentative hope of establishing a new relationship with it. It is the intrusion and badgering of her son and his friend that make her toss her typewriter and translation off the table in anger and frustration. Often these two Kafkaesque children play strange communication games – with walkie-talkies or with vaudevillian gestures of violence – which at once mirror and stand in ironic contrast to the mother's strained efforts to establish her own idiom for communication. As a reversal of the conventional structure of family and society, individuality in this family must begin as an outside image and can only then start to work its way into the communicative framework of a fresh language and restructured social relations.

With the full scope of its implications for film, this crisis of translation means, for Handke and his characters, finding a language to speak an image not as a language but as an authentic image. It means in effect creating a language as a negation of all that conventional language implies. Like the unemployed actor whom Marianne and her father meet at the photo booth (Rüdiger Vogler, a regular in Wenders's films), this image would have to discover the impossible formula for communicating intimately and naturally while being controlled by conventional rules. As Marianne's father tells the actor, "You always seem embarrassed by your lines. . . . You're posing." To show that he has understood this message about making a filmic image speak a natural language, the father asks the actor to make the image communicate intimately: "In your next film signal me that you understood." He concludes by suggesting that with these changes an authentic image can harmoniously enter a temporal order: "I look forward," he says, "to watching you grow older on the screen." Here as throughout the film, to become a viable language, the image must aim at a radical and discrete movement back into the human world: a movement by which the singularity of imagistic identity would use yet resist the conventions of discourse, a strained and balanced movement such as this barely visible and relatively static narrative structure which nonetheless remains very much a narrative and temporal order.

More specifically, this effort to translate the image takes the form of a tension between identity and allegory. Throughout the film there are obtrusive marks of allegory, such as street names like "rue Terre Neuve" or "rue de la Raison" (on which the woman lives). And Handke has remarked that these allegorical planes are central to the film's project, as they appear alongside those striking moments of imagistic identity to create a kind of friction. In his words: "The fact that names of this kind, completely casually, appear in the story, was not used as a device to show symbolic constriction — but rather served as a kind of distortion correcting pleasantness through the gestures of allegory."[14] This tension and dialectic is in short the tension of translation. Its unconstricted balance is clarified further when, in describing the image of the suburban houses that inspired the film, Handke uses the term "a separate togetherness."[15]

On the one hand, this tension between allegory and identity involves the life of the image itself which, for Handke, exists as a sort of pure and romantic identity, a self-sustaining pleasantness outside the abstractions and weight of any discourse or structure. On the other hand, there is the communal or social order which represents itself and its elements in terms of allegorical discourse, a language to be read and spoken through larger patterns of meaning, but one here without the stability and semantic unity of symbol. Unlike a symbolic discourse, with allegory there is no interpenetration of image and language; rather there is a slight distortion which in a curious way fits together the language and the image it appropriates, so that meaning lies in the dramatic gap between the two and the image speaks only as a slight negation of the language that surrounds it.

At one point in the film, Marianne walks down rue Elise and from a neighboring house we hear Beethoven's "Für Elise." Earlier, just after she has told Bruno of her illumination, she rushes home and, without explanation, walks around her living-room on stilts. In both cases, the image and action vibrate with a significance that comes from literal, allegorical *props* (romantic pathos, escape, etc.). Yet, in both cases, the singularity of the image and the artificiality of the allegory generate an attraction and repulsion which allow the image to speak through the allegory but as significantly more than it. In a way central to Handke's entire aesthetic, translation becomes a negation of its vehicular language (as allegory), since in appropriating the image the main service of this language is to create a friction (like balancing on stilts) between the allegorical props and the referent image, calling that image forward as meaningful while testifying to its own basic inability to claim that meaning. In *I Am an Inhabitant of the Ivory Tower* (*Ich bin ein Bewohner des Elfenbeinturms*, 1972) Handke explains this in different terms: "It is not only a question of unmasking clichés . . . but of entering into, with the help of clichés of reality, new conclusions concerning reality."[16] In translating the image, this negation therefore insinuates a positive meaning: like the shot of Marianne sitting in a small shed, looking defiantly up and shutting the door on the eye of the camera, the act of negation becomes a positive claim to the fundamental value of the image as self-contained meaning.

Stylistically and structurally, the most salient action with which Handke establishes this dialectic of translation is an imagistic montage, what Rentschler has called a "collision" of elements.[17] Thematically, this collision is present in the central predicament of the film: a German woman in a French city, displaced in her place. But usually this montage or collision works through a narrative or visual jolt, a surprise or friction, whose immediate consequence is a static charge. Connected with the abrasive stasis of those pillow-shot images set against the narrative flow or the friction created by the tension between allegory and identity, the indirect purpose of this charge is to generate meaning. More specifically, it locates within its tension and along its surfaces either a character depth or a radical interaction between characters. As a dramatic illustration of this, there is again the sequence at the photo booth. The actor and Marianne move tentatively toward each other to shake hands as they prepare to part, but, just at that moment, a static electric shock anticipates their fingertips. They quickly look up at each other, smile uncomfortably, and, in this way, communicate silently beyond the formal gesture that initiated the contact.

The narrative of *The Left-Handed Woman* is, in fact, disrupted continually by these jolts and collisions. The two children leaping unexpectedly from the suitcases, the awkward and peculiar confrontation with the publisher's chauffeur at her door, the café scenes with their disparate figures and angular visual planes, and especially the final party scene at Marianne's house: all describe simple social or visual shocks and unexpected collisions within the diegesis which make disturbingly apparent a world into which isolated characters and images must integrate themselves. The party scene is especially pertinent in this regard, for here one sees a gathering of all the character-images that have somewhat randomly gathered around Marianne through the course of the film. As alienated figures, these characters confront each other for the first time, and, in the clumsiness of their separate identities, they make an abrasive contact like the friction between the actor and Marianne. As summary of this contact and the communication it represents, the party ends with a fumbling fight between Bruno and the actor, which leads to the two men comforting each other as they leave. A more strictly visual version of these and other scenes is the striking shot of Marianne walking a path that parallels the path of a horse and rider which, in turn, forms a parallel with a speeding train: each moves along its own imagistic lines but in the contiguity of those lines there appear dramatic fissures which define both their differences and their shared space, their separate togetherness.

In *The Left-Handed Woman*, these moments of visual strain, friction, and confrontation become the film's center. They illustrate the action by which an identity (self and image) is distorted through the pressures of allegory (the discourse of society). They dramatize, above all else, how the pleasant integrity of the image – observed most readily in the stunning beauty of so many shots – becomes profitably distorted through the communal sense of allegory. In these distortions, the film and its images speak.

In *The Left-Handed Woman*, consequently, the singularity of the image continually and, at least from Handke's perspective, unavoidably translates itself through the force of its negations, into a discourse of meaning. More accurately, the pure image in Handke's film always teeters with a visible friction on the edge of a larger allegorical sense that, even in the ironic inadequacy of that sense, redeems the image from isolation. Usually, in this drama of the visual and the verbal, the static charge which is at its center serves, through its speaking, to illuminate the different sides of the dialectic. But, at least once, the film introduces a strange merger of the subjective and the objective, of allegory and identity. Here one witnesses Handke's dream of translation, an impossible and utopian making of image into an integrated discourse, freed of friction.

Of the significantly few times this utopian translation actually appears in Handke's work, the most striking in *The Left-Handed Woman* is a medium-long shot of Marianne looking out of a second-story window below her son who is in a parallel window on the third floor. It is a night shot, and the windows are brightly illuminated as sharply defined images of the two characters. As with much of the film, the shot is dramatically silent. Suddenly, the son tumbles from the window, across the gaze of the mother, and lands miraculously on his feet. The shot is unsettling since, like many of the shots in the film, it has a very tangential relation to the diegesis, but, more importantly, because the unexpectedly surreal nature of the shot makes it extremely difficult to locate in terms of the film's studied realism. This narrative jolt is clearly part of the disturbing friction that surfaces throughout the film, but the exceptional status of the shot indicates that it is also a central anchoring point in the film – against which the tension between allegory and identity can be measured. The content of the shot suggests itself a kind of wish fulfillment: a vision of the son, Marianne's potential link with new social relationships, saved from the disaster and tragedy this son and society could represent.[18] Formally, moreover, the same type of salvation is represented: just as Marianne's vision here metaphorically gathers up the image of the son as it crosses hers, the tension between the two internal frames is ultimately diffused into a very different image with an obviously new (surreal) look, an image which teases with the human significance of a *natural* discourse. Across the tense juxtaposition of these frames-within-the-frame, the extra-human vision of Marianne gives way to an imaginative interaction, a new kind of image which connects and integrates those previous oppositions. With this single shot, the collision between identity and allegory reconciles temporarily in a startling example of the utopian state that Marianne quietly seeks to translate herself into: where the self as singular image finds an apposite and *positive* idiom with which to speak that image to others, where image retains its identity while yet expressing itself in a social discourse. This, then, is a rare moment of true feeling.

Whether as a negative dialectic or a positive drama, this rigorous effort to translate an authentic image into a social discourse is the best indicator of Handke's distance from Bresson and Antonioni, two filmmakers to whom Handke is often compared. Despite resemblances between the work of Handke and that of these other filmmakers, Handke's style is not transcendent. As Rentschler has pointed out, observers who miss this point fail to recognize the socio-historical dimension in Handke's powerful individualism.[19] If Handke regularly focuses on the extra-human, it is only to return his characters and audience to a human integrity. Aptly, the publisher who gives Marianne work translating Flaubert is played by Bernhard Wicki, who once appeared in Antonioni's *La notte*. There Wicki plays a writer whose death early in the film introduces a dismally stark world of rigid images which overwhelm speech and any possibility of human society. Here, in Handke's film, Wicki is resurrected; and, fittingly, as a symbolic messenger of translation itself, he points the way to bringing those images of alienation back into human discourse. In brief, he brings the possibility of finding words to suit the radical difference of the image. Wicki, as the integrated presence of actor and man, thus indicates Handke's path through the alienation of Antonioni and Bresson (and, for that matter, Ozu) and toward a world where the individual subject isolated in images can translate him or herself back into history and social discourse.

For Handke, this possibility is an extremely tenuous one, its appearance often as tentative and awkward as any attempt to move between images and language. Yet, at the end of the film, Marianne does, through patience and endurance, finish her translation of a novel about human transcendence won through suffering. Shortly before, she makes a first, a prosaic gesture of friendship toward Bruno by buying him shoes. The final shots recall the opening pillow shots: blossoms on the sidewalk, Marianne watching her son swing, a train passing through an empty station, and commuters walking through a subway tunnel. But, in this ending, the images have begun to fill with a human and social content, not appropriate, strictly speaking, to a pillow shot. The final shot of the two children parting at the end of the tunnel to go their separate ways, moreover, is explicitly a summary image of promise: figures of a future dividing in the middle of the frame yet joined by the symmetrical tension of the otherwise static borders. The children move out of the frame, allegorizing a path for the spectator, and Handke underlines the direction of that path by closing the film with a written quotation from Vlado Kristl: "Have you noticed there's only room for those who make room for themselves?" Besides the telling irony of a verbal text having the last word in this film about imagistic identity, here is the central paradox and hope of *The Left-Handed Woman*: a definition of a *social* space only as it is produced by an individual's demand for a private space.

If *The Left-Handed Woman* has been (correctly) seen as a feminist film made by a man, it consequently can equally and perhaps more profitably be described as a story of images made by a man of prose. If it is a film of aggressive isolation and negation, it is also a social film precisely in the aggressiveness with which it speaks those negations. In this purposely difficult film, translation is achieved only by being adamantly and literally faithful to the original. Images are capable of joining the social allegory of language only by resisting as an identity apart. The chief, ironic revelation of the film is that the left-handed eccentric of the title is, in fact and by nature, a right-handed everywoman.

Notes

1. J. Hoberman, "She vants to be alone," *Village Voice*, 7 April 1980.
2. A list of Handke's literary achievements includes *Kaspar* (1967), *The Goalie's Anxiety at the Penalty Kick* (*Die Angst des Tormanns beim Elfmeter*, 1972), *Short Letter, Long Farewell* (*Der kurze Brief zum langen Abschied*, 1972), and *A Moment of True Feeling* (*Die Stunde der wahren Empfindung*, 1975).
3. See Stanley Kauffmann, "Notes on Handke's films," *The New Republic*, 8 March 1980.
4. Recently Handke and Wenders attempted another collaborative effort, a rendering of Handke's *The Slow Return Home* (*Die langsame Heimkehr*), but were unable to gain either government funding or television support.

5. Peter Handke *The Left-Handed Woman*, trans. Ralph Manheim (New York: Farrar, Straus & Giroux, 1977), p. 25.

6. Kauffmann, op. cit.

7. Given Handke's own social actions and his semi-autobiographical writings, it is not difficult to see the author as a reflection of his protagonist. See Eric Rentschler, *West German Film in the Course of Time* (Bedford Hills, NY: Redgrave, 1984), p. 169.

8. Noël Burch, *To the Distant Observer: Form and Meaning in the Japanese Cinema* (Berkeley: University of California Press, 1979), p. 161.

9. ibid., p. 161.

10. Handke, quoted in the press booklet prepared for the film by New Yorker Films.

11. Rentschler, p. 169.

12. The most celebrated analyses from this position are: Laura Mulvey, "Visual pleasure and narrative cinema," *Screen*, 16, No. 3 (Autumn 1975), 6–18; and Stephen Heath, "Difference," *Screen*, 19, No. 3 (Autumn 1978), 51–112. See also Annette Kuhn, *Women's Pictures: Feminism and Cinema* (London: Routledge & Kegan Paul, 1982).

13. See Ruth Perlmutter, "Visible narrative, visible woman," *Millennium Film Journal*, No. 6 (Spring 1980), 18–30.

14. Press booklet from New Yorker Films.

15. ibid.

16. Peter Handke, *Iche bin ein Bewohner des Elfenbeinturms* (Frankfurt am Main: Suhrkamp, 1972), p. 28.

17. Rentschler, p. 171.

18. In the novel the son to some extent parodies this utopian state when he reads a passage he has just written: "My idea of a better life: I would like the weather to be neither hot nor cold. There should always be a balmy breeze and once in a while a storm that makes people huddle on the ground. No more cars. All houses should be red. . . . I would know everything already, so I would not have to study. Everyone would live on islands. . . . Everything I don't know would disappear" (p. 4).

19. Rentschler, p. 173.

Selected Bibliography

Blumenberg, Hans C. "Kampf mit der Welt. Handke verfilmt Handke." *Die Zeit*, 4 November 1977.

Durzak, Manfred. *Peter Handke und die deutsche Gegenwartsliteratur*. Stuttgart: Kohlhammer, 1982.

Klinkowitz, Jerome and James Knowlton. *Peter Handke and the Postmodern Transformation: The Goalie's Journey Home*. Columbia, Mo.: University of Missouri Press, 1983.

Lenssen, Claudia. "*Die linkshändige Frau.*" *Frauen und Film*, No. 14 (December 1977), 42–4.

Linville, Susan and Kent Casper. "Reclaiming the self: Handke's *The Left-Handed Woman.*" *Literature/Film Quarterly*, 12, No. 1 (1984), 13–21.

Perlmutter, Ruth. "Visible narrative, visible woman." *Millennium Film Journal*, No. 6 (Spring 1980), 18–30.

Prümm, Karl. "Das Buch nach dem Film." In *Fernsehforschung und Fernsehkritik*. Ed. Helmut Kreuzer. Göttingen: Vandenhoeck & Ruprecht, 1980, pp. 54–74.

Pütz, Peter. *Peter Handke*. Frankfurt am Main: Suhrkamp, 1982.

Rentschler, Eric, "Peter Handke's *The Left-Handed Woman*: specularity and hunger for experience." In *West German Film in the Course of Time*. Bedford Hills, NY: Redgrave, 1984, pp. 166–73.

Strick, Philip. *"The Left-Handed Woman." Sight & Sound*, 48, No. 3 (Summer 1979), 195.

18

ANTON KAES

History, fiction, memory: Fassbinder's *The Marriage of Maria Braun* (1979)

Past and present: the functions of historical fiction

In one of his fragmentary notes written for the monumental *Passagen-Werk*, Walter Benjamin compared the representation of historical events with the production of photographic images.[1] Relating the work of a historian to that of a photographer, he distinguished between the "traditional" historian who simply looks through the camera like an amateur fascinated with the colorful pictures of the past, and the "dialectically trained," critical historian who is not satisfied with passively peering through the viewfinder, but insists on operating the camera in order to *control* the image he sees. Thus he may decide on a larger or smaller frame, or choose a harsher political lighting or a more subdued historical exposure before he pushes the button and arrests the historical moment in a snapshot. What the picture obviously captures is not only the image of an object at a certain moment, but more important, the attitude of the photographer toward his object. Likewise, an image of the past is not only inextricably bound to the particular bias and pre-understanding as well as to the specific time and place of the historian; it is also subject to the historian's conscious control. According to Benjamin, it is the task of the historian to take charge of tradition actively, to intervene in it, and, to use his metaphor, to operate and control the mechanisms with which we obtain our pictures of the past.

This image of a critical historiography will serve as the point of departure for my discussion of Fassbinder's fictional representation of German history in his film *The Marriage of Maria Braun* (*Die Ehe der Maria Braun*, 1979). Benjamin's critical "interventionist" hermeneutics and Fassbinder's Foucaultian project of writing a "history of the present"[2] intersect in their rejection of a kind of historicism based on the futile pursuit of an objective and timeless image of the past. "To articulate the past historically," said Benjamin in a famous passage from his "Theses on the philosophy of history," "does not mean to recognize it 'the way it really was' (Ranke). It means to seize hold of a memory as it flashes up at a moment of danger."[3] In this way history consists of an infinite series of fleeting images that irretrievably disappear if they are not seized by the present. History is perpetually constituted by an ever-changing constellation between the present and the past: historical writing inevitably contains the present perspective. Historical fictions are therefore themselves historical. They emerge from a particular politically and culturally determined moment which both circumscribes and shapes the representations of the past.

To the extent, then, that representations of the past are motivated and shaped by present concerns, it is necessary to examine first what these concerns were for Fassbinder when he made *The Marriage of Maria Braun* early in 1978. What explains the emergence of films like *The Marriage of Maria Braun*, *Lola*, and *Veronika Voss* (*Die Sehnsucht der Veronika Voss*), all made between 1978 and 1982 and called a "BRD-Trilogie" by Fassbinder himself? Why was Fassbinder suddenly interested in using German postwar history for the construction of his narratives? What, in short, were the questions to which these films were the answer?

The Marriage of Maria Braun, the first of his trilogy of films on West Germany's postwar and reconstruction period, was begun in January 1978, immediately following Fassbinder's contribution to the collective co-production *Germany in Autumn* (*Deutschland im Herbst*, 1978), which was shot in October 1977. His film *The Marriage of Maria Braun* can best be understood as a product of, and a response to, the political crisis which also brought forth *Germany in Autumn*. In other words, *The Marriage of Maria Braun* is Fassbinder's answer to the questions posed in his contribution to *Germany in Autumn*. The events of September and October 1977: the kidnapping and murder of the industrialist Hanns-Martin Schleyer, the Mogadishu hijacking of a Lufthansa jet by German terrorists, and the mysterious suicides of Andreas Baader, Gudrun Ensslin, and Jan-Carl Raspe in a maximum-security prison as well as the severe countermeasures of the government (such as the news blackout and the officially condoned witchhunt of leftist sympathizers) – these events of the fall of 1977 confronted the generation of Fassbinder (who was born in 1945) with the kind of rigid authoritarianism and disregard for individual democratic rights that could only be understood "historically" in the context of Germany's recent past. As Alexander Kluge has pointed out, the crisis of the fall of 1977 ruptured the collective amnesia and brought back memories of the psychological terrorism of the Hitler regime.[4] Fassbinder dramatizes this connection between the "German autumn" and the Third Reich when he has his mother admit (in his apparently scripted discussion with her in *Germany in Autumn*) that the political climate of Germany in October 1977 reminded her "a lot of the Nazi times when people simply were quiet in order to stay out of trouble." Fassbinder cuts away after this line, underscoring the poignancy of this constellation between past and present.

In another scene, Fassbinder reads a passage from Alfred Döblin's novel *Berlin Alexanderplatz*: "You know, we grabbed hold of the Jews, went to the courtyards and sang 'Watch on the Rhine,' I was so giddy. Then both Jews got hold of me and told me stories. Words are also good, Gottlieb, and what one says." The unexpected, narratively seemingly unmotivated reference to Jews and the nationalistic song "Watch on the Rhine" carry associations of past persecution and nationalistic power display simultaneously at work in the present. Even more resonant is the last remark made by his mother: "The best thing would be a kind of authoritarian ruler who is good and kind and orderly." Germany's recent past is represented here by Fassbinder as an ever-present repository of memories that – in the words of Benjamin – flash up in moments of danger. While the mother tries to marshal her memories of life under a dictatorship as a point of orientation in the crisis at hand, the son – obviously lacking his mother's memories – is visibly more shaken and perturbed by the events. With increasing agitation and aggression, he attacks her resigned equanimity and cowardly opportunism in the face of what he deems political injustice. He cannot understand why she or anybody else who has lived under fascism would condone intimidation and the violation of democratic principles. Why have his parents not learned from their experience? How did they *become* what they are? Could the crisis of the fall of 1977 not be seen as a revelation of precisely that kind of mentality which the terrorists meant to destroy? And, finally, how did (and does) political fascism intersect with fascism in the private realm?

These are some of the questions raised in Fassbinder's 25-minute segment in *Germany in Autumn* which could not be answered in sufficient complexity in the short contribution to a collective film. Fassbinder intended to explore these questions further in a film with the telling title "The Marriages of Our Parents." He was unable, however, to secure financing for this project.[5] Fassbinder then asked two professional scriptwriters, Peter Märthesheimer and Pea Fröhlich, to work his numerous ideas about "The Marriages of Our Parents" into a manageable scenario which, after further revisions by Fassbinder himself, would become *The Marriage of Maria Braun*.

In *The Marriage of Maria Braun*, Fassbinder wanted to write a history of the present, indeed his own history. Born at the end of the war, he saw himself as part of that history. He consciously reconstructs the past not in order to find out how it "really" was, but to explain how the present crisis came about. He uses the past to restore the temporal coherence which seemed suddenly to be ruptured in the fall of 1977. A series of still shots at the beginning and the end of *The Marriage of Maria Braun* shows the continuity of German leadership from Hitler (in the first frame) to Adenauer, Erhard, Kiesinger, and Helmut Schmidt (in the last frames), and thus boldly establishes a chronological nexus between the time depicted in the film (from 1944 to 1954) and the time of its production (early 1978). Willy Brandt's picture is conspicuously missing in the sequence – a deliberate omission, for Fassbinder considered Brandt an exception in the tradition of the authoritarian political leadership of postwar Germany.[6] This disjuncture between the make-believe world of the fictional character Maria Braun and the recognizable documentary photographs of the German chancellors foregrounds the story as a product and fabrication of a certain political and cultural milieu, namely that of the late 1970s which tended to romanticize the more liberal Brandt regime.

Only at the very end of the film does Fassbinder openly identify his fictional construction of the past as a construct of discourse which underlines, indeed makes transparent, its point of reference.[7] Other signs of directional enunciation such as self-conscious and artificial camera placement, theatrical choreography, often melodramatic lighting, defamiliarizing music, and even a recognizable appearance of Fassbinder in the role of a peddler on the black market trying to sell an edition of Heinrich von Kleist, the German romantic poet, who, like Fassbinder, dealt with the destructiveness of uncompromising love – these subtle signs of directorial intervention remind the spectator of the process of filmic enunciation and the discursive nature of the historical representation. Still Fassbinder is a far cry from the digressive post-modernist filmic discourse of other German filmmakers such as Alexander Kluge, Hans Jürgen Syberberg, or Werner Schroeter. Fassbinder likes to tell a good story. The historical fiction of *The Marriage of Maria Braun* seems therefore – at least on a first viewing – to unfold as a narrative from which a subject of enunciation is absent. In fact, the effacement of the speaking subject helps foster the referential illusion needed for the "realistic-historical effect." Any consideration of *The Marriage of Maria Braun* as a historical film very much depends on signifying conventions which create such a realistic-historical effect.

In *The Marriage of Maria Braun* the veracity of the image – from the faithfully rebuilt 1945 train station to the interior of a 1950s office, from the Allied uniforms to the changing styles of women's dresses – guarantees the veracity of the reconstructed historical period. The attention to the smallest detail constitutes the truth of the representation of the past. A historical period is evoked replete with *a priori* significations. Somehow we already know from old photographs and newsreels the visual images of returning soldiers, looking emaciated and haggard, of women clearing away the rubble, of well-fed American soldiers and German war brides. These images have over the years become conventionalized as valid representations of the immediate postwar years in Germany; they are used or, more precisely, re-used to persuade the audience to accept the film as an historical film. The realistic-historical effect, in other words, is determined by the visual memory of the spectator. The recognition effect of "that's the way it was" in a historical film is less a product of the historical plot than of the careful attention to the image: it must "look" historical.[8]

Plates 37 and 38   Historical verisimilitude in *The Marriage of Maria Braun:* the reality of shattered buildings and American occupation, the backdrop to the story in the foreground. Photos courtesy of Stiftung Deutsche Kinemathek.

Major political events such as the currency reform of 1948 and the founding of the Federal Republic of Germany in 1949 are not part of *The Marriage of Maria Braun*. The crucial political figure Konrad Adenauer is there only in radio broadcasts to which none of the characters pay attention. Fassbinder's historical interest does not lie in depicting the fate of great men or in reconstructing major political events. He focuses instead on a "history from below," on private events and emotions, on hopes and desires, frustration and despair, and the minute strategies of survival. He is interested in common people who do not participate in politics and are nevertheless at every moment dominated by it.

The private sphere is interwoven with the public and political sphere of the period by means of the soundtrack. We hear original recordings of Adenauer's radio speeches about rearmament; we listen to Fred Rauch's popular Wednesday *Wunschkonzert*; and we follow Herbert Zimmermann's original broadcast of the last seven minutes of the World Cup championship soccer match between Germany and Hungary on 4 July 1954. The structural importance of these historical markers cannot be overstated. They integrate the historical reality of public events into the story of a fictional character; they constitute the chronological time and authenticate, as it were, the historical truth of the fictional story. Fiction and documentary, two different and at the same time related modes of filmic representation, play off against each other in this film. The fictional framework gives meaning to the historical documents while the documentary adds the historical dimension to the fiction.[9] The period of postwar Germany not only becomes visible in terms of a carefully reconstructed space but also becomes narratively tangible in terms of reconstructed time.

History as story-telling

In his book *Instructions païennes* of 1977, the French poststructuralist critic Jean-François Lyotard defines history in the following way:

> History is made up of wisps of narratives, stories that one tells, that one hears, that one acts out; the people do not exist as a subject but as a mass of millions of insignificant and serious little stories that sometimes let themselves be collected together to constitute big stories and sometimes disperse into digressive elements.[10]

The story of Maria Braun is one of those many "wisps of narratives" that collectively constitute the "big story," namely the history of postwar Germany. Maria Braun's own story is embedded in an intricate web of numerous other stories. Her story unfolds as it traverses and crisscrosses these other stories; we see her life refracted in the life stories of the people around her. The plot is structured in such a way that even minor characters are given the opportunity to tell, however briefly, their own stories. For example, the

Red Cross nurse at the train station tells Maria Braun that she lost her husband in a crevasse of a glacier and as compensation the army headquarters sent her a mass-produced painting of the ocean (!) with the cynical inscription: "He died so Germany may live!" We also learn in the course of the film the various "stories" of Maria's mother, her sister Betti, and Betti's husband Willi; even the old disillusioned family doctor is given the chance to summarize his life in a brief monologue. Significantly we know least about Hermann Braun. Fassbinder deliberately leaves it to the spectator to construct Hermann's story, for he is only present in his absence, first in the war, then in prison, and finally in voluntary exile.

The film consists of a dense network of heterogeneous, irreducible private histories, full of contradictions, repetitions, and variations. To the extent that all the stories relate past experiences, they involve perpetual revelations and interpretations of the past in the light of the present. These stories intersect and in a sense subvert the notion of history as a sequence of events. History is presented as a complex web of endlessly interconnected little stories. Fassbinder de-emphasizes a straight narrative line in favor of a narrative space in which various "stories" coexist and comment on each other. These many "wisps of narratives" impart to the film the texture of social life as we experience it in everyday reality: fragmentary and inconclusive.

Maria, whose story is most closely bound to those of Hermann, her husband, and Karl Oswald, her lover, is probably the film's best story-teller. She tells everybody her life story, one organized around an obsessively idealized one-day marriage to Hermann Braun and a notion of absolute love. Like a story-teller, she invents and pretends; she makes up lies whenever it is expedient and she manipulates others through her image.[11] She is an expert in self-representation and disguise, the very figures of story-telling. Asked why she tells different stories to different people, she answers: "I'm a master of deceit. A capitalist tool by day, and by night an agent of the proletarian masses, the Mata Hari of the economic miracle."

Maria Braun's "story" unfolds like a traditional Hollywood melodrama of the 1940s and 1950s, a genre Fassbinder admired for its psychological realism and unabashed emotional power.[12] In film historical terms, *The Marriage of Maria Braun* bears a resemblance to such films as Douglas Sirk's *All That Heaven Allows* (1955) and Michael Curtiz's *Mildred Pierce* (1945) which dramatize the victimization of a female protagonist. Fassbinder once said that he preferred women as protagonists in his historical films (cf. also *Lola, Veronika Voss, Lili Marleen*) because he believed that their societal roles are less defined and restricted than those traditionally assumed by men.[13] In his view women are free to challenge or evade the rules and conventions of the dominant male discourse. The unpredictability of women's behavior in *The Marriage of Maria Braun* is echoed in the film's structure. The narrative is propelled by coincidence, chance encounters, sudden separations, and unexpected reunions. Maria Braun adapts to every new turn of events with resourcefulness, opportunism, and a strong will to succeed. "I don't wait for miracles – I prefer making them," she says at the height of a career which leads from poverty and an unrepented murder to wealth and public recognition.

Because she is such a consummate manipulator of her own story, Maria thinks she can keep the potentially conflicting stories of Hermann and Oswald apart. (She does not tell Oswald about Hermann.) Only after she learns that Oswald had made a secret deal with Hermann – to give him half of his fortune for Hermann's consent to relinquish his wife until Oswald's death – does she realize she had never been in command of her story at all, that in actual fact she was never more than an object of exchange in a transaction between two men.

Maria's private narrative is punctuated and amplified at regular intervals by the historical narrative that informs the story of the German nation from the end of the war to the so-called "economic miracle" of the 1950s. Political history is assimilated into the fictional space in a variety of representational modes. For instance, whenever we see Maria Braun waiting at the station for the return of her husband we hear a monotone radio voice reading names and numbers of displaced persons about whom information is available. The theme of reunification which is emphasized in the private narrative of Maria Braun is mirrored in the public discourse: a nation in disarray seeks to reunite its subjects who are homeless and scattered everywhere.

The question of national identity is broached later when a brief voice-over summarizes the Morgenthau Plan of 1944, a proposal according to which the German state was to be broken up and turned into farmland. Shortly thereafter, while the camera pans over destroyed buildings and the hustle and bustle of the black market, we hear a clumsy accordion rendition of the German national anthem, one that is interrupted twice by comments about the appropriateness of playing "Deutschland, Deutschland über alles" in a shattered Germany. The most significant intrusions of politics into the fictional world of Maria Braun are two speeches by Konrad Adenauer addressing the question of German rearmament. "I do not wish an army," he is heard saying on the radio, "we have had enough deaths already. Just think that now there are 160 women to 100 men." While Adenauer speaks, Maria Braun, her mother and grandfather, Betti and her husband are eating, and discussing ways to make the best potato salad. Nobody listens to Adenauer's speech. In this image Fassbinder dramatizes the complete lack of political awareness on the part of most German people during the reconstruction period when questions of food seemed to be more essential than those of politics.

Toward the end of the film, as Maria Braun dines alone after the death of Oswald, we hear Adenauer again, this time – four years later, in 1954 – arguing aggressively *for* the rearmament of Germany: "We have the right," he says emphatically, "to rearm as much as we can and as much as we want." It is left open whether Maria hears this fateful reversal of Adenauer's stance on rearmament, but immediately after the end of this broadcast we see her get up from her seat, stumble, and vomit. The tension in this scene between image and sound allows Fassbinder to correlate, however shockingly, public and private illness.

Adenauer's radio address is immediately followed by the live broadcast of the final game of the world soccer championship. The high-pitched, excruciatingly overwrought voice of the sports reporter is heard throughout the climax of the film where the narratives of all three protagonists come together. The public narrative – Germany fighting an eastern bloc country for national pride and self-esteem – accompanies and at times drowns out the denouement of the private narratives. The public narrative does not stop even after the private narratives have come to an abrupt end. Such disjuncture between private and public is also thematized in the first scene of the film: Hermann and Maria Braun's wedding takes place against the backdrop of air-raid sirens, explosions, and screams. We see Hermann Braun in uniform – it is still 1944 – and Maria Braun in a white wedding gown running from the bombarded city hall, squirming in a ludicrous posture on the ground, and forcing the official to sign the marriage certificate. Fassbinder insisted on deconstructing bourgeois conventions of marriage from the beginning, ensuring that Maria Braun's *idée fixe* is seen in a critical light. Maria and Hermann are presented from the start as victims of historical events over which they have no control. The dominance of the "big story" (in Lyotard's words) over millions of little private stories is forcefully established from the beginning.

Memory and the problem of historical representation

Film is a paradoxical medium. On the one hand, it is characterized by its principally ahistorical immediacy and presence. (There is no past tense in film language.) On the other hand, film consists of images which are always by necessity recorded, absent, and past. In this sense every film is a historical film. It is the burden of cinema to re-present images as memory traces of the past. In its very form, Fassbinder's *The Marriage of Maria Braun* foregrounds and problematizes these questions of presence and absence, of memory and historical re-presentation.

The Marriage of Maria Braun is constructed around acts of remembering and forgetting. Maria Braun's memory of a marriage which lasted only one night and half a day is the secret center of her narrative. Her persistence is put to various tests in which the price of memory goes up. She clings to this memory at a time when the country in which she lives seeks to forget its past. The disjuncture between the individual act of remembering and the collective act of forgetting becomes a source of contradiction and complications. Maria Braun legitimizes her ambition, her accumulation of money and her obsessive planning for the future, in terms of the past. A growing tension between past and future, which devalues the present, makes her distracted and forgetful.

In the end, the tension between remembering and forgetting (which informs the entire narrative) is quintessentialized in a climactic scene. Remembering or forgetting suddenly becomes a matter of life or death. As Maria Braun pulls a cigarette from the package, she hesitates, looks at it, asks her husband for a match, and then goes off to the kitchen where (as we remember from a previous scene) she has forgotten to turn the gas off. Fassbinder leaves it deliberately ambiguous whether she simply forgets or intentionally chooses not to remember. In either case, the ensuing death by fire of both protagonists grotesquely literalizes the tension between remembering and forgetting. This tension in turn may be read, within the code of filmic discourse, as a refraction of the larger tension that beset postwar Germany: that of remembering a past one would prefer to forget.

Memory functions on the basis of repetition, *déjà-vu*, and the kind of recognition that freezes the flow of time in a suddenly realized constellation between the present and the past. This Benjaminian notion of constellation which seeks to restore the non-sequential energy of subjective memory subverts the traditional concept of narrative as a sequence of events. Recurrent visual allusions and leitmotifs (such as Maria's habit of lighting her cigarette from the gas stove) form specific constellations of *déjà-vu* which transcend linear time and jog the memory of the spectator. Memory is likewise preserved by the very name of Maria Braun which resonates with associations of Eva Braun, Hitler's fiancée and wife, subtly suggesting a continuity between the Third Reich and the postwar period of ruthless reconstruction. Maria Braun herself associates her last name with the Nazi uniforms of the National Socialists whose members were nicknamed "brownshirts," when she remarks after looking at Bill, the black American soldier: "Better black than brown."

Memory draws on a multitude of signals and mediates between disjointed and often enigmatically cut scenes. In the end, the unexpected resurgence of Maria's past (which she had tried to hide from Oswald) disrupts the established order. The sudden revelation of this past reverses the situation and inverts the power relations: Maria recognizes that far from being an agent of her own fate, she was made the object of a financial transaction between her lover and her husband. The gesture of betrayal is projected and magnified from the private onto the public sphere: the German nation, if one follows the film's logic, was betrayed when Adenauer, despite painful memories of a military past, made a secret deal to rearm Germany. The explosion at the end of the film provides an escape from personal history, an abrupt closure which ironically undercuts the radio broadcast of the birth of a new national pride and identity ostensibly gained by the unexpected victory of Germany over Hungary. The last seven minutes of that final soccer match, presented uncut from the original broadcast, converge with the last seven minutes of the lives of Maria and Hermann Braun. For seven minutes, narrative time becomes identical with real time, private time identical with historical time. The mutually illuminating self-representation of Maria and the German nation is intimated and connoted throughout the film by the use of sound that lets public and political discourse enter the narrative space even though the protagonists are presented as unpolitical and oblivious to political discourse. By incorporating the public and political sphere as an audible background that can be ignored, Fassbinder convincingly fuses the discourse of the public with the discourse of the private. He also achieves a profusion of conflicting messages that deliberately plays on the multiplicity of meaning.

The very textuality of *The Marriage of Maria Braun* does not allow a single unified voice to emerge. Camera, *mise-en-scène*, framing, dialogue, music, lighting, radio news, and sound effects send out multiple, simultaneous, and often contradictory signs which cannot be separated and circumscribed. Film for Fassbinder at this point in his career was a mixture of diverse and stratified languages, conflicting voices, and different representational modes. His notion of film as the locus of many diverse stylistic unities is close to M. M. Bakhtin's concept of "heteroglossia," a term describing the conflicting plurality of voices in the discourse of the novel. In his essay "Discourse in the novel," Bakhtin argues: "The novel must represent all the social and ideological voices of its era, that is, all the era's languages that have any claim to be significant; the novel must be a microcosm of heteroglossia."[14] Fassbinder's attempt to include a multitude of heterogeneous voices in the narrative space of his historical film results in a crisis of representation. The sheer mass of messages tends to overwhelm the spectator. The multitude of interwoven signs and languages, all of them reflecting and commenting on each other, also results in ambiguities, double meanings, and indeterminacies which activate the spectator's search for the most persuasive reading. Fassbinder's own intention is refracted in the various voices that he presents in the film.

As a historian of postwar Germany, Fassbinder plays on the overcoded concreteness and symbolic amplitude of filmic discourse in order to represent the past in all its multi-layered and heterogeneous complexity. One might say that he developed the art of polyphonic speaking as a response to the challenge of representing the jumble of narratives that we call history. Like Fassbinder's films about contemporary Germany, *The Marriage of Maria Braun* concentrates on moments of rupture, discontinuity, and displacement. History itself is shown to be a story full of new beginnings, breaks, and unexpected reversals. If history is a story we tell ourselves about ourselves, then historical fictions do more than just represent the past: they shape our collective memory and constitute our present personal and national identity.

Notes

1. Walter Benjamin, "Fragment über Methodenfragen einer marxistischen Literaturanalyse," *Kursbuch*, No. 20 (March 1970), 1–3.

2. See Michael S. Roth, "Foucault's 'History of the Present,'" *History and Theory*, No. 20 (1981), 32–46. Foucault's position is most clearly formulated in *Discipline and Punish: The Birth of Prison*, trans. Alan Sheridan (New York: Pantheon, 1975).

3. Walter Benjamin, "Theses on the philosophy of history," in *Illuminations*, ed. Hannah Arendt, trans. Harry Zohn (New York: Schocken, 1969), p. 255.

4. Oskar Negt and Alexander Kluge, *Geschichte und Eigensinn* (Frankfurt am Main: Zweitausendeins, 1981), pp. 362ff. See also Miriam Hansen, "Cooperative auteur cinema and oppositional public sphere: Alexander Kluge's contribution to *Germany in Autumn*," *New German Critique*, Nos 24–5 (Fall/Winter 1981–2), 36–56. On the Fassbinder segment of *Germany in Autumn*, see Eric Rentschler, "Life with Fassbinder: the politics of fear and pain," *Discourse*, No. 6 (Fall 1983), 75–90.

5. See Fassbinder's account in the interview, "'Nur so entstehen bei uns Filme: indem man sie ohne Rücksicht auf Verluste macht,'" *Frankfurter Rundschau*, 20 February 1979.

6. ibid.

7. Cf. Christian Metz, "History/discourse: note on two voyeurisms," trans. Susan Bennett, *Edinburgh '76 Magazine*, 21–5. On the question of representation and representability of history in film, see Keith Tribe, "History and the production of memories," *Screen*, 18, No. 4 (Winter 1977/8), 9–22; Mark Nash and Steve Neale, "Film: 'history/production/memory,'" *Screen*, 18, No. 4 (Winter 1977/8), 77–91; Pierre Sorlin, *The Film in History: Restaging the Past* (Oxford: Blackwell, 1980); K. R. M. Short (ed.), *Feature Films as History* (London: Croom Helm, 1981).

8. In terms of the visual evocation of film, the historical film has a distinct advantage over the historical novel. This is made clear by Gerhard Zwerenz's novel based on the film, *Die Ehe der Maria Braun* (Munich: Goldmann, 1979). Zwerenz pays much less attention than Fassbinder to the historical reconstruction of the post-war period. He also leaves out the political and public dimension of the film (represented by sound documents) and thus reduces Fassbinder's intricate dialectics of private and national history to a love story. The novel was serialized in the illustrated weekly magazine *Stern*, beginning 22 February 1979, coinciding with the première of the film at the Berlin Film Festival. It may be assumed that the novelization of the film in a mass-media organ contributed to making *The Marriage of Maria Braun* the largest commercial success of the New German Cinema up to that point. For a brief comparison between Fassbinder's film and Zwerenz's novel, see Hans-Bernhard Moeller, "Das destruktive Ideal? Fassbinders Leinwand-Nationalcharakterologie in *Die Ehe der Maria Braun*," *German Studies Review*, 5, No. 1 (February 1982), 61.

9. Thomas Elsaesser speaks of a "parabolic" relation between Maria's story and German history in "Primary identification and the historical subject: Fassbinder and Germany," *Ciné-tracts*, No. 11 (Fall 1980), 51: "Why did West Germans rebuild such a conservative and conformist society? Democracy came to them imposed from without, and once again 'under alien control,' they reconstructed their Imaginary in the image of American consumer-capitalism. In parabolic fashion, this is the story of *The Marriage of Maria Braun*, whose heroine's ambiguous strength lies precisely in her 'inability to mourn.'" On Fassbinder's attitude toward postwar West German national identity and his "BRD-Trilogie," see also John O'Kane, "Rainer Werner Fassbinder: art cinema and the politics of culture," *Bennington Review*, No. 15

(Summer 1983), 56–64; and Howard Feinstein, "BRD 1–2–3: Fassbinder's postwar trilogy and the spectacle," *Cinema Journal*, 23, No. 1 (Fall 1983), 44–56.

10. Jean-François Lyotard, *Instructions païennes* (Paris: Galilee, 1977), p. 39.

11. Maria Braun is played by Hanna Schygulla, an actress whose rise as a leading star in German cinema is closely linked to Fassbinder's rise as a leading director. Her self-assured glamour in this film offers a strong potential for audience identification – an identification, however, which Fassbinder deliberately disturbs by emphasizing the manipulative opportunism with which she uses her looks.

12. On Fassbinder's use of melodrama in the construction of his narratives and in his dramaturgy, the most impressive account remains Thomas Elsaesser, "A cinema of vicious circles," in *Fassbinder*, ed. Tony Rayns, 3rd rev. edn (London: British Film Institute, 1980), pp. 24–36.

13. See "'Alles Vernünftige interessiert mich nicht.' Gespräch mit Rainer Werner Fassbinder," in Wolfgang Limmer, *Rainer Werner Fassbinder, Filmemacher* (Reinbek: Spiegel, 1982), p. 88.

14. M. M. Bakhtin, "Discourse in the novel," in *The Dialogic Imagination*, ed. Michael Holquist (Austin: University of Texas Press, 1982), p. 411.

Selected Bibliography

Dawson, Jan. "Women – present tense." *Take One*, July 1979, 10–12.

Elsaesser, Thomas, "Primary identification and the historical subject: Fassbinder and Germany." *Ciné-tracts*, No. 11 (Fall 1980), 43–52.

Feinstein, Howard. "BRD 1–2–3: Fassbinder's postwar trilogy and the spectacle." *Cinema Journal*, 23, No. 1 (Fall 1983), 44–56.

Jansen, Peter W. and Wolfram Schütte (eds). *Fassbinder*. 4th rev. edn. Munich: Hanser, 1983.

MacBean, James Roy. "The success and failure of Fassbinder." *Sight & Sound*, 52, No. 1 (Winter 1982/3), 42–8.

McCormick, Ruth. "*The Marriage of Maria Braun.*" *Cinéaste*, 10, No. 2 (Spring 1980), 34–6.

—— (ed.). *Fassbinder*. New York: Tanam, 1981.

Moeller, Hans-Bernhard. "Das destruktive Ideal? Fassbinders Leinwand-National-charakterologie in *Die Ehe der Maria Braun.*" *German Studies Review*, 5, No. 1 (1982), 57–66.

Noonan, Tom. "*The Marriage of Maria Braun.*" *Film Quarterly*, 33, No. 3 (Spring 1980), 40–5.

O'Kane, John. "Rainer Werner Fassbinder: art cinema and the politics of culture." *Bennington Review*, No. 15 (Summer 1983), 56–64.

Rayns, Tony (ed.). *Fassbinder*. 3rd rev. edn. London: British Film Institute, 1980.

Reimer, Robert C. "Memories from the past: a study of Rainer Werner Fassbinder's *The Marriage of Maria Braun.*" *Journal of Popular Film and TV*, 9, No. 3 (Fall 1981), 138–43.

Rentschler, Eric. "Life with Fassbinder: the politics of fear and pain." *Discourse*, No. 6 (Fall 1983), 75–90.

Zwerenz, Gerhard. *Die Ehe der Maria Braun: Roman.* Munich: Goldman, 1979.

19

E. ANN KAPLAN

The search for the Mother/Land in Sanders-Brahms's *Germany, Pale Mother* (1980)

Like many recent West German films by female directors, Helma Sanders-Brahms's *Germany, Pale Mother* (*Deutschland, bleiche Mutter*) is relatively unknown in America. Unable to promote themselves as successfully as their male counterparts, the critically acclaimed exponents of "New German Cinema," German women filmmakers have been producing their features in far from optimal conditions and often at expense to themselves. (The notable exception is, of course, Margarethe von Trotta, who has a considerable arthouse following in the US.) While Sanders-Brahms has been more fortunate than most of her peers, she has nonetheless not received the recognition she deserves.

Germany, Pale Mother, Sanders-Brahms's eighth feature film, belongs with a group of works by German ciné-feminists in the late 1970s which deal with mother–daughter relations.[1] Often basically realist, these films immediately provoke the questions that feminist film theorists have been debating ever since Claire Johnston's controversial 1973 essay, "Women's cinema as counter-cinema."[2] There Johnston pitted a realist cinema against an avant-garde one, declaring that to be feminist, a film had to interrogate Hollywood realist codes. While many filmmakers believe that making women's relationships and political struggles the center of a film narrative is itself revolutionary, the group rallying to Johnston's call argues that a feminist film has to address the very notion of the "feminine" as constructed under patriarchy.[3] The first position, often called "essentialist," assumes the category "woman" and proceeds to focus on women's specific needs (day care, abortion, equal pay, female bonding, sexual freedom); the second looks at the cinematic mechanisms through which the "feminine" (as a patriarchal construct) is produced on the screen, and at the relation of these mechanisms to woman as producer of desire in culture generally.

Viewed in this context, Sanders-Brahms's film can be seen on the one hand to move beyond the limitations of realism while still maintaining signs of an awkward essentialism. Perhaps over-ambitiously, Sanders-Brahms attempts to extend and deepen her exploration of mother–daughter relations by employing an historical address. In its dedication to Bertolt Brecht's poem, *"Deutschland"* (1933), the film pays homage to a German poetic tradition on which the filmmaker draws for a combined personal and historical address to the Mother:

> O Germany, pale mother!
> How soiled you are
> As you sit among the peoples.
> You flaunt yourself
> Among the besmirched.[4]

Since Sanders-Brahms's recourse to this tradition has problematic consequences in the film, it warrants some comment. The tradition of an address to a mother at once real and allegorical goes back through Brecht to Heinrich Heine's *"Nachtgedanken"* ("Night Thoughts").[5] This poem, written in 1843 during Heine's French exile, allegorizes the Mother, a ploy with a long tradition. At the same time, however, it already problematizes the Mother/Land trope. For here real and allegorical mothers are separated. Heine's longing for Germany, expressed in the first stanza, is distinguished from his yearning for his real mother, whom he describes in the next four verses:

> So many years have come and passed.
> Since I saw my old mother last
> Twelve years I have seen come and go
> My yearnings and my longing grow.

> My longing's grown since our farewell
> Perhaps she's cast on me a spell,
> The good old woman; I can't sleep
> And think of her – whom God may keep.

> From all her letters I must see
> How deep the love she feels for me . . .

> The Mother's always in my mind . . .
> Twelve long years since I did depart
> And clasped the mother to my heart.[6]

While the poet's address here reflects the deep longing of the son for the all-nurturing, protecting mother (something familiar in western representations), Heine sets it apart from a longing for his nation (i.e. "homeland"); this becomes a trope for the family presided over by the idealized Mother connoting security, nurturance, identity. In verse six, Heine contrasts healthy

Germany with a frail, infirm Mother, and in verse seven, notes that while Germany (now significantly called the "*Vaterland*") is eternal, his real mother may well die, as have many of his friends. The poem concludes with the entrance of his young foreign wife who, bringing the bright French day, scatters his "German" (both mother and homeland) sorrows.

Brecht's poem, on which Sanders-Brahms depends, provocatively reunites the real and allegorical mothers of the traditional trope. Presumably for political reasons, Brecht here undoes what Heine had effected. Relying on cultural valorization of the pure, saintly mother, Brecht compounds the horror at what has become of Germany by constructing a vile, besotted, and besmirched Mother-Germany. Her behavior, given the cultural myths, is all the more shocking, a violent wrenching of "what should be," a virulent expression of Brecht's chagrin about his native land. Writing in 1933, in exile (like Heine), but prior to the literal and psychological devastation that National Socialism was to wreak on Germany, Brecht turned to the original, unproblematized trope. Sanders-Brahms follows Brecht whole-heartedly; in so doing, she creates narrative and historical difficulties while conversely (because of her gender) and paradoxically opening up new space.

Some initial comments on the framing historical context and its problematic bearing on the original Mother/Land trope are in order. Working in a reconstructed Germany, Sanders-Brahms is fully aware of the Third Reich's disastrous effect on national tradition and identity. Indeed, this is one of the main themes of the film. Yet she does not foreground the difficulty of using the (essentially) nineteenth-century tradition of an address to the (ideal) Mother in the period following Nazism's abuse of that very tradition.

For, as Klaus Theweleit has shown, Nazism seized upon the notion of the "saintly" Mother, pushing it to an extreme and placing it in an aggressive, imperialistic, and racist ideology. Nazi representations focused on the "holy" Mother, set off against the "evil" sexual woman who was reviled as a dangerous seductress.[7] What was new, however, was how the Mother was placed in the service of the State rather than remaining a free-floating signifier of a nurture that could (if dwelt on too much) undermine male aggression. Founded on father–son bondings, Nazism parades a masculinity often said to contain repressed homosexual elements. Positioned at the periphery of the public sphere, woman is only relevant to that sphere as a begetter of sons who will serve in it. Longing for the Mother must be repressed while one stands at the beck and call of the Father's aggressive demands.[8]

By inserting Brecht's poem at the start of her film, Sanders-Brahms suggests that this trope of the ideal Mother Germany is still a viable one. The dedication is in no way called into question or undermined. Rather, it stands as homage. And, indeed, the film attempts to use the trope as if Nazism had not intervened – and not undermined whatever was originally innocent, even positive, about the worship of the Mother.

It is here that Sanders-Brahms's sense of history breaks down. For in other crucial ways, the film is deliberately constructed around an historical address of the younger generation to the older one, through the daughter's reconstructed appeal to her mother. But in her discourse about the Mother, Sanders-Brahms fails to historicize the trope. She does not reveal its nineteenth-century origins and implicit essentialism, nor its problematic status after being abused by the Third Reich.

A further way in which Sanders-Brahms's address to her mother takes on different proportions than that of Brecht's narrator lies in its being a *female* address, the address of a daughter rather than a son. Mother–daughter relationships have generally been repressed in dominant culture since the Industrial Revolution,[9] along with the repression of the Mother (or her relegation to object in a male address). In granting the daughter a voice, and in making the mother's experiences central to the narrative, Sanders-Brahms reclaims important space. I say "reclaims" because this space is not, in fact, new: nineteenth-century female writers (like Harriet Beecher Stowe) had already developed a subversive tradition that asserted the Mother's values and emotions as crucial for the preservation of civilization.[10] The tradition, however, had been eclipsed since the turn of the century, a development coinciding with Freud's articulation of a psychoanalytic theory that positioned women in negativity.

Like nineteenth-century women writers, twentieth-century filmmakers who give woman a voice transgress male codes and conventions. In doing so, they open up space hitherto closed to women, but nonetheless remain within the overall constraints imposed by patriarchy upon women. To validate women's values, to validate female–female bonding, does not raise questions about the sex-difference ideology inherent in patriarchy. Nor does it intervene in the notion of woman's body as the linchpin for desire in culture, rather keeping that body objectified and romanticized. Nevertheless, it does permit an interesting and significant shift in focus, enabling us to see both history and the present in new ways.

We turn now to *Germany, Pale Mother* to explore what Sanders-Brahms's shift in voice permits us to see about Nazi Germany and male–female relations. Crucial in this discussion is the question of what kind of realism she uses, the precise status of her cinematic enunciation, since it is here that we can judge the degree of transgression.

To begin with, it must be noted that the film's origins are unabashedly autobiographical. About Sanders-Brahms's own relationship to her mother, the film attempts to explore and understand the mother–daughter bond as it took shape through the historical events of the Third Reich and World War II.[11] This is compounded by the director's use of her own daughter as the fictional child in the film. The film is not a documentary, though, but rather an interesting mixture of fiction and fact.

The film thus constructs the fiction of an autobiographical intimacy, which works with varying success. At times, the voice-over is used transgressively, to open up a potentially new space that questions patriarchal constructs. At others, it falls into a sticky kind of sentimentalism caused by insufficient distance between the filmmaker and her material, the insistence of the *referent* (the author's real self and her real mother) in the filmic text. This destroys the text's effort to comment upon and to place the experiences of both Sanders-Brahms and her mother in a manner bearing on the concerns of representation, of enunciation, and of patriarchal constructs.

The film has three main parts: there is first a kind of prologue dealing with the period before the daughter's birth, when Nazism was getting under way; second, the war period, during which the family is dispersed; and finally, the postwar period in a reconstructed Germany, when the family is reunited.

In the first part of the film, the tradition of combining the personal mother and the allegorical Mother is neither obtrusive nor problematical. The daughter's address to her mother works on two levels simultaneously – on the level of the child's Oedipal link to her mother, and on that of the historical address. This latter address shows first how social institutions shape familial relationships, forcing them into constricting molds, and second, how, in exceptional periods, like war, relationships are suddenly freed from such constraints as a result of tremendous general social disruption. If the historical address manages to personalize the general, the personal address, in turn, manages to generalize the personal.

The opening and closing sections of the film are the ones most bound to the historical address, and in the last section, the mother is evoked in an awkwardly allegorical manner. The middle section, the war, deals most obviously with Oedipal issues, but these are also evident in the final scenes.

It makes sense for the start of the film to focus on the historical address, since the daughter's narration begins before her diegetic counterpart is born. The female voice-over works transgressively here and opens up a new "look" at Nazism and its effects on the "ordinary" German. We are spared the usual fetishistic Nazi iconography, and the obligatory conventions of expressionist-style camera work and lighting. Instead, the text presents Nazism as a pervasive background influence in the form of a huge Nazi flag that fills the screen at various points. The opening shot pictures the large flag strikingly reflected in a river across which Ulrich and Hans's boat floats. In the third scene, the camera focuses in extreme close-up on the flag (the shot is so close that we can see small insects clinging to the cloth before we really know what we are looking at), and then records characters dancing in a hall where the flag covers the walls. The Nazis themselves in this scene are shot in close-ups that humanize them. They are seen while eating and drinking innocently, clean-shaven young men looking around innocuously. In this way, the text brings Nazis down to the level of misled, simple folk while at the same time communicating the immense general impact of Nazism as a reality. People's lives are, as it were, drowned out by Nazism, symbolized through the ubiquitous flag. (A more familiar device is that of the constant, haranguing voice of the *Führer* flooding people's minds.)

The address to the Mother also functions as the address of a postwar generation to its elders who "allowed" Nazism to happen. While only a peripheral theme, quickly overtaken by the more personal address, this dimension is present in the scenes before the daughter is born. The film shows how the characters think about Nazism, not as a philosophy or political ideology, but as a tool to get what they want. They do not feel called upon to explore or even to fathom Nazism. Like most people anywhere, they readily push aside what they do not want to know. The film's non-judgmental, humanitarian stance towards the plight of the "ordinary" German results at least partly from the specifically female discourse of the narrator imagining how it must have been not only for her parents, but for others as well.

The historical address also comes into play through the use of documentary newsreel footage, combined with fictionalized documentary-style reconstructions. By transcending the boundary between documentary and fiction, Sanders-Brahms briefly problematizes her own historical address and interrupts the realistic cinematic illusion. At one moment, Sanders-Brahms splices together shots of Eva Mattes (playing Lene, the mother), and the director's own daughter (playing herself as a child) with documentary shots of a little boy. Mother and child supposedly "meet" the boy on the street, but it is clear that the boy occupies an entirely different space. The result is jarring, pulling the spectator away from the narrative, making us aware that the "history" is a reconstruction.

But this is a rare instance in the section of the film following the child's birth. In the main, it is only in the early part that the historical address is sufficiently distanced to break the cinematic illusion. This happens in part *against* Sanders-Brahms's intentions, as a result simply of the functioning of cinematic codes. In the classic system, the voice and image are usually synchronized for illusionist purposes; in the unusual voice-over situation (often flashbacks, as in *film noir*), the voice is anchored by the presence of the narrator in the image or in the diegesis.

In *Germany, Pale Mother*, however, when the diegetic child is not yet born, the voice often erupts into a scene in a way that breaks the illusion. Although the strategy connects the voice to the screen through a specific address to the mother in the image (it sets up an "I"/"You" situation), it nevertheless makes the spectator aware that the voice is *reconstructing* how things must have been for her parents, taking us out of a simply passive relation to the events. The comments of the speaker who is not herself (yet) present diegetically, open up an additional reflective dimension.

The following example demonstrates the kind of interruption that the voice causes, and shows that Sanders-Brahms was not deliberately creating this effect; it arose rather from her attempt to produce an honest, autobiographical film. In an early sequence, Hans and Lene fall in love, and then, rather quickly, marry. As the speaker reconstructs events, she seems to be struggling with the Oedipal enmeshment with her parents. This causes a kind of unintentional blockage in the narrative flow. Having difficulty imagining her parents falling in love, the narrator is more successful in recreating the sense of wonder and romance that her mother must have felt after the wedding, when Hans brings her to their new home. This sequence is delicately shot, and the over-exposed texture of the images conveys a dreamlike sense of unreality. The camera hugs Lene – lovely in cream dress, veil, and flowers – as she shyly explores the new home. At one point, she pricks her finger on a needle in an unfinished curtain, the image calling up the fairy-tale of Sleeping Beauty. Hans sucks the wound tenderly, turning the scene into an erotic moment. The camera focuses on Lene's hands as she tries out the phone, on her face as she sits at the mirror (her and Hans's images now reflected), on their embrace, also mirrored, and then on Hans's fingers clumsily unbuttoning her dress.

But something seems forced and strained here, as if an element were missing. When the speaker interrupts the love-making, we realize that she cannot take the fantasy any further. Breaking the illusion, the voice says: "I cannot imagine his entrance or how it felt." And then, in an attempt to separate herself from them and to assert her difference (and distance), she adds: "You are my parents. I am me." Yet the degree to which the narrator has really overcome her ties is called into doubt when she notes that she did not marry, having learned that from her mother. (Learned what, we may wonder? That marriage means misery? Possession? Powerlessness? It is not yet clear.)

In this sequence, the spectator is in the strange position of at once experiencing cinematic processes that break with classical codes, *and* sensing the attempt at transparency (the film is being used to explore the relationship between a "real" daughter and her "real" mother). These referents so close to the film prevent Sanders-Brahms from using cinematic mechanisms self-consciously. That is, the preoccupation with the level of lived experience makes difficult the distance necessary to raise problems of "representing" the female body on film in the first place (in the manner, say, of Helke Sander in *The All-Round Reduced Personality* – REDUPERS [*Die allseitig reduzierte Persönlichkeit* – REDUPERS, 1977].

What we have instead is the deliberate insertion into cinema of a female discourse, Sanders-Brahms taking "female" as an unproblematic category. But, as already noted, within the essentialist constraints, this strategy *does* open up new space. In the construction of her relationship to her mother, the narrator brings in the female imaginary closed off by psychoanalytic theory, and literary and filmic representations.[12] This opening up of female fantasies about mother–daughter relations is most obvious in the second section of the film, which deals with the war period. For, in the narrator's reconstruction,

Plates 39 and 40   Husband and wife, Hans and Lene, coupling during one of his leaves from the front. Another bond, though, that between mother and child, has become stronger: Anna takes over the father's place in the frame. Photos courtesy of Stiftung Deutsche Kinemathek.

Plate 40

the war becomes a moment of psychic liberation and joy for mother and daughter, now left alone without the intervening Father. Instead of being represented through realist codes as a period of distress, the flight of mother and baby girl takes on fairy-tale aspects of a pleasurable wandering and adventure.[13] Because of the war, the pair is totally freed from the constraining structures and daily routines which characterize the family in "normal" times. The culturally defined positions of mother, father, and child are destroyed by the war, permitting other bonds to form.

Mother and daughter increasingly find complete satisfaction in one another, while the father, Hans, is pushed further and further into the background. Born in an air raid while Hans is away fighting, the child barely knows her father and comes to expect having her mother to herself. After another air raid destroys their comfortable home, mother and daughter set off jauntily to Berlin to stay with relatives. Here the contrast between the illicit joy of mother and child, and the bickering, stiff, Nazi relatives highlights what mother and child have found. We see them playing happily together while bathing. The voice-over comments: "Lene and I loved one another."

They no longer need Hans. He is more present during his absence, as the figure for whose return they are ostensibly waiting, than when in fact there, at which time he seems merely in the way. This is evident when Hans comes on leave to the Berlin flat. In one shot, we see Lene and Anna happily playing on the bed, while Hans washes. When he comes out, Lene and the baby are dancing and singing together, while he watches them enviously. "What was I to do with a father?" the voice comments; "I wanted to be a witch, flying over the roofs with Lene." The fairy-tale reference suggests the sense of the forbidden around the bond with the mother. It is as if the speaker wanted to bewitch Lene, to capture and carry her away. And as if to demonstrate the fantasy flight, the camera cuts to documentary shots of a snow-covered city, sweeping along from a high angle over the silent, empty town.

Hans wants to dance too, but he cannot. Although he never speaks of the war, we know that his experiences have taken all joy out of him. When Lene speaks of giving birth during the air raid, and of her joy watching the child grow up, Hans only says: "We shall fight till the last man." For Lene, the war is a plot, and she tells Hans: "You've got to live, that's all."

As they begin to make love, the baby screams. "I was jealous of him, he of me," the voice tells us. When Lene goes to pick up Anna, and bring her to bed, the voice says: "Just what I wanted: her, but not him. I didn't know him." Hans looks on enviously as Lene cuddles the baby. "*I* wanted to hold you," he says, mournfully, the Oedipal triangles overlapping. In the morning, jealous of the breast-feeding, Hans blames the baby for "eating Lene up," and sadly leaves. The child has had her way, and symbolically replaces her father.

While the film records this transgression, it nevertheless presents Hans sympathetically. The adult voice-over never sees him as the enemy, whatever the little girl may fantasize. Hans also appears as a victim. Wanting only "peace and a girl with black hair," he is forced by society to leave his family and fight for something that he does not believe in. Early in the war, we see Hans and his mates kill a Polish woman (also played by Eva Mattes), who looks very much like Lene. To the scorn of his fellow soldiers, Hans breaks down and cries. Later he is ridiculed by his friends for refusing to take condoms, preferring to be faithful to Lene. (This makes Lene's refusal of sexual relations on his brief visit home all the more poignant, although Sanders-Brahms manages to convey Lene's side of this convincingly. His stored-up lust alienates her; he has become a stranger, her pleasure in her child fulfills her.) Instead of the usual war shots – battles, guns, trenches, violence – we see soldiers in their barracks, or, in one striking scene, Hans on a train at Christmas time, frozen, alone, pulling out a snapshot of Lene and the baby that he has not yet seen. Eschewing conventional war icon-ography (which establishes male heroism), Sanders-Brahms instead reveals the weakness of this male discourse, its vulnerability to powers beyond itself.[14]

The most transgressive section in terms of mother–daughter bonding is the long sequence of their trek through the war-torn German countryside. The sequence enacts the child's fantasy of flying witch-like over the roof-tops alone with Lene. And indeed there is a fairy-tale aspect to the way the shots are filmed. Time is elided through a series of overlapping shots showing the couple in different seasons, and at different times of day. These scenes seem to have no connection with one another and set the pair in another space. Further creating this dreamlike quality is the long fairy-tale about the Robber's betrothed that Lene tells the child along the way. The soundtrack alone connects these images of different stages of their wander-ing, and the tale's length, together with the offscreen narration, gives it a privileged place in the film.

Indeed, the story pulls together a number of central themes. First, as Sanders-Brahms has noted, the words "Turn round, turn round, young bride / You are in the house of a murderer," kept reverberating in her mind while she was making the film.[15] She decided on the spur of the moment to insert the tale because she realized its connection to Lene's increasing alienation and hatred of men during the flight with her child. Men come to symbolize both unbridled violence (the war; the dead bodies Lene and her child confront in natural settings, where they are grotesquely out of place), and uncontained lust (borne out finally during the rape of Lene by Ameri-cans once the war is over). Sanders-Brahms also saw the links between the tale and German history. Germany is like the "House of the Murderer." No better than robbers, the Nazis dismember citizens' bodies as in the fairy-tale. But mother and daughter are able to withstand the horror of the outside world as long as they remain alone in their fantasy – a dreamlike realm made possible by the abnormal conditions of war.

DEUTSCHLAND BLEICHE MUTTER
Ein Film von Helma Sanders-Brahms   Basis-Film Verleih Berlin

Plate 41   Flying like witches over the rooftops of Germany during the war: Lene and Anna's trek through the country. Photo courtesy of Stiftung Deutsche Kinemathek.

With the war's end, the mother–daughter idyll comes to an abrupt end, and its illicit quality emerges. The daughter's desire to possess the mother and to eliminate the father embodies an important (and culturally repressed) fantasy; its very foregrounding makes evident the oppression of women's desire that dominant heterosexual organization entails. This fantasy is by no means one-sided: the mother is also fulfilled by the child and no longer needs her husband even for sex. The wandering existence outside of home-as-institution, with all its sex-based routines, is what made possible the mutual pleasure of mother and daughter in one another.

The war's end signals the forced return to the family and the reinstitution of the heterosexual couple. The daughter's transgression of her (patriarchally) assigned place must now be corrected. The father, as third term, takes his socially sanctioned place between mother and daughter. The daughter is expected to turn to him in preparation for her future role as wife and bearer of children. On the surface, mother and child acquiesce to the new order. But extreme tension underlies the apparent return to normalcy, for "normalcy" means the effective silencing of both Lene's and Anna's voices. Cinematically, this is signalled by the silencing of the voice-over narrator and a return to a more conventional strategy of presentation. Dialogue is, however, minimal, as befits a culture that demanded denial/repression of all that had passed during the war.

Neither mother nor daughter consciously knows what has happened to them, but the repression of their joyful, illicit bonding takes its toll. In Lene's case, the repression returns in the form of bodily signs – her facial disfiguration. In Anna's case, the repression takes the form of sullen, hostile resentment toward the father who has come between her and her mother. (The father's irrational beating of Anna for little cause reflects *his* repressed resentment at the child for coming between him and Lene, for usurping his place during the war.) The cinematic enunciation expresses the daughter's attempt to retain her place between her parents, for the camera always cuts to the child between shots of Hans and Lene. With no one to talk to, mother and daughter retreat to their own spheres, the child going to school and doing her homework, Lene increasingly withdrawing into depression.

Germany, Pale Mother thus exposes the ways in which the forced re-institution of the heterosexual couple stifles female desire, nearly killing the mother, and damaging the child psychologically. But, having gone this far with the problematic, Sanders-Brahms does not seem to know exactly how to resolve it. How are we to read the film's ending? Lene's near-suicide on the one hand attests to her continued resistance to the place she has been assigned, but on the other bears out her powerlessness. The daughter's "saving" of the mother is poignant, and the final image of the two, with Anna's head on Lene's stomach, is touching. But what does it mean?

Even more problematic than the film's odd ending is Sanders-Brahms's attempt to retain the allegorical dimension of Lene's character in the whole final section. The combination of real and allegorical mothers that works well in Brecht's poem, simply does not succeed here. The insertion in a basically realist aesthetic of Lene's symbolic facial disfigurement is awkward, strained, artificial. Lene's distorted face cannot comfortably carry the idea of a divided, postwar Germany. And the teeth-pulling scene, equally symbolic of Germany's suffering, ends up being merely melodramatic. One experienced similar discomfort in an earlier scene intercutting Lene's birth pains with the bombing raid, thus linking artificially the personal and the political.

Sanders-Brahms's film is at its strongest when it functions in an unabashedly autobiographical manner. The autobiographical impulse does result in the insertion of a deliberately female discourse, and this produces an interesting rereading of Nazism, the war, and family relationships. The exploration of the mother–daughter relationship is important for what it shows about female desire, about the female Oedipal entanglement, and about the threat that mother–daughter bonding offers in patriarchy. But what is missing here is a framework enabling Sanders-Brahms to distance herself from the referents and to "place" her own and her mother's experiences in a larger context. The essentializing of a mother and daughter in post-Nazi Germany, without dealing with how Nazism has exploited images of "joyful" mothers and children, is a problem, as is the return to the trope of Mother/Germany. The material could easily have been used in a fascinating, non-realist manner to expose issues around female representation, the construction of the "female" in patriarchy and problems of cinematic enunciation, particularly in relation to the female voice and the female body.

What the film needed to foreground, from a theoretical point of view, is the mechanism whereby patriarchy represses woman's desire for the mother's body. The film *documents* this repression, but does not *reflect* upon it. Dominant sex-difference ideology forces the repression of the non-patriarchal feminine in culture that might work to free the focus on the female body as the obsessive object of male desire – as the linchpin for the whole desiring mechanism in the social formation. Only by such awarenesses will filmmakers avoid the reliance on woman as unproblematic referent in representation – a reliance that, while often transgressive in certain ways, can never move us beyond the impasse we have reached with our understanding of the "feminine" as a patriarchal construction.

Notes

1. Other films on the theme include Jutta Brückner's *Years of Hunger* (*Hungerjahre*, 1980), Recha Jungmann's *Something Hurts* (*Etwas tut weh*, 1979), and Jeanine Meerapfel's *Malou* (1980).
2. See Patricia Erens (ed.), *Sexual Stratagems: The World of Women in Film* (New York: Horizon, 1979), pp. 133–43.

3. This is basically Laura Mulvey's argument in her much-quoted article, "Visual pleasure and narrative cinema," *Screen*, 16, No. 3 (Autumn 1975), 6–18.

4. As translated by H. R. Hays in Bertolt Brecht, *Selected Poems* (New York: Grove, 1959), p. 113.

5. I am indebted to Miriam Hansen for this insight.

6. Heine's poem, "Nachtgedanken," as translated by Ernst Feise, in *Heinrich Heine: Lyric Poems and Ballads* (Pittsburgh: University of Pittsburgh Press, 1961), pp. 162–4.

7. Klaus Theweleit, *Männerphantasien 1: Frauen, Fluten, Körper, Geschichte* (Frankfurt am Main: Roter Stern, 1977), pp. 133–41.

8. See Rita Thalmann, *Frausein im Dritten Reich* (Munich: Hanser, 1984); and Renate Wiggershaus, *Frauen unterm Nationalsozialismus* (Wuppertal: Hammer, 1984).

9. Cf. Elisabeth Badinter, *The Myth of Motherhood: An Historical View of the Maternal Instinct*, trans. Roger DeGaris (London: Souvenir, 1981). For some notes on the literary and psychoanalytic repression of the Mother, see E. Ann Kaplan, "Missing mothers," *Social Policy*, 14, No. 2 (Fall 1983), 56–61.

10. Cf. Jane Tompkins, "Sentimental power: *Uncle Tom's Cabin* and the politics of literary history," *Glyph*, No. 8 (1981), 95–9.

11. See the "Exposé mit Vorrede" and the "Kleine Nachrede" in Helma Sanders-Brahms, *Deutschland, bleiche Mutter: Film-Erzählung* (Reinbek: Rowohlt, 1980), pp. 9–22 and pp. 115–19.

12. Cf. Sigmund Freud, essays collected in *Sexuality and the Psychology of Love*, ed. Philip Rieff (New York: Macmillan, 1963), especially, "A child is being beaten," "The passing of the Oedipus-complex," "Some psychological consequences of the anatomical distinction between the sexes," and "Female sexuality"; see also Juliet Mitchell, *Psychoanalysis and Feminism* (New York: Random House, 1974).

13. It is interesting in this light to note that many male critics missed this sense of liberation, reading the experience instead as one of hardship and suffering. See for example Alexander Walker's notice in *New Standard*, 6 April 1981.

14. But note that if Hans is as much a victim as Lene, the film insists that men like Ulrich, who are Nazis, are not victims.

15. See the interview with Sanders-Brahms in Renate Möhrmann, *Die Frau mit der Kamera: Filmemacherinnen in der Bundesrepublik Deutschland* (Munich: Hanser, 1980), pp. 155–6.

Script

Helma Sanders-Brahms. *Deutschland, bleiche Mutter. Filmerzählung*. Reinbek: Rowohlt, 1980.

Selected Bibliography

Berthommier, Vivian and Angelika Wittlich. "Cinéma Allemand. Journal de Voyage II. Femmes et Cinéastes à Berlin." *Cahiers du Cinéma*, No. 308 (February 1980), 29ff.

Blumenberg, Hans-Christoph. "*Deutschland, bleiche Mutter von Helma Sanders-Brahms*. Ein Brief an Lene." In *Gegenschuss: Texte über Filmemacher und Filme 1980–1983*. Frankfurt am Main: Fischer, 1984, pp. 51–3.

Hiller, Eva. "Mütter und Töchter. Zu *Deutschland, bleiche Mutter* (Helma Sanders-Brahms), *Hungerjahre* (Jutta Brückner), *Daughter Rite* (Michelle Citron)." *Frauen und Film*, No. 24 (June 1980), 29–33.

Höhne, Petra. "*Deutschland, bleiche Mutter.*" *Medium*, May 1980, 37.

Krininger, Doris and Claudia Cippitelli. "Distanz, nicht Distanzierung: *Deutschland, bleiche Mutter.*" *Medium*, February 1981, 45–6.

Möhrmann, Renate. *Die Frau mit der Kamera. Filmemacherinnen in der Bundesrepublik Deutschland*. Munich: Hanser, 1980, pp. 141–60.

Münzberg, Olaf. "'Schaudern vor der bleichen Mutter': Eine sozialpsychologische Analyse der Kritiken zum Film von Helma Sanders-Brahms." *Medium*, July 1980, 34–7.

Neubaur, Caroline. "Wenn du noch eine Mutter hast. Zu Helma Sanders Film *Deutschland, bleiche Mutter.*" *Freibeuter*, No. 4 (1980), 168–9.

Tast, Brigitte (ed.). *Helma Sanders-Brahms. Kulleraugen-Materialsammlung*, No. 8. Düsseldorf: Lory, 1980.

Zurmühl, Sabine. "Filme, die mir Angst nahmen." *Courage*, April 1980, 38–41.

20

ERIC RENTSCHLER

Terms of dismemberment: the body in/and/of Fassbinder's *Berlin Alexanderplatz* (1980)

Any attempt to sketch a topography of Rainer Werner Fassbinder's expansive and complex *Berlin Alexanderplatz* has a vast territory to cover. First of all, one must take into account the film's textual basis, Alfred Döblin's many-voiced urban epic of 1929, as well as Phil Jutzi's 1930 rendering of the novel starring Heinrich George, "an underworld drama with many documentary shots."[1] Second, Fassbinder's reception of the novel demands consideration. The filmmaker's life-long obsession with Döblin's book proved to be a dynamic relationship, one which Fassbinder depicted in a lengthy essay.[2] In the passionate article, the director openly admitted just how crucial *Berlin Alexanderplatz* had been for his own development, how the novel had left decisive marks on his impressionable young mind, and how these traces are to be found throughout his entire *oeuvre*. Finally, the most sizeable challenge remains Fassbinder's mammoth adaptation of the novel, a work of 15 hours 21 minutes. Accounting for the terms of this personal rendering of a work privileged by the *auteur* remains a strikingly imposing task, in 1984, two years after the filmmaker's death, four years since the film's controversy-ridden première on West German television,[3] a year following its resoundingly successful commercial release in American arthouses, at a time when the film is being aired on American cable outlets, marketed as a video cassette, and rescreened in Germany.[4] *Berlin Alexanderplatz* was in 1980 German television's most exorbitant undertaking ever, a 13 million DM investment supported by Westdeutscher Rundfunk (WDR) and the Italian Television Network (RAI), a film of thirteen episodes and an epilogue, a production with a cast of 100 lead and supporting actors besides 3000 extras, a work shot over 154 days between June 1979 and April 1980 on location in Berlin and in the Munich Bavaria Studio.[5]

Despite all the intense discussion the film has stimulated – be it the hurrahs of New York critics, the tributes that deem it to be Fassbinder's masterpiece, or the fierce attacks directed at the TV production in the West German press and equally impassioned vindications bemoaning the work's ill treatment in the FRG – one lacks reliable guides through the film, and still more a sense of orientation. The imposing body that is Fassbinder's *Berlin Alexanderplatz* remains for the most unexplored.[6] Outside of according the film the status of a crowning achievement ("a Mount Everest of modern cinema"[7]), commentators have not been able to situate it convincingly within the director's corpus.

The term "body" here dare not be only understood as metaphorical glibness, as a deconstructive indulgence. The word is to be taken literally, for Fassbinder's film, above all, exudes a stunning physicality. *Berlin Alexanderplatz* lingers in the mind, indeed haunts the viewer, as a markedly corporeal experience, a work that in equal measure brutalizes, fascinates, and moves its audience. Fassbinder's film is nothing less than an encyclopedia of bodies responding to modernity: street violence and domestic beatings; individuals in crowded spaces shrieking, moaning, rejoicing; an arm run over and a hand burned; people in transit, meeting and coupling in public places, having serious conversations while urinating or sexual intercourse in a toilet stall. One escapes from the city into small cubby holes – a smoke-filled bar or a rented room cluttered by a printing press and reddened by incessantly blinking neon lights. Fateful walks through the woods, the inescapable procession through the slaughterhouse: *Berlin Alexanderplatz* stands out as a film preoccupied with the force, possibility, and vulnerability of the human body within the constellations of modernity, a body not simply subject to natural workings, but one above all inscribed by historical process.

"The body," as Mary Ann Doane and many film theoreticians have pointed out in recent years, "is always a function of discourse."[8] And Fassbinder represents New German Film's most conscious and conspicuous exponent of the politics of the body (*Körperpolitik*), a visceral praxis that privileges direct impact over rhetoric, that places the tangible before the discursive. He once – in a sequence of *Germany in Autumn* (*Deutschland im Herbst*, 1978), where he played himself – sat without clothes before a camera and, oblivious to the spectator, masturbated. In other scenes, he alternately caressed, abused, and reviled his male lover while likewise haranguing his mother, sniffing cocaine, swilling liquor, refusing to eat, crying, screeching, retching. *Berlin Alexanderplatz* – the film the director works on during these scenes, a text that in essence arises out of Fassbinder's poignant self-disclosures – is an even more exhaustive and excruciating demonstration of the politics of the body. It is a film in which the bodies *in* the text very much have to do with the body *of* the text, a work of crucial importance in the personal history of postwar Germany's definitive epic filmmaker.

In talking of Fassbinder's adaptation, one must have recourse to the director's words as initial guideposts, but nonetheless refrain from letting these impressive documents overdetermine one's response to *Berlin Alexanderplatz*.

Fassbinder's "Introductory Notes" to the printed script of *Querelle* (1982) summarize his thinking on the art of literary adaptation cogently and succinctly. (In the space of several paragraphs he says what numerous scholars of film and literature have taken pages – or a book – to conclude.) Speaking about his rendering of Jean Genet's novel and drawing consequences from his numerous previous encounters with literary sources, Fassbinder insisted that an adaptation can only be successful when the adaptor has a subjective investment in the source. The only way to transform literature into film, maintained Fassbinder, was to find a personal relationship to the textual basis:

– through an unequivocal and single-minded questioning of the piece of literature and its language,
– by scrutinizing the substance and movement of the author's work,
– by developing an imagination instantly recognizable as unique,
– and by abandoning any vain attempt at "fulfilling" the work of literature.[9]

Confronting the special terms of fictional worlds estranges and enriches, luring the reader out of his or her own reality and ultimately back to a more profound sense of one's private world, "toward certain recognitions and decisions which, no matter how painful they may seem to be, bring us closer to our own lives."[10]

Another document, Fassbinder's crucial essay on Alfred Döblin's novel, "The cities of man and his soul" (1980), passionately details the central role *Berlin Alexanderplatz* played in the formation of the filmmaker's personal identity. In painfully intimate language, phrases sprinkled with ironic interjections, Fassbinder talks about his life-long grappling with the text, how it intervened to save him from a "murderous puberty," easing his burgeoning homosexuality, later becoming something like a life's script for him, a source of images and situations which he internalized, scenes that resurface in his films consistently and continually, unwittingly at times, intentionally at others. The encounter with the novel was an absolutely galvanizing experience, one that transpired "in the head, in the flesh, in the body as a whole and in my soul. . . ."[11] Döblin's modernistic narrative, a sprawling rendering of the thousand voices of the big city, a work redolent of John Dos Passos and possibly influenced by James Joyce's *Ulysses*, spoke in a variety of modalities, presenting the world through which its hero Franz Biberkopf moves and is driven, Berlin of 1927 and 1928, as a market-place of competing discourses, a polyphony of stimuli, a sensual overload where one constantly runs into the textuality of a mediated existence, a life surrounded by other forces seeking to enlist one. Out of Döblin's cinemorphic montage vision, Fassbinder derived a dominant interest, a story about two men, the possibility of a pure love between Franz and Reinhold, a love unfettered and undeterred by social constraints. This relationship ends in tragedy because the two lack the courage to recognize and act upon the fact "that they like each other in a curious way, that they somehow love each other, that something mysterious connects them, something more than is generally considered acceptable among men."[12]

Adaptations as personal displacements of a literary text into the life's world of an interpreter, Fassbinder's dialogue with Döblin's novel as a private psychodrama that recoded the original text as above all a love story between two men: this relationship between Fassbinder and *Berlin Alexanderplatz* has entranced, indeed predisposed, critics writing about the film. Wolfram Schütte, author of the most insightful essay thus far devoted to the work, grants it a monumental status, calling the film Fassbinder's *magnum opus*, "the great confession, the settlement of a debt, the fulfillment of a dream, and the summing up of all his previous artistic efforts."[13] Schütte's affective relationship to the film – and its creator[14] – replicates Fassbinder's passionate attachment to Döblin's novel. The Frankfurt critic champions the effort as "a self-willed, even narcissistic reading of this complex novel, an appropriation which projects into the work the desires, wishes, fears and utopian ideals of the reader."[15] These effusive phrases do much to capture – indeed to prolong verbally – the film's decisive impact on many viewers. The rhetoric does not, however, help to explain the special terms of Fassbinder's appropriation, except for taking the director's intentionality at face value. Schütte recounts the filmmaker's fascination with the Döblin novel and shows how this magnificent obsession took visual and aural shape. Schütte, and exuberant critics like him, extend the imaginary relationship of Fassbinder to Döblin's *Berlin Alexanderplatz*, ultimately becoming engulfed by that imaginary, limited to its terms. This lack of distance, for all the insights such sympathetic criticism can forward, has as a consequence crucial oversights – very singular ones, as we shall see.

When trying to understand the symbolic terms behind Fassbinder's rendering of *Berlin Alexanderplatz*, one does well to consider the film's origin in a way that does not only reproduce Fassbinder's account. As stated, the origin of the body of the film goes back to *Germany in Autumn*, to Fassbinder's chamber-room study of himself trying to write the scenario to *Berlin Alexanderplatz* during the frenzied German autumn of 1977 with its terrorist kidnappings, state-wide witchhunts, and an atmosphere of suspicion and anxiety. We watch the filmmaker dictating the script into a cassette player; we glimpse the dtv-paperback edition of the novel lying around the apartment; and we gain a sense of how Fassbinder incorporates this text into his own life. At one point he describes a medium close-up of Franz Biberkopf standing at a door looking lonely, precisely the shot we will see Fassbinder in later on: we witness Fassbinder as he sees Franz Biberkopf and as he sees himself as Biberkopf. Every bit as important, though, we see Fassbinder acting in ways we will come to associate with Reinhold. He beats

Arnim as Reinhold mistreats women, tormenting his male lover in the flat much as the petty gangster abuses Trude in episode six of *Berlin Alexanderplatz*.

The scenes of domestic violence documented in *Germany in Autumn* feature a creator who is at once the victim of larger socio-political constellations and the victimizer of those living in his near vicinity. Arnim Meier, the director's proletarian lover, committed suicide in a Munich apartment soon after the film was completed. Fassbinder's act of mourning, a tribute to Meier, the film *In a Year of 13 Moons* (*In einem Jahr mit 13 Monden*, 1978), is an outgrowth of *Germany in Autumn*. As a textual body it possesses compelling links to *Berlin Alexanderplatz*. The resemblances between the two works are manifold and striking: both feature protagonists who, by dint of an unhappy love for another man, lose an appendage. Each film takes place in a brutal urban landscape, a world of shadowy apartments, garish arcades, mean streets, a harsh reality that is likened in bloody explicitness to a slaughterhouse. Elvira, like the unravelled Franz of the epilogue, spends most of the film auditing her life, walking through previous stations, interviewing those who have been important to her, trying to take stock and find a reason to go on.[16] Both works involve people orphaned in the world. We hear a nun tell of Erwin's lonely youth in a convent; in episode one, we see Franz – of whose parents we never hear a word – carefully scrutinizing a cinema poster bearing the title, *Without Parents, the Fate of an Orphan Child*. *In a Year of 13 Moons* and *Berlin Alexanderplatz* are tales of lack, about desperate people who cannot live alone, but who cannot find lasting bonds with others either. Two characters seek to find their way through big cities, Berlin of the Weimar era, Frankfurt in the late 1970s, both trying to pose as the shapers of their own stories in the clamor of so many other voices and foreign desires.

Döblin's novel, as Fassbinder once said of Sirk's films, "tells you something about the world and what it does to you."[17] Every bit as significantly, though, Fassbinder's adaptation demonstrates what those living in this world do to others. To reduce the large and many-voiced novel and a rendering which is 15 hours 21 minutes long down to an impossible love between two men who bring disaster to each other is to leave out a central component, one obscured in Fassbinder's essay and one only peripherally broached by Schütte.[18] What is missing is precisely the means of exchange between the two, the third term in Franz and Reinhold's transactions: women. This is a curious omission, for in screenings of the film, the violence directed toward women (in the form of beatings, rapes, humiliation) invariably provokes extreme discomfort during showings and occasions vehement discussion afterwards. In fact, the film as a whole – unlike the novel! – is framed in a way to foreground acts of violence toward women wrought by the two protagonists. The first event in the narrative's chronology, a scene shown repeatedly and insistently throughout the film, is Franz's brutal murder of

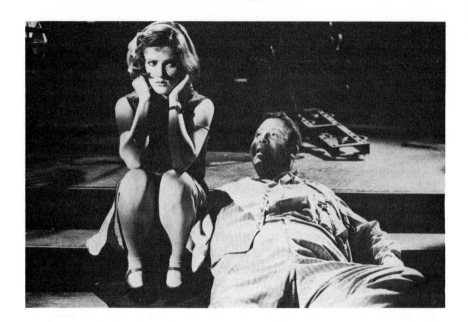

Plates 42 and 43 The tie that binds Franz (Günter Lamprecht, above) and Reinhold (Gottfried John, below): woman (Mieze, played by Barbara Sukowa). Biberkopf will beat his lover to a pulp in this space; Reinhold will later dispatch her in these woods. Photos courtesy of Stiftung Deutsche Kinemathek.

Ida. The film closes with a seemingly gratuitous flashback to Reinhold's attack on Mieze in Freienwalde. Coming at the end of the discursive epilogue, after Franz Biberkopf has exorcized his personal demons and we have taken leave of the resigned individual, this scene seems out of place, indeed superfluous. And how is one to account for the superimposed title over the frozen long-shot image of Reinhold strangling Mieze? "We know what we know, we had to pay dearly for it." Women – and violated women's bodies – would seem to be the dear price paid here: they serve as the means of exchange between Franz and Reinhold, the other that figures so crucially in their interactions, as well as in Fassbinder's interaction with Döblin's novel and German history.

The film's narrative chronology begins with Franz pummeling Ida with a shaving brush; the film's discursive finale closes with a reprise of Reinhold violating Mieze. Likewise, the three blows of fate which structure Franz's passion play, his great setbacks, all involve a similar constellation, a collision between two men at the middle of which stands a woman. Otto Lüders betrays Franz's friendship by terrorizing and robbing a lonely widow enamored of Franz. Reinhold becomes enraged when Franz refuses to continue to take in his discarded lovers. Angered as well by Biberkopf's attempts to reform him, Reinhold throws the unsuspecting chum out of a speeding car, an event that leaves Franz without an arm. Finally, Franz's insanity and near-death come in the wake of his grief after Reinhold's murder of Mieze. *Berlin Alexanderplatz* involves a triangulation of desire, in its story's beginning (Franz beats Ida after she threatens to leave him for another man) and its discourse's end, throughout the station drama's structure. In the textual body that is *Berlin Alexanderplatz*, women function as the main object in the play of differences which sustains the narrative's trajectory, as the vehicle of male desire which drives the film to its ultimate tragic conclusion. ("We know what we know. . . .") The film abounds with acts of violence toward the human body, ones that culminate in a vision of reality as a vast slaughterhouse and the human being as a helpless sacrificial beast. This body, more often than not, is that of a woman, and even when it is not, it is linked to woman in a curious – and disarming – way.

Bodies become texts in *Berlin Alexanderplatz*, sites of inscription and bearers of meaning. The camera gazes in relentless close-up shots at the wounds left by Franz on Ida's and Mieze's faces. Reinhold forces his victim-to-be to look at the anvil engraved on his chest and to fathom its significance. Physical signs betray one's past and one's person; people read others like a book. Lüders looks at Franz for the first time and – just as Lina had earlier intuited – knows he has an ex-convict before him. After losing his arm, Franz is thought by many to be a war veteran. (And he bows to this interpretation, buying an Iron Cross.) Not everyone, though, is a good or a close reader. From the beginning Franz misreads

Reinhold, viewing the fascinating stranger in the bar as a reflection of himself:

> FRANZ: I bet that you've done time, and I also bet that when you saw me you also thought right off that I'd done time too. And you're right, my boy, I've done time, four years in Tegel. Now you know it. And what's up now?
> REINHOLD: Sorry,but I've never done time, not once. I used to be political when I was younger. I wanted to blow up a gas factory, but someone blew the whistle on me. But they didn't get me.

The body of the text *Berlin Alexanderplatz* in the same way constantly incites us to read it, foregrounding its operations by such devices as an otherwise superfluous printing press we gaze on continually in Franz's rented room, a stand-in double for the film's own textuality, something that quite conspicuously gets in the spectator's way during several lovemaking sequences, demanding that we acknowledge its presence. Likewise, Fassbinder introduces – as is common to most of his films – spectator surrogates, characters like Frau Bast and Baumann (ones not to be found in the novel) who stand at doorways, peer through keyholes, and maintain a decidedly specular relationship to the events of Franz's life. Bodies in the text, the body of the text: both draw attention to themselves.

The story of Franz Biberkopf begins with the dazed and just-released prison inmate listening to the Jew Nachum tell the story of Stefan Zanowich, the tale of a man who shipwrecks on the world. A story that begins with a story: as if to ask, what effect do stories have, what can one learn from them? We will come to know Franz as a consummate recycler of even the most random experiences and fleeting impressions. At this point he is struck by one phrase in particular: "But the main thing about people is their eyes and their feet. One has to be able to see the world and walk up to it." As he readies to leave Nachum and his brother-in-law, Franz says portentously while smiling and shaking his head: "You talked about feet and eyes. I've still got them, no one has cut them off." Eyes and feet, seeing and walking, the observer of city life and the passer-by: herein lie two possibilities to which Franz will take constant recourse during the film – as will Xaver Schwarzenberger's camera, in its penetrating gazes and its exciting travelling shots. Within the phrase, though, also rests the threat of dismemberment. And to be sure, immediately after passing through the prison gate Franz is almost run over by a car. Franz is not just eyes and feet; he has powerful arms as well, the limbs he uses to beat Ida and Mieze; one arm is the appendage he loses under a car. Both butcher and sacrificial lamb, Biberkopf is victimizer and victim at once.

Franz's loss of an arm involves more than a symbolic castration. (Fassbinder had already – quite literally – made a definitive fantasy in this vein with *In a Year of 13 Moons*.) Biberkopf is disfigured at significant moments *prior* to the midnight accident where a car runs over his limb. As suggested earlier, the film concentrates on the physical nature of Franz Biberkopf's experience in the streets of Berlin during the late 1920s, focusing with special interest on his exchanges with women. In some way, as we have intimated, his treatment at the hands of reality has something to do with his own treatment of women. What, though, are the precise terms of dismemberment in Fassbinder's *Berlin Alexanderplatz*?

The scene in episode two where Franz stands on the street hawking ties is a crucial one. Unlike the corresponding passage in Jutzi's version, a sequence that becomes a performance vehicle for Heinrich George, one shot straight on and uninterrupted by cuts, Fassbinder frames Biberkopf eccentrically, from a series of curious angles, through a number of perspectives. On the soundtrack, Franz's hearty sales pitch ("Why doesn't the prole wear a tie?") is all but drowned out by the street noise. We first view Franz in long shot from across the street as he begins his speech; the camera then cuts in closer to a medium shot of him. The composition includes a bride mannequin in white standing behind him in the right-hand side of the frame. For the moment, the dismemberment of Franz takes place on the level of the film's editing, both visually and aurally: he does not command the center of attention on the city street, nor even within the confines of single frames. (Cf. the dominant presence of George in the 1931 version.) A later shot images Franz so that to the left of him a skinned chicken hangs in a store window, meat that has been processed in the slaughterhouse, anticipating the fate that lies in store for the sacrificial-animal-to-be.

Several cuts later, the camera now rests behind the bride mannequin, looking at Franz's back. We glimpse the bride's left hand – and, curiously, we do not see Franz's arm, for his hand rests in his pocket, out of view, as if he had already lost the arm. (At one juncture, Franz cries out to a young boy to stand back from the street, lest he be run over by a car: the recurring threat of coming under the wheels.) Eva, Franz's lover of many years before, enters the frame and also stands to the left of Franz. In essence, then, Franz is flanked by women, by his ex-bride and a figurative one, and as we come to learn, attended as well by his present "Braut," Lina, who lurks offscreen in a subway entrance. A small presence in the chimeric midst of the city, or as Franz put it when leaving prison: "All these people, and then the city and the world and me. . . ." Women become a source of solace in this confusion, a helping hand as it were. Franz does not consider himself restored to the world until after he has seduced/raped Ida's sister, Minna, rejoicing after their coupling, "What are the trumpets blowing, hussars come out, halleluja! Franz Biberkopf is back again! Franz is released! Franz Biberkopf is free!" In a drama of lack, the tale of one man trying to find substance and meaning, a life of his own, women become a crucial gap-filler, a second hand, the significant other.

Plate 44   The armband as a fetish object which at this point has little meaning for Franz, who will later lose an arm and join the National Socialists. Photo courtesy of Stiftung Deutsche Kinemathek.

A later scene in the same episode features another variation on the dismembered arm. Franz has taken a job selling the Nazi party organ, the *Völkischer Beobachter*, in the subway station at Potsdamer Platz. His new employer insists that Franz wear an armband with a swastika on it, something we see framed in extreme close-up, in a shot from the back which allows us only a view of Franz's arm and the party symbol, a cut, indeed, which reduces the arm to a fetish object. Soon he encounters a former comrade, the Communist Dreske with whom Franz used to run. Forced by his angry ex-chum to account for the change in his politics, Biberkopf summarizes his experience as a leftist during the early Weimar years:

We had inflation, paper bills, millions, billions, no meat, no butter. Nothing was there, how could it have been? And we? We just ran around and swiped potatoes from farmers. Revolution? Take the flagholder apart, hide the banner under a wax cover, and put the thing in a closet. Let your mother bring you your slippers and take off your fiery red ties. You always make revolution with your mouth, your republic – a disaster.

Red flags and ties, brown armbands: the objects become metonymical representations of the two major political forces in the Weimar Republic concerned with solving Germany's ills, with responding to a traumatized nation's feelings of insecurity, with posing alternative visions of well-being. For the men returning from the fronts of World War I to the cities of Germany, National Socialism offered compelling hopes, images of enchantment, promises of employment, plenitude, and order. "I don't know what will come of it," Franz says of the armband and what it represents as the camera tracks right, "but who knows?" As the shot ends, Franz once again appears with his arm truncated, just as he will at the end of the film, a one-armed garage attendant, who, as Fassbinder insists, will become a National Socialist.[19]

Döblin's novel is about a city and a man; its full title is *Berlin Alexanderplatz: The Story of Franz Biberkopf*. Similarly, Fassbinder's film deals with a public and a private history. As he once said in an interview: "I hope the things which will probably at first trouble a lot of people will ultimately make them more sensitive to that which is German history."[20] A lost world war and the nation that grew out of it, an individual disfigured by his experience in one of the nation's big cities: Fassbinder's epic work stresses the precariousness of the historical constellations framing Franz's story, constantly impressing upon the viewer the dent made by the public sphere on the small man, the way in which Biberkopf's existence is mediated by a multitude of socio-political forces. Public and private experience come together in the image of Franz's wound and the reactions it stimulates.

Franz visits Reinhold after the accident, seeking reconciliation. After an initially strained conversation, they make up. Reinhold then asks Franz to show him the stump and Biberkopf relents. The wound is pictured in un-abashed close-up, a shot that rhymes with previous images of Franz's arm. It looks very much like a vagina, prompting Reinhold to exclaim how it repulses him. He uses the word "eklig" to describe the stump, echoing the phrase he uttered earlier when expressing his disgust for Trude, whose presence he could no longer bear: "Versteh doch, die ekelt mich an, die ekelt mich ganz einfach an.'' Reinhold immediately talks of having Franz buy an artificial limb and then sets about frantically trying to stuff the empty sleeve with articles of clothing. Franz, in a different, but every bit as significant way, responds to his missing arm. Initially he creates a series of fictions to explain the loss. Later, after being repeatedly taken for an injured war veteran, he purchases an Iron Cross. In both cases what is at work is dis-avowal as described by Freud, the simultaneous denial and recognition of a traumatic absence. The stump becomes a fetish, something one would rather ignore, but cannot. By dint of the arm's very non-presence, one must talk about it and try to explain it away. The missing limb functions as a prop in the film, a major one, playing a role quite similar to *Berlin Alexanderplatz*'s other crucial stand-in and object of fascination, women.

The major confrontations between Franz and Reinhold, from their exchange of lovers and wares to the tragic string of events which ends in Mieze's death, have a woman at their center. The two express themselves through women, but women in turn are not allowed to express themselves. (Ida is murdered because she seeks to assert her will, to leave Franz for another man; Mieze, likewise, dies because Reinhold is angered to learn that she has strung him along, trying to sound him out about Franz.) In the discourse between the film's real romantic couple, Cilly, Fränze, Trude, and even Mieze forever remain the other, lacking their own voice – or even their own names. (Franz renames Mieze just as he once did Eva; both women allow their lover to determine what they should be called.) Feminist film theory has stressed the manner in which dominant – as well as much alterna-tive – cinema denies women a voice. The female presence becomes the object of narrative desire and visual pleasure, but women at the same time are denied their own volition, their own subject-hood. What strikes one so markedly about *Berlin Alexanderplatz* is the unabashed manner in which Fassbinder forefronts, indeed dramatizes, this perception. Likewise, one is equally confounded by the way previous (male) critics have sought to disavow this consideration. Women remain an auxiliary force in this film, to be sure, but in a much more compelling way than commentators have been willing to allow.[21]

Emmi's walk across a room (in episode seven) acts as an object lesson in semantics. The brash Willy asks the woman Franz has met in a bar to take a few steps and then questions the men standing in the night club to tell him what they have just seen. Did she walk, march, wiggle her ass, or dance? It's all in the mind of the beholder, according to Willy, which is his way of demonstrating the relative status of signifiers. Things are what words make them. In this scene, Emmi is present, yet absent, an object in the object lesson, lacking any independent existence – except for sticking out her tongue at the laughing male throng – and only there to prove someone else's point. She will disappear from the narrative after this scene, just as Lina, Fränze, and others before her.

Franz and Reinhold exchange women like chain letters, or as Franz describes the dynamics, it's just like "a transaction with a lot of middle men [*Kettenhandel*], just like during inflation." Women lack their own language and ultimate exchange value in the play of differences at the center of this discourse. At the same time, though, they act as the means of communication and expression between men. They have no meaning of their own and take on significance only in relation to male desire.[22] Women in *Berlin Alexanderplatz* are gap-fillers, sources of solace and simultaneous bearers of lack – hence the visual connection in the film between Franz's stump and the female vagina. Mieze and Eva function as helping hands for the wounded ex-soldier; they are not allowed, however, to transcend their subsidiary status as nurses who offer Franz succor, as prostitutes who care for his material and sexual needs. In essence, then, the reduction of women to empty signifiers reflects the precarious status of the phallic order in Fassbinder's film. This act amounts to one of projection and betrays the otherwise repressed element of trauma at work in male fantasy production. It is here that women, Franz's missing arm, and German history come together.

Franz's amputated limb becomes a monument for a lost world war as well as the embodiment of a forthcoming dismemberment. He compensates for his missing arm by wearing an Iron Cross, aligning himself with a generation of men who had – in their own memories – fought for a noble cause, losing only because they were "stabbed in the back" by incompetent leaders. Another means of compensating for this perceived lack was to be found in fascism. Have you lost the better part of yourself? the National Socialists asked in effect, consciously appealing to the wounded sensibilities of the World War I veterans. Not to worry: we have a whole new identity for you.[23] Döblin's novel was written at a time when a widespread war nostalgia was the rage in Germany, an attempt to restore the lost virility of life at the front, precisely at a moment when the fragmentation of political life made it hard for people to discern exactly where the front lay. Recollections of the war and common experience with other men – something evoked continually in Franz's singing of military songs – granted one an intact psychic identity, a remembrance of a period when things were clear-cut and one felt meaningfully engaged in a larger struggle.[24] Döblin's novel reflects the power of these male fantasies during the late 1920s in Weimar Germany.[25] Fassbinder's film goes further: it problematizes them.

Women in *Berlin Alexanderplatz* serve as functions of male fantasies, the go-between for men who cannot express their love for each other directly.

In the logic of the film, women and Nazism are second hands, gap-fillers for confused men with otherwise empty lives. In a variation on the Fassbinderian theme of oppression among the oppressed, men act out on women's bodies the violence they experience themselves at the hands of the everyday. The film, likewise, is Fassbinder's fantasy – not just the autobiographical epilogue, but the preceding thirteen parts as well. Here, as elsewhere in his work, women stand at the center of transactions between men who control the narrative action. (One finds this constellation already operative in the early gangster films.) Even in the case of Fassbinder's most forceful female protagonist, Maria Braun, we encounter a woman who serves as the unwitting object of exchange between two men, Hermann Braun and Karl Oswald, the true shapers of her fortune. A similar triangulation of desire informs *Lola* (1981) as well, where the night-club singer is a commodity passed between the city's two most influential men, the speculator Schuckert and the civic official von Bohm. Women act as vehicles in Fassbinder's tour through modern German history, the means by which one obtains a larger knowledge of cultural process – a knowledge for which one must pay dearly.

At one point toward the end of *Lili Marleen* (1981), we pass the site of Mieze's death and hear how a prostitute once was killed here. This is more than a cute bit of intertextuality, a precious moment of auteurist levity. Fassbinder, we recall, ended *Berlin Alexanderplatz*, the final moments of a film and personal epilogue $15\frac{1}{3}$ hours long, with a replay of Mieze's death at Reinhold's hands. That he reprises the event yet again in another film is neither superfluous nor coincidental. *Lili Marleen*, among other things, is a film that portrays one woman's career as a professional object of spectacle, a female body and voice in the service of fascism. This insistent repetition indicates that Fassbinder knew of the violence that comes of reducing women to "the blank page upon which history is written," [26] be it the inscriptions of simple men like Franz and Reinhold, be it the larger traces left by a national history controlled by male authors.

"We know what we know, we had to pay dearly for it." Franz Biberkopf loses an arm and ultimately his personality, appearing finally as a phantom devoid of will and emotion. He has paid a high price for his knowledge, so much that he has nothing left. The narrative, too, has extracted a dire toll: the deaths of two women which frame the film, the beatings and humiliations of others throughout its course, the denigration of female presence to a virtual cipher. Fassbinder knew well what it cost to stage male fantasies: German history and the classical narrative cinema, both of which fascinated and repelled him, had taught him considerable lessons in this regard. It stands to reason that when the director appears before the camera in the epilogue of *Berlin Alexanderplatz*, he, like his protagonist, is imaged in a way that pushes him to the side of the frame and cuts off his arm. German history, thus, is inscribed everywhere; we find traces of its undeniable violence in these images and in this narrative – and, not least, on the body of a director who wears his scars defiantly. Fassbinder recognized the terms of dismemberment: the same history he wished to re-present was the one that had (mis)shaped him. He knew what he knew; he, too, had to pay dearly for it.

Notes

1. Siegfried Kracauer, *From Caligari to Hitler: A Psychological History of the German Film* (Princeton: Princeton University Press, 1947), p. 223.
2. Rainer Werner Fassbinder, "Die Städte des Menschen und seine Seele. Alfred Döblins Roman *Berlin Alexanderplatz*." The article appeared originally in *Die Zeit*, 14 March 1980. It was reprinted in Rainer Werner Fassbinder and Harry Baer, *Der Film Berlin Alexanderplatz. Ein Arbeitsjournal* (Frankfurt am Main: Zweitausendeins, 1980), pp. 6–9, and in Rainer Werner Fassbinder, *Filme befreien den Kopf*, ed. Michael Töteberg (Frankfurt am Main: Fischer, 1984), pp. 81–90. Subsequent references are quoted from the latter source.
3. For Fassbinder's reflections on the many attacks directed against the film from, above all, conservative forces, see the interview between him and Klaus Eder, "Warum denn Ärger mit Franz Biberkopf: Ein Gespräch mit Rainer Werner Fassbinder über seinen Fernsehfilm *Berlin Alexanderplatz*," *Frankfurter Allgemeine Zeitung*, 29 December 1980.
4. The film was screened over four evenings on the third channel in Germany during late August and early September of 1984.
5. For a detailed account and documentation of the production, see the materials in *Der Film Berlin Alexanderplatz* put together by Fassbinder and Harry Baer (note 2).
6. Several dissertations, however, are currently being written in West Germany devoted to the film. As of October 1984, one still looked in vain for a lengthy article in English (besides Schütte's translated essay listed below) on the film.
7. This is Andrew Sarris's phrase, one used by the American distributor of the film, TeleCulture, in its advertising campaign. In a similar vein, see Vincent Canby's lengthy notice, "Is *Berlin Alexanderplatz* a vision of the movies' future?" *New York Times*, 10 July 1983.
8. Mary Ann Doane, "Woman's stake: filming the female body," *October*, No. 17 (Summer 1981), 26.
9. Rainer Werner Fassbinder, *Querelle: The Film Book*, ed. Dieter Schidor and Michael McLernon, trans. Arthur S. Wensinger and Richard H. Wood (Munich: Schirmer/Mosel/Grove, 1982), p. 11.
10. ibid.
11. Fassbinder, *Filme befreien den Kopf*, p. 81.
12. ibid., p. 83.
13. Wolfram Schütte, "Franz, Mieze, Reinhold, Death and the Devil. Rainer Werner Fassbinder's *Berlin Alexanderplatz*," in *Fassbinder*, ed. Ruth McCormick (New York: Tanam, 1981), p. 99.
14. Schütte was one of the few German film critics Fassbinder respected, so much so, indeed, that he admitted this regard unabashedly in an interview and even wrote a fragment about the journalist. See "Schütte: Von der Dialektik des Bürgers im Paradies der lähmenden Ordnung," in *Filme befreien den Kopf*, pp. 129–30.
15. Schütte, p. 102.
16. See Robert Burgoyne's article on *In a Year of 13 Moons*, "Narrative and sexual excess," *October*, No. 21 (Summer 1982), 56: "Erwin/Elvira's quest is to reconstruct the past and define his/her origins. Through this imaginary scenario Elvira

hopes to rescue herself from the nebulous zone in which she is bereft of sexual identity and to be restored to the system of clear definitions and polar organization, and thereby to the society which rejects her."

17. "Fassbinder on Sirk," trans. Thomas Elsaesser, *Film Comment*, 11, No. 6 (November–December 1975), 22.

18. Cf. Schütte, p. 108: "The women who cross Biberkopf's path, who stay with him for a while and then disappear, his friends and acquaintances, all have their mystery: they are living human beings."

19. Fassbinder, *Filme befreien den Kopf*, p. 88.

20. Klaus Eder, "Warum denn Ärger mit Franz Biberkopf" (note 3).

21. For a demonstration of the extreme denigration of women's presence in *Berlin Alexanderplatz*, see the description by Richard Corliss, "Germany without tears," *Time*, 15 August 1983, 64: Franz's second-hand lovers, according to the critic, amount to "a series of gross, silly and pathetic trollops."

22. Cf. Kaja Silverman, *The Subject of Semiotics* (New York: Oxford University Press, 1983), p. 173.

23. See Peter Sloterdijk, *Kritik der zynischen Vernunft* (Frankfurt am Main: Suhrkamp, 1983), II, 799. See also Rainer Stollmann, "Fascist politics as a total work of art: tendencies of the aesthetization of political life in National Socialism," trans. Ronald L. Smith, *New German Critique*, No. 14 (Spring 1978), 52: "It was, therefore, no coincidence that National Socialism referred to the 'soldiers' socialism' of the world war. The experience of the war, which was not adequately understood and worked out in the consciousness of the masses, could be flaunted once again, fifteen years later, as the transfigured image of a unified, no longer dismembered life, of alienation conquered. This was especially effective on the bourgeois youth and the young unemployed, who seemed to themselves useless and unfulfilled."

24. Sloterdijk, 748ff.

25. See Klaus Theweleit, *Männerphantasien* (Frankfurt am Main: Roter Stern, 1977), especially the section in volume two devoted to " 'Homosexualität' und weisser Terror."

26. This phrase is taken from Judith Mayne's unpublished paper, "Women, fascism and spectacle in *Lili Marleen*."

Script

Fassbinder, Rainer Werner and Harry Baer. *Der Film Berlin Alexanderplatz. Ein Arbeitsjournal.* Frankfurt am Main: Zweitausendeins, 1980.

Selected Bibliography

Burg, Vinzenz B. *"Berlin Alexanderplatz." Medien & Erziehung*, 25, No. 2 (1981), 97–104.

Burgoyne, Robert. "Narrative and sexual excess." *October*, No. 21 (Summer 1982), 51–61.

Fassbinder, Rainer Werner. *Filme befreien den Kopf*. Ed. Michael Töteberg. Frankfurt am Main: Fischer, 1984.

Greiner, Ulrich. "Die Schrecken der Liebe: Rainer Werner Fassbinders Verfilmung von Döblins *Berlin Alexanderplatz*." *Die Zeit*, 10 October 1980.

Jansen, Peter W. and Wolfram Schütte (eds). *Rainer Werner Fassbinder*. 4th rev. edn. Munich: Hanser, 1983.

Koch, Gertrud. "Die Frau vor der Kamera. Zur Rolle der Schauspielerin im Autorenfilm." *Frauen und Film*, No. 35 (October 1983), 92–6.

Kurath, Peter. "Döblins Atlanten neu aufgeschlagen: Dicht an der Vorlage: Fassbinders *Berlin Alexanderplatz*." *Film-Korrespondenz*, 9 September 1980, 1–4.

Pflaum, Hans Günther. "Rainer Werner Fassbinder: Ein Schwerarbeiter mit leichter Hand" (interview). *Kino* (Hamburg), No. 3 (15 May 1980), 27–42.

Schütte, Wolfram. "Franz, Mieze, Reinhold, Death and the Devil. Rainer Werner Fassbinder's *Berlin Alexanderplatz*." In *Fassbinder*. Ed. Ruth McCormick. New York: Tanam, 1981, pp. 99–109.

Schwarze, Michael. "Das Prinzip Hoffnung: Fassbinders *Berlin Alexanderplatz* auf der Film-Biennale." *Frankfurter Allgemeine Zeitung*, 3 September 1980.

Sontag, Susan. "Novel into film." *Vanity Fair*, September 1983, 86–90.

Der Spiegel. "Fassbinder: 'Der Biberkopf, das bin ich'" (cover story). 1 October 1980, 224–40.

Würker, Wolfgang. "Fassbinders *Berlin Alexanderplatz*: Franz Biberkopf sucht seinen Weg." *Frankfurter Allgemeine Zeitung*, 14 October 1980.

Appendix I

Credits of films discussed in the text

A list of rental sources for the following and other German feature films is on pp. 332–335.

Der Student von Prag – Ein romantisches Drama (The Student of Prague)

Released	1913
Producer	Deutsche Bioscop (Berlin)
Director	Stellan Rye
Screenplay	Hanns Heinz Ewers
Cinematography	Guido Seeber
Set decoration	Robert A. Dietrich and Klaus Richter
Music	Josef Weiss
Principal cast	Paul Wegener (Balduin)
	Grete Berger (Comtesse Margit)
	Lyda Salmonova (Lyduschka)
	John Gottowt (Scapinelli)
	Fritz Weidemann (Baron Waldis-Schwarzenberg)
	Lothar Körner (Count von Schwarzenberg)
Original length	1538 meters
Rental	Budget Films, West Glen Films

Nosferatu – Eine Symphonie des Grauens (Nosferatu)

Released	1922
Producer	Prana-Film (Berlin)
Director	F. W. Murnau
Screenplay	Henrik Galeen (based on Bram Stoker's novel *Dracula*)
Cinematography	Fritz Arno Wagner and Günther Krampf
Set decoration	Albin Grau
Original music	Hans Erdmann
Principal cast*	Max Schreck (Nosferatu)
	Gustav von Wangenheim (Jonathan Harker)

* These listings accord to the names used in American distribution copies, which vary systematically from those found in the more definitive recent German restoration of the original version.

Greta Schröder (Nina)
Alexander Granach (Renfield)
Max Nemetz (Captain of the *Demeter*)
John Gottowt (The Professor)
Georg Heinrich Schnell (Shipbuilder)
Ruth Landshoff (Ruth)
Gustav Botz (Town Doctor)
Wolfgang Heinz (First Mate of the *Demeter*)
Albert Venohr (Sailor)
Guido Herzfeld (Innkeeper)
Hardy von Francois (Doctor in Hospital)

Original length	1967 meters
Rental	Films Incorporated, Images Film Archive, West Glen Films

Die Büchse der Pandora (Pandora's Box)

Released	1929
Producer	Nero-Film (Berlin)
Director	G. W. Pabst
Screenplay	Ladislaus Vajda (from Frank Wedekind's plays *Der Erdgeist* and *Die Büchse der Pandora*)
Cinematography	Günther Krampf
Editing	Joseph R. Fliesler
Set decoration	Andrei Andreiev
Principal cast	Louise Brooks (Lulu)
	Fritz Kortner (Dr Peter Schön)
	Franz Lederer (Alwa Schön)
	Carl Goetz (Schigolch)
	Alice Roberts (Countess Anna Geschwitz)
	Daisy d'Ora (Marie de Zarniko)
	Krafft Raschig (Rodrigo Quast)
	Michael von Newlinsky (Marquis Casti-Piani)
	Siegfried Arno (Stage Manager)
	Gustav Diessl (Jack the Ripper)
Length	3254 meters
Rental	Films Incorporated

Der blaue Engel (The Blue Angel)

Released	1930
Producer	Ufa (Erich Pommer)
Director	Josef von Sternberg
Screenplay	Robert Liebmann, Carl Zuckmayer, and Karl Vollmöller (from Heinrich Mann's novel, *Professor Unrat*)
Cinematography	Günther Rittau and Hans Schneeberger
Editing	Sam Winston
Set decoration	Otto Hunte and Emil Hasler
Music and songs	Friedrich Hollaender
Song lyrics	Robert Liebmann
Sound	Fritz Thiery
Principal cast	Emil Jannings (Professor Immanuel Rath)
	Marlene Dietrich (Lola)
	Kurt Gerron (Kiepert)

	Rosa Valetti (Guste)
	Hans Albers (Mazeppa)
	Reinhold Bernt (Clown)
	Eduard von Winterstein (Headmaster)
	Rolf Müller (Angst)
	Roland Varno (Lohmann)
	Carl Balhaus (Ertzum)
	Robert Klein-Lörk (Goldstaub)
	Karl Huszar-Puffy (Innkeeper)
	Wilhelm Diegelmann (Captain)
	Gerhard Bienert (Policeman)
	Ilsa Fürstenberg (Rath's Landlady)
	Hans Roth (Caretaker)
Length	108 minutes
Rental	Films Incorporated, Images Film Archive, West Glen Films

Liebelei

Released	1933
Producer	Elite-Tonfilm (Berlin)
Director	Max Ophüls
Screenplay	Curt Alexander, Hans Wilhelm, and Max Ophüls, with the assistance of Felix Salten (from the play by Arthur Schnitzler)
Cinematography	Franz Planer
Editing	Friedel Buckow
Set decoration	Gabriel Pellon
Music supervision	Theo Mackeben (with compositions by Mozart, Johannes Brahms, Beethoven, and Josef Lanner)
Sound	Hans Grimm
Principal cast	Magda Schneider (Christine Weiring)
	Wolfgang Liebeneiner (Fritz Lobheimer)
	Willy Eichberger (Theo Kaiser)
	Luise Ullrich (Mizzi Schlager)
	Gustaf Gründgens (Baron von Eggersdorf)
	Olga Tschechowa (Baroness von Eggersdorf)
	Paul Hörbiger (Hans Weiring, Christine's Father)
Length	88 minutes*
Rental	Images Film Archive

Der zerbrochene Krug (The Broken Jug)

Released	1937
Producer	Tobis-Magna (Berlin)
Director	Gustav Ucicky and Emil Jannings
Screenplay	Thea von Harbou (from the play by Heinrich von Kleist)
Cinematography	Fritz Arno Wagner
Set decoration	Robert Herlth
Music	Wolfgang Zeller
Principal cast	Emil Jannings (Adam)
	Friedrich Kayssler (Walter)
	Max Gülstorff (Licht)

* Original length in Austria, 1933: 93 minutes

Lina Carstens (Marthe Rull)
Angela Salloker (Eve)
Bruno Hübner (Veit Tümpel)
Paul Dahlke (Ruprecht)
Elisabeth Flickenschildt (Brigitte)
Walter Werner (Servant)
Erich Dunskus (Bailiff)
Gisela von Collande (First Maid)
Lotte Rausch (Second Maid)

Length	86 minutes
Rental	Trans-World Films, West Glen Films

Das Fräulein von Barnhelm

Released	1940
Producer	Bavaria (Munich)
Director	Hans Schweikart
Screenplay	Ernst Hasselbach and Peter Francke (from the comedy *Minna von Barnhelm* by G. E. Lessing)
Cinematography	Carl Hoffmann and Heinz Schnackertz
Set decoration	Ludwig Reiber and Rudolf Pfenninger
Music	Alois Melichar
Sound	Carl Becker-Reinhardt
Principal cast	Käthe Gold (Minna von Barnhelm)
	Ewald Balser (Major von Tellheim)
	Fita Benkhoff (Franziska)
	Paul Dahlke (Just)
	Fritz Kampers (Werner)
	Erich Ponto (Innkeeper)
	Theo Lingen (Riccaut de la Marlinière)
Length	91 minutes
Rental	Trans-World Films

The Seventh Cross

Released	1944
Producer	MGM (Pandro S. Berman)
Director	Fred Zinnemann
Screenplay	Helen Deutsch (based on Anna Seghers's novel)
Cinematography	Karl Freund
Set design	Edwin B. Millis and Mac Alper
Music	Roy Webb
Principal cast	Spencer Tracy (George Heisler)
	Signe Hasso (Toni)
	Hume Cronyn (Paul Roeder)
	Jessica Tandy (Liesel Roeder)
	Agnes Moorehead (Madame Marelli)
	Felix Bressart (Poldi Schlamm)
	Katherine Locke (Mrs Sauer)
	George Macready (Bruno Sauer)
	Paul Guilfoyle (Fiedler)
	George Zucco (Fahrenberg)
Length	112 minutes
Rental	Films Incorporated

Wozzeck

Released	1947
Producer	DEFA (Berlin)
Director	Georg C. Klaren
Screenplay	Georg C. Klaren (based on Georg Büchner's dramatic fragment, *Woyzeck*)
Cinematography	Bruno Mondi
Editing	Lena Neumann
Set decoration	Hermann Warm and Bruno Monden
Costume design	Walter Schulze-Mittendorf
Music	Herbert Trantow
Sound	Klaus Jungk
Principal cast	Kurt Meisel (Wozzeck)
	Helga Zülch (Marie)
	Max Eckard (Büchner)
	Richard Häussler (Drum Major)
	Arno Paulsen (Captain)
	Willi Rose (Andres)
	R. Lieffertz-Vincenti (Petty Officer)
	Kläre Reigwart (Margarete)
	Max Drahn (Fool)
Length	100 minutes
Rental	Films Incorporated

Der Untertan (The Subject)

Released	1951
Producer	DEFA (Berlin/GDR)
Director	Wolfgang Staudte
Screenplay	Wolfgang and Fritz Staudte (from the novel by Heinrich Mann)
Cinematography	Robert Baberske
Editing	Johanna Rosinski
Set design	Erich Zander and Karl Schneider
Costume design	Walter Schulze-Mittendorf
Music	Horst Hanns Sieber
Sound	Erich Schmidt
Principal cast	Werner Peters (Diederich Hessling)
	Paul Esser (President von Wulkow)
	Blandine Ebinger (President's Wife)
	Sabine Thalbach (Agnes Göpel)
	Friedrich Maurer (Mr Göpel)
	Renate Fischer (Guste Daimchen)
	Ernst Legal (Pastor Zillich)
	Hans-Georg Laubenthal (Mahlmann)
	Gertrud Bergmann (Mother Hessling)
	Emmy Burg (Magda Hessling)
	Carola Braunbock (Emmi Hessling)
	Eduard von Winterstein (Old Buck)
	Raimund Schelcher (Dr Wolfgang Buck)
	Friedrich Gnass (Napoleon Fischer)
Length	108 minutes
Rental	Films Incorporated

Der Hauptmann von Köpenick (The Captain of Köpenick)

Released	1956
Producer	Gyula Trebitsch for Real-Film (Hamburg)
Director	Helmut Käutner
Screenplay	Carl Zuckmayer and Helmut Käutner (based on Zuckmayer's play)
Cinematography	Albert Benitz
Editing	Klaus Dudenhöfer
Set decoration	Herbert Kirchhoff and Albrecht Becker
Costume design	Erna Sander
Music	Bernhard Eichhorn
Sound	Werner Schlagge
Principal cast	Heinz Rühmann (Wilhelm Voigt)
	Hannelore Schroth (Mathilde Obermüller)
	Martin Held (Mayor Obermüller)
	Erich Schellow (Captain von Schlettow)
	Willy A. Kleinau (Friedrich Hoprecht)
	Wolfgang Neuss (Kalle)
	Helmut Käutner (Street Singer)
	Erica Balqué (Street Singer)
Length	93 minutes. Color
Rental	Budget Films, Films Inc., Kit Parker Films

Der junge Törless (Young Törless)

Released	1966
Producer	Franz Seitz (Munich)/Nouvelles Editions de Film (Paris)
Director	Volker Schlöndorff
Screenplay	Volker Schlöndorff and Herbert Asmodi (from the novel *Die Verwirrungen des Zöglings Törless* by Robert Musil)
Cinematography	Franz Rath
Editing	Claus von Boro
Set decoration	Maleen Pacha
Music	Hans Werner Henze
Sound	Klaus Eckelt
Principal cast	Matthieu Carrière (Törless)
	Bernd Tischer (Beineberg)
	Marian Seidowsky (Basini)
	Alfred Dietz (Reiting)
	Lotte Ledl (Innkeeper)
	Hanne Axmann-Rezzori (Frau Törless)
	Herbert Asmodi (Herr Törless)
	Fritz Gehlen (School Director)
	Barbara Steele (Božena)
	Jean Launay (Teacher)
Length	87 minutes
Rental	New Yorker Films, West Glen Films

Abschied von gestern (Yesterday Girl)

Released	1966
Producer	Kairos-Film (Munich) and Independent-Film (Berlin)
Director	Alexander Kluge

Screenplay	Alexander Kluge (based on the short story "Anita G." in his collection *Lebensläufe*)
Cinematography	Edgar Reitz and Thomas Mauch
Editing	Beate Mainka-Jellinghaus
Sound	Hans-Jörg Wicha, Klaus Eckelt, and Heinz Pusel
Principal cast	Alexandra Kluge (Anita G.)
	Günther Mack (Manfred Pichota)
	Eva Maria Meineke (Frau Pichota)
	Hans Korte (Judge)
	Edith Kuntze-Peloggio (Parole Officer Treiber)
	Peter Staimmer (Young Man)
	Josef Kreindl (Head of Record Company)
	Ursula Dirichs (Mother)
	E. O. Fuhrmann (Parachutist)
	Karl-Heinz Peters (Gentleman)
	Palma Falck (Frau Budek)
	Ado Riegler (Priest)
	Käthe Ebner (Wife of Record Company Head)
	Hans Brammer (Professor)
	Fritz Werner (Manager of Fur Store)
	Hedwig Wissing (Cleaning Woman)
	Nathan Gnath (Hotel Director)
	Maria Schäfer (Maid)
	Harald Patzer (Full Professor)
	Alfred Edel (Teaching Assistant)
	Gottfried Gerhard Bowin-Schlegel (Hotel Porter)
	Adam Delle (Dog Trainer)
	Fritz Bauer (State Prosecutor)
	Irma Kolmhuber (Prison Nurse)
	Erna Bepperling (Prison Therapist)
	Alexander Kluge (Voice-over Narrator)
Length	88 minutes
Rental	West Glen Films

Lebenszeichen (Signs of Life)

Released	1968
Producer	Werner Herzog Filmproduktion (Munich)
Director	Werner Herzog
Screenplay	Werner Herzog (based loosely on Achim von Arnim's novella *Der tolle Invalide auf dem Fort Ratonneau*)
Cinematography	Thomas Mauch and Dietrich Lohmann
Editing	Beate Mainka-Jellinghaus and Maximiliane Mainka
Music	Stavros Xarchakos
Sound	Herbert Prasch
Principal cast	Peter Brogle (Stroszek)
	Wolfgang Reichmann (Meinhard)
	Athina Zacharopoulos (Nora)
	Wolfgang von Ungern-Sternberg (Becker)
	Wolfgang Stumpf (Captain)
	Henry van Lyck (Lieutenant)
	Julio Pinheiro (Gypsy)

Florian Fricke (Pianist)
Dr Heinz Usener (Physician)
Werner Herzog (Soldier)
Achmed Hafiz (Villager)

Length	90 minutes
Rental	New Yorker Films

Geschichtsunterricht (History Lessons)

Released	1972
Producer	Straub-Huillet (Rome) and Janus Film und Fernsehen (Frankfurt)
Directors	Jean-Marie Straub and Danièle Huillet
Screenplay	Straub/Huillet (based on Bertolt Brecht's novel fragment, *Die Geschäfte des Herrn Julius Caesar*)
Cinematography	Renato Berta and Emilio Bestetti
Editing	Straub/Huillet
Sound	Jeti Grigioni
Principal cast	Gottfried Boldt (Banker)
	Johann Unterpertinger (Farmer)
	Henri Ludwig (Lawyer)
	Carl Vaillant (Writer)
	Benedikt Zulauf (Young Man)
Length	88 minutes. Color
Rental	New Yorker Films

Lotte in Weimar

Released	1975
Producer	DEFA (Berlin/GDR)
Director	Egon Günther
Screenplay	Egon Günther (from the novel by Thomas Mann)
Cinematography	Erich Gusko
Editing	Rita Hiller
Set decoration	Harald Horn
Costume design	Christiane Dorst
Music supervision	Vaclav Neumann (selections from Gustav Mahler's Sixth Symphony)
Sound	Wolfgang Höfer and Gerhard Ribbeck
Principal cast	Lilli Palmer (Lotte)
	Martin Hellberg (Goethe)
	Hilmar Baumann (August)
	Monika Lennartz (Charlotte, Lotte's Daughter)
	Jutta Hoffmann (Adele Schopenhauer)
	Katharina Thalbach (Ottilie von Pogwisch)
	Rolf Ludwig (Mager)
	Angelika Ritter (Klärchen)
	Hilmar Eichhorn (Young Goethe)
	Martina Wilke (Young Lotte)
	Thomas Thieme (Young Kestner)
Length	124 minutes. Color
Rental	Film Library of the German Democratic Republic

Die linkshändige Frau (The Left-Handed Woman)

Released	1977
Producer	Road Movies (Berlin) and Wim Wenders Produktion (Munich), WDR (Cologne)
Director	Peter Handke
Screenplay	Peter Handke
Cinematography	Robby Müller
Editing	Peter Przygodda
Costumes	Domenica Kaesdorf
Sound	Ulrich Winkler
Principal cast	Edith Clever (The Woman)
	Markus Mühleisen (Stefan)
	Bruno Ganz (Bruno)
	Michel Lonsdale (Waiter)
	Angela Winkler (Franziska)
	Ines de Longchamps (Woman with Child)
	Philippe Caizergues (Stefan's Friend)
	Gérard Depardieu (Man with T-Shirt)
	Bernhard Wicki (Publisher)
	Nicolas Novikoff (Chauffeur)
	Jany Holt (Woman at the Meeting)
	Bernhard Minetti (The Father)
	Rüdiger Vogler (The Actor)
Length	119 minutes. Color
Rental	New Yorker Films

Die Ehe der Maria Braun (The Marriage of Maria Braun)

Released	1979
Producer	Albatros Produktion (Munich), Trio-Film (Duisburg), WDR (Cologne)
Director	Rainer Werner Fassbinder
Screenplay	Peter Märthesheimer, Pea Fröhlich (based on an idea of Rainer Werner Fassbinder's)
Cinematography	Michael Ballhaus
Editing	Franz Walsch (Rainer Werner Fassbinder) and Juliane Lorenz
Set decoration	Helga Ballhaus
Set design	Norbert Scherer
Costume design	Barbara Baum
Music	Peer Raben
Sound	Jim Willis
Principal cast	Hanna Schygulla (Maria Braun)
	Klaus Löwitsch (Hermann)
	Ivan Desny (Oswald)
	Gottfried John (Willi)
	Gisela Uhlen (Mother)
	Günter Lamprecht (Wetzel)
	George Byrd (Bill)
	Elisabeth Trissenaar (Betti)
	Isolde Barth (Vevi)
	Peter Berling (Bronski)
	Sonja Neudorfer (Red Cross Nurse)

Liselotte Eder (Frau Ehmke)
Volker Spengler (Conductor)
Karl-Heinz von Hassel (Prosecuting Attorney)
Michael Ballhaus (Lawyer)
Christine Hopf-de Loup (Notary)
Hark Bohm (Senkenberg)
Dr Horst-Dieter Klock (Man with Car)
Günther Kaufmann (American GI in Train)
Bruce Low (American at Conference)
Rainer Werner Fassbinder (Black Marketeer)
Claus Holm (Physician)
Anton Schirsner (Grandpa Berger)
Hannes Kaetner (Justice of the Peace)
Martin Häussler (Reporter)
Norbert Scherer (Prison Guard I)
Rolf Bührmann (Prison Guard II)
Arthur Glogau (Prison Guard III)

Length	120 minutes. Color
Rental	New Yorker Films

Deutschland, bleiche Mutter (Germany, Pale Mother)

Released	1980
Producer	Helma Sanders-Brahms, Literarisches Colloquium (Berlin), WDR (Cologne)
Director	Helma Sanders-Brahms
Screenplay	Helma Sanders-Brahms
Cinematography	Jürgen Jürges
Editing	Elfi Tillack and Uta Periginelli
Set decoration	Götz Heymann
Costumes	Janken Janssen
Music	Jürgen Knieper
Sound	Gunther Kortwich
Principal cast	Eva Mattes (Helene)
	Ernst Jacobi (Hans)
	Elisabeth Stepanek (Hanne)
	Angelika Thomas (Lydia)
	Rainer Friedrichsen (Ulrich)
	Gisela Stein (Aunt Ihmchen)
	Fritz Lichtenhahn (Uncle Bertrand)
	Anna Sanders/Sonja Lauer/Miriam Lauer (Anna)
Length	123 minutes.* Color
Rental	New Yorker Films, West Glen Films

Berlin Alexanderplatz

Released	1980
Producer	Bavaria Studios (Munich), RAI (Italian Television Network) in collaboration with WDR (Cologne)
Director	Rainer Werner Fassbinder
Screenplay	Rainer Werner Fassbinder (from the novel by Alfred Döblin)

* There is also a longer version of 145 minutes

Cinematography	Xaver Schwarzenberger
Editing	Juliane Lorenz and Franz Walsch (Rainer Werner Fassbinder)
Set decoration	Helmut Gassner, Werner Achmann, and Jürgen Henze
Costumes	Barbara Baum
Music	Peer Raben
Sound	Karsten Ulrich
Sound editing	Milan Bor
Principal cast	Günter Lamprecht (Franz Biberkopf)
	Hanna Schygulla (Eva)
	Barbara Sukowa (Mieze)
	Gottfried John (Reinhold)
	Franz Buchrieser (Meck)
	Claus Holm (Barkeeper)
	Brigitte Mira (Frau Bast)
	Roger Fritz (Herbert)
	Karin Baal (Minna)
	Barbara Valentin (Ida)
	Hark Bohm (Lüders)
	Ivan Desny (Pums)
	Annemarie Düringer (Cilly)
	Liselotte Eder (Frau Pums)
	Irm Hermann (Trude)
	Peter Kollek (Nachum)
	Angela Schmid (Widow)
	Volker Spengler (Bruno)
	Elisabeth Trissenaar (Lina)
	Helen Vita (Fränze)
	Gerhard Zwerenz (Baumann)
Length	13 episodes and an epilogue. 15 hours 21 minutes. Color
Rental	TeleCulture Films

Rental sources for films discussed in the text

Budget Films
4590 Santa Monica Blvd
Los Angeles, California 90029
(213) 660–0187

Embassy of the German Democratic Republic
1717 Massachusetts Avenue N.W.
Washington, DC 20036

Films Incorporated
440 Park Avenue South
New York, New York 10016
(212) 889–7910
Northeast: (800) 223–6246; Central: (800) 323–1406;
Southeast: (800) 241–5530; West: (800) 421–0612;
Alaska: (907) 272–1408

Images Film Archive, Inc.
300 Phillips Park Road
Mamaroneck, New York 10543
(914) 381–2993
(800) 431–1774

Kit Parker Films
1245 Tenth Street
Monterey, California 93940
(408) 649–5573

New Yorker Films
16 West 61st Street
New York, New York 10023
(212) 247–6110

TeleCulture, Inc.
82 Greene Street
New York, New York 10012
(212) 219–2500

Trans-World Films, Inc.
332 South Michigan Avenue
Chicago, Illinois 60604
(312) 922–1530

West Glen Films
1430 Broadway
New York, New York 10001
(212) 921–0966

Other non-theatrical sources for German feature films

Almi/Libra/Cinema 5
1585 Broadway
New York, New York 10036
(212) 975–0550

The Cinema Guild
1697 Broadway, Suite 802
New York, New York 10019
(212) 246–5522

Cine World
177 Sound Beach Avenue
Old Greenwich, Connecticut 06870
(203) 637–4319

Gray City, Inc.
853 Broadway, Room 1711
New York, New York 10003
(212) 473–3600

Grove Press
Film Division
196 West Houston Street
New York, New York 10014
(212) 242–4900

International Spectra Films
29 West 43rd Street, 12th Floor
New York, New York 10001
(212) 947–0888

Ivy Films/16
165 West 46th Street
New York, New York 10036
(212) 765–3940

Kino International
250 West 57th Street
New York, New York 10019
(212) 586–8720

The Museum of Modern Art
Circulating Film Library
11 West 53rd Street
New York, New York 10019
(212) 708–9530

New Line Cinema
575 Eighth Avenue, 16th Floor
New York, New York 10018
(212) 239–8880

New World Pictures
250 West 57th Street
New York, New York 10019
(212) 247–3240
(213) 551–1444

Orion Classics
711 Fifth Avenue
New York, New York 10022
(212) 758–5100

Promovision International/
Cinevista
353 West 39th Street
New York, New York 10018
(212) 947–4373

Arnold Pressburger
140 West 57th Street
New York, New York 10019
(212) 757–2509

Swank Motion Pictures, Inc.
60 Bethpage Road
Hicksville, New York 11801
(516) 931–7500

Tamarelle's French Film House
110 Cohasset Stage Road
Chico, California 95926
(916) 895–3429

United Artists/MGM
1350 Avenue of the Americas
New York, New York 10019
and
5890 West Jefferson Blvd
Los Angeles, California 90016
(800) 223–0933

Universal/16
445 Park Avenue
New York, New York 10022
(212) 759–7500

Appendix II

Adaptations in German film history: a basic guide (1913–85)

The following inventory lists the most important film adaptations made in Germany since the advent of narrative feature-length production through mid-1985. The catalogue includes films based on classical sources as well as popular titles. It does not claim to be exhaustive. It stresses hallmarks of German cinema, but also remakes of popular sources; it includes selected short films and television productions, and tries to mention all films available in the USA as well as the adaptations made by more recognized figures. It has become considerably easier to track down filmographical references since the initial and unfortunately often quite inaccurate effort of Alfred Estermann (in his book, *Die Verfilmung literarischer Werke*) to provide a catalogue of literary adaptations made in Germany. For the sake of consistency, I have listed films according to the date of their first public showing. This will, of course, differ in many cases from the actual date of production. Hans-Michael Bock and Jörg Schöning were of invaluable assistance in putting together this inventory: they checked over an initial version, providing numerous corrections, clarifications, and additions. The following reference works also proved to be helpful in compiling this basic guide:

Bauer, Alfred. *Deutscher Spielfilm Almanach 1929–1950*. 3rd edn. Berlin: Film-blätter, 1965.
—— *Deutscher Spielfilmalmanach 1946–1955*. Munich: Winterberg, 1981.
Baum, Heinz and Hermann Herlinghaus (eds). *20 Jahre DEFA-Spielfilm*. Berlin (GDR): Henschel, 1968.
Bucher, Felix. *Germany*. Screen Series. London/New York: Zwemmer/Barnes, 1970.
CineGraph: Lexikon zum deutschsprachigen Film. Ed. Hans-Michael Bock. Munich: Edition Text und Kritik, 1984ff.
Estermann, Alfred. *Die Verfilmung literarischer Werke*. Bonn: Bouvier, 1965.
Hembus, Joe and Christa Bandmann. *Klassiker des deutschen Tonfilms 1930–1960*. Munich: Goldmann, 1980.
Hembus, Joe and Ilona Brennicke. *Klassiker des deutschen Stummfilms 1910–1930*. Munich: Goldmann, 1983.
Hembus, Joe and Robert Fischer. *Der Neue Deutsche Film 1960–1980*. Munich: Goldmann, 1981.
Jahrbuch Film. Ed. Hans Günther Pflaum. Munich: Hanser, 1977ff.
Jansen, Peter W. and Wolfram Schütte (eds). *Film in der DDR*. Munich: Hanser, 1977.

Lamprecht, Gerhard. *Deutsche Stummfilme.* 9 vols and an index. Berlin: Stiftung Deutsche Kinemathek, 1967–70.

Pflaum, Hans Günther and Hans Helmut Prinzler. *Film in der Bundesrepublik Deutschland.* Munich: Hanser, 1979.

Prisma. Kino- und Fernseh-Almanach. Ed. Horst Knietzsch. Berlin (GDR): Henschel, 1970ff.

Prochnow, Christoph (ed.). "Literaturverfilmungen." In *Theorie und Praxis des Films,* No. 2 (1983).

Schriftsteller und Film. Dokumentation und Bibliographie. Ed. Erika Pick. Berlin (GDR): Henschel, 1979.

6000 Filme: Kritische Notizen aus den Kinojahren 1948–58. Ed. Klaus Brüne. 4th edn. Düsseldorf: Altenberg, 1980.

Tadikk, Hans and Silvia Ellner (eds). *Katalog der Literaturvorlagen im Film und Fernsehen.* Wiesbaden-Breckenheim: Deutsche Gesellschaft für Filmdokumentation, 1973.

Items with an asterisk in the lists below indicate short films, i.e. ones with a running length of less than an hour.

Early German film (1913–17)

1913 Max Mack, *Der Andere/The Other Man,* based on Paul Lindau's drama.

1914 Stellan Rye, *Erlkönigs Töchter/Erlking's Daughters,* based loosely on J. W. von Goethe's poem, "Der Erlkönig".

1915 Urban Gad, *Vordertreppe und Hintertreppe/Front Stairs and Back Stairs,* based on Hermann Sudermann's drama, *Die Ehre.*

Max Mack, *Der Katzensteg/The Cat Walk,* based on Hermann Sudermann's novel.

1916 Richard Oswald, *Hoffmanns Erzählungen/Tales of Hoffmann,* based on E. T. A. Hoffmann's stories.

1917 Alexander von Antalffy, *Lulu,* based loosely on motifs from Frank Wedekind's dramas, *Der Erdgeist* and *Die Büchse der Pandora.*

Ernst Lubitsch, *Das fidele Gefängnis/The Jolly Prison,* based on motifs from C. Haffner's and Richard Genée's operetta, *Die Fledermaus.*

Classical German film (1918–32)

1918 Ernst Lubitsch, *Carmen,* based on Prosper Mérimée's novella.

Richard Oswald, *Das Tagebuch einer Verlorenen/The Diary of a Lost Woman* (2 parts), first part based on Margarete Böhme's novel.

1919 Alfred Halm, *Rose Bernd,* based on Gerhart Hauptmann's drama.

Ernst Lubitsch, *Rausch/Intoxication,* based on August Strindberg's drama, *Brott och brott.*

Joe May/Uwe Jens Krafft/Karl Gerhardt, *Die Herrin der Welt/The Mistress of the World,* based on Karl Figdor's novel.

Richard Oswald, *Die Reise um die Erde in 80 Tagen/The Trip around the Earth in 80 days,* based on Jules Verne's novel, *Around the World in 80 Days.*

—— *Unheimliche Geschichten/Uncanny Tales,* based on stories by Edgar Allan Poe ("The Black Cat"), Selma Heine ("Die Erscheinung"), Robert Liebmann ("Die Hand"), Robert Louis Stevenson ("The Suicide Club"), and Richard Oswald ("Der Spuk").

Conrad Veidt, *Wahnsinn/Madness,* based on Kurt Münzer's novella.

1920 Carl Froelich, *Die Brüder Karamasoff/The Brothers Karamazov*, based on Feodor Dostoevsky's novel.

Rochus Gliese, *Der verlorene Schatten/The Lost Shadow*, loosely based on Adalbert von Chamisso's story, *Peter Schlemihls wundersame Geschichte*.

Ernst Lubitsch, *Sumurun*, based on the pantomime drama by Friedrich Freska.

Max Mack, *Figaros Hochzeit/The Marriage of Figaro*, based on the comedy by Pierre Augustin Caron de Beaumarchais.

Karl Heinz Martin, *Von morgens bis mitternachts/From Morning to Night*, based on Georg Kaiser's drama.

F. W. Murnau, *Der Bucklige und die Tänzerin/The Hunchback and the Dancer*, based on Carl Mayer's manuscript, "Der grüne Kuss".

——*Der Januskopf/Janus Head*, based on Robert Louis Stevenson's novel, *The Strange Case of Dr Jekyll and Mr Hyde*.

Richard Oswald, *Manolescus Memoiren/Manolescu's Memoirs* (alternate title: *Fürst Lahovary, der König der Diebe*), based on the autobiography of George Manolescu.

Lupu Pick, *Der Dummkopf/The Blockhead*, based on Ludwig Fulda's play.

Friedrich Zelnik, *Anna Karenina*, based on Leo Tolstoy's novel.

1921 Dimitri Buchowetzki, *Danton*, based on Georg Büchner's drama, *Dantons Tod*.

E. A. Dupont, *Die Geier-Wally/Vulture Wally*, based on Wilhelmine von Hillern's novel.

Sven Gade and Heinz Schall, *Hamlet*, based on Shakespeare's play.

Fritz Lang, *Kämpfende Herzen/Battling Hearts*, based on Rolf E. Vanloo's play, *Vier um die Frau*.

Paul Leni, *Die Verschwörung zu Genua/The Genoa Conspiracy*, based loosely on Friedrich Schiller's drama, *Die Verschwörung des Fiesko zu Genua*.

F. W. Murnau, *Schloss Vogelöd/The Haunted Castle*, based on Rudolf Stratz's novel.

1922 Felix Basch, *Fräulein Julie*, based on August Strindberg's drama, *Frolzen Julie*.

Dimitri Buchowetzki, *Othello*, based loosely on Shakespeare's drama and Cinthio's novella.

Carl Theodor Dreyer, *Die Gezeichneten/The Stigmatized*, based on Aage Madelung's novel, *I Dyreham*.

Carl Froelich, *Der Taugenichts/The Good-for-Nothing*, based on Joseph von Eichendorff's novella, *Aus dem Leben eines Taugenichts*.

—— *Luise Millerin*, based on Friedrich Schiller's drama, *Kabale und Liebe*.

Urban Gad, *Hanneles Himmelfahrt/Hannele's Trip to Heaven*, based on Gerhart Hauptmann's drama.

Arthur von Gerlach, *Vanina*, based on Stendhal's novella.

Fritz Lang, *Dr Mabuse, der Spieler/Dr Mabuse, the Gambler* (2 parts), based on Norbert Jacques's novel.

F. W. Murnau, *Marizza, genannt die Schmuggler-Madonna/Marizza, the Smugglers' Madonna*, based on Wolfram Geiger's manuscript, "Grüne Augen".

—— *Nosferatu – Eine Symphonie des Grauens/Nosferatu*, based on Bram Stoker's novel, *Dracula*.

—— *Phantom*, based on Gerhart Hauptmann's novel.

Richard Oswald, *Lucrezia Borgia*, based on Harry Scheff's novel.

Carl Wilhelm, *Der böse Geist Lumpaci-Vagabundus/The Evil Spirit Lumpaci-Vagabundus*, based on Johann Nestroy's comedy, *Der böse Geist Lumpazivagabundus oder Das liederliche Kleeblatt*.

1923 Hans Behrendt, *Alt-Heidelberg*, based on Wilhelm Meyer-Förster's play.

Ludwig Berger, *Ein Glas Wasser/A Glass of Water*, based on Eugène Scribe's play, *Le Verre d'eau*.

—— *Der verlorene Schuh/The Lost Shoe*, based on the fairy-tale "Cinderella" and motifs from E. T. A. Hoffmann and Clemens Brentano.

Peter Paul Felner, *Der Kaufmann von Venedig/The Merchant of Venice*, based on Shakespeare's drama.

Rochus Gliese, *Brüder/Brothers*, based on Otto Ludwig's novel, *Zwischen Himmel und Erde*.

Kurt Götz (Curt Goetz), *Friedrich Schiller*, based on the early years of the writer's life.

Leopold Jessner, *Erdgeist/Earth Spirit*, based on Frank Wedekind's drama, *Der Erdgeist*.

Gerhard Lamprecht, *Die Buddenbrooks*, based on Thomas Mann's novel, *Buddenbrooks*.

Ernst Lubitsch, *Die Flamme/The Flame*, based on Hans Müller's play.

F. W. Murnau, *Die Austreibung/The Expulsion*, based on Carl Hauptmann's play.

Manfred, Noa, *Nathan der Weise/Nathan the Wise*, based on G. E. Lessing's drama.

G. W. Pabst, *Der Schatz/The Treasure*, based on Rudolf Hans Bartsch's novella.

Berthold Viertel, *Nora – Ein Puppenheim/A Doll's House*, based on Henrik Ibsen's drama, *Et dukkehjem*.

Robert Wiene, *Raskolnikow*, based on Feodor Dostoevsky's novel, *Crime and Punishment*.

1924 Paul Czinner, *Nju*, based on Osip Dymov's play.

Carl Theodor Dreyer, *Michael*, based on Herman Bang's novel, *Mikaël*.

Carl Froelich, *Mutter und Kind/Mother and Child*, based on Friedrich Hebbel's epic poem.

F. W. Murnau, *Die Finanzen des Grossherzogs/The Finances of the Grand Duke*, based on Frank Heller's novel, *Storhertigens Finanser*.

Robert Wiene, *Orlacs Hände/The Hands of Orlac*, based on Maurice Renard's novel, *Les Mains d'Orlac* (Austrian production).

1925 Ludwig Berger, *Ein Walzertraum/A Waltzer's Dream*, based on Hans Müller's novella, *Nux, der Prinzgemahl*, and the operetta, *Ein Walzertraum*, by Felix Dörrmann, Leopold Jacobsen, and Oscar Strauss.

E. A. Dupont, *Varieté*, based on motifs from Felix Hollaender's novel, *Der Eid des Stephan Huller*.

Arthur von Gerlach, *Zur Chronik von Grieshuus/The Chronicle of the Grey House*, based on Theodor Storm's novella.

Gerhard Lamprecht, *Die Verrufenen/The Notorious Ones*, based on the experiences of Heinrich Zille.

F. W. Murnau, *Tartüff*, based on Molière's comedy, *Tartuffe*.

Hans Neumann, *Ein Sommernachtstraum/A Midsummer Night's Dream*, based on Shakespeare's comedy.

G. W. Pabst, *Die freudlose Gasse/The Joyless Street*, based on Hugo Bettauer's novel.

1926 Alexander Korda, *Madame wünscht keine Kinder/Madame Does Not Want Any Children*, based on Clément Vautel's novel, *Pas d'Enfants*.

F. W. Murnau, *Faust*, based on Christopher Marlowe's drama, *Doctor Faustus*, the Faust legend, and J. W. von Goethe's drama.

G. W. Pabst, *Geheimnisse einer Seele/Secrets of a Soul*, based on a case study by Sigmund Freud.

Arthur Robison, *Manon Lescaut*, based on Abbé Prévost's novel, *Histoire du Chevalier des Grieux et de Manon Lescaut*.

Rudolf Walther-Fein, *Die Gesunkenen/The Sunken Ones*, based on Luise Westkirch's novel, *Diebe*.

1927   Hans Behrendt, *Die Hose/Royal Scandal*, based on Carl Sternheim's comedy.

Kurt Bernhardt, *Kinderseelen klagen euch an/The Souls of Children Accuse You*, based on Paul Keller's story, "Die drei Ringe".

Gerhard Lamprecht, *Der Katzensteg/The Cats' Walk*, based on Hermann Sudermann's novel.

F. W. Murnau, *Sunrise*, based on Hermann Sudermann's novella, *Die Reise nach Tilsit*.

Richard Oswald, *Gehetzte Frauen/Agitated Women*, based on Annie von Brabenetz's novel, *Brettlfliegen*.

G. W. Pabst, *Die Liebe der Jeanne Ney/The Love of Jeanne Ney*, based on Ilya Ehrenburg's novel, *Ljubov' Žanny Nej*.

Bruno Rahn, *Dirnentragödie/Tragedy of the Street*, based on Wilhelm Braun's play.

—— *Kleinstadtsünder/Small Town Troublemaker*, based on Hans Alfred Kihn's play, *Meiseken*.

Friedrich Zelnik, *Die Weber/The Weavers*, based on Gerhart Hauptmann's drama.

1928   Kurt Bernhardt, *Schinderhannes*, based on Carl Zuckmayer's play.

Wilhelm Dieterle, *Die Heilige und ihr Narr/The Saint and Her Fool*, based on Agnes Günther's novel.

Henrik Galeen, *Alraune/Mandrake*, based on Hanns Heinz Ewers's novel.

Joe May, *Heimkehr/Homecoming*, based on Leonhard Frank's novella, *Karl und Anna*.

1929   Kurt Bernhardt, *Die Frau, nach der man sich sehnt/The Woman One Desires*, based on Max Brod's novel.

Paul Czinner, *Fräulein Else*, based on Arthur Schnitzler's novella.

Karl Grune, *Katharina Knie*, based on Carl Zuckmayer's play.

Phil Jutzi, *Mutter Krausens Fahrt ins Glück/Mother Krause's Trip to Happiness*, based on Heinrich Zille's stories as told by Otto Nagel.

G. W. Pabst, *Die Büchse der Pandora/Pandora's Box*, based on Frank Wedekind's plays, *Der Erdgeist* and *Die Büchse der Pandora*.

—— *Das Tagebuch einer Verlorenen/The Diary of a Lost Woman*, based on Margarete Böhme's novel.

1930   Richard Oswald, *Alraune/Mandrake*, based on Hanns Heinz Ewers's novel.

—— *Dreyfus*, based on Bruno Weil's book, *Der Prozess des Hauptmanns Dreyfus*.

G. W. Pabst, *Westfront 1918*, based on Ernst Johannsen's novel, *Vier von der Infanterie*.

Josef von Sternberg, *Der blaue Engel/The Blue Angel*, based on Heinrich Mann's novel, *Professor Unrat*.

Hans Tintner, *Cyankali/Cyanide*, based on Friedrich Wolf's play.

Gustav Ucicky, *Hokuspokus*, based on Curt Goetz's play.

1931   Paul Czinner, *Ariane*, based on Claude Anet's novel, *Ariane, jeune fille russe*.

Carl Froelich, *Luise, Königin von Preussen/Luise, Queen of Prussia*, based on Walter von Molo's novel, *Luise*.

Phil Jutzi, *Berlin-Alexanderplatz*, based on Alfred Döblin's novel.

Fritz Kortner, *Der brave Sünder/The Good Sinner*, based on Alfred Polgar's drama, *Die Defraudanten*, and Valentin Kataev's novel, *Die Hochstapler*.

Carl Lamac, *Die Fledermaus*, based on Johann Strauss's operetta.

Gerhard Lamprecht, *Emil und die Detektive/Emil and the Detectives*, based on Erich Kästner's novel.

Fritz Lang, *M*, based on an article by Egon Jacobsen.

Richard Oswald, *Der Hauptmann von Köpenick/The Captain of Köpenick*, based on Carl Zuckmayer's drama.

Fedor Ozep, *Der Mörder Dimitri Karamasoff/The Murderer Dimitri Karamazov*, based on Feodor Dostoevsky's novel, *The Brothers Karamazov*.

G. W. Pabst, *Die Dreigroschenoper/The Threepenny Opera*, based on the play by Bertolt Brecht and Kurt Weill.

Leontine Sagan, *Mädchen in Uniform*, based on Christa Winsloe's drama, *Gestern und Heute*.

1932   Hans Behrendt, *Grün ist die Heide/Green Is the Heather*, based on motifs from Hermann Löns's novel, *Dahinten in der Heide*.

Paul Czinner, *Der träumende Mund/The Dreaming Mouth*, based on Henry Bernstein's play, *Mélo*.

Carl Theodor Dreyer, *Vampyr*, based on Sheridan Le Fanu's novel, *In a Glass Darkly*.

E. A. Dupont, *Peter Voss, der Millionendieb/Peter Voss, the Thief of Millions*, based on Ewald Gerhard Seeliger's novel.

Erich Engel, *Fünf von der Jazzband/Five from the Jazz Band*, based on Felix Joachimson's comedy.

Karl Hartl, *F. P. 1 antwortet nicht/F.P. 1 Doesn't Answer*, based on Curt Siodmak's novel.

Leopold Lindtberg, *Wenn zwei sich streiten/When Lovers Quarrel*,* based on J. W. von Goethe's poem, "Gutmann und Gutweib".

Max Ophüls, *Die verkaufte Braut/The Bartered Bride*, based on Bedrich Smetana's opera.

Richard Oswald, *Unheimliche Geschichten/Uncanny Tales*, based on Edgar Allan Poe's stories, "The Black Cat" and "The System of Doctor Tarr and Professor Feather", and Robert Louis Stevenson's story "The Suicide Club".

G. W. Pabst, *Die Herrin von Atlantis/L'Atlantide/The Mistress of Atlantis*, based on Pierre Benoit's novel, *L'Atlantide*.

German film during the Third Reich (1933–45)

1933   Kurt Bernhardt, *Der Tunnel/The Tunnel*, based on Bernhard Kellermann's novel.

Carl Froelich, *Der Choral von Leuthen/The Hymn of Leuthen*, based on Walter von Molo's novel, *Fridericus*.

Georg Jakoby, *Das 13. Weltwunder/The 13th Wonder of the World*,* based on Georg Belly's comedy, *Monsieur Herkules*.

Max Ophüls, *Liebelei*, based on Arthur Schnitzler's play.

Richard Oswald, *Ganovenehre/Honor among Thieves*, based on Charles Rudolph's play.

Hasso Preiss, *Mister Herkules*,* based on Georg Belly's comedy, *Monsieur Herkules*.

Robert Siodmak, *Brennendes Geheimnis/Burning Secret*, based on Stefan Zweig's novella.

Hans Steinhoff, *Hitlerjunge Quex/Hitler Youth Quex*, based on Kurt Aloys Schenzinger's novel.

Gustav Ucicky, *Flüchtlinge/Refugees*, based on Gerhard Menzel's novel.

Fritz Wendhausen, *Kleiner Mann – was nun?/Little Man – What Now?*, based on Hans Fallada's novel.

Franz Wenzler, *Hans Westmar*, based on Hanns Heinz Ewers's novel, *Horst Wessel*.

Georg Zoch, *Schwarzwaldmädel/Black Forest Girl*, based on the operetta by August Neidhart and Leon Jessel.

1934 Hans Deppe, *Schloss Hubertus/Castle Hubertus*, based on Ludwig Ganghofer's novel.

—— *Ferien vom Ich/Vacation from Myself*, based on Paul Keller's novel.

Gustaf Gründgens, *Die Finanzen des Grossherzogs/The Finances of the Grand Duke*, based on Frank Heller's novel, *Storhertigens Finanser*.

Curt Oertel/Hans Deppe, *Der Schimmelreiter/The Rider on the White Horse*, based on Theodor Storm's novella.

Heinz Paul, *Wilhelm Tell*, based on Friedrich Schiller's drama.

R. A. Stemmle, *So ein Flegel/Such a Lout*, based on Heinrich Spoerl's novel, *Die Feuerzangenbowle*.

Erich Waschnek, *Regine*, based on Gottfried Keller's novel.

Fritz Wendhausen, *Peer Gynt*, based on Henrik Ibsen's drama.

1935 Erich Engel, *Pygmalion*, based on George Bernard Shaw's play.

Werner Hochbaum, *Vorstadtvarieté/Music Hall on the Outskirts of Town*, based on Felix Salten's play, *Der Gemeine*.

—— *Die ewige Maske/The Eternal Mask*, based on Leo Lapaire's novel.

—— *Leichte Kavallerie/Light Cavalry*, based on Heinz Lorenz-Lambrecht's novel, *Umwege zur Heimat*.

Carl Hoffmann, *Viktoria*, based on Knut Hamsun's novel, *Victoria*.

Carl Lamac, *Im Weissen Rössl/The Inn of the White Horse*, based on Ralph Benatzky's operetta.

Curt Oertel, *Pole Poppenspäler*,* based on Theodor Storm's novella.

Reinhold Schünzel, *Amphitryon*, based on Heinrich von Kleist's comedy.

Herbert Selpin, *Ein idealer Gatte/The Ideal Husband*, based on Oscar Wilde's comedy.

Detlef Sierck, *Das Mädchen von Moorhof/The Girl from the Marsh Croft*, based on Selma Lagerlöf's novel, *Tösen från Stormyrtorpet*.

—— *Stützen der Gesellschaft/Pillars of Society*, based on Henrik Ibsen's play, *Samfundets støter*.

1936 Richard Eichberg, *Der Kurier des Zaren/The Czar's Courier*, based on Jules Verne's novel, *Michel Strogoff*.

Erich Engels, *Donner, Blitz und Sonnenschein/Thunder, Lightning, and Sunshine*, based on Max Neal's and Max Ferner's play, *Der Hunderter im Westentaschl*.

Carl Froelich, *Wenn wir alle Engel wären/If We All Were Angels*, based on Heinrich Spoerl's novel.

—— *Traumulus*, based on Arno Holz's and Oskar Jerschke's drama.

Rolf Hansen and Carl Froelich, *Das Schönheitsfleckchen/The Little Beauty Mark*, based on Alfred de Musset's novella, *La Mouche*.

Johannes Meyer, *Fridericus*, based on Walter von Molo's novel.

Franz Seitz, *Waldfrieden/Forest Quiet*,* based on Ludwig Thoma's short play.

Detlef Sierck, *Das Hofkonzert/The Court Concert*, based on the play by Paul Verhoeven and Toni Impekoven, *Das kleine Hofkonzert*.

Frank Wysbar, *Die Unbekannte/The Unknown Woman*, based on Reinhold Conrad Muschler's novella.

Hans H. Zerlett, *Truxa*, based on Heinrich Seiler's novel, *Programm mit Truxa*.

1937 Fritz Peter Buch, *Der Katzensteg/The Cat Walk*, based on Hermann Sudermann's novel.

Willi Forst, *Serenade*, based on Theodor Storm's novella, *Viola tricolor*.

Carl Froelich, *Die ganz tollen Torheiten/The Completely Mad Insanities*, based on Marianne von Angern's novel.

Gustaf Gründgens, *Capriolen/Caprioles*, based on Jochen Huth's play, *Himmel auf Erden*.

Veit Harlan/Emil Jannings, *Der Herrscher/The Ruler*, based on Gerhart Hauptmann's play, *Vor Sonnenuntergang*.

Werner Hochbaum, *Man spricht über Jacqueline/They're Talking about Jacqueline*, based on Katrin Holland's novel.

Phil Jutzi, *Wiederseh'n macht Freude/Meeting Again Is Fun*,* based on K. R. Neubert's novella, *Paul, der Jugendfreund*.

Max W. Kimmich, *Doppelselbstmord/Double Suicide*,* based on Ludwig Anzengruber's play.

Gerhard Lamprecht, *Madame Bovary*, based on Gustave Flaubert's novel.

Detlef Sierck, *Zu neuen Ufern/To New Shores*, based on Lovis Hans Lorenz's novel.

Hans Steinhoff, *Ein Volksfeind/An Enemy of the People*, based on Henrik Ibsen's play, *En folkefiende*.

Luis Trenker, *Der Berg ruft/The Mountain Calls*, based on Carl Haensel's novel, *Der Kampf ums Matterhorn*.

Gustav Ucicky/Emil Jannings, *Der zerbrochene Krug/The Broken Jug*, based on Heinrich von Kleist's comedy.

Frank Wysbar, *Ball im Metropol*, based on Theodor Fontane's novel, *Irrungen, Wirrungen*.

1938 Carl Boese, *Fünf Millionen suchen einen Erben/Five Million Look for an Heir*, based on Harald Baumgarten's novel.

Richard Eichberg, *Das indische Grabmal & Der Tiger von Eschnapur/The Indian Tomb and The Tiger of Eschnapur*, based on Thea von Harbou's novel, *Das indische Grabmal*.

E. W. Emo, *13 Stühle/13 Chairs*, based on the novel by Eugeny P. Petrov and Ilya A. Ilf, *Dvenadacat' stul'ev*.

Erich Engel, *Der Maulkorb/The Muzzle*, based on Heinrich Spoerl's novel.

Carl Froelich, *Heimat/Homeland*, based on Hermann Sudermann's drama.

Veit Harlan, *Jugend/Youth*, based on Max Halbe's drama.

Wolfgang Liebeneiner, *Yvette*, based on Guy de Maupassant's novella.

Paul Ostermayr, *Der Edelweisskönig/The Edelweiss King*, based on Ludwig Ganghofer's novel.

Hans Schweikart, *Das Mädchen mit dem guten Ruf/The Girl with the Good Reputation*, based on Carlo Goldoni's comedy, *La Locandiera*.

Alfred Stöger, *Glück im Winkel/Happiness in a Small Corner*,* based on Johann Nestroy's play, *Hinüber – Herüber*.

Viktor Tourjansky, *Der Blaufuchs/The Blue Fox*, based on Ferenc Herczeg's play, *Akék róka*.

1939 Willi Forst, *Bel Ami*, based on Guy de Maupassant's novel.

Gustaf Gründgens, *Der Schritt vom Wege/Off the Beaten Track*, based on Theodor Fontane's novel, *Effi Briest*.

Veit Harlan, *Die Reise nach Tilsit/The Journey to Tilsit*, based on Hermann Sudermann's novella.

—— *Das unsterbliche Herz/The Immortal Heart*, based on Walter Harlan's play, *Das Nürnbergisch Ei*.

Kurt Hoffmann, *Paradies der Junggesellen/Bachelors' Paradise*, based on Johannes Boldt's novel.

Helmut Käutner, *Kitty und die Weltkonferenz/Kitty and the International Conference*, based on Stefan Donat's comedy, *Weltkonferenz*.

Wolfgang Liebeneiner, *Der Florentiner Hut/The Florentine Hat*, based on Eugène Labiche's comedy, *Un Chapeau de paille d'Italie*.

Arthur Maria Rabenalt, *Johannisfeuer/St John's Fire*, based on Hermann Sudermann's drama.

Herbert Selpin, *Wasser für Canitoga/Water for Canitoga*, based on G. Turner Krebs's play.

Georg Zoch, *Die drei Smaragde/The Three Emeralds*,* based on Norbert Jacques's novella.

1940   Georg Jacoby, *Kora Terry*, based on Hans-Caspar von Zobeltitz's novel.

Helmut Käutner, *Kleider machen Leute/Clothes Make the Man*, based on Gottfried Keller's novella.

Herbert Maisch, *Friedrich Schiller*, based on the writer's life.

Hans Schweikart, *Das Mädchen von Fanö/The Girl from Fanö*, based on Günther Weisenborn's novel.

—— *Das Fräulein von Barnhelm*, based on G. E. Lessing's comedy, *Minna von Barnhelm*.

Herbert Selpin, *Trenck, der Pandur*, based on O. E. Groh's play.

Hans Steinhoff, *Die Geierwally/Vulture Wally*, based on Wilhelmine von Hillern's novel.

Gustav Ucicky, *Der Postmeister/The Postmaster*, based on Alexander Pushkin's novella, *Stancionnyi Smotritel*.

1941   Peter Paul Brauer, *Die schwedische Nachtigall/The Swedish Nightingale*, based on Friedrich Forster's play, *Gastspiel in Kopenhagen*.

Kurt Hoffmann, *Quax, der Bruchpilot/Quax, the Crash Pilot*, based on Hermann Grote's story.

Wolfgang Liebeneiner, *Ich klage an!/I Accuse!*, based on Hellmuth Unger's novel, *Sendung und Gewissen*.

G. W. Pabst, *Komödianten/Theater People*, based on Olly Boeheim's novel, *Philine*.

Hans Steinhoff, *Ohm Krüger*, based on Arnold Krieger's novel, *Mann ohne Volk*.

1942   Erich Engels, *Dr Crippen an Bord/Dr Crippen on Board*, based on W. Ebert's eyewitness account.

Walter Felsenstein, *Ein Windstoss/A Gust of Wind*, based on Giovacchino Forzano's play, *Un colpo di vento*.

Veit Harlan, *Die goldene Stadt/The Golden City*, based on Richard Billinger's play, *Der Gigant*.

Helmut Käutner, *Wir machen Musik/We're Making Music*, based on Manfried Rössner's play, *Karl III. und Anna von Österreich*.

Herbert Maisch, *Andreas Schlüter*, based on Alfons von Czibulka's novel, *Der Münzturm*.

Hans Steinhoff, *Rembrandt*, based on Valerian Tornius's novel, *Zwischen Hell und Dunkel*.

1943   Boleslav Barlog, *Wenn die Sonne wieder scheint/When the Sun Shines Again*, based on Stijn Steuvels's novel, *De vlaschaard*.

Hans Deppe, *Der kleine Grenzverkehr/The Small Border Traffic*, based on Erich Kästner's novel, *Georg und die Zwischenfälle*.

Veit Harlan, *Immensee*, based on Theodor Storm's novella.

Kurt Hoffmann, *Ich vertraue dir meine Frau an/I Entrust You with My Wife*, based on Johann von Vaszary's play.

G. W. Pabst, *Paracelsus*, based on Pert Peternell's novel, *König der Ärzte*.
Heinz Rühmann, *Sophienlund*, based on the comedy by Helmut Weiss and Fritz Woedtke.
Hans Schweikart, *Der unendliche Weg/The Neverending Road*, based on Walter von Molo's novel, *Ein Deutscher ohne Deutschland*.
Hans Steinhoff, *Gabriele Dambrone*, based on Richard Billinger's play.
R. A. Stemmle, *Johann*, based on Theo Lingen's comedy.

1944 Harald Braun, *Nora*, based on Henrik Ibsen's drama, *Et dukkehjem*.
Carl Froelich, *Familie Buchholz/The Buchholz Family*, based on Julius Stinde's novel.
—— *Neigungsehe/Love Match*, based on Jochen Kulmey's play.
Veit Harlan, *Opfergang/Sacrifice*, based on Rudolf G. Binding's novella.
Peter Pewas, *Der verzauberte Tag/The Enchanted Day*, based on Franz Nabl's story, *Die Augen*.
Helmut Weiss, *Die Feuerzangenbowle/The Punch Bowl*, based on Heinrich Spoerl's novel.

Postwar German film (1945–61)

1947 Hans Müller, *Und finden dereinst wir uns wieder/And If We Should Meet Again*, based on Hertha von Gebhardt's novella.
1948 Josef von Baky, *Via mala*, based on John Knittel's novel.
Karl Hartl, *Der Engel mit der Posaune/The Angel with the Trumpet*, based on Ernst Lothar's novel.
G. W. Pabst, *Der Prozess/The Trial*, based on Rudolf Brunngraber's novel, *Prozess auf Leben und Tod* (Austrian production).
Arthur Maria Rabenalt, *Morgen ist alles besser/Everything Will Be Better in the Morning*, based on Annemarie Selinko's novel.
1949 Wolfgang Liebeneiner, *Liebe 47/Love 47*, based on Wolfgang Borchert's radio play and drama, *Draussen vor der Tür*.
Harald Reinl, *Bergkristall/Rock Crystal*, based on Adalbert Stifter's novella, *Der Wildschütz von Tirol*.
Karl Heinz Stroux, *Begegnung mit Werther/Meeting with Werther*, based on J. W. von Goethe's novel, *Die Leiden des jungen Werthers*.
1950 Josef von Baky, *Das doppelte Lottchen/The Two Little Lottas*, based on Erich Kästner's novel.
Hans Deppe, *Schwarzwaldmädel/Black Forest Girl*, based on the operetta by August Neidhart and Leon Jessel.
Curt Goetz and Karl Peter Gillmann, *Frauenarzt Dr Prätorius/Woman's Dr Prätorius*, based on Curt Goetz's play, *Dr med. Hiob Prätorius*.
Rudolf Jugert, *Es kommt ein Tag/A Day Will Come*, based on Ernst Penzoldt's novella, *Korporal Mombour*.
Helmut Käutner, *Unter den Brücken/Under the Bridges*, based on Leo Laforgue's manuscript, *Unter den Brücken von Paris*.
1951 Hans Deppe, *Grün ist die Heide/Green Is the Heather*, based on motifs from the novels of Hermann Löns.
Curt Goetz, *Das Haus in Montevideo/The House in Montevideo*, based on Curt Goetz's play.
Veit Harlan, *Unsterbliche Geliebte/Immortal Lover*, based on Theodor Storm's novella, *Aquis submersus*.
1952 Harald Braun, *Herz der Welt/Heart of the World*, based on the life of Bertha von Suttner.
Erich Engel, *Der fröhliche Weinberg/The Merry Vineyard*, based on Carl Zuckmayer's comedy.

Willi Forst, *Im Weissen Rössl/The White Horse Inn*, based on Ralph Benatzky's operetta.

Arthur Maria Rabenalt, *Alraune/Mandrake*, based on Hanns Heinz Ewers's novel.

1953 Josef von Baky, *Der träumende Mund/The Dreaming Mouth*, based on Henry Bernstein's Play, *Mélo*.

Harald Braun, *Königliche Hoheit/His Royal Highness*, based on Thomas Mann's novel.

Thomas Engel and Erich Engel, *Pünktchen und Anton/Spot and Anton*, based on Erich Kästner's novel.

Kurt Hoffmann, *Musik bei Nacht/Night Music*, based on Curt Johannes Braun's play, *Die grosse Kurve*.

—— *Hokuspokus*, based on Curt Goetz's comedy.

—— *Moselfahrt aus Liebeskummer/Heartbroken on the Mosel*, based on Rudolf G. Binding's novella.

Helmut Käutner, *Käpt'n Bay-Bay*, based on the play by Iva Vanya, Fritz Grasshoff, and Norbert Schultze.

1954 Harald Braun, *Der letzte Sommer/The Last Summer*, based on Ricarda Huch's novella.

Kurt Hoffmann, *Das fliegende Klassenzimmer/The Flying Classroom*, based on Erich Kästner's novel.

Wolfgang Liebeneiner, *Und ewig bleibt die Liebe/And Love Lasts Forever*, based on Hermann Sudermann's drama, *Johannisfeuer*.

Paul May, *08/15*, based on Hans Hellmut Kirst's novel.

G. W. Pabst, *Das Bekenntnis der Ina Kahr/The Confession of Ina Kahr*, based on Hans Emil Dits's novel.

R. A. Stemmle, *Emil und die Detektive/Emil and the Detectives*, based on Erich Kästner's novel.

Alfred Weidenmann, *Canaris*, based on a manuscript by Erich Ebermayer.

1955 Rolf Hansen, *Teufel in Seide/Devil in Silk*, based on Gina Kaus's novel, *Der Teufel nebenan*.

Günter Hess, *Peter Schlemihl* (TV), based on Adalbert von Chamisso's novella, *Peter Schlemihls wundersame Geschichte*.

Kurt Hoffmann, *Ich denke oft an Piroschka/I Often Think of Piroschka*, based on Hugo Hartung's novel and radio play.

Rudolf Jugert, *Rosen im Herbst/Roses in Autumn*, based on Theodor Fontane's novel, *Effi Briest*.

Helmut Käutner, *Ludwig II*, based on Kadidya Wedekind's story.

—— *Des Teufels General/The Devil's General*, based on Carl Zuckmayer's drama.

Robert Siodmak, *Die Ratten/The Rats*, based on Gerhart Hauptmann's drama.

Rolf Thiele, *Die Barrings/The Barrings*, based on William von Simpson's novel.

1956 Josef von Baky, *Fuhrmann Henschel/Driver Henschel*, based on Gerhart Hauptmann's drama (Austrian production).

Kurt Hoffmann, *Heute heiratet mein Mann/My Husband's Getting Married Today*, based on Annemarie Selinko's novel.

—— *Salzburger Geschichten/Salzburg Tales*, based on Erich Kästner's novel, *Der kleine Grenzverkehr oder Georg und die Zwischenfälle*.

Helmut Käutner, *Ein Mädchen aus Flandern/A Girl from Flanders*, based on Carl Zuckmayer's story, *Das Engele von Loewen*.

—— *Der Hauptmann von Köpenick/The Captain of Köpenick*, based on Carl Zuckmayer's drama.

Wolfgang Liebeneiner, *Die Trapp-Familie/The Trapp Family*, based on the memoirs of Baroness Maria von Trapp.

Gottfried Reinhardt, *Vor Sonnenuntergang/Before Sunset*, based on Gerhart Hauptmann's drama.

Georg Tressler, *Die Halbstarken/The Hooligans*, based on Will Tremper's story.

Alfred Weidenmann, *Kitty und die grosse Welt/Kitty and the Whole Wide World*, based on Stefan Donat's comedy, *Weltkonferenz*.

1957 Rolf Hansen, . . . *und führe uns nicht in Versuchung/And Lead Us Not into Temptation*, based on Ödön von Horváth's drama, *Der jüngste Tag*.

Kurt Hoffmann, *Bekenntnisse des Hochstaplers Felix Krull/Confessions of the Confidence Man Felix Krull*, based on Thomas Mann's novel.

Helmut Käutner, *Die Zürcher Verlobung/The Engagement in Zürich*, based on Barbara Noack's novel.

—— *Monpti*, based on Gabor von Vaszary's novel.

Robert Siodmak, *Nachts, wenn der Teufel kam/The Devil Strikes at Midnight*, based on Will Berthold's eyewitness account.

Wolfgang Staudte, *Rose Bernd*, based on Gerhart Hauptmann's drama.

Rolf Thiele, *El Hakim*, based on John Knittel's novel.

Franz Josef Wild, *Zwischen Meer und Himmel/Between Sea and Sky* (TV), based on Herman Melville's story, *Benito Cereno*.

Frank Wysbar, *Haie und kleine Fische/Sharks and Small Fish*, based on Wolfgang Ott's novel.

1958 Gustav Burmester, *Stunde der Wahrheit/Hour of Truth* (TV), based on Heinrich Böll's radio play, *Bilanz*.

Falk Harnack, *Unruhige Nacht/Restless Night*, based on Albrecht Goes's novella.

Kurt Hoffmann, *Das Wirtshaus im Spessart/The Spessart Inn*, based on Wilhelm Hauff's novel.

—— *Wir Wunderkinder/Aren't We Wonderful?*, based on Hugo Hartung's novel.

Helmut Käutner, *Der Schinderhannes*, based on Carl Zuckmayer's drama, *Schinderhannes*.

Geza von Radvanyi, *Der Arzt von Stalingrad/The Doctor of Stalingrad*, based on Heinz G. Konsalik's novel.

—— *Mädchen in Uniform*, based on Christa Winsloe's drama, *Gestern und Heute*.

Wolfgang Staudte, *Der Maulkorb/The Muzzle*, based on Heinrich Spoerl's novel.

Alfred Weidenmann, *Scampolo*, based on Dario Niccodemi's play.

Franz Peter Wirth, . . . *und nichts als die Wahrheit/And Nothing But the Truth*, based on Ricarda Huch's novella.

—— *Helden/Heroes*, based on George Bernard Shaw's comedy, *Arms and the Man*.

1959 Kurt Hoffmann, *Das schöne Abenteuer/The Wonderful Adventure*, based on Antonia Ridge's novel, *Family Album*.

Helmut Käutner, *Der Rest ist Schweigen/The Rest Is Silence*, based on motifs from Shakespeare's tragedy, *Hamlet*.

Robert Siodmak, *Dorothea Angermann*, based on Gerhart Hauptmann's drama.

Rolf Thiele, *Labyrinth der Leidenschaft/Labyrinth of Passion*, based on Gladys Baker's novel, *Our Hearts Are Restless*.

Victor Vicas, *Jons und Erdme*, based on Hermann Sudermann's novella.

Alfred Weidenmann, *Buddenbrooks* (2 parts), based on Thomas Mann's novel.

Bernhard Wicki, *Die Brücke/The Bridge*, based on Manfred Gregor's novel.

Franz Peter Wirth, *Konto ausgeglichen/Closed Account* (TV), based on James M. Cain's novel, *The Embezzler*.

Frank Wysbar, *Hunde, wollt ihr ewig leben?/You Dogs, Do You Want To Live Forever?*, based on Fritz Wöss's novel and Heinz Schröter's books, *Stalingrad "bis zur letzten Patrone"* and *Letzte Briefe aus Stalingrad*.

1960   Harald Braun, *Die Botschafterin/The Lady Ambassador*, based on Hans Wolfgang's novel.

Alberto Cavalcanti, *Herr Puntila und sein Knecht Matti/Puntila and His Servant Matti*, based on Bertolt Brecht's play.

Wilhelm Dieterle, *Die Fastnachtsbeichte/The Lenten Confession*, based on Carl Zuckmayer's novella.

Peter Gorski/Gustaf Gründgens, *Faust*, based on J. W. von Goethe's drama, *Faust I*.

Rolf Hansen, *Gustav Adolfs Page*, based on Conrad Ferdinand Meyer's novella (Austrian production).

Helmut Käutner, *Das Glas Wasser/The Glass of Water*, based on Eugène Scribe's play, *Le Verre d'eau*.

Gerd Oswald, *Schachnovelle/Chess Novella*, based on Stefan Zweig's novella.

Harald Philipp, *Strafbataillon 999/Punishment Batallion 999*, based on Heinz G. Konsalik's novel.

Harald Reinl, *Die Bande des Schreckens/The Band of Terror*, based on Edgar Wallace's novel, *The Terrible People*.

Wolfgang Staudte, *Der letzte Zeuge/The Final Witness*, based on Maximilian Vernberg's report.

Rolf Thiele, *Der liebe Augustin/Dear Augustin*, based on Horst Wolfram Geissler's novel.

Alfred Weidenmann, *An heiligen Wassern/On Holy Waters*, based on Jakob Christoph Herr's novel (Swiss production).

Frank Wysbar, *Fabrik der Offiziere/The Officer Factory*, based on Hans Hellmut Kirst's novel.

1961   Rolf Hädrich, *Brennpunkt/Focal Point* (TV), based on Arthur Miller's novel, *Focus*.

Kurt Hoffmann, *Die Ehe des Herrn Mississippi/The Marriage of Mr Mississippi*, based on Friedrich Dürrenmatt's play.

Werner Klinger, *Lebensborn*, based on Will Berthold's magazine article.

Geza von Radvanyi, *Es muss nicht immer Kaviar sein/It Doesn't Always Have To Be Caviar* and *Diesmal muss es Kaviar sein/This Time It Has To Be Caviar*, based on Johannes Mario Simmel's novels.

Jürgen Roland, *Der Transport/The Transport*, based on Wolfgang Altendorf's novel.

Helmut Weiss, *Drei Mann in einem Boot/Three Men in a Boat*, based on Jerome K. Jerome's novel *Three Men in a Boat*.

Bernhard Wicki, *Das Wunder des Malachias/Father Malachy's Miracle*, based on Bruce Marshall's novel.

Rainer Wolffhardt, *Sansibar* (TV), based on Alfred Andersch's novel, *Sansibar oder der letzte Grund*.

New German Film (1962–85)

1962   Ludwig Cremer, *Die sündigen Engel/The Wicked Angels* (TV), based on Henry James's story, *The Turn of the Screw*.

Sylvain Dhomme, *Das Schloss/The Castle* (TV), based on Franz Kafka's unfinished novel.

Rolf Hädrich, *Der Schlaf der Gerechten/The Sleep of the Just* (TV), based on Albrecht Goes's novella, *Das Brandopfer.*

Falk Harnack, *Jeder stirbt für sich allein/Everyone Dies Alone* (TV), based on Hans Fallada's novel.

Helmut Käutner, *Die Rote/The Red Cat*, based on Alfred Andersch's novel.

Egon Monk, *Anfrage/Inquiry* (TV), based on Cristian Geissler's novel.

Harald Reinl, *Der Schatz im Silbersee/The Treasure in Silver Lake*, based on Karl May's novel.

Robert Siodmak, *Tunnel 28/Escape from East Berlin*, based on a story by Gabriele Upton and Peter Berneis.

Wolfgang Staudte, *Die Rebellion/The Rebellion* (TV), based on Joseph Roth's story.

—— and John Olden, *Die glücklichen Jahre der Thorwalds/The Happy Years of the Thorwald Family*, based on J. B. Priestley's play, *Time and the Conways.*

Rolf Thiele, *Lulu*, based on Frank Wedekind's dramas, *Der Erdgeist* and *Die Büchse der Pandora* (Austrian production).

Herbert Vesely, *Das Brot der frühen Jahre/The Bread of the Early Years*, based on Heinrich Böll's novel.

Alfred Vohrer, *Das Gasthaus an der Themse/The Inn on the River*, based on Edgar Wallace's novel, *The India Rubber.*

1963   Kurt Hoffmann, *Schloss Gripsholm/Gripsholm Palace*, based on Kurt Tucholsky's novel.

Helmut Käutner, *Das Haus in Montevideo/The House in Montevideo*, based on Curt Goetz's play.

Gerhard Klingenberg, *Unterm Birnbaum/Under the Pear Tree* (TV), based on Theodor Fontane's novel.

John Olden, *Lieutenant Gustl* (TV), based on Arthur Schnitzler's novella.

Harald Reinl, *Winnetou I*, based on Karl May's novel.

Wolfgang Staudte, *Die Dreigroschenoper/The Threepenny Opera*, based on the play by Bertolt Brecht and Kurt Weill.

Jean-Marie Straub/Danièle Huillet, *Machorka-Muff,** based on Heinrich Böll's story, *Hauptstädtisches Journal.*

Ladislao Vajda, *Das Feuerschiff/The Fire Ship*, based on Siegfried Lenz's story.

Paul Verhoeven, *Kleider machen Leute/Clothes Make the Man* (TV), based on Gottfried Keller's novella.

Alfred Weidenmann, *Das grosse Liebesspiel/The Great Game of Love*, based on Arthur Schnitzler's drama, *Reigen.*

Franz Josef Wild, *Die Legende vom heiligen Trinker/The Legend of the Holy Drinker* (TV), based on Joseph Roth's story.

1964   Thomas Fantl, *Zeit der Schuldlosen/Age of the Innocent*, based on Siegfried Lenz's drama and radio play.

Helmut Käutner, *Lausbubengeschichten/Stories of Little Rascals*, based on Ludwig Thoma's stories.

Michael Pfleghar, *Die Tote von Beverly Hills/The Dead Woman from Beverly Hills*, based on Curt Goetz's novel.

Harald Reinl, *Winnetou II*, based on Karl May's novel.

Robert Siodmak, *Der Schut/The Bandit Schut*, based on Karl May's novel.

Wolfgang Staudte, *Das Lamm/The Lamb*, based on Willy Kramp's story.

Rolf Thiele, *Tonio Kröger*, based on Thomas Mann's novella.

Alfred Vohrer, *Unter Geiern/Under Vultures*, based on Karl May's novel.

Alfred Weidenmann, *Verdammt zur Sünde/Damned To Sin*, based on Henry Jaeger's novel, *Die Festung*.

Bernhard Wicki, *Der Besuch/The Visit*, based on Friedrich Dürrenmatt's play, *Der Besuch der alten Dame*.

Claus Peter Witt, *Wie in schlechten Romanen/Just Like in Bad Novels* (TV), based on Heinrich Böll's story.

1965 Rolf Hädrich, *Dr Murkes gesammeltes Schweigen/Dr Murke's Collected Silences* (TV), based on Heinrich Böll's story.

Kurt Hoffmann, *Dr med. Hiob Prätorius*, based on Curt Goetz's comedy.

—— *Das Haus in der Karpfengasse/The House on Carp Street* (TV – 3 parts), based on Moscheh Yaakov Ben-gavriêl's novel.

—— *Hokuspokus – oder: wie lasse ich meinen Mann verschwinden/Hocuspocus – or: How Do I Make My Husband Disappear?*, based on Curt Goetz's comedy, *Hokuspokus*.

Michael Kehlmann, *Radetzkymarsch/Radetzky March* (TV – 2 parts), based on Joseph Roth's novel.

Jean-Marie Straub/Danièle Huillet, *Nicht versöhnt/Not Reconciled*, based on Heinrich Böll's novel, *Billard um halbzehn*.

Rolf Thiele, *DM-Killer*, based on Peter Norden's novel (Austrian production).

—— *Wälsungenblut/Blood of the Walsungs*, based on Thomas Mann's story.

Fritz Umgelter, *Der Sündenbock/The Scapegoat*, based on Luise Rinser's novel.

Alfred Vohrer, *Old Surehand, 1. Teil/Old Surehand, Part One*, based on Karl May's novel.

Claus Peter Witt, *Im Schlaraffenland/In the Land of Milk and Honey* (TV), based on Heinrich Mann's novel.

1966 Alexander Kluge, *Abschied von gestern/Yesterday Girl*, based on Kluge's story, "Anita G."

Rudolf Noelte, *Irrungen – Wirrungen/Mistakes – Confusions* (TV), based on Theodor Fontane's novel.

Jürgen Roland, *Vier Schlüssel/Four Keys*, based on Max Pierre Schaeffer's novel.

Peter Schamoni, *Schonzeit für Füchse/Closed Season on Fox Hunting*, based on Günter Seuren's novel, *Das Gatter*.

Volker Schlöndorff, *Der junge Törless/Young Törless*, based on Robert Musil's novel, *Die Verwirrungen des Zöglings Törless*.

Will Tremper, *Sperrbezirk/Blockade Area*, based on Ernst Neubach's novel.

1967 Peter Beauvais, *Peter Schlemihls wundersame Geschichte/Peter Schlemihl's Strange Story* (TV), based on Adalbert von Chamisso's novella.

Ludwig Cremer, *Die Mission/The Mission* (TV), based on Hans Habe's novel.

Wilm ten Haaf, *Stine* (TV), based on Theodor Fontane's novel.

George Moorse, *Der Findling/The Foundling* (TV), based on Heinrich von Kleist's novella.

Hansjürgen Pohland, *Katz und Maus/Cat and Mouse*, based on Günter Grass's novella.

Johannes Schaaf, *Der Mann aus dem Bootshaus/The Man from the Boathouse* (TV), based on John C. Mortimer's novel, *The Narrowing Stream*.

Michael Verhoeven, *Paarungen/Couplings*, based on August Strindberg's drama, *The Dance of Death*.

1968 Günther Anders, *Pole Poppenspäler* (TV), based on Theodor Storm's novella.

Max Friedmann, *Eine Krankheit genannt Leben/A Sickness Named Life* (TV), based on Italo Svevo's novel, *La coscienza di Zeno*.

Hans W. Geissendörfer, *Der Fall Lena Christ/The Case of Lena Christ* (TV), based on Lena Christ's autobiography, *Erinnerungen einer Überflüssigen* and Peter Bendix's book, *Der Weg der Lena Christ*.

Werner Herzog, *Lebenszeichen/Signs of Life*, based on Achim von Arnim's novella, *Der tolle Invalide auf dem Fort Ratonneau*.

Helmut Käutner, *Bel ami* (TV – 2 parts), based on Guy de Maupassant's story, "Boule de Suif".

Rudolf Noelte, *Das Schloss/The Castle*, based on Franz Kafka's unfinished novel.

Johannes Schaaf, *Lebeck* (TV), based on Günter Seuren's novel.

Willi Schmidt, *Romeo und Julia auf dem Dorfe/A Country Romeo and Juliet* (TV), based on Gottfried Keller's novella.

Hans Dieter Schwarze, *Madame Bovary* (TV), based on Gustave Flaubert's novel.

Wolfgang Staudte, *Die Klasse/The Class* (TV), based on Hermann Ungar's novel, *Lehrer Blau*.

Rolf von Sydow, *Der Idiot/The Idiot* (TV – 3 parts), based on Feodor Dostoevsky's novel.

Claus Peter Witt, *Mathilde Möhring* (TV), based on Theodor Fontane's novel.

1969 Zbynek Brynych, *Amerika oder der Verschollene/America* (TV), based on Franz Kafka's unfinished novel, *Amerika*.

Rainer Werner Fassbinder, *Katzelmacher*, based on Fassbinder's drama.

Peter Fleischmann, *Jagdzenen aus Niederbayern/Hunting Scenes from Lower Bavaria*, based on Martin Sperr's drama.

Eberhard Itzenplitz, *Nur der Freiheit gehört unser Leben/Our Life Only Belongs To Freedom* (TV), based on Ödön von Horváth's novel, *Jugend ohne Gott*.

Helmut Käutner, *Christoph Kolumbus oder Die Entdeckung Amerikas/Christopher Columbus or The Discovery of America* (TV), based on the comedy by Walter Hasenclever and Kurt Tucholsky.

Volker Schlöndorff, *Michael Kohlhaas – Der Rebell/Michael Kohlhaas*, based on Heinrich von Kleist's novella, *Michael Kohlhaas*.

Hans Dieter Schwarze, *Die missbrauchten Liebesbriefe/The Misused Love Letters* (TV), based on Gottfried Keller's novella.

Peter Zadek, *Ich bin ein Elefant, Madame/I Am an Elephant, Madame*, based on Thomas Valentin's novel, *Die Unberatenen*.

1970 Wolfgang Glück, *Traumnovelle/Dream Novella* (TV), based on Arthur Schnitzler's novella.

Vojtech Jasny, *Nicht nur zur Weihnachtszeit/Not Only at Christmas Time* (TV), based on Heinrich Böll's story.

Gerhard Klingenberg, *Friede den Hütten! Krieg den Palästen!/Peace to the Cottages! War to the Palaces!* (TV), based in part on Kasimir Edschmid's novel, *Georg Büchner – Eine deutsche Revolution*.

Edgar Reitz, *Cardillac*, based on E. T. A. Hoffmann's novella, *Das Fräulein von Scudéri*.

Volker Schlöndorff, *Baal* (TV), based on Bertolt Brecht's drama.

Wolfgang Staudte, *Die Person/The Person* (TV), based on Manfred Bieler's story, *Der junge Roth*.

Robert Stratil, *Krebsstation/Cancer Ward* (TV – 2 parts), based on Alexander Solzhenitsyn's novel.

Jean-Marie Straub/Danièle Huillet, *Othon*, based on Pierre Corneille's play.

Hans Jürgen Syberberg, *San Domingo*, based on Heinrich von Kleist's novella, *Die Verlobung in San Domingo*.

Herbert Vesely, *Das Bastardzeichen/The Sign of the Bastard* (TV), based on Vladimir Nabokov's novel, *Bend Sinister*.

1971 Peter Beauvais, *Deutschstunde/The German Lesson* (TV – 2 parts), based on Siegfried Lenz's novel.

Horst Bienek, *Die Zelle/The Cell*, based on Bienek's novel.

Rainer Werner Fassbinder, *Pioniere in Ingolstadt/Pioneers in Ingolstadt* (TV), based on Marieluise Fleisser's drama.

Hans W. Geissendörfer, *Carlos*, based loosely on Friedrich Schiller's drama, *Don Carlos*.

Reinhard Hauff, *Offener Hass gegen Unbekannt/Open Hatred against Persons Unknown* (TV), based on Heine Schoof's book, *Erklärung*.

Peter Lilienthal, *Jakob von Gunthen* (TV), based on Robert Walser's novel.

Ferry Radax, *Der Italiener/The Italian* (TV), based on Thomas Bernhard's story.

Johannes Schaaf, *Trotta*, based on Joseph Roth's novel, *Die Kapuzinergruft*.

Maximilian Schell, *First Love/Erste Liebe*, based on Ivan Turgenev's novella.

Volker Schlöndorff, *Der plötzliche Reichtum der armen Leute von Kombach/The Sudden Wealth of the Poor People of Kombach*, based on a chronicle from the year 1825 about the post robbery in the Subach Valley.

Peter Schulze-Rohr, *Davor/Before* (TV), based on Günter Grass's play, *Davor*, and his novel, *Örtlich betäubt*.

Hans-Dieter Schwarze, *Ende einer Dienstfahrt/The End of a Business Trip* (TV), based on Heinrich Böll's story.

Wolfgang Staudte, *Der Seewolf/The Sea Wolf* (TV – 4 parts), based on Jack London's stories and his novel, *The Sea Wolf*.

Bernhard Wicki, *Das falsche Gewicht/The False Measure* (TV), based on Joseph Roth's novel.

1972 Oswald Döpke, *Deutsche Novelle/German Novella* (TV), based on Leonhard Frank's novella.

Rainer Werner Fassbinder, *Die bitteren Tränen der Petra von Kant/The Bitter Tears of Petra von Kant*, based on Fassbinder's drama.

—— *Wildwechsel/Jail Bait*, based on Franz Xaver Kroetz's drama.

Rolf Hädrich, *Erinnerung an einen Sommer in Berlin/Memory of One Summer in Berlin* (TV), based on a chapter of Thomas Wolfe's novel, *You Can't Go Home Again*.

Klaus Kirschner, *La Jalousie* (TV), based on Alain Robbe-Grillet's novel.

Jean-Marie Straub/Danièle Huillet, *Geschichtsunterricht/History Lessons*, based on Bertolt Brecht's novel fragment, *Die Geschäfte des Herrn Julius Caesar*.

Wim Wenders, *Die Angst des Tormanns beim Elfmeter/The Goalie's Anxiety at the Penalty Kick*, based on Peter Handke's novel.

1973 Wolfgang Petersen, *Van der Valk und die Reichen/Van der Valk and the Rich People* (TV), based on Nicolas Freeling's novel, *King of the Rainy Country*.

Johannes Schaaf, *Traumstadt/Dream City*, based on Alfred Kubin's novel, *Die andere Seite*.

Michael Verhoeven, *Ein unheimlich starker Abgang/Apotheosis*, based on Harald Sommer's drama.

Wim Wenders, *Der scharlachrote Buchstabe/The Scarlet Letter* (TV), based on Nathaniel Hawthorne's novel.

1974 Rainer Werner Fassbinder, *Fontane Effi Briest*, based on Theodor Fontane's novel, *Effi Briest*.

Michael Fengler, *Output* (TV), based on Ulf Miehe's novel, *Ich hab' noch einen Toten in Berlin*.

Hans W. Geissendörfer, *Perahim – die zweite Chance/Perahim – The Second Chance* (TV), based on C. V. Gheorghiu's novel, *Gangster Maximilian Perahim*.

Falk Harnack, *Der Verfolger/The Pursuer* (TV), based on Günther Weisenborn's novel.

Reinhard Hauff, *Zündschnüre/Fuses* (TV), based on Franz Josef Degenhardt's novel.

Eberhard Itzenplitz, *Der Abituriententag/Class Reunion* (TV), based on Franz Werfel's novel.

Wolfgang Petersen, *Einer von uns beiden/One of the Two of Us*, based on -ky's novel.

Ottokar Runze, *Der Lord von Barmbeck/The Lord of Barmbeck*, based on the memoirs of Julius Adolf Petersen.

1975   Eberhard Fechner, *Tadellöser & Wolff/Right or Wrong: My Country* (TV – 2 parts), based on Walter Kempowski's novel.

Rolf Hädrich, *Der Stechlin* (TV – 3 parts), based on Theodor Fontane's novel.

Ulf Miehe, *John Glückstadt*, based on Theodor Storm's novella, *Ein Doppelgänger*.

Wolfgang Petersen, *Stellenweise Glatteis/Occasional Patches of Ice* (TV – 2 parts), based on Max von der Grün's novel.

Manfred Purzer, *Das Netz/The Net*, based on Hans Habe's novel.

Helma Sanders-Brahms, *Erdbeben in Chili/The Earthquake in Chile* (TV), based on Heinrich von Kleist's novella, *Das Erdbeben in Chili*.

Volker Schlöndorff, *Georginas Gründe/Georgina's Reasons* (TV), based on Henry James's story.

—— (with Margarethe von Trotta), *Die verlorene Ehre der Katharina Blum/ The Lost Honor of Katharina Blum*, based on Heinrich Böll's story.

Jean-Marie Straub/Danièle Huillet, *Moses und Aron/Moses and Aaron*, based on Arnold Schönberg's opera.

Rudolf Thome, *Tagebuch/Diary*, based loosely on J. W. von Goethe's novel, *Die Wahlverwandtschaften*.

Wim Wenders, *Falsche Bewegung/Wrong Move*, based loosely on motifs from J. W. von Goethe's novel, *Wilhelm Meisters Lehrjahre*.

1976   Lutz Büscher, *Das Fräulein von Scudéri* (TV), based on E. T. A. Hoffmann's novella.

Rainer Werner Fassbinder, *Ich will doch nur, dass ihr mich liebt/I Only Want You to Love Me* (TV), based on a story in *Lebenslänglich* by Klaus Antes and Christiane Ehrhardt.

Hans W. Geissendörfer, *Sternsteinhof/Sternstein Manor*, based on Ludwig Anzengruber's novel, *Der Sternsteinhof*.

—— *Die Wildente/The Wild Duck*, based on Henrik Ibsen's drama, *Vildanden*.

Wolf Gremm, *Die Brüder/The Brothers*, based on Septimus Dale's short story, "The Little Girl Eater".

Werner Herzog, *Herz aus Glas/Heart of Glass*, based on a story in Herbert Achternbusch's *Die Stunde des Todes*.

Vojtech Jasny, *Ansichten eines Clowns/The Clown*, based on Heinrich Böll's novel.

—— *Fluchtversuch/Attempted Escape*, based on W. J. M. Wippersberg's story.

Roland Klick, *Lieb Vaterland, magst ruhig sein/Rest Thou Tranquil, Beloved Country*, based on Johannes Mario Simmel's novel.

Alexander Kluge, *Der starke Ferdinand/Strong Man Ferdinand*, based on Kluge's story, "Ein Bolschewist des Kapitals".

Thomas Koerfer, *Der Gehülfe/The Assistant*, based on Robert Walser's autobiographical novel.

Peter Lilienthal, *Hauptlehrer Hofer/Schoolmaster Hofer*, based on Günter Herburger's story.

Manfred Purzer, *Die Elixiere des Teufels/The Devil's Elixirs*, based on E. T. A. Hoffmann's novel.

Eric Rohmer, *Die Marquise von O . . ./The Marquise of O . . .*, based on Heinrich von Kleist's novella.

Volker Schlöndorff, *Der Fangschuss/Coup de Grâce*, based on Marguerite Yourcenar's novel, *Coup de Grâce*.

Daniel Schmid, *Schatten der Engel/Shadows of the Angels*, based on Rainer Werner Fassbinder's drama, *Der Müll, die Stadt und der Tod*.

Peter Stein, *Sommergäste/Summer Guests*, based on Maxim Gorki's drama.

Jean-Marie Straub/Danièle Huillet, *Fortini Cani*, based on Franco Fortini's book, *The Dogs of Sinai*.

1977 Robert Van Ackeren, *Belcanto oder Darf eine Nutte weinen?/Belcanto*, based on Heinrich Mann's novel, *Empfang bei der Welt*.

Alf Brustellin/Bernhard Sinkel, *Der Mädchenkrieg/The Three Sisters*, based on Manfred Bieler's novel.

Dagmar Damek, *Cécile* (TV), based on Theodor Fontane's novel.

Ingemo Engström/Gerhard Theuring, *Fluchtweg nach Marseille/Escape Route to Marseilles* (TV – 2 parts), based in part on motifs from Anna Seghers's novel, *Transit*.

Rainer Werner Fassbinder, *Bolwieser/The Station Master's Wife* (TV – 2 parts), based on Oskar Maria Graf's novel.

—— *Frauen in New York/Women in New York* (TV), based on Clare Booth's drama, *The Women*.

Horst Flick, *Die Aula/The Auditorium* (TV), based on Hermann Kant's novel and play.

Heidi Genée, *Grete Minde – Der Wald ist voller Wölfe/Grete Minde*, based on Theodor Fontane's novel, *Grete Minde*.

Peter Handke, *Die linkshändige Frau/The Left-Handed Woman*, based on Handke's story.

Michael Haneke, *Drei Wege zum See/Three Ways to the Sea* (TV), based on Ingeborg Bachmann's story.

Theodor Kotulla, *Aus einem deutschen Leben/Death Is My Trade*, based on Robert Merle's novel, *La Mort est mon métier*.

Wolfgang Petersen, *Die Konsequenz/The Consequence*, based on Alexander Ziegler's autobiographical novel.

Alexander Petrović, *Gruppenbild mit Dame/Group Portrait with Lady*, based on Heinrich Böll's novel.

Ottokar Runze, *Die Standarte/The Standard*, based on Alexander Lernet-Holenia's novel.

Helma Sanders-Brahms, *Heinrich*, based on the life and letters of Heinrich von Kleist.

Daniel Schmid, *Violanta*, based on Conrad Ferdinand Meyer's novella, *Die Richterin*.

Franz Seitz, *Unordnung und frühes Leid/Disorder and Early Sorrow*, based on Thomas Mann's novella.

Wim Wenders, *Der amerikanische Freund/The American Friend*, based on Patricia Highsmith's novel, *Ripley's Game*, and motifs from her novel, *Ripley Underground*.

Bernhard Wicki, *Die Eroberung der Zitadelle/The Conquest of the Citadel*, based on Günter Herburger's story.

1978   Herbert Ballmann, *Ein Mann will nach oben/A Man Wants to Rise* (TV – 13 parts), based on Hans Fallada's novel.

Hajo Baumgärtner, *Die Flucht/The Escape*, based on Adalbert Stifter's novella, *Der Hochwald*.

Axel Corti, *Die beiden Freundinnen/The Two Girlfriends* (TV), based on Alfred Döblin's report, "Die beiden Freundinnen und ihr Giftmord".

Ulrich Edel, *Der harte Handel/The Brutal Barter* (TV), based on Oskar Maria Graf's novel.

Klaus Emmerich, *Heinrich Heine* (TV – 2 parts), based on the poet's life.

Harun Farocki, *Zwischen zwei Kriegen/Between Two Wars*, based on Farocki's radio play, *Das grosse Verbindungsrohr*.

Rainer Werner Fassbinder, *Despair – Eine Reise ins Licht/Despair*, based on Vladimir Nabokov's novel.

Eberhard Fechner, *Winterspelt 1944*, based on Alfred Andersch's novel, *Winterspelt*.

Hans W. Geissendörfer, *Die gläserne Zelle/The Glass Cell*, based on Patricia Highsmith's novel.

Wolf Gremm, *Tod oder Freiheit/Death or Liberty*, based in part on motifs from Friedrich Schiller's drama, *Die Räuber*.

Helmut Käutner, *Mulligans Rückkehr/Mulligan's Return* (TV), based on Hans Frick's novel.

Gaudenz Meili, *Kneuss* (TV), based on Beat Brechbühl's novel.

Peter Patzak, *Das Einhorn/The Unicorn*, based on Martin Walser's novel.

Volker Schlöndorff and Heinrich Böll, "Die verschobene Antigone"/"The Rescheduled Antigone", sequence in *Deutschland im Herbst/Germany in Autumn*, based on Sophocles' tragedy.

Bernhard Sinkel, *Taugenichts/Good-for-Nothing*, based on Joseph von Eichendorff's novella, *Aus dem Leben eines Taugenichts*.

Peter Stein, *Trilogie des Wiedersehens/Trilogy of Farewell*, based on Botho Strauss's drama.

Michael Verhoeven, *Das Männerquartett/The Male Quartet* (TV), based on Leonhard Frank's novel, *Das Ochsenfurter Männerquartett*.

Herbert Vesely, *Der kurze Brief zum langen Abschied/Short Letter, Long Farewell* (TV), based on Peter Handke's novel.

Alfred Weidenmann, *Der Schimmelreiter/The Rider on the White Horse*, based on Theodor Storm's novella.

Christian Ziewer, *Aus der Ferne sehe ich dieses Land/From the Distance I See This Country*, based on Antonio Skármeta's story, *Nix passiert*.

1979   Alf Brustellin, *Der Sturz/The Fall*, based on Martin Walser's novel.

Gustav Ehmck, *Neues vom Räuber Hotzenplotz/Further Adventures of the Robber Hotzenplotz*, based on Otfried Preussler's novel, *Der Räuber Hotzenplotz*.

Klaus Emmerich, *Die erste Polka/The First Polka*, based on Horst Bienek's novel.

Horst Flick, *Kotte* (TV), based on Klaus Schlesinger's novel, *Alte Filme*.

Hans W. Geissendörfer, *Theodor Chindler* (TV – 8 parts), based on Bernard von Brentano's novel.

Wolf Gremm, *Die Schattengrenze/Frontiers of Darkness* (TV), based on Dieter Wellershoff's novel.

Werner Herzog, *Nosferatu – Phantom der Nacht/Nosferatu – the Vampire*, based on Bram Stoker's novel, *Dracula*.

Werner Herzog, *Woyzeck*, based on Georg Büchner's dramatic fragment.
Norbert Kückelmann, *Die letzten Jahre der Kindheit/The Last Years of Child-hood*, based on Kückelmann's report, "Der Fall R."
Wolfgang Liebeneiner, *Götz von Berlichingen mit der eisernen Hand/Götz von Berlichingen with the Iron Hand*, based on J. W. von Goethe's drama, *Götz von Berlichingen*.
Peter Lilienthal, *David*, based on Joel König's book, *Den Netzen entronnen*.
Marianne Lüdcke, *Die grosse Flatter/The Big Flutter* (TV – 3 parts), based on Leonie Ossowski's novel.
Theo Mezger, *Gefangen in Frankreich/Prisoner in France* (TV), based on Theodor Fontane's report, *Kriegsgefangen*.
Ottokar Runze, *Der Mörder/The Murderer*, based on Georges Simenon's novel, *L'Assassin*.
Maximilian Schell, *Geschichten aus dem Wienerwald/Tales from the Vienna Woods*, based on Ödön von Horváth's drama.
Volker Schlöndorff, *Die Blechtrommel/The Tin Drum*, based on Günter Grass's novel.
Wolfgang Staudte, *Der eiserne Gustav/Iron Gustav* (TV – 7 parts), based on Hans Fallada's novel.
Jean-Marie Straub/Danièle Huillet, *Dalla nube alle resistanza/From the Cloud to the Resistance*, based on Cesare Pavese's books, *Dialoghi con Levcò* and *La luna et il falò*.
Franz Peter Wirth, *Buddenbrooks* (TV – 11 parts), based on Thomas Mann's novel.
Claus Peter Witt, *Ein Mord, den jeder begeht/A Murder Committed by Everyone* (TV), based on Hemito von Doderer's novel.
1980 Luc Bondy, *Die Ortliebschen Frauen/The Women of Ortlieb*, based on Franz Nabl's novel, *Das Grab des Lebendigen*.
Walerian Borowczyk, *Lulu*, based on Frank Wedekind's dramas, *Der Erdgeist* and *Die Büchse der Pandora*.
Rainer Werner Fassbinder, *Berlin Alexanderplatz* (TV – 13 parts and an epilogue), based on Alfred Döblin's novel.
Eberhard Fechner, *Ein Kapitel für sich/A Long Story* (TV – 3 parts), based on Walter Kempowski's novels, *Uns geht's ja noch Gold*, *Im Block*, and *Ein Kapitel für sich*.
Karl Fruchtmann, *Der Boxer/The Boxer* (TV), based on Jurek Becker's novel.
Wolf Gremm, *Fabian*, based on Erich Kästner's novel.
Klaus Michael Gruber/Ellen Hammer, *Winterreise im Olympiastadion/Winter's Journey in the Olympic Stadium*, based on Friedrich Hölderlin's novel, *Hyperion*.
Reiner Kunze, *Die wunderbaren Jahre/The Wonderful Years*, based on Kunze's book.
Helma Sanders-Brahms, *Deutschland, bleiche Mutter/Germany, Pale Mother*, based on an image from Bertolt Brecht's poem, "Deutschland".
Peter Stein, *Gross und klein/Large and Small*, based on Botho Strauss's drama.
Michael Verhoeven, *Sonntagskinder/Sunday's Children* (TV), based on Gerlind Reinshagen's drama.
—— *Die Ursache/The Cause* (TV), based on Leonhard Frank's story.
—— *Am Südhang/The South Slope* (TV), based on Eduard von Keyserling's story.
1981 Percy Adlon, *Céleste*, based on Céleste Albaret's memoirs, *Monsieur Proust*.
Frank Beyer, *Der König und sein Narr/The King and His Jester* (TV), based on Martin Stade's novel.

Lutz Büscher, *Pseudonym Hans Fallada* (TV), based on the life and work of the poet (Rudolf Ditzen).

Ulrich Edel, *Christiane F. – Wir Kinder vom Bahnhof Zoo/Christiane F.*, based on the book by Kai Hermann and Horst Rieck.

Alexander von Eschwege, *Flächenbrand/Widespread Fire* (TV), based on Max von der Grün's novel.

Rainer Werner Fassbinder, *Lili Marleen*, based on Lale Andersen's autobiography, *Der Himmel hat viele Farben*.

—— *Theater in Trance*, which includes texts from Antonin Artaud's book, *Le Theâtre et son double*.

Radu Gabrea, *Fürchte dich nicht, Jakob!/Don't Be Afraid, Jacob!*, based on Ion Luca Caragiale's story, *Die Osterkerze*.

Wolf Gremm, *Kein Reihenhaus für Robin Hood/No Tract Home for Robin Hood*, based on -ky's novel.

—— *Nach Mitternacht/After Midnight*, based on Irmgard Keun's novel.

Egon Günther, *Exil/Exile* (TV – 7 parts), based on Lion Feuchtwanger's novel.

Klaus Holldack, *Vor den Vätern sterben die Söhne/The Sons Die before the Fathers* (TV), based on Thomas Brasch's story, "Und über uns schliesst sich ein Himmel aus Stahl".

Stephan Kayser, *Magma – Reise von hier nach dort/Magma – A Trip from Here to There*, which includes texts from Max Frisch's story, *Bin oder Die Reise nach Peking*, the novels *Homo faber* and *Mein Name sei Gantenbein*, and the book, *Der Mensch erscheint im Holozän*.

Theodor Kotulla, *Der Fall Maurizius/The Maurizius Case* (TV – 5 parts), based on Jakob Wassermann's novel.

Wolfgang Petersen, *Das Boot/The Boat*, based on Lothar-Günther Buchheim's book.

Ottokar Runze, *Stern ohne Himmel/Star without a Sky*, based on Leonie Ossowski's novel.

Volker Schlöndorff, *Die Fälschung/Circle of Deceit*, based on Nicolas Born's novel.

Peter Schulze-Rohr, *Collin* (TV – 2 parts), based on Stefan Heym's novel.

István Szábo, *Mephisto*, based on Klaus Mann's novel.

1982   Stanislav Barabas, *Ich werde warten/I'll Be Waiting* (TV), based loosely on Raymond Chandler's story, "I'll Be Waiting".

Alf Brustellin/Bernhard Sinkel, *Bekenntnisse des Hochstaplers Felix Krull/Confessions of the Confidence Man Felix Krull* (TV – 5 parts), based on Thomas Mann's novel.

Rainer Werner Fassbinder, *Querelle – Ein Pakt mit dem Teufel/Querelle*, based on Jean Genet's novel, *Querelle de Brest*.

Hans W. Geissendörfer, *Der Zauberberg/The Magic Mountain*, based on Thomas Mann's novel.

Heidi Genée, *Kraftprobe/Test of Strength*, based on Dagmar Kekulé's novel, *Ich bin eine Wolke*.

Wolf Gremm, *Kamikaze 1989*, based on Per Wahlöö's novel, *Murder on the Thirty-First Floor*.

Hartmut Griesmayer, *Leben im Winter/Life in Winter* (TV), based on Klaus Schlesinger's novel.

Reinhard Hauff, *Der Mann auf der Mauer/The Man on the Wall*, based on Peter Schneider's book.

Helmut Herbst, *Eine deutsche Revolution/A German Revolution*, based on Kasimir Edschmid's novel, *Georg Büchner – Eine deutsche Revolution*.

Michael Kehlmann, *Tarabas* (TV – 2 parts), based on Joseph Roth's novel, *Tarabas, ein Gast auf dieser Erde*.

Thomas Koerfer, *Die Leidenschaftlichen/The Passionate Ones* (TV), based on J. W. von Goethe's novel, *Die Leiden des jungen Werthers*, and on the poet's life.

Horst Königstein, *Das Beil von Wandsbek/The Ax of Wandsbek* (TV), based on Arnold Zweig's novel.

Werner Nekes, *Uliisses*, based on Homer's epic *The Odyssey*, James Joyce's novel, *Ulysses*, and Neil Oram's play, *The Warp*.

Rosa von Praunheim, *Rote Liebe/Red Love*, based on Alexandra Kollontai's novel, *Wassilissa Malegyna*.

Werner Schroeter, *Liebeskonzil/Lovers' Council*, based on Oskar Panizza's drama.

Franz Seitz, *Doktor Faustus*, based on Thomas Mann's novel.

Hans Jürgen Syberberg, *Parsifal*, based on Richard Wagner's opera.

Wim Wenders, *Hammett*, based on Joe Gores's novel.

Franz Josef Wild, *Frau Jenny Treibel* (TV), based on Theodor Fontane's novel.

1983 Percy Adlon, *Die Schaukel/The Swing*, based on Annette Kolb's novel.

Walter Bockmayer/Rolf Bührmann, *Kiez*, based on Peter Greiner's drama.

Hans W. Geissendörfer, *Ediths Tagebuch/Edith's Diary*, based on Patricia Highsmith's novel.

Michael Kehlmann, *Mich wundert, dass ich so fröhlich bin/I Wonder Why I'm So Happy* (TV), based on Johannes Mario Simmel's novel.

Egon Monk, *Die Geschwister Oppermann/The Oppermann Siblings* (TV – 2 parts), based on Lion Feuchtwanger's novel.

Hans Neuenfels, *Heinrich Penthesilea von Kleist – Träumereien über eine Inszenierung/Heinrich Penthesilea von Kleist – Reveries about a Production*, based on Heinrich von Kleist's drama, *Penthesilea*.

Wolfgang Staudte, *Satan ist auf Gottes Seite/Satan Is on God's Side* (TV), based on Hans Herlin's novel.

Peter Stein, *Klassenfeind/Class Enemy*, based on Nigel Williams's drama.

Wolfgang Storch, *Reifenwechsel/A Change of Tires* (TV), based on Georges Simenon's novel, *Feux rouges*.

Andrzej Wajda, *Eine Liebe in Deutschland/A Love in Germany*, based on Rolf Hochhuth's novel.

Claus Peter Witt, *Fremdes Land/Strange Country* (TV), based on Arno Surminski's novel.

Peter Zadek, *Die wilden Fünfziger/The Wild Fifties*, based loosely on Johannes Mario Simmel's novel, *Hurra, wir leben noch*.

1984 Peter Beauvais, *Die ewigen Gefühle/The Eternal Feelings* (TV), based on Bernard von Brentano's novel.

Karin Brandauer, *Der Weg ins Freie/The Way Out into the Open* (TV – 2 parts), based on Arthur Schnitzler's novel.

Wolf-Eckart Bühler, *Der Havarist*, based on Sterling Hayden's novel, *Wanderer*.

Burkhard Driest, *Annas Mutter/Anna's Mother*, based on Heiko Gebhardt's book.

Ulrich Edel, *Eine Art von Zorn/A Kind of Anger* (TV), based on Eric Ambler's novel.

Oliver Herbrich, *Wodzeck*, based on Georg Büchner's dramatic fragment, *Woyzeck*.

Claus Hubalek, *Lenin in Zürich* (TV), based on Alexander Solzhenitsyn's book.

Eberhard Itzenplitz, *Feuer für den grossen Drachen/Fire for the Big Dragon* (TV), based on -ky's novel.

Erwin Keusch, *Kerbels Flucht/Kerbel's Escape* (TV), based on Uwe Timm's novel.

—— *Das leise Gift/The Slow Poison* (TV), based on Marcus P. Nester's novel.

Peter Lilienthal, *Das Autogramm/The Autograph*, based on Osvaldo Soriano's novel, *Cuarteles de Invierno*.

Marianne Lüdcke, *Liebe ist kein Argument/Love Is No Excuse*, based on Leonie Ossowski's novel.

Wolfgang Petersen, *Die unendliche Geschichte/The Neverending Story*, based on Michael Ende's novel.

Chris Petit, *Fluchtpunkt Berlin/Flight to Berlin*, based on Jennifer Potter's unpublished novel, *Strange Days*.

Volker Schlöndorff, *Eine Liebe von Swann/Swann in Love*, based on a chapter from Marcel Proust's novel, *A la recherche du temps perdu*.

Wolfgang Staudte, *Der Snob/The Snob* (TV), based on Carl Sternheim's comedy.

Jean-Marie Straub/Danièle Huillet, *Klassenverhältnisse/Class Relations*, based on Franz Kafka's unfinished novel, *Amerika*.

Franz Peter Wirth, *Vor dem Sturm/Before the Storm* (TV – 8 parts), based on Theodor Fontane's novel.

Krzysztof Zanussi, *Blaubart/Bluebeard*, based on Max Frisch's story.

1985 Peter F. Bringmann, *Der Schneemann/The Snow Man*, based on Jörg Fauser's novel.

Egon Günther, *Morenga*, based on Uwe Timm's novel.

Elfi Mikesch/Monika Treut, *Verführung: Die grausame Frau/Seduction: The Brutal Woman*, based loosely on Leopold von Sacher-Masoch's novel, *Venus im Pelz*.

Hans Neuenfels, *Die Schwärmer/The Dreamers*, based on Robert Musil's play.

Bernhard Wicki, *Die Grünstein-Variante/Grünstein's Clever Move*, based on Wolfgang Kohlaase's radio play and inspired by Ludwig Turek's stories.

East German film

1947 Georg C. Klaren, *Wozzeck*, based on Georg Büchner's dramatic fragment, *Woyzeck*.

Kurt Maetzig, *Ehe im Schatten/Marriage in the Shadows*, based on Hans Schweikart's novella, *Es wird schon nicht so schlimm*.

1949 Erich Engel, *Der Biberpelz/The Beaver Coat*, based on Gerhart Hauptmann's comedy.

Kurt Maetzig, *Die Buntkarierten/The Colorful Checked Dress*, based on Berta Waterstradt's radio play, *Während der Stromsperre*.

1950 Hans Müller, *Bürgermeister Anna/Mayor Anna*, based on Friedrich Wolf's drama.

1951 Falk Harnack, *Das Beil von Wandsbek/The Ax of Wandsbek*, based on Arnold Zweig's novel.

Wolfgang Staudte, *Der Untertan/The Subject*, based on Heinrich Mann's novel.

1952 Georg C. Klaren/Hans-Georg Rudolph, *Karriere in Paris/Career in Paris*, based on Honoré de Balzac's novel, *Père Goriot*.

1953 Wolfgang Staudte, *Die Geschichte vom kleinen Muck/The Story of Little Muck*, based on Wilhelm Hauff's fairy-tale.

1954 Artur Pohl, *Pole Poppenspäler*, based on Theodor Storm's novella.

1955 Martin Hellberg, *Der Ochse von Kulm/The Ox of Kulm*, based on W. K. Schweickert's novel.

Eugen York, *Das Fräulein von Scudéri*, based on E. T. A. Hoffmann's novella.

1956 Konrad Wolf, *Genesung/Convalescence*, based on the radio play by Karl Georg Egel and Paul Wiens.

1957 Martin Hellberg, *Wo Du hingehst/Wherever You Go*, based on Eduard Claudius's novel, *Grüne Oliven und nackte Berge*.

Kurt Jung-Alsen, *Betrogen bis zum jüngsten Tag/Betrayed to the Final Judgment*, based on Franz Fühmann's novella, *Kameraden*.

Konrad Wolf, *Lissy*, based on F. C. Weiskopf's novel, *Die Versuchung*.

1958 Martin Hellberg, *Emilia Galotti*, based on G. E. Lessing's drama.

Joachim Kunert, *Der Lotterieschwede/The Lottery Swede*, based on Martin Andersen Nexö's novella.

1959 Martin Hellberg, *Kabale und Liebe/Love and Intrigue*, based on Friedrich Schiller's drama.

1960 Kurt Maetzig, *Der schweigende Stern/The Silent Planet*, based on Stanislaw Lem's novel, *Milczaca gwiazda*.

1961 Ralf Kirsten, *Steinzeitballade/A Stone Age Ballad*, based on Ludwig Turek's novel, *Anna Lubitzke*.

Peter Palitzsch and Manfred Wekwerth, *Mutter Courage und ihre Kinder/Mother Courage and Her Children*, based on Bertolt Brecht's drama.

Konrad Wolf, *Professor Mamlock*, based on Friedrich Wolf's play.

1962 Martin Hellberg, *Minna von Barnhelm*, based on G. E. Lessing's comedy.

1963 Frank Beyer, *Nackt unter Wölfen/Naked among Wolves*, based on Bruno Apitz's novel.

Ralf Kirsten, *Beschreibung eines Sommers/Description of a Summer*, based on Karl-Heinz Jakobs's story.

1964 Heiner Carow, *Die Hochzeit von Länneken/The Wedding in Länneken*, based on Herbert Nachbar's novel.

Kurt Maetzig, *Preludio 11*, based on Wolfgang Schreyer's novel.

Werner W. Wallroth, *Alaskafüchse/Alaska Foxes*, based on Wolfgang Schreyer's story.

Konrad Wolf, *Der geteilte Himmel/The Divided Sky*, based on Christa Wolf's novel.

1965 Joachim Hasler, *Chronik eines Mordes/Chronicle of a Murder*, based on Leonhard Frank's novel, *Die Jünger Jesu*.

Joachim Kunert, *Die Abenteuer des Werner Holt/The Adventures of Werner Holt*, based on volume one of Dieter Noll's novel.

Kurt Maetzig, *Das Kaninchen bin ich/I Am the Rabbit*, based on Manfred Bieler's novel.

1966 Frank Beyer, *Spur der Steine/Path of the Stones*, based on Erik Neutsch's novel.

Heiner Carow, *Die Reise nach Sundevit/The Trip to Sundevit*, based on Benno Pludra's story.

Heinz Thiel/Horst E. Brandt, *Irrlicht und Feuer/Will-o'-the-Wisp and Fire* (TV – 2 parts), based on Max von der Grün's novel.

1967 Hans-Joachim Kasprzik, *Kleiner Mann – was nun?/Little Man – What Now?* (TV – 2 parts), based on Hans Fallada's novel.

Rolf Losansky, *Der Revolver des Corporals/The Corporal's Revolver*, based on motifs from Eberhard Panitz's story.

Kurt Maetzig, *Die Fahne von Kriwoj Rog/The Flag of Kriwoj Rog*, based on Otto Gotsche's novel.

1968   Egon Günther, *Abschied/Farewell*, based on Johannes R. Becher's novel.
Joachim Kunert, *Die Toten bleiben jung/The Dead Stay Young*, based on Anna Seghers's novel.
Wolfgang Luderer, *Alchemisten/Alchemists* (TV – 2 parts), based on Eduard Klein's novel.
Helmut Schiemann, *Der Streit um den Sergeanten Grischa/The Dispute about Sergeant Grischa* (TV – 2 parts), based on Arnold Zweig's novel.
Horst Seemann, *Schüsse unterm Galgen/Shots under the Gallows*, based on Robert Louis Stevenson's novels, *Kidnapped* and *Catriona*.
Ulrich Thein, *Mitten im kalten Winter/In the Middle of a Cold Winter* (TV), based on Hermann Kant's story, "Ein bisschen Südsee".

1969   Günter Reisch, *Jungfer, sie gefällt mir/The Maid Pleases Me*, based on Heinrich von Kleist's comedy, *Der zerbrochene Krug*.
Herrmann Zschoche, *Weite Strassen – stille Liebe/Wide Streets – Quiet Love*, based on Hans-Georg Lietz's story, *Endlose Strassen*.

1970   Egon Günther, *Junge Frau von 1914/A Young Woman of 1914* (TV – 2 parts), based on Arnold Zweig's novel.
Hans-Joachim Kaprzik, *Jeder stirbt für sich allein/Everyone Dies Alone* (TV – 3 parts), based on Hans Fallada's novel.
Ralf Kirsten, *Zwei Briefe an Pospischiel/Two Letters to Pospischiel* (TV – 2 parts), based on Max von der Grün's novel.
Wolfgang Luderer, *Effi Briest* (TV), based on Theodor Fontane's novel.
Günter Reisch, *Unterwegs zu Lenin/On the Way to Lenin*, based on Alfred Kurella's memoirs.

1971   Heiner Carow, *Karriere/Career*, based on Egon Richter's story, "Die Anzeige".
Ralf Kirsten, *Der verlorene Engel/The Lost Angel*, based on Franz Fühmann's novella, *Das schlimme Jahr*.
Siegfried Kühn, *Zeit der Störche/Time of the Storks*, based on Herbert Otto's story.
Georg Leopold, *Verwandte und Bekannte/Relatives and Acquaintances* (TV – 3 parts), based on Willi Bredel's novel, *Die Väter*.
Ingrid Reschke, *Kennen Sie Urban?/Do You Know Urban?*, based on Gisela Karau's reports.
Rainer Simon, *Männer ohne Bart/Men without Beards*, based on Uwe Kant's novel, *Das Klassenfest*.
Konrad Wolf, *Goya*, based on Lion Feuchtwanger's novel, *Goya oder der arge Weg der Erkenntnis*.

1972   Lothar Bellag, *Der Regimentskommandeur/The Regiment Commander* (TV), based on Walter Flegel's novel.
Klaus Gendries, *Florentiner 73* (TV), based on Renate Holland-Moritz's story, "Das Durchgangszimmer".
Egon Günther, *Der Dritte/The Third Husband*, based on Eberhard Panitz's story, "Unter den Bäumen regnet es zweimal".
Peter Hagen, *Das Licht der schwarzen Kerze/The Light of the Black Candle* (TV – 3 parts), based on Wolfgang Held's novel.
Joachim Kunert, *Die grosse Reise der Agathe Schweigert/The Long Journey of Agathe Schweigert* (TV), based on Anna Seghers's story, "Agathe Schweigert".
Lothar Oehme, *Der Mann, der nach der Oma kam/The Man Who Came after Granny*, based on Renate Holland-Moritz's story, "Graffunda räumt auf".

1973   Frank Beyer, *Die sieben Affären der Doña Juanita/The Seven Affairs of Doña Juanita* (TV – 4 parts), based on Eberhard Panitz's novel.

Celino Bleiweiss, *Aus dem Leben eines Taugenichts/The Life of a Good-for-Nothing*, based on Joseph von Eichendorff's novella.

Egon Günther, *Erziehung vor Verdun/Education before Verdun* (TV), based on Arnold Zweig's novel.

Hans-Joachim Kaprzik, *Die Brüder Lautensack/The Lautensack Brothers* (TV – 2 parts), based on Lion Feuchtwanger's novel.

Ralf Kirsten, *Die Elixiere des Teufels/The Devil's Elixirs*, based on E. T. A. Hoffmann's novel.

—— *Unterm Birnbaum/Under the Pear Tree*, based on Theodor Fontane's novel.

1974   Frank Beyer, *Jakob der Lügner/Jakob the Liar*, based on Jurek Becker's novel.

Siegfried Kühn, *Die Wahlverwandtschaften/The Elective Affinities*, based on J. W. von Goethe's novel.

Joachim Kunert, *Das Schilfrohr/The Reed* (TV), based on Anna Seghers's story.

Rolf Losansky, *. . . verdammt, ich bin erwachsen/Damn, I'm Grown Up*, based on Joachim Novotny's novel, *Der Riese im Paradies*.

1975   Horst E. Brandt, *Zwischen Tag und Nacht/Between Day and Night*, based on Erich Weinert's life and on his notebooks and poems.

Egon Günther, *Lotte in Weimar*, based on Thomas Mann's novel.

Kurt Jung-Alsen, *Im Schlaraffenland/In the Land of Milk and Honey* (TV), based on Heinrich Mann's novel.

Ralf Kirsten, *Eine Pyramide für mich/A Pyramid for Me*, based on Karl-Heinz Jakobs's novel.

Joachim Kunert, *Steckbrief eines Unerwünschten/Wanted Poster for an Unwanted Man* (TV – 3 parts), based on Günter Wallraff's reports.

Rainer Simon, *Till Eulenspiegel*, based on Christa and Gerhard Wolf's reworking of the folk tale.

Manfred Wekwerth, *Die unheilige Sophia/Unholy Sophia* (TV), based on Eberhard Panitz's novel.

1976   Walter Beck, *Trini*, based on Ludwig Renn's novel.

Egon Günther, *Die Leiden des jungen Werthers/The Sorrows of Young Werther*, based on J. W. von Goethe's novel.

Kurt Maetzig, *Mann gegen Mann/Man against Man*, based on Kurt Biesalski's novel, *Das Duell*.

Helmut Nitzschke, *Das Licht auf dem Galgen/Light on the Gallows*, based on Anna Seghers's story.

Helmut Schiemann, *Auf der Suche nach Gatt/Looking for Gatt* (TV – 2 parts), based on Erik Neutsch's novel.

Kurt Veth, *Sein letzter Fall/His Last Case* (TV), based on Bernt Engelmann's report, "Grosses Bundesverdienstkreuz".

Werner W. Wallroth, *Liebesfallen/Love Traps*, based on Ludwig Turek's book.

1977   Peter Deutsch, *Auftrag für M & S/A Job for M & S* (TV), based on Hasso Grabner's novel, *Die Zelle*.

Richard Engel, *Schach von Wuthenow* (TV), based on Theodor Fontane's story.

Joachim Kunert, *Das Verhör/The Interrogation* (TV), based on the first chapter of the story by Georg Egel and Oscar Kurganow, "Der erste Frühling".

Christa Mühl, *Tod und Auferstehung des Wilhelm Hausmann/Death and Resurrection of Wilhelm Hausmann* (TV), based on Bertolt Brecht's story,

"Der Arbeitsplatz oder Im Schweisse deines Angesichts sollst du kein Brot essen".

Roland Oehme, *Ein irrer Duft von frischem Heu/An Incredible Aroma of Fresh Hay*, based on Rudi Strahl's comedy.

Helmut Schiemann, *Die Verführbaren/The Pliable Ones* (TV), based on Heinrich Mann's novel, *Ein ernstes Leben*.

Kurt Veth, *Auftrag: Überleben/Mission: Survival* (TV), based on Erich Hanke's book, *Erinnerungen eines Illegalen*.

Manfred Wekwerth, *Happy End* (TV), based on Dorothy Lane's play.

1978   Horst E. Brandt, *Brandstellen/Patches of Fire*, based on Franz Josef Degenhardt's novel.

Klaus Gendries, *Wie soll sich eine Frau entscheiden?/How Is a Woman Supposed to Decide?* (TV), based on Erich Schlossarek's radio play, *Der Tadel*.

Egon Günther, *Ursula* (TV), based on Gottfried Keller's novella.

Rainer Hausdorf, *Gefährliche Fahndung/Dangerous Search* (TV – 7 parts), based on Julius Mader's novel, *Sepp Plieseis – Partisan der Berge*.

Ralf Kirsten, *Ich zwing dich zu leben/I Force You to Live*, based on Karl Sewart's story, "Gambit".

Thomas Langhoff, *Stine* (TV), based on Theodor Fontane's novel.

Horst Seemann, *Fleur Lafontaine* (TV – 2 parts), based on Dinah Nelken's novel, *Das angstvolle Heldenleben einer gewissen Fleur Lafontaine*.

Erwin Stranka, *Sabine Wulff*, based on Heinz Kruschel's novel, *Gesucht wird die freundliche Welt*.

Hans Werner, *Über sieben Brücken musst Du gehn/You Have to Cross Seven Bridges* (TV), based on Helmut Richter's story.

1979   Hans-Joachim Kaprzik, *Abschied vom Frieden/Taking Leave of Peace* (TV – 3 parts), based on F. C. Weiskopf's novel.

Georgi Kissimov, *Hochzeit in Weltzow/Wedding in Weltzow* (TV), based on Günter de Bruyn's story.

Christa Mühl, *Die Rache des Kapitäns Mitchell/The Revenge of Captain Mitchell* (TV), based on Bertolt Brecht's story, "Safety First".

Peter Vogel, *Die Birke da oben/The Birch Up There* (TV), based on Joachim Knappe's novel.

Ulrich Weiss, *Blauvogel/Bluebird*, based on Anna Jürgen's story.

1980   Celino Bleiweiss, *Meines Vaters Strassenbahn/My Father's Tram* (TV – 2 parts), based on Eberhard Panitz's story.

Klaus Gendries, *Am grauen Stand, am grauen Meer/On the Gray Beach, on the Gray Sea* (TV), based on Theodor Fontane's story, "Hans und Heinz Kirch".

Jurij Kramer, *Ende vom Lied/End of the Song* (TV – 2 parts), based on Leonhard Frank's novels, *Das Ochsenfurter Männerquartett* and *Von drei Millionen drei*.

Thomas Langhoff, *Guten Morgen, du Schöne!/Good Morning, You Pretty One!* (TV – 3 parts), based on Maxi Wander's book.

—— *Muhme Mehle* (TV), based on Ruth Werner's story.

Günther Rücker/Günter Reisch, *Die Verlobte/The Fiancée*, based on Eva Lippold's trilogy, *Haus der schweren Tore*.

Horst Seemann, *Levins Mühle/Levin's Mill*, based on Johannes Bobrowski's novel.

Herrmann Zschoche, *Glück im Hinterhaus/Happiness in the Back Building*, based on Günter de Bruyn's novel, *Buridans Esel*.

—— *Und nächstes Jahr am Balaton/And Next Year on Balaton*, based on Joachim Walther's story, "Ich bin nun mal kein Yogi".

1981   Jürgen Brauer, *Pugowitza*, based on Alfred Wellm's novel, *Pugowitza oder Die silberne Schlüsseluhr*.

Helmut Dziuba, *Als Unku Edes Freundin war . . ./When Unku Was a Friend of Ede's*, based on Alex Wedding's novel, *Ede und Unku*.

Gerd Keil, *Suturp – Eine Liebesgeschichte/Suturp – A Love Story* (TV), based on Heinrich Mann's novella.

Wolf-Dieter Panse, *Adel im Untergang/The Declining Nobility* (TV – 2 parts), based on Ludwig Renn's novel.

Christian Steinke, *Kippenberg* (TV – 2 parts), based on Dieter Noll's novel.

Peter Vogel, *Der Leutnant Yorck von Wartenburg/Lieutenant Yorck von Wartenburg* (TV), based on Stephan Hermlin's story.

Lothar Warnecke, *Unser kurzes Leben/Our Short Life*, based on Brigitte Reimann's novel, *Franziska Linkerhand*.

Herrmann Zschoche, *Bürgschaft für ein Jahr/Security Deposit for a Year*, based on Tine Schulze-Gerlach's novel.

1982   Celino Bleiweiss, *Wilhelm Meisters theatralische Sendung/Wilhelm Meister's Theatrical Apprenticeship* (TV – 2 parts), based on J. W. von Goethe's novel.

Gunter Friedrich, *Das grosse Abenteuer des Kaspar Schmeck/The Great Adventure of Kaspar Schmeck* (TV – 3 parts), based on Alex Wedding's novel.

Roland Gräf, *Märkische Forschungen/Researches in the Marches*, based on Günter de Bruyn's story.

Hans-Joachim Kasprzik, *Bahnwärter Thiel/Station Master Thiel* (TV), based on Gerhart Hauptmann's novella.

Georgi Kissimov, *Emil der Versager/Emil the Loser* (TV), based on Ludwig Turek's story, "Emil Bierstedt".

Thomas Langhoff, *Stella. Nach Goethe* (TV), based on J. W. von Goethe's play, *Stella*.

—— *Melanie van der Straaten* (TV), based on Theodor Fontane's novella, *L'Adultera*.

Ulrich Thein, *Romanze mit Amélie/Romance with Amélie*, based on Benito Wogatzki's novel.

Ulrich Weiss, *Dein unbekannter Bruder/Your Unknown Brother*, based on Willi Bredel's novel.

1983   Frank Beyer, *Der Aufenthalt/The Sojourn*, based on a chapter of Hermann Kant's novel.

Konrad Herrmann, *Rublark*, based on Jurij Koch's story, "Landvermesser".

Rainer Simon, *Das Luftschiff/The Sky Ship*, based on Fritz Rudolf Fries's novel.

Herrmann Zschoche, *Insel der Schwäne/Swan Island*, based on Benno Pludra's novel.

1984   Frank Beyer, *Bockshorn*, based on Christoph Meckel's novel.

Helmut Dziuba, *Erscheinen Pflicht!/Attendance is Obligatory*, based on Gerhard Holtz-Baumert's stories, "Erscheinen Pflicht" and "Aber das Leben . . ."

Jörg Foth, *Das Eismeer ruft/The Sea of Ice Calls*, based on Alex Wedding's novel.

Klaus Gendries, *Der Schimmelreiter/The Rider on the White Horse* (TV), based on Theodor Storm's novella.

Joachim Hasler, *Der Mann mit dem Ring im Ohr/The Man with the Ring in His Ear*, loosely based on Bernhard Seeger's novel, *Der Harmonikaspieler*.

Siegfried Kühn, *Romeo und Julia auf dem Dorfe/A Country Romeo and Juliet*, based on Gottfried Keller's novella.

Horst Seemann, *Ärztinnen/Women Doctors*, based on Rolf Hochhuth's play.

Peter Vogel, *Zeit der Einsamkeit/The Lonely Time* (TV), based on Stephan Hermlin's story.

1985 Christa Mühl, *Franziska* (TV), based on Theodor Fontane's novel, *Graf Petöfy*.

Roland Oehme, *Meine Frau Inge und meine Frau Schmidt/My Wife Inge and My Wife Schmidt*, based on Joachim Brehmer's radio play.

Horst Seemann, *Besuch bei van Gogh/A Visit at van Gogh's*, loosely based on Sewer Gansowski's novella.

Rainer Simon, *Die Frau und der Fremde/The Woman and the Stranger*, based on Leonhard Frank's novella, *Karl und Anna*.

Appendix III

Selected bibliography

The references to be found on the following pages provide a basic guide to the massive body of scholarship devoted to German film history and to the interrelations between German film and literature as well as research on cinematic adaptation and the exchanges between film and literature in general. Given the extremely substantial amount of material available on these subjects, choices had to be made. (Nonetheless, the most comprehensive bibliographies on film and literature have been noted for those seeking further references.) The catalogue above all intends to serve as an initial point of orientation within this growing sub-discipline. It tends to privilege English-language materials, although it does include the most important German writing on the subject. (Considerations of space unfortunately demanded that I neglect the French and Italian scholarship in this area.) Studies that have been listed in the bibliographies at the end of individual chapters (except for general works) are not duplicated here. This selected bibliography takes into account books and articles published prior to October 1984.

1. German film history

General
Bandmann, Christa and Joe Hembus. *Klassiker des deutschen Tonfilms 1930–1960*. Munich: Goldmann, 1980.
Borde, R., F. Buache, and F. Courtade. *Le Cinéma réaliste allemand*. Lyon: SERDOC, 1965.
Bredow, Wilfried von and Rolf Zurek (eds). *Film und Gesellschaft in Deutschland. Dokumente und Materialien*. Hamburg: Hoffmann & Campe, 1975.
Bucher, Felix. *Germany*. Screen Series. London/New York: Zwemmer/Barnes, 1970.
Fraenkel, Heinrich. *Unsterblicher Film – Die grosse Chronik – Von der Laterna Magica bis zum Tonfilm*. Munich: Kindler, 1956.
Grafe, Frieda and Enno Patalas. *Im Off. Filmartikel*. Munich: Hanser, 1974.
Gregor, Ulrich. *Geschichte des Films ab 1960*. Munich: Bertelsmann, 1978.
—— and Enno Patalas. *Geschichte des Films*. Munich, Gütersloh and Vienna: Bertelsmann, 1973.
Holba, Herbert, Günter Knorr and Peter Spiegel. *Reclams deutsches Filmlexikon*. Stuttgart: Reclam, 1984.

Kalbus, Oskar. *Vom Werden deutscher Filmkunst*. 2 vols. Altona-Bahrenfeld: Cigaretten-Bilderdienst, 1935.
Manvell, Roger and Heinrich Fraenkel. *The German Cinema*. New York: Praeger, 1971.
Marquardt, Axel and Heinz Rathsack (eds). *Preussen im Film*. Reinbek: Rowohlt, 1981.
Wollenberg, H. H. *Fifty Years of German Cinema*. New York: New York Times/ Arno, 1972.

From the beginnings through Weimar (1895–1933)
Barlow, John D. *German Expressionist Film*. Boston: Twayne, 1982.
Brennicke, Ilona and Joe Hembus. *Klassiker des deutschen Stummfilms 1910–1930*. Munich: Goldmann, 1983.
Eisner, Lotte H. *The Haunted Screen*. Trans. Roger Greaves. Berkeley: University of California Press, 1969.
Elsaesser, Thomas. "Film history and visual pleasure: Weimar cinema." In *Cinema Histories, Cinema Practices*. Ed. Patricia Mellencamp and Philip Rosen. Frederick, Md.: University Publications, 1984, pp. 47–84.
—— "Social mobility and the fantastic: German silent cinema." *Wide Angle*, 5, No. 2 (1982), 14–25.
Güttinger, Fritz. *Der Stummfilm im Zitat der Zeit*. Frankfurt am Main: Deutsches Filmmuseum, 1984.
Hansen, Miriam B. "Early silent cinema: whose public sphere?" *New German Critique*, No. 29 (Spring/Summer 1983), 147–84.
Korte, Helmut (ed.). *Film und Realität in der Weimarer Republik*. Munich: Hanser, 1978.
Kracauer, Siegfried. *From Caligari to Hitler: A Psychological History of the German Film*. Princeton: Princeton University Press, 1947.
—— *Von Caligari zu Hitler*. Trans. Ruth Baumgarten and Karsten Witte. Frankfurt am Main: Suhrkamp, 1979.
Kühn, Gertraude, Karl Tümmler and Walter Wimmer (eds). *Film und revolutionäre Arbeiterbewegung in Deutschland 1918–1932*. 2 vols. Berlin (GDR) Hochschule für Film und Fernsehen der DDR, 1975.
Kurtz, Rudolf. *Expressionismus und Film*. Berlin: Verlag der Lichtbildbühne, 1926.
Manz, H. P. *Ufa und der frühe deutsche Film*. Zürich: Sanssouci, 1963.
Monaco, Paul. *Cinema & Society. France & Germany During the Twenties*. New York: Elsevier, 1976.
Plummer, Thomas *et al.* (eds). *Film and Politics in the Weimar Republic*. New York: Holmes & Meier, 1982.
Prawer, S. S. *Caligari's Children: The Film as Tale of Terror*. London: Oxford University Press, 1980.

Nazi cinema
Albrecht, Gerd (ed.). *Der Film im Dritten Reich. Eine Dokumentation*. Karlsruhe: Schauburg & Doku, 1979.
Belach, Helga (ed.). *Wir tanzen um die Welt. Deutsche Revuefilme 1933–1945*. Munich: Hanser, 1979.
Cadars, Pierre and Francis Courtade. *Le Cinéma Nazi*. Paris: Losfeld, 1972.
Friedländer, Saul. *Reflections of Nazism: An Essay on Kitsch and Death*. Trans. Thomas Weyr. New York: Harper & Row, 1984.
Hull, David Stewart. *Film in the Third Reich*. Berkeley: University of California Press, 1969. New York: Simon & Schuster, 1973.

Kurowski, Ulrich (ed.). *Deutsche Spielfilme 1933–1945. Materialien*. 3 vols. Munich: Filmmuseum, 1978ff.

Leiser Erwin. *"Deutschland, erwache!" Propaganda im Film des Dritten Reiches*. 2nd rev. edn. Reinbek: Rowohlt, 1978.

—— *Nazi Cinema*. Trans. Gertrud Mander and David Wilson. New York: Collier, 1975.

Petley, Julian. *Capital and Culture: German Cinema 1933–45*. London: British Film Institute, 1979.

Welch, David. *Propaganda and the German Cinema 1933–1945*. Oxford: Clarendon Press, 1983.

Wetzel, Kraft and Peter Hagemann. *Liebe, Tod und Technik. Kino des Phantastischen 1933–1945*. Berlin: Spiess, 1977.

—— *Zensur: Verbotene deutsche Filme 1933–1945*. Berlin: Spiess, 1978.

Wulf, Joseph (ed.). *Theater und Film im Dritten Reich. Eine Dokumentation*. Frankfurt am Main: Ullstein, 1966.

Postwar German film (1945–62)

Gramann, Karola, Gertrud Koch and Heide Schlüpmann (eds). "Die Fünfziger Jahre." Special issue of *Frauen und Film*, No. 35 (October 1983).

Hembus, Joe. *Der deutsche Film kann gar nicht besser sein*. Bremen: Schünemann, 1961.

Höfig, Willi. *Der deutsche Heimatfilm 1947–1960*. Stuttgart: Enke, 1973.

Kreimeier, Klaus. *Kino und Filmindustrie in der BRD. Ideologieproduktion und Klassenwirklichkeit nach 1945*. Kronberg: Scriptor, 1973.

Kurowski, Ulrich *et al.* (eds). *nicht mehr fliehen. Das Kino der Ära Adenauer*. 3 vols. Munich: Filmmuseum, 1979ff.

Pleyer, Peter. *Deutscher Nachkriegsfilm 1946–1948*. Münster: Fahle, 1965.

Schmieding, Walther. *Kunst oder Kasse. Der Ärger mit dem deutschen Film*. Hamburg: Rütten & Loening, 1961.

Schnurre, Wolfdietrich. *Rettung des deutschen Films. Eine Streitschrift*. Stuttgart: Deutsche Verlags Anstalt, 1950.

New German Film

Bathrick, David and Miriam B. Hansen (eds). "Special double issue on New German Cinema." *New German Critique*, Nos 24–5 (Fall/Winter 1981–2).

Corrigan, Timothy. *New German Film: The Displaced Image*. Austin: University of Texas Press, 1983.

Fischer, Robert and Joe Hembus. *Der Neue Deutsche Film 1960–1980*. Munich: Goldmann, 1981.

Franklin, James. *New German Cinema: From Oberhausen to Hamburg*. Boston: Twayne, 1983.

Jahrbuch Film. Ed. Hans Günther Pflaum. Munich: Hanser, 1977ff.

Kino: German Film. Ed. Ronald and Dorothea Holloway. Berlin, 1979ff.

Neuer Deutscher Film. Eine Dokumentation. Ed. Verband der deutschen Filmclubs. Mannheim: Internationale Filmwoche, 1967.

Pflaum, Hans Günther and Hans Helmut Prinzler. *Film in der Bundesrepublik Deutschland*. Munich: Hanser, 1978.

—— *Cinema in the Federal Republic of Germany*. Bonn: Inter Nationes, 1983.

Phillips, Klaus (ed.). *New German Filmmakers: From Oberhausen through the 1970s*. New York: Ungar, 1984.

Rayns, Tony (ed.). *Fassbinder*. 2nd rev. edn. London: British Film Institute, 1979.

Rentschler, Eric. *West German Film in the Course of Time*. Bedford Hills, NY: Redgrave, 1984.

Rentschler, Eric (ed.). "West German film in the 1970s." Special issue of *Quarterly Review of Film Studies*, 5, No. 2 (Spring 1980).
Sandford, John. *The New German Cinema*. Totowa, NJ: Barnes & Noble, 1980.

East German film
Albrecht, Hartmut *et al.* (ed.). *Sozialistisches Menschenbild und Filmkunst. Beiträge zu Kino und Fernsehen*. Berlin (GDR): Henschel, 1970.
Baumert, Heinz and Hermann Herlinghaus (eds). *20 Jahre DEFA-Spielfilm*. Berlin (GDR): Henschel, 1968.
Film- und Fernsehkunst der DDR. Traditionen, Beispiele, Tendenzen. Ed. Hochschule für Film und Fernsehen der DDR. Berlin (GDR): Henschel, 1979.
Jansen, Peter W. and Wolfram Schütte (eds). *Film in der DDR*. Munich: Hanser, 1977.
Kersten, Heinz. *Das Filmwesen in der sowjetischen Besatzungszone Deutschlands*. 2nd rev. edn. Berlin and Bonn: Bundesministerium für Gesamtdeutsche Fragen, 1963.
Liehm, Mira and Antonin J. *The Most Important Art: East European Film After 1945*. Berkeley: University of California Press, 1977.
Prisma. Kino- und Fernseh-Almanach. Ed. Horst Knietzsch. Berlin (GDR): Henschel, 1970ff.
Richter, Rolf (ed.). *DEFA-Spielfilm-Regisseure und ihre Kritiker*. 2 vols. Berlin (GDR): Henschel, 1981 and 1983.

2. Literature and film

General background literature
Andrew, Dudley. *Concepts in Film Theory*. London: Oxford University Press, 1984.
Armes, Roy. *The Ambiguous Image: Narrative Style in Modern European Cinema*. Bloomington: Indiana University Press, 1976.
Barthes, Roland. *S/Z*. Trans. Richard Miller. New York: Hill & Wang, 1974.
—— *Writing Degree Zero*. Trans. Annette Lavers and Colin Smith. Boston: Beacon, 1967.
Bazin, André. *What Is Cinema?* Ed. Hugh Gray. 2 vols. Berkeley: University of California Press, 1971.
Beja, Morris. *Film and Literature*. New York: Longmans, 1979.
Bluestone, George. *Novels into Film*. Berkeley: University of California Press, 1957.
Bresson, Robert. *Notes on Cinematography*. Trans. Jonathan Griffin. New York: Urizen, 1975.
Burch, Noël. *Theory of Film Practice*. Trans. Helen R. Lane. Princeton: Princeton University Press, 1981.
Caughie, John (ed.). *Theories of Authorship*. London: Routledge & Kegan Paul, 1981.
Cavell, Stanley. *The World Viewed: Reflections on the Ontology of Film*. Rev. edn. Cambridge, Mass.: Harvard University Press, 1979.
Chatman, Seymour. *Story and Discourse: Narrative Structure in Fiction and Film*. Ithaca, NY: Cornell University Press, 1978.
Cohen, Keith. *Film and Fiction: The Dynamics of Exchange*. New Haven, Conn.: Yale University Press, 1979.
Conger, Syndy and Janice Welsch (eds). *Narrative Strategies: Essays in Film and Prose Fiction*. Macomb, Ill.: Western Illinois University Press, 1980.
Dick, Bernard. "Authors, auteurs and adaptations: literature as film/film as literature." *Yearbook of Comparative and General Literature*, No. 27 (1978), pp. 72–6.

Edel, Leon. "Novel and camera." In *The Theory of the Novel: New Essays*. Ed. John Halperin. New York: Oxford University Press, 1974, pp. 177–88.

Eidsvik, Charles. *Cineliteracy: Film Among the Arts*. New York: Random House, 1978.

—— "Toward a 'Politique des Adaptations.'" *Literature/Film Quarterly*, 3, No. 3 (1975), 255–63.

Eisenstein, Sergei. *The Film Sense*. Trans. and ed. Jay Leyda. New York: Praeger, 1947.

Ellis, John. "The literary adaptation – an introduction." *Screen*, 23, No. 1 (May–June 1982), 3–5.

Fell, John L. *Film and the Narrative Tradition*. Norman, Ok.: Oklahoma University Press, 1974.

Geduld, Harry M. (ed.). *Authors on Film*. Bloomington: Indiana University Press, 1972.

Goodwin, James. "Literature and film: a review of criticism." *Quarterly Review of Film Studies*, 4, No. 2 (Spring 1979), 227–46.

Guzzetti, Alfred. "Narrative and the film image." *New Literary History*, 6 (1975), 379–92.

—— "The role of theory in films and novels." *New Literary History*, 3 (1972), 547–58.

Harrington, John (ed.). *Film and/as Literature*. Englewood Cliffs, NJ: Prentice-Hall, 1976.

Heath, Stephen. *Questions of Cinema*. Bloomington: Indiana University Press, 1981.

—— and Patricia Mellencamp (eds). *Cinema and Language*. Frederick, Md.: University Publications, 1984.

Horton, Andrew S. and Joan Magretta (eds). *Modern European Filmmakers and the Art of Adaptation*. New York: Ungar, 1981.

Hulseberg, R. A. "Novels and films: a limited inquiry." *Literature/Film Quarterly*, 6, No. 1 (1978), 57–65.

Jinks, William. *The Celluloid Literature: Film in the Humanities*. Riverside, NJ: Glencoe, 1971.

Johnson, William C. "Literature, film, and the evolution of consciousness." *Journal of Aesthetics and Art Criticism*, 38 (1979), 29–38.

Kawin, Bruce. "Authorial and systemic self-consciousness in literature and film." *Literature/Film Quarterly*, 10, No. 1 (1982), 3–12.

—— *Mindscreen: Bergman, Godard, and First-Person Film*. Princeton: Princeton University Press, 1978.

—— *Telling It Again and Again: Repetition in Literature and Film*. Ithaca, NY: Cornell University Press, 1972.

Kittredge, William. *Stories into Film*. New York: Harper & Row, 1979.

Lindell, Richard L. "Literature/ film bibliography." *Literature/Film Quarterly*, 8, No. 4 (1980), 169–276.

Lindsay, Vachel. *The Art of the Moving Picture*. New York: Macmillan, 1952.

McConnell, Frank D. *Storytelling and Mythmaking*. New York: Oxford University Press, 1979.

—— *The Spoken Seen: Film and the Romantic Imagination*. Baltimore: Johns Hopkins University Press, 1975.

Magny, Claude-Edmonde. *The Age of the American Novel: The Film Aesthetic of Fiction between the Two Wars*. Trans. Eleanor Hochman. New York: Ungar, 1972.

Mast, Gerald and Marshall Cohen (eds). *Film Theory and Criticism*. 2nd rev. edn. New York: Oxford University Press, 1979.

Mayer, Peter C. "Film ontology and the structure of the novel." *Literature/Film Quarterly*, 8, No. 3 (1980), 204–12.

Metz, Christian. *Film Language*. Trans. Michael Taylor. New York: Oxford University Press, 1974.
—— *The Imaginary Signifier*. Trans. Celia Britton *et al*. Bloomington: Indiana University Press, 1982.
Morrissette, Bruce. "Aesthetic response to novel and film: parallels and differences." *Symposium*, 27 (1973), 137–51.
—— "Post-modern generative fiction: novel and film." *Critical Inquiry*, 2 (1975), 253–62.
Morse, Margaret. "Paradoxes of realism: the rise of film in the train of the novel." *Ciné-tracts*, No. 13 (Spring 1981), 27–37.
Murray, Edward. *The Cinematic Imagination: Writers and the Motion Pictures*. New York: Ungar, 1972.
Peary, Gerald and Roger Shatzkin (eds). *The Classical American Novel and the Movies*. New York: Ungar, 1977.
Poague, Leland A. "Literature vs cinema: the politics of aesthetic definition." *Journal of Aesthetic Education*, 10, No. 1 (1976), 75–91.
Praz, Mario. *Mnemosyne: The Parallel between Literature and the Visual Arts*. Princeton: Princeton University Press, 1967.
Richardson, Robert. *Literature and Film*. Bloomington: Indiana University Press, 1969.
Ropars-Wuilleumier, Marie-Claire. *De la littérature au cinéma: genèse d'une écriture*. Paris: Colin, 1970.
—— *L'Écran de la mémoire: essais de lecture cinématographique*. Paris: Seuil, 1970.
Schneider, Harold W. "Literature and film: marking out some boundaries." *Literature/Film Quarterly*, 3, No. 1 (1975), 30–44.
Shattuck, Roger. "Fact in film and literature." *Partisan Review*, 44 (1977), 539–50.
Silverstein, Norman. "Film and language, film and literature." *Journal of Modern Literature*, 2 (1971), 154–60.
Small, Edward S. "Literary and film genres: toward a taxonomy of film." *Literature/Film Quarterly*, 7, No. 4 (1979), 290–9.
Sontag, Susan. *Against Interpretation*. New York: Dell, 1972.
Spiegel, Alan. *Fiction and the Camera Eye: Visual Consciousness in Film and the Modern Novel*. Charlottesville, Va.: University of Virginia Press, 1975.
Von Abele, Rudolph. "Film as interpretation: a case study of *Ulysses*." *Journal of Aesthetics and Art Criticism*, 31 (1973), 487–500.
Wagner, Geoffrey. *The Novel and the Cinema*. Cranbury, NJ: Fairleigh Dickinson University Press, 1975.
Welch, Geoffrey Egan. *Literature and Film: An Annotated Bibliography 1909–1977*. London: Garland, 1981.
Wendell, Daniel. "A researcher's guide and selected checklist to film as literature and language." *Journal of Modern Literature*, 3, No. 2 (April 1973), 323–50.
Wicks, Ulrich. "Literature/film: a bibliography." *Literature/Film Quarterly*, 6, No. 2 (1978), 135–43.
Winston, Douglas Garrett. *The Screenplay as Literature*. Rutherford, NJ: Fairleigh Dickinson University Press, 1973.

Special studies on German film and literature
Acuff, Skip. "Excerpts from 'Big Business Bolshevik': the genesis of Alexander Kluge's *Strong Man Ferdinand*." *Quarterly Review of Film Studies*, 5, No. 2 (Spring 1980), 193–204.
—— "Towards a realistic method: commentaries on the notion of antagonistic realism. A translation of Alexander Kluge's *Zur realistischen Methode*." M. A. thesis. University of Texas, 1980.

Acuff, Skip and Hans-Bernhard Moeller. "Selected writings by Alexander Kluge: theory and literary-cinematic practice of the auteur film." *Wide Angle*, 3, No. 4 (1980), 26–33.

Adam, Gerhard. *Literaturverfilmungen*. Munich: Oldenbourg, 1984.

Adorno, Theodor W. "Transparencies on film." Trans. Thomas Y. Levin. *New German Critique*, Nos 24–5 (Fall/Winter 1981–2), 199–205.

Albersmeier, Franz-Josef. *Bild und Text: Beiträge zu Film und Literatur (1976–1982)*. Frankfurt am Main: Lang, 1982.

—— "Der Einfluss des Films auf die Literatur." *Universitas*, 33, No. 9 (1978), 951–5.

Andersch, Alfred. "Für ein Fernsehen der Autoren?" *Merkur*, 17 (1963), 508–12.

—— "Das Kino der Autoren." *Merkur*, 15 (1961), 332–48.

Arnheim, Rudolf. *Film as Art*. Berkeley: University of California Press, 1957.

—— *Kritiken und Aufsätze zum Film*. Ed. Helmut H. Diederichs. Munich: Hanser, 1977.

Bachmann, Gideon. "*Nicht versöhnt*." *Film Quarterly*, 19, No. 4 (Summer 1966), 51–5.

Balázs, Béla. *Theory of the Film: Character and Growth of a New Art*. Trans. Edith Bone. New York: Dover, 1970.

Bauschinger, Sigrid, Susan L. Cocalis and Henry A. Lea (eds). *Film und Literatur: Literarische Texte und der neue deutsche Film*. Berne and Munich: Francke, 1984.

Belach, Helga *et al.* (eds). *Das Kino und Thomas Mann: Eine Dokumentation*. Berlin: Stiftung Deutsche Kinemathek, 1975.

Berman, Russell A. "The recipient as spectator: West German film and poetry of the seventies." *German Quarterly*, 55, No. 4 (November 1982), 499–510.

Bloom, Michael. "*Woyzeck* and *Kaspar*: the congruities in drama and film." *Literature/Film Quarterly*, 8, No. 4 (1980), 225–31.

Blumenberg, Hans-Christoph. *Gegenschuss: Texte über Filmemacher und Filme 1980–1983*. Frankfurt am Main: Fischer, 1984.

—— *Kinozeit: Aufsätze und Kritiken zum modernen Film 1976–1980*. Frankfurt am Main: Fischer, 1980.

Boll, Karl Friedrich. "Über die Verfilmung von Werken Fontanes and Storms." *Schriften der Theodor Storm Gesellschaft*, 25 (1976), 61–74.

Borchardt, Edith. "Leitmotif and structure in Fassbinder's *Effie Briest*." *Literature/Film Quarterly*, 7, No. 3 (1979), 201–7.

Brock, D. Heyward. "Dürrenmatt's *Der Besuch der alten Dame*: stage and screen adaptations." *Literature/Film Quarterly*, 4, No. 1 (Winter 1976), 60–7.

Bronner, Stephen Eric and Douglas Kellner (eds). *Passion and Rebellion: The Expressionist Heritage*. South Hadley, Mass.: Bergin, 1983.

Buchka, Peter. *Augen kann man nicht kaufen. Wim Wenders und seine Filme*. Munich: Hanser, 1983.

Buchloh, Paul G. "Literatur in filmischer Darstellung: Methodische Möglichkeiten zur philologischen Erschliessung verfilmter Literatur." *Literatur in Wissenschaft und Unterricht*, 13, No. 1 (1980), 47–73.

Budd, Michael. "Retrospective narration in film: rereading *The Cabinet of Dr Caligari*." *Film Criticism*, 4, No. 1 (Fall 1979), 35–43.

Cardullo, Bert. "Expressionism and the real *Cabinet of Dr Caligari*." *Film Criticism*, 6, No. 2 (Winter 1982), 28–34.

Carroll, Noël. "Welles and Kafka." *Film Reader*, No. 3 (1978), 180–8.

Cerf, Steven R. "Diverse screenings: coordinating film and text in German." *Unterrichtspraxis*, 12, No. 2 (Fall 1979), 12–19.

Conley, Tom. "Writing *Scarlet Street*." *Modern Language Notes*, 98, No. 5 (1983), 1085–120.

Corrigan, Timothy. "On the edge of history: the radiant spectacle of Werner Schroeter." *Film Quarterly*, 37, No. 4 (Summer 1984), 6–18.

—— "Werner Schroeter's operatic cinema." *Discourse*, No. 3 (Spring 1981), 46–59.

Dawson, Jan (ed.). *The Films of Hellmuth Costard*. London: Riverside Studios, 1979.

—— *Wim Wenders*. Toronto: Festival of Festivals, 1976.

Denk, Rudolf (ed.). *Texte zur Poetik des Films*. Stuttgart: Reclam, 1978.

Dietrich, Isolde. *Das Buch als Film: Ein Verzeichnis von Büchern, die verfilmt wurden*. Wolfsburg: Stadtbücherei, 1959.

Drews, Jörg (ed.). *Herbert Achternbusch*. Frankfurt am Main: Suhrkamp, 1983.

Durzak, Manfred. "Herman Broch und der Film." *Der Monat*, No. 212 (1966), 68–75.

Elsaesser, Thomas. "Achternbusch and the German avant-garde." *Discourse*, No. 6 (Fall 1983), 92–112.

—— "Myth as the phantasmagoria of history: H. J. Syberberg, cinema and representation." *New German Critique*, Nos 24–5 (Fall/Winter 1981–2), 108–54.

Erffmeyer, Thomas E. "*I Only Want You to Love Me*: Fassbinder, melodrama, and Brechtian form." *Journal of Film and Video*, 35, No. 1 (Winter 1983), 37–43.

Eschenbach, Achim and Wendelin Rader. *Film Semiotik. Eine Bibliographie*. Munich: Saur, 1978.

Estermann, Alfred. *Die Verfilmung literarischer Werke*. Bonn: Bouvier, 1965.

Faber, Marion. "Carl Mayer's *Sylvester:* the screenplay as literature." *Monatshefte*, 70, No. 2 (Summer 1978), 159–70.

—— "Hofmannsthal and the film." *German Life and Letters*, 32, No. 3 (April 1979), 187–95.

Fassbinder, Rainer Werner. *Schatten der Engel*. Munich: Zweitausendeins, 1976.

Faulstich, Werner. *Einführung in die Filmanalyse*. 3rd rev. edn. Tübingen: Narr, 1980.

—— and Ingeborg Faulstich. *Modelle der Filmanalyse*. Munich: Fink, 1977.

Faupel, Gunther. *Medien im Wettstreit: Film und Fernsehen*. Münster: Regensburg, 1979.

Figge, Richard. "The use of film in teaching German culture." *Unterrichtspraxis*, 10, No. 2 (1977), 88–93.

Film und Fernsehen in Forschung und Lehre. Berlin: Stiftung Deutsche Kinemathek, 1978ff.

Finger, Ellis. "Kaspar Hauser doubly portrayed: Peter Handke's *Kaspar* and Werner Herzog's *Every Man for Himself and God Against All*." *Literature/Film Quarterly*, 7, No. 3 ((1979), 235–43.

Franklin, J. C. "Alienation and the retention of the self: the heroines of *Der gute Mensch von Sezuan*, *Abschied von gestern*, and *Die verlorene Ehre der Katharina Blum*." *Mosaic*, 13, No. 4 (Summer 1979), 87–98.

—— "Metamorphosis of a metaphor: the shadow in early German cinema." *German Quarterly*, 54, No. 2 (March 1980), 176–88.

—— "Teaching culture through film: *Der letzte Mann*." *Unterrichtspraxis*, 13, No. 1 (Spring 1980), 31–8.

Freisburger, Walther. *Theater im Film*. Emsdetten: Heinr. & J. Leuchte, 1936.

Friedman, Lester D. "Cinematic techniques in *The Lost Honor of Katharina Blum*." *Literature/Film Quarterly*, 7, No. 3 (1979), 244–52.

Frisch, Shelley. "The disenchanted image: from Goethe's *Wilhelm Meister* to Wenders' *Wrong Movement*." *Literature/Film Quarterly*, 7, No. 3 (1979), 208–14.

Geist, Kathe. "The cinema of Wim Wenders 1967–1977." Dissertation. University of Michigan, 1981.

Gerlack, John. "Rohmer, Kleist, and *The Marquise of O.*" *Literature/Film Quarterly*, 8, No. 2 (1980), 84–91.

Gersch, Wolfgang. *Film bei Brecht*. Munich: Hanser, 1976.

Gittelman, Sol. "Fritz Lang's *Metropolis* and Georg Kaiser's *Gas I*: film, literature, and the crisis of technology." *Unterrichtspraxis*, 12, No. 2 (Fall 1979), 27–30.

Greve, Ludwig, Margot Pehle and Heidi Westhoff. *Hätte ich das Kino! Die Schriftsteller und der Stummfilm*. Stuttgart: Klett, 1976.

Grob, Norbert. *Wenders: Die frühen Filme*. Berlin (FRG): Filmland Presse, 1984.

Grund, Uwe. *Die Verwandlung. Audiovisuelle und literarische Erzähltechnik – ein Kursmodell zu Kafka*. Tübingen: Narr, 1982.

Halliday, Jon. *Sirk on Sirk*. New York: Viking, 1972.

Hamburger, Käte. "Zur Phänomenologie des Films." *Merkur*, 10 (1956), 873–80.

Handke, Peter. *Ich bin ein Bewohner des Elfenbeinturms*. Frankfurt am Main: Suhrkamp, 1972.

Hansen, Miriam B. "Introduction to Adorno, 'Transparencies on film' (1966)." *New German Critique*, Nos 24–5 (Fall/Winter 1981–2), 186–98.

Harrigan, Renny. "*Effi Briest. The Marquise of O* . . . Women oppressed!" *Jump Cut*, No. 15 (July 1977), 3–5.

Harvey, Sylvia. "Whose Brecht? Memories for the eighties: a critical recovery." *Screen*, 23, No. 1 (May–June 1982), 45–59.

Head, David. "'Der Autor muss respektiert werden' – Schlöndorff/Trotta's *Die verlorene Ehre der Katharina Blum* and Brecht's critique of film adaptation." *German Life and Letters*, 32, No. 3 (April 1979), 248–64.

—— "Volker Schlöndorff's *Die Blechtrommel* and the 'Literaturverfilmung' debate." *German Life and Letters*, 36, No. 4 (July 1983), 347–67.

Heidtmann, Frank and Paul S. Ulrich. *Wie finde ich film- und theaterwissenschaftliche Literatur?* Berlin (FRG): Berlin, 1978.

Heimann, Bodo and Angela Kandt. "Film und deutsche Gegenwartsliteratur." In *Deutsche Gegenwartsliteratur: Ausgangspositionen und aktuelle Entwicklungen*. Ed. Manfred Durzak. Stuttgart: Reclam, 1981, pp. 424–43.

Heining, Heinrich. *Goethe und der Film*. Baden-Baden: Neue Verlags-Anstalt, 1949.

Hellberg, Martin. *Bühne und Film*. Berlin (GDR): Henschel, 1955.

Heller, Heinz-B. "Literatur und Film." In *Zwischen den Weltkriegen*. Ed. Thomas Koebner. Wiesbaden: Athenaion, 1982, pp. 161–94.

Herkenrath, Michael (ed.). "Film als Requisit der Literatur?" *Film Forum*, March 1979, 86–103.

Hickethier, Knut and Joachim Paech (eds). *Modelle der Film- und Fernsehanalyse*. Stuttgart: Metzler, 1979.

Holloway, Ronald. "The backbone of German cinema." *Kino: German Film*, No. 3 (Summer 1980), 22–5.

Horak, Jan-Christopher. "*Threepenny Opera*: Brecht vs Pabst." *Jump Cut*, No. 15 (July 1977), 17–21.

Huyssen, Andreas. "The vamp and the machine: technology and sexuality in Fritz Lang's *Metropolis*." *New German Critique*, Nos 24–5 (Fall/Winter 1981–2), 221–37.

Imfeld, Justus. *Der Film als Kunstwerk*. Basel: Hanschin, 1958.

Isaacs, Neil D. "Lubitsch and the filmed-play syndrome." *Literature/Film Quarterly*, 3, No. 4 (Fall 1975), 299–308.

Jahn, Wolfgang. "Kafka und die Anfänge des Kinos." *Jahrbuch der deutschen Schillergesellschaft*, 9 (1962), 353–368.

Jameson, Frederic. "'In the destructive element immerse': Hans-Jürgen Syberberg and cultural revolution." *October*, No. 17 (Summer 1981), 99–118.

Jenkins, Stephen (ed.). *Fritz Lang: The Image and the Look*. London: British Film Institute, 1981.

Johnson, Catherine. "The imaginary & *The Bitter Tears of Petra von Kant*." *Wide Angle*, 3, No. 4 (1980), 20–5.

Johnston, Sheila (ed.). *Wenders*. London: British Film Institute, 1982.

Jubak, James. "Lang and parole: character and narrative in *Doktor Mabuse, der Spieler*." *Film Criticism*, 4, No. 1 (Fall 1979), 25–34.

Kaes, Anton (ed.). *Kino-Debatte. Texte zum Verhältnis von Literatur und Film 1909–1929*. Tübingen: Niemeyer, 1978.

—— "The expressionist vision in theater and cinema." In *Expressionism Reconsidered. Affinities and Relationships*. Ed. Gertrud Bauer Pickar and Karl Eugen Webb. Munich: Fink, 1979, pp. 89–98.

—— "Verfremdung als Verfahren: Film und Dada." In *Sinn aus Unsinn: Dada International*. Ed. Wolfgang Paulsen and Helmut G. Hermann. Berne and Munich: Francke, 1982, pp. 71–83.

Knilli, Friedrich, Knut Hickethier and Wolf Dieter Lützen (eds). *Literatur in den Massenmedien: Demontage von Dichtung?* Munich: Hanser, 1976.

Kracauer, Siegfried. *Theory of Film: The Redemption of Physical Reality*. London: Oxford University Press, 1960.

Kreuzer, Helmut (ed.). "Film- und Fernsehforschung." Special issue of *LiLi* (*Zeitschrift für Literaturwissenschaft und Linguistik*), No. 29 (1978).

—— "Filmtheorie und Filmanalyse." Special issue of *LiLi* (*Zeitschrift für Literaturwissenschaft und Linguistik*), No. 36 (1979).

—— *Literaturwissenschaft – Medienwissenschaft*. Heidelberg: Quelle & Meyer, 1977.

—— and Karl Prümm (eds). *Fernsehsendungen und ihre Formen*. Stuttgart: Reclam, 1979.

Lamb, Stephen. "The place of film in a German Studies course." *University Vision*, No. 14 (March 1976), 5–14.

Lensing, Leo A. "'Kinodramatisch': cinema in Karl Kraus' *Die Fackel* and *Die letzten Tage der Menschheit*." *German Quarterly*, 55, No. 4 (November 1982), 480–98.

Loiperdinger, Martin. "*Nathan der Weise*: Faschistische Filmzensur, Antisemitismus und Gewalt anno 1923." *Lessing Yearbook*, 14 (1982), 61–9.

Lukács, Georg. "Thoughts on an aesthetic for the cinema." Trans. Barrie Ellis-Jones. *Framework*, No. 14 (Spring 1981), 2–4.

MacCabe, Colin. "Realism and the cinema: notes on some Brechtian theses." *Screen*, 15, No. 2 (Summer 1974), 7–27.

Magisos, Melanie. "*Not Reconciled*: the destruction of visual pleasure." *Wide Angle*, 3, No. 4 (1980), 35–41.

Mayne, Judith. "Fassbinder and spectatorship." *New German Critique*, No. 12 (Fall 1977), 61–74.

—— "Female narration, women's cinema: Helke Sander's *The All-Round Reduced Personality/Redupers*." *New German Critique*, Nos 24–5 (Fall/Winter 1981–2), 155–71.

Mellencamp, Patricia. "Oedipus and the robot in *Metropolis*." *Enclitic*, 5, No. 1 (Spring 1981), 20–42.

Mitgutsch, Waltraud. "Faces of dehumanization: Werner Herzog's reading of Büchner's *Woyzeck*." *Literature/Film Quarterly*, 11, No. 3 (1981), 152–60.

Moeller, Hans-Bernhard. "Brecht and 'epic' film medium: the cinéaste, playwright, film theoretician and his influence." *Wide Angle*, 3, No. 4 (1980), 4–11.

—— "Literatur und Film im medienüberschreitenden Produktionskontext." In *Deutsche Literatur in der Bundesrepublik seit 1965: Untersuchungen und Berichte*.

Ed. Paul Michael Lützeler and Egon Schwarz. Königstein: Athenäum, 1980, pp. 85–98.

—— "Literature in the vicinity of film: on German and *noveau roman* authors." *Symposium*, 28 (Winter 1974), 314–33.

—— "Die Rolle des Films in der Gegenwartsdichtung." *Basis*, No. 2 (1971), 53–70.

Nash, Mark. "*Vampyr* and the fantastic." *Screen*, 17, No. 3 (Autumn 1976), 29–67.

Paech, Joachim (ed.). *Literatur und Film: Mephisto*. Frankfurt am Main: Diester-weg, 1984.

—— *Methodenprobleme der Analyse verfilmter Literatur*. Münster: MAkS, 1984.

Pettifer, James. "The limits of naturalism (on *Mutter Krausens Fahrt ins Glück* and *Kuhle Wampe*)." *Screen*, 16, No. 4 (Winter 1975/6), 5–15.

Phillips, Klaus. "Teaching a course in the German cinema." *Modern Language Journal*, 62 (1978), 414–19.

Pick, Erika (ed.). *Schriftsteller und Film. Dokumentation und Bibliographie*. Berlin (GDR): Henschel, 1979.

Pinthus, Kurt (ed.). *Das Kinobuch*. Frankfurt am Main: Fischer, 1983 (reprint).

Polan, Dana B. "Brecht and the politics of self-reflexive cinema." *Jump Cut*, No. 17 (April 1978), 29–32.

Prawer, Siegbert. "A new muse climbs Parnassus: German debates about literature and the cinema 1909–1929." *German Life and Letters*, 32, No. 3 (April 1979), 196–205.

Prodolliet, Ernst. *Faust im Kino. Die Geschichte des Faustfilms von den Anfängen bis in die Gegenwart*. Freiburg (Switzerland): Universitätsverlag, 1978.

Prokop, Dieter (ed.). *Materialien zur Theorie des Films*. Munich: Hanser, 1971.

Rach, Rudolf. *Literatur und Film: Möglichkeiten und Grenzen der filmischen Adaption*. Cologne: Grote, 1964.

Rauh, Reinhold. "Worte und Blicke im Film." *Sprache im technischen Zeitalter*, No. 89 (15 March 1984), 30–53.

Reif, Monika I. *Film und Text*. Tübingen: Narr, 1984.

—— "Film versus Roman? Erzählen – Lesen – Zuschauen. Überlegungen zu einer rezeptionstheoretischen Filmbetrachtung." Dissertation. University of Constance, 1977.

Reimer, Robert C. "Movies in the literature class." *Unterrichtspraxis*, 12, No. 2 (Fall 1979), 3–12.

Reitz, Edgar. *Liebe zum Kino: Utopien und Gedanken zum Autorenfilm 1962–1983*. Cologne: Köln, 1984.

Renner, Karl Nikolaus. *Der Findling. Eine Erzählung von Heinrich von Kleist und ein Film von George Moorse. Prinzipien einer adäquaten Wiedergabe narrativer Strukturen*. Munich: Fink, 1984.

Rentschler, Eric. "*Deutschland im Vorherbst:* literature adaptation in West German film." *Kino: German Film*, No. 3 (Summer 1980), 11–19.

—— "Hans W. Geissendörfer: from genre films to *The Magic Mountain*." *Kino: German Film*, No. 11 (Summer 1983), 50–9.

—— "How American is it: the US as image and imaginary in German film." *German Quarterly*, 57, No. 4 (1984), 603–20.

—— "Reopening the cabinet of Dr Kracauer: teaching German film as film." *Modern Language Journal*, 64, No. 3 (1980), 318–28.

Rich, B. Ruby. "*Maedchen in Uniform*." *Jump Cut*, Nos 24/5 (March 1981), 44–50.

—— "She says, he says: the power of the narrator in modernist film politics." *Discourse*, No. 6 (Fall 1983), 31–46.

Richter, Hans. *Filmgegner von heute – Filmfreunde von morgen*. Frankfurt am Main: Fischer, 1981.

—— *Der Kampf um den Film*. Ed. Jürgen Römhild. Munich: Hanser, 1976.

Rohmer, Eric. *Murnaus Faustfilm: Analyse und szenisches Protokoll*. Ed. and trans. Frieda Grafe and Enno Patalas. Munich: Hanser, 1980.

Roud, Richard. *Straub*. New York: Viking, 1972.

Rundell, Richard J. "Keller's *Kleider machen Leute* as *Novelle* and film." *Unterrichtspraxis*, 13, No. 2 (Fall 1980), 156–65.

Ruppert, Peter. "Applying reader-response analysis in literature and film classes." *Unterrichtspraxis*, 14, No. 1 (Spring 1981), 20–6.

—— "Fassbinder's *Despair*: Hermann Hermann through the looking-glass." *Post Script*, 3, No. 2 (Winter 1984), 48–64.

Sandford, John. "*Literaturverfilmung* and the New German Cinema." *Publications of the English Goethe Society*, 52 (1981–2), 67–89.

Schlöndorff, Volker. "*Die Blechtrommel*": *Tagebuch einer Verfilmung*. Darmstadt: Luchterhand, 1979.

Schlunk, Jürgen E. "The images of America in German literature in the New German Cinema: Wim Wenders' *The American Friend*." *Literature/Film Quarterly*, 7, No. 3 (1979), 215–22.

Schneider, Irmela. *Der verwandelte Text. Wege zu einer Theorie der Literaturverfilmung*. Tübingen: Niemeyer, 1981.

Schütte, Wolfgang (ed.). *Klassenverhältnisse*. Frankfurt am Main: Fischer, 1984.

Seitz, Gabriele. "Film als Rezeptionsform von Literatur, dargestellt an der Verfilmung von Erzählungen Thomas Manns." Dissertation. University of Munich, 1978.

Sharrett, Christopher. "Epiphany for modernism: anti-illusionism and theatrical tradition in Syberberg's *Our Hitler*." *Millennium Film Journal*, Nos 10/11 (Fall/Winter 1981–2), 141–57.

Silverman, Kaja. "Helke Sander and the will to change." *Discourse*, No. 6 (Fall 1983), 10–30.

—— "Kaspar Hauser's 'terrible fall' into narrative." *New German Critique*, Nos 24–5 (Fall/Winter 1981–2), 73–93.

Sontag, Susan. "Syberberg's *Hitler*." In *Under the Sign of Saturn*. New York: Vintage, 1980, pp. 135–65.

Stepun, Fedor. *Theater und Film*. Munich: Hanser, 1953.

—— *Theater und Kino*. Berlin: Bühnenvolksbund, 1932.

Stiles, Victoria M. "The Siegfried legend and the silent screen: Fritz Lang's interpretation of a hero saga." *Literature/Film Quarterly*, 8, No. 4 (1980), 232–6.

Thal, Ortwin. *Realism und Fiktion: Literatur- und filmtheoretische Beiträge von Adorno, Lukács, Kracauer und Bazin*. Dortmund: Nowotny, 1985.

Titfold, J. S. "Object-subject relationships in German expressionist cinema." *Cinema Journal*, 13, No. 1 (Fall 1973), 17–24.

Todd, Janet M. "The class-ic vampire." In *The English Novel and the Movies*. Ed. Michael Klein and Gillian Parker. New York: Ungar, 1981, pp. 197–210.

Tomasulo, Frank. "*The Cabinet of Dr Caligari*: history/psychoanalysis/cinema." *On Film*, No. 11 (Summer 1983), 2–7.

Waldman, Diane. "Critical theory and film: Adorno and 'the culture industry' revisited." *New German Critique*, No. 12 (Fall 1977), 39–60.

Walker, William. "GDR film in cultural context." *Unterrichtspraxis*, 15, No. 2 (Fall 1982), 194–206.

—— "Masterpieces of German literature and film in English translation." *Unterrichtspraxis*, 14, No. 2 (Fall 1981), 277–85.

Walsh, Martin. *The Brechtian Aspect of Radical Cinema*. London: British Film Institute, 1981.

Welsh, James M. and Gerald R. Barrett. "Graham Greene's *Ministry of Fear*: the transformation of an entertainment." *Literature/Film Quarterly*, 2, No. 4 (Fall 1974), 310–23.

Welsh, James M. and Richard C. Keenan. "Wim Wenders and Nathaniel Haw-thorne: from *The Scarlet Letter* to *Der scharlachrote Buchstabe.*" *Literature/Film Quarterly*, 6, No. 2 (Spring 1978), 175–9.

Wenders, Wim. *Texte zu Filmen und Musik*. Berlin: Freunde der Deutschen Kine-mathek, 1975.

White, J. J. "Horst Bienek's *Die Zelle* – novel and film." *German Life and Letters*, 32, No. 3 (April 1979), 229–47.

Williams, Alan. "Structures of narrativity in Fritz Lang's *Metropolis.*" *Film Quarterly*, 27, No. 4 (Summer 1974), 17–24.

Wolff, Jürgen. "Literaturverfilmungen im Deutschunterricht." *Mitteilungen des Deutschen Germanistenverbandes*, 28, No. 2 (1982), 32–48.

Zipes, Jack. "The political dimensions of *The Lost Honor of Katharina Blum.*" *New German Critique*, No. 12 (Fall 1977), 75–84.

Zischler, Hanns. "Masslose Unterhaltung. Franz Kafka geht ins Kino." *Freibeuter*, No. 16 (1983), 33–47.

Index